ENCYCLOPEDIA OF
AMERICAN
IMMIGRATION

Volume 4

James Ciment
Editor

 SHARPE REFERENCE
An imprint of M.E. Sharpe, INC.

SHARPE REFERENCE

Sharpe Reference is an imprint of *M.E. Sharpe*, INC.

M.E. Sharpe, INC.
80 Business Park Drive
Armonk, NY 10504

© 2001 by *M.E. Sharpe*, INC.

All rights reserved.

Library of Congress Cataloging-in-Publication Data

Encyclopedia of American Immigration / James Ciment, editor
p. cm.
Includes bibliographical references and index.
ISBN 0-7656-8028-9 (set; alk. paper)
1. United States—Emigration and immigration—Encyclopedias. 2. Immigrants—United States—Encyclopedias. I. Ciment, James.

JV6465.E53 2000
304.8′73′03—dc21

00-026560

Printed and bound in the United States of America

The paper used in this publication meets the minimum requirements of American National Standard for Information Sciences—Permanence of Paper for Printed Library Materials, ANSI Z 39.48-1984.

BM (c)   10   9   8   7   6   5   4   3   2   1

CONTENTS

OCEANIA

Natives of Oceania have a long history of immigration to the United States. Inhabitants from the region include Australians, Melanesians (Fiji, Irian Jaya, New Caledonia, Papua New Guinea, Solomon Islands, and Vanuatu), Micronesians (Commonwealth of the Northern Mariana Islands, Federated States of Micronesia, Guam, Kiribati, Marshall Islands, Nauru, and Palau), and Polynesians (American Samoa, Cook Islands, French Polynesia, New Zealand, Niue, Pitcairn, Easter Island, Western Samoa, Tokelau, Tonga, Tuvalu, and Wallis and Furtuna Islands). Like other immigrants to the United States, those from this region came to America searching for greater economic opportunities.

EARLY OCEANIC IMMIGRANTS

The earliest immigrants from the region were Polynesians, Micronesians, and Australians who worked as whalers and sealers and settled in San Francisco. The first documented immigrant is a male Australian who came to the United States in 1839. The people of the Oceanic region have a strong seafaring tradition, and various area folktales depict much migration and crossings to foreign lands. In the 1830s, Polynesians and Micronesians were among the first to leave for destinations such as Hawaii and Massachusetts, where they found work within the shipping industry. While the main motivation for immigration among Australians, Polynesians, Micronesians, and Melanesians are similar, there are remarkable differences. A distinction should be made among the areas of the region, including New Zealand, which, while officially classified under "Polynesia," merits a separate mention due to its large white settler population, advanced economy, and similarities with Australia.

The most popular destinations for Islanders were Hawaii and the West Coast, while Australians and New Zealanders (or "Kiwis") settled throughout the mainland United States. Since Australia was settled by English convicts beginning in 1788, it is likely that a few convicts from the continent immigrated to the United States. The discovery of gold in California in the 1840s brought more immigrants into the country. The gold rush also brought criminal elements to the state, and notorious crime groups came to California to take advantage of the sudden wealth that emerged. During the late nineteenth century, between five hundred and one thousand immigrants from Australia and New Zealand left for North America each year, with Canada being a primary destination as well. From 1861 to 1976, 133,299 immigrants arrived from Australia and New Zealand, with roughly 60 to 90 percent Australians.

By the end of World War I, about ten thousand Australians were living in the United States. During the 1930s, the Great Depression brought a decline in immigration from the region, and by the beginning of World War II, it is estimated that only about fifteen thousand Australians were settled in the United States. Very little movement from the islands occurred, but the numbers increased after World War II, with the majority of immigrants hailing from Polynesia and Micronesia. During World War II, about five hundred thousand U.S. servicemen were stationed in the Oceania region, many of whom married local women. By the early 1940s, Australian "war brides," who eventually numbered 15,000, began to arrive in the United States. Since World War II, immigration from the region as a whole has steadily increased, with females outnumbering males. A high rate of intermarriage also occurred between native Islander women and American men, who eventually returned to the United States with their spouses. The war brides from the region reported dissatisfaction with their new country; many were deserted by their husbands or found themselves in impoverished conditions because their newly returned husbands found difficulty secur-

The Los Angeles area is home to a thriving Pacific Islander community, which includes these two Samoan-American construction workers at the naval shipyard in Long Beach. *(Shades of L.A. Archives, Los Angeles Public Library)*

ing employment. Many women found that their experience of America fell short of the illusions they had seen from Hollywood movies. A poll taken in 1947 indicated that 80 percent of the 10,000 Australian war brides wanted to return to their country with their families, citing impoverished conditions and the desire to restore familial ties as primary reasons.

NEW OCEANIC IMMIGRANTS

From 1988 to 1994, 35,278 immigrants from the region arrived, representing 0.5 percent of total immigration. During the decade of 1881–90, the United States admitted 5.25 million immigrants, of which Oceania represented 12,500. One hundred years later, in the period of 1981–90, the United States accepted slightly over 7 million immigrants, with those from the Oceania region numbering 45,000. Thus, while present-day immigration has risen slightly, the region accounts for a very small percentage of immigrants to the United States. Figures from 1994 estimate that 85,000 Samoans were living in the United States, followed closely by Tongans at 30,000 and Fijians at 15,000, while immigrants from Federated States of Micronesia numbered 11,000. The total number of immigrants from Melanesia, Micronesia, and Polynesia (except New Zealand) living in the United States was estimated at 150,000 in 1994.

Australia and New Zealand served as settler colonies of England, and many continue to emigrate to

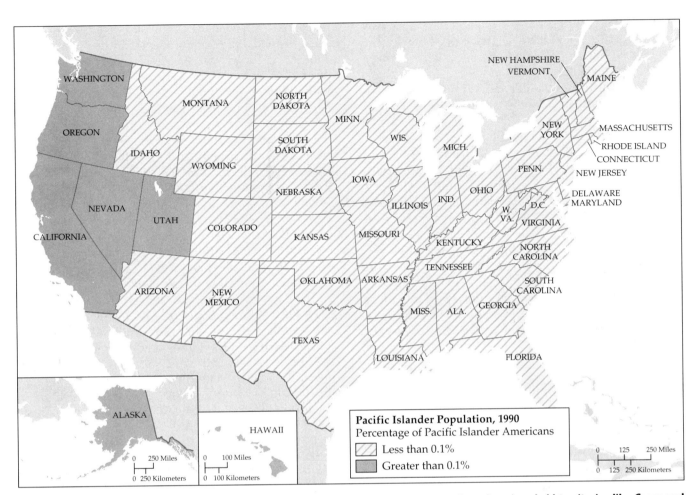

Originating in the Pacific Ocean basin, most Pacific Islander immigrants (and migrants from American-held territories like Guam and Samoa) have settled in California, Hawaii, and other Pacific states. *(CARTO-GRAPHICS)*

Great Britain as an alternative to the United States. Their shared cultural heritage and ancestral ties are one reason for the high rate of immigration to England, and favorable schemes such as work opportunities for young Australians and New Zealanders encourage many to emigrate there. Despite this, many prefer to emigrate to the United States, as it is generally believed that economic opportunities in the United States are greater than in England or other European countries. From the media, books, and returned immigrants' own accounts, most immigrants have notions of America as a country of immense wealth. The cultural life in large cities such as Los Angeles and New York continues to draw people from the region.

Push factors cited for immigration from Australia include a high rate of taxation, government ineffectiveness, the influence of labor unions, and the high cost of living. Additionally, the isolated location of the continent continues to be a factor, with many Australians seeking to experience the more metropolitan cultures of America and Europe. A varied climate and landscape have also been cited as reasons for immigration from the Oceania region as a whole, as well as marriage to an American spouse and family reunification. The chance to attend American schools and universities is also cited as another draw for immigration. Australia itself attracts immigrants from within the region, as it enjoys a considerably stronger economy than the smaller, island countries. The vast geographical distance and the high cost of emigration have not been helpful in the movement of Oceanic immigrants to the United States and have limited migratory movement within the region, drawn by the stronger economy found in Australia.

Among the Islander immigrants, different push factors encouraged migration to the United States. For instance, religion played a major role in the decision of many to immigrate to the United States. Many converted to the Mormon Church, whose main communities were located in Hawaii and Utah. Other Islanders were eager to leave their small island environment with its limited opportunities for economic and personal growth. They were anxious to share in the wealth and high living standards projected by American television programs and movies.

The majority of Islander immigrants continue to settle in Hawaii. The Polynesian presence in Hawaii has been documented long before the arrival of European explorers and before the annexation of the islands to the United States in 1898. Hawaii, officially classified under the Polynesian cultural area designation, is popular due to its close proximity to the rest of the islands in the Oceania region. Many Samoans and Guamanians serve in the U.S. naval service in Hawaii. Both American Samoa and Guam had a large military base that served as the largest area employer. When the American naval base on Samoa closed in 1951, many Samoans emigrated in search of work, as they had depended entirely on military employment and had cultivated no other industries. The U.S. Navy relocated about one thousand Samoans to work in Pearl Harbor.

SETTLEMENT PATTERNS AND CULTURAL ADAPTATION

Although the most popular destination among Polynesians, Melanesians, and Micronesians is Hawaii, Los Angeles also saw its share of Islander immigrants. Independence is one of the traits of Australians and New Zealanders, and they did not settle in an established community, in sharp contrast to those immigrants from the rest of the region, who come from close-knit communities. Those from the islands tend to live in established communities, with the exception of Samoans, who having had a long presence in the United States, do not restrict themselves to living within a Samoan community.

Australians and New Zealanders find many similarities between their countries and the United States, with the common language being a significant factor. Like the United States, Australia and New Zealand were both colonized by England and share a similar cultural heritage. Additionally, Australia and to some extent, New Zealand attract a large immigration population from within the region, as well as from the nearby Asian countries. Thus transition and adjustment were easier for them than other immigrants from the region, who did not speak English as a first language, and who were not accustomed to living with a diverse population.

Professionals such as college professors, bankers, physicians, engineers, and employees of multinational firms formed a majority of the Australian immigrants. Americans have received Australian influences in a positive manner; since 1976, a Chair of Australian Studies has been established at Harvard University. Among the Polynesians, Melanesians, and Micronesians, military service was a popular career. During the Vietnam War, the United States was eager to recruit as many personnel as possible, and many Islanders volunteered for the service. After the war, they were granted American citizenship. Most of the civilians who came to the United States were students and church ministers. Others found work that utilized traditional skills such as therapeutic masseurs and tattoo artists. Some Samoans were engaged in sporting careers in football or sumo wrestling, taking full advantage of their large physical size.

Samoans represent the largest group of Polynesians in the United States, but no distinction is made between those from American Samoa, a U.S. territory, and Western Samoa, an independent country. According to U.S. census figures, 62,962 Samoans were residing in the United States in 1990, but other sources estimate there were 65,000 Samoans residing in California alone and about 20,000 in Hawaii in 1989. Some Western Samoans use American Samoa to gain easier access into the United States. Many women purposely traveled to American Samoa so that their children would be born on American territory. The problem became so widespread that legislation was passed to prevent Western Samoan women over six months pregnant from entering Western Samoa. The Samoan population in the United States continues to grow, due to a high rate of reproduction. The second largest presence of Pacific Islanders in the United States are Tongans. While the 1990 census recorded 16,000 Tongans in the United States, it is estimated that the real figure numbered over 30,000. Most Tongans arrived in the country as students at Brigham Young University campuses in Hawaii and Utah. After their studies, many remained in the United States by marrying American citizens or securing permanent employment. The low salaries, shortages of land and jobs, and limited opportunities in Tonga encourage many to emigrate.

The French consulate general estimates that about one thousand Tahitians live in Hawaii, either studying at Brigham Young University or performing for its affiliated Polynesian Cultural Center. Islanders from French Polynesia are French citizens and are allowed to visit the United States without a visa. French Polynesians have not been as eager to emigrate to the United States as other Islanders in the region, because France provides massive government subsidies and promotes heavy tourism throughout the islands, so that French Polynesians enjoy a relatively high standard of living. Those who do emigrate and become naturalized American citizens usually retain their French citizenship as well. When the Northern Mariana Islands became a United States Commonwealth in 1979, its inhabitants earned the right to live and work in the United States, along with Guamanians and American Samoans.

Although 96 percent of Pacific Islanders choose to settle in an urban environment, most came from rural villages, with the exception of Guamanians and Northern Mariana Islanders. Many Pacific Islanders start their own small businesses that cater to the needs of their immigrant communities, in popular industries such as landscape design, travel agencies, food imports, and ship repair. Religion continues to be a big factor in the Islanders' decision to emigrate and a compelling reason to remain in the United States. Cultural, social, and welfare groups were created by various church ministries, forming a support system and providing a sense of community for the Islander immigrants. Other civic groups have also been formed, including regional associations like the Office of Polynesian Affairs, based in Salt Lake City, and national groups such as the National Office of Samoan Affairs and the Association of Pacific Island Educators.

While some Islander immigrants find success with small business operations, many others obtain work as low-skilled workers. English is their second language, which has affected their ability to fully integrate into their new country, and while Islanders adapted many aspects of American culture well, they have had disastrous results with its diet. The excessively high fat and sugar content that constitute the American diet caused many Islanders in the United States to develop diabetes, obesity, heart and other related diseases. These lifestyle diseases are a direct result of immigration and are the immigrants' response to a remarkably different environment.

While the number of Australians who emigrate to the United States has steadily increased from the 1950s to the 1970s, statistics show that there is a general decline in the rate of naturalization, with most Australians taking up to eight years with the natural-

ization process. The return rate of migration to Australia has been high. Statistics show that many who emigrate to the United States eventually return to their homeland. From 1971 to 1974, about fifteen thousand Australian immigrants returned home. Return migration rates are also high for the Islander immigrants. Since a large number were employed in the U.S. military, they return to their native lands with savings and pensions that allow them to retire comfortably. Another factor in return migration is that some Islanders are entitled to land or noble titles, which are forfeited when not claimed. Others simply want to be reunited with their extended families. A strong sense of family is important to the Pacific Islanders' ethnic and national identity, and the notion of lineage, clan, and group membership remain significant. In the United States, economic survival becomes the prevailing concern, but after immigrants have established themselves financially, attention returns to issues of cultural identity and community life, with the long-term goal of returning home for retirement and family reunification.

Grace Ebron

See also: Los Angeles, San Francisco (Part II, Sec. 12); Immigration to Australia (Part II, Sec. 13).

BIBLIOGRAPHY

Barkan, Elliott Robert. *Asian and Pacific Islander Migration to the United States.* Westport, CT: Greenwood Press, 1992.

Crocombe, Ron G. *The Pacific Islands and the USA.* Suva and Honolulu: Institute of Pacific Studies, University of the South Pacific and Pacific Islands Development Program, 1995.

Cuddy, Dennis Laurence. "Australian Immigration to the United States: From Under the Southern Cross to 'The Great Experiment.'" In *Contemporary American Immigration: Interpretive Essays.* Boston: G. K. Hall & Co., 1982.

Immigration and Naturalization Service. *1997 Statistical Yearbook of the Immigration and Naturalization Service.* Washington, DC: Government Printing Office, 1999.

Moore, J. H., ed. *Australians in America, 1876–1976.* St. Lucia: University of Queensland Press, 1977.

Price, Charles. "Migration to and from Australia." In *Commonwealth Migration: Flows and Policies,* ed. T. E. Smith, et al. London: Macmillan, 1981.

PHILIPPINES

The Philippines, a nation in Southeast Asia, consists of a cluster of islands in the Pacific Ocean. Filipinos, sometimes also referred to as Pilipinos, made up the second largest Asian group in the United States at the end of the twentieth century. Approximately 1.4 million people in the United States claimed Filipino ancestry in the 1990 census. Filipinos live in every state but are most heavily concentrated in California.

THE FIRST FILIPINOS IN AMERICA

Most Filipino immigration to the United States has taken place in the twentieth century. But some historians believe that Filipino settlement in America may date back to as early as the 1600s. From 1570 to 1898, the Philippines was a colony of Spain, and Filipino seamen served on ships sailing between the Philippines and Mexico. It seems likely that some Filipinos stayed in Mexico and moved into the Spanish-speaking territories of North America.

The earliest known Filipino community in the United States was established in Louisiana during the first half of the nineteenth century. In the 1830s, Filipino fisherfolk and trappers began to appear in the region south of New Orleans. The earliest of these settlers were probably seamen from Spanish ships. The port city of New Orleans, with its close business connections to Mexico and South America, provided a point of entry for other Filipinos after the first pioneers from Southeast Asia had made Louisiana a possible destination.

After the Louisiana Filipino fishing village of St. Malo was destroyed by a hurricane in the 1890s, the Filipino seaman Quentin de la Cruz founded a second colony, Manila Village, about forty miles south of New Orleans near the mouth of the Mississippi River. By 1933, Manila Village had a population of about fifteen hundred people, most of whom lived by shrimping, fishing, and fur trapping. Popularly known as "Manila men," the Louisiana Filipinos did maintain a sense of ethnic distinctiveness, even though they also intermarried with the local population.

Manila Village disappeared by the end of World War II. Few of the descendants of the Manila men could speak any Filipino languages by the 1950s. Still, many of the old Filipino families of the New Orleans area have retained a sense of their heritage, and as the twentieth century ended, some of the Louisiana Filipinos were still trying to preserve their cultural heritage through social clubs and Catholic religious organizations.

THE UNITED STATES–PHILIPPINES CONNECTION

Western influences on Filipino culture established deep roots during the three hundred years that the Philippines was a colony of Spain. Most Filipinos became Roman Catholics in the Spanish period, although Muslims in the south successfully resisted Spanish control and Spanish efforts at conversion. Many Filipinos took Spanish names. Speakers of Philippine languages adopted many Spanish words, although, in contrast with the Spanish colonies of Latin America, Filipinos did not adopt Spanish but retained their own local languages. Tagalog, the language of the area around Manila, became the dominant and most widely spoken language. Regional differences in language and culture made it difficult for the Philippines to create national unity.

At the end of the nineteenth century, many Filipinos began to try to cast off Spanish domination through guerrilla warfare. At the same time, Cuba, also a Spanish colony, began a similar struggle for independence. Public feeling in the United States,

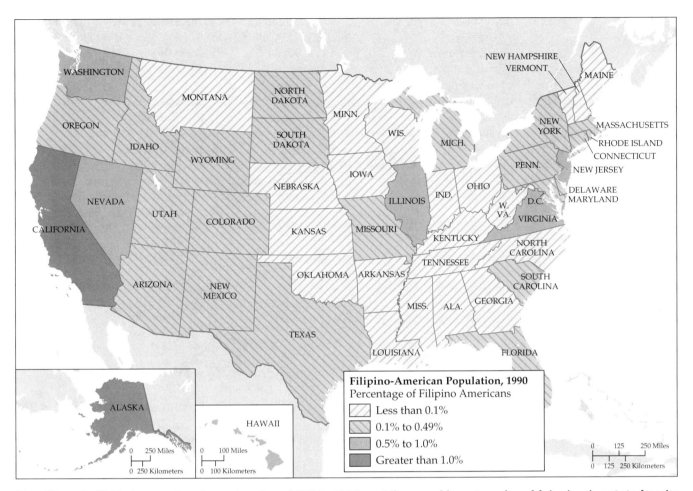

Filipino-American Population, 1990
Percentage of Filipino Americans
- ▨ Less than 0.1%
- ▨ 0.1% to 0.49%
- ▨ 0.5% to 1.0%
- ■ Greater than 1.0%

After China, the Philippines, an American colony from 1898 to 1946, sent the second-largest number of Asian immigrants to America in the twentieth century. (CARTO-GRAPHICS)

stirred up by newspaper reporting, favored the Cuban rebels. American businessmen in Cuba also strongly favored Cuban independence, and a number of American military men and politicians favored war as a means of transforming their country into a world power. In 1898, after a mysterious explosion that sank an American naval ship in the Havana harbor, the United States declared war on Spain.

A U.S. naval fleet, following secret orders from Assistant Secretary of the Navy Theodore Roosevelt, attacked the Spanish in Manila Bay. Already weakened by their fight against the Filipino insurgents, the Spanish were quickly defeated. At first the Filipinos, who had already set up their own independent government, welcomed the Americans. However, the United States, for reasons that are still debated, decided to keep the Philippines for itself. The Filipino fighters for independence resisted, and America sent its soldiers into a full-scale war of conquest. American history textbooks frequently overlook this conflict altogether or refer to it only briefly as "the Philippine Insurgency." Filipino historians, however, usually refer to the fighting as "the

Philippine-American War" (1900–1905), arguing that it was a major struggle between two nations. Reliable records on the casualties are not available, but scholarly estimates suggest that approximately two hundred thousand to five hundred thousand Filipinos died in the conflict with the United States.

Once it had defeated the guerrilla forces of the Philippines, the United States proceeded to govern its new possession with a combination of racial prejudice, desire for economic advantage, and democratic idealism. The natives of the Philippines were treated as second-class citizens in their own country, and their economy was dominated by American investors. At the same time, though, the Americans built roads, schools, universities, and public buildings. Filipino political institutions were established on the U.S. model. The use of English in high schools and the viewing of American movies in theaters brought American culture into the Philippines even before large numbers of Filipinos settled in the United States. Filipinos often describe their colonial history under Spain and the United States with the saying, "Three hundred years in a convent, followed by fifty years in Hollywood."

In World War II, Filipino soldiers fought against the invading Japanese, either in the American army or as guerrillas. The experience of having faced a common enemy, combined with an intimate familiarity with American popular culture, created a special feeling among Filipinos for the large country across the ocean. Even after the Philippines became an independent nation in 1946, Filipinos continued to be heavily influenced by the United States both culturally and politically.

AGRICULTURAL IMMIGRATION

A few immigrants from the Philippines began to arrive in the United States shortly after American forces finally suppressed the independence fighters in 1899. William Howard Taft, who later became president of the United States, was appointed governor-general of the Philippine Islands. Taft was committed to a program of education as a strategy for bringing economic and political development to the new colony. Teachers from the United States arrived in the Philippines, and students from the Philippines were sent to America. These Filipino students were called *pensionados* because the American government paid the costs of their education. The first pensionados arrived on American shores in 1903, and the program continued until 1938.

The pensionados were relatively few in number. Probably only about fourteen thousand Filipinos entered the United States under this educational program during the entire thirty-five years that it was in existence. The first true wave of Filipino immigration was largely a result of the growing American demand for agricultural labor, as large-scale agriculture became an increasingly important part of the American economy in the early twentieth century.

Most of the early agricultural laborers who emigrated from the Philippines went to what was then the American territory of Hawaii rather than to the mainland. American sugarcane planters in Hawaii rapidly expanded their exports in the first decade of the twentieth century and needed workers for the fields. In 1906, the Hawaii Sugar Planters Association (HSPA) hired attorney A. F. Judd to travel to the Philippines to recruit field-workers and to make legal arrangements for bringing the workers to Hawaii. Small numbers of workers migrated from the Philippines to Hawaii over the following three years. In 1909, however, Japanese plantation workers in Hawaii went on strike, and recruiting efforts in the Philippines became

more intensive. About four thousand workers left the Philippine Islands for Hawaii each year from 1909 to 1914. These numbers became somewhat smaller after 1915 because the legislature of the Philippines passed laws regulating the recruitment and treatment of Filipino workers. The numbers picked up again in the 1920s, though, and by 1925, Filipinos made up about half of all plantation workers in Hawaii. Five years later, an estimated three out of every four agricultural workers in Hawaii were Filipinos.

Filipino workers in Hawaii came from different regions in their native country, and they spoke different languages. Many of them initially had difficulty communicating with one another. They began to develop pidgin languages, simplified languages based on their varied tongues. For this reason, the sugarcane fields of Hawaii have long been of interest to linguists interested in the study of pidgin and creole languages, the languages that emerge when pidgin languages take root in a population and become fully developed systems of speech.

Farmers in California and canning factories in Alaska also started to recruit Filipino workers in large numbers. An estimated forty-five thousand Filipinos reached the West Coast of the mainland United States during the 1920s. Improved transportation and refrigeration had made it possible to grow fruits and vegetables on large farms in one part of the nation for export to all other regions. The resulting demand for cheap agricultural labor on the West Coast led to rapid growth of the Filipino population on the mainland, from 5,603 people in 1920 to 45,372 in 1930. Filipinos worked as migrant laborers, following the harvest seasons of crops around California as well as Oregon and Washington. Working ten hours each day almost every day of the month, these workers harvested grapes, lettuce, potatoes, strawberries, carrots, beets, and asparagus.

Most of the Filipino migrant laborers were single men, a fact that contributed to racial tensions between the Filipinos and local whites. Gambling and cockfighting were popular activities among the hard-working bachelors when they did have free time. Dance halls, where Filipino men met white women, often became focal points of racial conflict in California. On October 24, 1929, an anti-Filipino riot erupted in Exeter, a farming community in the San Joaquin Valley of southern California. A mob attacked the local labor camp where Filipino workers lived and burned it to the ground. In early 1930, another anti-Filipino riot occurred in Watsonville, California, where a mob of about five hundred white youths marched on a Filipino dance hall. On January 22, 1930, about four hundred white vigilantes attacked the Northern Monterey Filipino Club, severely beating a large number of Filipinos. When policemen attempted to halt the beatings, the vigilantes called the officers "Goo Goo lovers," using a racist term for Filipinos that had originated among American soldiers at the end of the nineteenth century.

Between agricultural seasons, Filipino agricultural laborers often sought work as dishwashers, gardeners, and domestic workers in American cities. This led to the creation of Filipino communities in Chicago, New York, Philadelphia, and New Jersey during the 1920s and 1930s.

Labor contractors from canneries in Alaska hired Filipino workers on the West Coast throughout much of the first half of the twentieth century. The canneries brought in thousands of Filipino workers to work three-month and six-month seasons in Alaska. Typically, the contractors were considered the direct employers and provided the workers with transportation, food, and wages, while the canneries provided only housing.

The period from 1906 to World War II is generally regarded as the first wave of Filipino immigration to the United States, in which immigration centered around labor, particularly agricultural labor. During this period, the United States passed several laws severely limiting immigration. Owing to the status of the Philippines as an American colony, Filipinos were the only Asians permitted to enter the United States in significant numbers. This wave of Filipino immigration began to draw to a close in 1934, when the U.S. Congress passed the Tydings-McDuffie Act, creating the Philippine Commonwealth. Although this

Filipinos, like these cannery workers in central California, have been immigrating to the United States since the American takeover of their country in 1898. *(Wing Luke Asian Museum)*

A Filipina student expresses her allegiance to her new home through the ROTC program at her San Francisco high school. *(David Maung, Impact Visuals)*

increased the self-government of the Philippines and placed the colony on the road to independence, it also meant that Filipinos ceased to be considered American nationals and became aliens. With this new piece of legislation, immigration from the Philippines to the United States was limited to only fifty persons a year.

With the limitation in new workers, Filipinos gradually became less of a presence in American agriculture. In the 1960s, Filipino migrant farm laborers under the leadership of Larry Dulay Itliong played a prominent part in the creation of the United Farm Workers union, but the number of Filipino migrant workers on the West Coast was steadily decreasing.

MARRIAGE AND IMMIGRATION

During World War II, when Japanese forces occupied the Philippines, there was no migration to the United States from the Philippines. In 1946, the Philippines became officially independent of the United States.

The number of Filipino immigrants allowed to enter the United States was raised to 100, but this was still too small to contribute substantially to the Filipino-American population. Spouses of U.S. citizens were not subject to the national quota, however.

During the second wave of Filipino immigration from 1946 to 1965, the migrants were overwhelmingly wives of U.S. servicemen. After recognizing Philippine independence, the United States kept two large military bases in the Philippines. Subic Naval Base was located on Bataan Peninsula across Manila Bay from Manila, and Clark Air Force Base was located in the mountains north of Manila. Most American servicemen at these bases were young and single, and marriages between them and Filipinas became fairly common. Of the 19,307 Filipinos who were admitted to the United States from the Philippines from 1951 to 1960, 71 percent were women who were admitted as nonquota immigrants.

This second wave of immigration, during which marriage was the primary route from the Philippines to the United States, ended in 1965 when Congress liberalized American immigration legislation and it became easier for other Filipino immigrants to enter. Migration through marriage did not cease, though. American military personnel continued to be stationed at Subic and Clark until 1991, when the Philippine government decided not to renew the lease on the bases.

Nonmilitary spouses of U.S. citizens also continued to enter the United States. The close cultural and political ties between the United States and the Philippines provided many opportunities for Filipinos and Americans to meet. During the 1970s, the Philippines became a major source of "mail-order brides" for the United States. These were women who met their husband by correspondence through the mail. Filipino and American entrepreneurs set up introduction services to put American men in search of wives in contact with Filipinas in search of financially stable husbands. Most often, the international introduction services put potential spouses in contact with each other by marketing catalogs that contained photographs of the women along with addresses and information. By the late 1990s, several of these catalogs were available by Internet as well as by regular mail.

A marriage fraud provision of the 1986 U.S. Immigration Reform and Control Act prohibited foreigners from coming to the United States to marry people they had never met. This meant that prospective American husbands would usually have to travel to the Philippines to meet the women with whom they had corresponded before a marriage could take place. Still, Philippine-American marriages stemming from correspondence continued. In some cases, brides from the Philippines would arrive in the United States on tourist or other temporary visas in order to meet with future husbands. In 1997, the social scientist Concepcion Montoya identified Filipina mail-order brides, who often established social networks among themselves, as a rapidly emerging American community. Researchers have found that popular stereotypes of these women as uneducated peasants are misleading. At the end of the twentieth century, fewer than 10 percent of the brides came from the countryside or held menial jobs in their home country. The majority were college students, and about 30 percent held professional, managerial, or clerical jobs that required fairly high levels of education.

THE POST-1965 WAVE OF FILIPINO IMMIGRATION

In 1965, the United States passed a new immigration law that ended a bias against non-European countries

and greatly expanded the opportunities for migration from Asia and other areas outside of Europe. The result was a rapid growth in the Asian-American population in general and in the Filipino-American population in particular. The number of Filipinos living in the United States roughly doubled in each ten-year period from 1960 to 1990: from 176,000 in the census of 1960 to 343,000 in that of 1970, to 775,000 in 1980, to over 1.4 million in the 1990 census.

Under the 1965 immigration law, those who were most likely to be admitted to the United States were immediate family members of American citizens, followed by immediate family members of legal residents of the United States. This means that as more Filipinos established residence in the United States, they were able to bring over members of their families as well. Thus, immigration along family lines created something of a snowball effect in the growth of the Filipino-American population.

The largest numbers of people from the Philippines arrived in the 1980s and 1990s. Data from the U.S. Immigration and Naturalization Service (INS) show that only 14 percent of people born in the Philippines living in the United States in 1996 had entered before 1970. One in four Filipino immigrants had entered during the decade 1970–79. Well over one-third (39 percent) of the Filipinos living in the United States in 1996 arrived in the 1980s. The first six years of the 1990s saw continued high levels of immigration from the Philippines: 22 percent of Filipinos living in the States in 1996 had arrived since 1990.

While immigrants who arrived before 1965 were mostly laborers from rural parts of the Philippines or wives of American citizens, immigrants after 1965 were frequently highly educated professionals, including engineers, doctors, nurses, and teachers. The post-1965 Filipino immigrants were also much more likely to come from cities. This may have created "brain drain" problems for the Philippines, which lost many of its professionals, executives, and technicians to the United States, but it was a benefit to the American economy. It became common, for example, to find Filipino doctors and nurses working in American hospitals.

FILIPINO IMMIGRATION AT THE END OF THE TWENTIETH CENTURY

Following the change in immigration law in 1965, legal immigrants allowed into the United States as permanent residents were admitted under a system of preference categories, with a quota of immigrants allowed to each country. Husbands and wives of citizens were not under the quota system. This means that marrying a U.S. citizen continued to be one of the easiest legal ways to settle permanently in the United States. Refugees were also not under the quota system. These were people who were forced to flee their native countries because of political oppression. For other immigrants, the first preference under the 1965 act consisted of unmarried children, of any age, of U.S. citizens. Spouses of holders of green cards (people with documents entitling them to legal residence) and unmarried children of green card holders fell into the second preference. This means that after the unmarried children of U.S. citizens who applied for U.S. residence in a given year were granted visas, quota slots began to be filled by spouses and unmarried children of green card holders. The third preference went to professionals and persons of exceptional ability in the arts and sciences coming to the United States to work for an American employer. Married children, of any age, of U.S. citizens received fourth preference. The fifth preference went to noncitizen sisters and brothers of U.S. citizens. Skilled and unskilled workers coming to take jobs for which American workers are in short supply were classified as sixth preference.

A majority of Filipinos entering the United States in the 1990s were admitted as immediate relatives of U.S. citizens. In 1997, for example, 52 percent of all Filipino immigrants were immediate relatives of citizens, compared with 40 percent of all immigrants. Although Filipinos often entered as spouses of U.S. citizens, they were more likely to be admitted as children or parents of citizens. While 10 percent of all immigrants to the United States came in as children of citizens and 9 percent came in as parents of citizens, 14 percent of Filipino immigrants arrived as children of citizens and 17 percent as parents. This trend resulted largely because Filipinos were more likely than other groups to become U.S. citizens. Although spouses of American citizens had made up the majority of those arriving from the Philippines from the end of World War II to the early 1960s, by the end of the twentieth century, Filipinos were no more likely than other immigrants to be admitted as husbands and wives of citizens. One in five Filipino immigrants and one in five of all immigrants were allowed into the United States because they were married to citizens.

Those who were not admitted as immediate relatives of citizens were most likely to be allowed into the United States because of other family connections. Thirty-four percent of Filipino immigrants were sponsored by other family members, while 27 percent of all immigrants had family members as sponsors. Family connections, then, offered the primary route to immigration to the United States for people from all nations, but these connections were particularly important for Filipinos.

There were also large numbers of illegal immigrants from the Philippines. In October 1996, the INS estimated that ninety-five thousand people from the Philippines were residing illegally in the United States. This meant that Filipinos made up the country's sixth largest illegal immigrant population, after those from Mexico, El Salvador, Guatemala, Canada, and Haiti. Most of the Filipino illegal immigrants had entered on nonimmigrant visas, such as tourist or student visas, and overstayed their allowed time limits. One consequence of this trend is that individuals applying for visas at the U.S. embassy in Manila are scrutinized very closely, and tourist visas are particularly difficult to obtain for young, unattached, employable people.

CHARACTERISTICS OF THE FILIPINO-AMERICAN POPULATION

One result of the close historical and cultural ties between the United States and the Philippines is that Filipino immigrants have very high rates of naturalization as U.S. citizens. While only 35 percent of all immigrants were naturalized citizens in 1997, 58 percent of Filipino immigrants were citizens. In thinking about these percentages, one should keep in mind that most Filipinos were extremely recent immigrants, most having arrived since 1980. If we take this recency of immigration into consideration, Filipino rates of taking U.S. citizenship are even higher. According to INS records, 65.4 percent of immigrants admitted to the United States from the Philippines in 1982 had become citizens by 1997. This was the second highest rate of naturalization of all countries, and it far exceeded the overall rate of naturalization of 48.2 percent.

The fact that professionals, especially medical professionals, made up such a large proportion of immigrants from the Philippines since 1965 has meant that many Filipino Americans hold middle-class jobs at the beginning of the twenty-first century. A majority of employed Filipinos in the United States (55 percent) were in white-collar jobs in 1990. Almost one of four employed Filipino Americans over the age of sixteen worked in health services. By contrast, fewer than one of ten employed Americans of all backgrounds worked in hospitals or in health-related jobs in that year.

Immigrants from the Philippines in 1990 tended to be better educated than Filipino Americans born in the United States and better educated than other native-born Americans. Data from the 1990 census show that 42 percent of foreign-born Filipinos were college graduates, compared with just over 22 percent of U.S.-born Filipinos and just under 22 percent of America's white population. Young Filipinos, both foreign-born and native-born, were more likely than most people in the United States to pursue higher educations. Among foreign-born Filipinos aged twenty to twenty-four, 50 percent were enrolled in educational institutions. Among U.S.-born Filipinos, 44 percent of those in this age group were currently enrolled, whereas only 35 percent of white Americans of the same ages were enrolled in that census year.

The professional specialization of so many Filipino Americans tended to make them a relatively prosperous group. The median household income of Filipino Americans in 1990 was $43,780 in 1990, compared with $30,056 among Americans in general. Further, while 10 percent of all American families lived below the poverty level in 1990, only slightly over 5 percent of Filipino families in the United States lived in poverty.

Filipinos live in every state in the United States. Middle-class, professional Filipino immigrants are especially likely to live in areas where members of other ethnic groups predominate. Nevertheless, Filipinos do have a few major concentrations. The states of New York and New Jersey are home to about 8 percent of all people of Filipino ancestry in the United States. Nearly two-thirds (71 percent) live in the West, with over half (52 percent) concentrated in California. Hawaii holds the second largest population of Filipinos (12 percent).

These concentrations are due to the continuing influence of history. Once a group is established in a location, other members of that group are drawn to the same place. Although Filipinos are no longer heavily involved in agriculture in California and Hawaii, the early agricultural immigrants did create the beginnings of communities that would grow over time. The cities where early Filipino laborers went looking for work in agricultural off-seasons became major areas of Filipino settlement outside of the West. Because immigrants in general and Filipinos in particular tend to enter the United States along the lines of family connections, family reunification contributes to the growth of ethnic concentrations.

New Filipino immigrants to the United States, then, are most likely to settle where there are already large numbers of people in their ethnic group. In 1997, immigrants from the Philippines interviewed by INS gave every state in the United States as intended places of residence. However, California was by far the most popular destination: over 44 percent of all those legally admitted to the United States from the Philippines gave this as their intended state of residence. Hawaii was the second most favored state, with 9 percent of new immigrants in 1997 planning to settle there. Other popular destinations included Illinois (6 percent), New York (5 percent), New Jersey (5 percent), Texas (3 percent), Washington (3 percent), and Florida (3 percent).

Filipinos in the United States have historically had high rates of marriage to people outside their own ethnic group. This was partly due to the heritage of the second period of immigration, when marriage to U.S. citizens was the primary way that people moved from this Southeast Asian nation to America. It was also partly due to the familiarity of Filipinos with American culture.

There is some evidence that rates of marriage of Filipinos to non-Filipinos may actually have grown proportionately smaller as the Filipino population of the United States grew. Social scientists Sharon Lee and Marilyn Fernandez have estimated that 30 percent of all married Filipinos in the United States in 1980 were married to non-Filipinos. By 1990, though, only 18 percent of Filipinos in the United States were married to people outside their own ethnic group.

Because the Filipino population of the United States grew so rapidly during the 1980s, this population consisted increasingly of new arrivals. New immigrants are more likely than people born and reared in the United States to choose marriage partners in their own ethnic group, for they are more likely to be attached to the culture of their homeland. Moreover, as the size of an ethnic group grows, more partners are available within that group. Therefore, heavy immigration from the Philippines at the end of the twentieth century meant not only that the Filipino-American population grew larger but also that both the continuing influx of new arrivals and the increase in in-group marriage were likely to maintain the ethnic distinctiveness of Filipinos in the United States.

Carl Bankston III

See also: Los Angeles, San Francisco (Part II, Sec. 12); Immigration to Australia (Part II, Sec. 13).

BIBLIOGRAPHY

Agbayani-Siewert, Pauline, and Linda Revilla. "Filipino Americans." In *Asian Americans: Contemporary Trends and Issues*, ed. Pyong Gap Min, pp. 95–133. Thousand Oaks, CA: Sage, 1995.

Almirol, Edwin B. *Ethnic Identity and Social Negotiation: A Study of a Filipino Community in California*. New York: AMS Press, 1985.

Anderson, Robert N., with Richard Coller, and Rebecca F. Pestano. *Filipinos in Rural Hawaii*. Honolulu: University of Hawaii Press, 1984.

Bickerton, Derek. "Creole Languages." *Scientific American* (July 1983), pp. 116–22.

Crouchett, Lorraine Jacobs. *Filipinos in California: From the Days of the Galleons to the Present*. El Cerrito, CA: Downey Place, 1982.

Department of the Census. *Current Population Survey, March 1997*. Washington, DC: Government Printing Office, 1997.

———. *Current Population Survey, March 1996*. Washington, DC: Government Printing Office, 1996.

———. *1990 Census of Population, Asians and Pacific Islanders in the United States*. Washington, DC: Government Printing Office, 1993.

———. *1990 Census of Population, General Population Characteristics, the United States*. Washington, DC: Government Printing Office, 1993.

Espina, Maria E. *Filipinos in Louisiana*. New Orleans: A. F. Laborde, 1988.

Immigration and Naturalization Service. *1997 Statistical Yearbook of the Immigration and Naturalization Service*. Washington, DC: Government Printing Office, 1999.

Karnow, Stanley. *In Our Image: America's Empire in the Philippines*. New York: Random House, 1989.

Le Espiritu, Yen. *Filipino American Lives*. Philadelphia: Temple University Press, 1995.

Lee, Sharon M., and Marilyn Fernandez. "Trends in Asian American Racial/Ethnic Intermarriage: A Comparison of 1980 and 1990 Census Data." *Sociological Perspectives* 41:2 (1998); 323–42.

Mangiafico, Luciano. *Contemporary American Immigrants: Patterns of Filipino, Korean, and Chinese Settlement in the United States*. New York: Praeger, 1988.

Mitchell, Don. *The Lie of the Land: Migrant Workers and the California Landscape*. Minneapolis: University of Minnesota Press, 1996.

Okamura, Jonathan Y. *Imagining the Filipino American Diaspora: Transnational Relations, Identities, and Communities*. New York: Garland, 1998.

Pido, Antonio J. A. *The Pilipinos in America: Macro/Micro Dimensions of Immigration and Integration*. New York: Center for Migration Studies, 1985.

Root, Maria P. P., ed. *Filipino Americans: Transformation and Identity*. Thousand Oaks, CA: Sage, 1997.

SOUTH ASIA

Immigration from the subcontinent of South Asia began early in U.S. history but did not acquire significant dimensions until the late twentieth century. Changes in U.S. immigration law, admissions and citizenship policies in other countries, and political and economic conditions in South Asia have all contributed to the enormous post-1965 growth in the number of immigrants from India, Pakistan, Afghanistan, and Bangladesh. As a result, by fiscal year 1998 India was the third-largest national source of immigration to the United States, behind only Mexico and mainland China. Arrivals from the other nations of South Asia—Sri Lanka, Nepal, and Bhutan—have been much fewer and will figure less in the discussion below.

HISTORICAL PERSPECTIVE

The earliest record of a South Asian presence on American soil is that of a traveler from Madras who visited Massachusetts in 1790. Soon after, Indian seamen began to work on the wharves of Salem and other eastern ports. Although the sailors were often distinctive in their dress, their dark skin meant they were sometimes considered as African Americans in early American slaveholding society. For some, this led to marriage with black women; for others, it resulted tragically in enslavement.

In the nineteenth century, small numbers of Indians arrived as merchants, entertainers, religious leaders, and miners headed for the California gold rush. The 1900 national census registered 2,050 individuals from India, which then incorporated the territories that are now Pakistan and Bangladesh. At this time roughly five hundred Indian traders were estimated to reside in the United States, largely Parsees located in New York, Missouri, and a few southern cities. The first Indian student in the United States arrived on the West Coast in the winter of 1901–2, and the following

year a Lahore mathematics professor entered from Japan.

In the first decade of the twentieth century, two significant migration streams from India developed. The first was composed of a small core of nationalists who sought political refuge and support for their goal of driving the British colonial government out of India. In 1906, the Pan-Aryan Association and the Indo-American Association were founded by Indians in New York, and the Home Rule League was established in 1910. The first issue of *Free Hindustan* was published in the United States in 1908. And the Ghadr (Revolutionary) Party, formed in 1913 in San Francisco by a Stanford professor, launched a 1917 mission to foment rebellion in the Punjab. The attempt failed, and fourteen of the twenty-nine Ghadr leaders subsequently arrested in California for violating American neutrality laws were convicted.

The second and larger turn-of-the-century immigrant stream was made up of Punjabi, largely Sikh, workers who entered Washington State via Canada. Many were originally recruited from Asia to work on the Canadian Pacific Railway and later ventured south in search of railroad, lumber, and orchard work. After only 20 Indians entered the United States in 1903, 258 in 1904, and 145 in 1905, 600 applied for admission in 1906, primarily from Vancouver. Whereas fewer than 700 Indians were estimated to have immigrated to the United States during the entire nineteenth century, approximately 4,713 Indian immigrants arrived in the first decade of the twentieth century alone.

Hostility toward the Sikh immigrants plagued them in the United States as well as in Canada. Both racism and labor-market conflict were behind this aggression. Since Indians often worked for lower wages than European immigrants, the latter accused them of taking away jobs and undercutting worker efforts to negotiate better pay. As a result of this conflict, roughly a thousand Indians were expelled from lum-

While Indian immigrants once headed for former colonial ruler Britain, many, like this Philadelphia mother and child, have come to the United States in recent decades. *(Harvey Finkle/Impact Visuals)*

bering areas in a series of riots in the American Northwest in 1907. Many retreated inland to the agricultural communities of central California, working in the Sacramento, San Joaquin, and Imperial Valleys during the summer, and in Yuba City, Stockton, and El Centro in the winter. With few Indian women in the country, these Punjabi farmers frequently married Mexican women, and the community they founded in California, which can be said to be the first significant South Asian settlement in the United States, was in fact a bicultural one. To this day Sikhs are prominent in the agriculture of that region; this group, which numbers about ten thousand, has been called the largest South Asian agricultural community outside India.

In addition to labor strife, the early immigrants faced other forms of discrimination, many of which targeted Asians in general regardless of nationality. Anti-Hindu housing covenants materialized, and in 1913 California passed the Alien Land Law, prohibiting noncitizens from owning or leasing land. The 1917 federal Asiatic Barred Zone provision cut off new im-

migration from Asia. And in 1923, the U.S. Supreme Court decided not only that Indians could not be granted citizenship because they were not white (a prerequisite for naturalization based on a 1790 law), but that those who had previously been naturalized should be stripped of their U.S. citizenship. Although the 1927 Supreme Court decision *United States v. Sakaram Ganesh Pandit* halted denaturalization proceedings, Indians would not be allowed to become citizens or own property until the 1946 passage of the Luce-Celler bill. Despite such restrictions, some of the early Punjabi farmers prospered, but their community dwindled once the barriers to new immigration from South Asia were put in place. Emigration was the major cause of this decline; some forty-five hundred Indians left the United States between 1911 and 1930. The numbers of South Asians in the United States, which had probably never exceeded six thousand even during the 1904–23 influx, shrank to roughly fifteen hundred by midcentury.

IMMIGRATION TO THE UNITED STATES AS PART OF A DIASPORA

Although South Asian immigration to the United States would not become large-scale until the last quarter of the twentieth century, emigration from the South Asian subcontinent to other destinations was already sizable in the nineteenth century. Thus South Asian immigration to the United States can be seen as simply one stream—albeit an important one today—of a long-standing and varied outflow from the subcontinent. Accordingly, it should be kept in mind that not all immigrants of South Asian origin enter the United States directly from India, Pakistan, and their neighbors. Instead, South Asian immigrants move from the Caribbean, East Africa, and the United Kingdom, among other places. It has been estimated that Indians overseas numbered 15 to 20 million in the early 1990s and that approximately 1 million people of South Asian descent lived in the United States in 1999.

The global web of South Asian communities, often referred to as a diaspora, has its roots in the British colonial occupation of India (1757–1947). Imperial rule entailed not only political control, but also economic command, the imposition of internal boundaries, and intervention in social hierarchies. Moreover, decolonization resulted in the 1947 partition of the territory into India and Pakistan, which in turn split in 1971 into today's Pakistan and Bangladesh. Together, all these factors contributed to the dislocation and migration of large segments of the subcontinental population. Some of the colonial measures that most directly provoked outmigration, however, were the system of indentured servitude, the employment of Indians as middlemen in other British colonies, and the assignment of certain occupations to particular groups.

Once slavery was abolished in Britain in 1834, the English sought Indian and Chinese laborers to replace slaves in sugar cane fields, mines, and other colonial projects. Between 1834 and 1934, an estimated 30 million indentured servants were exported from India to Mauritius, Guyana, Trinidad, Surinam, Fiji, Malaysia, and South Africa. Indians were also sent to East Africa to serve as clerks and bureaucrats in the colonial administration. Finally, the British favored certain caste or regional groups for specific occupations. For example, Punjabi Sikhs formed the backbone of the native army and were sent abroad to put down rebellions and serve as policemen elsewhere in the empire.

It was these Sikh former soldiers, whose employment in East Asia positioned them for recruitment by Canadian railroad officials, who would form the nucleus of the early-twentieth-century South Asian community in California.

The British further influenced South Asian emigration even after decolonization through the establishment of the British Commonwealth, which originally facilitated movement to Canada, Australia, and the United Kingdom.

CONTEMPORARY SOUTH ASIAN IMMIGRATION TO THE UNITED STATES

In 1946, the same Luce-Celler bill that permitted Indians to become American citizens and own property also opened up the possibility of bringing family members into the country. A quota on Indian immigration was established. While from 1931 to 1940, only 496 Indian immigrants entered the United States, some 1,760 arrived between 1941 and 1950, and about 1,970 came in the 1951–60 decade.

It was not until the Immigration Act of 1965 (P.L. 89–236) took effect in 1968, however, that immigration from South Asia began its swift upward trajectory. The 1965 act eliminated the old system based on national origin that had favored certain European countries as sources of immigration, and instead established a preference system that allowed immigrants to enter based either on family ties or occupational skills or as refugees. Since the South Asian community in the United States at the time was too small to sponsor much family-reunification immigration, the first wave of new immigrants from the subcontinent came largely for professional reasons.

From a total of less than 600 Indian immigrants in 1965, over 10,000 entered the United States in 1970, nearly 23,000 in 1980, and 30,700 in 1990. The latest figures from the U.S. Immigration and Naturalization Service (INS) (shown in Table 1) record 36,483 legal immigrants from India in 1998, as well as 13,094 from Pakistan and 8,621 from Bangladesh. Over the 1981–98 period, legal immigration from India has been over twice as great as that from the rest of South Asia: Nearly 573,000 immigrants arrived from India during this time, compared to 158,000 from Pakistan and 68,000 from Bangladesh.

South Asian illegal immigrants are also numerous. The INS has estimated that in 1996, 41,000 Pakistani

Table 1
South Asian Immigration to the United States, Fiscal Years 1981–1998*

Time Period	India	Pakistan	Number of Immigrants from: Bangladesh	Afghanistan	Sri Lanka	Nepal	Bhutan
1981–1990	261,841	61,300	15,200	26,600	6,125	NA	NA
1991–1995	191,609	57,968	27,213	12,296	5,516	1,212	9
1996	44,859	12,519	8,221	1,263	1,277	431	8
1997	38,071	12,967	8,681	1,129	1,128	447	6
1998	36,482	13,094	8,621	NA	NA	NA	NA
Total	572,862	157,848	67,936	41,288	14,046	2,090	23

*The figures above do not include persons entering as refugees, asylees, or illegal immigrants; this table uses fiscal years ending on September 30.
Sources:
Gall and Gall, *Statistical Record of Asian Americans,* 1993, Tables 515 and 517.
Helweg and Helweg, *An Immigrant Success Story: East Indians in America,* 1990, Table 4.
Bureau of the Census, *Statistical Abstract of the United States: 1998,* Tables 8 and 11.
Department of Justice (Immigration and Naturalization Service), *Office of Policy and Planning Annual Report,* 1999.
Department of Justice (Immigration and Naturalization Service), *1997 Statistical Yearbook of the Immigration and Naturalization Service,* 1999.

illegal aliens resided in the United States, as did 33,000 Indians and 50,000 from Trinidad and Tobago, which has a large Indian-origin population. In fact, in 1986 Indians were estimated to make up the largest non-Hispanic group to illegally cross the U.S.-Mexico border, continuing a strategy used by Indian immigrants in the 1920s.

South Asians also frequently become permanent residents after having arrived as students (Indians make up the fourth-largest contingent of international students in the United States) or as refugees or political asylees. While the latter category has been applied in connection with civil war in Sri Lanka and separatist struggles in Kashmir and the Punjab, it was most heavily used in the 1980s in connection with the conflict in Afghanistan. From 1981 to 1990, nearly 23,000 Afghan refugees and asylees entered the United States, and 9,065 more came in the 1991–96 period.

Altogether, the South Asian–origin population of the United States, including both immigrants and their American-born descendants, has been estimated at 1 million in 1999, or 0.36 percent of the total population of nearly 274 million. This represents more than a doubling of their numbers since 1980, when the census enumerated 387,223 individuals of Asian Indian ancestry and 15,792 of Pakistani origin. Ancestry and race reports from the 1990 U.S. census suggest that in a total South Asian–origin population of approximately 840,000, 80 percent were of Indian origin, 12 percent of Pakistani ancestry, and 4 percent of Afghan origin. See also Table 2 for 1960–90 Census Bureau estimates of the share of the U.S. population born in South Asia (though not necessarily of South Asian ancestry).

The South Asian community in the United States is not only a small one compared to the larger national population, but it is also fairly geographically dispersed. In 1996, 17 percent of new Indian immigrants intended to settle in California, 14 percent in New Jersey, 13 percent in New York, 9 percent in Illinois, and 7 percent in Texas. This is a much less geographically concentrated inflow than the two larger immigrant streams in that year; 40 percent of both Mexican and Filipino immigrants that year planned to settle in a single state (California). However, it should be noted that other South Asian immigrant groups tend to greater spatial concentration than Indians; in 1991, over 60 percent of Bangladeshi immigrants and 33 percent of Pakistani arrivals were headed for New York City alone, compared to 16 percent of Indians.

As the American South Asian–origin population has grown, family reunification immigration has made up an increasing share of new inflows. From 1972 to 1977, 57 percent of Indian immigrants entered the United States with employment preference visas, while only 14 percent did so in the 1978–91 period. In 1992–94, this share rose to 26 percent. The changing balance in the basis for admission among Indian immigrants has raised questions about the characteristics of recent arrivals compared to those of the early 1970s, particularly in terms of occupation. However, these fluctuations in visa type do not translate directly into changes in the percentage of immigrants arriving with

Table 2
U.S. Population Born in South Asia, 1960–1990

Country	Census Year			
	1960	1970	1980	1990
India	12,296	51,000	206,087	450,406
Pakistan	1,708	6,182	30,774	91,889
Afghanistan	NA	NA	3,760	28,444
Bangladesh	NA	NA	4,989	21,414
Sri Lanka	NA	NA	5,576	14,022
Nepal	NA	NA	844	2,262
Total:	14,004	57,182	252,030	608,437
Total U.S. Population:	179,325,671	203,210,158	226,545,805	248,709,873
% born in S. Asia:	0.008	0.028	0.111	0.245

Source: Gibson, Campbell J., and Emily Lennon. "Historical Census Statistics on the Foreign-born Population of the United States: 1850–1990." U.S. Census Bureau Population Division, Working Paper No. 29 (February 1992). Tables 1, 3.
URL: http://www.census.gov/population/www/documentation/twps0029/twps0029.html
Notes: Until 1947, India included the territories that are now Pakistan and Bangladesh. In 1947, Pakistan was established, incorporating both present-day Pakistan (then known as West Pakistan) and Bangladesh (formerly East Pakistan). In 1971, East Pakistan seceded to form Bangladesh.
"NA" indicates either that the country in question was not yet in existence, or the number of its immigrants in the United States was negligible.
These figures exclude U.S.-born individuals of South Asian ancestry, and they include individuals who do not have South Asian ancestry but who were born on the subcontinent.

professional occupations, since professionals and managers frequently choose to enter with family preference visas. Indeed, the proportion of Indian immigrants who held professional or managerial occupations declined only slightly, from 84 percent of those reporting an occupation over the 1972–77 period, to 73 percent in 1992–94.

As noted above, the Immigration Act of 1965 encouraged South Asian immigration to take on the shape of labor migration, because the U.S.-based community was too small at the time to provoke much family-reunification immigration. Moreover, the change in U.S. law came at a time when the United Kingdom's admissions policies were becoming increasingly restrictive. However, the highly professional nature of immigration from the subcontinent was also determined both by a shortage in the United States of medical personnel, lasting through the mid-1970s, and by the severe unemployment problem in India for engineers, physicians, and scientists, among others. The number of unemployed engineers alone has been put in the hundreds of thousands, both for the 1970s and today. It is not surprising, then, that India has become the archetypal example of "brain drain" emigration, and that Indian immigrants have consistently included a larger percentage of professionals than any other large immigrant group.

SOUTH ASIANS IN THE UNITED STATES

The South Asian–origin community in the United States is unusual in its relatively high average socioeconomic levels. However, it is also a heterogeneous grouping, both in terms of occupation, education, and income, and with respect to national origin, language, religion, caste, and regional affiliation. As the second and third generations grow, some of this cultural diversity may become less salient for their sense of identity—or it may be further nurtured by new immigrants from the subcontinent.

SOCIOECONOMIC STATUS

Asian Indians in particular have come to be considered something of a "model minority" in the United States, given their high educational, occupation, and income levels. In 1990, 70 percent of Indians over age twenty-five in the United States held a bachelor's degree, 34 percent had a master's, 8 percent had professional degrees, and 9 percent held doctorates. In the same year, only 20 percent of the national population held a bachelor's or higher degree. Indian high-school students had the highest mean grade-point average (GPA = 3.8) of all Asian groups, and the lowest drop-out rate.

In terms of income, the 1990 census revealed Indians to have higher family and per capita incomes than any other foreign-born group. Their annual median household income, $43,320, was considerably higher than the national figure of $35,894. The related propensity of Indian immigrants to have professional occupations has already been noted above. Another way to consider their predominance in the professions, however, is to note that although South Asians have been estimated to make up only 0.3 percent of the U.S. population, they furnished an estimated 4 percent of all U.S. doctors in 1997.

At the same time, it is frequently asserted that self-employment has become more prevalent among South Asian immigrants. In addition to the Gujarati domination of the American small-hotel/motel industry, South Asian employees, managers, and owners have become familiar sights in newspaper stands, taxicabs, convenience stores and gas stations, restaurants, and ethnic businesses that sell groceries, clothing, and jewelry.

SOCIOCULTURAL DIVERSITY

The socioeconomic diversity of the South Asian community is accompanied by tremendous heterogeneity in language, caste, religious, regional, and national affiliation, which constitute important markers of identity. As noted above, South Asians of Indian origin constitute the largest segment of this population, but their common nationality hardly guarantees a sense of community across linguistic, regional, and other lines. In 1990, Helweg and Helweg estimated that 60 percent of the Indians in the United States were of Gujarati origin, roughly 30 percent were Punjabi, and 10 percent were from the state of Kerala. Similarly, the Pakistani community includes Punjabi-speakers (about half), a third who use Urdu as their mother tongue, and speakers of Gujarati, Sindhi, Baluchi, and Pashto. Most Pakistanis in the United States are Sunni Muslims, but Shiite Muslims, Ahmadis, Hindus, Christians, Buddhists, and Parsees have also settled here.

These layers of complex identities can be described beginning at the global level and working downward to the local. Thus South Asian–origin immigrants may come from South Asia or from elsewhere (e.g., the Caribbean, East Africa, East Asia, the United Kingdom, or Canada), and those from South Asia may hail from a variety of nations (e.g., India, Pakistan, Afghanistan, Bangladesh, Sri Lanka). Furthermore, immigrants from the same country depart from different regions and bring different languages, caste and class identifications, and religious practices. In sum, the South Asian–origin population of the United States is a decidedly less homogeneous one than the much smaller early-twentieth-century California-based Punjabi community.

In addition, the distinction between first-generation immigrants and their second-generation offspring has important implications for South Asian identity formation, as it does for all immigrant groups in the United States. At present, the South Asian community in the United States is overwhelmingly a foreign-born one; 1990 census data show 77 percent to be immigrants. The predominance of the immigrant population influences the political orientation of the South Asian American community and the strength of its ties to the subcontinent; the continued importance of the national, regional, linguistic and other social divisions described above; and the process of assimilation to American society, particularly in terms of race and ethnicity.

POLITICAL AFFILIATION AND ETHNIC IDENTITY

Given the large share of immigrants, it is not surprising that only 50 percent of South Asian–origin individuals are U.S. citizens. The limitations that a low citizenship rate places on political participation in the United States do not necessarily imply domestic political disengagement, however. South Asians have strongly mobilized around certain issues—for example, immigration reform and (in the 1970s and 1980s) their official classification as racial minorities eligible for special equal-opportunity consideration. South Asian–origin politicians have also served broad constituencies, beginning with Dalip Singh Saund, who became the first Indian-born U.S. congressman in 1956. More recently, Cochin native Joy Cherian served as head of the Equal Employment Opportunity Commission in the 1988–92 administration of President George H. Bush. Other South Asian Americans have held high-ranking positions in the Republican and Democratic Parties and contributed strongly to political fund-raising.

Nevertheless, events in South Asia continue to command the attention of many, particularly in the immigrant first generation. It is telling that the agendas of large organizations such as the National Federation of Indian-American Associations and the Association of Indians in America demonstrate an abiding concern for political and economic developments in India—promoting, for example, exchanges of technology and investment—and for the state of

U.S.-India relations. The hopes that many immigrants nurture of returning to their native countries—whether realized or not—encourage a continued vested interest in the evolution of politics at home. Some governments, moreover, actively court such sentiment. India has established a Non-Resident Indian (NRI) category that offers privileges such as competitive-rate bank accounts, reserved apartments, and admission for children to top schools, in exchange for foreign-currency deposits or investment. Although these privileges have provoked resentment from some in India, they have also encouraged emigrant investment, the results of which can be seen in new hospitals, roads, libraries, schools, and emigrant-serving businesses, particularly in Gujarat and the Punjab.

Just as links to South Asia may exert a stronger pull on the immigrant first generation than on their children, the salience of religious, regional, linguistic, caste, and national divisions that are important to their parents may wane among the second generation. The establishment of pan-national South Asian student associations on college campuses around the country speaks to such a breaking down of traditional dividing lines. Moreover, Helweg and Helweg point out that some national associations, such as the Association of Indians in America, aim to foster "an Indian identity with an American commitment" that would take precedence over more parochial identities. The future marriage patterns of the growing second generation will offer telling evidence of the extent to which the divisions that shaped the social world of their parents continue to color their own.

Furthermore, the second generation of South Asians in America has to contend with growing up in a society that places enormous emphasis on race. This presents them with a challenge not only because it calls into play an omnipresent set of classifications that is foreign to their parents, but also because there is a lack of consensus, both within the South Asian community and outside it, about how South Asians should be classified in racial terms. Historically, respondents of South Asian origin have been classified variously as Hindu, white, other, and Asian in the U.S. census. In the early years of the twentieth century, when being white was a prerequisite for naturalization, American courts vacillated on the question of whether Indians were white or not. In contrast to Mexicans and Armenians, who were deemed white for the purposes of citizenship acquisition, and Japanese, Chinese, and Filipino applicants, who were not, the verdict on the racial classification of Indians changed from case to case. Considerable confusion stemmed from the question of whether being Caucasian or Aryan by the anthropological conventions of

the day was synonymous with being white; American courts tended to think not when it came to Indian petitioners.

As a result of Indian-American lobbying in the 1970s, South Asians have come to be included within the Asian/Pacific Islander racial category on the U.S. census. This official designation, however, has not ensured a feeling of common cause among Americans of South Asian and East Asian descent. Moreover, the relatively dark coloring of some South Asians causes other Americans to associate them at times with blacks and/or Hispanics. Many observers have claimed that South Asian Americans face the same discrimination as other minorities. In a 1975 statement to the U.S. Civil Rights Commission, the Association of Indians in America contended, "It is undeniable that Indians are different in appearance; they are equally dark-skinned as other non-white individuals and are, therefore, subject to the same prejudices." A memorable example of such prejudice comes from the experience of Nobel laureate Rabindranath Tagore, who was subjected to segregationist hotel policies when visiting California in the early 1940s. Finally, the sense of similarity between anti–South Asian prejudice and antiblack racism is reinforced by the British practice, familiar to some, of referring to South Asians as "black."

However, it should be noted that the most egregious outburst of recent violence against South Asians—namely, the Jersey City, New Jersey, "dotbuster" series of attacks in 1987, which resulted in one death and several injuries—was not the handiwork solely, or even primarily, of whites. Instead, Puerto Ricans, blacks, whites, and other Asians also participated in what has been interpreted by many as assaults grounded in economically motivated resentment. Although such harassment has been infrequent, it has materialized in Chicago, Long Island, and New York City as well, and it may become more prevalent as the South Asian community grows in size.

Recent immigration flows from South Asia to the United States have given rise to a community that on the whole faces promising prospects for adaptation to American society. The high levels of human capital that many immigrants from the subcontinent bring facilitates their integration at higher levels of the U.S. labor market than is true for almost any other significant foreign-born group. However, potential changes in immigration flows could have important effects on future assimilation.

Future numbers of immigrants and their resulting impact on the size of the South Asian American community will affect its relations with other ethnic groups. Geographic dispersion may give way to greater concentration, also influencing intergroup relations. Furthermore, changes in the characteristics of immigrants—occupational, educational, income, cultural—would have repercussions for where they settle and thus the groups with whom they interact. Finally, the generational balance will also color attitudes toward U.S. society and shape marriage patterns. In sum, all the factors above will affect South Asians' relationships with other Americans, with each other, and with important political, social, and cultural institutions.

Ann Morning

See also: New Jersey and Suburban America, New York City (Part II, Sec. 12); Immigration to Canada, Immigration to Western Europe (Part II, Sec. 13); *United States v. Bhagat Singh Thind*, 1923 (Part IV, Sec. 1).

BIBLIOGRAPHY

Bureau of the Census. *Statistical Abstract of the United States: 1998.* Washington, DC, 1998.

Bureau of the Census (Housing and Household Economic Statistics Division). "Changes in Median Household Income: 1969 to 1996." Washington, DC, 1999.

Bureau of the Census (Population Estimates Program, Population Division). "Resident Population Estimates of the United States by Age and Sex: April 1, 1990 to November 1, 1999." Washington, DC, 1999.

Davis, Floyd James. *Who Is Black? One Nation's Definition.* University Park: Pennsylvania State University Press, 1991.

Department of Education. *Digest of Education Statistics 1998.* Washington, DC, 1999.

Department of Justice (Immigration and Naturalization Service). "Legal Immigration, Fiscal Year 1998." Washington, DC, 1999.

———. *Office of Policy and Planning Annual Report.* Washington, DC, 1999. www.ins.usdoj.gov/graphics/aboutins/statistics/index.htm.

———. 1997 *Statistical Yearbook of the Immigration and Naturalization Service.* Washington, DC, 1999. www.ins.usdoj.gov/graphics/aboutins/statistics/ybpage.htm.

Gall, Susan B., and Timothy L. Gall, eds. *Statistical Record of Asian Americans.* Detroit: Gale, 1993.

George, Rosemary Marangoly. " 'From Expatriate Aristocrat to Immigrant Nobody': South Asian Racial Strategies in the Southern California Context." *Diaspora* 6 (1997): 31–60.

Haney López, Ian F. "White by Law." In *Critical Race Theory: The Cutting Edge,* ed. Richard Delgado, pp. 542–50. Philadelphia: Temple University Press, 1995.

Helweg, Arthur, and Usha Helweg. *An Immigrant Success Story: East Indians in America.* Philadelphia: University of Pennsylvania Press, 1990.

Jensen, Joan M. *Passage from India: Asian Indian Immigrants in North America.* New Haven: Yale University Press, 1988.

Kotkin, Joel. *Tribes: How Race, Religion, and Identity Determine Success in the New Global Economy.* New York: Random House, 1993.

La Brack, Bruce. "South Asians." In *A Nation of Peoples: A Sourcebook on America's Multicultural Heritage,* ed. Elliott Robert Barkan, pp. 482–504. Westport, CT: Greenwood Press, 1999.

Lee, Sharon M. "Racial Classifications in the U.S. Census: 1890–1990." *Ethnic and Racial Studies* 16 (1993): 75–94.

Lobo, Arun Peter, and Joseph J. Salvo. "Changing U.S. Immigration Law and the Occupational Selectivity of Asian Immigrants." *International Migration Review* 32 (1998): 737–60.

Misir, Deborah N. "The Murder of Navroze Mody: Race, Violence, and the Search for Order." *Amerasia Journal* 22 (1996): 55–76.

Morning, Ann. "The Racial Self-Identification of South Asians in the United States." Manuscript.

Petersen, William. *Ethnicity Counts.* New Brunswick, NJ: Transaction, 1997.

Portes, Alejandro, and Rubén G. Rumbaut, eds. *Immigrant America: A Portrait.* Berkeley: University of California Press, 1996.

Shankar, Lavina Dhingra, and Rajini Srikanth, eds. *A Part, Yet Apart.* Philadelphia: Temple University Press, 1998.

Takaki, Ronald. *Strangers at the Gates Again: Asian American Immigration After 1965.* New York: Chelsea House, 1995.

Varadarajan, Tunku. "A Patel Motel Cartel?" *New York Times Magazine,* July 4, 1999, pp. 36–39.

SOUTHEAST ASIA

Southeast Asians are relative newcomers to American soil. No Southeast Asian countries were reported specifically in the Immigration and Naturalization Service's statistical summaries until the 1950s. During that decade only 335 persons of Vietnamese origin were specifically mentioned. Just over 4,000 Vietnamese were admitted in the 1960s. With the fall of Saigon in April 1975, the number of Vietnamese and other Southeast Asians mushroomed—most entering as refugees from Vietnam, Laos, and Cambodia, with immigrants from other countries coming through normal immigration channels. It is not fanciful to estimate that over 2 million persons from Southeast Asia and their American-born offspring now reside in the United States. Forces of war, takeovers by totalitarian dictatorships, economic deprivation, lack of opportunity, and political alliances have been key forces in this migration.

The geographic region of Southeast Asia is composed of nations that are members of the Association of Southeast Asian Nations (ASEAN), a regional alliance founded in 1967 to foster stability and economic growth. Malaysia, Thailand, Indonesia, Singapore, and the Philippines were the original members (1967); Brunei joined upon its independence in 1984; Vietnam became a member in 1995; Laos and Burma (Myanmar) joined in 1997; and Cambodia was admitted in 1999. From an immigration perspective, these countries fall into three major categories: (1) low immigrant inflows (countries with few immigrants to the United States—Brunei, Singapore, Malaysia, Indonesia, and Burma); (2) moderate immigrant inflows (Thailand); and (3) refugees (Vietnam, Laos, and Cambodia). Approximately 1.5 million Southeast Asians have been officially recorded as emigrating since 1974. Refugees make up over 90 percent of all Southeast Asian entries, and the Vietnamese alone account for two-thirds of the inflow from the region (see Table 1).

LOW IMMIGRANT INFLOW COUNTRIES

Five Southeast Asian countries—Brunei, Singapore, Malaysia, Indonesia, and Myanmar (formerly Burma)—have traditionally had small numbers of immigrants entering the United States. However, two different dynamics, namely stable or struggling economies and political isolation, can aid in understanding each country's immigrant flow.

BRUNEI

Brunei Darussalam (the country's official name) is a small, oil-rich country, slightly larger than the state of Delaware, wedged between the two Malaysian provinces of Sabah and Sarawak on the island of Borneo. Ruled by a hereditary nobility, its fifteenth- through seventeenth-century empire once ranged from all of Borneo up into the southern Philippines. In 1888, Brunei became an official British protectorate (which means it ruled its own internal affairs, while Great Britain handled foreign relations), and remained so until its peaceful independence in 1984.

Oil wealth has allowed Brunei to maintain one of the highest standards of living in the region, with a life expectancy of 74 years, a literacy rate of 90 percent, and an infant mortality rate comparable with that of the United States. In short, a stable economy and a high standard of living produce few "push" factors for Brunei citizens to leave their country. Immigration to the United States has numbered less than two dozen persons per year. The number of Bruneians in the United States is so small that the country is not listed in a recent release of foreign-born persons. Based on immigration statistics, it is reasonable to estimate that no more than 400 Bruneians currently reside in the United States.

Table 1
Immigrants Admitted to the United States from Southeast Asia by Country, 1974–1997

	1974	1975	1976	1977	1978	1979	1980	1981	1982	1983	1984	1985
Brunei	9	22	20	11	17	11	13	31	13	18	—	—
Burma	558	734	726	1,101	1,188	1,534	1,211	1,083	820	723	719	990
Cambodia	40	98	103	126	2,677	1,432	2,801	12,749	13,438	18,120	11,656	13,563
Indonesia	443	44	529	778	694	820	977	1,006	1194	952	1,113	1,269
Laos	61	96	3,603[b]	237	4,369	3,565	13,970	15,805	36,528	23,662	12,279	9,133
Malaysia	311	332	378	455	577	623	795	1,033	1,046	852	879	939
Singapore	176	203	220	308	320	321	322	408	390	362	377	460
Thailand	4,956	4,217[a]	6,923	3,945	3,574	3,194	4,115	4,799	5,568	5,875	4,885	5,239
Vietnam	3,192	133,433[a]	14,048[c]	6,512[d]	88,543	22,546	43,485	55,631	72,553	37,560	37,236	31,895
Total	9,746	139,179	26,550	6,961	101,959	34,046	67,689	92,545	131,550	88,124	69,144	63,488

	1986	1987	1988	1989	1990	1991	1992	1993	1994	1995	1996	1997	Total
Brunei	29	12	12	16	16	15	17	26	14	14	20	—	356
Burma	863	941	803	1,170	1,120	946	816	849	938	1,233	1,320	1,081	23,467
Cambodia	13,501	12,460	9,629	6,076	5,179	3,251	2,573	1,639	1,404	1,492	1,568	1,683	137,258
Indonesia	1,183	1254	1,342	1,513	3,498	2,223	2,916	1,767	1,367	1,020	1,084	906	29,892
Laos	7,842	6,828	10,667	12,524	10,446	9,950	8,696	7,285	5,089	3,936	2,847	1,935	207,593
Malaysia	886	1,016	1,250	1,506	1,867	1,860	2,235	2,026	1,480	1,223	1,414	1,051	26,034
Singapore	480	469	492	566	620	535	77	3,798	542	399	561	—	12,406
Thailand	6,204	6,733	6,888	9,332	8,914	7,397	7,090	6,654	5,489	5,136	4,310	3,094	134,531
Vietnam	29,993	24,231	25,789	37,739	48,792	55,307	77,735	59,614	41,345	41,752	42,067	38,519	1,069,517
Total	60,981	53,944	56,872	70,442	80,452	81,484	102,155	83,658	57,668	56,205	55,191	41,613	1,483,869

Sources: Immigration and Naturalization Service, *Statistical Yearbook of the Immigration and Naturalization Service, 1983–97* (Washington, DC: Government Printing Office, 1984–98); Paul James Rutledge, *The Vietnamese Experience in America* (Bloomington: Indiana University Press, 1992).

a Includes refugees resettled under the Special Parole Program of 1975 and the Humanitarian Parole Program of 1975; includes ethnic Lao, Hmong, and Cambodians.
b Includes refugees resettled under the Special Lao Program of 1976.
c Includes refugees resettled under the Expanded Parole Program of 1976; includes refugees from several countries.
d Includes refugees resettled under "Boat Cases" Program as of August 1, 1977.

SINGAPORE

The Republic of Singapore (once a British colony) is an island city-state and the most commercialized economy in Southeast Asia. One of the most densely populated countries of the world, its citizens have an average life expectancy of 75 years (male) and 79 years (female), with an infant mortality rate lower than that of the United States. In spite of the Asian economic crisis in the late 1990s, it continues to attract investments from more than three thousand multinational corporations and enjoys virtually full employment.

Citizenship is highly protected, and foreigners wishing to give birth in Singapore must go through an extensive screening process and renounce rights of Singaporean citizenship. Hence, very few seek to leave the thriving economy and a government that is committed to cooperation between management, labor, and government. Immigration to the United States has averaged just over 500 persons per year over the last two and a half decades, and the census reported 12,889 Singaporeans residing in the United States in 1990.

MALAYSIA

Unlike Brunei and Singapore, the other Southeast Asian countries with low immigrant flow to the United States experience struggling economies. Malaysia is a multiethnic Muslim nation with uneven population distribution spread over the Malay Peninsula and the northern part of the island of Borneo, with a high birth rate and over one-third of its population under fifteen years of age. The country has experienced rule by Portugal, Britain, and Japan (which occupied it during World War II) and confrontation with Indonesia until 1966. In addition, communist guerrillas operated in northern Malaysia until signing a peace agreement in 1989, and a small-scale communist insurgency plagued the province of Sarawak in northern Borneo until a peace accord was signed in October 1990. Malaysia suffered from the Asian economic crisis in 1997–98 but is showing signs of recovery. The United States is Malaysia's largest trading partner.

Despite an economy on the upswing, much poverty exists in Malaysia. Emigration is also tightly controlled. One area of outflow of Malaysians is that of college students. With about fourteen thousand Malaysians studying at American universities, it has one of the largest foreign student populations in the United States. Some of these students end up staying legally in the United States after graduation. Since the 1980s, Malaysian immigrants have been admitted at the rate of 1,000 to 2,000 per year. In 1996, approximately half of these were granted residence due to relatives' sponsorship. Over 40 percent were allowed entry under employment provisions. There were an estimated 33,834 persons of Malaysian origin living in the United States in 1990.

INDONESIA

Although Indonesia has over nine times the population of Malaysia (201 million, making it the fourth largest nation in the world), its immigration rates to the United States are essentially the same. Spread out over 13,000 islands with over 300 languages, Indonesia has a lower life expectancy and higher infant mortality rate (ten times that of Brunei, over six times that of Malaysia) than the other nations discussed above. A Dutch possession for 300 years, Indonesia provided a rich source of spices and other natural resources for the colonial traders. Japanese occupation during World War II stifled the Netherlands's control of the islands and gave birth to an independence movement, which succeeded after only a brief struggle in 1945.

Since then, Indonesia's political and economic condition has been precarious and has included an attempted communist coup in 1965, followed by a strictly controlled, semidemocratic state run essentially by the military. The country's external public sector debt is in the range of $70 billion, while private external debt is over $80 billion. Per capita income in 1998 was estimated at only $448 (compared with Malaysia's $3,272). This means that most Indonesians are too poor to even consider the expensive proposition of emigration to the United States. The government strictly controls exit visas.

Slightly more than 48,000 Indonesians resided in the United States in 1990. In 1996, the majority of immigrants (64 percent) were admitted under provisions of family preference (they had sponsoring relatives in the United States). In 1996, only 20 percent of all Indonesians entered under employment provisions. A small number of Indonesian students study in American institutions of higher education.

BURMA

Burma, renamed Myanmar in 1989 (which is an English spelling of the country's official name; the United States and many other governments still use "Burma" as the country's name), has been one of the least accessible countries in Southeast Asia. Foreign journalists and visitors were banned from the country between 1989 and 1990. The policies of this tightly structured socialist state, controlled almost exclusively by the military, has sent the country's economy into a downward spiral. For example, Myanmar's proportion of the world's rice trade dropped from a former high of 28 percent to only 2 percent by 1970. In 1987, the United Nations declared Myanmar one of the world's least developed nations, along with Chad and Ethiopia in Africa and Bangladesh and Nepal in South Asia.

Repeatedly since its independence from Britain in 1948, oppressive measures have been used against dissidents, students, and minority groups throughout the country. The State Department characterizes Myanmar's government as a highly authoritarian regime and in 1998 had "decertified" Myanmar as an ally in the war on drugs for the seventh consecutive year. Myanmar is the principal source of heroin that reaches American streets, and drug money props up the current regime financially.

Estimates are that up to 80 percent of Myanmar's economy is connected to the drug trade and "black market" products, which provide jobs and an economic safety valve for the country and help avert outright armed revolution. The increasing use of drugs has led to a serious Acquired Immunodeficiency Syndrome (AIDS) epidemic in the country. Drug use is reported high among university students, and some reports indicate that as many as 200 people share the same needle. Though the United States has put some punitive measures in place in response to human rights violations (such as restrictions on the import of Myanmar textiles to the United States and the banning of new investments), total sanctions are avoided, as the United States continues to seek cooperation with Myanmar on the issue of drug control policy and interdiction.

In a dramatic staging of civil pressure, an election in 1990 resulted in the pro-democracy party, the National League for Democracy (spearheaded by Aung San Suu Kyi, daughter of Aung San, the independence war hero and first democratically elected official who was assassinated in 1947), winning 392 of 485 seats in the Myanmar parliament. The military government in power immediately annulled the election results and put Suu Kyi under house arrest, where she remained through 1998. In May 1999, Suu Kyi delivered the commencement address at Bucknell University in Pennsylvania, continuing to gather U.S. support for a free Myanmar.

Despite poor economic conditions, continued repressive measures by the government, and restrictions on emigration, a small number of people from Myanmar—roughly 1,000 each year—make their way to the United States. In 1996, three-quarters of these persons came in under immigration provisions that allow for family reunification. Over 100 refugees were admitted that year. Increasing support for Myanmar by the United States could result in an increase in the number of immigrants from Myanmar. There were just under 20,000 Myanmar residents in the United States counted in 1990.

MODERATE IMMIGRANT INFLOW COUNTRIES

THAILAND

Thailand became a unified kingdom in 1350, and unlike all other Southeast Asian nations, it was never colonized and has remained independent throughout its history. The Thai nation never developed an "inferiority complex" in regard to the West, nor did it outright reject Western ways, resulting in more flexibility and adaptability economically. As a result, Thailand has produced a vibrant regional and global economy, including close ties with the United States and other Western nations. The country has successfully managed to slow its population growth, which has also added to its economic stability. Thailand is also experiencing growing democratization.

Part of the explanation for the relatively higher number of Thai immigrants to the United States can be found in Thailand's long-standing political and military relationship with the United States. An original signatory of the Manila Pact, which formed the Southeast Asia Treaty Organization (the military alliance which bound several countries in the struggle against communist expansion in the region and which dissolved in 1977), Thailand maintains close military ties with the United States. The Thai Air Force has participated in joint military exercises not only with the United States but also with Australia, Japan, the Philippines, and South Korea. Thailand was a key staging area for the United States during the Vietnam War.

The United States is also Thailand's largest trading partner, accounting for 20 percent of its exports. The Thai government cooperates extensively with the United States and the United Nations to control drug trafficking through the Golden Triangle, where Burma, Laos, and Thailand intersect. These factors, along with the presence of the American military in Thailand and extensive tourism by Westerners, as exemplified in the motion picture *The Beach* (2000), have created some "pull" factors toward the United States. Annual immigration ranged from a low of 3,194 persons in 1979 to a peak of 9,332 entries in 1989. Immigrant flows have slowed each year through the 1990s, with 4,310 Thai immigrants reported for 1996. Forty-five percent of those immigrants entered under family preferences, while just less than half entered as refugees. Because of Thailand's geographic location between the war-torn countries of Cambodia, Laos, and Vietnam on the east and troubled Burma on the west, numerous refugee camps accommodating many different Southeast Asian nationalities and minorities have been in place for several decades. This "intermediate position" accounts for some of the refugee flow from this country.

As of 1990, Thai immigrants follow a typical pattern of settling in large metropolitan areas. One-third of all Thai immigrants (30,500) live in California, and one in four (23,300) have settled in the Los Angeles-Orange-Riverside-San Bernardino County metropolitan area. Eight percent (7,400) have settled in the vicinity of New York City, while about 4,600 (5 percent) have made the Chicago metropolitan area their home. Washington, D.C., is home to over 4,300 Thais (see Table 2). Despite the fact that there are large clusters on the West Coast and in metropolitan areas, Thai immigrants are more evenly dispersed throughout the United States than any of the other major Southeast Asian groups, with families living in every single state. The popularity of Thai cuisine in the 1990s is raising the awareness of many Americans to these newcomers.

Taking into consideration the 91,000 Thai residents reported in the 1990 census, the 35,000 recorded immigrants from 1991 to 1996, and continued immigration and U.S. births, it is not unreasonable to estimate that over 160,000 persons of Thai origin reside in the United States in the year 2000. Steady inflows of 3,000 to 4,000 people a year can be expected.

SOUTHEAST ASIAN REFUGEES

Without question, the largest impact of immigrants from Southeast Asia has been made by the Vietnamese, Cambodians, and Laotians who fled their homelands for fear of their life and future following U.S. involvement in Vietnam and the fall of Saigon in April 1975. Numerically, almost 1 million persons from these three countries were counted in the 1990 census (which is probably an undercount). They make up over 14 percent of all Asians living in the United States, 42 percent of all Southeast Asians (including Filipinos), and 80 percent of all Southeast Asians from the countries discussed in this entry. This national trio

accounts for 85 percent of all Southeast Asian immigration between the years 1974 and 1996, with Vietnamese refugees and immigrants alone being responsible for over two-thirds of the Southeast Asian total.

VIETNAM

The first sojourners from Vietnam were students who came to study in the United States immediately following World War II. This period also saw the arrival of some Catholic priests to assist primarily the Vietnamese student population. In addition, some civilians and military personnel from the newly demarcated territory of South Vietnam came for short periods of time for training. Many of these early visitors would flee their home decades later, reconnecting with persons and places of these initial experiences. Most of these immigrants stayed a few months to a few years and then returned to Vietnam. Only 335 persons from Vietnam were recorded as immigrants in the 1950s.

With American involvement in Vietnam, the numbers of Vietnamese relocating to the United States increased, many as "war brides." These women were placed in a precarious position socially. They were often not fully accepted by their new American neighbors, being perceived as "the enemy" or derisively called "gooks" as the war in Southeast Asia was heating up and many of the Americans' family members and friends were being drafted to fight in this confusing and brutal conflict. At the same time, other Vietnamese, including some of their relatives, saw these women as weak or disloyal for taking the "easy way out" of Vietnam. Their initial experience somewhat paralleled the experience of Korean war brides, but this alienation would intensify with the first wave of refugees. The presence of students, priests, civilian and military personnel, and war brides was hardly noted by the American populace. Less than 3,500 Vietnamese were present in the United States before May 1975.

For many Vietnamese, the flight to the United States was not their first refugee experience. Eight hundred and fifty thousand northerners sought to escape the fledgling Communist regime in Hanoi and other cities by heading south when Vietnam was partitioned in 1954. That year, Nguyen Thut Thanh (better known as Ho Chi Minh) helped defeat the French, who had occupied Vietnam as well as Laos and Cambodia since the mid-nineteenth century. Many European elements entered Vietnamese culture during this century of occupation, blending with a complex mix of Chinese traditional beliefs and indigenous language and values. The Vietnamese people have al-

Table 2
Residence of Selected Southeast Asian Groups by Metropolitan Area, 1990

Metropolitan Area	Population	Percentage[a]	Metropolitan Area	Population	Percentage[a]
Southeast Asians (Vietnamese, Cambodian, Laotian, Hmong, Thai)			**Vietnamese**		
1990 Population—1,075,434			*1990 Population—593,213*		
Los Angeles, CA[b]	214,975	20.0	Los Angeles, CA[b]	145,464	24.5
San Francisco, CA[b]	110,945	10.3	San Francisco, CA[b]	84,981	14.3
Central Valley, CA[c]	106,341	9.9	Houston, TX[b]	32,964	5.6
Houston, TX[b]	38,903	3.6	Washington, D.C.	23,484	4.0
San Diego, CA	35,248	3.3	Central Valley, CA[c]	20,986	3.5
Washington, D.C.	34,289	3.2	San Diego, CA	20,561	3.5
Minneapolis-St. Paul, MN-WI	33,272	3.1	Dallas-Fort Worth, TX[b]	19,095	3.2
Dallas-Ft. Worth, TX[b]	30,323	2.8	New York, NY-NJ-CT[b]	15,766	2.7
Seattle-Tacoma, WA[b]	29,922	2.8	Seattle-Tacoma, WA[b]	14,210	2.4
New York, NY-NJ-CT[b]	28,596	2.7	Boston, MA[b]	11,117	1.9
Boston, MA[b]	27,073	2.5	New Orleans, LA	10,842	1.8
Chicago, IL-IN-WI[b]	17,848	1.7	Philadelphia, PA-NJ-DE-MD[b]	9,894	1.7
Philadephia, PA-DE-NJ-MD[b]	17,117	1.6	Minneapolis-St. Paul, MN-WI	8,107	1.4
Portland, OR[b]	13,916	1.3	Portland, OR[b]	7,599	1.3
New Orleans, LA	11,253	1.0	Chicago, IL-IN-WI[b]	7,259	1.2
Cambodian			**Laotian**		
1990 Population—149,047			*1990 Population—147,375*		
Central Valley, CA[c]	18,727	12.6	Central Valley, CA[d]	28,170	19.1
Boston, MA[b]	11,966	8.0	San Francisco, CA[b]	10,502	7.1
San Francisco, CA[b]	11,595	7.8	Los Angeles, CA[b]	8,790	6.0
Seattle-Tacoma, WA[b]	9,056	6.1	San Diego, CA	7,159	4.9
Philadelphia, PA-NJ-DE-MD[b]	4,844	3.2	Dallas-Fort Worth, TX[b]	5,611	3.8
Providence, RI[b]	4,623	3.1	Minneapolis-St. Paul, MN-WI	5,214	3.5
San Diego, CA	4,404	3.0	Seattle-Tacoma, WA[b]	4,441	3.0
Washington, DC[b]	4,136	2.8	Chicago, IL-IN-WI[b]	3,216	2.2
New York, NY-NJ-CT[b]	3,412	2.3	Portland, OR[b]	2,971	2.0
Dallas-Fort Worth, TX[b]	3,027	2.0	Atlanta, GA	2,917	2.0
Houston, TX[b]	2,895	1.9	Boston, MA[b]	2,819	1.9
Chicago, IL-IN-WI[b]	2,405	1.6	Washington, D.C.	2,318	1.6
Minneapolis-St. Paul, MN-WI	2,228	1.5	Milwaukee-Racine, WI[b]	2,311	1.6
Portland, OR[b]	2,187	1.5	Nashville, TN	2,288	1.6
Atlanta, GA	1,701	1.1	Providence, RI[b]	2,249	1.5
Hmong			**Thai**		
1990 Population—94,439			*1990 Population—91,360*		
Central Valley, CA[d]	39,800	42.1	Los Angeles, CA[b]	23,305	25.5
Minneapolis-St. Paul, MN-WI	17,317	18.3	New York, NY-NJ-CT[b]	7,423	8.1
Milwaukee-Racine, WI[b]	3,713	3.9	Chicago, IL-IN-WI[b]	4,599	5.0
Yuba City, CA	2,611	2.8	Washington, D.C.	4,344	4.8
San Diego, CA	2,035	2.2	San Francisco, CA[b]	3,779	4.1
La Crosse, WI	2,022	2.1	Dallas-Fort Worth, TX[b]	2,500	2.7
Appleton-Oshkosh, WI	2,014	2.1	Seattle-Tacoma, WA[b]	1,859	2.0
Wausau, WI	1,986	2.1	Houston, TX[b]	1,542	1.7
Detroit, MI[b]	1,691	1.8	Las Vegas, NV	1,528	1.7
Green Bay, WI	1,678	1.8	Boston, MA[b]	1,171	1.3

Table 2
Residence of Selected Southeast Asian Groups by Metropolitan Area, 1990 (continued)

Metropolitan Area	Population	Percentage[a]	Metropolitan Area	Population	Percentage[a]
Hmong (continued)			**Thai** (continued)		
Eau Claire, WI	1,661	1.8	Honolulu, HI	1,113	1.2
Los Angeles, CA[b]	1,562	1.7	San Diego, CA	1,089	1.2
Chico, CA	1,232	1.3	Miami, FL	1,080	1.2
Denver, CO[b]	1,207	1.3	Sacramento, CA	985	1.1
Providence, RI[b]	1,185	1.3	Tampa-St. Petersburg, FL	969	1.1

Source: Bureau of the Census. *Statistical Abstract of the United States.* Washington, DC: Bureau of the Census, 1990.
[a] Percentage of group living in the given geographic area.
[b] Combined metropolitan statistical areas.
[c] Includes Sacramento, Stockton, Merced, and Fresno metropolitan areas.
[d] Includes Sacramento, Stockton, Merced, Fresno, and Visalia-Tulare-Porterville metropolitan areas.

ways retained a strong sense of nationalism, having an identity apart from the Chinese as early as 111 B.C., and they date the birth of their country back to A.D. 939, the year they shed Chinese occupation. This historic sense of identity helped them defeat the French but also enabled them to wage an internal war that would propel the exodus of millions.

Longing for one Vietnam, the Communists of the north were convinced that a socialist state was the wave of Vietnam's future. Figuring that the government of nationalist prime minister Ngo Dinh Diem in the south would collapse under the pressure of a fragile, unstable economy and the weight of over three-quarters of a million refugees from the north, the Communists were poised to take over the entire country. However, the Diem government was able to consolidate various factions in the south and enlist U.S. military and economic aid. Ho Chi Minh then activated cadres of Communists who remained in the south—the Viet Cong—to attempt to destabilize and derail progress there. The United States stepped up military aid to South Vietnam when in December 1961 President John F. Kennedy sent military advisers to help the army deal with the increasing insurgence by the Viet Cong and aggression from the north. In 1964, President Lyndon Johnson sent soldiers to protect U.S. bases in Vietnam, and in 1965, he committed 125,000 troops to the region. By 1969, the United States had reached the height of its military presence at over 500,000 soldiers.

To bring the conflict to a swift end, the United States began bombing North Vietnam in 1965. Peace talks between the United States, North Vietnam, and other interests began in May 1968. The bombing of North Vietnam was halted on November 1 of that year, and the United States began a slow troop withdrawal, giving the South Vietnamese a larger role in their own defense, interpreting Hanoi's presence at the slow-moving peace talks as a sign of good faith. The United States continued to provide air support for Vietnamese troops until the peace agreement was signed in January 1973.

While feigning peace, North Vietnam continued to send massive amounts of equipment and personnel into South Vietnam. In 1975, with American troops gone and insurgents well armed, the North Vietnamese army mounted a major campaign and pushed into South Vietnam.

On April 29, 1975, the Communist Army marched into Saigon, South Vietnam's capital. All feared that the northern army would take captive, torture, imprison, or execute all remaining Americans in the Saigon embassy and any Vietnamese who had ties with the United States, the South Vietnamese government, or the military. (This fear was founded: While 58,000 Americans perished in Vietnam, over 1.5 million Vietnamese lost their life in the conflict, and another 3 million eventually fled for their life.) For weeks prior to Saigon's capture, an exodus took place, with over 50,000 Americans and Vietnamese leaving the city. The fast pace of the North Vietnamese army required what was to be the largest helicopter evacuation in history—seventy helicopters airlifted 1,000 Americans and 5,000 Vietnamese from the embassy complex. Those who were not airlifted and had resources escaped by any means possible. Officers in the Vietnamese navy loaded up their ships with evacuees and "stole" their own vessels. Others rushed to rivers and beaches, searching for any seaworthy vessel they could find. Still others tried to escape overland, through Cambodia to Thailand.

Those who were airlifted were initially taken to Clark Air Force Base and Subic Bay Naval Station in the Philippines, then on to Guam for processing.

Since their mass exodus from Southeast Asia following the Vietnam War in the late 1970s and 1980s, immigrants from Vietnam, Cambodia, and Laos have settled all over the United States, including Lowell, Massachusetts. *(Kenneth Martin/Impact Visuals)*

Many were picked up at sea during the next few weeks and transported to holding camps in the Philippines. France, Canada, and other nations agreed to accept refugees as well, and some Vietnamese immigrated to those countries. This "first wave" of refugees to the United States were initially transported to four military sites set up for processing the newcomers: Camp Pendleton, California; Fort Indiantown Gap, Pennsylvania; Fort Chaffee, Arkansas; and Fort Eglin, Florida. By the end of 1975, more than 130,000 refugees had been processed, more than four times the number anticipated. This partially accounts for why California, Pennsylvania, Florida, Texas, and Louisiana (the last, a neighbor of Arkansas) are five of the top eight locations where the highest concentrations of Vietnamese are found. By 1990, the United States had accepted over half of all refugees who had fled Indochina—Vietnam, Laos, and Cambodia.

In 1975, the United States had no uniform policy for refugees, so the Vietnamese were granted admission through the parole powers given to the U.S. attorney general. The Southeast Asian refugee situation, and especially the boat people crisis beginning in 1978, pushed the U.S. government to formalize policy in the Refugee Act of 1980.

The Office of Refugee Resettlement (ORR) was hastily formed under the Department of Health, Education, and Welfare to oversee the mammoth task of integrating the Vietnamese into American society. The strategy was to find sponsors, who could be either individuals or organizations, to take responsibility for the incoming refugees. The policy was to try to spread the resettlement of the Vietnamese over as many locales as possible, so no one city or state would have to carry the financial burdens of resettlement. Most Vietnamese entered with little or no wealth at all, due primarily to their hasty exits. There was no conscious effort to keep extended families, villages, or friends together. This strategy was minimally successful. Some of the Vietnamese engaged in "secondary migration" as soon as they were financially able and joined larger Vietnamese communities rather than live in isolation. Some used contacts with Americans they had befriended in Vietnam to help them with resettlement. Most of the first wave of Vietnamese refugees were relatively educated and urban and ended up in major cities. Three years of financial support was extended to refugees, including opportunities to study English and take vocational training courses.

The restructuring of Vietnamese society by the new Communist government precipitated the "second wave" of Vietnamese, the so-called boat people. Ethnic Chinese, merchants and businesspeople who had lived in Vietnam for generations, held an inordinate amount of wealth in comparison with the general Vietnamese population. Border disputes with China were also heating up, so the government resettled many urban Chinese Vietnamese to farms and pressured, sometimes even assisted—that is, forced— these Vietnamese citizens to "escape." Between 1978 and 1982, 12,000 ethnic Chinese and Vietnamese left their homeland each month, many by small boat. According to some estimates, pirates attacked as many as 70 percent of these boats. Many refugees were robbed, raped, and sometimes murdered. Boats often capsized or were destroyed. The experiences of living under the Communist regime, the traumatic nature of their departures and journeys, their ethnic makeup, and the fact that this group of Vietnamese was generally poorer and possessed fewer skills and American contacts than the first wave made them unique (see Table 3). Very soon, Americans—even the well-meaning not-for-profit organizations—began to "burn out" at what seemed an endless flow of refugees. Governmental monetary assistance to refugees was incrementally cut from a duration of three years for 1975 arrivals to only eight months for those arriving in 1991.

To encourage the Vietnamese and other refugee groups to take charge of their own affairs and build supportive communities, the ORR provided guidelines for these groups to establish their own organizations. Officially known as Mutual Assistance Associations (MAAs, though most groups renamed their organizations), these organizations became conduits for certain types of funding. In many cases, these entities indeed provided a minimal amount of money for community events and aid to group members. However, MAAs were controlled by early arrivals and exhibited a bias toward those of higher social classes and more prestige. In at least one city, a decision was made by a few not to form such an organization for the benefit of the community—an action that has caused some tension among the Vietnamese in the area.

Vietnamese refugees entered a somewhat hostile American climate. Though many church groups and not-for-profit organizations worked diligently to find places for Vietnamese families, a Gallup poll indicated that 54 percent of the American public opposed resettlement, and a Harris survey found that only 36 percent of Americans thought Indochinese refugees should be allowed to enter the country. Conflicts between Vietnamese and other groups have occasionally been reported over the past two decades. These included altercations between Vietnamese and Anglo-American shrimp fishermen on the Gulf Coast, violent acts by the Ku Klux Klan, Vietnamese residents being chased from a Denver housing project by Hispanics with bricks and bottles, and beatings of Vietnamese youth.

Under pressure from the United States (along with several other countries and international organizations) for relief from the massive exodus of boat people, the Vietnamese agreed in 1979 to the Orderly Departure Program for emigrants. Shortly thereafter a Humanitarian Order to release certain Vietnamese prisoners and detainees who had former ties with the United States was instituted, as well as a program to allow Amerasians, or mixed-race Vietnamese children whose fathers were purportedly American, to come to this country. These "half-breeds" were often rejected by Vietnamese society and ended up on the streets in many cases. Emigrants under these programs do not go through the horrors of escape that the first and second waves experienced and are sometimes looked down upon by the earlier waves of refugees after they arrive in the United States.

Another component of the third and ongoing wave of Vietnamese is immigration provisions for family reunification. The nature of refugee departures left numerous families fragmented, many of whom seek now to be reunited. About 25 percent of all 1996 immigrants from Vietnam were admitted under family preference provisions, yet even more than twenty years after the initial wave of refugees from that country, 70 percent were still admitted as refugees. Inflows are slowly declining but remained at over 40,000 in 1997.

Determining exactly how many Vietnamese are currently in the United States is somewhat problematic. Figures from the Office of Refugee Resettlement, the Immigration and Naturalization Service (INS), and the Census Bureau do not agree. This is because "Vietnamese" is a term that can refer either to ethnicity, nationality, or residence. For instance, a Vietnamese person of Chinese descent might mark "Chinese" on the census form but have been a Vietnamese citizen. And there are Vietnamese who were living across the border in Cambodia or Laos who may have been counted in that country's statistic, even though they are ethnically Vietnamese. The 1990 census counted 593,213 Vietnamese in the United States at that time. The total number that the INS admitted to the United States from 1974 to 1996 was 887,721. Assuming 1997–99 flows reflected 1994–96 flows (averaging about 40,000) and figuring in new births, it can be estimated that the Vietnamese population in the year 2000 is slightly more than 1 million.

The Vietnamese, more than any other Southeast Asian group, has gravitated toward selected states and large U.S. cities. Almost half (46.7 percent) had settled in California by 1990: One in five Vietnamese in the United States live in the greater Los Angeles area; one in ten live in the San Francisco Bay area; and one in ten live in several adjacent counties and metropolitan areas in California's Central Valley (Sacramento, Stockton, and Fresno, in that order). "Little Saigon" in the Westminster–Garden Grove area of Southern California is the largest Vietnamese business concentration in the United States, and 850 businesses in the Los Angeles area have banded together to form the Vietnamese Chamber of Commerce.

Houston had almost forty thousand Vietnamese residents, and sizable populations can be found in San Diego, Washington, D.C., Minneapolis-St. Paul, Dallas-Fort Worth, Seattle, New York, and Boston. Southeast Asians, with the aid of money from the new Chinese immigrant community, have revitalized Argyle Street between Broadway and Sheridan into the "New Asia" district in Chicago, where large crowds of Indochinese flock from all over the Midwest to shop on the weekend.

Religion has played an important role in the settlement of the Vietnamese in America. While only about 10 percent of the population in Vietnam were Roman Catholic, half the Vietnamese refugees in the United States confess allegiance to the Catholic Church. The other half are predominantly Buddhist of Vietnamese Mahayana or Zen traditions. Most of the larger cities have a Catholic church with at least one Vietnamese priest. This venue provides an environment in which Vietnamese youth can be raised in the context of their cultural community and can often find mates that meet with the approval of their parents. The Vietnamese have their own Catholic seminary in Carthage, Missouri; every August, over 10,000 Vietnamese overwhelm this small town for a ritual procession in honor of the Virgin Mary. This connects, on an annual basis, Vietnamese community leaders from across the country.

The Vietnamese have been cited as a "model minority." In many respects, their adjustment and achievements have been remarkable. It is not an un-common practice for Vietnamese family members to all work and pool their resources to send one member to university or professional school full-time. Upon graduation, that person would enter his or her career (many in engineering, medicine, dentistry, and even law) and continue pooling money to send others, until all the children in the family had completed their education. Children of Vietnamese refugees are often highlighted as valedictorians of their high school classes. The Vietnamese clearly display greater gains in all socioeconomic measures as compared with other Southeast Asian refugee groups (see Table 3).

However, this "model minority" stereotype is flawed. The Vietnamese population seems to be bifurcating, that is, breaking into two parts—those who are "making it" and those who are not. Vietnamese gangs in major urban areas have reputations of being particularly brutal, and many Vietnamese still struggle with speaking English and holding down a living-wage job. Assimilation and adjustment among the Vietnamese does not occur evenly throughout the population or at the same rate. Stereotypes and overgeneralizations are unwarranted.

CAMBODIA

The Oscar Award–winning motion picture *The Killing Fields* (1984) has perhaps most dramatically portrayed the plight of Cambodian refugees under the ruthless regime of Pol Pot and the Communist Khmer Rouge takeover of Cambodia shortly after the fall of Saigon in 1975. By the time of the film's release, over 50,000 Cambodian refugees had already resettled in the United States.

A French protectorate since 1863, Cambodia did not receive its full independence until ninety years later. The country attempted to remain neutral in the 1950s and 1960s but found the North Vietnamese army and Viet Cong establishing bases inside its border with South Vietnam, which set the stage for a growing antipathy between the two nations. The United States began bombing bases inside Cambodia in 1969, thus complicating the domestic political struggle between rightist and leftist elements.

Following several interim governments, the Khmer Republic (one of Cambodia's frequent name changes) was established. The United States supported the new government against both the North Vietnamese and the Communist Khmer Rouge ("Red Khmer"—Khmer is the designation of the major ethnic group that makes up Cambodia). This latter faction, supported militarily by North Vietnam, continued to gain strength. By 1973, the Khmer Rouge controlled 60 percent of Cambodia (but only 25 per-

Table 3
Selected Social and Economic Characteristics of Southeast Asian Refugee Groups, 1980 and 1990

	Total U.S.		Vietnamese		Cambodian	Laotian	Hmong
	1980	1990	1980	1990	1990	1990	1990
Total Persons	226,545,805	248,908,873	261,729	593,213	149,047	147,375	94,439
Foreign-born	6.2	7.9	90.5	79.9	79.1	79.4	65.2
Median age	30.0	33.0	21.2	25.6	19.7	20.5	12.7
Fertility per female 35–44 years of age	2.6	2.0	2.7	2.5	3.4	3.5	6.1
% Female householder	18.9	16.0	14.2	15.9	25.4	11.3	13.6
% Not speaking English "very well"	4.8	6.1	45.5	60.8	70.0	67.8	76.1
% < High school diploma (over 25 years old)	33.5	24.8	35.8	38.8	65.1	60.0	68.9
% In labor force	62.0	65.3	66.6	64.5	46.5	58.0	29.3
% White collar	53.0	58.1	45.6	47.1	33.1	20.2	31.7
Median family income	$19,917	$35,225	$12,840	$30,550	$18,126	$23,101	$14,327
% Below poverty level	12.4	13.1	16.8	25.7	42.6	34.7	63.6
% Receiving public assistance	8.0	7.5	28.1	24.5	51.1	35.4	67.1
% Owning home	65.6	64.2	27.2	40.1	19.7	24.0	11.1

Sources: Barrington, Herbert R., Robert W. Gardner, and Michael J. Levin. *Asians and Pacific Islanders in the United States.* New York: Russell Sage Foundation, 1993; Min, Pyong Gap, ed. *Asian Americans: Contemporary Trends and Issues.* Thousand Oaks, CA: Sage Publications, 1995; Bureau of the Census. *Statistical Abstract of the United States.* Washington, DC: Bureau of the Census, 1980, 1990.

cent of its population). However, over 2 million villagers from the countryside sought refuge in the capital, Phnom Penh. On New Year's Day 1975, the Khmer Rouge forces launched an offensive toward the capital city and in four months—just two weeks before the fall of Saigon—had taken control of the country and renamed it the Democratic Republic of Kampuchea. Their leader, Pol Pot, then began to "restructure" Cambodian society, amassing one of the worst human rights records of any nation in history. An estimated 1 to 3 million Cambodians were killed in this civil war.

Though communist in orientation and formerly supported by North Vietnam, the Khmer Rouge regime was staunchly anti-Vietnamese. China backed Kampuchea, whereas the Soviet Union backed Vietnam. Border skirmishes escalated, and in 1978 Vietnam invaded Kampuchea to "liberate" it, establishing the People's Republic of Kampuchea. Six hundred thousand Cambodians fled westward toward Thailand as the Vietnamese army approached, holding up in refugee camps on either side of the Thai border. It was not until thirteen years later, in 1991, that the United Nations would supervise a cease-fire between insurgent Cambodians and the Vietnamese, oversee Vietnam's withdrawal, and attempt the repatriation of

Cambodians in Thai refugee camps. The country's name reverted back to Cambodia.

This complex and bloody history has led to several waves of Cambodians seeking refuge in other countries. The largest influx of Cambodians to the United States followed Vietnam's invasion, producing a flow of an average of 20,000 refugees a year between 1980 and 1985. In 1990, 149,047 persons from Cambodia (these include some persons of Hmong, Laotian, and Vietnamese ethnicity) were reported living in the United States—over six times the U.S. Cambodian population of 20,175 counted in 1980.

Cambodians are among the most dispersed of all Southeast Asian immigrant groups. About one in five Cambodians have settled in the Central Valley and San Francisco areas of California. However, outside of California, Boston boasts the largest population of Cambodians—almost 12,000. Thirty thousand Cambodians reside on the East Coast in the "Bos-Wash" (Boston-to-Washington) corridor, with sizable populations in Washington, D.C., Philadelphia, New York City–New Jersey area, Connecticut, and Providence, Rhode Island. Cambodians, Laotians, Hmong, and Vietnamese are culturally and linguistically distinct and tend not to interact extensively with one another, forming their own communities. Settlement patterns for Vietnamese and Thais are similar, and Laotians and Hmong tend to share the same spaces. Cambodians, while also favoring the West Coast, have carved out niches for themselves in all regions of the United States.

Socially and economically, Cambodians resemble the Hmong in terms of social characteristics: young population, low command of English, low levels of income, high rates of poverty and welfare dependency (over 50 percent), and the highest incidence of female heads of household. On the other hand, they have greater workforce participation and lower birth rates than their Hmong counterparts. Though initially disadvantaged, prospects for second-generation Cambodians appear hopeful.

LAOS

The long, narrow country of Laos shares its eastern border with Vietnam in a way that spans both the North and the South, which ultimately involved Laos in the Vietnam conflict. This nation of 5 million people has been at war virtually the entire twentieth century, first under Thai rule, then French, Japanese, and again French occupation. Its 1962 independence resulted in a civil war between communist, neutralist, and rightist groups. With the fall of Saigon to the Vietnamese Communists in 1975 and the fall of Phnom Penh in Cambodia to the Communists the same year, the Lao People's Revolutionary Party gained momentum and in December established a socialist state in that country. The new government's harsh and totalitarian policies and its already poor and declining economy sent over 10 percent of Laos's population into Thailand as refugees. The United States resettled over 250,000 Laotians between 1975 and 1996.

Two major groups have emigrated from Laos and are categorized separately in the U.S. census—Laotians and Hmong (the Mien people, another Laotian group, are similar to the Hmong). There are several reasons for this distinction. The Hmong are a unique ethnic group—people from an agricultural tribal society with no written language until the mid-twentieth century—who inhabited the highlands along with border of Vietnam, through which the Ho Chi Minh trail ran (which the North Vietnamese used to supply the Viet Cong in the South). The U.S. Agency for International Development and the Central Intelligence Agency enlisted leaders of Hmong villages to recruit their young men to fight on behalf of the Americans, in an attempt to interrupt supply lines. Hmong immigrants have reported that virtually every able-bodied Hmong male was pressed into service. About fifteen thousand Hmong were killed in

Many Southeast Asian immigrants, including this elderly Laotian refugee in Oakland, California, have found the cultural adjustment to life in America difficult. *(Lonny Shavelson/Impact Visuals)*

combat, and when the Lao Communist government (Pathet Lao) seized power, they set out to systematically exterminate the Hmong for their collaboration with anti-communist forces. The U.S. government felt an obligation to keep its promises of protection to these people and arranged for their emigration from Thai refugee camps. A population of 94,439 Hmong was reported in 1990 census. Over 40 percent have settled in the agriculturally rich Central Valley of California (52.1 percent of the Hmong population resided in California generally) but many have experienced difficulties because of vast differences in farming technology. About 30,000 have settled in Minnesota and Wisconsin, the epicenter being the Minneapolis-St. Paul area.

The Hmong were introduced suddenly to modern American culture without much psychological preparation and few social tools for the transition. Their strong animistic beliefs (including belief in spirits) and group orientation put them at odds with individualistic and high-tech American society. Many Hmong have become suicidal after their supposed failure to adapt to these new situations (including fairly "simple" issues such as receiving a traffic ticket). A well-documented "sudden death syndrome" has occurred among males, in which they go to sleep in a depressed state and never wake up. Some analysts have suggested that these people die of "broken hearts." Table 3 highlights social and economic characteristics, which can be interpreted as disadvantaging the Hmong. After two and a half decades, many Hmong still experience intense isolation and difficulty in assimilating to American life.

Most Laotians, however, are Lao Loum and other lowland Lao, the majority ethnic groups in Laos. Interestingly, this group has been less studied than the Hmong and Vietnamese. More literate and somewhat urban, their adjustment to American life—while not easy—has been smoother than that of their tribal counterparts, the Hmong. While many Laotians have settled near their Hmong neighbors in central California and Minneapolis-St. Paul, they are (along with Cambodians) a more diverse group in terms of geographic resettlement than the Vietnamese and Hmong. Dallas has become home to over 5,000 Laotians, and over 4,000 have settled in the Seattle area. Chicago, Portland, Atlanta, and Boston have Lao populations of around 3,000. After the Vietnamese, Laotians appear to have made the best adjustment to America. Though the Lao seem to have a strong family structure (the percentage of female heads of household is lower than other Southeast Asian refugee groups and the U.S. population as a whole), over one-third were below the official poverty line and receiving public assistance in 1990.

Altogether, over 170,000 persons from Laos—Hmong, Mien, and lowland Laotians—reside in the United States. Their population has nearly tripled since 1980.

Refugees from the war-torn countries of Vietnam, Laos, and Cambodia account for the majority (85 percent) of Southeast Asian immigrants to the United States. In addition, more than 100,000 newcomers from Thailand add to an already diverse array of peoples from the region. The stable or growing economies of Brunei and Singapore provide incentives for their citizens to remain in those countries, resulting in small numbers of immigrants to the United States. Indonesia's poverty and instability, strict emigration policies, and colonial ties with Europe have prevented large-scale emigration. Burma's political isolation and its

unfavorable status with the United States over the drug trade, as well as very tightly controlled exit visas, have resulted in low levels of immigration.

Emigration from the region has peaked three times: (1) in 1975 as a result of the fall of South Vietnam and the Communist takeovers of Laos and Cambodia, (2) in the early 1980s due to the exodus of boat people, the takeover of Cambodia by Vietnam, and Orderly Departure and Humanitarian programs, and (3) in the early 1990s, due to continuing resettlement of refugees, family reunification, and growing normalization of relations between the United States and Vietnam. Inflows from Southeast Asia have been gradually decreasing since 1993.

N. Mark Shelley

See also: Southeast Asian Refugee Crisis (Part I, Sec. 5); Political, Ethnic, Religious, and Gender Persecution, Wars and Civil Unrest (Part II, Sec. 1); Houston, Los Angeles, Rural America (Part II, Sec. 12); Immigration to Western Europe (Part II, Sec. 13).

BIBLIOGRAPHY

Barrington, Herbert R., Robert W. Gardner, and Michael J. Levin. *Asians and Pacific Islanders in the United States.* New York: Russell Sage Foundation, 1993.

Bureau of the Census. *1990 Census Data, STF3A and STF3C.*

Bureau of the Census. *Table 3. Region and Country or Area of Birth of Foreign-Born Population, 1960–1990,* Internet release March 9, 1999.

Caplan, Nathan S., Marcella H. Choy, and John K. Whitmore. *Children of the Boat People: A Study of Educational Success.* Ann Arbor: University of Michigan Press, 1991.

Caplan, Nathan S., John K. Whitmore, and Marcella H. Choy. *The Boat People and Achievement in America: A Study of Family Life, Hard Work, and Cultural Values.* Ann Arbor: University of Michigan Press, 1989.

Department of State. *Background Notes: Brunei.* Washington, DC: Department of State, August 1999.

———. *Background Notes: Cambodia.* Washington, DC: Department of State, January 1996.

———. *Background Notes: Indonesia.* Washington, DC: Department of State, August 1999.

———. *Background Notes: Laos.* Washington, DC: Department of State, August 1998.

———. *Background Notes: Malaysia.* Washington, DC: Department of State, August 1999.

———. *Background Notes: Singapore.* Washington, DC: Department of State, August 1999.

———. *Background Notes: Thailand.* Washington, DC: Department of State, August 1999.

————. *Background Notes: Vietnam*. Washington, DC: Department of State, August 1999.

Immigration and Naturalization Service. *Statistical Yearbook of the Immigration and Naturalization Service 1997*. Washington, DC: Government Printing Office, 1998.

Karnow, Stanley. *Vietnam: A History*. New York: Foreign Policy Association, 1983.

Kean, Leslie, and Dennis Bernstein. "Aung San Suu Kyi." *The Progressive*, March 1997 (vol. 61), pp. 32–35.

Kitano, Harry H. L., and Roger Daniels. *Asian Americans: Emerging Minorities*. 2d ed. Englewood Cliffs, NJ: Prentice Hall, 1995.

Knoll, Tricia. *Becoming Americans: Asian Sojourners, Immigrants, and Refugees in the Western United States*. Portland, OR: Coast to Coast Books, 1982.

Min, Pyong Gap, ed. *Asian Americans: Contemporary Trends and Issues*. Thousand Oaks, CA: Sage Publications, 1995.

Neher, Clark D. *Southeast Asia in the New International Era*. Boulder, CO: Westview Press, 1991.

Parrillo, Vincent N. *Strangers to These Shores*. Boston: Allyn and Bacon, 2000.

Rutledge, Paul James. *The Vietnamese Experience in America*. Bloomington: Indiana University Press, 1992.

Shelley, N. Mark. "Rebuilding Community from 'Scratch': Forces at Work among Urban Vietnamese Refugees." *Sociological Inquiry* (Spring 2001).

Silverstein, Ken. "A Kinder, Gentler Burma?" *Washington Monthly*, May 1988, pp. 28–31.

Takaki, Ronald. *Strangers from a Different Shore*. Boston: Back Bay Books, 1998.

TAIWAN AND HONG KONG

Among individuals of Chinese ancestry in the United States, two major groups came from Taiwan, an island about one hundred miles from mainland China. One group, identifying themselves as Taiwanese, are descendents of Chinese who migrated to the island many generations ago. The 1990 census shows that there are 73,778 Taiwanese in the United States. The great majority of Taiwanese Americans are foreign-born (79 percent) and came to the United States after 1965 (77 percent). In the late 1940s, when the Communists were rapidly gaining control over mainland China, more than 1 million Chinese, together with the retreating Nationalist (Kuomintang) government, moved to Taiwan. This second group and their offspring always see themselves as Chinese and regard Taiwan as a province of China, a view shared by the communist government on the mainland but not by the Taiwanese. The island, about the size of Maryland and Delaware combined, also has its own indigenous people of Malay-Polynesian descent, of which the Amis, Atayal, Saisiat, Bunun, Paiwan, Rukai, Yami, Tsou, and Puyuma are the nine officially recognized tribes. Of the 22 million people in Taiwan, about 2 percent are aborigine, 84 percent Taiwanese, and 14 percent Chinese.

TAIWANESE AND TAIWAN CHINESE

The total Taiwan-born population in the United States, counting both Taiwanese and Chinese, was 244,102 in 1990. Taiwanese Americans are a highly educated group. The 1990 U.S. census shows that roughly 60 percent of the Taiwanese, age twenty-five or over, have a college degree, which is significantly higher than both the national average (20 percent) and all Chinese Americans in general (41 percent). In terms of work, Taiwanese are also more likely to be in the managerial and professional specialty (48 per-

cent) than the average American (26 percent) and the average Chinese (36 percent). The next most common type of work for Taiwanese is in the technical, sales, and administrative support areas (34 percent).

Politically, Taiwanese and Chinese from Taiwan are divided on the issues of nationhood for Taiwan and past oppressions of Taiwanese by the Nationalist government. Another distinction is that many Taiwanese call their island Formosa (meaning "beautiful"), a name that was given by the Portuguese in the 1600s. There is also a push among the Taiwanese toward the use of the Taiwan language, Holo, instead of using the mainland Mandarin. The younger generation of Taiwanese Americans has been particularly visible in emphasizing their unique identity. On many college campuses, Taiwanese students have formed their own support groups. On the national level, organizations such as the Intercollegiate Taiwanese American Students Association (ITASA), Society of Taiwanese Americans (SOTA), and North America Taiwanese Professors' Association (NATPA) have similar aims in promoting the uniqueness of Taiwanese and Taiwanese-American heritages. While Taiwanese and Taiwan Chinese may differ on political issues, they share the same problems and successes in their adaptations to American society. The younger generations of both groups also have something else in common: fondness for Japanese popular culture. They are attracted to the contemporary Japanese lifestyle such as fashion, music, books, and other consumer items. The acceptance of Japanese popular culture can be traced from its Taiwan origins where the trend first started. While Taiwan, which was under Japan's rule from 1895 to 1945, has a culture that is already blended with Japanese elements, the Taiwan youths in the United States seem to have embraced Japanese popular culture more conspicuously. Besides boutiques, bookstores, and novelty shops where Japanese influence is evident, a new type of café or teahouse with considerable Japanese overtones has become popular in the Taiwan community in the United States. Styled after the modern-looking Japanese *kissaten* (tea/coffee houses), these restaurants cater mainly to the younger crowd. They serve only non-alcoholic beverages and light meals, but offer a great variety of tea and coffee drinks with exotic names such as "Happy Paradise" and "The Fragrant Tree of Paris." The signature item on every menu is an iced drink called BoBa ("Balls Colossal," in literal translation). The beverage consists of large tapioca balls, about half the size of marbles, in tea or coffee flavored with milk and syrup. Originated in Taiwan about fifteen years ago, the BoBa phenomenon spread to the United States in the mid-1990s. This type of café is more than a drinking and eating place; it is an important social venue where young people come to meet their friends, do homework, play cards and chess, watch MTV, or just relax and read comic books. Many of the reading materials are adaptations of Japanese *manga* (comic books).

Many prominent "Chinese Americans" came originally from Taiwan. Some came in adulthood for advanced education or for work; others emigrated with their families in childhood. Among them are Nobel Prize–winning chemist Yuan Tseh Lee, ViewSonic Corporation's James Chu, Kingston Technology cofounder David Sun, Vitria Technology CEO JoMei Chang, forensic expert Henry Lee, Hollywood director Ang Lee, special effects specialist Dough Chiang, AIDS researcher David D. Ho, Yahoo cocreator Jerry Yang, Watson Pharmaceuticals founder Allen Chao, and former deputy secretary of the Department of Transportation (1989–91) and president of United Way of America (1992–96) Elaine L. Chao.

HONG KONG CHINESE

Another island that has been a major source of Chinese immigration to the United States is Hong Kong. The island of Hong Kong and its adjacent territories were under British control from the 1840s until 1997, when they were returned to the People's Republic of China. After regaining Hong Kong's sovereignty, China has designated it as a Special Administrative Region, with its own law and a high degree of autonomy. Hong Kong has a history of being both a departure point for Chinese emigration and a destination point for immigration from within China. In the past, the majority of Chinese immigrants in the United States, regardless of place of origin, came by way of Hong Kong. Since the 1970s, the pattern has changed, but Hong Kong continues to be an impor-

tant gateway for Chinese emigrating to the United States. Between 1983 and October 1999, the American consulate general in Hong Kong has issued a total of 176,498 visas for immigration to the United States, both to those born in Hong Kong and those born elsewhere. Most of the Chinese in the United States who came from Hong Kong in the 1980s and 1990s are middle-class professional, technical, and managerial personnel. Some are wealthy investors and entrepreneurs. One conservative estimate is that Hong Kong Chinese had invested $2 billion in California as of 1994, concentrating in real estate such as industrial buildings, apartment houses, and hotels. The flow of Hong Kong capital and people to the United States is partly related to the change in government in 1997. In the decade or so before 1997, anxiety over reversion to Chinese sovereignty had prompted many Hong Kong professionals and those with substantial wealth to either emigrate immediately or make investments abroad in preparation for possible future emigration.

Using the place of birth as criterion, the 1990 census counted 147,131 Hong Kong Chinese in the United States. The actual number, however, is much greater because the term "Hong Kong Chinese" is used in the Chinese community very broadly to refer to all individuals who identify with Hong Kong as a result of residence and not only birth. One major difference between Hong Kong Chinese and Chinese from mainland China and Taiwan is the spoken dialect. Hong Kong Chinese speak Cantonese, whereas Chinese from mainland China and Taiwan speak Mandarin. Since many Chinese in Hong Kong attended English-speaking schools, they are generally more fluent in English than the other Chinese. There are also more Christians among the Hong Kong Chinese because Catholic and Protestant missionaries operate some of the better-known schools in the former British territory. Hong Kong Chinese are less interested in politics in general, especially in matters concerning China, Taiwan, or Chinese Americans.

Like immigrants from Taiwan, Hong Kong Chinese have a special cuisine that differentiates them from the other Chinese. A type of restaurant, billing itself "Hong-Kong western cuisine," serves a variation of European and American dishes such as sandwiches and steaks. To the uninitiated, including non–Hong Kong Chinese, they might find the look and taste of the food odd, even though the names do not appear to be unusual. Instead of "BoBa," these Hong Kong restaurants have an equivalent signature beverage called "Yin-Yeung milk tea," which is a mixture of coffee and tea sweetened with condensed milk. Ethnic niche restaurants appealing to the tastes and lifestyles of subpopulations within the larger Chinese-

American community have become an important social marker for identifying the different groups of Chinese. In addition to Hong Kong Chinese and Taiwan Chinese restaurants, there are also mainland Chinese and Vietnam Chinese restaurants.

NEWS FOR DIFFERENT GROUPS

There are four major Chinese newspapers and a few others with smaller circulation published in the United States. Although all carry local and national news, they differ in their coverage of mainland China, Taiwan, and Hong Kong. *Sing Tao Daily,* which has a long history of publication in Hong Kong, has a strong following among individuals from that region. While the paper has separate sections devoted to each of the three Chinese territories, its entertainment and business pages are heavily tilted toward Hong Kong. Aiming for readers who emigrated from Taiwan are the *Chinese L.A. Daily News* (known as *Taiwan Daily* in Chinese), which has the most complete coverage of events on that island. A number of dailies specialize in news from mainland China. They are relatively new compared to the others and have yet to attract a stable readership. Two major papers that take a more balanced approach in coverage are the *International Daily News* and the *Chinese Daily News (World Daily News* in Chinese). These two have the largest circulation in the United States. All the major Chinese newspapers are published in the traditional written characters used in Hong Kong and Taiwan. On the other hand, the newer ones that cover mainly mainland news use the simplified characters that are familiar to those recently immigrated from mainland China. Both writing systems, however, have enough similarity to be at least partially understood by most Chinese.

PARACHUTE KIDS AND ASTRONAUTS

Since the 1980s, a special problem has surfaced in the Chinese-American community. Many wealthy parents from Taiwan and Hong Kong simply drop off their children for schooling in the United States and go back home. These children, nicknamed "parachute kids" by the media, usually come during their junior high school years; they either stay alone at a house bought by their parents or are placed with their relatives or paid caretakers. Their parents may visit them once or twice a year; the rest of the time parents and children communicate by phone, fax, or e-mail. Estimates of these unaccompanied children range as high as thirty thousand, with about ten thousand in California, five thousand in New York, and the rest in Texas and other states. While parachute kids usually do well in school and have no financial worries, they often suffer from depression and homesickness. Some cannot handle the situation and turn to gangs for social support. Most of these children come as bona fide immigrants, but some are illegal, overstaying their tourist visas. While there are no statistics on unaccompanied children from Hong Kong, it is believed that the numbers are not as high as of those from Taiwan.

A slightly different phenomenon, called "astronauting," is more common among the Hong Kong Chinese. Many men do not stay with their wives and children after immigration. They return to Hong Kong for work after escorting their families to the United States. The fathers may visit their families a few times a year and keep in touch by phone and other high-tech means on a more regular basis. The estimate is that as many as 12 percent of the Hong Kong Chinese immigrants have returned to Hong Kong to work. It is called astronauting by the Hong Kong press because of the double meaning of the word, which implies flying and is pronounced exactly as "wife-empty person" *(tai hung yan)* in Cantonese Chinese. While astronauting is also found among immigrants from Taiwan, it is not as common as "parachuting," where the children are left alone in the United States without both parents.

The causes of immigration in the 1980s and 1990s are quite different from the push-pull model of an earlier era. The economies in Hong Kong and Taiwan are robust, with low unemployment rates and high wages. Individuals from Hong Kong and Taiwan, therefore, are emigrating not because of poor economic conditions at home; they emigrate for the perceived benefits to their children, believing that they would have a better future in the United States. For many people in Hong Kong and Taiwan there is a lingering fear that the social and political situations may not be as good for the next generation due to reunification with communist China, which has already occurred for Hong Kong and may happen to Taiwan in the future. Hence, astronauting is seen as a necessary sacrifice for the sake of the children. Psychologists George K. Hong and MaryAnna D. Ham observed that these families are paying a high price for maintaining a split household across two continents because of the enormous stress placed on the family relationships. In the long run, cultural gaps may divide not only father and children but also husband and wife as a result of the children and wife becoming more Americanized than the father who stays back home in Hong Kong or Taiwan.

Lawrence K. Hong

See also: Political, Ethnic, Religious, and Gender Persecution (Part II, Sec. 1); Los Angeles, San Francisco (Part II, Sec. 12); Immigration to Australia, Immigration to Canada, Immigration to Western Europe (Part II, Sec. 13); Page Act, 1875, Angell Treaty, 1881, Chinese Exclusion Act, 1882, Contract Labor Act (Foran Act), 1885, Scott Act, 1888, Repeal of Chinese Exclusion Acts, 1943 (Part IV, Sec. 1).

BIBLIOGRAPHY

Chung, E. C. "An Investigation of the Psychological Well-Being of Unaccompanied Taiwanese Minors/Parachute Kids in the United States." Dissertation, University of Southern California, 1994.

Deane, D. "Have Job, Will Travel; They're Called 'Astronauts' . . ." *Los Angeles Times*, March 31, 1993.

Hamilton, D. "A House, Cash—No Parents." *Los Angeles Times*, June 24, 1993.

Hong, G. K., and M. D. Ham. "Impact of Immigration on the Family Life Cycle: Clinical Implications for Chinese Americans." *Journal of Family Psychotherapy* 3:3 (1992): 27–40.

Hong, L. K. "Japanese Pop Culture on the New Silk Road." *Japan Quarterly* (April-June 1998): 54–60.

Watanabe, T. " 'Child-Dumping'—Taiwan Teens Left to Struggle in U.S." *San Jose Mercury News*, March 26, 1989.

EUROPE

Introduction

Eastern Europe
John Radzilowski

Former Soviet Union
Michelle Stem Cook

Great Britain
John Herschel Barnhill

Ireland
John Herschel Barnhill

Western and Southern Europe
Daniel James

INTRODUCTION

The entries in Part III, Section 4 of the *Encyclopedia of American Immigration* are devoted to immigration and immigrants from Europe and the nations of the former Soviet Union. Most of the articles in this section are devoted to regions, including Eastern Europe, the former Soviet Union, and Western Europe. In addition, there are two national entries on Great Britain and Ireland.

In his entry on Eastern Europe—described as the former communist nations east of the Iron Curtain, including the nations emerging out of the former Yugoslavia—John Radzilowski begins with a history of migration patterns within the region going back to the Middle Ages. The author discusses the early history of immigration from the region to the United States through the immigration restriction acts of the 1920s. Next, Radzilowski looks at the settlement patterns and work experiences of immigrants from Eastern Europe before going on to an examination of their ethnic communities and cultures in the United States. The author concludes with a discussion of post–World War II Eastern European immigration to America.

Michelle Stem Cook's entry on immigrants and immigration from the nation-states of the former Soviet Union begins with a history of causes of immigration, particularly for the many Jews who have left this region for the United States. She then discusses settlement patterns, adaptation, and the culture that immigrants from the former Soviet Union have created in the United States.

John Herschel Barnhill's entry on Great Britain explores the long history of immigration from that country to the United States, beginning with a discussion of the colonial era. He then goes on to discuss British immigration in the nineteenth century—when numbers peaked—and its decline in the twentieth century. Barnhill also details immigration from the West Indies when they were under British rule, as well as the British war brides of American soldiers during World War II. Finally, the author concludes with a discussion of the impact of recent British immigrants on American life.

As with his entry on Great Britain, Barnhill's article on Ireland begins with the long history of that country's immigrants in America, beginning with a discussion of the early nineteenth century and the great wave of Irish immigration following the potato famine of the mid-nineteenth century. Next, the author offers an examination of the so-called new Irish immigrants since the end of the 1960s.

In his entry on Western and Southern Europe—defined as the countries of the European Union, as well as others that lie west of the former Iron Curtain—Daniel James begins with an exploration into the long history of immigration from that region to the United States, going back to the early days of exploration and the colonial era. He then discusses western European immigration during the nineteenth and early twentieth centuries. Finally, he offers a picture of the historical and contemporary immigration situation of a variety of Western European ethnic and national groups, including Basques, Dutch, French, Germans, Greeks, Italians, Portuguese, Scandinavians, Spanish, and Swiss.

EASTERN EUROPE

The countries between Russia and Germany, the Baltic Sea and Greece, often called, somewhat inaccurately, Eastern Europe, present a picture of great geographic, linguistic, and ethnic diversity. There are perhaps three distinct regions that fall under the Cold War–era rubric of Eastern Europe: east-central Europe (modern-day Poland, Slovakia, Hungary, and the Czech Republic), the Balkans, and the old Polish-Russian borderlands or Kresy (modern Ukraine, Belarus, Lithuania, and Latvia).

The majority of its inhabitants are Slavs, including West Slavs (Poles, Czechs, Slovaks, and Serbians), East Slavs (Ukrainians, Russians, Belarussians, and Carpatho-Rusyns), and South Slavs (Croatians, Slovenes, Serbs, Bosnians, Macedonians, and Bulgarians). In addition, there are Balts (Latvians and Lithuanians), Magyars (commonly called Hungarians), Romanians, and Albanians who make up a majority population in many areas. Minorities are and were scattered throughout the regions, the largest being ethnic Germans, Jews, and Romani (Gypsies). Smaller minorities abound, including Armenians, Vlachs, Tatars, and Karaites. In addition, many groups that are majorities in one area are minorities in other areas. Polish minorities were historically found as far east as Russia and as far south as Bosnia. Magyar minorities lived for centuries in Slovakia, eastern Austria, northern Serbia, and Transylvania. This brief tally does not even begin to account for many strong local and regional identities and distinct religious minorities, such as Old Believers or Mariavites.

MIGRATION IN EASTERN, EAST-CENTRAL, AND SOUTHEASTERN EUROPE

Given this complexity, eastern Europe does not have one single migration experience but many. Despite this, it is possible to discern some broad patterns in the region's migration history. In the Middle Ages and early modern period, eastern Europe was rich in resources but relatively sparsely populated. As a result, it was the destination of migrants from western and central Europe and to a lesser extent from central Asia and the Mediterranean. In addition, there was significant migration among the indigenous population as well into the early 1600s. Such movement was encouraged by monarchs and local lords who needed skilled labor and were willing to provide economic and political incentives to migrants. Germans were the largest group, settling in towns and cities and some rural enclaves as well. Jews received special rights of communal self-government and came in large numbers. Other migrants included Flemings, Irish, Scots, Armenians, Italians, and Tatars. At various times, both Poland and Austria pursued a policy that encouraged the settlement of military populations along hostile borders.

The region's migration complexity is demonstrated by the experience of the so-called Bukovinian Poles. In the fifteenth and sixteenth century, these people migrated from the highlands of Austria-ruled Silesia into northern Slovakia. At the beginning of the nineteenth century, they migrated east to Bukovina (today northern Romania and southwestern Ukraine). As mass emigration swept eastern Europe at the end of the nineteenth century, many opted to immigrate to Brazil or the United States. Another large group migrated into Bosnia. At the end of World War II, many of the Bosnian Poles (now speaking both Serbo-Croatian and an archaic form of Polish) "returned" to Silesia (placed under Poland as a result of the Yalta agreement), thus completing "the Great Circle" in the space of a mere 500 years! From Silesia, many opted to join relatives living in the West.

Beginning in the nineteenth century, eastern Europe became an exporter rather than an importer of people. Serfdom, which had been gradually imposed

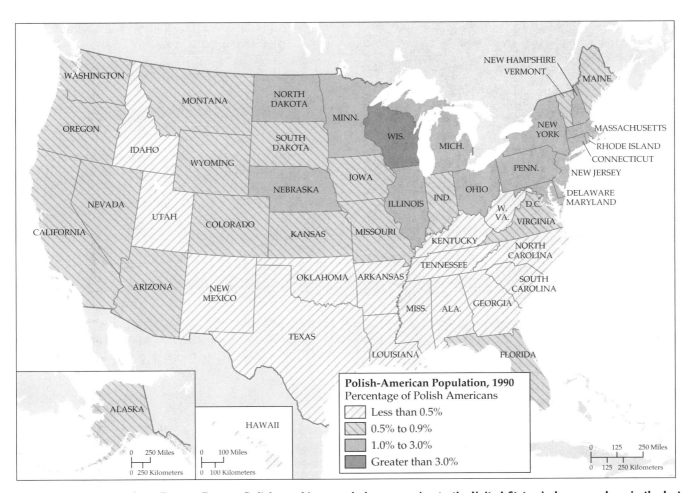

Like other immigrants from Eastern Europe, Polish-speaking people began coming to the United States in large numbers in the last two decades of the nineteenth century, with most settling in the industrial states of the Northeast and Upper Midwest. *(CARTO-GRAPHICS)*

on the region's peasants in the period between the mid-sixteenth century and the late seventeenth century, was lifted throughout eastern Europe. Beginning in the Austrian Empire in 1781, in Prussia in 1807, and czarist Russia in 1861, the end of serfdom transformed peasants' labor obligations into cash rents. This simultaneously freed the peasants and impoverished them. As the Polish scholar Aleksander Gella put it, the end of serfdom removed the shackles from the peasants' ankles and removed the shoes from their feet. Only in a few places, such as Bulgaria, did peasants receive land in quantities sufficient to sustain their family as it grew. Local studies confirm numerous lawsuits filed by peasants against former landlords and against each other over the ownership and traditional use of pastures and forestland.

Finding themselves in need of cash, which had formerly been a scarce but rarely needed commodity, peasants began to look for wage labor. At first, this often meant going to work for their former landlords.

Later, however, peasants began to venture further afield. As they did so, they began to see new possibilities in the world beyond the village that would allow economic advancement rather than mere subsistence. As the peasants' mental and geographic horizons expanded, the old notion that economics was a zero-sum game receded, replaced by the new idea that the material world was infinitely expandable.

In addition to the need for cash and the lure of opportunity, peasant migrants faced other motivations for migration. Rising populations in eastern Europe, caused by gradually improving health and nutrition and a general absence of major wars, put pressure on peasant smallholders, especially in the last half of the nineteenth century. (Despite the improvement in health and nutrition, however, child mortality rates for eastern Europe remained at or below late-twentieth-century "third world" child mortality rates.) This was exacerbated by inheritance patterns common in many parts of eastern Europe in

The wars in the former Yugoslavia sent tens of thousands of refugees to the United States in the 1990s, including these two Bosnian laundry workers in Utica, New York. *(Mel Rosenthal)*

Armenian tradesmen, merchants, and peddlers. Such groups helped spread knowledge of the wider world among the peasants. Studies from east-central Europe indicate that ethnically heterogeneous areas experienced higher rates of migration than ethnically homogeneous areas. In other words, "migration fever" was spread by interaction among different ethnic groups.

Early migration patterns were focused on the needs of large agricultural concerns. Poles from Austrian Galicia and the Russian-controlled Congress Kingdom of Poland followed potato and sugar beet harvests in Prussia, Denmark, and Sweden. Migrants from Bohemia, Slovakia, and Hungary traveled to Austria and Germany. Although overseas migration for industrial labor would take primarily young men, seasonal agricultural migration involved both men and women.

MIGRATION TO AMERICA

Scattered individuals from eastern Europe began arriving in North America as early as the 1600s. Their numbers were too tiny to be of great significance, although a number of Poles and Hungarians served in the Revolutionary War, and Slovenian Catholic missionaries were active among Native Americans in the Great Lakes region in the first half of the nineteenth century. Longer and more permanent migrations to the Americas originated on the western edges of eastern Europe. Czechs, Sorbs, and Polish Silesians and Kaszubs began following their German neighbors to the New World by the 1850s. In 1854, the first permanent Polish community in the United States was created by a group of Silesians at Panna Maria on the Texas gulf coast.

These antebellum immigrants were almost exclusively settler migrants who came with their families in search of available farmland. Czechs and Sorbs followed the German settlement pattern and as a result became the most rural of all the east European immigrant groups. Almost half of all first-generation Czech immigrants took up farming, compared with about 10 percent for Poles, the next most rural of the east European groups.

Significant economic immigration from eastern Europe began in the 1870s and 1880s. Czechs, Sorbs, and Poles from the eastern marches of Prussia were soon joined by Jews, Hungarians, Slovaks, Poles from Austrian Galicia and the Congress Kingdom, and Carpatho-Rusyns and Ukrainians from Galicia. Although emigration from Russia was illegal until 1891,

which parents divided their property up evenly among surviving children. This led to the creation of progressively smaller landholdings and the emergence of a class of "dwarf holders" who often had less than 2 hectares (5 acres) of land that was divided among several widely dispersed parcels. This tendency was especially pronounced in regions such as Galicia. The Polish census of 1921 found that 34 percent of all farms consisted of 2 hectares (5 acres) or less, and nearly 65 percent were 5 hectares (12.5 acres) or less.

Peasant migration in eastern Europe began as a short-term response to local and family needs but quickly took on a more permanent character as migration became the preferred way to fulfill family economic strategies. Of course, certain groups had always had a higher degree of mobility than the population at large. Among these were Jewish and

The politics of the old country continue to interest many immigrants, including these Polish arrivals in Chicago. Note the photo of former Polish president Lech Walesa on the left. *(AP/Wide World Photos)*

special guides were available, for a price, to conduct illegal emigrants across the frontier.

North America was not the only destination for the migrants. In the early 1890s, "Brazil fever" swept parts of Poland, only to subside when reports of the harsh tropical conditions circulated among likely emigrants. Prussian citizens, both Jews and Poles, could move freely throughout reunited Germany, and many found jobs in the coal-mining regions of the Ruhr or the growing German industrial cities. Small groups of Jews also journeyed to England. Further south, Czechs, Hungarians, Slovenians, and Croatians were attracted to the industries of upper Austria. As a general rule, those living further away from European industrial centers were more likely to choose migration to the Americas, where wages were higher. The fever for migration swept from central Europe eastward

and southward as immigrants were drawn into the expanding Atlantic economy. The main exception were ethnic Russians, whose migration focused primarily on Siberia and the eastern steppe.

Although settler migrants coming with their families tended to predominate in the earliest stages of immigration, a different pattern emerged by the 1880s and 1890s as ever more massive waves of people left eastern Europe. The new immigrants were, at least to begin with, predominantly men, traveling alone, pursuing the relatively short-term goal of making as much money as possible in a short time to bolster the overall economic situation of the family.

Return migration was common, even among the early waves of Jewish migration, with some immigrants making two, three, or even four trips across the Atlantic. Return migration was especially pronounced among the South Slavic groups such as Bulgarians, of whom 85 percent returned. The returning migrants and the money they sent home created a whole new sector of the economy. Many returnees built American-style homes. In Slovakia, the money from America sent or brought back by unskilled workers created a demand for and migration of skilled labor to build new houses. Small villages sometimes saw dramatic increases in their total wealth. After impoverished Poland regained independence in 1918, emigrant remittances remained the number one source of foreign exchange throughout the interwar period.

SETTLEMENT AND LABOR

In the United States, early east European immigrant communities first emerged in midwestern agricultural areas and around some extractive industries, such as lumber and coal mining. Changes in industrial practice dramatically raised the demand for unskilled and semiskilled labor, so that by the late 1880s and 1890s, the flow of immigrant labor from eastern Europe became a flood. Between 1900 and the start of World War I in 1914, east Europeans, mainly from Austria-Hungary and Russia, poured into the United States in unprecedented numbers, dominating the overall immigrant flow and contributing to the largest per capita influx yet recorded in U.S. history, with 1907 being the peak year. East European communities grew dramatically. In 1870, for example, there were an estimated 50,000 Poles in the United States. By 1880, that number had grown tenfold to half a million. By 1890, the number of Poles had doubled to 1 million, then doubled again to 2 million in 1900, then grew by 50 percent to 3 million in 1910.

There were some attempts to settle these new arrivals in rural areas, and some agricultural colonies and settlements were created for Poles, Czechs, Ukrainians, and Carpatho-Rusyns. There were also efforts to set up Jewish farming communities in North Dakota and Montana. Yet, for a variety of reasons, the new immigrants settled in and remained in urban and industrial settings, especially on the eastern seaboard and in the Midwest and Great Lakes states. Cities such as New York, Chicago, Cleveland, Detroit, Buffalo, Milwaukee, and Pittsburgh attracted large east European immigrant populations. So, too, did mining regions: Pennsylvania's anthracite regions, the copper mines of Michigan's Upper Peninsula, and Minnesota's Iron Range. From these mining areas, some immigrants journeyed to similar jobs further west. Poles and Slovenes could be found in Colorado's coal and

lead mines, while Serbs, Montenegrin Serbs, and Croatians could be found in the copper mines of southeast Arizona.

Immigrants took industrial wage labor jobs because they were, in most cases, the only position open to unskilled, non-English-speaking foreigners. In addition, wage labor fit the immigrants' economic and personal strategies. By the standards of the places they had come from, wages for even an unskilled American worker were high, allowing them to amass what in their homeland was a significant amount of money. Yet, the very act of immigration and exposure to the larger world changed the immigrants' self-perception and their ideas of what the good life meant. The old standard of well-being was soon discarded, and the newcomers began to judge themselves more by the yardstick of the new urban, industrial world of which they were rapidly making themselves a part. The attraction of short-term employment for limited goals related to Old Country concerns became less and the pressure to remain permanently in the industrial labor force became greater.

The one significant exception to the preference for wage labor among most east European immigrants was the tendency of Jewish immigrants to open small businesses. In major cities, such as New York, Jews did enter industrial wage labor in large numbers, especially in the textile industry. Yet, with a long tradition in Europe of operating small businesses, Jewish immigrants were frequently attracted to the more independent existence of commercial life. This often led Jewish immigrants beyond major Jewish centers. Many American small towns, from the rural South, where a genre of establishments called "Jew stores" existed, to the new railroad towns of the Upper Midwest, had a small cluster of Jewish families who operated Main Street businesses. Would-be Jewish merchants were often attracted to towns with large populations of east European gentile immigrants, such as Johnstown, Pennsylvania. Thus, the two groups often resumed an Old Country relationship that, while sometimes fraught with friction, was at least familiar.

The entry of so many east European immigrants into the nation's industrial life put them at the forefront of the struggles over labor and the rights of workers. Established craft unions, often dominated by Protestants of northern and western European ancestry, saw the immigrants as a threat to their craft. With the notable exception of coal mining, there were few sustained, systematic attempts to bring immigrant workers into the established unions until the 1930s. Although east European immigrant workers were sometimes used as strikebreakers, in most communities a strong feeling against strikebreaking was the norm by the 1890s. A major reason for this was the abuse that the immigrant workers felt they received at the hands of employers. East European immigrants routinely received the lowest pay and worked the most difficult and dangerous jobs in any given industry. Accidents were commonplace, and deaths from mine cave-ins, workers getting smashed and mangled by machinery, and disasters like the Triangle Shirt Waist Factory Fire claimed the lives of countless east European workers. Immigrants were the first to be fired and were subject to manipulative practices, de facto debt peonage in company towns, unannounced pay cuts, and, in the case of female workers, rampant sexual harassment.

Pay cuts and mass firings struck at the very basis of the immigrants' goals and economic strategies. As a result, east European immigrants engaged in series of intense labor struggles from the late 1880s to the 1930s. In most cases, these were conducted with little support from established unions, forcing the communities to rely on their own limited resources. Although local, temporary successes were possible, it was not until the 1930s when major, permanent gains were made. By then, east European immigrants were a dominant presence in many heavy industries. Their mass movement of the 1930s, which was harnessed by the leadership of such new unions as the Congress of Industrial Organizations, United Mine Workers, and the United Automobile Workers, with the help of organizers who spoke the immigrants' languages, brought about major changes in the treatment of all American workers.

This result was not achieved easily, and east European workers were often the victims of bloody reprisals by police and company-hired thugs. The Lamont Canal Strike Massacre of 1893 and the Lattimer Massacre of 1897 were but the most notable of these tragedies. Support for violence against east European immigrants was common. During a strike by Polish workers at a Bayonne, New Jersey, oil refinery in 1915, an oil company executive, supported by the mayor of Bayonne, said: "Get me 250 husky men who can swing clubs. If they're not enough, get a thousand, two thousand. I want them to march up East Twenty-second street through the guts of Polacks." Such sentiments were supported by the dominant view of the time, which saw east and south European immigrants as culturally and racially inferior. In 1891, the president of Massachusetts Institute of Technology, Francis Amasa Walker, described east Europeans as miserable, broken, corrupt, abject, unlucky, thriftless, and worthless, "representing the utterest failures of civilization, the worst defeats in the struggle for existence,

the lowest degradation of human nature." In a later article, he wrote: "The entrance into our political, social, and industrial life of such vast masses of peasantry, degraded below our utmost conceptions, is a matter which no intelligent patriot can look upon without the gravest apprehension and alarm."

IMMIGRANT COMMUNITIES, ETHNIC CULTURE

While the mainstream society looked down on the east European immigrants and many Americans were often unable to distinguish one group from another, the immigrants themselves were in the process of developing an intense community and cultural life. Hundreds of east European immigrant newspapers flourished, representing almost every political and cultural current in the various communities. Some of these papers were ephemeral, but others were not. Under the leadership of publisher Antoni Paryski, Toledo's Polish-language daily *Ameryka-Echo* achieved a national circulation of over 110,000 prior to World War I. Several east European newspapers, founded in the 1880s or 1890s, continue to publish at the beginning of the twenty-first century. Although little researched, immigrant publishing houses also flourished, producing reprints of Old Country classics as well as works by immigrant authors themselves, usually in an inexpensive paperbound format. A partial catalog of Paryski-published books released during the interwar period listed some 10,000 titles. By the 1920s, there were also east European immigrant recording companies, film companies, and radio stations.

Theater was a vital cultural component of immigrant life. Although New York's Yiddish-language theatrical tradition was unequaled, it had its counterpart in virtually every east European immigrant community. Nearly every local community, school, fraternal lodge, parish, congregation, or political party sponsored amateur theater productions. Similar vitality was found in music, art, and architecture. It is no surprise that renowned Czech composer Antonín Dvořák found a welcoming climate among his immigrant compatriots when he wrote his symphony entitled *From the New World* (1893).

Immigrant community life arose within the geographic confines of urban neighborhoods and, to a lesser extent, rural enclaves. The center of such communities was almost always a parish church or a synagogue. Although they performed a vital religious function, these institutions were also community gathering points, social halls, self-help mechanisms, and cultural centers whose importance cannot be underestimated. A yearly cycle of religious and cultural rituals were enacted with particular intensity within the confines of immigrant parishes and synagogues.

Another important institution was the immigrant saloon, which doubled as men's clubs for east European immigrants. Often apart from the priest, the saloonkeeper was the most respected individual in the community. Some saloonkeepers served as bankers and ticket agents. Immigrants often preferred to leave their money with the saloonkeeper—a fellow ethnic—than with banks. In addition, saloonkeepers were often the conduit through which political patronage could be distributed.

After 1924, when the United States enacted restrictions on immigration from eastern Europe—whose people were considered racially and culturally undesirable—a cultural change began to take hold in many east European-American communities. The creation of several new nations in Europe—Poland, Czechoslovakia, Yugoslavia, Lithuania, Latvia, and Estonia—meant free and independent homelands. Despite some initial enthusiasm for return migration and, in the case of Polish Americans, the creation of a large army to fight for Polish independence, most immigrants decided to stay in North America. Although overjoyed at the independence of their homelands, the nations of eastern Europe, especially the new ones created from the wreckage left behind by World War I, were often unstable, hungry, and impoverished. They were not the ideal nations envisioned by prewar émigré leaders. Nor did reemigrants fit in especially well. Whereas in America, they were seen as "foreigners," in "their" homeland, they were viewed as "Americans," as interlopers with too much money and too many alien ideas. For these reasons, the east European Americans felt that only in their ethnic enclaves in America would they be truly at home.

The interwar years also brought new cultural forms to east European ethnic communities as ethnic media adapted to new technology and styles. Mainstream advertisers began to take an interest in ethnic niche markets. Second-generation young people, faced with a conservative, traditional American culture and the new styles and movements of the Jazz Age, chose the latter and helped introduce new cultural forms to the mainstream. At the same time, they actively participated in the creation and re-creation of hybrid ethnic cultures that combined elements of American and Old Country culture into something new and unique.

Table 1
East European Ancestry Groups in America, 1990

Group	Rank	Number
Polish	9	9,366,106
East European Jewish	n/a	6,000,000 (estimate)
Russian[a]	16	2,952,987
Slovak	21	1,882,897
Hungarian	24	1,582,302
Czech	27	1,296,411
Lithuanian	37	811,865
Ukrainian	38	740,803
Croatian	45	544,270
Romanian	53	365,544
Czechoslovakian[b]	56	315,285
Yugoslavian[b]	60	257,994
Slovene	74	124,437
Serbian	75	116,795
Latvian	79	100,331
Slavic[b]	88	76,931
Albanian	105	47,710
Bulgarian	119	29,595
Estonian	121	26,762
Macedonian	128	20,365
Soviet Union[a]	152	7,729
Carpatho-Rusyn	156	7,602
Belarusian	178	4,277
Moravian	184	3,781
Ruthenian	185	3,776
Wendish	191	3,189
Total		20,659,744

Source: 1990 Census of the Population. *Supplementary Reports: Detailed Ancestry Groups for States,* CD-5-1-2 (Washington, DC: Government Printing Office, 1992).

[a]The categories "Russian" and "Soviet Union," contain a significant proportion of Jewish Americans with roots in Russia and the former Soviet Union. More recent Russian Jewish émigrés show a greater tendency to identify with Russian culture. The "Russian" category also contains many Carpatho-Rusyns who have come to identify themselves as Russian. The actual number of ethnic Great Russians in the United States is unknown. The census does not report Jewish ancestry numbers. The number shown is a commonly accepted estimate from Jewish-American community organizations.

[b]Categories such as these tend to be amalgamations of more than one identity. It is probable that most of those identifying as "Slavic" are of Carpatho-Rusyn ancestry and most of those identifying as Czechoslovakian are of Czech ancestry.

POST-WORLD WAR II IMMIGRATION

Significant new immigration from the region did not occur until after World War II. The destruction of eastern Europe, the Holocaust and other genocides, the huge number of displaced persons, and the Soviet takeover of the region impelled the United States to admit many refugees and displaced persons. Large numbers of Jews, Poles, Ukrainians, Latvians, Lithuanians, and others arrived in the late 1940s and early 1950s. Following the 1956 Hungarian Revolution, some 60,000 Hungarian refugees were admitted.

After the lifting of immigration restrictions in the 1960s, growing numbers of east European immigrants came to America. Some came under the auspices of reuniting families; others, such as the Soviet Jewish refuseniks, fled political repression. After the imposition of martial law in Poland in 1981, over 34,000 Polish refugees were admitted. This was but a harbinger of larger flows. By the end of the 1980s, as communist rule in eastern Europe decayed and then collapsed, more and more east Europeans followed the path laid down by earlier immigrants. Several U.S. cities, such as New York, Chicago, Detroit, Los Angeles, and San Francisco, have seen the largest influx. Poles continue to be the largest of these groups and the largest single group of immigrants from Europe. Russians (most often Russian Jews) and Ukrainians have also arrived in large numbers. Following the deadly conflicts in the Balkans in the 1990s, there has been an increasing flow of Bosnian, Croatian, and Albanian refugees and immigrants, although their overall numbers remain small compared with the larger east European groups.

Such immigrants have not always fit seamlessly into their respective ethnic communities. Although the older ethnic communities played a major role in lobbying the U.S. government to allow in refugees and immigrants from the Old Country, the arrival of the newcomers was not always happy. Differing notions of what it meant to be Polish or Ukrainian or Jewish, different social and educational backgrounds, life goals, and expectations of America, led many of the newer immigrants to form separate ethnic institutions. These "new-new immigrants" often existed in uneasy alliance with their second-, third-, and fourth-generation counterparts. The experience of the post–World War II refugees has shown, however, that time tends to break down such divisions, even though the process can be slow and painful.

Academic and media pundits have frequently predicted the demise of many east European American ethnic communities over the course of the last century.

Yet, this has failed to occur. Although the nature and meaning of east European ethnicity has changed significantly since the first immigrants arrived in the Americas, these diverse communities continue to be a vital component of a multicultural America.

John Radzilowski

See also: Collapse of Communism (Part I, Sec. 5); Political, Ethnic, Religious, and Gender Persecution (Part II, Sec. 1); New York City (Part II, Sec. 12); Immigration to Canada, Immigration to Western Europe (Part II, Sec. 13); President Truman's Directive on European Refugees, 1945 (Part IV, Sec. 1); *Whom We Shall Welcome*, 1953 (Part IV, Sec. 1); The Immigrant and the Community, 1917 (Part IV, Sec. 2).

BIBLIOGRAPHY

Allen, James Paul, and Eugene James Turner. *We the People: An Atlas of America's Ethnic Diversity*. New York: Macmillan, 1988.

Altankov, Nicolay. *The Bulgarian Americans*. Palo Alto, CA: Ragusan Press, 1979.

Barton, Josef J. *Peasants and Strangers: Italians, Rumanians, and Slovaks in an American City, 1890–1950*. Cambridge, MA: Harvard University Press, 1975.

Bukowczyk, John J. *And My Children Did Not Know Me: A History of the Polish Americans*. Bloomington, IN: Indiana University Press, 1987.

———, ed. *Polish Americans and Their History*. Pittsburgh: University of Pittsburgh Press, 1996.

Colakovic, Branko M. *The South Slavic Immigration in America*. New York: Twayne, 1978.

———. *Yugoslav Migrations to America*. San Francisco: Ragusan Press, 1973.

Donia, Robert J., and John V. A. Fine Jr. *Bosnia and Hercegovina: A Tradition Betrayed*. New York: Columbia University Press, 1994.

Fainhauz, David. *Lithuanians in the U.S.A.: Aspects of Ethnic Identity*. Chicago: Lithuanian Library Press, 1991.

Feingold, Henry L. *The Jewish People in America*. 5 vols. Baltimore: Johns Hopkins University Press, 1992.

Greene, Victor R. *For God and Country: The Rise of Polish and Lithuanian Ethnic Consciousness in America, 1860–1910*. Madison, WI: State Historical Society of Wisconsin, 1975.

———. *The Slavic Community on Strike: Immigrant Labor in Pennsylvania Anthracite*. Notre Dame: Notre Dame University Press, 1968.

Habenicht, Jan. *History of Czechs in America*. St. Paul: Czech and Slovak Genealogical Society of Minnesota, 1910. Reprint, 1996.

Kipel, Vituat. *Belarusy u ZshA* (Belarusians in the U.S.). Minsk, Belarus: Belaruski instytut navuki i mastatstva, 1993.

Kostash, Myrna. *All of Baba's Children*. Edmonton: NeWest Press, 1977.

Kruszka, Waclaw. *History of Poles in America to 1908*. 4 vols. 1908–11. Reprint, Washington, DC: Catholic University Press, 1993–2000.

Kuropas, Myron B. *Ukrainian-American Citadel: The First One Hundred Years of the Ukrainian National Association*. Boulder, CO: East European Monographs, 1997.

———. *The Ukrainian Americans: Roots and Aspirations, 1884–1954*. Toronto: University of Toronto Press, 1991.

Magosci, Paul Robert. *Our People: Carpatho-Rusyns and Their Descendants in North America*. 3d ed. Toronto: University of Toronto Press, 1994.

Morawska, Ewa. "East Europeans on the Move." In *The Cambridge Survey of World Migration*. Cambridge: Cambridge University Press, 1996.

———. *For Bread with Butter: The Life Worlds of East-Central Europeans in Johnstown, Pennsylvania, 1880–1940*. Cambridge: Cambridge University Press, 1985.

———. *Insecure Prosperity: Small-Town Jews in Industrial America, 1890–1940*. Princeton: Princeton University Press, 1996.

Pipic, George J. *The Croatian Immigrants in America*. New York: Philosophical Library, 1971.

Pula, James S. *Polish Americans: An Ethnic Community*. New York: Twayne, 1995.

Puskás, Julianna, ed. *Overseas Migration from East-Central and Southeastern Europe, 1880–1940*. Budapest: Hungarian Academy of Science, 1990.

Radzilowski, John. *The Eagle and the Cross: A History of Polish Roman Catholic Union of America, 1873–1998*. Boulder, CO: East European Monographs (forthcoming).

Sachar, Howard M. *A History of the Jews in America*. New York: Knopf, 1992.

Stolarik, M. Mark. *Immigration and Urbanization: The Slovak Experience, 1870–1918*. Minneapolis, MN: AMS Press, 1974.

Vecoli, Rudolph J., and Suzanne Sinke, eds. *A Century of European Migrations, 1830–1930*. Urbana, IL: Illinois University Press, 1991.

Wolkovich-Valkavicius, William. *Lithuanian Religious Life in America: A Compendium of 150 Roman Catholic Parishes and Institutions*. Norwood, MA: Corporate Fulfillment Systems, 1991.

Wyman, Mark. *Round Trip to America: The Immigrants Return to Europe, 1880–1930*. Ithaca, NY: Cornell University Press, 1993.

FORMER SOVIET UNION

Scholars describing immigrants and immigration from Russia and the former Soviet Union to the United States speak in terms of four waves. The first wave peaked in the early twentieth century and ended soon after the Bolshevik revolution in 1917. The second wave stretched over the half century from when Joseph Stalin came to power in the 1920s, through the first years of the Cold War following World War II, and ended in the 1970s. The third wave arrived in the late 1970s during a time when the politics of the Cold War made it politically advantageous for the Soviet Union to allow Soviet Jews to emigrate. The collapse of communism recently ushered in the fourth wave in the 1990s and early twenty-first century. With the exception of the second wave, the overwhelming majority of these immigrants have been Jewish.

THE FIRST WAVE: IMMIGRATION PRIOR TO 1925

The first wave of immigrants consisted of more than 3 million persons who came to the United States between 1881 and 1917 from the geographic territories that ultimately made up the Soviet Union. (This total includes immigrants from the Baltic states and other areas that were not annexed to the Soviet Union until World War II.) Radical social, political, and economic changes occurring in the Russian empire at the close of the nineteenth and the beginning of the twentieth century gave rise to a resurgence of anti-Semitic violence in the form of pogroms. Most of the immigrants of the first wave were Jews seeking to escape these pogroms and the impoverished Pale of Settlement, a geographic region to which most Jews in the empire were confined.

In the 1880s, Jews from the Russian empire began arriving in the United States in large numbers, desti-tute and unable to speak English. In response to their plight, the established community of Jews in New York formed what is now known as the Hebrew Immigrant Aid Society. This organization has facilitated the emigration of Jews from Russia, eastern Europe, and other areas of the world from the 1880s to the present. In addition to providing shelter, language training, money for transportation, help with finding employment, kosher meals, and other forms of assistance, American Jews secured the release of many initially detained immigrants by helping them locate the friends and relatives who would claim them. The wave peaked in 1913 with the admission of almost 300,000 immigrants in that year alone. These Jewish immigrants differed significantly from those who later followed them: Whereas first-wave immigrants largely came from rural villages where the dominant language was Yiddish and where Judaic traditions predominated, most of those arriving from 1925 to the present have been highly educated urban professionals, profoundly assimilated to Russian culture.

From 1914 to 1920, emigration from the region that became the Soviet Union sharply attenuated owing to the First World War, the Bolshevik revolution in 1917, and the civil war that followed. In the wake of these catastrophic events, a brief period of relative freedom followed from 1921 to 1924 under the New Economic Policy; anxious about the future, more than 70,000 Soviet citizens immigrated to the United States in the four years leading up to Vladimir Lenin's death in 1924.

EMIGRATION FROM BEHIND THE IRON CURTAIN

Following Stalin's ascension to power, emigration became nearly impossible until the years of détente in

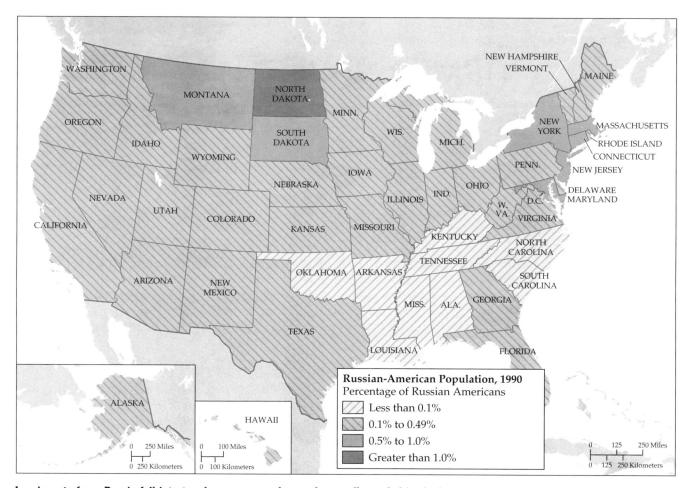

Immigrants from Russia fall into two large groups—Jews, who usually settled in the large cities of the Northeast and Upper Midwest, and Christians, who often headed for rural areas in the Great Plains states. *(CARTO-GRAPHICS)*

the 1970s. The second wave refers primarily to the thousands of Soviet citizens who, finding themselves in Germany and other countries at the end of World War II, chose to immigrate to the United States. During World War II, virtually no one immigrated to the United States from the Soviet Union. After the war, Soviet authorities mounted an intense propaganda campaign to coax all Soviet citizens abroad to return to their homeland, all the while treating those who did return as traitors and sending them to concentration camps. Recognizing the risks of repatriation, thousands of Soviet citizens abroad chose not to return to the Soviet Union after the war. Among these were many prisoners of war and Holocaust survivors. The U.S. Immigration and Naturalization Service reports that more than 120,000 immigrant aliens native to the Soviet Union and the Baltic states were admitted to the United States between 1945 and 1952, but this number only approximates the size of this wave.

Apart from displaced persons who emigrated during the postwar years, only approximately fifty thousand former Soviets immigrated to the United States between 1925 and 1974, relatively few of whom were Jews. These included famed ballet star Mikhail Baryshnikov, United Nations Undersecretary General Arkady Shevchenko, film director Andrey Tarkovsky, and other prominent defectors whose exceptional talents or high levels of advancement in the Communist Party earned them the opportunity to represent the Soviet Union abroad. Among the defectors were several sailors who literally "jumped ship" at different points in time.

JEWISH LIFE IN THE SOVIET UNION

Notwithstanding the ways in which the Soviet system violated the basic human rights of citizens of all ethnic

Table 1
Immigration from the Soviet Union and Former Soviet Union, 1881–Present

Wave	Approximate number of refugee, asylee, and immigrant arrivals[1] (excludes parolees)	Years	Dominant characteristics of immigrants in each wave (these apply to most but not all immigrants arriving in these time frames)	Country of origin
I	More than 3 million (an average of more than 175,000 per year during the peak period between 1901 and 1914)	1881–1917	Jews emigrating primarily from small, rural villages in the impoverished Pale of Settlement, fleeing pogroms, whose first language was Yiddish and who were observant of Judaic traditions	Russian empire and the Baltic states[2]
Between I and II	Less than 3,000 per year	1918–20	Immigrants and defectors of various ethnic origins	Soviet Union[3] and Baltic states
	More than 70,000 (an average of 18,000 per year)	1921–24		
II	Approximately 50,000 (an average of less than 1,000 per year)	1925–40, and 1945–74		
	Less than 150 per year	1941–45 (WWII)		
	Thousands	Postwar years	Displaced Soviet citizens of various ethnic origins who did not return to the Soviet Union at the end of World War II	Nations outside the Soviet Union and Baltic states
III	Approximately 65,000	1975–82	Jews emigrating primarily from large cities, who were highly educated and experienced in professional occupations, whose first language was Russian, and who identified with Russian culture and knew little about Judaic tradition	Soviet Union and Baltic states
Between III and IV	Approximately 5,000 per year	1983–86	Immigrants and defectors of various ethnic origins	
IV	Nearly 1 million	1987–91	Armenians, ethnic Germans, victims of the 1986 Chernobyl disaster, and Jewish refugees received as "free cases"	
		1992–2000	Jewish immigrants arriving under the auspices of family reunification	Former Soviet Union[4] and Baltic states

Sources: Bureau of the Census, "Series C 89-119. Immigrants by Country: 1820–1870." In *Historical Statistics of the United States.* White Plains, NY: Kraus International, 1989; Immigration and Naturalization Service, *Annual Reports* and *Statistical Yearbooks for Fiscal Years Ending 1965–1998.* Washington, DC: Government Printing Office, 1999.

[1] Compiled from census statistics for immigration from the geographic regions that ultimately comprised the USSR, excluding Finland, and excluding Asian USSR between 1931 and 1963, and from the annual reports and statistical yearbooks of the Immigration and Naturalization Service for the years 1965–98.

[2] Latvia, Lithuania, and Estonia. Although they were incorporated into the Russian empire and the Soviet Union at various points in time, they are listed separately in all time frames presented here for the sake of clarity.

[3] The Union of Soviet Socialist Republics was not officially founded until 1922, as the region was embroiled in civil war up to that time.

[4] The Soviet Union ceased to exist in December 1991. "Former Soviet Union and Baltic states" serves as a constant category for assemblage and comparison of this kind of data.

Religious freedom was often a reason for leaving the Soviet Union. Here immigrants from Latvia living in Syracuse, New York, attend mass. *(Mel Rosenthal)*

backgrounds, anti-Semitic policies and anti-Semitism among the general populace made Jews the targets of unique forms of repression and discrimination. Bolsheviks initially denounced anti-Semitism with vehemence, but they simultaneously denounced Judaism, and repression of religious Jews soon encompassed secular Jews as well. Although such institutions as the Moscow State Yiddish Theater continued to exist until after World War II within the framework of the "nationalist in form, socialist in content" policy, in practice, Yiddish language and other expressions of Jewish culture attracted the condemnation of teachers, employers, and other authority figures. Beginning in 1933, all Soviet citizens were required to carry internal passports that displayed their nationality on the fifth line, and these passports perpetuated discrimination against Jews long after the Yiddish language and Jewish culture had ceased to set Jews apart from other Soviet citizens.

Anti-Semitism escalated after World War II. Propaganda alleged that Jews had not fought, when in actuality Jews were disproportionately represented among Soviet partisans and soldiers who died in the battle against fascism. Furthermore, the Soviet Union did not acknowledge that more than half of the prewar population of Soviet Jews had perished as Holocaust victims of the Nazi invaders. (Estimates of the number of Soviet Jews killed during the Holocaust

range between 2.5 million and 3.3 million.) Stalin's anti-Semitic excesses culminated when he alleged that Soviet Jewish doctors were responsible for the murder of several high Soviet officials. He intended for this "Doctors' Plot" to lay the foundation for massive deportation of Jews to Siberia, but he died before it could be realized. Under Nikita Khrushchev and Leonid Brezhnev, the Soviet government continued to institute anti-Semitic policies barring Jews from high positions and placing quotas on Jewish admissions to universities. When Jewish identity began to afford the opportunity to emigrate, some former Soviet Jews remarked with surprise that they had never thought they would see the day when Russians would wish for a Jewish passport, because in the Soviet Union, the consequences of having a Jewish passport had been so onerous. Nevertheless, almost all Soviet Jews cherish their "Jewishness" and would never renounce it.

Soviet and American conceptions of what it means to be Jewish differ in fundamental ways. These differences can be accounted for by the historical contexts in which these conceptions developed. "Jewishness" in the Soviet Union was powerfully constrained by government-sponsored anti-Semitism, whereas "Jewishness" in the United States was not constrained by the government. Therefore, Soviet Jews are more likely to associate "Jewishness" with a duty to withstand and overcome external pressure, whereas American Jews are more likely to associate it with a duty to adhere willfully to a code of behavior and a set of beliefs. The label "Russian" is uncomfortable for many former Soviet Jews in the United States. From their perspective, though they speak Russian, they are and have always been Jews, not Russians. Service providers in the American Jewish community refer to immigrants from the former Soviet Union as "New Americans."

THE THIRD AND FOURTH WAVES: IMMIGRATION SINCE 1974

In the wake of the Holocaust, the American Jewish community used its influence on the U.S. Congress, Soviet interest in normative relations with the West, and the dynamics of the Cold War to effectively aid Soviet Jewry. A pivotal moment came in 1974 when Congress passed the Freedom of Emigration Amendment to the Trade Act of 1974, which made commercial credit and Most Favored Nation status for the Soviet Union contingent on liberalization of emigration policies. Thus, in the mid-1970s, the confluence of détente and political pressure applied by the American Jewish community on behalf of Soviet Jewry made it possible for tens of thousands of Soviet Jews to emigrate from the Soviet Union to the United States and Israel. This third wave of emigration from the Soviet Union to the United States culminated in the late 1970s and early 1980s. Most of the third wave passed through Vienna and spent time waiting in Rome for permission to enter the United States. The third wave left behind their coapplicants, who, although denied permission to emigrate, suffered severe consequences for having publicly declared their intention to emigrate, including aggressive KGB surveillance and loss of employment. Jews who were denied permission to emigrate were referred to as "refuseniks."

Due to tense relations between the Soviet Union and the United States in the mid-1980s, relatively few people succeeded in emigrating from the Soviet Union. During the time between the third and fourth waves, the American Jewish community continued to raise awareness of injustices against refuseniks and other Jews in the Soviet Union in a variety of ways, and in 1989, Mikhail Gorbachev's administration suddenly allowed large numbers of Jews to emigrate. In response, local Jewish communities across the United States launched a fund-raising campaign called Operation Exodus, raising millions of dollars to fund local services as well as services in Israel. There was also an outpouring of volunteer support. By the mid-1990s, the number of refugees applying for admission was declining, and most American Jewish communities stopped receiving "free cases," as refugees without anchor relatives were called. Since the fourth wave peaked in the early 1990s, most former Soviets have been admitted under the auspices of family reunification programs, and anchor relatives have accepted much of the responsibility for resettling them.

Although only a decade separated those arriving in the 1970s and early 1980s from those arriving after 1988, the two groups differed in several ways. Most fourth-wave immigrants were Jewish, but the wave also included many ethnic Germans fleeing decades of brutal persecution and Armenians fleeing the war between Armenia and Azerbaijan. The third wave arriving in the late 1970s had different needs from the fourth wave due to changing conditions in the former Soviet Union, changes in legislation affecting assistance to refugees in the United States, and changes brought about in the receiving community by the increasing numbers of refugees resettled. The fourth wave overall had greater resources than the third wave because of the streamlining of resettlement services in the United States, the awaiting presence of refugees that preceded them, and the increased funding for resettlement that resulted from the Refugee Act of 1980.

ENCLAVES AND OTHER AREAS OF CONCENTRATED SETTLEMENT

Immigrants from the former Soviet Union have settled primarily in large urban areas on the East and West Coasts. More than half of all the third- and fourth-wave immigrants from the former Soviet Union live in New York City. The New York Association for New Americans (NYANA) considered the same factor when selecting areas for resettlement that Jewish resettlement agencies in other cities considered as well: the need for inexpensive housing in locations where an infrastructure of services to Jewish elderly was already in place. Consequently, in New York, Chicago, Los Angeles, San Francisco, Baltimore, and elsewhere, the immigrants of the third and fourth waves were resettled for the most part into the same neighborhoods that had received Jews from Russia and eastern Europe since the middle of the nineteenth century. Since the 1970s, former Soviet Jews have revitalized and transformed these neighborhoods both culturally and economically. The quintessential enclave of former Soviet émigré entrepreneurship is Brighton Beach, a neighborhood in Brooklyn, New York. West Rogers Park in Chicago and Skokie, Illinois, and West Hollywood and the Fairfax district in Los Angeles are other examples of historically Jewish neighborhoods that have become Russian-speaking enclaves.

Brighton Beach is by far the most populous Russian-speaking enclave in the United States. The streets are filled with sights and sounds of Russian language and culture, such as storefronts labeled with Russian names written with Cyrillic letters. By catering to coethnic customers and hiring coethnic laborers, ex-Soviet immigrants to Brighton Beach and other enclaves have achieved success as entrepreneurs without having to master the English language. In the 1980s, news media coverage of the Russian-speaking mafia corrupted the image of Brighton Beach, leaving it with a reputation for mob violence and crime. Therefore, many immigrants of the fourth wave tried to resettle elsewhere.

The 1990s marked an increasing trend toward suburban settlement of Jewish émigrés from the former Soviet Union, particularly those wanting to integrate into the mainstream U.S. economy. Many economically successful immigrants with children have migrated to suburban areas in pursuit of homeowner-ship, quality education for their children, and other aspects of the American dream. Younger immigrants who remain in the old inner-city neighborhoods into which they were initially resettled often stay because they cannot afford to do otherwise, whereas many older immigrants choose to stay because they derive the benefits of services to older adults and the companionship of their older coethnic peers.

ÉMIGRÉ CULTURE

Whereas their predecessors had expressed their Jewish identity by establishing religious institutions, Jews arriving from the former Soviet Union since 1970 have expressed themselves by establishing institutions and schools that promote the fine arts. Jewish families often celebrate and enact ritual rites of passage in Russian restaurants. Jewish parents who wish for their child to publicly experience his or her own bar mitzvah or bat mitzvah might feel uncomfortable in a synagogue setting, but the enactment of the ceremony in a nonkosher Russian restaurant enables them to reconcile and unite "three powerful aspects of their sense of self—their Jewish, Russian, and American identities." Russian-language poetry readings, plays, and concerts, meetings of Soviet veterans of World War II, and various other cultural events held in local synagogues and Jewish community centers also resolve the tension between who Soviet Jews were in the past, who they are becoming now in the United States, and who they might have been had they been free under Soviet rule to observe evolving Judaic traditions.

In addition to publishing many Russian-language newspapers in the United States, former Soviet immigrants maintain innumerable Web sites on the Internet. These newspapers and Web sites provide practical information about adaptation and naturalization, advertise businesses that cater to Russian-speaking clients, feature domestic and international news stories, and promote communication between former Soviet immigrants.

Among former Soviet Jewish émigrés, three minority groups stand out because of their ancient origins in Central Asia, their persistent religiosity, and their distinct cultural practices. During the Soviet era, destruction of religious institutions did not occur on the same scale in these remote areas as it did in the western republics and in such large cities as Alma-Ata and Baku. These three groups of indigenous central Asian Jews are concentrated in the ethnic enclave encompassing Rego Park and Forest Hills in Queens,

New York. The first group, Bukharan Jews, emigrated primarily from Uzbekistan, Tajikistan, and Kazakhstan in central Asia, where their ancestors developed a culture that blended Judaism and the Hebrew language with the Persian language and central Asian culture. Bukharan Jews have been exceptionally successful in building family businesses through the hard work of all family members. Many Bukharan Jews have embraced the Orthodox practice of Judaism and have formed close ties with the Hasidic community. Devout Jews from the former republic of Georgia comprise the second distinct group, and "Tats," as Jews from the Caucasus Mountains of Azerbaijan are sometimes called, make up the third.

THE ADAPTATION OF FORMER SOVIET IMMIGRANTS IN THE UNITED STATES

"A century ago it took more than one generation to integrate into American society," announced a spokesperson for the Research Institute for New Americans (RINA), an organization founded by former Soviet immigrants. "Now it's six years." Based on data obtained between August 1998 and October 1999 from a survey of more than one thousand ex-Soviet immigrants living in New York City, RINA asserted that ex-Soviet households achieve levels of income comparable with those in American households within six years of the immigrants' arrival in the United States, on average. The data showed an 82 percent rate of employment among those surveyed who were under the age of sixty-five and who had been in the United States for nine years or longer.

A 1998 survey conducted by the Office of Refugee Resettlement found that refugees from the former Soviet Union coming to the United States between 1993 and 1998 had twelve years of education on average, the highest level of education among all the refugee populations studied. Rates of unemployment and welfare participation among the ex-Soviet population are relatively high because the population is disproportionately older compared with other immigrant populations. Most immigrants over the age of sixty-five rely on Supplemental Security Income (SSI) pensions for income. These pensions have indirectly enabled their children to achieve economic self-sufficiency more quickly.

Studies of former Soviet Jews in the United States show that age at time of arrival, gender, number of dependent children, republic of origin, level of education, former occupation, and present occupation are significant sources of variation within the ex-Soviet émigré community. Age at arrival emerges as the most powerful variable affecting the economic adaptation of refugees in this community. Men between the ages of fifty-five and sixty-five have experienced the most difficulty in finding employment, particularly employment that utilizes their expertise and experience. Consequently, men in this age range have suffered the greatest incidence of psychiatric and physical illnesses. In general, loss of professional status seems to be the greatest trauma for former Soviets in the United States, as many of them left behind jobs which, though poorly paid, were complex and intellectually interesting. A large proportion of this highly educated population furthers their education in the United States in order to qualify to practice former professions or to change professions entirely. Many ex-Soviet immigrants have found a niche in the computer industry after completing programming courses offered by community colleges or by schools founded by former Soviet immigrants.

Since the inception of the Soviet Union, the United States has been greatly enriched by the contributions of former Soviet immigrants in a variety of professions, including those made by brilliant scientists, engineers, doctors, musicians, and artists, as well as hardworking entrepreneurs. Those who have decried the "brain drain" from the former Soviet Union understand that the Soviet loss became American gain.

Michelle Stem Cook

See also: Impact of Immigration on the American Economy (Part II, Sec. 7); Social Services, Welfare and Public Benefits (Part II, Sec. 9); Illegal Immigration Reform and Immigrant Responsibility Act, 1996, Personal Responsibility and Work Opportunity Reconciliation Act, 1996, California Proposition 187, 1994 (Part IV, Sec. 1); Title IV: Restricting Welfare and Public Benefits for Aliens, 1996 (Part IV, Sec. 2).

BIBLIOGRAPHY

Altshuler, Mordechai. *Soviet Jewry Since the Second World War: Population and Social Structure*. New York: Greenwood Press, 1987.

Bureau of the Census. "Series C 89–119. Immigrants by Country: 1820–1970." In *Historical Statistics of the United States*. White Plains, NY: Kraus International Publishers, 1989.

Chervyakov, Valeriy, Zvi Gitelman, and Vladimir Shapiro. "Religion and Ethnicity: Judaism in the Ethnic Consciousness of Contemporary Russian Jews." *Ethnic and Racial Studies* 20 (1997): 280–305.

Cook, Michelle Stem. "The Impossible Me: Misconstruing Structural Constraint and Individual Volition." In *Self and Identity Through the Life Course in Cross-Cultural Perspective*, ed. Zena Smith Blau, pp. 55–76. Stanford, CT: JAI Press, 2000.

Fein, Isaac M. *The Making of an American Jewish Community: The History of Baltimore Jewry from 1773 to 1920*. Philadelphia: Jewish Publication Society of America, 1971.

Friedman, Murray, and Albert D. Chernin, eds. *A Second Exodus: The American Movement to Free Soviet Jews*. Hanover, NH: University Press of New England for Brandeis University Press, 1999.

Gitelman, Zvi. *A Century of Ambivalence*. New York: Schocken Press, 1988.

Gold, Stephen J. *From the Workers' State to the Golden State: Jews from the Former Soviet Union in California*. Boston, MA: Allyn and Bacon, 1995.

———. *Refugee Communities: A Comparative Field Study*. Edited by J. Stanfield. Newbury Park, CA: Sage Publications, 1992.

Hebrew Immigrant Aid Society Web site: www.hias.org

Immigration and Naturalization Service. *Annual Reports and Statistical Yearbooks for the Fiscal Years Ending 1965–1998*. Washington, DC: Government Printing Office, 1999.

Immigration and Naturalization Service. "Table 13 Immigrant Aliens Admitted by Country or Region of Birth, Years Ended June 30, 1945 to 1954." In *Annual Report of the INS for the Fiscal Year Ending June 30, 1954*. Washington, DC: Government Printing Office, 1954.

Jacobs, Dan N., and Ellen Frankel Paul, eds. *Studies of the Third Wave: Recent Migration of Soviet Jews to the United States*. Boulder, CO: Westview Press, 1981.

Krasnov, Vladislav. *Soviet Defectors: The KGB Wanted List*. Stanford, CA: Hoover Institution Press, 1985.

Levin, Nora. *The Jews in the Soviet Union Since 1917: Paradox of Survival*. New York: New York University Press, 1988.

Litwin, Howard. "The Social Networks of Elderly Immigrants: An Analytic Typology." *Journal of Aging Studies* 9 (1995): 155–74.

MacKenzie, David, and Michael W. Curran. *A History of Russia and the Soviet Union*. Belmont, CA: Wadsworth, 1987.

Markowitz, Fran. *A Community in Spite of Itself: Soviet Jewish Emigrés in New York*. Washington, DC: Smithsonian Institution Press, 1993.

———. "Rituals as Keys to Soviet Immigrants' Jewish Identity." In *Between Two Worlds: Ethnographic Essays on American Jewry*, ed. Jack Kugelmass, pp. 128–47. Ithaca: Cornell University Press, 1988.

Office of Refugee Resettlement Web site: www.acf.dhhs.gov/programs/orr

Orleck, Annelise. *The Soviet Jewish Americans*. Westport, CT: Greenwood Press, 1999.

Pinkus, Benjamin. *The Jews of the Soviet Union*. Cambridge, MA: Cambridge University Press, 1988.

Ro'i, Yaacov. *The Struggle for Soviet Jewish Emigration, 1948–1967*. Cambridge, MA: Cambridge University Press, 1991.

Shapiro, Gershon. *Under Fire: The Stories of Jewish Heroes of the Soviet Union*. Jerusalem: Yad Vashem, 1988.

Simanovsky, Stanislav, Margarita P. Strepetova, and Yuriy G. Naido. *Brain Drain from Russia: Problems, Prospects, and Ways of Regulation.* New York: Nova Science Publishers, 1996.

Wiener, Julie. "Russian Jewish Immigrants Go to the Head of the Class." *Jewish Telegraphic Agency,* http://www.jta.org, 2000.

Yurganov, Oleg. Personal communication, November 2000.

Zborowski, Mark, and Elizabeth Herzog. *Life Is with People: The Culture of the Shtetl.* New York: Schocken Books, 1952.

Zolatarev, Semeon. *Lyudi i Sydbi* (People and Fates). Baltimore: Vestnik Information Agency, 1997.

GREAT BRITAIN

The British immigration to America is unique because the English laid the foundation for American culture. As the dominant group from the early colonial period, they defined the society to which later immigrants came. Because they arrived in a familiar environment, later British immigrants experienced a smoother transition than the one endured by those without common ties of religion, language, and culture, whether Huguenot or Hmong. Historically, over 5 million British immigrants have come to the United States, a number that ranks third behind Germany and Italy.

COLONIAL ERA

The colonial era (1607–1776) saw the beginnings of European settlement and the definition of the American society that later immigrant groups would join. During the seventeenth century, the colonial population included Walloons, Dutch, Swedes, and French, but these small groups were overshadowed by the larger populations of Germans and British—the English, the Scots, and the Scots-Irish. The English had settled Virginia in 1607 and the New England colonies from the 1620s, with the great Puritan migration of 20,000 people taking place between 1629 and 1640. The English civil war stopped migration, but the Restoration under Charles II stabilized England, and by 1689 there were over 200,000 people in the British colonies. New England and the southern colonies were already homogeneously English Protestant, but the middle colonies, established in the late seventeenth century, began existence culturally and religiously diverse. The eighteenth-century influx of Germans and Scots-Irish helped to increase the population tenfold between 1689 and 1776. In 1776, the population included 1.2 million English. There were half that many African Americans and 600,000–700,000 Native Amer-

icans. More important culturally were the 300,000 Scots-Irish and 250,000 Germans. The remaining 200,000 were French, Dutch, Belgian, Scottish, Welsh, and Jewish, mostly in the middle colonies.

In the colonial era, the English Protestant majority had reservations about non-English immigrants. The Scots, both highland and lowland, and the Germans did not adapt to the dominant culture. Instead, they removed themselves into ethnic enclaves where they preserved their own customs. The Celtic Irish were a concern to the anti-Catholic English. As for the Scots-Irish, they seemed obnoxious, narrow-minded, and everywhere. Although clannish with a common Presbyterian church, they lacked strong family ties and willingly removed from their community. They were restlessly mobile movers of the frontier westward. Still, they had a common language with the English. By the time of the American Revolution, they were well along the way to acculturation.

NINETEENTH CENTURY

In the late eighteenth and early nineteenth centuries, the British attempted to reduce emigration. To keep the skills needed for their industrial revolution, the British prohibited emigration of skilled artisans. The British Passenger Act of 1803 limited the number of people a ship could carry, making the indentured servant trade unprofitable and reducing Irish immigration to only a few thousand a year. Further discouraging immigration was the British habit of impressing immigrants into the navy, a major deterrent from 1810 until the end of the Napoleonic Wars in 1815. It was also a source of friction; impressment of American citizens was one cause of the War of 1812. The Treaty of Ghent in 1814 recognized the right of British individuals to renounce their citizenship in favor of American citizenship. Dual citizenship also became British law. From that point Britain and the United States generally had a special friendship, even though there was occasional conflict, as in their competing claims in Oregon by the late 1830s and 1840s.

Between 1815 and 1860, 5 million immigrants flooded America, more immigrants than the total population of the United States in 1790. Over half came from the British Isles. Two million were Irish, but another 750,000 came from England, Wales, and Scotland. For the 1820s through the 1890s, total English immigration was only 1.8 million out of a total of 14.39 million immigrants; Scotland added another 368,012 individuals, and Wales, 42,076. These British immigrants, like their counterparts elsewhere in western Europe, were leaving due to rapid population growth (Europe grew from 140 million in 1750 to over 400 million by World War I), which reduced agricultural opportunity, and due to industrialization, which altered the occupational structure. British immigrants were mostly ambitious and status-conscious small farmers and workers who sought higher wages or cheaper farmland in America. Protestant and English-speaking, educated and skilled, immigrants fit readily into a predominantly Protestant, English-speaking country committed to education, ambition, and exploitation. The major Welsh immigration occurred between 1820 and 1900, when 40,000 left Wales and another 50,000 left England, mostly in search of land or jobs in mines or industry. Although sharing a common religious and cultural heritage, the Welsh had a distinct language. They settled initially in their own communities with Welsh-language institutions, switched to English in the second generation, and moved easily into the mainstream.

In the 1890s, a changed American economy needed less skilled labor; the old immigrants gave way to the new immigrants who came to the cities and labored to build the Gilded Age industrial America. For the British, the island nation's commercial empire provided ample opportunity both at home and around the world. British capital was a major contribution to the rapid development of the United States after the American Civil War.

TWENTIETH-CENTURY DECLINE

Between 1901 and 1912, British and Irish emigrants choosing the United States declined from 61 percent to 25 percent of emigrants. England, Scotland, and Wales combined for 1.3 million immigrants out of a total of 18.3 million from the turn of the century through the 1930s. Commonwealth ties attracted the majority of emigrants, who chose to move to Canada, Australia, and South Africa. After the turn of the century, America had become a land of no frontier, and competition for jobs as unskilled labor was strong from the new southern and eastern European immigrants.

Restrictive immigration laws of the 1920s reduced immigration from 800,000 in 1921 to less than 150,000 by 1929. The national origins system, which was in full effect by 1929, also reduced immigration while shifting its composition. The British quota doubled, while those of Germany, Scandinavia, and the Irish Free State dropped markedly. These three areas had sent almost three times as many immigrants as Britain, but the new British quota was larger than that for all the rest of northwest Europe combined.

BRITISH WEST INDIES

The British quota under the Quota Act of 1921 and the Immigration Act of 1924 included the British West Indies. Black immigrants benefited from the pro-European bias of the 1920s legislation until the McCarran-Walter Act of 1952 set a quota of 100 immigrants per year from the European dependencies. The West Indian migration shifted to England until the mid-1960s, when the West Indian countries won their independence and American law once again favored those excluded by the 1920s laws. West Indians were prominent in the Harlem Renaissance and American cultural, political, and intellectual life from the 1920s. Prominent among them were the writer Claude McKay and the black nationalist Marcus Garvey. Also noteworthy from the late twentieth century are Stokely Carmichael, who coined the phrase, "Black is beautiful," and Shirley Chisholm, the first African-American woman elected to Congress. By the 1990 census, there were 682,418 West Indians in the United States.

GREAT DEPRESSION

Despite relatively favorable American legislation, the Great Depression of the 1930s basically killed British immigration. Between 1926 and 1930, there were only 121,000 British immigrants; between 1931 and 1935, that number fell to less than 15,000 (the 1933 total from all sources was only 23,000 new immigrants, the lowest total since 1830). The next surge came during and after World War II.

WAR BRIDES

The War Brides Act of 1945 and the 1947 Fiancée Act authorized entry of aliens married or engaged to veterans regardless of quota. The two laws produced the largest immigration, especially of women, since the 1920s, and the largest immigration of women in the 1940s was from Britain. Thousands were deserted, widowed, or held up by immigration laws for years. Also, thousands of GIs immigrated to their wives' homeland. The first war brides in Britain and Australia immigrated in 1942; the last, Japanese who had to wait for repeal of the Oriental Exclusion Act, did not begin immigrating until 1952.

The British normally welcomed American GIs. They shared a common language. Local men were away (sometimes marrying local women themselves, including Americans). Britain had a shortage of men and a surplus of women. GIs found themselves in close proximity to local women who were independent and sociable. These circumstances produced the 115,000 war brides and grooms who immigrated under the postwar legislation. In addition, approximately thirty thousand came from Britain during the war on standby with the wounded and prisoners of war. A total of 100,000 brides had come from Britain by 1947.

Government policy was to discourage marriage, even though an estimated 80 percent of several thousand World War I marriages had worked out. The red tape involving getting a soldier's wife into the United States could take up to a year and required one or more interviews, including one with the Red Cross. Marriage without permission could result in court martial or transfer to the war zone.

In 1945, the Married Women's Association, a British women's organization, picketed the American embassy, protested in Hyde Park, and finally met with the American ambassador's representative. But troop transport had first priority, especially with pressure from wives and members of Congress in the United States to bring the soldiers back home. At the time of the demonstration, there were 60,000 British and 6,000 Australian and New Zealand brides awaiting transportation, some of whom had been separated from their husband for two to three years.

On December 28, 1945, Public Law 271, the War Brides Act, granted nonquota status (the current ceiling was 150,000 immigrants per year) for three years. In January 1946, preparations began for transport of the brides on thirty ships, mostly troopships and hospital ships but also the *Queen Elizabeth*, the *Argentina*, and especially the speedy, 2,500-passenger-capacity

Queen Mary. Priority was given to dependents of military above classification E-4, those on orders to America, former prisoners of war, those wounded in action, and those hospitalized in the United States.

Paperwork required included a visa, proof of the spouse's support, commander's approval of the spouse's affidavit, and from the spouse's family guarantee of a place to stay if traveling ahead of the spouse. Also required were a passport, marriage certificate, birth certificate, police record and discharge papers if applicable, and proof that on arrival he/she would have or could buy a railroad ticket. The visa fee was $10. British currency restrictions limited all overseas travelers to £10.

Some tried to make their own way but were generally turned back. Brides and fiancées of nonwhite GIs were discouraged because a majority of the states did not recognize their marriages. These women had to apply under the quota, which could have taken up to ten years to allow them into the United States. And once in the antimiscegenation states, the brides were at risk for becoming public charges, because they would not be allowed to live with their husbands, or going to jail for violation of the antimiscegenation laws. Either situation was grounds for revocation of a visa or deportation. The final ship out was the *Henry Gibbons*, which sailed in October 1946.

The Fiancée Act, public law 4712, of June 1947, authorized nonimmigrant visitors visas good for three months for those from a nationality eligible for immigration and possessing proof of intent to marry. The law was to last for one year. Failure to marry was grounds for deportation. Covered by this law were an estimated 1,500 Australians, 1,000 Europeans, and 15,000 in the United Kingdom. It included recognized children of an American citizen; stepchildren had a separate visa process, but they had priority. Fiancées, with a lower priority, sometimes got married by proxy if their destination was one of the nineteen states that recognized proxy. Some flew military transport. Some brides paid their own way, but commercial airfare could be £100 ($403).

Once in the United States, they were not automatically citizens because of the immigration law of 1922. Still, the five-year wait was waived, and they could begin the citizenship process in two years. Most eventually became citizens.

Some were incomplete immigrants. In July 1947, the American Red Cross reported 1,133 brides in England who did not want to emigrate. Divorce and desertion happened in England, but it was not an issue, so it was probably uncommon. In December 1945, the British government estimated there were 550 mixed-race children deserted by their mothers. And as early as 1944, the Red Cross was dealing with brides who found out after arrival in the United States that either their husband or his family did not want them. And inevitably reunion resulted sometimes in divorce, or homesickness overpowered love. The first-year return rate was perhaps 5 percent, or 3,500 people.

Averaging age twenty-three on arrival, these brides had generally completed the mandatory schooling to age fourteen. They were working or lower middle class, and they did not settle in ethnic enclaves because they did not come in groups. They were the beneficiaries of the first special nonrestrictive American immigration laws in the twentieth century. Also, they were welcomed and received a great deal of publicity, mostly favorable. Still, they experienced alienation and loneliness. As with other immigrant groups, they established social and cultural clubs and organizations. The Episcopal Church was of assistance. British war brides set up networks to replicate the extended families they had sacrificed for the American nuclear family. Not surprisingly, fifty years later, most retained strong British identification and had not fully assimilated. British war brides under the War Brides Act and the Fiancée Act were the most publicized of all war brides. And it was a stable group: approximately 86 percent remained married 40 years later.

POSTWAR DOWNTURN

Even with the war brides, between 1945 and 1955 more than 80 percent of British emigrants went to other Commonwealth nations, primarily Canada and Australia. The United States was choice number three.

In the second half of the twentieth century, there was an upsurge after World War II and another in the 1960s. In the 1950s Great Britain was adjusting to the diminished role that resulted from two world wars, the Korean War, and the end of its empire. With wartime rationing still in place as late as 1956, the future appeared brighter elsewhere, especially for those who were skilled, educated, and ambitious. Britain feared the adverse impact of a "brain drain," as many of its best-trained and brightest technical and professional people migrated out in search of better opportunity in the commonwealth and in the United States. In 1966, Britain lost 4,200 engineers and technologists, half to North America; scientists and engineers were drawn by salaries triple the British level and research budgets four times as large. Still, by historical standards, the British economy was good: gross domestic product grew by an annual rate of 2.7 percent be-

tween 1948 and 1968, and unemployment held at 3 percent or less from 1945 to 1970. But the rest of Europe grew much faster, and by the late 1970s, England's standard of living was no better than Italy's. Then, in the general economic malaise of the 1970s, Britain's long-standing problems—among them low productivity, obsolete infrastructure, and high welfare costs—revealed its noncompetitiveness and resulted in the first decline in living standards since 1945. Britain climbed back in the 1980s, but not without a struggle. High unemployment peaked at 13 percent in 1983, the worst since the depression; inflation was 21 percent in 1979; industrial output fell more in 1979–81 than it did in 1929–32. But Margaret Thatcher denationalized and sold off many state-owned assets, North Sea oil came in, and American tourism rose from $120 million in 1960 to more than $1 billion in the early 1980s. Britain reestablished itself not as an economic miracle but as a significant European state.

By the mid-1960s, some English feared they were becoming an economic and cultural colony of the United States because of the inroads made by American businesses, movies, and service personnel. When John Lennon and Paul McCartney launched the "British Invasion," returning rock and roll to America as ramped-up skiffle music draped in the Union Jack, they led a cultural transformation from Carnaby Street to Haight-Ashbury to the end of the century. Gerry and the Pacemakers, the Animals, the Kinks, Petula Clark, Tom Jones, Ian Whitcomb, and many others exchanged British-accented music for American dollars. James Bond novels and movies and English fashion, including Twiggy, swept the colonies.

Neither the brain drain nor the British Invasion significantly affected immigration, which had already become a trickle that would be less than 2 percent of the annual total in the late 1990s. By the mid-1980s, Great Britain ranked twelfth in the number of immigrants coming to the United States. Ahead of Great Britain were Mexico, the Philippines, Korea, Cuba, India, China, the Dominican Republic, Vietnam, Jamaica, Haiti, and Iran. In the 1990s, British immigration was minimal. In 1995, only 12,326 immigrated—more than 7,000 were relatives or family sponsored. Less than 4,000 came under the employment provision (special skills or more than $1 million in capital and employer of ten or more people), and 1,169 were diversity immigrants, those from countries underrepresented in recent annual immigration totals. In 1998, the United Kingdom contributed only 9,011 of 660,477 total legal immigrants.

IMPACT

Although the numbers were small, the impact of the British in America was out of proportion to the total. Despite divergence over time, American society was originally and remains more English than anything else, this despite its incorporation of elements of the diverse cultures brought by the large numbers of immigrants from other countries. And Americans throughout their history have been receptive to all things English, from George Whitefield's fiery preaching in the eighteenth century through the Shakespearean performances that were a strong element of nineteenth-century popular culture through James Bond to the British Invasion and *Masterpiece Theater*. And British expatriates, as most other groups in America, maintain ties to home through newspapers and Web sites devoted to their interests. Such Web sites as *britishinamerica.com* provide links to information on visas, British goods, food, news and sports, jobs, immigration lawyers, and so on. In hard copy or online, the homesick can access such publications as the *American Scottish Gazette, British Heritage,* and *Ninnau* (Welsh and Welsh immigrant news in Wales, Canada, and the United States).

John Herschel Barnhill

See also: Los Angeles (Part II, Sec. 12); Immigration to Australia, Immigration to Canada, Immigration to Western Europe (Part II, Sec. 13); History of the English Settlement in Edwards County, Illinois, 1818 (Part IV, Sec. 3).

BIBLIOGRAPHY

Cose, Ellis. *A Nation of Strangers.* New York: William Morrow and Company, 1992.

Dimbleby, David, and David Reynolds. *An Ocean Apart.* New York: Vintage Books, 1989.

Jones, Maldwyn Allen. *American Immigration.* 2d ed. Chicago: University of Chicago Press, 1992.

Olson, James Stuart. *The Ethnic Dimension in American History.* New York: St. Martin's Press, 1979.

Palmer, Ransford W. *Pilgrims from the Sun: West Indian Migration to America.* Twayne's Immigrant Heritage of America Series. New York: Twayne Publishers, 1995. Thomas J. Archdeacon, General Editor.

Shukert, Elfrieda, and Barbara Smith. *War Brides of World War II.* Novato, CA: Presidio Press, 1988.

Virden, Jenel. *Goodbye Piccadilly: British War Brides in America.* Statue of Liberty-Ellis Island Centennial Series. Urbana: University of Illinois Press, 1996.

IRELAND

hether in exile or in search of opportunity, the Irish have long been in America. In the colonial era of the seventeenth and eighteenth centuries, they came, as did many other groups, as indentured servants. In 1788, Britain prohibited emigration of skilled artisans from Ireland. The British Passenger Act of 1803 made the servant trade unprofitable, and Irish immigration fell to only a few thousand individuals a year. At the same time and especially through the Napoleonic Wars (1810–12), the British navy impressed immigrants into service, another disincentive to ship to America.

Between the War of 1812 and the American Civil War (1861–65), more immigrants entered the United States than the total U.S. population had numbered in 1790. Two million, or 40 percent of them, were Irish. In the 1820s and 1830s, the Irish were approximately 35 percent of the total immigrants, and in the famine immigration of the 1840s, more Irish immigrated than in all previous U.S. history. Many of these Irish settled in northeastern U.S. cities, where they labored as cartmen, dockworkers, and other unskilled occupations. Some were put to work constructing the Erie Canal. For all of their contributions to the northern economy, however, the large influx of Catholic Irish immigrants into a predominantly Protestant country triggered antiforeign nativism. Indeed, one of the largest political parties of the period—the American Party, or Know-Nothings—was fundamentally an anti-Catholic, anti-immigrant organization.

During the Civil War, the United States needed immigrant workers to take the places of American workers who had entered the Union army. Simultaneously, the British government encouraged emigration of the Irish and English poor. Secretary of State William Seward even published letters in Irish newspapers promoting emigration to the United States. Also, the rumor was that Ireland was planning to outlaw emigration. Although there was a perception in some quarters that the United States was recruiting foreigners to immigrate and join its armies, the Irish still came. Most entered at the low end of the socioeconomic structure and often competed with blacks for the lowest-paying jobs. When Congress enacted draft legislation, it exempted foreigners, but not those in the process of becoming citizens. It also exempted blacks as well as those who could pay their way out or provide a substitute. When the draft lottery began in New York City in July 1863, a riot ensued; its main target became blacks, and its main participants were Irish. The riot left at least 100 dead, perhaps as many as thousands injured. Irish Catholics for years after felt on the fringe of society. But the post–Civil War years began to see a new trend in Irish-American history. While many remained on the bottom rungs of the economic ladder, more and more were able to succeed in politics, the police, and private industry.

Between 1860 and 1890, the number of Irish immigrants declined, though there were temporary upswings such as the one after another agricultural crisis (and another Irish famine) in 1882, when Irish immigration reached 179,000 in 1882. This number was still less than the number of immigrants from Germany (250,000). The late-nineteenth-century Scots-Irish immigration included individuals with industrial skills, such as coal miners, iron puddlers, and the like. (The Scots Irish were Protestants from what is now Northern Ireland; originally they had come from Scotland.)

Between the late nineteenth century and the 1980s, immigration from Ireland continued at a slow but steady pace. Under the quota law of 1924—which allowed persons from a given nation to immigrate to the United States at a rate equal to 2 percent of their total in the United States in 1890—Irish were largely free to enter, since there were so many in the United States by 1890. But with Irish freedom from Britain in 1921, followed by the Great Depression and World War II, immigration from the island nation declined.

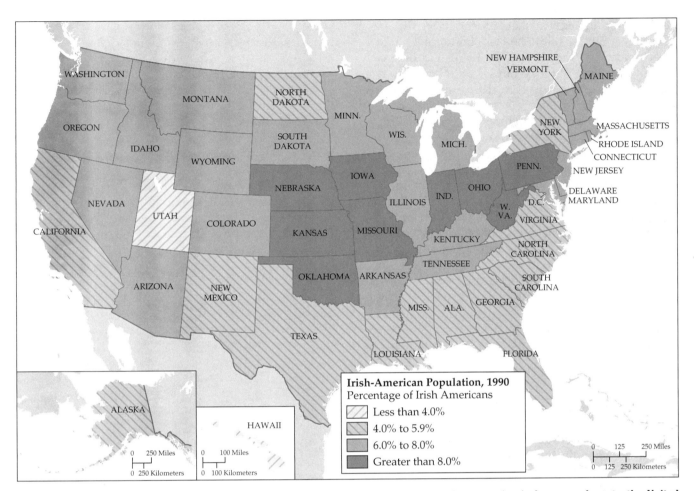

Irish-American Population, 1990
Percentage of Irish Americans

- Less than 4.0%
- 4.0% to 5.9%
- 6.0% to 8.0%
- Greater than 8.0%

The Irish—that is, the Catholic Irish, as opposed to the Protestant Scots-Irish—have been coming in large numbers to the United States since the mid-nineteenth century. Most settled in the large cities of the Northeast and Midwest. *(CARTO-GRAPHICS)*

NEW IRISH

In the 1980s, another wave of emigrants left Ireland, heading as they had for so many decades for the United States. From before the American Revolution, North America has been a major influence in Irish life, and there is a long history of immigration to the new world. Continuing the long pattern, between 100,000 and 150,000 undocumented Irish entered the United States in the 1980s, and they tended to end up predominantly in New York City and Boston, where long-established networks were in place and opportunity was strong.

In the mid-1960s, Ireland attempted to discourage emigration, seeking to develop its own homegrown economic miracle. The 1965 immigration reform act, which shifted immigration criteria to encourage the reunification of families, largely foreclosed immigration by the Irish. But at that time it was not a concern, and those Irish who wished to emigrate had outlets in England and Australia. A few thousand students came to the United States each year, but most Irish went elsewhere.

By the 1980s, the Irish economy had hit hard times, with unemployment rising to 19 percent by the end of 1986 and no relief in sight; Irish industry and exports faltered. For the young Irish, America was once again the land of opportunity. When they learned of the 1965 immigration reforms, they refused to accept American immigration law.

The few thousand Irish immigrants who entered the United States legally with visas were overshadowed by the thousands more who came as tourists, visitors, or students and then chose to stay, disappearing into the Irish community. These illegal aliens, who preferred to be known as "undocumenteds," tended to be young, educated, and the "cream" of the Irish population. They were not like their nineteenth-century predecessors, Catholic or Protestant, who had been integral to the building of America. Nor were they like most other twentieth-century illegal aliens, who tended to be from the lower end of the economic and educational ladder. Rather, the New Irish were ambitious, middle-class immigrants with a good education. And they spoke English as opposed to many other immigrant groups. In the 1980s, no one knew exactly how many New Irish undocumenteds were in the United States. The Immigration and Naturalization Service (INS) estimated them at 40,000, while the advocates of special legislation for the undocumented Irish preferred to toss out numbers ranging to 500,000. No matter their number, the Irish illegally in the United States did not qualify for the amnesty provided to other illegal aliens under the Immigration Reform and Control Act (IRCA) of 1986. The act gave permanent residency to illegal aliens who had entered the country before January 1, 1982, and who had been continuously in residence since then. Those Irish who had emigrated because of the economic downturn in Ireland after 1982 were too new to qualify.

The Irish had already been hit once by adverse immigration policy and could not qualify under the family preference rules of the 1960s. Still they came, and although better educated and more urban than those who had arrived in the nineteenth century, they often ended up in unskilled jobs. Because they could not get the documents required for a middle-class life, they ended up bussing tables, tending children, and generally handling the low-end labor for which documentation was less expected. Thus they could not obtain social security cards, driver's licenses, and home loans, some of the basic means by which individuals enter mainstream American life. At the same time, they were cut off from the Irish political process because overseas Irish could not vote. They were also highly vulnerable to exploitation by those who provided them with low-end jobs in the underground economy. And they were not willing to accept second-class status. In the aftermath of the amnesty program, the INS tightened enforcement; illegal aliens faced a real threat of deportation. The undocumenteds were unwilling to accept such a situation, and they did not have to because they had other resources.

What the New Irish had was support, protection, and advocacy from the Irish-American and Irish immigrant communities, which lobbied for changes in America's immigration laws. Boston mayor Raymond Flynn wanted to establish an agency especially to help them, and Representative Joseph Kennedy (D-MA) floated an amnesty bill specifically for the pre-1987 illegal Irish, but that measure died.

The Immigration Reform and Control Act of 1986 set aside 10,000 visas for "adversely affected" countries, that is, those countries that were negatively im-

pacted by the 1965 immigration reform act. The provision was included by Representative Brian Donnelly (D-MA) of Boston, whose district was considered the most Irish in the United States, with as many as 10,000 illegal Irish. Donnelly believed there were so many illegal, because the Irish received so few visas. Between 1840 and 1860, the Irish composed 37 percent of the nation's 4.3 million immigrants; in 1986, they made up less than 2 percent of the over 600,000 legal immigrants. One reason for the small percentage of Irish was the immigration reform legislation of 1965, which favored Asian immigrants over European ones because more and more of the former could claim family ties. Those squeezed out were deemed "adversely affected" and competed in the lottery of 1987. The lottery was designed to allow immigrants from countries adversely affected by the 1965 immigration law to receive more visas. Applicants filed for visas and were then chosen by lottery. In that lottery, 1.4 million Irish applied for the 10,000 slots. Irish received more than one-third of the visas.

In 1987, Representative Donnelly, Senator Edward Kennedy (D-MA), and Senator Daniel Patrick Moynihan (D-NY) introduced legislation to set aside 50,000 visas for old sources of immigrants such as Western Europe and Canada, with special emphasis on attracting young, well-educated, English-speaking individuals from the adversely affected countries. After negotiation, the final legislation, known as the Kennedy-Donnelly Act of 1988, deleted the preference for those who spoke English, but it set aside 16,000 visas per year for the Irish while opening the immigration door wider for a range of constituencies that had been ignored or excluded in the 1920s.

Aside from politicians, the New Irish had strong support from Old Irish and Irish-American institutions in the mid-1980s. Most noticeable was the Irish Immigration Reform Movement (IIRM). Established by Patrick Hurley and Sean Minihane, the IIRM was the principal lobby for the New Irish with sympathetic politicians, the old-guard Irish Americans and the Irish immigrants of the 1950s, the church, and the media. One of the key players in the IIRM was Adrian Flannelly, a New York radio personality and critic of the Catholic failure to do more for the undocumenteds. Flannelly spearheaded the effort to establish Project Irish Outreach, which imported Irish priests to help undocumenteds with problems; with approval from John Cardinal O'Connor, the first priests arrived in early 1988. Flannelly also influenced Irish politicians to set up Immigration Working Committees in all Irish consulates, and in 1988, he founded the Emerald Isle Immigration Center (EIIC) in New York City, the prototype for immigration centers elsewhere in the United States. Funding for the EIIC came from the Irish government, New York State, New York City, and several boroughs.

Also important in publicizing the plight of the New Irish were two newspapers, the *Irish Echo,* voice of the older community, and the *Irish Voice,* established in 1987 by the IIRM. Other media also tended to be supportive in part due to the significant presence in them of New Irish immigrants.

In 1990, the Bush administration raised the annual immigration ceiling from 490,000 to 700,000. The ceiling decreased to 675,000 in 1995 once an initial adjustment for spouses and children had occurred. For the first three years under this legislation, more than half of the slots were set aside for relatives of those already in the United States, signifying no major departure from the 1960s approach. The big change was that nearly 140,000 visas (almost triple what had been available before) were based on possession of a needed skill. And there was a set-aside of 40,000 visas (increasing to 55,000 in 1995) for immigrants from traditional source countries in Europe and Africa, including Ireland. But there was no absolute guaranteed allotment for the Irish; in this, Irish and Irish-American lobbying efforts had failed.

All this activity by Congress, social and religious groups, the press, and other molders of public opinion was brought about by the perceived need to compensate for the miscalculation of those who designed the 1960s legislation. When shifting the focus to bringing in family members, legislators expected that most family members would be European. To their surprise, most came from Asia.

By the time of the Bush adjustment, the Irish economy had rebounded and appeared able to accommodate those who had previously emigrated. Rather than emigrating, many of the New Irish commuted, visited, or established themselves as world business people without fixed location in either Ireland or the United States. Although the *Irish Echo* in 1999 was decrying the tightened INS enforcement against illegals, for the most part the pressures for better treatment of the New Irish abated. In combination, the immigration legislation of the 1980s had produced 72,000 visas; presumably, there remained undocumented Irish in the United States, but probably at nowhere near the 1980s level.

John Herschel Barnhill

See also: New York City (Part II, Sec. 12); Immigration to Australia, Immigration to Canada, Immigration to Western and Southern Europe (Part II, Sec. 13); Stimulating Emigration from Ireland, 1837, Emigration, Emigrants, and Know-Nothings, 1854, Irish Response to Nativism, 1854, Four Years of Irish History, 1845–1849 (Part IV, Sec. 3).

BIBLIOGRAPHY

Cose, Ellis. *A Nation of Strangers: Prejudice, Politics, and the Populating of America.* New York: William Morrow, 1992.

Jones, Maldwyn Allen. *American Immigration.* 2d ed. Chicago: University of Chicago Press, 1992.

Miller, Kerby A. *Emigrants and Exiles: Ireland and the Irish Exodus to North America.* New York: Oxford University Press, 1985.

O'Hanlon, Ray. *The New Irish Americans.* Niwot, CO: Roberts Rinehart, 1998.

Web sites:

Culturefront Online   www.culturefront.org

Emerald Isle Immigration Center of
New York   www.eiic.org

Irish Echo Newspaper Online   www.irishecho.com

WESTERN AND SOUTHERN EUROPE

Native Americans aside, western Europeans were the first people to emigrate to and settle in the territory that is now the United States.* While the first to arrive and colonize North America came from the British Isles in the early seventeenth century, they were soon followed by western Europeans, most notably those from the Netherlands and the German-speaking states of central Europe. (Germany, as a national entity, did not come into existence until the mid-nineteenth century.) Meanwhile, the Spanish had arrived earlier, in the sixteenth century, and settled in what is now Florida and the Southwest, but in relatively tiny numbers. The French moved into Canada in the early seventeenth century, even as the English were settling the Atlantic colonies to the south.

The first important western European settlement in the United States was organized by the Dutch. Beginning in the early 1600s, the Dutch West India Company established a number of trading posts along the Hudson, Delaware, and Connecticut Rivers, with their headquarters at New Amsterdam (now New York). Several thousand Dutch settled the land as well, mostly in the Hudson River Valley, where they established large estates known as patroonships in a failed attempt to re-create feudal-style manors in America. The project was ultimately doomed, as few wanted to labor on another's land where there was so much available for their own. The colony was eventually absorbed by Britain in 1664. (Sweden also established a tiny colony in what is now Delaware, but it was soon swallowed by the larger Dutch settlements.)

A contingent of French Protestants settled in the English colonies following the revocation of the religiously liberal Edict of Nantes. Fears of renewed per-

secution by the government and the Catholic majority of France sent hundreds of thousands out of the country, with small contingents arriving in Britain's North American colonies. Several thousand German-speaking people from the Palatinate, fleeing warfare, settled in Pennsylvania in the early 1700s. Going under the name of "Pennsylvania Dutch," a corruption of *Deutsch*, the German word for "German," many of these were religious dissenters, including Amish, Mennonites, and Moravians, drawn by the Quaker colony's reputation for religious tolerance.

While small numbers of various western European nationalities made their way to America during the revolutionary and early republic periods, the next great wave to arrive on American shores came in the mid-nineteenth century. These were peoples from the German-speaking states of central Europe. While many were artisans and crafts workers displaced by economic modernization, a minority consisted of political radicals escaping persecution following a series of failed revolutions in 1848. At the same time, several thousand western Europeans from a variety of nations made their way to California in these years in search of gold.

Although the Civil War briefly disrupted immigration from western Europe, the flow of migrants quickly revived in the late 1860s and 1870s, with large contingents arriving from the German-speaking states of central Europe. But beginning in the 1880s, a new and much larger wave of western European immigrants began arriving in America, particularly through the port of New York. During this decade, approximately 5 million immigrants arrived on U.S. shores. Most notable among these were several million Italians, mostly from the impoverished southern reaches of the country. Displaced by agricultural modernization and finding few economic opportunities in urban Italy, they fled to the United States and settled in the large metropolitan areas and small industrial cities, primarily in the Northeast and Midwest.

*For the purposes of this entry, "western and southern Europe" covers the area that was outside the Soviet sphere of influence during the Cold War: Austria, Belgium, France, Germany, Greece, Italy, Netherlands, Portugal, Scandinavia, Spain, Switzerland, and other, smaller countries. Britain and Ireland are covered in separate entries in this section.

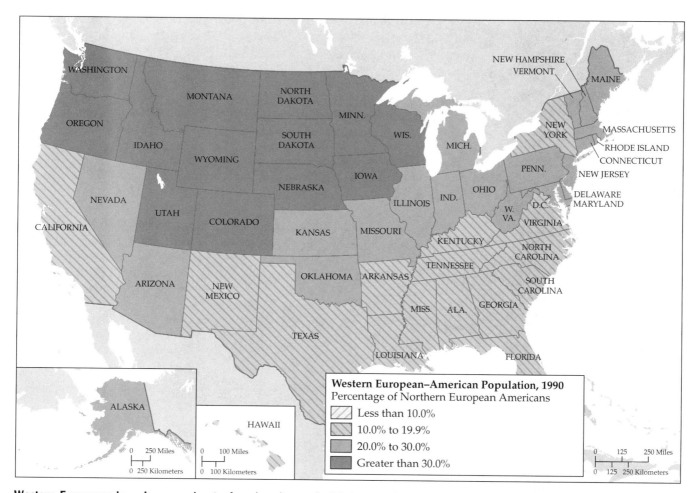

Western European–American Population, 1990
Percentage of Northern European Americans

Less than 10.0%	
10.0% to 19.9%	
20.0% to 30.0%	
Greater than 30.0%	

Western Europeans have been coming to America since colonial times and settling in virtually all sections of the country. *(CARTO-GRAPHICS)*

A smaller contingent of Greeks, facing a similar situation in their native country, also fled to the United States at this time. Meanwhile, it is important to remember, traditional sources of Western European immigration to America—particularly Germany—continued to send large numbers of people here throughout this period. All in all, some 26 million immigrants came to America between the end of the Civil War and the beginning of World War I, although a large portion of these had origins in eastern Europe. While World War I cut off the flow of people dramatically, it was doings on the other side of the Atlantic that ended much of the new immigration.

But the large numbers of Italians, Greeks, and Slavic east European immigrants created a political backlash among native-born Americans, who feared that their Protestant republic would be overwhelmed by Catholic, Jewish, and Eastern Orthodox "hordes" who were unable or unwilling to assimilate. Beginning with an act to ban illiterate immigrants in 1917, the U.S. government passed increas-

ingly harsh immigration laws aimed at Europeans. (Earlier anti-immigration laws had been aimed mainly at Asians.) In 1924, the final and the most restrictive of these laws was passed. The Quota Act of 1924, popularly called the "National Origins Act," followed a related act, the Immigration Act of 1921, popularly called "the Emergency Quota Act." The 1921 act temporarily restricted the number of immigrants entering the United States to 3 percent of the size of a particular nationality group based on the census of 1910, with an annual quota of 357,802. This policy preferred Europeans, who made up a large percentage of the population in 1910, while discriminating against Asians. Because many felt that the Emergency Quota Act of 1921 was not exclusive enough of Asians, Congress implemented a permanent immigration policy in 1924 that allowed 2 percent of a particular nationality based on the 1890 census with an annual quota that dropped from 358,000 to 164,000. The Quota Act of 1924 established the first true immigration quota in Ameri-

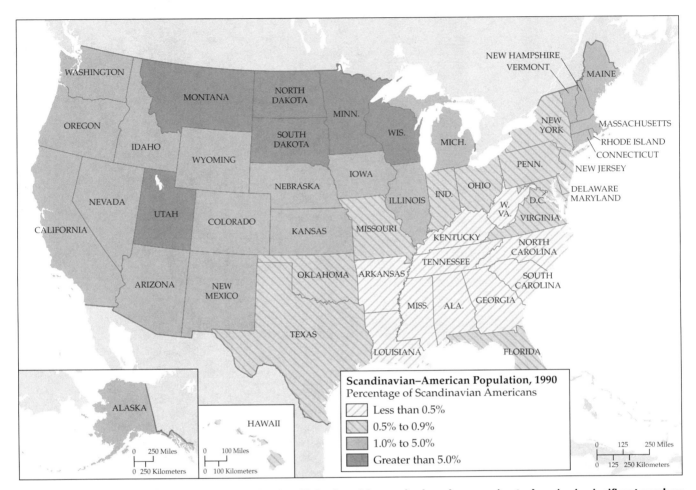

| Scandinavian–American Population, 1990 |
Percentage of Scandinavian Americans

Less than 0.5%
0.5% to 0.9%
1.0% to 5.0%
Greater than 5.0%

Scandinavians—including people from Norway, Sweden, Finland, and Denmark—have been coming to America in significant numbers since the late nineteenth century, with most settling in the states of the Upper Midwest and Great Plains. *(CARTO-GRAPHICS)*

can history based on a national origins system and, as of July 1924, required all aliens emigrating to the United States to carry a visa. By basing this system on the 1890 census, southern and eastern Europeans were practically denied entry altogether. The new law cut the quota for northern and western European countries by 29 percent, but cut that for southern and eastern Europe by 87 percent.

Meanwhile, those western Europeans who were already here in large numbers in the 1880s—notably those from the German-speaking states, who were seen by many American xenophobes as more assimilable—continued to be allowed in large numbers, though the Great Depression and World War II contributed to the drastic overall reduction in immigration to America in the mid-twentieth century.

While the U.S. government was not particularly open to immigrants or refugees in the 1930s and early 1940s, turning its back on many Jews fleeing Nazi Germany, it did open up its gates after World War II to allow in a number of displaced persons, particu-

larly from the former combat zones of central Europe. In addition, thousands of western European war brides of U.S. soldiers were permitted by special legislation as well. Still, immigration from the western part of Europe has remained limited since the 1950s, a decline that can largely be attributed to the miraculous economic recovery achieved on the Continent in the past fifty years. With per capita incomes equivalent and even superior to those in the United States—as well as the enviable social welfare systems on much of the Continent—few Europeans are driven to American shores by economic want, though thousands continue to come here for educational, cultural, or personal reasons.

BASQUES

A stateless people from southwestern France and northern Spain, the Basques were among the earliest

Like the late John Lennon, many recent immigrants from Western Europe come to America with skills or artistic talents. With his radical politics, however, Lennon was denied legal status for years by a suspicious U.S. government. *(Associated Press)*

DUTCH

As noted above, the Dutch presence in North America goes back to the colonization of New Netherlands (New York State) in the early seventeenth century. Throughout the eighteenth and nineteenth centuries, the Dutch continued to come in small numbers, settling throughout the country in no discernible pattern, though, like most immigrants, they largely avoided the antebellum South. If there was a place that Dutch immigrants were likely to head to, however, it was New York State and the upper midwestern states of Iowa, Michigan, and Wisconsin. Most Dutch who came to this country in these years were relatively prosperous members of the middle class, not fleeing poverty but seeking greater economic opportunities.

In the years following World War II, the Dutch government—fearing overpopulation—began to encourage emigration. In 1953, it passed the Refugee Relief Act, which provided assistance to the tens of thousands of Netherlanders forced to flee the former Dutch colony of Indonesia after the latter won its independence in 1949. Ultimately, about eighty thousand of these colonists made their way to the United States. Still, with increased economic prosperity and a shortage of labor in the 1960s and 1970s, the Netherlands has sent few immigrants to the United States. According to the 1990 census, the United States had approximately 3.5 million persons of Dutch descent.

FRENCH

Like the Dutch, the French presence in North America goes back to the early seventeenth century, although significant numbers did not settle in what is now the United States until the last years of that era, when thousands of French Protestants, or Huguenots, fled renewed religious persecution in their native country. In the wake of the French and Indian Wars of the 1750s and 1760s, the victorious British exiled thousands of French-speaking—and hence potentially treasonous—settlers from what are now the maritime provinces of Canada, or Acadia, to Louisiana. These Cajuns (the name is a variant on *Acadians*) continue to maintain their cultural distinctiveness. Following the French Revolution in 1789, a number of French nobles made their way to America, though most went back after the return of the monarchy in 1815.

There has been no great wave of French immigration to the United States since the late 1600s, although French immigrants came in small but steady numbers

groups of Spanish settlers in the American Southwest in the seventeenth century. Bolstered by a small contingent who arrived for the California gold rush in the mid-nineteenth century, many Basques ended up becoming sheepherders and ranchers in the West in the late nineteenth century. Affected negatively by grazing restrictions around the turn of the twentieth century, many Basques were forced to give up their independent economic existence and go to work for larger ranchers who were able to gain grazing rights on federal lands. In the 1950s, Basques won exemptions from the very restricted quotas on Spanish immigrants—effected by the quota laws of the 1920s—and a number came over under three-year "herder contracts," but then stayed on and settled in the West, most notably in northern Nevada and Idaho. The modernization of the sheepherding industry saw a dramatic decline in Basque herders in the late twentieth century, with most Basques moving to the cities of California and other western states. According to the 1990 census, there were 47,956 people of Basque descent living in the United States, approximately 20,000 of them in California and another 5,000 in both Nevada and Idaho.

throughout the nineteenth and early twentieth centuries. By 1920, there were approximately 153,000 persons of French descent living in the United States. (This figure does not include the larger numbers of French-speaking Canadian immigrants who have settled in the New England states.) The Quota Act of 1924 limited French immigration to three thousand per year. That law, followed by the Great Depression and World War II, greatly diminished French immigration to the United States in the mid-twentieth century. Economic prosperity at home has continued to limit the numbers of French coming to the United States in the late twentieth century. It is estimated that there are approximately 6.2 million persons of French descent living in the United States today, excluding those from Canada. There are approximately 2.2 French Canadians in the United States.

GERMANS

The largest European immigrant group in the United States, after the English and Irish, the Germans have been coming to this country in large numbers since the eighteenth century. The first contingent came as religious dissenters in the mid-1700s and settled largely in Pennsylvania. The American Revolution and the wars following the French Revolution disrupted German immigration for a time, but it soon revived in the mid-nineteenth century. In 1834, most of the German-speaking states of central Europe adopted the *Zollverein,* or customs union, which allowed people and goods to pass freely between the multitude of ministates that then constituted Germany. This allowed people to travel easily from the interior parts of Germany to the great emigration ports of Bremen and Hamburg. This law, which stimulated the economic modernization that displaced many artisans and crafts workers, contributed to an increased flow of German-speaking people across the Atlantic, where many of them settled in the newer states of the upper Midwest, most notably Wisconsin. The failed revolutions of 1848 also sent a number of political radicals to the United States, where many of them became active in the American labor movement. Although Germans faced some persecution during the nativist, or anti-immigrant, reaction of the 1850s, the brunt of this xenophobic political movement was directed at the Catholic Irish. In general, the largely Protestant German immigrants were viewed more favorably, as more hardworking and assimilable than the Celts.

Germans continued to emigrate to America in large numbers during the late nineteenth and early twentieth centuries and were, for the most part, easily assimilated into the urban and rural areas of the upper Midwest, where most of them settled. This, of course, changed with World War I. With America at war with Germany, anti-German sentiment grew dramatically, and many descendants of German immigrants tried to hide their identities by changing their names and dropping other national customs. But by the 1920s, immigration from Germany resumed. Some half a million Germans emigrated to the United States in that decade, most fleeing the economic turmoil of the interwar years. The rise of Nazism and the onset of World War II greatly reduced German immigration to the United States beyond a handful of leftist intellectuals and Jews persecuted by the Nazi government.

In the wake of World War II, tens of thousands of German refugees made their way to the United States, some under liberalized refugee laws. Most of these Germans did not come from Germany proper, however, but from Slavic states to the east, where they were driven out by anti-German sentiment after the war. Since the 1950s, the so-called German economic miracle—combined with a general social welfare system—has seen the number of German immigrants to this country decline dramatically. On average, just seven thousand come to the United States annually today, mostly for educational, cultural, or personal reasons. Overall, since 1820, approximately 7 million people from Germany or the German-speaking states of central Europe have come to the United States.

GREEKS

Virtually no Greeks emigrated to the United States before the great wave of immigration in the late nineteenth century. Economic modernization, better transport, and increased access to information about opportunities in the United States fed the upsurge in Greeks fleeing impoverished agricultural conditions to come to America in the approximately thirty years between 1890 and the quota laws of the 1920s. In addition, the expulsion of Greeks from Turkey following World War I contributed thousands to the flow.

Most Greeks who came during this period were men, and they came as individuals, initially hoping to raise enough capital to return to their native country and buy land or a small business. But, as the achievement of that dream proved more difficult than expected, many sent for their wives and families, eventually establishing a significant and permanent

Greek presence, largely in the industrial cities of the Northeast and Midwest. Significant Greek communities exist in Boston, Chicago, Detroit, Philadelphia, and Queens (New York).

Like other southern European nationalities, Greeks were hard hit by the quota laws of the 1920s, which limited immigration to a trickle. Those laws—as well as the Great Depression and World War II—cut immigration numbers from Greece to about fifteen hundred a year through 1945. In the postwar era, however, there has been a significant revival of Greek immigration. In contrast to nations in the western part of Europe, Greece remained poor and relatively economically backward through much of the postwar era. Along with the liberalization of American immigration law in 1965, which saw an end to national quotas, this aspect of the Greek economy has sent waves of immigrants to this country. Since that year, approximately two hundred thousand Greeks have come to America, though the number has been steadily diminishing as Greece itself modernizes. Still, the continued flow has helped keep many Greek communities in the United States alive. Altogether, it is estimated that about 1 million Americans have Greek ancestry, with about one-fourth of those living in the New York metropolitan area.

ITALIANS

While Italians have been coming to the United States in small numbers since colonial times, it was not until the 1880s that large groups arrived here. Several factors contributed to the upsurge in Italian immigration between 1880 and the passage of the restrictive American quota laws of the early 1920s. First, with the development of large-scale agriculture in California and Florida in the late nineteenth century, the United States cut its imports of citrus crops—a major part of the economy of southern Italy, which was the source of most Italian immigration to the United States. Around the same time, France introduced restrictive tariffs on grape imports. These developments, combined with an infestation of phylloxera that attacked grapevines, had a catastrophic effect on the southern Italian economy. But there were long-term trends as well. Economic modernization, including the consolidation of large, commercially oriented agricultural holdings, threw tens of thousands of subsistence-level Italian peasants off the land. Most headed for Italian cities first. But limited economic opportunities there—along with better transport and a concerted advertis-

ing effort by U.S. railroad and land companies to encourage immigration—produced the massive wave of Italian immigration that marked the decades between 1880 and the onset of World War I in 1914.

Like the Greeks, most of the more than 4 million Italians who came to America in these years were male. First, coming largely as individuals, they hoped to amass enough capital to return to Italy and buy land or open businesses of their own. Ultimately, over half of all Italian immigrants, popularly known as "birds of passage," would return to their native land. But for those who found wealth elusive or enjoyed life in America, bringing families followed. By about 1900, large Italian communities were thriving in cities across the Northeast, Midwest, and Far West, though the first of these accounted for about 50 percent of the Italian-American population. Most ended up working as industrial workers in America's growing factories. Others wound up in garment sweatshops in New York.

World War I and restrictive quota laws virtually cut off Italian immigration after 1914. Only a small trickle came into the United States during the 1920s, Great Depression, and World War II eras. At the same time, economic prosperity was luring many Italians out of the old ghettos of the inner city for suburbia, a trend accelerated by the numerous highway and urban renewal projects that destroyed many inner-city neighborhoods. By the 1960s, most of the so-called Little Italys of America had disappeared, shrunk, or been transformed into tourist meccas. Renewed Western European prosperity after World War II also affected Italian immigration to the United States. While southern Italy remained impoverished, the economic revival elsewhere on the Continent offered closer and often more lucrative opportunities for southern Italians than America. Today, approximately 11 million Americans trace their ancestry back to Italy.

PORTUGUESE

Among the very first immigrants to America were a group of Portuguese Jews. Fleeing persecution under the Inquisition, a small number settled in religiously tolerant Rhode Island, where they built what many historians recognize as the nation's first synagogue. Despite these early origins, there has never been any large-scale Portuguese immigration to the United States, and for one simple reason: Brazil, Portugal's massive colony in South America, has drawn the lion's share of immigrants. Of the approximately 1.5 million persons leaving Portugal in the great southern

European immigration period from 1880 to 1914, just 4 percent headed for the United States.

Following in the steps of those early Portuguese Jews, most have settled in New England, though not for the same reasons. A seafaring people, the Portuguese—including people from the Azore Islands—have found their economic niche in the fishing communities of that region. In addition, small numbers settled on the Pacific Coast, while a number were imported to Hawaii around the turn of the twentieth century as contract laborers on the sugar and pineapple plantations. Overall, some 225,000 Portuguese immigrated to the United States between 1870 and 1920. Quota laws and world wars greatly diminished Portuguese immigration despite the fact that the country remained neutral in World War II. While, like Greece, Portugal remained impoverished in the first decades after World War II, most emigrants headed for Brazil, Portugal's African colonies (most notably Angola and Mozambique), or more prosperous countries in Western and northern Europe.

SCANDINAVIANS

Scandinavian immigrants began making their way to the United States in significant numbers in the mid- to late nineteenth century. Unlike many other Europeans of that period, most did not head for urban areas, choosing instead to homestead the prairies of the upper Midwest and Great Plains. Most of these immigrants were farmers and they helped settle such states as Minnesota, Iowa, and the Dakotas. There they made their political presence felt. Liberal and tolerant by tradition, they became engaged in the left-wing politics of the Progressive and Depression eras. Still, by the 1880s, however, the demographics of Scandinavian immigration began to change, with about half now coming from urban areas and choosing to settle in the cities of the upper Midwest and Great Plains. By 1920, approximately 120,000 Swedes and Norwegians—always the two largest Scandinavian contingents—lived in Chicago.

While Scandinavian immigrant groups were somewhat less affected than southern and eastern Europeans by the quota laws of the 1920s—having already established a moderate presence in the population—fewer and fewer emigrated here after 1920. This was due, in part, to the Great Depression and world wars, but it also had much to do with the growing economic prosperity of the Scandinavian homeland and the elaborate social welfare states created there.

SPANISH

The Spanish, of course, were the first western Europeans to settle in what is now the United States, establishing colonies in Florida and the American Southwest as early as the mid-sixteenth century, fully fifty years before the first English colonies. Still, their numbers remained small. Even in New Mexico, the most populous Spanish colony in North America, the Spanish population numbered less than ten thousand in 1821, when Mexico achieved its independence, and barely more than that in 1848, when the northern territory was officially ceded to the United States. Even smaller settlements existed in Arizona, California, and Texas.

Spanish immigration to the United States—as opposed to the immigration of Latin Americans of full or partial Spanish descent—has remained limited. As in the case of the Portuguese, this can be explained by the fact that Spanish immigrants had other options. Indeed, of the 3.5 million Spanish to emigrate to the Americas in the decades between 1880 and 1930, a small fraction came to the United States, with most preferring to settle in the culturally and linguistically familiar former colonies of the Caribbean, Central America, Mexico, and South America. Less than 135,000 Spaniards emigrated to the United States between 1890 and 1930.

Because there were significant numbers of people of Spanish descent in the United States in the quota law base year of 1890, quotas on Spanish immigrants were not particularly restrictive. Still, few came, preferring Latin America instead. The outbreak of the Spanish civil war in 1936 further restricted immigration, at least at first. The late 1930s, however, saw a small but renewed wave of Spanish immigration, both to Latin America and to the United States, as persons with leftist political leanings were forced to flee the country during and after the civil war, which brought the fascist Francisco Franco regime to power in 1939.

Like other southern European countries, Spain was slow to achieve economic prosperity in the post–World War II era. Continued poverty sent hundreds of thousands of Spanish abroad, though most did not come to the United States. The vast majority either settled in Latin America or else took up residency in the expanding economies of Western and northern Europe.

SWISS

Like some areas of the German-speaking region to the north, parts of Switzerland were affected by the religious wars of the mid-seventeenth century. These conflicts sent small numbers of Swiss to America. But it was continued economic hard times that sent some twenty-five thousand Swiss to America before 1776, a trend that continued in the nineteenth century. Overpopulation, land shortages, and a lack of economic opportunities in their homeland caused some 250,000 Swiss to emigrate to the United States by 1820. During the next 100 years, an additional 265,000 immigrants arrived, although some did not remain permanently. Like other German-speaking people, many of the first Swiss to come in the eighteenth century settled in Pennsylvania and the back country of the Carolinas. By the 1800s, the preferred destination was farmland in the midwestern states of Illinois, Missouri, Ohio, and Wisconsin. Hardly affected by the quota laws—since their population in the United States for the quota law base year of 1890 was significant—the Swiss continued to come in significant numbers in the early twentieth century, with approximately twenty-five thousand arriving in the 1920s alone. But the Great Depression and World War II (Switzerland remained a neutral island in war-torn Europe) cut immigration dramatically, and it has barely revived. The unprecedented prosperity of Switzerland in the postwar era reduced the number of people leaving the country to a trickle. Indeed, during this era, Switzerland has instead become home to vast numbers of immigrants and foreign workers.

Daniel James

See also: Immigration to Western Europe (Part II, Sec. 13); President Truman's Directive on European Refugees, 1945 (Part IV, Sec. 1).

BIBLIOGRAPHY

Barkan, Elliott R. *A Nation of Peoples: A Sourcebook on America's Multicultural Heritage.* Westport, CT: Greenwood, 1999.

De Jong, G. F. *The Dutch in America, 1609–1974.* Boston: Twayne, 1974.

Douglass, W. A., and Jon Bilbao. *Amerikanuak: Basques in the New World.* Reno: University of Nevada Press, 1975.

Gallo, Patrick. *Old Bread, New Wine: A Portrait of Italian Americans.* Chicago: Nelson-Hall, 1981.

Gomez, R. A. "Spanish Immigration to the United States." *The Americas* 19 (1962): 59–77.

von Grueningen, J. P. *The Swiss in the United States.* Madison, WI: Swiss-American Historical Society, 1940.

Jones, O. L., ed. *The Spanish Borderlands: A First Reader.* Los Angeles: Lorrin L. Morrison, 1974.

Kessner, Thomas. *The Golden Door: Italians and Jewish Immigrant Mobility in New York City, 1880–1915.* New York: Oxford University Press, 1977.

Louder, Dean, and Eric Waddell. *French America: Mobility, Identity, and Minority Experience Across the Continent.* Baton Rouge: Louisiana State University Press, 1993.

Luebke, F. C. *Germans in the New World: Essays in the History of Immigration.* Champaign: University of Illinois Press, 1990.

Moskos, Charles. *Greek Americans: Struggle and Success.* New Brunswick, NJ: Transaction, 1988.

Nelli, Humberto. *Italians in Chicago, 1880–1930.* New York: Oxford University Press, 1975.

Norman, Hans, and Harald Runblom. *Transatlantic Connections: Nordic Migration to the New World after 1800.* Oslo: Norwegian University Press, 1987.

Pap, Leo. *The Portuguese-Americans.* New York: Twayne, 1981.

Scourby, Alice. *The Greek Americans.* New York: Twayne, 1984.

Trefousse, Hans, ed. *Germany and America: Essays on Problems of International Relations and Immigration.* Brooklyn, NY: Brooklyn College Press, 1980.

Urza, Monique. *The Deep Blue Memory.* Reno: University of Nevada Press, 1993.

Part

IMMIGRATION DOCUMENTS

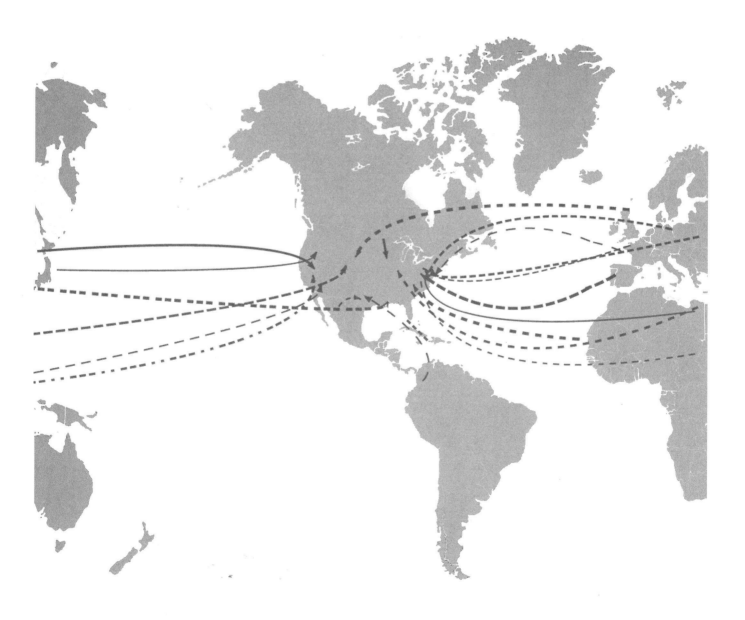

LEGAL DOCUMENTS

A. Laws and Treaties

B. Executive Orders, Directives, and Statements

C. Supreme Court Cases

D. Referenda

$\mathcal{I}$NTRODUCTION

$\mathcal{S}$ection 1 of Part IV of the *Encyclopedia of American Immigration* is devoted to legal documents. These documents are then divided into four subsections: laws and treaties; executive orders, directives, and statements; court cases; and referenda. They range in time from the founding of the American Republic through the late 1990s.

Subsection 1A (Laws and Treaties) consists largely of laws regulating immigration to the United States. Under the Constitution (appropriate passages of which make up the first document in this subsection), Congress is given the power to pass laws determining the rules of naturalization, powers that were later extended to immigration as well. The first laws passed by Congress on the subject concerned naturalization—first, the 1790 law setting the overall rules for naturalization and then, in 1798, the Alien Act, which temporarily made naturalization more difficult.

Most of the immigration laws that have been passed by Congress over the years, however, have involved restrictions on immigration, including the Chinese Exclusion Act, the Literacy Act of 1917, and the quota acts of 1921 and 1924. Others have redressed previous restrictions. Such pieces of legislation include the repeal of the Chinese Exclusion Act in 1943 and the Immigration and Nationality Act of 1965, which overturned the national quota rules established in the 1920s.

In more recent years, Congress has passed laws to regulate immigration in more indirect ways. For example, the 1986 Immigration Reform and Control Act aimed to strengthen the enforcement of laws against illegal immigration, while the 1996 Illegal Immigration Reform and Immigrant Responsibility Act tried to dissuade immigrants from coming by limiting the social services available to them. More specialized legislation included here includes the granting of citizenship to Puerto Ricans and Native Americans, as well as a series of labor laws aimed at immigrant agricultural workers.

The main treaties in this subsection are concerned with citizenship rights of Mexicans living in territories ceded to America after the Mexican-American War of the 1840s (Treaty of Guadalupe Hidalgo) and the Angell Treaty of 1881, designed to limit Chinese immigration to the United States.

Subsection 1B pertains to orders, directives, and statements issued by the executive branch of the government. These include a wide range of documents, such as the 1907 Gentlemen's Agreement whereby President Theodore Roosevelt received assurances from the imperial government of Japan that it would limit immigration to the United States; President Franklin Roosevelt's executive order interning Japanese Americans for the duration of World War II; President Harry Truman's directive on post–World War II European refugees; a report issued by the Eisenhower administration calling for more open immigration laws; and various presidential statements from the 1980s and 1990s concerning Cuban, Haitian, and other immigrants.

Subsection 1C concerns critical Supreme Court cases pertaining to immigration. Documents here include decisions on the immigration of Asian Indians (*United States v. Bhagat Singh Thind*, 1923); the legitimacy of Japanese-American internment (*Hirabayashi v. United States*, 1943); bilingual education (*Lau v. Nichols*, 1974); education for illegal immigrant children (*Plyler v. Doe*, 1982); the provision of social services to illegal immigrants (*LULAC et al. v. Wilson et al.*, 1995); and a lower court ruling on Haitian refugees (*District Court on Admissions of Haitians*, 1993). Finally, subsection 1D includes two key California referenda—one calling for the limitation of social services available to illegal immigrants (Proposition 187, 1994) and the other concerning bilingual education (Proposition 227, 1998).

A. Laws and Treaties

U.S. Constitution: Article I, Section 8, Clause 4, 1787

*U*nder the Constitution of the United States, the Congress is given the power to regulate naturalization. In recent years, this power has been challenged by states enacting laws cutting off social services to immigrants, most of which have been overturned in federal courts. In addition, the Constitution permitted the slave trade to continue for another twenty years after ratification.

ARTICLE I, SECTION 8

The Congress shall have the power.... To establish a uniform Rule of Naturalization . . .

ARTICLE I, SECTION 9

The Migration of Importation of such Persons as any of the States now existing shall think proper to admit, shall not be prohibited by the Congress prior to the Year one thousand eight hundred and eight but a tax or duty may be imposed on such Importation, not exceeding ten dollars for each person.

Source: U.S. Constitution.

An Act to Establish a Uniform Rule of Naturalization, 1790

The Constitution gave Congress the right to establish laws concerning naturalization and citizenship. On March 26, 1790, Congress enacted the nation's first legislation dealing with naturalization, and President George Washington signed it into law. This law, excerpted below, introduced requirements based on race and years of residency in the United States.

Section 1: Be it enacted by the Senate and House of Representatives of the United States of America in Congress assembled, That any alien, being a free white person, who shall have resided within the limits and under the jurisdiction of the United States for the term of two years, may be admitted to become a citizen thereof, on application to any common court of record, in any one of the states wherein he shall have resided for the term of one year at least, and making proof to the satisfaction of such court, that he is a person of good character, and taking the oath of affirmation prescribed by law, to support the constitution of the United States, which oath or affirmation such court shall administer; and the clerk of such court shall record such application, and the proceedings thereon; and thereupon such person shall be considered as a citizen of the United States. And the children of such persons so naturalized, dwelling within the United States, being under the age of twenty-one years at the time of such naturalization, shall also be considered as citizens of the United States. And the children of citizens of the United States, that may be born beyond sea, or out of the limits of the United States, shall be considered as natural born citizens; Provided, That the right of citizenship shall not descend to persons whose fathers have never been resident in the United States; Provided also, That no person heretofore proscribed by any state, shall be admitted a citizen as aforesaid, except by an act of the legislature in the state in which such person was proscribed.

Source: 1 Stat. 103.

Alien Act, 1798

In the late 1790s, tensions between Federalists and Democratic Republicans in Congress reached a critical point. The two parties differed on many issues, including foreign policy, free speech, and immigration. On June 18, 1798, President John Adams, a Federalist, signed the Naturalization Act, lengthening the period of residence required for admission to citizenship from five to fourteen years. One week later he signed the Alien Act, which gave the president broad authority to remove foreigners from the country. The Alien Act remained in force for two years.

Be it enacted by the Senate and the House of Representatives of the United States of America in Congress assembled, That it shall be lawful for the President of the United States at any time during the continuance of this act, to order all such aliens as he shall judge dangerous to the peace and safety of the United States, or shall have reasonable grounds to suspect are concerned in any treasonable or secret machinations against the government thereof, to depart out of the territory of the United States within such time as shall be expressed in such order, which order shall be served to the alien by delivering a copy thereof, or leaving the same at his usual abode, and returned to the office of the Secretary of State, by the marshal or other person to whom the same shall be directed. And in case any alien, so ordered to depart, shall be found at large within the United States after the time limited in such order for his departure, and not having obtained a license from the President to reside therein, or having obtained such license shall not have conformed thereto, every such alien shall, on conviction thereof, be imprisoned for a term not exceeding three years, and shall never after be admitted to become a citizen of the United States. Provided always, and be it further enacted, that if any alien so ordered to depart shall prove to the satisfaction of the President, by evidence to be taken before such person or persons as the President shall direct, who are for that purpose hereby authorized to administer oaths, that no injury or danger to the United States will arise from suffering such alien to reside therein, the President may grant a license to such alien to remain within the United States for such time as he shall judge proper, and at such place as he may designate. And the President may also re-quire of such alien to enter into a bond to the United States, in such penal sum as he may direct, with one or more sufficient sureties to the satisfaction of the person authorized by the President to take the same, conditioned for the good behavior of such alien during his residence in the United States, and not violating his license, which license the President may revoke, whenever he shall think proper.

Sec. 2. And be it further enacted, That it shall be lawful for the President of the United States, whenever he may deem it necessary for the public safety, to order to be removed out of the territory thereof, any alien who may or shall be in prison in pursuance of this act; and to cause to be arrested and sent out of the United States such of those aliens as shall have been ordered to depart therefrom and shall not have obtained a license as aforesaid, in all cases where, in the opinion of the President, public safety requires a speedy removal. And if any alien so removed or sent out of the United States by the President shall voluntarily return thereto, such alien on conviction thereof, shall be imprisoned so long as, in the opinion of the President, the public safety may require. . . .

Sec. 4. And be it further enacted, That the circuit and district courts of the United States, shall respectively have cognizance of all crimes and offenses against this act. And all marshals and other officers of the United States are required to execute all precepts and orders of the President of the United States issued in pursuance or by virtue of this act.

Sec. 5. And be it further enacted, That it shall be lawful for any alien who may be ordered to be removed from the United States, by virtue of this act, to take with him such part of his goods, chattels, or other property, as he may find convenient; and all property left in the United States by any alien, who may be removed, as aforesaid, shall be, and remain subject to his order and disposal, in the same manner as if this act had not been passed.

Sec. 6. And be it further enacted, That this act shall continue and be in force for . . . two years.

Source: 1 Stat. 566.

Manifest of Immigrants Act, 1819

The Manifest of Immigrants Act, passed on March 2, 1819, is the first piece of legislation dealing directly with immigrants in United States history. Calling on shipowners and masters to supply information to the government on the passengers aboard and their intentions upon arrival in the United States, it is also the nation's first attempt at gathering immigrant statistics.

Be it enacted by the Senate and the House of Representatives of the United States of America in Congress assembled . . .

Sec. 4. And be it further enacted, That the captain or master of any ship or vessel arriving in the United States or any of the territories thereof, from any foreign place whatever, at the same time that he delivers a manifest of all cargo, and, if there be no cargo, then at the time of making a report or entry of the ship or vessel, pursuant to the existing laws of the United States, shall also deliver and report, to the collector of the district in which such ship or vessel shall arrive, a list or manifest of all passengers taken on board of the said ship or vessel at any foreign port or place; in which list or manifest it shall be the duty of the said master to designate, particularly, the age, sex, and occupation, of the said passengers, respectively, the country to which they severally belong, and that of which it is their intention to become inhabitants; and shall further set forth whether any, and what number, have died on the voyage; which report and manifest shall be sworn to by the said master, in the same manner as is directed by the existing laws of the United States, in relation to the manifest of the cargo, and that the refusal or neglect of the master aforesaid, to comply with the provisions of this section, shall incur the same penalties, disabilities, and forfeitures, as are at present provided for a refusal or neglect to report and deliver a manifest of the cargo aforesaid.

Source: 3 Stat. 489.

Treaty of Guadalupe Hidalgo, 1848

Following the Mexican-American War of 1846–1848, in which the United States seized the northern third of Mexico, the two countries signed the Treaty of Guadalupe Hidalgo. Article 8 of the treaty, reprinted below, granted full U.S. citizenship to any of the thousands of Mexicans living in those territories, including the modern-day states of California, Arizona, Nevada, and Utah, and parts of New Mexico, Colorado, and Wyoming.

Mexicans now established in territories previously belonging to Mexico, and which remain for the future within the limits of the United States as defined by the present treaty, shall be free to continue where they now reside, or to remove at any time to the Mexican republic, retaining the property which they possess in the said territories, or disposing thereof, and removing the proceeds wherever they please, without their being subjected on this account, to any contribution, tax, or charge whatever.

Those who shall prefer to remain in the said territories, may either retain the title and rights of Mexican citizens, or acquire those of citizens of the United States. But they shall be under the obligation to make their election within one year from the date of the exchange of ratifications of this treaty, and those who shall remain in the said territories after the expiration of that year, without having declared their intention to retain the character of Mexicans, shall be considered to have elected to become citizens of the United States.

Source: William Malloy, ed. *Conventions, International Acts, Protocols, and Agreements Between the United States of America and Other Powers, 1776–1909.* Volume 1. Holmes Beach, FL: Gaunt, 1996.

Page Act, 1875

During the Gold Rush of the late 1840s and 1850s and the building of the transcontinental railroad in the 1860s, tens of thousands of Chinese emigrated to the West Coast of the United States. They encountered vast hostility from white immigrants and settlers, and California enacted numerous anti-Chinese statutes. In 1875 Congress passed the first national law aimed at limiting Chinese immigration. Named after its sponsor, Representative Horace F. Page (R-CA), the Page Act had two aims: to prevent Chinese immigrants from coming to America under contract or obligation without their free and voluntary consent; and to prevent Asian prostitutes from coming to America. The law ultimately made it difficult for any Asian—and especially Chinese—women to emigrate, and thus hindered Chinese immigrants from forming families in the United States.

Be it enacted . . . , That in determining whether the immigration of any subject of China, Japan, or any Oriental country, to the United States, is free and voluntary . . . it shall be the duty of the consul-general or consul of the United States residing at the port from which it is proposed to convey such subjects, in any vessel enrolled or licensed in the United States, or any port within the same, before delivering to the masters of any such vessels the permit or certificate provided for in such section, to ascertain whether such immigrant has entered into a contract or agreement for a term of service within the United States, for lewd and immoral purposes; and if there be such contract or agreement, the said consul-general or consul shall not deliver the required permit or certificate.

Sec. 2. That if any citizen of the United States, or other person amenable to the laws of the United States, shall take, or cause to be taken or transported, to or from the United States any subject of China, Japan, or any Oriental country, without their free and voluntary consent, for the purpose of holding them to a term of service, such citizen or other person shall be liable to be indicted therefor, and, on conviction of such offense, shall be punished by a fine not to exceed two thousand dollars and be imprisoned not exceeding one year; and all contracts and agreements for a term of service of such persons in the United States, whether made in advance or in pursuance of such illegal importation, and whether such importation shall have been in American or other vessels, are hereby declared void.

Sec. 3. That the importation into the United States of women for the purposes of prostitution is hereby forbidden; and all contracts and agreements in relation thereto, made in advance or in pursuance of such illegal importation and purposes are hereby declared void; and whoever shall knowingly and willfully import, or cause any importation of, women to the United States for purposes of prostitution, or shall knowingly and willfully hold, or attempt to hold, any woman to such purposes, in pursuance of such illegal importation and contract or agreement, shall be deemed guilty of a felony, and on conviction thereof, shall be imprisoned not exceeding five years and pay a fine not exceeding five thousand dollars. . . .

Source: 18 Stat. 477; 8 United States Code.

Angell Treaty, 1881

*I*n 1868 the United States ratified the Burlingame Treaty with China. The treaty led to increased trade between the two countries and gave Chinese individuals the right to emigrate to America. Eleven years later, Congress passed a law restricting Chinese immigration, which President Rutherford B. Hayes vetoed because it conflicted with the Burlingame Treaty. However, he appointed a commission headed by University of Michigan president James B. Angell to go to China and negotiate a new treaty that would give the United States authority to restrict Chinese immigration. The Angell Treaty, as it came to be called, was negotiated in 1880 and ratified in 1881.

Whenever in the opinion of the Government of the United States, the coming of Chinese laborers to the United States, or their residence therein, affects or threatens to affect the interests of that country, or to endanger the good order of the said country or any locality within the territory thereof, the Government of China agrees that the Government of the United States may regulate, limit, or suspend such coming or residence, but may not absolutely prohibit it. The limitation or suspension shall be reasonable, and apply only to Chinese who may go to the United States as laborers, other classes not being included in the limitations. Legislation taken in regard to Chinese laborers will be of such a character only as is necessary to enforce the regulation, limitation, or suspension of immigration, and immigrants shall not be subject to personal maltreatment or abuse.

ARTICLE II

Chinese subjects, whether proceeding to the United States as teachers, students, merchants, or from curiosity, together with their body and household servants, and Chinese laborers who are now in the United States shall be allowed to go and come of their own free will and accord, and shall be accorded all the rights, privileges, immunities, and exemptions which are accorded to citizens and subjects of the most favored nation.

ARTICLE III

If Chinese laborers, or Chinese of any other class, now either permanently or temporarily residing in the territory of the United States, meet with ill treatment at the hands of any other persons, the Government of the United States will exert all its powers to devise measures for their protection and to secure to them the same rights, privileges, immunities, and exemptions as may be enjoyed by the citizens or subjects of the most favored nation, and to which they are entitled by treaty.

Source: 22 Stat. L., 826.

Chinese Exclusion Act, 1882

After ratification of the Angell Treaty with China in 1881, Congress began drafting legislation to restrict Chinese immigration. The first version of the Chinese Exclusion Act, which Congress passed in March 1882, would have excluded all Chinese laborers from emigrating to the United States for twenty years. President Chester Arthur vetoed the bill, claiming that the twenty-year provision was excessive and a violation of the Angell Treaty. Congress reduced the length of exclusion to ten years and passed the bill overwhelmingly: 201 to 37 in the House of Representatives, 32 to 15 in the Senate. On May 6, 1882, President Arthur signed the bill into law. The Chinese Exclusion Act, which barred practically all Chinese from American shores, was the first federal law ever passed banning a group of immigrants solely on the basis of race or nationality. The law also denied the more than 100,000 Chinese immigrants already in the United States the right to become citizens. Reenacted in 1892, 1902, and made permanent in 1904, the Chinese Exclusion Act remained in effect for sixty-one years. It was repealed in 1943 when China became an ally of the United States during World War II.

Whereas, in the opinion of the Government of the United States the coming of Chinese laborers to this country endangers the good order of certain localities within the territory thereof: Therefore, *Be it enacted by the Senate and the House of Representatives of the United States of America in Congress assembled,* That from and after the expiration of ninety days next after the passage of this act, and until the expiration of ten years next after the passage of this act, the coming of Chinese laborers to the United States be, and the same is hereby, suspended; and during such suspension it shall not be lawful for any Chinese laborer to come, or having so come after the expiration of said ninety days, to remain within the United States.

Sec. 2. That the master of any vessel who shall knowingly bring within the United States on such vessel, and land or permit to be landed, any Chinese laborer, from any foreign port or place, shall be deemed guilty of a misdemeanor, and on conviction thereof shall be punished by a fine of not more than five hundred dollars for each and every such Chinese laborer so brought, and may also be imprisoned for a term not exceeding one year. . . .

Sec. 4. That for the purpose of properly identifying Chinese laborers who were in the United States . . . or shall come into the same before the expiration of ninety days next after the passage of this act, and in order to furnish them with the proper evidence of their right to go from and to come to the United States of their own free will and accord, as provided by the treaty of the United States and China . . . the collector of customs of the district from which any such Chinese laborer shall depart from the United States shall, in person or by deputy, go on board each vessel having on board any such Chinese laborer and cleared or about to sail from his district for a foreign port, and on such vessel make a list of all such Chinese laborers, which shall be entered in registry-books to be kept for that purpose, in which shall be stated the name, age, occupation, last place of residence, physical marks or peculiarities, and all facts necessary for the identification of each of such Chinese laborers, which books shall be kept in the custom-house; and every such Chinese laborer so departing from the United States shall be entitled to, and shall receive free of any charge or cost upon application thereof, from the collector or his deputy, at the time such a list is taken, a certificate, signed by the collector or his deputy and attested by his seal of office, in such form as the Secretary of the Treasury shall prescribe, which certificate shall contain a statement of the name, age, occupation, last place of residence, personal description, and facts of identification of the Chinese laborer to whom the certificate is issued, corresponding with the said list and registry in all particulars. . . . The certificate herein provided for shall entitle the Chinese laborer to whom the same is issued to return to and re-enter the United States upon producing and delivering the same to the collector of customs of the district at which the Chinese laborer shall re-enter; and upon delivery of such certificate by such Chinese laborer to the collector of customs at the time of re-entry in the United States, said collector shall cause the same to be filed in the custom-house and duly canceled. . . .

Sec. 6. That in order to the faithful execution of articles one and two of the treaty in this act before mentioned, every Chinese person other than a laborer who may be entitled by said treaty to come within the United States, and who shall be about to come to the United States, shall be identified as so entitled by the Chinese government in each case, such identity to be evidenced by a certificate issued under the authority of said government, which certificate shall be in the English language . . . stating such right to come, and which certificate shall state the name, title, or official rank, if any, the age, height, and all physical peculiarities, former and present occupation or profession, and place of residence in China of the person to whom the certificate is issued. . . . Such certificate shall be prima-facie evidence of the fact set forth therein. . . .

Sec. 7. That any person who shall knowingly and falsely alter or substitute any name for the name written in such certificate or forge any such certificate, or knowingly utter any forged or fraudulent certificate, or falsely personate any person named in any such certificate, shall be deemed guilty of a misdemeanor; and upon conviction thereof shall be fined in sum not exceeding one thousand dollars, and imprisoned in a penitentiary for a term of not more than five years.

Sec. 8. That the master of any vessel arriving in the United States from any foreign port or place shall, at the same time he delivers a manifest of the cargo, . . . deliver and report to the collector of customs of the district in which such vessel shall have arrived a separate list of all Chinese passengers on board the vessel at that time. Such list shall show the names of such passengers . . . and such list shall be sworn to by the master in the manner required by law in relation to the manifest of the cargo. Any willful refusal or neglect of any such master to comply with the provisions of this section shall incur the same penalties and forfeiture as are provided for a refusal or neglect to report and deliver a manifest of cargo.

Sec. 9. That before any Chinese passengers are landed from any such vessel, the collector, or his deputy, shall proceed to examine such passengers, comparing the certificates with the list and with the passengers; and no passenger shall be allowed to land in the United States from such vessel in violation of law.

Sec. 10. That every vessel whose master shall knowingly violate any of the provisions of this act shall be deemed forfeited to the United States, and shall be liable to seizure and condemnation in any district of the United States into which such vessel may enter or in which she may be found.

Sec. 11. That any person who shall knowingly bring into or cause to be brought into the United States by land, or who shall knowingly aid and abet the same, or aid and abet the landing in the United States from any vessel of any Chinese person not lawfully entitled to enter the United States, shall be deemed guilty of a misdemeanor, and shall, on conviction thereof, be fined in a sum not exceeding one thousand dollars, and imprisoned for a term not exceeding one year.

Sec. 12. That no Chinese person shall be permitted to enter the United States by land without producing the certificate in this act required of Chinese persons seeking to land from a vessel. And any Chinese person found unlawfully within the United States shall be caused to be removed therefrom to the country from whence he came . . . after being brought before some justice, judge, or commissioner of a court of the United States and found to be one not lawfully entitled to be or remain in the United States.

Sec. 13. That this act shall not apply to diplomatic and other officers of the Chinese Government traveling upon the business of that government . . . and shall exempt them and their body and household servants from the provisions of this act as to other Chinese persons.

Sec. 14. That hereafter no State court or court of the United States shall admit Chinese to citizenship; and all laws in conflict with this act are hereby repealed.

Sec. 15. That the words "Chinese laborers," wherever used in this act, shall be construed to mean both skilled and unskilled laborers and Chinese employed in mining.

Source: 22 Stat. 58; 8 United States Code.

Contract Labor Act (Foran Act), 1885

*C*ontract labor involves the importation of foreign workers— usually in groups—by a business or contracting firm. The workers' passage to the country is paid for by the contractor, with the worker required to pay off that passage by his or her labor. Since the Civil War, American workers and unions fought to outlaw contract labor, which threatened both their power and their wages. In 1885, Congress passed the Contract Labor Act, also known as the Foran Act, after its sponsor, Representative Martin A. Foran (D-OH), prohibiting the practice of contract labor.

Be it enacted by the Senate and House of Representative of the United States of America in Congress assembled, That from and after the passage of this act it shall be unlawful for any person, company, partnership, or corporation, in any manner whatsoever, to prepay the transportation, or in any way assist or encourage the importation or migration of any alien or aliens, any foreigner or foreigners, into the United States, its Territories, or the District of Columbia, under contract or agreement, parol [sic] from or special, express or implied, made previous to the importation or migration of such alien or aliens, foreigner or foreigners, to perform labor or service of any kind in the United States, its Territories, or the District of Columbia.

Sec. 2. That all contracts or agreements, express or implied, parol, or special, which may hereafter be made by and between any person, company, partnership, or corporation, and any foreigner or foreigners, alien or aliens, to perform labor or service or having reference to the performance of labor or service by any person in the United States, its Territories, or the District of Columbia previous to the migration or importation of the person or persons whose labor or service is contracted for into the United States, shall be utterly void and of no effect.

Sec. 3. That for every violation of any of the provisions of section one of this act the person, partnership, company, or corporation violating the same, by knowingly assisting, encouraging or soliciting the migration or importation of any alien or aliens, foreigner or foreigners, into the United States

. . . shall forfeit and pay for every such offense the sum of one thousand dollars. . . .

Sec. 4. That the master of any vessel who knowingly brings within the United States on any such vessel and land, or permit to be landed, from any foreign port or place, any alien laborer, mechanic, or artisan, who, previous to embarkation on such vessel, had entered into contract or agreement, parol or special, express or implied, to perform labor or service in the United States, shall be deemed guilty of a misdemeanor, and on the conviction thereof, shall be punished by a fine of not more than five hundred dollars for each and every such alien laborer, mechanic, or artisan so brought as aforesaid, and may also be imprisoned for a term not exceeding six months.

Sec. 5. That nothing in this act shall be so construed as to prevent any citizen or subject of any foreign country temporarily residing in the United States, either in private or official capacity, from engaging, under contract or otherwise, persons not residents or citizens of the United States to act as private secretaries, servants, or domestics for such foreigner temporarily residing in the United States as aforesaid; nor shall this act be construed so as to prevent any person, or persons, partnership, or corporation from engaging, under contract or agreement, skilled workmen in foreign countries to perform labor in the United States in or upon any new industry not at present established in the United States; Provided, That the skilled labor for that purpose cannot be otherwise obtained; nor shall the provisions of this act apply to professional actors, artists, lecturers, or singers, nor to persons employed strictly as the personal or domestic servants, nor to ministers of any recognized religious denomination, nor persons belonging to any recognized profession, nor professors for colleges and seminaries; Provided, That nothing in this act shall be construed as prohibiting any individual from assisting any member of his family to migrate from any foreign country to the United States for the purpose of settlement here. . . .

Source: 23 Stat. 332; 8 United States Code.

Scott Act, 1888

The Scott Act, passed by Congress on September 13, 1888, added new restrictions to the Chinese Exclusion Act of 1882. Previously, Chinese workers already in the United States could come and go to China as they pleased. Under the Scott Act, named after its sponsor, Representative William Scott (D-PA), Chinese immigrants were required to get certificates to do so in advance, and the certificates were not easy to come by.

Be it enacted by the Senate and the House of Representatives of the United States of America in Congress assembled, That from and after the date of the exchange of ratifications of the pending treaty between the United States of America and His Imperial Majesty the Emperor of China, signed on the twelfth day of March, anno Domini eighteen hundred and eighty-eight, it shall be unlawful for any Chinese person, whether a subject of China or any other power, to enter the United States except as hereinafter provided.

Sec. 2. That Chinese officials, teachers, students, merchants, or travelers for pleasure or curiosity, shall be permitted to enter the United States, but in order to entitle themselves to do so, they shall first obtain the permission of the Chinese Government, or other Government of which they may at the time be citizens or subjects. Such permission and also their personal identity shall in such case be evidenced by a certificate to be made out by the diplomatic representative of the United States in that country, or of the consular representative of the United States at the port or place from which the person therein named comes. The certificate shall contain a full description of such person, of his age, height, and general physical features, and shall state his former and present occupation or profession and place of residence, and shall be made out in duplicate. One copy shall be delivered open to the person named and described, and the other copy shall be sealed up and delivered by the diplomatic or consular officer as aforesaid to the captain of the vessel on which the person named in the certificate sets sail for the United States, together with the sealed certificate, which shall be addressed to the collector of customs at the port where such person is to land.... And any captain who

lands or attempts to land a Chinese person in the United States, without having in his possession a sealed certificate, as required in this section, shall be liable to the penalties prescribed in section nine of this act.

Sec. 3. That the provisions of this act shall apply to all persons of the Chinese race, whether subjects of China or other foreign power, excepting Chinese diplomatic or consular officers and their attendants; and the words "Chinese laborers," whenever used in this act, shall be construed to mean both skilled and unskilled laborers and Chinese employed in mining.

Sec. 4. That the master of any vessel arriving in the United States from any foreign port or place with any Chinese passengers on board shall, when he delivers his manifest of cargo, and if there be no cargo, when he makes legal entry of this vessel, and before landing or permitting to land any Chinese person (unless a diplomatic or consular officer, or attendant of such officer) deliver to the collector of customs of the district in which the vessel shall have arrived the sealed certificates and letters as aforesaid, and a separate list of all Chinese persons taken on board of his vessel at any foreign port or place, and of all such persons on board at the time of the arrival as aforesaid. Such list shall show the names of such persons and other particulars as shown by their open certificates, or other evidences required by this act, and such list shall be sworn to by the master in the manner required by law in relation to the manifest of the cargo.

The master of any vessel as aforesaid shall not permit any Chinese diplomatic or consular officer or attendant of such officer to land without having first been informed by the collector of customs of the official character of such officer or attendant. Any refusal or willful neglect of the master of any vessel to comply with the provisions of this section shall incur the same penalties and forfeitures as are provided for a refusal or neglect to report and deliver a manifest of the cargo.

Sec. 5. That from and hereafter the passage of this act, no Chinese laborer in the United States shall be permitted, after having left, to return thereto, except under the conditions stated in the following sections.

Sec. 6. That no Chinese laborer within the purview of the preceding section shall be permitted to return to the United States unless he has a lawful wife, child, or parent in the United States, or property therein of the value of one thousand dollars, or debts of like amount due him and pending settlement. The marriage to such wife must have taken place at least one year prior to the application of the laborer for a permit to return to the United States, and must have been followed by the continuous cohabitation of the parties as man and wife.

If the right to return be claimed on the ground of property or of debts, it must appear that the property is bona fide and not colorably acquired for the purpose of evading this act, or that the debts are unascertained and unsettled, and not promissory notes or other similar acknowledgments of ascertained liability.

Sec. 7. That a Chinese person claiming the right to be permitted to leave the United States and return thereto on any of the grounds stated in the foregoing section, shall apply to the collector of customs of the district from which he wishes to depart at least one month prior to the time of his departure, and shall make an oath before the said collector a full statement descriptive of his family, or property, or debts, as the case may be, and shall furnish to the said collector such proofs of the facts entitling him to return as shall be required by the rules and regulations prescribed from time to time by the Secretary of the Treasury, and for any false swearing in relation thereto he shall incur the penalties of perjury. He shall also permit the collector to take a full description of his person, which description the collector shall retain and mark with a number. And if the collector, after hearing the proofs and investigating all the circumstances of the case, shall decide to issue a certificate of return, he shall at such time and place as he may designate, sign and give to the person applying a certificate containing the number of the description last aforesaid, which shall be the sole evidence given to such person of his right to return. If the last named certificate be transferred, it shall become void, and the person to whom it was given shall forfeit his right to return to the United States. The right of return under said certificate shall be limited to one year; but it may be extended for an additional period, not to exceed a year, in cases where, by reason of sickness or other cause of disability beyond his control, the holder thereof shall be rendered unable sooner to return, which facts shall be fully reported to and investigated by the consular representative of the United States at the port or place from which such laborer departs for the United States, and certified by such representatives of the United States to the satisfaction of the collector of customs at the port where such Chinese person shall seek to land in the United States, such certificate to be delivered by said representative to the master of the vessel on which he departs for the United States. And no Chinese laborer shall be permitted to re-enter the United States without producing to the proper officer of the customs of the port of such entry the return certificate herein required. A Chinese laborer possessing a certificate under this section shall be admitted to the United States only at the port from which he departed therefrom. . . .

Sec. 13. That any Chinese person, or persons of Chinese descent, found unlawfully in the United States, or its Territories, may be arrested upon a warrant issued upon a complaint, under oath, filed by any party on behalf of the United States, by any justice, judge, or commissioner of any United States court, returnable before any justice, judge, or commissioner of a United States court, or before any United States court, and when convicted, upon a hearing, and found and adjudged to be one not lawfully entitled to be or remain in the United States, such person shall be removed from the United States to the country from whence he came. . . . And in all such cases the person who brought or aided in bringing such person into the United States shall be liable to the Government of the United States for all necessary expenses incurred in such investigation and removal; and all peace officers of the several States and Territories of the United States are hereby invested with the same authority in reference to carrying out the provisions of this act, as a marshal or deputy marshal of the United States, and shall be entitled to like compensation, to be audited and paid by the same officers.

Sec. 14. That the preceding sections shall not apply to Chinese diplomatic or consular officers or their attendants, who shall be admitted to the United States under special instructions of the Treasury Department, without production of other evidence than that of personal identity.

Source: 25 Stat. 476; 8 United States Code.

Act Banning Naturalization of Anarchists, 1903

Although the Red Scare of the post–World War I era was still nearly two decades away, fear of anarchists rose in the United States in the late nineteenth and early twentieth centuries, especially following the assassination of President William McKinley in 1901 by self-proclaimed anarchist Leon Czolgosz. Anarchists believed in both individual freedom and an end to all governments, and some advocated violence to achieve their ends. On March 3, 1903, Congress passed legislation banning the naturalization and citizenship of alleged anarchists.

Sec. 39. That no person who believes in or who is opposed to all organized government, or who is a member of or affiliated with any organization entertaining and teaching such disbelief in or opposition to all organized government, or who advocates or teaches the duty, necessity, or propriety of the unlawful assaulting or killing of any officers, either of specific individuals or of officers generally, of the Government of the United States or of any other government, because of his or their official character, or who has violated the provisions of this Act, shall be naturalized or be made a citizen of the United States. All courts and tribunals and all judges and officers thereof having jurisdiction of naturalization proceedings or duties to perform in regard thereto shall, on the final application for naturalization, make careful inquiry into such matters, and before issuing the final order or certificate of naturalization cause to be entered of record the affidavit of the applicant and of his witnesses so far as applicable, reciting and affirming the truth of every material requisite for naturalization. All final orders and certificates of naturalization hereafter made shall show on their face specifically that said affidavits were duly made and recorded, and all orders and certificates that fail to show such facts shall be null and void.

That any person who purposely procures naturalization in violation of the provisions of this section shall be fined not more than five thousand dollars, or shall be imprisoned not less than one nor more than ten years, or both, and the court in which such conviction is had shall thereupon adjudge and declare the order or decree and all certificates admitting such person to citizenship null and void. Jurisdiction is hereby conferred on the courts having jurisdiction of the trial of such offense to make such adjudication.

That any person who knowingly aids, advises, or encourages any such person to apply for or to secure naturalization or to file the preliminary papers declaring an intent to become a citizen of the United States, or who in any naturalization proceeding knowingly procures or gives false testimony as to any material fact, or who knowingly makes an affidavit false as to any material fact required to be proved in such proceeding, shall be fined not more than five thousand dollars, or imprisoned not less than one nor more than ten years, or both.

Source: 32 Stat. 1222.

White Slave Traffic Act (Mann Act), 1910

*A*lthough *it is hard to say how serious the problem was, Congress moved to outlaw the importation of women for the purposes of prostitution by passing the so-called White Slave Traffic Act of 1910. Many historians believe the law—also called the Mann Act, after its sponsor, Representative James R. Mann (R-IL)—offered a politically expedient way for Congress to appear that it was doing something about the overwhelming numbers of immigrants pouring into the country in the early twentieth century—a flow that was beginning to arouse opposition among native-born Americans.*

Sec. 1. That the term "interstate commerce" as used in this Act, shall include transportation from any State or Territory or the District of Columbia to any other State or Territory or the District of Columbia, and the term "foreign commerce," as used in this Act, shall include transportation from any State or Territory or the District of Columbia to any foreign country and from any foreign country to any State or Territory or the District of Columbia.

Sec. 2. That any person who shall knowingly transport or cause to be transported, or aid or assist in obtaining transportation for, or in transporting, in interstate or foreign commerce, or in any Territory or in the District of Columbia, any woman or girl for the purpose of prostitution or debauchery, or for any other immoral purpose, or with the intent and purpose to induce, entice, or compel such woman or girl to become a prostitute or to give herself up to debauchery, or to engage in any other immoral practice; or who shall knowingly procure or obtain, or cause to be procured or obtained, or aid or assist in procuring or obtaining, any ticket or tickets, or any form of transportation or evidence of the right thereto, to be used by any woman or girl in interstate or foreign commerce, or in any Territory or the District of Columbia, in going to any place for the purpose of prostitution or debauchery, or for any other immoral purpose, or with the intent or purpose on the part of such person to induce, entice, or compel her to give herself up to the practice of prostitution, or to give herself up to debauchery, or any other immoral purpose, whereby such woman or girl shall be transported in interstate or foreign commerce, or in any Territory or the District of Columbia, shall be deemed guilty of a felony, and upon conviction thereof shall be punished by a fine not exceeding five thousand dollars, or by imprisonment of not more than five years, or by both such fine and imprisonment, in the discretion of the court. . . .

Sec. 3. That any person who shall knowingly persuade, induce, entice, or coerce, or cause to be persuaded, induced, enticed, or coerced, or aid or assist in persuading, inducing, enticing, or coercing any woman or girl to go from one place to another in interstate or foreign commerce . . . for the purpose of prostitution or debauchery, or for any other immoral purpose . . . shall be deemed guilty of a felony and on conviction thereof, shall be punished by a fine of not more than five thousand dollars, or by imprisonment for a term not exceeding five years, or by both such fine and imprisonment. . . .

Sec. 6. That for the purpose of regulating and preventing the transportation in foreign commerce of alien women and girls for the purpose of prostitution and debauchery, and in pursuance of and for the purpose of carrying out the terms of the agreement or project of arrangement for the suppression of the white-slavery traffic . . . the Commissioner of Immigration and Naturalization is hereby designated as the authority of the United States to receive and centralize information concerning the procuration of alien women and girls with a view to their debauchery, and to exercise supervision over such alien women and girls. . . .

Every person who shall keep, maintain, control, support, or harbor in any house or place for the purpose of prostitution, or for any other immoral purpose, any alien woman or girl within three years after she shall have entered the United States from any country . . . shall be deemed guilty of a felony, and on conviction thereof shall be punished by a fine of not more than ten thousand dollars, or by imprisonment for a term of not exceeding ten years, or by both such fine and imprisonment, in the discretion of the court.

Source: 36 Stat. 825; United States Code.

Immigration Act, 1917

Popularly referred to as the "Literacy Act," the Immigration Act of 1917 was the first American piece of restrictive legislation aimed at all immigrants, including those from Europe. While the act called for the exclusion of persons with physical and mental diseases—as well as those with allegedly dangerous political convictions—it also included a clause that banned immigrants who were illiterate in English or their native tongue. Finally, the law banned most Asians from emigrating to the United States.

Sec. 1. That the word "alien" wherever used in this Act shall include any person not a native-born or naturalized citizen of the United States; but this definition shall not be held to include Indians of the United States not taxed or citizens of the islands under the jurisdiction of the United States. That the term "United States" as used in the title as well as in the various sections of this Act shall be construed to mean the United States, and any waters, territory, or other place subject to the jurisdiction thereof, except the Isthmian Canal Zone. . . .

Sec. 2. That there shall be levied, collected, and paid a tax of $8 for every alien, including alien seamen regularly admitted as provided in this Act, entering the United States. . . .

Sec. 3. That the following classes of aliens shall be excluded from admission into the United States: All idiots, imbeciles, feeble-minded persons, epileptics, insane persons . . . persons with chronic alcoholism; paupers; professional beggars; vagrants; persons afflicted with tuberculosis in any form or a loathsome or dangerous contagious disease; persons not comprehended within any of the foregoing excluded classes who are found to be and are certified by the examining surgeon as being mentally or physically defective, such physical defect being of a nature which may affect the ability of such alien to earn a living; persons who have been convicted . . . of a felony or other crime or misdemeanor involving moral turpitude; polygamists, or persons who practice polygamy or believe in and advocate the practice of polygamy; anarchists, or persons who advocate the overthrow by force or violence of the Government of the United States, or of all forms of law . . . or who advocate the assassination of public officials, or who advocate and teach the unlawful destruction of property . . . ; prostitutes, or persons coming to the United States for the purpose of prostitution or immoral purposes . . . ; persons hereinafter called contract laborers . . . ; persons likely to become public charges . . . ; persons whose ticket or passage is paid for with the money of another; persons whose ticket or passage is paid for by any corporation, association, society, municipality, or foreign government, either directly or indirectly; stowaways . . . ; all children under sixteen years of age unaccompanied by or not coming to one or both of their parents . . . unless otherwise provided for by existing treaties, persons who are natives of islands not possessed by the United States adjacent to the continent of Asia, situate [*sic*] south of the twentieth parallel latitude north, west of the one hundred and sixtieth meridian of longitude east from Greenwich, and north of the tenth parallel of latitude south, or who are natives of any country, province, or dependency situate on the Continent of Asia west of the one hundred and tenth meridian of longitude east from Greenwich and east of the fiftieth meridian of longitude east from Greenwich and south of the fiftieth parallel of latitude north, except that portion of said territory situate between the fiftieth and sixty-fourth and thirty-eighth parallels of latitude north, and no alien now in any way excluded from, or prevented from entering the United States shall be admitted to the United States. . . .

That after three months from the passage of this Act in addition to the aliens who are by law now excluded from admission into the United States, the following persons shall also be excluded:

All aliens over sixteen years of age, physically capable of reading, who cannot read the English language, or some other language or dialect, including Hebrew or Yiddish: Provided, That any admissible alien, or any alien heretofore or hereafter legally admitted, or any citizen of the United States, may bring in or send for his father or grandfather over fifty-five years of age, his wife, his mother, his grandmother, or his unmarried or widowed daughter, if otherwise admissible, whether such relative can read or not; and such relative shall be permitted to enter. That for the purpose of ascertaining whether aliens can read the immigrant inspectors shall be furnished with slips of uniform size, prepared under the direction of the Attorney General, each containing not less than thirty nor more than forty words in ordinary use, printed in plainly legible type in some one of the various languages or dialects of immigrants. Each alien may designate the particular language or dialect in which he desires the examination to be made, and shall be rejquired to read the words printed on the slip in such language or dialect. . . .

Provided, That nothing in this Act shall exclude, if otherwise admissible, persons convicted, or who admit to the commission, or who teach or advocate the commission, of an offense purely political. . . .

Provided further, That skilled labor, if otherwise admissible, may be imported if labor of the kind unemployed can not be found in this country, and the question of the necessity of importing such skilled labor in any particular instance may be determined by the Attorney General upon the application of any person interested, such application to be made before such importation, and such determination by the Attorney General to be reached after a full hearing and an investigation into the facts of the case. . . .

It shall also be unlawful for any person to bring to any port of the United States any alien who is excluded by the provisions of section 3 of this Act because unable to read, or who is excluded by the terms of section 3 of this Act as a native of that portion of the Continent of Asia and the islands adjacent thereto described in said section. . . .

Sec. 27. That for the preservation of the peace and in order that arrests may be made for crimes under the laws of the States and Territories of the United States where the various immigration stations are located, the officers in charge of such stations, as occasion may require, shall admit therein the proper State and municipal officers charged with the enforcement of such laws, and for the purpose of this section the jurisdiction of such officers and of the local courts shall extend over such stations. . . .

Sec. 29. That the President of the United States is authorized, in the name of the Government of the United States, to call, in his discretion, an international conference, to assemble at such point as may be agreed upon, or to send special commissioners to any foreign country, for the purpose of regulating by international agreement, subject to the advice and consent of the Senate of the United States, the immigration of aliens to the United States; of providing for the mental, moral, and physical examination of such aliens by American consuls or other officers of the United States Government at the ports of embarkation, or elsewhere; of securing the assistance of foreign Governments in their own territories to prevent the evasion of the laws of the United States governing immigration to the United States; of entering into such international agreements as may be proper to prevent the immigration of aliens who, under the laws of the United States, are or may be excluded from entering the United States, and of regulating any matters pertaining to such immigration. . . .

Source: 39 Stat. 874; 8 United States Code.

Puerto Rico Citizenship Act, 1917

*F*ollowing the Spanish-American War in 1898, the United States annexed Puerto Rico as a colony. Nineteen years later, Congress acted to extend a limited form of citizenship to the people of Puerto Rico. Many historians say the 1917 act was passed in order to draft Puerto Ricans to serve in the military as U.S. entry into World War I loomed.

Sec. 5. That all citizens of Puerto Rico, as defined by section seven of the Act of April twelfth, nineteen hundred, "temporarily to provide revenues and a civil government for Puerto Rico, and for other purposes," and all natives of Puerto Rico, who were temporarily absent from that island on April eleventh, eighteen hundred and ninety-nine, and have since returned and are permanently residing in that island, and are not citizens of any foreign country, are hereby declared, and shall be deemed and held to be, citizens of the United States: *Provided,* That any person hereinbefore described may retain his present political status by making a declaration, under oath, of his decision to do so within six months of the taking effect of this Act before a district court in which he resides, the declaration to be in form as follows:

"I, _____, being duly sworn, hereby declare my intention not to become a citizen of the United States as provided in the Act of Congress conferring United States citizenship upon citizens of Puerto Rico and certain natives permanently residing in said island." . . .

After making such declaration and submitting such proofs, such persons shall be admitted to take the oath of allegiance before the court, and thereupon shall be considered a citizen of the United States.

Source: 39 Stat. 951; 48 United States Code 733 a-1.

Quota Act of 1921

As its name implies, the Quota Act of 1921 was the first legislation designed to restrict immigrants on a quota system. Under the 1921 system, the allowable number of immigrants from a given country would be set at 3 percent of the total number of persons from that country living in the United States in 1910.

Be it enacted by the Senate and the House of Representatives . . . ,

Sec. 2. (a) That the number of aliens of any nationality who may be admitted under the immigration laws to the United States in any fiscal year shall be limited to 3 per centum of the number of foreign-born persons of such nationality resident in the United States as determined by the United States census of 1910. This provision shall not apply to the following, and they shall not be counted in reckoning any of the percentage limits provided in this Act: (1) Government officials, their families, attendants, servants, and employees; (2) aliens in continuous transit through the United States; (3) aliens lawfully admitted to the United States who later go in transit . . . to another foreign contiguous territory; (4) aliens visiting the United States as tourists or temporarily for business or pleasure; (5) aliens from countries immigration from which is regulated in accordance with treaties or agreements relating solely to immigration; (6) aliens from the so-called Asiatic barred zone . . . (7) aliens who have resided continuously for at least five years immediately preceding the time of their application for admission . . . in the Dominion of Canada, Newfoundland, the Republic of Cuba, the Republic of Mexico, countries of Central and South America, or adjacent islands; or (8) aliens under the age of eighteen who are children of citizens of the United States.

(b) For the purposes of this Act nationality shall be determined by country of birth, treating as separate countries the colonies or dependencies for which separate enumeration was made in the United States census of 1910;

(c) That the Secretary of State, the Secretary of Commerce, and the Attorney General, jointly, shall, as soon as feasible after enactment of this Act, prepare a statement showing the number of persons of the various nationalities resident in the United States as determined by the census of 1910, which statement shall be the population basis for the purposes of this Act. . . .

(d) When the maximum number of aliens from any nationality who may be admitted in any fiscal year under this Act shall have been admitted all other aliens of such nationality, except as otherwise provided for by this Act . . . shall be excluded. . . .

Provided further, That in the enforcement of this Act preference shall be given so far as possible to the wives, parents, brothers, sisters, children under eighteen years of age, and fiancees, (1) of citizens of the United States, (2) of aliens now in the United States who have applied for citizenship in the manner provided by law, or (3) of persons eligible to United States citizenship who served in the military or naval forces of the United States at any time between April 6, 1917 and November 11, 1918 . . . and have been separated from such forces under honorable conditions.

Sec. 3. That the Commissioner of Immigration and Naturalization, with the approval of the Attorney General, shall as soon as feasible after the enactment of this Act, and from time to time hereafter, prescribe rules and regulations necessary to carry the provisions of this Act into effect. He shall, as soon as feasible . . . publish a statement showing the number of aliens of the various nationalities who may be admitted to the United States. . . . Thereafter he shall publish monthly statements during the time this Act remains in force showing the number of aliens of each nationality already admitted under provisions of this Act . . . and the number who may be admitted . . . during the then current fiscal year . . . but when 75 per centum of the maximum number of any nationality . . . shall have been admitted such statements shall be issued weekly thereafter. . . . The Attorney General shall also submit such statements to the Secretary of State, who shall transmit the information contained therein to the proper diplomatic and consular officials of the United States, which officials shall make the same available to persons intending to emigrate to the United States and to others who may apply.

Sec. 5. That this Act shall take effect and be enforced 15 days after its enactment . . . and shall continue in force until June 30, 1924 [originally "1922" but extended for two more years], and the number of aliens of any nationality who may be admitted during the remaining period of the current fiscal year, from the date when this Act becomes effective until June 30, shall be limited in proportion to the number admissible during the fiscal year 1922.

Sec. 6. That it shall be unlawful for any person, including any transportation company other than railway lines entering the United States from foreign contiguous territory, or the owner, master, agent, or consignee of any vessel, to bring to the United States either from a foreign country or any insular possession of the United States any alien not admissible under the terms of this Act or regulations made thereunder.

Source: 42 Stat. 5; 8 United States Code 229.

Quota Act of 1924

hree years after passing the first quota act in 1921, Congress moved to restrict immigration even further through the Quota Act of 1924. The 1921 bill had set a limit on annual immigration from a given country at 3 percent of the total number of persons of that nationality living in the United States in 1910; the 1924 act lowered the percentage to 2 percent. More importantly, it set the base year at 1890. Because much of the immigration from Eastern and Southern Europe had come after that year, the quotas for countries in those regions were correspondingly lowered to a significant degree.

Sec. 2. (a) A consular officer upon the application of any immigrant . . . may . . . issue to such an immigrant an immigration visa which shall consist of one copy of the application provided for in section 7, visaed by such consular officer. Such visa shall specify (1) the nationality of the immigrant; (2) whether he is a quota immigrant (as defined in section 5) or a non-quota immigrant (as defined in section 4); (3) the date on which the validity of the immigration visa shall expire; and (4) such additional information necessary to the proper enforcement of the immigration laws and the naturalization laws as may be by regulation prescribed.

Sec. 6. (a) Immigration visas to quota immigrants shall be issued in each fiscal year as follows:

(1) Fifty per centum of the quotas of each nationality for such year shall be made available . . . to the following classes of immigrants, without priority of preference as between such classes: (A) Quota immigrants who are the fathers or mothers of citizens of the United States . . . or who are the husbands of citizens of the United States by marriages occurring on or after May 31, 1928, of citizens who are citizens of the United States who are twenty-one years of age or over; and (B) in the case of any nationality the quota of which is three hundred or more, quota immigrants who are skilled in agriculture, and the wives, and the dependent children under the age of eighteen years, of such immigrants skilled in agriculture, if accompanying or following to join them.

(2) The remainder of the quota of each nationality for such year . . . shall be made available in such year for the issuance of immigration visas to quota immigrants of such nationality who are the unmarried children under twenty-one years of age, or the wives, of alien residents of the United States who were lawfully admitted to the United States for permanent residence. . . .

Sec. 10. (a) Any alien about to depart temporarily from the United States may make application to the Commissioner of Immigration and Naturalization for a permit to reenter the United States stating the length of his intended absence, and the reasons therefor. . . .

Sec. 11. (a) The annual quota of any nationality shall be 2 per centum of the number of foreign-born individuals of such nationality resident in continental United States as determined by the United States census of 1890, but the minimum quota of any nationality shall be 100. . . .

Sec. 12. (a) For the purpose of this Act nationality shall be determined by country of birth, treating as separate countries the colonies, dependencies, or self-governing dominions for which separate enumeration was made in the United States census of 1890 and which was not included in the enumeration for the country to which such colony or dependency belonged. . . .

Sec. 13. (a) No immigrant shall be admitted . . . unless he (1) has an unexpired immigration visa . . . ; (2) is of the nationality specified in the visa; (3) is a nonquota immigrant if specified in the visa as such; (4) is a preference-quota immigrant if specified . . . as such; and (5) is otherwise admissible under the immigration laws. . . .

(c) No alien ineligible to citizenship shall be admitted to the United States unless such alien (1) is admissible as a non-quota immigrant under the provisions of subdivisions (b), (d) or (e) of section 4, or (2) is the wife, or the unmarried child under 18 years of age, of an immigrant admissible . . . , and is accompanying or following to join him, or (3) is not an immigrant as defined in section 3. . . .

(e) No quota immigrant shall be admitted under subdivision (d) if the entire number of immigrant visas which may be issued to quota immigrants of the same nationality for the fiscal year has already been issued. . . .

Sec. 18. If a quota immigrant of any nationality having an immigration visa is excluded from admission to the United States under the immigration laws and deported, or does not apply for admission to the United States before the expiration of the validity of the immigration visa, or if any alien of any nationality having an immigration visa issued to him as a quota immigrant is found not to be a quota immigrant, no additional immigration visa shall be issued in lieu thereof to any other immigrant.

Sec. 19. No alien seaman excluded from admission . . . shall be permitted to land . . . except temporarily for medical treatment, or pursuant to such regulations as the Attorney General may prescribe for the ultimate departure, removal, or deportation of such alien from the United States.

Sec. 23. Whenever any alien attempts to enter the United States the burden of proof shall be upon the alien to establish that he is not subject to exclusion under any of the provisions of the immigration laws.

Source: 43 Stat. 153; 8 United States Code 201.

Act Conferring United States Citizenship on American Indians, 1924

Although Native Americans were the first people to live in what eventually became the United States, those living on reservations were the very last to become full citizens. They received that status by act of Congress on June 2, 1924. The law also declared the third Sunday in May as Citizenship Day.

Be it enacted by the Senate and House of Representatives of the United States of America in Congress assembled, That all non-citizen Indians born within the territorial limits of the United States be and they are hereby, declared to be citizens of the United States: *Provided,* That the granting of such citizenship shall not in any manner impair or otherwise affect the right of any Indian to tribal or other property. (43 Stat. 253; 8 U. S. C. 3.)

Source: Immigration and Nationality Laws and Regulations as of March 1, 1944. Washington, DC: United States Government Printing Office, 1944.

Repeal of Chinese Exclusion Acts, 1943

Beginning in 1882, Congress passed a series of laws that virtually excluded all Chinese immigration into the United States. During World War II, however, China became a critical ally of the United States in the struggle against the Japanese Empire. As part of that alliance—and as a reflection of diminishing anti-Chinese racism in the United States—Congress repealed the Chinese Exclusion Acts in December 1943. It established a quota of 105 Chinese immigrants per year.

Be it enacted by the Senate and House of Representatives of the United States of America in Congress assembled, That the following Acts or parts of Acts relating to the exclusion or deportation of persons of the Chinese race are hereby repealed: [The Act then lists every Act or part of an Act passed since 1882.] *Provided,* That all charges for the maintenance or return of Chinese persons applying for admission to the United States shall hereafter be paid or reimbursed to the United States by the person, company, partnership, or corporation bringing such Chinese to a port of the United States as applicants for admission. . . .

Sec. 2. With the exception of Chinese wives of American citizens and those Chinese aliens coming under subsections (b), (d), (e) and (f) of section 4, Immigration Act of 1924 . . . all Chinese persons entering the United States annually as immigrants shall be allocated to the quota for the Chinese computed under the provisions of section 11 of the said Act. A preference up to 75 per centum of the quota shall be given to Chinese born and resident in China.

Source: 57 Stat. 600; 8 United States Code 212(a).

"Bracero Program" Act, 1949

To assure a steady and adequate supply of agricultural workers, the United States moved to allow Mexican workers into the country in 1949. Under the so-called Bracero Program, workers were allowed to come into the United States on a temporary basis. While the act contained sections designed to prevent abuse of workers, critics complained that these continued anyway. The program was ended in 1964.

Be it enacted by the Senate and House of Representatives of the United States of America in Congress assembled, That this Act may be cited as the "Agricultural Act of 1949."

Sec. 501. For the purpose of assisting in such production of agricultural commodities and products as the Secretary of Agriculture deems necessary, by supplying agricultural workers from the Republic of Mexico . . . the Secretary of Labor is authorized—

(1) to recruit workers . . .

(2) to establish and operate reception centers at or near places of actual entry of such workers into the continental United States for the purpose of receiving and housing such workers for their employment in, or departure from, the continental United States;

(3) to provide transportation for such workers . . .

(4) to provide workers with such subsistence . . . at reception centers;

(5) to assist such workers and employers in negotiating contracts for agricultural employment . . .

(6) to guarantee the performance by employers of provisions of such contracts. . . .

Sec. 502. No workers shall be made available under this title to any employer unless such employer enters into an agreement with the United States—

(1) to indemnify the United States against loss . . .

(2) to reimburse the United States for essential expenses . . .

(3) to pay to the United States, in any case in which a worker is not returned [costs]. . . .

Sec. 505. Workers recruited under this title who are not citizens of the United States shall be admitted to the United States subject to the immigration laws. . . .

Sec. 506.(c) Workers recruited under the provisions of this title shall not be subject to the head tax levied under section 2 of the Immigration Act of 1917. . . .

Source: 63 Stat. 1051.

Immigration and Nationality Act (McCarran-Walter Act), 1952

As the Cold War and anti-communist sentiment intensified in the late 1940s and early 1950s, Congress moved to alter immigration and naturalization laws to fit national security interests. The massive Immigration and Nationality Act of 1952, also known as the McCarran-Walter Act after its sponsors Senator Patrick McCarran (D-NY) and Representative Francis Walter (D-PA), was largely a reiteration of the 1917 and 1924 literacy and quota acts, with some increase of immigration from Asia. The section below, however, sought to block the naturalization of persons deemed a threat to national security. The law was passed over President Harry S. Truman's veto.

CHAPTER 2—NATIONALITY THROUGH NATURALIZATION

Sec. 311. The right of a person to become a naturalized citizen of the United States shall not be denied or abridged because of race or sex or because such a person is married. Notwithstanding section 405(b), this section shall apply to any person whose petition for naturalization shall hereafter be filed, or shall have been pending on the effective date of this Act.

Sec. 312. No person except as otherwise provided in this title shall hereafter be naturalized as a citizen of the United States upon his own petition who cannot demonstrate—

(1) an understanding of the English language, including the ability to read, write, and speak words in ordinary usage in the English language. . . .

(2) a knowledge and understanding of the fundamentals of the history, and of the principles and form of government, of the United States.

Sec. 313. (a) Notwithstanding the provisions of section 405(b), no person shall be naturalized as a citizen of the United States—[the act lists subsections (1) through (6) which prohibit the naturalization of anarchists, communists, totalitarians, and those who believe or publish such, etc.]. . . .

Sec. 316. (a) No person, except as otherwise provided for in this title, shall be naturalized unless such petitioner, (1) immediately preceding the date of filing his petition for naturalization has resided continuously, after being lawfully admitted for permanent residence, within the United States for at least five years and during the five years . . . has been physically present therein for periods totaling at least half of that time, and who has resided within the State in which petition is filed for at least six months, (2) has resided continuously within the United States from the date of the petition up to the time of admission to citizenship, and (3) during all the periods referred to in this subsection has been and still is a person of good moral character, attached to the principles of the Constitution of the United States, and well disposed to the good order and happiness of the United States. [The subsection then specifies when and how absences are accepted as exceptions to the "continuous" residing provision.] . . .

Sec. 337. (a) A person who has petitioned for naturalization shall, in order to be and before being admitted to citizenship, take in open court an oath (1) to support the Constitution of the United States; (2) to renounce and abjure absolutely and entirely all allegiance and fidelity to any foreign prince, potentate, state, or sovereignty of whom or which the petitioner was before a subject or citizen; (3) to support and defend the Constitution and laws of the United States against all enemies, foreign and domestic; (4) to bear true faith and allegiance [to] the same; and (5) (A) to bear arms on behalf of the United States when required by law, or (B) to perform non-combatant service in the Armed Forces of the United States when required by law, or (C) to perform work of national importance under civilian direction when required by law. . . .

Sec. 349. (a) From and after the effective date of this Act a person who is a national of the United States whether by birth or naturalization, shall lose his nationality by—

(1) obtaining naturalization in a foreign state upon his own application, upon an application filed in his behalf by a parent, guardian, or duly authorized agent, or through the naturalization of a parent having legal custody of such person. . . .

(2) taking an oath or making an affirmation or other formal declaration of allegiance to a foreign state or a political subdivision thereof . . .

(3) entering, or serving in, the armed forces of a foreign state . . . unless [prior to doing so] authorized by the Secretary of State and the Secretary of Defense . . .

(4) accepting, serving in, or performing the duties of any office, post, or employment under the government of a foreign state or a political subdivision thereof . . .

(5) voting in a political election in a foreign state . . .

(6) making a formal renunciation of nationality before a diplomatic or consular officer of the United States in a foreign state, in such form as may be prescribed by the Secretary of State . . .

(7) making in the United States a formal written renunciation of nationality in such form as may be prescribed by . . . the Attorney General . . .

(8) deserting the military, air, or naval forces of the United States in a time of war, if and when he is convicted thereof by court martial and as the result of such conviction is dismissed or dishonorably discharged from the service . . .

(9) committing any act of treason against, or attempting to overthrow, or bearing arms against, the United States . . .

(10) departing from or remaining outside of the jurisdiction of the United States in time of war . . . for the purpose of evading or avoiding . . . service in the military. . . .

Source: 66 Stat. 163.

Immigration and Nationality Act, 1965

*I*n 1952, Congress passed the Immigration and Nationality Act, also known as the McCarran-Walter Act. The McCarran-Walter Act removed the ban against immigration of Asian and Pacific peoples, but kept in place most of the quota system established in the 1920s. Spurred by a booming economy, the civil rights movement, and rising liberal sentiment in the 1950s and 1960s, the public's attitude toward immigration changed to a more welcoming position. In 1965, Congress passed and President Lyndon Johnson signed a new law, the Immigration and Nationality Act, which carried the same name as the 1952 law. The 1965 act amended the 1952 act and virtually eliminated the old quota system of immigrant entry.

Be it enacted by the Senate and House of Representatives of the United States of America in Congress assembled, That section 201 of the Immigration and Nationality Act [of 1952] . . . be amended to read as follows:

Sec. 201. (a) Exclusive of special immigrants defined in section 101 (a) (27), and of the immediate relatives of United States citizens specified in subsection (b) of this section, the number of aliens who may be issued immigrant visas or who may otherwise acquire the status of an alien lawfully admitted to the United States for permanent residence, or who may, pursuant to section 203 (a) (7) enter conditionally, (i) shall not in any of the first three quarters of any fiscal year exceed a total of 45,000 and (ii) shall not in any fiscal year exceed a total of 170,000.

(b) The "immediate relatives" referred to in subsection (a) of this section will mean the children, spouses, and parents of a citizen of the United States: *Provided,* That in the case of parents, such citizen must be at least twenty-one years of age. . . .

(d) Quota numbers not issued or otherwise used during the previous fiscal year, as determined in accordance with subsection (c) hereof, shall be transferred to an immigration pool. Allocation of numbers from the pool and from national quotas shall not together exceed in any fiscal year the numerical limitations in subsection (a) of this section. The immigration pool shall be made available to immigrants otherwise admissible under the provisions of this Act who are unable to obtain prompt issuance of a preference visa due to oversubscription of their quotas, or subquotas as determined by the Secretary of State. . . .

(e) The immigration pool and the quota areas shall terminate June 30, 1968. Thereafter immigrants admitted under the provisions of this Act who are subject to the numerical limitations of subsection (a) of this Act will be admitted in accordance with the percentage limitations and in the order of priority specified in section 203.

Sec. 2. Section 202 of the Immigration and Nationality Act [of 1952] . . . is amended to read as follows:

"(a) No person shall receive any preference or priority or be discriminated against in the issuance of an immigrant visa because of his race, sex, nationality, place of birth, or place of residence, except as specifically provided in section 101 (a) (27), section 201 (b), and section 203: *Provided,* That the total number of immigrant visas and the number of conditional entries made available to natives of any single foreign state . . . shall not exceed 20,000 in any fiscal year. . . .

"(b) Each independent country, self-governing dominion, mandated territory, and territory under the international trusteeship of the United Nations, other than the United States and its outlying possessions, shall be treated as a separate foreign state for the purposes of the numerical limitation set forth in the proviso to subsection (a) of this section when approved by the Secretary of State. All other inhabited lands shall be attributed to a foreign state specified by the Secretary of State. For the purposes of this Act the foreign state to which an immigrant is chargeable shall be determined by birth within such foreign state." . . .

Sec. 3. Sec. 203 of the Immigration and Nationality Act [of 1952] . . . is amended as follows:

"Sec. 203. (a) Aliens who are subject to the numerical limitations . . . shall be allotted visas or their conditional entry authorized, as the case may be, as follows:

"(1) Visas shall be first made available, in a number not to exceed 20 per centum of the number specified in section 201 (a) (ii), to qualified immigrants who are the unmarried sons or daughters of citizens of the United States.

"(2) Visas shall next be made available, in a number not to exceed 20 per centum of the number specified in section 201 (a) (ii), plus visas not required to be classes specified in paragraph (1), to qualified immigrants who are spouses, unmarried sons or unmarried daughters of an alien admitted for permanent residence.

"(3) Visas shall next be made available, in a number not to exceed 10 per centum . . . to qualified immigrants who are members of the professions, or who because of their exceptional ability in the sciences or arts will substantially benefit prospectively the national economy, cultural interests, or welfare of the United States.

"(4) Visas shall next be made available, in a number not to exceed 10 per centum . . . to qualified immigrants who are the married sons or married daughters of citizens of the United States.

"(5) Visas shall next be made available, in a number not to exceed 24 per centum . . . to qualified immigrants who are the brothers or sisters of citizens of the United States.

"(6) Visas shall next be made available, in a number not to exceed 10 per centum of the number specified . . . to qualified immigrants who are capable of performing specified skilled or unskilled labor, not of a temporary or seasonal nature, for which a shortage of employable and willing persons exists in the United States.

"(7) Conditional entries shall next be made available by the Attorney General, pursuant to such regulations as he may prescribe and in a number not to exceed 6 per centum . . . to aliens who satisfy an Immigration and Naturalization Service officer at an examination in any non-Communist or non-Communist-dominated country, (A) that (i) because of persecution or fear of persecution on account of race, religion, or political opinion they have fled (I) from any Communist or Communist-dominated country or area, or (II) from any country within the general area of the Middle East, and (ii) are unable or unwilling to return to such country or area on account of race, religion, or political opinion, and (iii) are not nationals of the countries or areas in which their application for conditional entry is made; or (B) that they are persons uprooted by catastrophic natural calamity as defined by the President who are unable to return to their usual place of abode. For the purposes of the foregoing the term 'general area of the Middle East' means the area between and including (1) Libya on the west, (2) Turkey on

the north, (3) Pakistan on the east, and (4) Saudi Arabia and Ethiopia on the south. . . .

"(8) Visas authorized in any fiscal year, less those required for issuance to the classes specified in paragraphs (1) through (6) and less the conditional entries and visas made available pursuant to paragraph (7), shall be made available to other qualified immigrants strictly in the chronological order in which they qualify. Waiting lists of applicants shall be maintained in accordance with regulations prescribed by the Secretary of State. No immigrant visa shall be issued to a nonpreference immigrant under this paragraph, or to an immigrant with a preference under paragraph (3) or (6) of this subsection, until the consular officer is in receipt of a determination made by the Secretary of Labor in pursuant to the provisions of section 212 (a) (14).

"(9) A spouse or child as defined in section 101 (b) (1) (A), (B), (C), (D), or (E) shall, if not otherwise entitled to an immigrant status and the immediate issuance of a visa, or to conditional entry under paragraph (1) through (8), be entitled to the same status, and the same order of consideration provided in subsection (b), if accompanying, or following . . . his spouse or parent. . . .

"(d) Every immigrant shall be presumed to be a nonpreference immigrant until he establishes to the satisfaction of the consular officer and the immigration officer that he is entitled to a preference status." . . .

Sec. 8. Section 101 of the Immigration and Nationality Act [of 1952] . . . is amended as follows:

(a) Paragraph (27) of subsection (a) is amended to read as follows:

"(27) The term 'special immigrant' means—

"(A) an immigrant who was born in any independent foreign country of the Western Hemisphere or in the Canal Zone and the spouse and children of any such immigrant, if accompanying, or following to join him . . .

"(B) an immigrant, lawfully admitted for permanent residence, who is returning from a temporary visit abroad;

"(C) an immigrant who was a citizen of the United States and may, under section 324 (a) or 327 of title III, apply for reacquisition of citizenship;

"(D) (i) an immigrant who continuously for at least two years immediately preceding the time of his application for admission . . . has been, and who seeks to enter the United States solely for the purpose of carrying on the vocation of minister of a religious denomination, and whose services are needed by such religious denomination having a bona fide organization in the United States; and (ii) the spouse or the child of any such immigrant, if accompanying or following to join him; or

"(E) an immigrant who is an employee, or an honorably retired former employee, of the United States Government abroad, and who has performed faithful service for a total of fifteen years or more, and his accompanying spouse and children. . . ."

Sec. 10. Section 212 (a) of the Immigration and Nationality Act [of 1952] . . . is amended as follows: (a) Paragraph (14) is amended to read as follows: "Aliens seeking to enter the United States, for the purpose of performing skilled or un-skilled labor, unless the Secretary of Labor has determined and certified to the Secretary of State and to the Attorney General that (A) there are not sufficient workers in the United States who are able, willing, qualified, and available at the time of the application for a visa and admission to the United States and at the place to which the alien is destined to perform such skilled or unskilled labor, and (B) the employment of such aliens will not adversely affect the wages and working conditions of the workers in the United States similarly employed. . . ."

Sec. 11 (a) Section 221 (a) is amended by deleting the words "the particular nonquota category in which the immigrant is classified, if a nonquota immigrant," and substituting in lieu thereof the words "the preference, nonpreference, im-mediate relative, or special immigration classification to which the alien is charged." . . .

Sec. 20. This Act shall become effective on the first day of the first month after the expiration of thirty days following the date of its enactment except as provided herein.

Source: 79 Stat. 911.

California's Farm Labor Law, 1975

ollowing years of strikes, boycotts, and labor strife in the farmlands of California, the state legislature passed and Governor Edmund "Jerry" Brown Jr. signed into law the California Farm Labor Act, the first such law in the nation's industry protecting the rights of farm workers to bargain collectively. Enacted in June 1975, the law essentially followed the National Labor Relations Act of the 1930s and represented a major victory for the United Farm Workers union and its president, Cesar Chavez.

The following document includes excerpts from the legislation.

The people of the State of California do enact as follows:

SEC. 1. In enacting this legislation the people of the State of California seek to ensure peace in the agricultural fields by guaranteeing justice for all agricultural workers and stability in labor relations.

This enactment is intended to bring certainty and a sense of fair play to a presently unstable and potentially volatile condition in the state. The Legislature recognizes that no law in itself resolves social injustice and economic dislocations.

However, in the belief the people affected desire a resolution to this dispute and will make a sincere effort to work through the procedures established in this legislation, it is the hope of the Legislature that farm laborers, farmers, and all the people of California will be served by the provisions of this act.

SEC. 1.5. It is the intent of the Legislature that collective-bargaining agreements between agricultural employers and labor organizations representing the employees of such employers entered into prior to the effective date of this legislation and continuing beyond such date are not to be automatically canceled, terminated, or voided on that effective date; rather, such a collective-bargaining agreement otherwise lawfully entered into and enforceable under the laws of this state shall be void upon the Agricultural Labor Relations Board certification of that election after the filing of an election petition by such employees pursuant to Section 1156.3 of the Labor Code.

SEC. 2. Part 3.5 (commencing with Section 1140) is added to Division 2 of the Labor Code, to read:

PART 3.5. AGRICULTURAL LABOR RELATIONS
CHAPTER 1. GENERAL PROVISIONS AND DEFINITIONS
1140. This part shall be known and may be referred to as the Alatorre-Zenovich-Dunlap-Berman Agricultural Labor Relations Act of 1975.

1140.2. It is hereby stated to be the policy of the State of California to encourage and protect the right of agricultural employees to full freedom of association, self-organization, and designation of representatives of their own choosing, to negotiate the terms and conditions of their employment, and to be free from the interference, restraint, or coercion of employers of labor, or their agents, in the designation of such representatives or in self-organization or in other concerted activities for the purpose of collective bargaining or other mutual aid or protection. For this purpose this part is adopted to provide for collective-bargaining rights for agricultural employees. . . .

1140.4. As used in this part:

(a) The term "agriculture" includes farming in all its branches, and, among other things, includes the cultivation and tillage of the soil, dairying, the production, cultivation, growing, and harvesting of any agricultural or horticultural commodities (including commodities defined as agricultural commodities in Section 1141j(g) of Title 12 of the United States Code), the raising of livestock, bees, fur-bearing animals, or poultry, and any practices (including any forestry or lumbering operations) performed by a farmer or on a farm as an incident to or in conjunction with such farming operations, including preparation for market and delivery to storage or to market or to carriers for transportation to market.

(b) The term "agricultural employee" or "employee" shall mean one engaged in agriculture, as such term is defined in subdivision (a). However, nothing in this subdivision shall be construed to include any person other than those employees excluded from the coverage of the National Labor Relations Act, as amended, as agricultural employees, pursuant to Section 2(3) of the Labor Management Relations Act (Section 152(3), Title 29, United States Code), and Section 3(f) of the Fair Labor Standards Act (Section 203(f), Title 29, United States Code).

Further, nothing in this part shall apply, or be construed to apply, to any employee who performs work to be done at the site of the construction, alteration, painting, or repair of a building, structure, or other work (as these terms have been construed under Section 8(e) of the Labor Management Relations Act, 29 USC Section 158(e)) or logging or timber-clearing operations in initial preparation of land for farming, or who does land leveling or only land surveying for any of the above.

As used in this subdivision, "land leveling" shall include only major land moving operations changing the contour of the land, but shall not include annual or seasonal tillage or preparation of land for cultivation.

(c) The term "agricultural employer" shall be liberally construed to include any person acting directly or indirectly in the interest of an employer in relation to an agricultural employee, any individual grower, corporate grower, cooperative grower, harvesting association, hiring association, land management group, any association of persons or cooperatives engaged in agriculture, and shall include any person who owns or leases or manages land used for agricultural purposes, but shall exclude any person supplying agricultural workers to an employer, any farm labor contractor as defined by Section 1682, and any person functioning in the capacity of a labor contractor. The employer engaging such labor contractor or person shall be deemed the employer for all purposes under this part.

(d) The term "person" shall mean one or more individuals, corporations, partnerships, associations, legal representatives, trustees in bankruptcy, receivers, or any other legal entity, employer, or labor organization having an interest in the outcome of a proceeding under this part.

(e) The term "representatives" includes any individual or labor organization.

(f) The term "labor organization" means any organization of any kind, or any agency or employee representation committee or plan, in which employees participate and which exists, in whole or in part, for the purpose of dealing with employers concerning grievances, labor disputes, wages, rates of pay, hours of employment, or conditions of work for agricultural employees.

(g) The term "unfair labor practice" means any unfair labor practice specified in Chapter 4 (commencing with Section 1153) of this part.

(h) The term "labor dispute" includes any controversy concerning terms, tenure, or conditions of employment, or concerning the association or representation of persons in negotiating, fixing, maintaining, changing, or seeking to arrange terms or conditions of employment, regardless of whether the disputants stand in the proximate relation of employer and employee.

(i) The term "board" means Agricultural Labor Relations Board.

(j) The term "supervisor" means any individual having the authority, in the interest of the employer, to hire, transfer, suspend, lay off, recall, promote, discharge, assign, reward, or discipline other employees, or the responsibility to direct them, or to adjust their grievances, or effectively to recommend such action, if, in connection with the foregoing, the exercise of such authority is not of a merely routine or clerical nature, but requires the use of independent judgment.

CHAPTER 2. AGRICULTURAL LABOR RELATIONS BOARD

ARTICLE 1. AGRICULTURAL LABOR RELATIONS BOARD: ORGANIZATION

1141. (a) There is hereby created in state government the Agricultural Labor Relations Board, which shall consist of five members.

(b) The members of the board shall be appointed by the Governor with the advice and consent of the Senate. The term of office of the members shall be five years, and the terms shall be staggered at one-year intervals. Upon the initial appointment, one member shall be appointed for a term ending January 1, 1977, one member shall be appointed for a term ending January 1, 1978, one member shall be appointed for a term ending January 1, 1979, one member shall be appointed for a term ending January 1, 1980, and one member shall be appointed for a term ending January 1, 1981. Any individual appointed to fill a vacancy of any member shall be appointed only for the unexpired term of the member to whose term he is succeeding. The Governor shall designate one member to serve as chairperson of the board. Any member of the board may be removed by the Governor, upon notice and hearing, for neglect of duty or malfeasance in office, but for no other cause.

CHAPTER 3. RIGHTS OF AGRICULTURAL EMPLOYEES

1152. Employees shall have the right to self-organization, to form, join, or assist labor organizations, to bargain collectively through representatives of their own choosing, and to engage in other concerted activities for the purpose of collective bargaining or other mutual aid or protection, and shall also have the right to refrain from any or all of such activities except to the extent that such right may be affected by an agreement requiring membership in a labor organization as a condition of continued employment as authorized in subdivision (c) of Section 1153.

CHAPTER 4. UNFAIR LABOR PRACTICES AND REGULATION OF SECONDARY BOYCOTTS

1153. It shall be an unfair labor practice for an agricultural employer to do any of the following:

(a) To interfere with, restrain, or coerce agricultural employees in the exercise of the rights guaranteed in Section 1152.

(b) To dominate or interfere with the formation or administration of any labor organization or contribute financial or other support to it. However, subject to such rules and regulations as may be made and published by the board pursuant to Section 1144, an agricultural employer shall not be prohibited from permitting agricultural employees to confer with him during working hours without loss of time or pay.

(c) By discrimination in regard to the hiring or tenure of employment, or any term or condition of employment, to encourage or discourage membership in any labor organization.

Nothing in this part, or in any other statute of this state, shall preclude an agricultural employer from making an agreement with a labor organization (not established, maintained, or assisted by any action defined in this section as an unfair labor practice) to require as a condition of employment, membership therein on or after the fifth day following the beginning of such employment, or the effective date of such agreement whichever is later, if such labor organization is the representative of the agricultural employees as provided in Section 1156 in the appropriate collective-bargaining unit covered by such agreement. No employee who has been required to pay dues to a labor organization by virtue of his employment as an agricultural worker during any calendar month, shall be required to pay dues to another labor organization by virtue of similar employment during such month. For purposes of this chapter, membership shall mean the satisfaction of all reasonable terms and conditions uniformly applicable to other members in good standing; provided, that such membership shall not be denied or terminated except in compliance with a constitution or bylaws which afford full and fair rights to speech, assembly, and equal voting and membership privileges for all members, and which contain adequate procedures to assure due process to members and applicants for membership.

(d) To discharge or otherwise discriminate against an agricultural employee because he has filed charges or given testimony under this part.

(e) To refuse to bargain collectively in good faith with labor organizations certified pursuant to the provisions of Chapter 5 (commencing with Section 1156) of this part.

(f) To recognize, bargain with, or sign a collective-bargaining agreement with any labor organization not certified pursuant to the provisions of this part.

1154. It shall be an unfair labor practice for a labor organization or its agents to do any of the following:

(a) To restrain or coerce:

(1) Agricultural employees in the exercise of the rights guaranteed in Section 1152. This paragraph shall not impair the right of a labor organization to prescribe its own rules with respect to the acquisition or retention of membership therein.

(2) An agricultural employer in the selection of his representatives for the purposes of collective bargaining or the adjustment of grievances.

(b) To cause or attempt to cause an agricultural employer to discriminate against an employee in violation of subdivision (c) of Section 1153 or to discriminate against an employee with respect to whom membership in such organization has been denied or terminated for reasons other than failure to satisfy the membership requirements specified in subdivision (c) of Section 1153.

(c) To refuse to bargain collectively in good faith with an agricultural employer, provided it is the representative of his employees subject to the provisions of Chapter 5 (commencing with Section 1156) of this part.

(d) To do either of the following: (i) To engage in, or to induce or encourage any individual employed by any person to engage in, a strike or a refusal in the course of his employment to use, manufacture, process, transport, or otherwise handle or work on any goods, articles, materials, or commodities, or to perform any services; or (ii) to threaten, coerce, or restrain any person; where in either case (i) or (ii) an object thereof is any of the following:

(1) Forcing or requiring any employer or self-employed person to join any labor or employer organization or to enter into any agreement which is prohibited by Section 1154.5.

(2) Forcing or requiring any person to cease using, selling, transporting, or otherwise dealing in the products of any other producer, processor, or manufacturer, or to cease doing business with any other person, or forcing or requiring any other employer to recognize or bargain with a labor organization as the representative of his employees unless such labor organization has been certified as the representative of such employees. Nothing contained in this paragraph shall be construed to make unlawful where not otherwise unlawful, any primary strike or primary picketing.

(3) Forcing or requiring any employer to recognize or bargain with a particular labor organization as the representative of his agricultural employees if another labor organization has been certified as the representative of such employees under the provisions of Chapter 5 (commencing with Section 1156) of this part.

(4) Forcing or requiring any employer to assign particular work to employees in a particular labor organization or in a particular trade, craft, or class unless such employer is failing to conform to an order or certification of the board determining the bargaining representative for employees performing such work.

CONSUMER BOYCOTTS PERMITTED

Nothing contained in this subdivision (d) shall be construed to prohibit publicity including picketing for the purpose of truthfully advising the public, including consumers, that a product or products or ingredients thereof are produced by an agricultural employer with whom the labor organization has a primary dispute and are distributed by another employer, as long as such publicity does not have an effect of inducing any individual employed by any person other than the primary employer in the course of his employment to refuse to pick up, deliver, or transport any goods, or not to perform any services at the establishment of the employer engaged in such distribution, and as long as such publicity does not have the effect of requesting the public to cease patronizing such other employer.

However, publicity which includes picketing and has the effect of requesting the public to cease patronizing such other employer shall be permitted only if the labor organization is currently certified as the representative of the primary employer's employees.

Further, publicity other than picketing, but including peaceful distribution of literature which has the effect of requesting the public to cease patronizing such other employer, shall be permitted only if the labor organization has not lost an election for the primary employer's employees within the preceding 12-month period, and no other labor organization is currently certified as the representative of the primary employer's employees.

Nothing contained in this subdivision (d) shall be construed to prohibit publicity, including picketing, which may not be prohibited under the United States Constitution or the California Constitution.

Nor shall anything in this subdivision (d) be construed to apply or be applicable to any labor organization in its representation of workers who are not agricultural employees. Any such labor organization shall continue to be governed in its intrastate activities for nonagricultural workers by Section 923 and applicable judicial precedents.

(e) To require of employees covered by an agreement authorized under subdivision (c) of Section 1153 the payment, as a condition precedent to becoming a member of such organization, of a fee in an amount which the board finds excessive or discriminatory under all circumstances. In making such a finding, the board shall consider, among other relevant factors, the practices and customs of labor organizations in the agriculture industry and the wages currently paid to the employees affected.

(f) To cause or attempt to cause an agricultural employer to pay or deliver, or agree to pay or deliver, any money or other thing of value, in the nature of an exaction, for services which are not performed or not to be performed.

(g) To picket or cause to be picketed, or threaten to picket or cause to be picketed, any employer where an object thereof is either forcing or requiring an employer to recognize or bargain with a labor organization as the representative of his employees, or forcing or requiring the employees of an employer to accept or select such labor organization as their collective bargaining representative, unless such labor organization is currently certified as the representative of such employees, in any of the following cases:

(1) Where the employer has lawfully recognized in accordance with this part any other labor organization and a question concerning representation may not appropriately be raised under Section 1156.3.

(2) Where within the preceding 12 months a valid election under Chapter 5 (commencing with Section 1156) of this part has been conducted.

Nothing in this subdivision shall be construed to prohibit any picketing or other publicity for the purpose of truthfully advising the public (including consumers) that an employer does not employ members of, or have a contract with, a labor organization, unless an effect of such picketing is to induce an individual employed by any other person in the course of his employment, not to pick up, deliver, or transport any goods or not to perform any services.

Nothing in this subdivision (g) shall be construed to permit any act which would otherwise be an unfair labor practice under this section.

(h) To picket or cause to be picketed, or threaten to picket or cause to be picketed, any employer where an object thereof is either forcing or requiring an employer to recognize or bargain with the labor organization as a representative of his employees unless such labor organization is currently certified as the collective-bargaining representative of such employees.

(i) Nothing contained in this section shall be construed to make unlawful a refusal by any person to enter upon the premises of any agricultural employer, other than his own employer, if the employees of such employer are engaged in a strike ratified or approved by a representative of such employees whom such employer is required to recognize under this part. . . .

CHAPTER 5. LABOR REPRESENTATIVES AND ELECTIONS

1156. Representatives designated or selected by a secret ballot for the purposes of collective bargaining by the majority of the agricultural employees in the bargaining unit shall be the exclusive representatives of all the agricultural employees in such unit for the purpose of collective bargaining with respect to rates of pay, wages, hours of employment, or other conditions of employment. Any individual agricultural employee or a group of agricultural employees shall have the right at any time to present grievances to their agricultural employer and to have such grievances adjusted, without the intervention of the bargaining representative, as long as the adjustment is not inconsistent with the terms of a collective-bargaining contract or agreement then in effect, if the bargaining representative has been given opportunity to be present at such adjustment.

1156.2. The bargaining unit shall be all the agricultural employees of an employer. If the agricultural employees of the employer are employed in two or more contiguous geographical areas, the board shall determine the appropriate unit or units of agricultural employees in which a secret ballot election shall be conducted.

1156.3. (a) A petition which is either signed by, or accompanied by authorization cards signed by, a majority of the currently employed employees in the bargaining unit may be filed in accordance with such rules and regulations as may be prescribed by the board, by an agricultural employee or group of agricultural employees, or any individual or labor organization acting in their behalf alleging all the following:

(1) That the number of agricultural employees currently employed by the employer named in the petition, as determined from his payroll immediately preceding the filing of the petition, is not less than 50 percent of his peak agricultural employment for the current calendar year.

(2) That no valid election pursuant to this section has been conducted among the agricultural employees of the employer named in the petition within the 12 months immediately preceding the filing thereof.

(3) That no labor organization is currently certified as the exclusive collective-bargaining representative of the agricultural employees of the employer named in the petition.

(4) That the petition is not barred by an existing collective-bargaining agreement.

Upon receipt of such a signed petition, the board shall immediately investigate such petition, and, if it has reasonable cause to believe that a bona fide question of representation exists, it shall direct a representation election by secret ballot to he held, upon due notice to all interested parties and within a maximum of seven days of the filing of the petition. If at the time the election petition is filed a majority of the employees in a bargaining unit are engaged in a strike, the board shall, with all due diligence, attempt to hold a secret ballot election within 48 hours of the filing of such petition. The holding of elections under strike circumstances shall take precedence over the holding of other secret ballot elections.

The board shall make available at any election under this chapter ballots printed in English and Spanish. The board may also make available at such election ballots printed in any other language as may be requested by an agricultural labor organization, or agricultural employee eligible to vote under this part. Every election ballot, except ballots in runoff elections where the choice is between labor organizations, shall provide the employee with the opportunity to vote against representation by a labor organization by providing an appropriate space designated "No Labor Organizations."

(a) Any other labor organization shall be qualified to appear on the ballot if it presents authorization cards signed by at least 90 percent of the employees in the bargaining unit at least 24 hours prior to the election.

(b) Within five days after an election, any person may file with the board a signed petition asserting that allegations made in the petition filed pursuant to subdivision (a) were incorrect, that the board improperly determined the geographical scope of the bargaining unit, or objecting to the conduct of the election or conduct affecting the results of the election.

(c) Upon receipt of a petition under this subdivision, the board, upon due notice, shall conduct a hearing to determine whether the election shall be certified. Such hearing may be conducted by an officer or employee of a regional office of the board. He shall make no recommendations with respect thereto. If the board finds, on the record of such hearing, that any of the assertions made in the petition filed pursuant to this subdivision are correct, or that the election was not conducted properly, or misconduct affecting the results of the election occurred, the board may refuse to certify the election. Unless the board determines that there are sufficient grounds to refuse to do so, it shall certify the election.

(d) If no petition is filed pursuant to subdivision (c) within five days of the election the board shall certify the election.

(e) The board shall decertify a labor organization if the United States Equal Employment Opportunity Commission has found, pursuant to Section 2000(e) (5) of Title 42 of the United States Code, that the labor organization engaged in discrimination on the basis of race, color, national origin, religion, sex or any other arbitrary or invidious classification in violation of Subchapter Vl of Chapter 21 of Title 42 of the United States Code during the period of such labor organization's present certification.

HARVEST-TIME STRIKES

1156.4. Recognizing that agriculture is a seasonal occupation for a majority of agricultural employees, and wishing to provide the fullest scope for employees' enjoyment of the rights included in this part, the board shall not consider a representation petition or a petition to decertify as timely filed unless the employer's payroll reflects 50 percent of the peak agricultural employment for such employer for the current calendar year for the payroll period immediately preceding the filing of the petition.

In this connection, the peak agricultural employment for the prior season shall alone not be a basis for such determination, but rather the board shall estimate peak employment on the basis of acreage and crop statistics which shall be applied uniformly throughout the State of California and upon all other relevant data.

1156.5. The board shall not direct an election in any bargaining unit where a valid election has been held in the immediately preceding 12-month period.

1156.6. The board shall not direct an election in any bargaining unit which is represented by a labor organization that has been certified within the immediately preceding 12-month period or whose certification has been extended pursuant to subdivision (b) of Section 1155.2.

1156.7. (a). No collective-bargaining agreement executed prior to the effective date of this chapter shall bar a petition for an election.

(b) A collective-bargaining agreement executed by an employer and a labor organization certified as the exclusive bargaining representative of his employees pursuant to this chapter shall be a bar to a petition for an election among such employees for the term of the agreement, but in any event such bar shall not exceed three years, provided that both the following conditions are met:

(1) The agreement is in writing and executed by all parties thereto.

(2) It incorporates the substantive terms and conditions of employment of such employees.

(c) Upon the filing with the board by an employee or group of employees of a petition signed by 30 percent or more of the agricultural employees in a bargaining unit represented by a certified labor organization which is a party to a valid collective-bargaining agreement, requesting that such labor organization be decertified, the board shall conduct an election by secret ballot pursuant to the applicable provisions of this chapter, and shall certify the results to such labor organizations and employer.

However, such a petition shall not be deemed timely unless it is filed during the year preceding the expiration of a collective-bargaining agreement which would otherwise bar the holding of an election, and when the number of agricultural employees is not less than 50 percent of the employer's peak agricultural employment for the current calendar year.

(d) Upon the filing with the board of a signed petition by an agricultural employee or group of agricultural employees, or any individual or labor organization acting in their behalf, accompanied by authorization cards signed by a majority of the employees in an appropriate bargaining unit, and alleging all the conditions of paragraphs (1), (2), and (3), the board shall immediately investigate such petition and, if it has reasonable cause to believe that a bona fide question of representation exists, it shall direct an election by secret ballot pursuant to the applicable provisions of this chapter:

(1) That the number of agricultural employees currently employed by the employer named in the petition, as determined from his payroll immediately preceding the filing of the petition, is not less than 50 percent of his peak agricultural employment for the current calendar year.

(2) That no valid election pursuant to this section has been conducted among the agricultural employees of the employer named in the petition within the 12 months immediately preceding the filing thereof.

(3) That a labor organization, certified for an appropriate unit, has a collective-bargaining agreement with the employer which would otherwise bar the holding of an election and that this agreement will expire within the next 12 months.

1157. All agricultural employees of the employer whose names appear on the payroll applicable to the payroll pe-

riod immediately preceding the filing of the petition of such an election shall be eligible to vote. An economic striker shall be eligible to vote under such regulations as the board shall find are consistent with the purposes and provisions of this part in any election, provided that the striker who has been permanently replaced shall not be eligible to vote in any election conducted more than 12 months after the commencement of the strike.

In the case of elections conducted within 18 months of the effective date of this part which involve labor disputes which commenced prior to such effective date, the board shall have the jurisdiction to adopt fair, equitable, and appropriate eligibility rules, which shall effectuate the policies of this part, with respect to the eligibility of economic strikers who were paid for work performed or for paid vacation during the payroll period immediately preceding the expiration of a collective-bargaining agreement or the commencement of a strike; provided, however, that in no event shall the board afford eligibility to any such striker who has not performed any services for the employer during the 36-month period immediately preceding the effective date of this part.

1157.2. In any election where none of the choices on the ballot receives a majority, a runoff shall be conducted, the ballot providing for a selection between the two choices receiving the largest and second largest number of valid votes cast in the election.

1157.3. Employers shall maintain accurate and current payroll lists containing the names and addresses of all their employees, and shall make such lists available to the board upon request.

1158. Whenever an order of the board made pursuant to Section 1160.3 is based in whole or in part upon the facts certified following an investigation pursuant to Sections 1156.3 to 1157.2 inclusive, and there is a petition for review of such order, such certification and the record of such investigation shall be included in the transcript of the entire record required to be filed under Section 1160.8 and thereupon the decree of the court enforcing, modifying, or setting aside in whole or in part the order of the board shall be made and entered upon the pleadings, testimony, and proceedings set forth in such transcript.

1159. In order to assure the full freedom of association, self-organization, and designation of representatives of the employees own choosing, only labor organizations certified pursuant to this part shall be parties to a legally valid collective-bargaining agreement.

CHAPTER 6. PREVENTION OF UNFAIR LABOR PRACTICES AND JUDICIAL REVIEW AND ENFORCEMENT

1160. The board is empowered, as provided in this chapter, to prevent any person from engaging in any unfair labor practice, as set forth in Chapter 4 (commencing with Section 1153) of this part.

1160.2. Whenever it is charged that any person has engaged in or is engaging in any such unfair labor practice, the board, or any agent or agency designated by the board for such purposes, shall have power to issue and cause to be served upon such person a complaint stating the charges in that respect, and containing a notice of hearing before the board or a member thereof, or before a designated agency or agencies, at a place therein fixed, not less than five days after the serving of such complaint. No complaint shall issue based upon any unfair labor practice occurring more than six months prior to the filing of the charge with the board and the service of a copy thereof upon the person against whom such charge is made, unless the person aggrieved thereby was prevented from filing such charge by reason of service in the armed forces, in which event the six-month period shall be computed from the day of his discharge. Any such complaint may be amended by the member, agent, or agency conducting the hearing, or the board in its discretion, at any time prior to the issuance of an order based thereon. The person so complained against shall have the right to file an answer to the original or amended complaint and to appear in person or otherwise and give testimony at the place and time fixed in the complaint. In the discretion of the member, agent, or agency conducting the hearing or the board, any other person may be allowed to intervene in the proceeding and to present testimony. Any such proceeding shall, so far as practicable, be conducted in accordance with the Evidence Code. All proceedings shall be appropriately reported.

1160.3. The testimony taken by such member, agent, or agency, or the board in such hearing shall be reduced to writing and filed with the board. Thereafter, in its discretion, the board, upon notice, may take further testimony or hear argument. If, upon the preponderance of the testimony taken, the board shall be of the opinion that any person named in the complaint has engaged in or is engaging in any such unfair labor practice, the board shall state its findings of fact and shall issue and cause to be served on such person an order requiring such person to cease and desist from such unfair labor practice, to take affirmative action, including reinstatement of employees with or without backpay, and making employees whole, when the board deems such relief appropriate, for the loss of pay resulting from the employer's refusal to bargain, and to provide such other relief as will effectuate the policies of this part. Where an order directs reinstatement of an employee, backpay may be required of the employer or labor organization, as the case may be, responsible for the discrimination suffered by him. Such order may further require such person to make reports from time to time showing the extent to which it has complied with the order. If, upon the preponderance of the testimony taken, the board shall be of the opinion that the person named in the complaint has not engaged in or is not engaging in any unfair labor practice, the board shall state its findings of fact and shall issue an order dismissing the complaint. No order of the board shall require the reinstate-

ment of any individual as an employee who has been suspended or discharged, or the payment to him of any backpay, if such individual was suspended or discharged for cause. In case the evidence is presented before a member of the board, or before an administrative law officer thereof, such member, or such administrative law officer, as the case may be, shall issue and cause to be served on the parties to the proceedings a proposed report, together with a recommended order, which shall be filed with the board, and, if no exceptions are filed within 20 days after service thereof upon such parties, or within such further period as the board may authorize, such recommended order shall become the order of the board and become effective as therein prescribed.

Until the record in a case shall have been filed in a court, as provided in this chapter, the board may, at any time upon reasonable notice and in such manner as it shall deem proper, modify or set aside, in whole or in part, any finding or order made or issued by it.

1160.4. The board shall have power, upon issuance of a complaint as provided in Section 1160.2 charging that any person has engaged in or is engaging in an unfair labor practice, to petition the superior court in any county wherein the unfair labor practice in question is alleged to have occurred, or wherein such person resides or transacts business, for appropriate temporary relief or restraining order. Upon the filing of any such petition, the board shall cause notice thereof to be served upon such person, and thereupon the court shall have jurisdiction to grant to the board such temporary relief or restraining order as the court deems just and proper.

1160.5. Whenever it is charged that any person has engaged in an unfair labor practice within the meaning of paragraph (4) of subdivision (d) of Section 1154, the board is empowered and directed to hear and determine the dispute out of which such unfair labor practice shall have arisen, unless within 10 days after notice that such charge has been filed, the parties to such dispute submit to the board satisfactory evidence that they have adjusted, or agreed upon methods for the voluntary adjustment of the dispute. Upon compliance by the parties to the dispute with the decision of the board or upon such voluntary adjustment of the dispute, such charge shall be dismissed.

1160.6. Whenever it is charged that any person has engaged in an unfair labor practice within the meaning of paragraph (1), (2), or (3) of subdivision (d), or of subdivision (g), of Section 1154, or of Section 1155, the preliminary investigation of such charge shall be made forthwith and given priority over all other cases except cases of like character in the office where it is filed or to which it is referred. If, after such investigation, the officer or regional attorney to whom the matter may be referred has reasonable cause to believe such charge is true and that a complaint should issue, he shall, on behalf of the board, petition the superior court in the county in which the unfair labor practice in question has occurred, is alleged to have occurred, or where the person alleged to have committed the unfair labor practice resides or transacts business, for appropriate injunctive relief pending the final adjudication of the board with respect to the matter. The officer or regional attorney shall make all reasonable efforts to advise the party against whom the restraining order is sought of his intention to seek such order at least 24 hours prior to doing so. In the event the officer or regional attorney has been unable to advise such party of his intent at least 24 hours in advance, he shall submit a declaration to the court under penalty of perjury setting forth in detail the efforts he has made. Upon the filing of any such petition, the superior court shall have jurisdiction to grant such injunctive relief or temporary restraining order as it deems just and proper. Upon the filing of any such petition, the board shall cause notice thereof to be served upon any person involved in the charge and such person, including the charging party, shall be given an opportunity to appear by counsel and present any relevant testimony. For the purposes of this section, the superior court shall be deemed to have jurisdiction of a labor organization either in the county in which such organization maintains its principal office, or in any county in which its duly authorized officers or agents are engaged in promoting or protecting the interests of employee members. The service of legal process upon such officer or agent shall constitute service upon the labor organization and make such organization a party to the suit. In situations where such relief is appropriate, the procedures specified herein shall apply to charges with respect to paragraph (4) of subdivision (d) of Section 1154.

1160.7. Whenever it is charged that any person has engaged in an unfair labor practice within the meaning of subdivision (c) of Section 1153 or subdivision (b) of Section 1154, such charge shall be given priority over all other cases except cases of like character in the office where it is filed or to which it is referred and cases given priority under Section 1160.6.

1160.8. Any person aggrieved by the final order of the board granting or denying in whole or in part the relief sought may obtain a review of such order in the court of appeal having jurisdiction over the county wherein the unfair labor practice in question was alleged to have been engaged in, or wherein such person resides or transacts business, by filing in such court a written petition requesting that the order of the board be modified or set aside. Such petition shall be filed with the court within 30 days from the date of the issuance of the board's order. Upon the filing of such petition, the court shall cause notice to be served upon the board and thereupon shall have jurisdiction of the proceeding. The board shall file in the court the record of the proceeding, certified by the board within 10 days after the clerk's notice unless such time is extended by the court for good cause shown. The court shall have jurisdiction to grant to the board such temporary relief or restraining order it deems just and proper and in like manner to make and enter a decree enforcing, modifying and enforcing as so modified, or setting aside in whole or in part, the order of the board. The findings of the board with respect to questions of fact if supported by substantial evidence on the record considered as a whole shall in like manner be conclusive.

An order directing an election shall not be stayed pending review, but such order may be reviewed as provided in Section 1158.

If the time for review of the board order has lapsed, and the person has not voluntarily complied with the board's order, the board may apply to the superior court in any county in which the unfair labor practice occurred or wherein such person resides or transacts business for enforcement of its order. If after the hearing, the court determines that the order was issued pursuant to procedures established by the board and that the person refuses to comply with the order, the court shall enforce such order by writ of injunction or other proper process. The court shall not review the merits of the order.

1160.9. The procedures set forth in this chapter shall be the exclusive method of redressing unfair labor practices.

Source: Congressional Quarterly. *Historic Documents of 1975.* Washington, DC: Congressional Quarterly, Inc., 1976.

Refugee Act of 1980

During much of the Cold War, United States immigration policy was largely designed to offer refuge to persons fleeing communist countries, especially those coming from Cuba. In 1980, Congress passed the Refugee Act, which enlarged the scope of people considered refugees. Under the new law, the meaning of "refugee" was changed toward the United Nations definition of the word: any person with a "well-founded fear of persecution" due to race, religion, politics, or nationality.

Be it enacted by the Senate and House of Representatives of the United States of America in Congress assembled, That this Act may be cited as the "Refugee Act of 1980."

Sec. 101. (a) The Congress declares that it is the historic policy of the United States to respond to the urgent needs of persons subject to persecution in their homelands, including, where appropriate, humanitarian assistance for their care and maintenance in asylum areas, efforts to promote opportunities for resettlement or voluntary repatriation, aid for necessary transportation and processing, admission to this country of refugees for special humanitarian concern to the United States, and transitional assistance to refugees in the United States. The Congress further declares that it is the policy of the United States to encourage all nations to provide assistance and resettlement opportunities to refugees to the fullest extent possible.

(b) The objectives of this Act are to provide permanent and systematic procedures for the admission to this country of refugees of special humanitarian concern to the United States, and to provide comprehensive and uniform provisions for the effective resettlement and absorption of those refugees who are admitted. . . .

(42) The term "refugee" means (A) any person who is outside any country of such person's nationality or, in the case of a person having no nationality, is outside any country in which such person last habitually resided, and who is unable or unwilling to return to, and is unable or unwilling to

avail himself or herself of the protection of, that country because of persecution or a well-founded fear of persecution on account of race, religion, nationality, membership in a particular social group, or political opinion, or (B) in such special circumstances as the President after appropriate consultation . . . may specify. . . . The term "refugee" does not include any person who ordered, incited, assisted, or otherwise participated in the persecution of any person on account of race, religion, nationality, membership in a particular social group, or political opinion. . . .

Sec. 207. (a) (1) Except as provided in subsection (b), the number of refugees who may be admitted under this section in fiscal year 1980, 1981, or 1982, may not exceed fifty thousand unless the President determines, before the beginning of the fiscal year and after appropriate consultation . . . , that admission of a specific number of refugees in excess of such number is justified by humanitarian concerns or is otherwise in the national interest.

(2) Except as provided in subsection (b), the number of refugees who may be admitted under this section in any fiscal year after fiscal year 1982 shall be such number as the President determines, before the beginning of the fiscal year and after appropriate consultation, is justified by humanitarian concerns or is otherwise in the national interest.

(3) Admissions under this subsection shall be allocated among refugees of special humanitarian concern to the United States in accordance with a determination made by the President after appropriate consultation.

(b) If the President determines, after appropriate consultation, that (1) an unforeseen emergency refugee situation exists, (2) the admission of certain refugees in response to the emergency refugee situation is justified by grave humanitarian concern or is otherwise in the national interest, and (3) the admission to the United States of these refugees cannot be accomplished under subsection (a), the President may fix a number of refugees to be admitted to the United States during the succeeding period (not to exceed twelve months) in response to the emergency refugee situation and such admissions shall be allocated among refugees of special humanitarian concern to the United States in accordance with a determination made by the President after the appropriate consultation provided under this subsection. . . .

(4) The refugee status of any alien (and of the spouse or child of the alien) may be terminated by the Attorney General pursuant to such regulations as the Attorney General may prescribe if the Attorney General determines that alien was not in fact a refugee within the meaning of subsection 101 (a) (42) at the time of the alien's admission. . . .

(d)(l) Before the start of each fiscal year the President shall report to the Committees of the Judiciary of the House of Representatives and of the Senate regarding the foreseeable number of refugees who will be in need of resettlement during the fiscal year and the anticipated allocation of refugee admissions during the fiscal year. . . .

(3)(B) After the President initiates appropriate consultation prior to making a determination, under subsection (b), that the number of refugee admissions should be increased because of an unforeseen emergency refugee situation, to the extent that time and the nature of the emergency refugee situation permit, a hearing to review the proposal to increase refugee admissions shall be held unless public disclosure of the details of the proposal would jeopardize the lives or safety of individuals. . . .

Sec. 208. (a) The Attorney General shall establish a procedure for an alien physically present in the United States or at a land border or port of entry, irrespective of such alien's status, to apply for asylum, and the alien may be granted asylum at the discretion of the Attorney General if the Attorney General determines that such alien is a refugee within the meaning of section 101(a)(42)(a). . . .

Sec. 209. (b) Not more than five thousand of the refugee admissions authorized under section 207(a) in any fiscal year may be made available by the Attorney General, in the Attorney General's discretion and under such regulations as the Attorney General may prescribe, to adjust to the status of an alien lawfully permitted for permanent residence the status of any alien granted asylum who—(1) applies for such adjustment;

(2) has been physically present in the U.S. for at least one year after being granted asylum,

(3) continues to be a refugee in the meaning of section 101(a)(42)(a) or a spouse or child of such refugee,

(4) is not firmly resettled in any foreign country, and

(5) is admissible (except as otherwise provided for under subsection (c) as an immigrant under this Act at the time of examination for adjustment of such alien. . . .

Sec. 203 . . . (a) Exclusive of special immigrants in section 101(a)(27), immediate relatives specified in subsection (b) of this section, and aliens who are admitted or granted asylum under section 207 or 208, the number of aliens born in any foreign country or dependent area who may be issued immigrant visas or who may otherwise acquire the status of an alien lawfully admitted to the United States for permanent residence, shall not in any of the first three quarters of any fiscal year exceed a total of seventy-two thousand and shall not in any fiscal year exceed two hundred and seventy thousand. . . .

(h)(1) The Attorney General shall not deport or return any alien (other than an alien described in section 241(a)(19)[)] to a country if the Attorney General determines that such alien's life or freedom would be threatened in such country on account of race, religion, nationality, membership in a particular social group, or political opinion. . . .

Sec. 204. (2) The Attorney General shall establish the asylum procedure referred to in section 208(a) of the Immigration and Nationality Act (as added by section 201(b) of this title) not later than June 1, 1980. . . .

Sec. 301. (a) The President shall appoint, by and with the advice and consent of the Senate, a United States Coordinator for Refugee Affairs (hereinafter referred to as the "Coordinator"). The Coordinator shall have the rank of Ambassador-at-Large.

Source: 94 Stat. 102.

Immigration Reform and Control Act, 1986

With the rising tide of immigration following the Immigration and Naturalization Act of 1965, sentiment against open immigration began to turn in the United States, particularly during the conservative Reagan era of the 1980s. In 1986, Congress passed and President Ronald Reagan signed the Immigration Reform and Control Act. A lengthy piece of legislation, the critical elements included efforts to punish employers who hired illegal aliens. In addition, a major amnesty program was offered to those illegal aliens who had lived in the United States for a number of years.

TITLE I—CONTROL OF ILLEGAL IMMIGRATION

SEC. 101. CONTROL OF UNLAWFUL EMPLOYMENT OF ALIENS

(a) In General

  (1) In General—It is unlawful for a person or other entity to hire, or to recruit or refer for a fee, for employment in the United States—
     (A) an alien knowing the alien is an unauthorized alien (as defined in subsection (h)(3)) . . .
     (B) an individual without complying with the requirements of subsection (b).

  (2) Continuing employment—It is unlawful for a person or other entity, after hiring an alien for employment in accordance with paragraph (1), to continue to employ the alien in the United States knowing the alien is (or has become) an unauthorized alien with respect to such employment.

  (3) Defense—A person or entity that establishes that it has complied in good faith with the requirements of subsection (b) with respect to the hiring, recruiting, or referral for employment of an alien in the United States who has established an affirmative de-

fense that the person or entity has not violated paragraph (1)(A) with respect to such hiring, recruiting, or referral.

  (4) Use of Labor Through Contract—For the purposes of this section, a person or other entity who uses a contract, subcontract, or exchange, entered into, renegotiated, or extended after the date of the enactment of this section, to obtain the labor of an alien in the United States knowing that the alien is an unauthorized alien . . . with respect to performing such labor, shall be considered to have hired the alien for employment in the United States in violation of paragraph (1)(A).

  (5) Use of State Employment Agency Documentation—For the purposes of paragraph (1)(B) and (3), a person or entity shall be deemed to have complied with the requirements of subsection (b) with respect to the hiring of an individual who was referred for such employment by a State employment agency. . . .

(b) Employment Verification System—The requirements referred to in paragraphs (1)(B) and (3) are, in the case of a person or other entity hiring, recruiting, or referring an individual for employment in the United States, the requirements specified in the following three paragraphs:

  (1) Attestation After Examination of Documentation—
     (A) In General—The person or entity must attest, under penalty of perjury and on a form designated or established by the Attorney General by regulation, that it has verified that the individual is not an unauthorized alien by examining—
        (i) a document described in subparagraph (B), or
        (ii) a document described in subparagraph (C) and (D).
     (B) Documents Establishing Both Employment Authorization and Identity—A document described in this subparagraph is an individual's—

(i) United States passport;

(ii) certificate of United States Citizenship;

(iii) certificate of naturalization;

(iv) unexpired foreign passport, if the passport has an appropriate, unexpired endorsement of the Attorney General authorizing the individual's employment in the United States; or

(v) resident alien card or other alien registration, if the card—

    (I) contains a photograph of the individual . . .

    (II) is evidence of authorization of employment in the United States

(C) Documents Evidencing Employment Authorization—A document described . . . is [a]

(i) social security account number card . . .

(ii) certificate of birth in the United States or establishing United States nationality at birth;

(iii) other documents evidencing authorization of employment in the United States which Attorney General finds, by regulation, to be acceptable for the purposes of this section.

(D) Documents establishing identity of an individual—A document described in this subparagraph is an individual's

(i) driver's license or similar document issued for the purpose of identification by a State, if it contains a photograph of the individual . . .

(ii) in the case of individuals under 16 years of age or in a State which does not provide for issuance of an identification document . . . referred to in clause (i), documentation of personal identity of such type as the Attorney General finds, by regulation, provides a reliable means of identification. . . .

(3) Definition of Unauthorized Alien—As used in this section, the term "unauthorized alien" means, with respect to the employment of an alien at a particular time, that the alien is not at that time either (A) an alien lawfully admitted for permanent residence, or (B) authorized to be so employed by this Act or by the Attorney General. . . .

DEFERRAL OF ENFORCEMENT WITH RESPECT TO SEASONAL AGRICULTURAL SERVICES—

(A) In General—Except as provided in subparagraph (B), before the end of the application period, it is unlawful for a person or entity (including a farm labor contractor) or an agent of such a person or entity, to recruit an unauthorized alien (other than an alien described in clause (ii)) who is outside the United States to enter the United States to perform seasonal agricultural services.

(ii) Exception—Clause (i) shall not apply to an alien who the person or entity reasonably believes to meet the requirements of section 210(a)(2) of this Act (relating to the performance of seasonal agricultural services).

(j) GENERAL ACCOUNTING OFFICE REPORTS—

(1) In General—Beginning one year after the date of enactment of this Act, and at intervals of one year thereafter for a period of three years after such date, the Comptroller General of the United States shall prepare and transmit to the Congress and to the taskforce established under subsection (k) a report describing the results of a review of the implementation and enforcement of this section during the preceding twelve-month period, for the purpose of determining if—

(A) such provisions have been carried out satisfactorily;

(B) a pattern of discrimination has resulted against citizens or nationals of the United States or against eligible workers seeking employment; and

(C) an unnecessary regulatory burden has been created for employers hiring such workers.

(k) REVIEW BY THE TASKFORCE—

(1) Establishment of Taskforce—The Attorney General, jointly with the Chairman of the Commission on Civil Rights and the Chairman of the Equal Employment Opportunity Commission, shall establish a taskforce to review each report of the Comptroller General transmitted under subsection (j)(1).

(2) Recommendations to Congress—If the report transmitted includes a determination that the implementation of this section has resulted in a pattern of discrimination in employment (against other than unauthorized aliens) on the basis of national origin, the taskforce shall, taking into consideration any recommendations in the report, report to Congress recommendations for such legislation as may be appropriate to deter or remedy such discrimination. . . .

(1) TERMINATION DATE FOR EMPLOYER SANCTIONS—

(1) If Report of Widespread Discrimination and Congressional Approval—The provisions of this section shall terminate 30 days after receipt of the last report required to be transmitted under subsection (j), if—

(A) the Comptroller General determines, and so reports . . . that a widespread pattern of discrimination has resulted against citizens or nationals of the United States or against eligible workers seeking employment solely from the implementation of this section; and

(B) there is enacted, within such period of 30 calendar days, a joint resolution stating in substance that the Congress approves the findings of the Comptroller General contained in such report.

(2) Senate Procedures for Consideration—Any joint resolution referred to in clause (B) of paragraph (1) shall be considered in the Senate in accordance with subsection (n). . . .

Sec. 111.(b) Increased Authorization of Appropriations for INS and EOIR—In addition to any other amounts authorized to be appropriated, in order to carry out this Act, there are authorized to be appropriated to the Department of Justice—

(1) for the Immigration and Naturalization Service, for fiscal year 1987, $12,000,000, and for fiscal year 1988, $15,000,000 . . . to provide for an increase in the border patrol personnel of the INS so that the average level of such personnel in each fiscal year 1987 and 1988 is at least 50 per cent higher than such level for fiscal year 1986. . . .

TITLE II—LEGALIZATION

SEC. 201. LEGALIZATION OF STATUS. . . .

Sec. 245A. (a) Temporary Resident Status—The Attorney General shall adjust the status of an alien to that of an alien lawfully admitted for temporary residence if the alien meets the following requirements:

(1) Timely Application—

(A) During Application Period—Except as provided in subparagraph (B), the alien must apply for such adjustment during the 12-month period beginning on a date (not later than 180 days after the date of enactment of this section) designated by the Attorney General. . . .

(2) Continuous Lawful Residence Since 1982—

(A) In General—The alien must establish that he entered the United States before January 1, 1982, and that he has resided continuously in the

United States in an unlawful status since such date and through the date the application is filed under this subsection.

(B) Non-immigrants—In the case of an alien who entered the United States as a non-immigrant before January 1, 1982, the alien must establish that the alien's period of authorized stay as a non-immigrant expired before such date through the passage of time or the alien's unlawful status was known to the Government as of such date. . . .

(4) Admissible as Immigrant—For the purposes of this subsection, an alien in the status of a Cuban and Haitian entrant described in paragraph (1) or (2)(A) of section 501(e) of Public Law 96–422 shall be considered to have entered the United States and to be in an unlawful status in the United States.

(b) Subsequent Adjustment to Permanent Residence and Nature of Temporary Resident Status—

(1) Adjustment to Permanent Residence—The Attorney General shall adjust the status of any alien provided lawful temporary resident status under subsection (a) to that of an alien lawfully admitted for permanent residence if the alien meets the following requirements:

(A) Timely Application After One Year's Residence—The alien must apply for such adjustment during the one-year period beginning with the nineteenth month that begins after the date the alien was granted such temporary status.

(B) Continuous Residence—The alien must establish that he has continuously resided in the United States since the date the alien was granted such temporary resident status.

(C) Admissible as Immigrant—The alien must establish that he—

(i) is admissible to the United States as an immigrant, except as otherwise provided under subsection (d)(2), and

(ii) has not been convicted of any felony or three or more misdemeanors committed in the United States.

(D) Basic Citizenship Skills—The alien must demonstrate that he either—

(I) meets the requirements of section 312 (relating to minimal understanding of ordinary English and a knowledge and understanding of the history and government of the United States. . . .

(II) is satisfactorily pursuing a course of study (recognized by the Attorney General) to achieve an understanding of English and such knowledge and understanding of the history and government of the United States. . . .

(h) Temporary Disqualification of Newly Legalized Aliens from Receiving Certain Public Welfare Assistance—

(1) In General—During the five year period beginning

on the date an alien was granted lawful temporary resident status under subsection (a), and notwithstanding any other provision of law—

(A) except as provided in paragraphs (2) and (3), the alien is not eligible for—

(i) many programs of financial assistance furnished under Federal law . . .

(ii) medical assistance under a State plan approved under Title XIX of the Social Security Act; and

(iii) assistance under the Food Stamp Act of 1977; and

(B) a State or political subdivision therein may, to the extent consistent with paragraph (A) and paragraphs (2) and (3), provide that an alien is not eligible for the programs of financial assistance or for medical assistance described in subparagraph (A) (ii) furnished under the law of that State or political subdivision . . .

Unless otherwise specifically provided by this section or other law, an alien in temporary lawful residence status granted under subsection (a) shall not be considered (for purposes of any law of a State or political subdivision providing for a program of financial assistance) to be permanently residing in the United States under color of law.

(2) Exceptions.—Paragraph (1) shall not apply—

(A) to a Cuban and Haitian entrant (as defined in paragraph (1) or (2)(A) of section 501(e) of Public Law 96–422, as in effect on April 1, 1983) . . .

TITLE III—REFORM OF LEGAL IMMIGRATION, PART A—TEMPORARY AGRICULTURAL WORKERS

SEC. 301. H-2A AGRICULTURAL WORKERS

(a) Providing New "H-2A" Nonimmigrant Classification for Temporary Agricultural Labor—Paragraph (15)(H) of section 101 (a) (8 U.S.C. 1101(a)) is amended by striking out "to perform temporary services or labor," in clause (ii) and inserting in lieu thereof, "(a) to perform agricultural labor or services, as defined by the Secretary of Labor in regulations and including agricultural labor defined in section 3121(g) of the Internal Revenue Code of 1954 and agriculture as defined in section 3(f) of the Fair Labor Standards Act of 1938 . . . or a temporary or seasonal nature, or (b) to perform other temporary service or labor."

(b) Involvement of Departments of Labor and Agriculture in H-2A Program—Section 214(c) (8 U.S.C. 1184(c)) is amended by adding to the end the following: "For purposes of this subsection with respect to non-immigrants described in section 101(a)(15)(H)(ii)(a), the term 'appropriate agencies of Government' means the Department of Labor and includes the Department of Agriculture. The provisions of section 216 shall apply to the question of importing any alien as non-immigrant under section 101(a)(15)(H)(ii)(a)."

(c) Admission of H-2A Workers—Chapter 2 of Title II is amended by adding after section 215 the following new section:

"SEC. 216(A) CONDITIONS FOR APPROVAL OF H-2A PETITIONS—(1)

A petition to import an alien as an H-2A worker . . . may not be approved by the Attorney General unless the petitioner has applied to the Secretary of Labor for a certification that—

"(A) there are not sufficient workers who are able, willing, and qualified, and who will be available at the time and place needed, to perform the labor or services involved in the petition, and

"(B) the employment of the alien in such labor or services will not adversely affect the wages and working conditions of workers in the United States similarly employed."

[Title IV of the act specifies various reports to Congress over the next three years dealing with comprehensive reports on immigration, unauthorized alien employment, the H-2A program, the legalization program, evidence of discrimination, and the visa waiver pilot program.]

Source: 100 Stat. 3360.

Immigration Act of 1990

On November 29, 1990, Congress passed legislation to modify the Immigration Reform and Control Act of 1986. The changes largely involved the preference system, making family reunification easier for immigrants. In addition, the new legislation opened up immigration levels for persons with specialized skills and occupations. Finally, it added an entirely new category intended to increase ethnic and geographic diversity among immigrants.

Sec. 201. (a) In General—Exclusive of aliens described in subsection (b), aliens born in a foreign state or dependent area who may be issued immigrant visas or who may otherwise acquire the status of an alien lawfully admitted to the United States for permanent residence are limited to

(1) family-sponsored immigrants described in section 203(a) . . . in a number not to exceed in any fiscal year the number specified in subsection (c) for that year, and not to exceed in any of the first three quarters of any fiscal year 27 percent of the worldwide level under such subsection for all such fiscal year;

(2) employment-based immigrants described in subsection 203(b) . . . in a number not to exceed in any fiscal year the number specified in subsection (d) for that year, and not exceed in any of the first 3 quarters of any fiscal year 27 percent of the worldwide level under such subsection for all of such fiscal year; and

(3) for fiscal years beginning with fiscal year 1995, diversity immigrants described in section 203(c) . . . in a number not to exceed in any fiscal year the number specified in subsection (e) for that year, and not to exceed in any of the first three quarters of any fiscal year 27 percent of the worldwide level under such subsection for all such fiscal year.

(2)(A)(i) Immediate Relatives—For purposes of this subsection, the term "immediate relatives" means the children, spouses, and parents of a citizen of the United States, except that, in the case of parents, such citizens be at least 21 years of age. In the case of an alien who was the spouse of a citizen of the United States for at least 2 years at the time of the citizen's death and was not legally separated from the citizen at the time of the citizen's death, the alien shall be considered, for the purpose of this subsection, to remain an immediate relative after the date of the citizen's death but only if the spouse files a petition under section 204(a)(1)(A) within 2 years after such date and only until the date the spouse remarries.

(c) Worldwide Level of Family-Sponsored Immigrants—(1)(A) The worldwide level of family-sponsored immigrants under this subsection for a fiscal year is, subject to subparagraph (B) equal to—

(i)   480,000 minus
(ii) the number computed under paragraph (2), plus
(iii) the number (if any) computed under paragraph (3).

(B)(i) For each of fiscal years 1992, 1993, and 1994, 465,000 shall be substituted for 480,000 in subparagraph (A)(i).

(ii) In no case shall the number computed under subparagraph (A) be less than 226,000 . . .

(d) Worldwide Level of Employment-Based Immigrants—(1) The worldwide level of employment-based immigrants under this subsection for a fiscal year is equal to—

(A) 140,000 plus

(B) the number computed under paragraph (2).

(2) The number computed under this paragraph for a fiscal year is the difference (if any) between the maximum number of visas which may be issued in section 203(a) . . . during the previous fiscal year and the number of visas issued under that section during that year.

(e) Worldwide Level of Diversity Immigrants—The worldwide level of diversity immigrants is equal to 55,000 for each fiscal year.

Sec. 102. Per Country Levels.

Sec. 202 (8 U.S.C. 1152) is amended—(1) by amending subsection (a) to read as follows:

(a) Per Country Level—
   (1) Nondiscrimination—Except as specifically provided in paragraph (2) and in sections 101(a)(27), 201(b)(2)(A)(i), and 203, no person shall receive any preference or priority or be discriminated against in the issuance of an immigrant visa because of a person's race, sex, nationality, place of birth, or place of residence.
   (2) Per Country Levels for Family-Sponsored and Employment-Based Immigrants—Subject to paragraphs (3) and (4), the total number of immigrant visas made available to natives of any single foreign state or dependent area under subsections (a) and (b) of section 203 in any fiscal year may not exceed 7 percent (in the case of a single foreign state) or 2 percent (in the case of a dependent area) of the total number of such visas made available under such subsection in that fiscal year.

SUBTITLE B—PREFERENCE SYSTEM

PART 1—FAMILY-SPONSORED IMMIGRANTS
SEC. 111. FAMILY-SPONSORED IMMIGRANTS

Sec. 203 (8 U.S.C. 1153) is amended—

(1) by redesignating subsections (b) and (e) as subsections (d) through (g), respectively, and (2) by striking subsection (a) and inserting the following:

(a) Preference Allocation for Family-Sponsored Immigrants—Aliens subject to the worldwide level specified in section 201(c) for family-sponsored immigrants shall be allotted visas as follows:
   (1) Unmarried sons and daughters of citizens . . . in a number not to exceed 23,400 plus any visas required for the class specified in paragraph (4).
   (2) Spouses and unmarried sons and unmarried daughters of permanent resident aliens . . . shall be allocated visas in a number not to exceed 114,200 plus the number (if any) by which such worldwide level exceeds 226,000 plus any visas not required for the class specified in paragraph (1); except that not less

than 77 percent of such visa numbers shall be allocated to aliens described in subparagraph (A).
   (3) Married sons and married daughters of immigrants—in a number not to exceed 23,400, plus any visas not required for the classes specified in paragraphs (1) and (2).
   (4) Brothers and sisters of citizens—in a number not to exceed 65,000, plus any visas not required for the classes specified in paragraphs (1) through (3) . . .
(c) Legalized Alien Defined—In this section, the term "legalized alien" means an alien lawfully admitted for temporary or permanent residence who was provided—
   (1) temporary or permanent residence status under section 210 of the Immigration and Nationality Act,
   (2) temporary or permanent residence status under section 245A of the Immigration and Nationality Act, or
   (3) permanent residence status under section 202 of the Immigration Reform and Control Act of 1986.

PART 2—EMPLOYMENT-BASED IMMIGRANTS
SEC. 121. EMPLOYMENT-BASED IMMIGRANTS

(a) In General—Section 203 (8 U.S.C. 1153) is amended by inserting after subsection (a), as inserted by section 111, the following new subsection:
(b) Preference Allocation for Employment-Based Immigrants—Aliens subject to the worldwide level specified in section 201(d) for employment-based immigrants in a fiscal year shall be allocated visas as follows:
   (1) Priority Workers—Visas shall first be made available in a number not to exceed 40,000, plus any visas not required for the classes specified in paragraphs (4) and (5), to qualified immigrants who are aliens described in any of the following subparagraphs (A) through (C):
      (A) Aliens with extraordinary ability—in sciences, arts, education, business, or athletics which has been demonstrated by sustained national or international acclaim and whose achievements have been recognized in the field through extensive documentation.
      (B) Outstanding Professors and Researchers. . . .
      (C) Certain Multinational Executives and Managers. . . .
   (2) Alien members of Professions holding advanced degrees or aliens of exceptional ability. . . .
   (3) Skilled workers, professionals, and other workers. . . .
   (4) Certain special immigrants—Visas shall be made available, in a number not to exceed 10,000 to qualified special immigrants described in section 101 (a)(27) . . . of which not more than 5,000 may be made available in any fiscal year to special immigrants described in subclause (II) or (III) of section 101 (a) (27)(C)(ii).
   (5) Employment Creation—
      (A) In General—Visas shall be made available, in a

number not to exceed 10,000, to qualified immigrants seeking to enter the United States for the purpose of engaging in a new commercial enterprise—

(i)   which the alien has established,

(ii) in which such alien has invested . . . or is actively in the process of investing, capital in an amount not less than the amount specified in subparagraph (C), and

(iii) which will benefit the United States economy and create full-time employment for not fewer than 10 United States citizens or aliens lawfully admitted for permanent residence or other immigrants lawfully authorized to be employed in the United States (other than the immigrant and the immigrant's spouse, sons, or daughters).

PART 3—DIVERSITY IMMIGRANTS
SEC. 131. DIVERSITY IMMIGRANTS

Sec. 203, as amended by sections 111 and 121 of this Act, is further amended by inserting after subsection (b) the following new subsection:

(c) Diversity Immigrants—

(1) In General—Except as provided in paragraph (2), aliens subject to the worldwide level specified in section 201(e) for diversity immigrants shall be allotted visas each fiscal year as follows:

(A) Determination of Preference Immigration—The Attorney General shall determine for the most recent previous 5-year period for which data are available, the total number of aliens who are natives of each foreign state and who (i) were admitted or otherwise provided lawful permanent resident status . . . and (ii) were subject to the numerical limitations of section 201(a) . . . or who were admitted or otherwise provided lawful permanent resident status as an immediate relative or other alien described in section 201(b)(2) . . . (iv) Redistribution of Unused Visa Numbers—If the Secretary of State estimates that the number of immigrant visas to be issued to natives in any region for the fiscal year under this paragraph is less than the number of immigrant visas made available to such natives under this paragraph for the fiscal year, subject to clause (v), the excess visa numbers shall be made available to natives (other than the natives of a high-admission state) of the other regions in proportion to the percentages otherwise specified in clauses (ii) and (iii).

SUBTITLE C—COMMISSION AND INFORMATION

SEC. 141. COMMISSION OF LEGAL IMMIGRATION REFORM.

(a) Establishment and Composition of Commission—(1) Effective October 1, 1991, there is established a Commission on Legal Immigration Reform . . . which shall be composed of 9 members . . .

TITLE III—FAMILY UNITY AND TEMPORARY PROTECTED STATUS

SEC. 301. FAMILY UNITY.

(a) Temporary Stay of Deportation and Work Authorization for Certain Eligible Immigrants—

The Attorney General shall provide that in the case of an alien who is an eligible immigrant . . . who has entered the United States before [May 5, 1988], who has resided in the United States on such date, and who is not lawfully admitted for permanent residence, the alien—. . . .

(2) The term "legalized alien" means an alien lawfully admitted for temporary or permanent residence who was provided—

(A) such under section 210 of the Immigration and Nationality Act;

(B) temporary or permanent residence status under section 245A of the Immigration and Nationality Act, or

(C) permanent residence status under section 202 of the Immigration Reform and Control Act of 1986. . . .

Sec. 302. Temporary Protected Status.

(a) In General—The Immigration and Nationality Act is amended by inserting after section 244 the following new section:

"Sec. 244 A. (a) Granting of Status—

"(1) In General—In the case of an alien who is a national of a foreign state . . . under subsection (b) and who meets the requirements of subsection (c), the Attorney General—

"(A) may grant the alien temporary protected status in the U.S. and shall not deport the alien from the U.S. during the period in which such status is in effect, and

"(B) shall authorize the alien to engage in employment in the U.S. and to provide the alien with an 'employment authorized' endorsement or other appropriate work permit.

(b) Designations—

"(1) In General—The Attorney General, after consultation with appropriate agencies . . . may designate any foreign state . . . under this subsection only if—

"(A) the Attorney General finds that there is an ongoing armed conflict within the state, and, due to such conflict, requiring the return of aliens who are nationals of that state . . . would pose a serious threat to their personal safety.

"(B) the Attorney General finds that—

(i) there has been an earthquake, flood, drought, epidemic, or other environmental disaster in the state resulting in a substantial, but temporary, disruption of living conditions in the area affected,

(ii) the foreign state is unable, temporarily, to handle adequately the return to the state of aliens who are nationals of the state, and

(iii) the foreign state officially has requested designation under this paragraph; or

"(C) the Attorney General finds that there exists extraordinary and temporary conditions in a foreign state that prevent aliens who are nationals from the state from returning to the state safely. . . ."

(c) No effect on Executive Order 12711—Notwithstanding subsection (g) of section 244 A of the Immigration and Nationality Act . . . such section shall not supersede or affect Executive Order 12711 (April 11, 1990), relating to policy implementation with respect to nationals of the People's Republic of China.

Sec. 303. Special Temporary Protected Status for Salvadorans.

(a) Designation—

(1) In General. El Salvador is hereby designated under section 244(b) of the Immigration and Nationality Act, subject to the provisions of this section.

(2) Period of Designation—Such designation shall take effect on the date of the enactment of this section and shall remain in effect until the end of the 18-month period beginning January 1, 1991.

TITLE IV—NATURALIZATION

SEC. 401. ADMINISTRATIVE NATURALIZATION.

(a) Naturalization Authority.—Section 310 (8 U.S.C. 1421) is amended to read as follows: "Sec. 310. (a) Authority in Attorney General—The sole authority to naturalize persons as citizens of the United States is conferred upon the Attorney General.

"(b) Administration of Oaths.—An applicant for naturalization may choose to have the oath of allegiance under section 337 (a) administered by the Attorney General or by any District Court of the United States for any State or by any court of record in any State having a seal, clerk, and jurisdiction in actions in law or equity, or law and equity, in which the amount in controversy is unlimited. . . .

Sec. 402. Substituting 3 Months residence in INS District or State for 6 months residence in a State.

Section 316(a)(1) (8 U.S.C. 1427(a)(1)) is amended by striking "and who has resided within the State in which the petitioner filed the petition for at least six months" and inserting "and who has resided within the State or within the district of the Service in the United States in which the applicant filed the application for at least three months."

Sec. 403. Waiver of English Language Requirement for Naturalization.

Section 312(1) (8 U.S.C. 1423(1)) is amended by striking "is over fifty years of age and has been living in the United States for periods totaling at least twenty years subsequent to a lawful admission for permanent residence" and inserting "either (A) is over fifty years of age and has been living in the United States for periods totaling at least 20 years subsequent to a lawful admission for permanent residence, or (B) is over 55 years of age and has been living in the U.S. for periods totaling at least 15 years subsequent to a lawful admission for permanent residence."

Sec. 405. Naturalization of Natives of the Philippines Through Certain Active Duty Service During World War II.

(a) Waiver of Certain Requirements.—(1) Clauses (1) and (2) of section 329(a) of the Immigration and Nationality Act . . . shall not apply to the naturalization of any person—

(A) who was born in the Philippines and who was residing in the Philippines before the service described in subparagraph (B);

(B) who served honorably—

(i) in an active-duty status under the command of the United States Armed Forces in the Far East, or

(ii) within the Philippine Army, the Philippine Scouts, or recognized guerilla units, at any time during the period beginning September 1, 1939, and ending December 31, 1946;

(C) who is otherwise eligible for naturalization under section 329 of such Act; and

(D) who applies for naturalization during the 2-year period beginning on the date of the enactment of this Act.

Sec. 406. Public Education regarding naturalization benefits. Section 332 (8 U.S.C. 1443) is amended by adding at the end the following subsection:

"(h) In order to promote the opportunities and responsibilities of United States citizenship, the Attorney General shall broadly distribute information concerning the benefits which persons may receive under this title and the requirements to obtain such benefits. In carrying out this subsection, the Attorney General shall seek the assistance of appropriate community groups, private voluntary agencies, and other relevant organizations. . . ."

Source: 104 Stat. 4981.

Illegal Immigration Reform and Immigrant Responsibility Act, 1996

ven as Congress was grappling with welfare reform legislation in 1996, it was also working on new legislation concerning immigration. The welfare reform legislation's restrictions on legal immigrants' access to social services created a political uproar. Less sensitive—and largely unprotested—was the Illegal Immigration Reform and Immigrant Responsibility Act of 1996 aimed at curbing illegal immigration and illegal immigrants' rights to social services. The following is a Congressional Quarterly *summary of the 1996 Illegal Immigration Reform and Immigrant Responsibility Act.*

1. Border agents. Authorize funding to increase the number of Border Patrol agents by 1,000 per year through fiscal 2001, doubling the total force from 5,000 to 10,000. The bill also authorized funds to increase the number of clerical workers and other support personnel at the border by 300 per year through fiscal 2001.

The bill ordered the INS [Immigration and Naturalization Service] to relocate as many agents as possible to border areas with the largest number of illegal immigrants and to coordinate relocation plans with local law enforcement agencies. The INS was required to report to Congress on these activities within six months of enactment.

2. Other INS employees. Authorize funding of 900 additional INS agents to investigate and prosecute cases of smuggling, harboring or employing illegal aliens and 300 new agents to investigate people who overstay their visas.

3. Border fence. Authorize $12 million for the second and third tiers of a triple fence along a 14-mile strip at the U.S.-Mexico border south of San Diego, and for roads surrounding the fence. The project was exempt from the strictures of the 1973 Endangered Species Act and the 1969 Environmental Policy Act if either would prevent expeditious construction. It allowed the Attorney General to acquire land through condemnation for the fence.

4. Border Crossing Cards. Require the INS to develop alien identification cards that include a biometric identifier, such as a fingerprint, that could be read by machine, and for future cards that could use such devices as retina scanners.

5. Fleeing through checkpoints. Create a penalty up to five years in prison for fleeing through an INS checkpoint and deportation of those convicted.

6. Entry-Exit system. Order the Attorney General, within two years of enactment, to create a data base of information gathered from the documents people filled out as they legally entered and left the country which would allow the INS to match entry and exit records to identify people who overstayed their visas.

7. Pre-inspection. Require the INS to establish "pre-inspection" stations at five of the 10 foreign airports that were the departure points for the largest number of inadmissible immigrants to screen people who did not have proper documents.

8. State-federal cooperation. Allow the INS to enter into agreements with state and local governments for help in investigating, arresting, detaining and transporting illegal immigrants.

DOCUMENT FRAUD AND ALIEN SMUGGLING

9. Wiretaps. Grant wiretap authority to the criminal division of the Justice Department for investigating cases of immigration document fraud.

10. Penalties for alien smuggling. Create felonies for alien smuggling for up to 10 years in prison for the first and sec-

ond offenses, and 15 years for subsequent offenses; and make it a crime with up to five years in prison for employers who knowingly hired 10 people or more who were smuggled into the United States.

11. Prosecutors. Create 25 positions for Assistant United States Attorneys to prosecute cases of alien smuggling and document fraud.

12. Undercover operations. Grant broad authority for the INS to conduct undercover operations to track organized illegal immigration rings, including allowing the INS to establish or acquire companies, deposit funds in bank accounts without regard to federal regulations, and use profits from such front companies to offset expenses.

13. Document fraud. Increase penalty for document fraud from 5 years to 10 or 15 years in most cases; and, if fraud was used in facilitating a drug trafficking crime, a new penalty of 20 years in prison, and if involving terrorism, the penalty is 25 years.

14. Assisting in document fraud. Create a civil penalty for hiring someone to make a false application for public benefits such as food stamps. It further created a criminal penalty for "knowingly and willfully" failing to disclose it. This offense is punishable by up to 15 years.

15. False attestation of citizenship. Create a criminal penalty of up to five years in prison for falsely claiming U.S. citizenship.

16. Illegal voting. Create a criminal penalty for up to one year in prison for unlawfully voting in a federal election.

17. Seizure of assets. Allow courts in imposing sentences against violators of immigration statutes, to seize vehicles, boats, airplanes, and real estate if they were used in the commission of a crime or profit from the proceeds of a crime.

18. Involuntary servitude. Increase the penalty from five years in prison to 10 years for employers who kept workers in a state of involuntary servitude.

19. Subpoenas and evidence. Allow INS agents to subpoena witnesses and to videotape testimony at deportation proceedings.

DETENTION AND DEPORTATION

20. Readmission of deported aliens. Bar any alien who had been deported from re-entry into the United States for five years; and up to 10 years if the alien left while deportation proceedings were in progress or attempted to re-enter the country unlawfully; and bar repeat offenders for two years, as well as people convicted of aggravated felonies.

21. Status of illegal aliens. Deny legal status to anyone who resided in the United States unlawfully for at least 180 days; and persons so convicted could not gain legal status for three years. People in the country illegally for a year or more could not become legal for ten years, except for minors or persons with a pending application for asylum, or were battered women and children, or were people granted protection under the family unity provision of the 1990 Act, or spouses and minor children granted amnesty under the Immigration Reform and Control Act of 1986 to stay in the United States even if they entered illegally, while their application for legal status was pending.

22. Inadmissibility of arriving aliens. Allow people who arrived in the United States without legitimate documentation to be detained and deported without hearing unless they could demonstrate a credible fear of persecution back home. An asylum officer was to screen each case. An officer who decided there was no credible fear could deport the applicant. The applicant could request a review by an immigration judge within seven days, during which time the applicant had to remain in detention. The review could take place by telephone or teleconference.

23. Detention of certain aliens. Require the detention of most illegal aliens serving criminal sentences after their prison terms were completed. The attorney general could release certain illegal immigrants from detention centers if there was insufficient space if he determined their release did not pose a security risk or a risk of fleeing, or who came from countries that would not take them back.

24. Deportation proceeding. Streamline deportation by replacing multiple proceedings with one, allowing proceedings by telephone or teleconference, and after 10 day notice of a hearing.

25. Departure. Require aliens be deported within 90 days of a deportation order, with mandatory detention during that period. Violent criminals would have to complete their prison terms before being deported; some non-violent criminal aliens could be deported before their term was up.

26. Deportation appeals. Limit judicial review of deportation orders. The state department could discontinue all visas for countries that declined to take back their deported nationals.

27. Criminal alien tracking. Authorize $5 million for a criminal alien tracking center using criminal alien data base authorized in the 1994 crime law (PL 103–322) to be used to assist local governments in identifying criminals who might be deportable.

28. Prisoner transfer treaties. Advise the president to negotiate bilateral prisoner transfer treaties to allow criminals to serve their terms in their home countries; and for the Secretary of State and Attorney General to report to Congress by April 1, 1997, on the potential for such treaties.

29. Vaccinations. Make a potential immigrant who did not have proof of proper vaccinations inadmissible to the United States.

30. Stalking. Add stalking, domestic violence, and child abuse to the list of crimes that made someone deportable.

31. Benedict Arnold's language. Permanently bar from entry anyone who renounced his or her citizenship to avoid taxes.

32. Delegation of authority. Allow the attorney general to authorize local law enforcement officials to perform the duties of an immigration officer in the event of a mass influx of immigrants.

33. Judicial deportation. Broaden authority of judges to issue deportation orders, allowing someone deported as part of probation or a plea agreement.

34. Military bases. Create a pilot program on the use of closed military bases as INS detention centers.

EMPLOYEE VERIFICATION

35. Employment verification programs. Order the attorney general to create three pilot programs—a basic pilot program, a Citizen Attestation Program, and the so-called Machine-Readable Document Pilot Program—to test the effectiveness of workplace verification systems, participation in which by employers would be voluntary; and the attorney general was to choose the states where each program would be tested, though in some cases employers in non-selected states could participate. All federal departments and agencies within the chosen states were required to participate in the program.

36. Basic pilot program. Allow participating employers to contact the INS via telephone, fax, or e-mail, to check job applicant's immigration status. INS to maintain a data base of names, Social Security numbers, and other information useful to verify an applicant's eligibility to work; and the INS to respond to inquiries within 3 days, and if the tentative response was that the person was not legal, the INS to have 10 days to confirm that determination. The program was to be tested in five of the seven states with the largest number of illegal immigrants.

37. Citizen attestation program. Create a similar program that would allow applicants to bypass the check if they at-

tested that they were U.S. citizens; the penalty for false claims set at up to five years in prison being presumed sufficient to prevent widespread abuse.

38. Machine-readable documentation program. Allow employers to scan a card into a machine, which would verify the owner's Social Security number with the INS data base; to be placed in states selected by the attorney general in which driver's licenses or other state documents included Social Security numbers that could be read by machine.

39. Non-discrimination. Make it harder for the government to sue employers who used immigration laws to discriminate against certain workers, job applicants or other individuals by placing the burden on the government to show that the employer "acted for the purpose, or with the intent to discriminate" against the individual.

PUBLIC BENEFITS

40. Public charges. Allow any consular agent to deny an immigrant visa on the basis that the person was likely to become a public charge.

41. Income requirement. Require sponsors of legal immigrants to earn at least 25 percent more than the federal poverty level and to sign an affidavit that they would be financially responsible for the people they sponsored.

42. Driver's license pilot program. Allow states to create pilot programs to explore the feasibility of denying driver's licenses to illegal immigrants; the attorney general to report to Congress on these programs after three years.

43. Social Security. Clarify that Social Security benefits were not to be paid to illegal immigrants.

44. Student aid. Order the General Accounting Office to study the use of student aid by illegal immigrants and to report on such to Congress within one year of enactment.

45. Welfare. Require the GAO to report to Congress within 180 days on the unlawful use of means-tested benefits—such as food stamps and cash welfare—by illegal immigrants.

46. Battered women and children. Amend the new welfare law to permit certain illegal immigrants who were victims of domestic violence to qualify for public benefits.

47. Nonprofit organizations. Amend the welfare law so that non-profit charitable organizations were no longer required to verify the immigration status of applicants to determine their eligibility for benefits.

48. Food stamps. Allow legal immigrants who were receiving food stamps, and who would lose them under provisions of the new welfare law, to continue receiving them until April 1, 1997, and as long as August 22, 1997—when the process of certifying people for food stamps was complete.

49. Falsely applying for benefits. Allow judges to double the monetary penalty and triple the prison terms for anyone who forged or counterfeited any United States seal to make a false application for public benefits.

50. Reimbursement for medical care. Allow reimbursement to states and localities for emergency medical care of illegal immigrants, if the care was not already reimbursed via existing federal programs in an amount subject to appropriations.

51. Assisted housing. Require the Secretary of Housing and Urban Development to deny financial assistance through subsidized housing programs to families in which all members were illegal immigrants. If families were split between legal and illegal immigrants, HUD could adjust the size of the benefit to match the percentage of family members who were in the United States legally.

OTHER PROVISIONS

52. Forced population control. Stipulate that anyone who had been forced to undergo sterilization or an abortion, or who had been persecuted for failure to do so, could be eligible for asylum or refugee status—up to 1,000 persons per year to be admitted to the United States under the program.

53. Parole. Limit the ability of the INS to use parole of detainees to facilitate mass immigration. When the government did use parole to facilitate immigration, the parolees would count toward caps on legal immigration.

54. Asylum. Require that asylum applications from people already in the United States be filed no later than one year after entry; asylum interviews to take place within 45 days of application; a ruling within 180 days, and an appeal to be filed within 30 days of the ruling. The provision allowed asylum to be denied for many reasons, and asylum could be rescinded if the circumstances changed, such as if a new

government came to power in the home country of the person granted asylum.

55. Public education. Deny visas to immigrants whose intention was to attend a public elementary or secondary school for more than one year.

56. Visas. Clarify that a short-term visa was void as soon as the person stayed longer than its term; requiring a new visa to be issued in the home country of the applicant.

57. Buddhist monks. Allow the State Department unlimited authority to determine the procedures and locations for processing immigrant visa applications—allowing them to require Vietnamese monks and nuns of the An Quang Buddhist sect in Thailand to return to Vietnam to apply for visas to the United States.

58. Genital mutilation. Create a crime punishable by prison for performing female genital mutilation.

59. Mail-order brides. Require "international matchmaking organizations" to disseminate to their clients information about U.S. immigration laws under penalty of a $20,000 fine for failure to do so; and require the Attorney General to prepare a report to Congress on the mail-order bride business within a year of enactment.

60. Temporary agriculture workers. Require the INS to report by the end of 1996 whether or not the United States had an adequate number of temporary agricultural workers.

61. State issued documents. Set national standards for birth certificates, driver's licenses and other identification documents. The Department of Transportation was to set standards for IDs which had to include Social Security numbers, and agencies issuing them had to keep these numbers on file and confirm their accuracy with the Social Security Administration. The standards were intended to make such documents more tamper-resistant; were to be issued within one year; and to be complied with by October 1, 2000.

62. Tamper-proof Social Security cards. Require the Social Security Administration to develop a prototype tamper-proof identity card.

Source: Congressional Quarterly Almanac, Volume 52 (1996). Washington, DC: Congressional Quarterly, 1997: 5-8-5-10.

Personal Responsibility and Work Opportunity Reconciliation Act, 1996

In 1996 Congress passed and President Bill Clinton signed the Personal Responsibility and Welfare Act, otherwise known as the Welfare Reform Act. While the law covered welfare arrangements for all Americans, it had provisions aimed specifically at immigrants. In effect, those provisions of the bill that pertained to immigrants reflected much that was in California Proposition 187 passed two years earlier. Essentially, the Welfare Reform Act severely limited access of legal and illegal immigrants to social welfare and other programs of the federal government. The following is a summary produced by the Congressional Quarterly *of the immigrant-related portions of the Personal Responsibility and Welfare Act of 1996.*

The new welfare law imposed new restrictions on both legal and illegal immigrants, including provisions to:

ILLEGAL ALIENS

1. Restrictions. Restrict the federal benefits for which illegal aliens and legal non-immigrants, such as travelers and students, could qualify. The benefits denied were those provided by a federal agency or federal funds for:

—Any grant, contract, loan, professional license or commercial license.

—Any retirement, welfare, health, disability, food assistance or unemployment benefit.

2. Exceptions. Allow illegal aliens and legal non-immigrants to receive:

—Emergency medical services under Medicaid, but denied coverage for pre-natal or delivery assistance that was not an emergency.

—Short-term, non-cash emergency disaster relief.

—Immunizations and testing for treatment for the symptoms of communicable diseases.

—Non-cash programs identified by the attorney general that were delivered by community agencies such as soup kitchens, counseling, and short-term shelter, that were not conditioned on the individual's income or resources and were necessary for the protection of life and safety.

—Certain housing benefits (for existing recipients only).

—Licenses and benefits directly related to work for which a non-immigrant had been authorized to enter the United States.

—Certain Social Security retirement benefits protected by treaty or statute.

3. State and local programs. Prohibit states from providing state or local benefits to most illegal aliens, unless a state law was enacted after August 22, 1996, the day the bill was enacted, that explicitly made illegal aliens eligible for the aid. However, illegal aliens were entitled to receive a school lunch and/or breakfast if they were eligible for a free public education under state or local law. A state could also opt to provide certain other benefits related to child nutrition and emergency food assistance.

LEGAL IMMIGRANTS

4. Current immigrants. Make most legal immigrants, including those already in the United States, ineligible for SSI and food stamps until they became citizens; existing recipients to have an eligibility review by August 1997. This ban was exempt for:

—Refugees, those granted asylum and aliens whose deportation was being withheld.

—Those who had worked in the United States for ten years.

—Veterans and those on active military duty, as well as their spouses and unmarried children.

5. Future immigrants. Bar legal immigrants who arrived in the United States after August 22, 1996, from receiving most low-income federal benefits for five years after their arrival. Individuals exempt from this ban were:

—Refugees and those granted asylum and aliens whose deportation had been withheld, as well as Cuban and Haitian entrants.

—Veterans and those on active military duty, their spouses and minor children.

—Programs exempt from this ban were:

—Emergency medical service under Medicaid.

—Short-term, non-cash emergency disaster relief.

—Child nutrition, including school lunch programs, WIC [Women, Infant, and Children program], etc.

—Immunization and testing for treatment of symptoms of communicable diseases.

—Foster care and adoption assistance.

—Non-cash programs identified by Attorney General [soup kitchens, etc.].

—Loans and grants for higher education.

—Elementary and secondary education.

—Head Start program for pre-school children.

—Assistance from the Job Training Partnership Act.

6. State options. Allow states to deny benefits from the welfare block grant, Medicaid and social service block grants to most legal immigrants, with exemptions the same as for SSI and Food Stamps; future immigrants subject to the five-year ban noted above.

—Existing recipients to be continued until January 1, 1997.

—Exemptions granted to refugees, those granted asylum, etc.; those who worked in U.S. for ten years; veterans and those on active military duty, their spouses and minor children.

7. Sponsors. Expand circumstances under which an immigrant's sponsor would be financially responsible for that individual, generally affecting those entering the United States sponsored by a member of their immediate family. Affidavits of support would be legally enforceable for up to ten years after the immigrant last received benefits. Programs exempted were the same as those exempted from the five-year ban on benefits to future immigrants.

8. Reporting and verifying. Requires agencies that administer SSI, housing assistance or the welfare block grant to report quarterly to the INS the names and addresses of people they knew were unlawfully in the United States. Charged the Attorney General to issue regulations requiring within 18 months that anyone applying for federal benefits be in the United States legally and that States administering federal benefits would have to comply with the verification system within 24 months after they were issued.

Source: Congressional Quarterly Almanac, Volume 52 (1996). Washington, DC: Congressional Quarterly, 1997: 6-17-6-8.

Amerasian Children Act, 1997

During the Vietnam War, it is estimated that tens of thousands of children born to Vietnamese mothers were sired by American military personnel. Often forgotten or lost track of by their fathers, many of the so-called Amerasian children were scorned and discriminated against by their fellow Vietnamese. In 1997, legislation was passed exempting many of these persons (now young adults)—along with their spouses and children—from certain restrictions on immigration.

The following document includes excerpts from the legislation.

Sec. 584 of Pub. L. 100-202, in part, as amended by Pub. L. 101-167, Pub. L. 101-513 and Pub. L. 101-649
Sec. 584. AMERASIAN IMMIGRATION
(TL:VISA-170; 10-01-1997)

(a)(1) Notwithstanding any numerical limitations specified in the Immigration and Nationality Act, the Attorney General may admit aliens described in subsection (b) to the United States as immigrants if—

(A) they are admissible (except as otherwise provided in paragraph (2)) as immigrants, and

(B) they are issued an immigrant visa and depart from Vietnam on or after March 22, 1988.

(2) The provisions of paragraphs (4), (5), and (7)(A) of section 212(a) of the Immigration and Nationality Act shall not be applicable to any alien seeking admission to the United States under this section, and the Attorney General on the recommendation of a consular officer may waive any other provision of such section (other than paragraph (2)(C) or subparagraph (A), (B), (C), or (E) of paragraph (3)) with respect to such an alien for humanitarian purposes, to assure family unity, or when it is otherwise in the public interest. Any such waiver by the Attorney General shall be in writing and shall be granted only on an individual basis following an investigation by a consular officer.

(3) Notwithstanding section 221(c) of the Immigration and Nationality Act, immigrant visas issued to aliens under this section shall be valid for a period of one year.

(b)(1) An alien described in this section is an alien who, as of the enactment of this Act, is residing in Vietnam and who establishes to the satisfaction of a consular officer or an officer of the Immigration and Naturalization Service after a face-to-face interview, that the alien—(A) (i) was born in Vietnam after January 1, 1962, and before January 1, 1976, and (ii) was fathered by a citizen of the United States (such an alien in this section referred to as a "principal alien");

(B) is the spouse or child of a principal alien and is accompanying, or following to join, the principal alien; or

(C) subject to paragraph (2), either (i) is the principal alien's natural mother (or is the spouse or child of such mother), or (ii) has acted in effect as the principal alien's mother, father, or next-of-kin (or is the spouse or child of such an alien), and is accompanying, or following to join, the principal alien.

(2) An immigrant visa may not be issued to an alien under paragraph (1) (C) unless the officer referred to in paragraph (1) has determined, in the officer's discretion, that (A) such an alien has a bona fide relationship with the principal alien similar to that which exists between close family members and (B) the admission of such an alien is necessary for humanitarian purposes or to assure family unity. If an alien described in paragraph (1)(C)(ii) is admitted to the United States, the natural mother of the principal alien involved shall not, thereafter, be accorded any right, privilege, or status under the Immigration and Nationality Act by virtue of such parentage.

(3) For purposes of this section, the term "child" has the meaning given such term in section 101(b)(1) (A), (B), (C), (D), and (E) of the Immigration and Nationality Act.

(c) Any alien admitted (or awaiting admission) to the United States under this section shall be eligible for benefits under chapter 2 of title IV of the Immigration and Nationality Act to the same extent as individuals admitted (or awaiting admission) to the United States under section 207 of such Act are eligible for benefits under such chapter.

(d). . . .

(e) Except as otherwise specifically provided in this section, the definitions contained in the Immigration and Nationality Act shall apply in the administration of this section and nothing contained in this section shall be held to repeal, amend, alter, modify, effect, or restrict the powers, duties, functions, or authority of the Attorney General in the administration and enforcement of such Act or any other law relating to immigration, nationality, or naturalization. The fact that an alien may be eligible to be granted the status of having been lawfully admitted for permanent residence under this section shall not preclude the alien from seeking such status under any other provision of law for which the alien may be eligible.

Source: 9 Fam. 42.24, Related Statutory Provisions.

B. Executive Orders, Directives, and Statements

Gentlemen's Agreement, 1907

*A*lthough not as numerous as the Chinese, Japanese immigrants to the West Coast of the United States sparked anti-Asian hostility as well. But unlike China, Japan was a major world power and had to be dealt with as more or less an equal. In March 1907, President Theodore Roosevelt negotiated the so-called Gentlemen's Agreement calling for the Japanese government to impose voluntary restrictions on the emigration of its citizens (and those of Korea, then in the process of becoming a Japanese colony) to the United States.

Whereas, by the act entitled "An Act to regulate the immigration of aliens into the United States," approved February 20, 1907, whenever the President is satisfied that passports issued by any foreign Government to its citizens to go to any country other than the United States or to the Canal Zone, are being used for the purpose of enabling the holders to come to the continental territory of the United States from such country or from such insular possession or from the Canal Zone;

AND WHEREAS, upon sufficient evidence produced before me by the Department of Commerce and Labor, I am sat-

isfied that passports issued by the Government of Japan to citizens of that country or Korea and who are laborers, skilled or unskilled, to go to Mexico, to Canada and to Hawaii, are being used for the purpose of enabling the holders thereof to come to the continental territory of the United States to the detriment of labor conditions therein;

I hereby order that such citizens of Japan or Korea, to wit: Japanese and Korean laborers, skilled and unskilled, who have received passports to go to Mexico, Canada, or Hawaii, and come therefrom, be refused permission to enter the continental territory of the United States.

It is further ordered that the Secretary of Commerce and Labor be, and he hereby is, directed to take, through the Bureau of Immigration and Naturalization, such measures and to make and enforce such rules and regulations as may be necessary to carry this order into effect.

Source: Executive Order Number 589, March 14, 1907.

President Roosevelt's Executive Order 9066 (Japanese Internment), 1942

Following the December 7, 1941, attack on the navy base at Pearl Harbor in Hawaii by the forces of the Japanese Empire, the United States declared war on Japan. As the United States entered World War II, widespread panic hit the West Coast that an invasion was imminent. Rumors circulated that Japanese agents were at work preparing the region for the attack. Although no proof of such a conspiracy was ever found, Japanese Americans came under suspicion. On February 19, 1942, President Franklin Roosevelt issued Executive Order 9066 calling for internment of all Japanese Americans (citizens of the U.S. or not) living in the western United States. Ironically, the most vulnerable U.S. territory—Hawaii—never applied such a measure.

NOW, THEREFORE, by virtue of the authority vested in me as President of the United States, and Commander in Chief of the Army and Navy, I hereby authorize and direct the Secretary of War, and the Military commanders whom he may from time to time designate, whenever he or any designated Commander deems such action necessary or desirable, to prescribe military areas in such places and of such extent as he or the appropriate Military Commander may determine, from which any and all persons may be excluded, and with respect to which, the right of any person to enter, remain in, or leave shall be subject to whatever restrictions the Secretary of War or the appropriate Military Commander may impose in his discretion. The Secretary of War is hereby authorized to provide for residents of any such area who are excluded therefrom, such transportation, food, shelter, and other accommodations as may be necessary, in the judgment of the Secretary of War, of the said Military Commander, and until other arrangements are made, to accomplish the purpose of this order. The designation of military areas in any region or locality shall supersede designations of prohibited or restricted areas by the Attorney General under the proclamations of December 7 and 8, 1941, and shall supersede the responsibility and authority of the Attorney General under the said Proclamation in respect of such prohibited and restricted areas.

I hereby further authorize and direct the Secretary of War and the said Military Commanders to take such other steps as he or the appropriate Military Commander may deem advisable to enforce compliance with the restrictions applicable to each Military area hereinabove authorized to be designated, including the use of Federal troops and other Federal Agencies, with authority to accept assistance of state and local agencies.

I hereby further authorize and direct all Executive commanders in carrying out this Executive Order, including the furnishing of medical aid, hospitalization, food, clothing, transportation, use of land, shelter, and other supplies, equipment, utilities, facilities, and services.

This order shall not be construed as modifying or limiting in any way the authority granted under Executive Order 8972, dated December 12, 1941, nor shall it be construed as limiting or modifying the duty and responsibility of the Federal Bureau of Investigation, with respect to the investigation of alleged acts of sabotage or the duty and responsibility of the Attorney General and the Department of Justice under the Proclamations of December 7, and 8, 1941, prescribing regulations for the conduct and control of alien enemies, except as such duty and responsibility is superseded by the designation of military areas hereunder.

Source: Federal Register, Volume VII, number 38.

President Truman's Directive on European Refugees, 1945

Before and during World War II, the United States often refused to accept refugees—particularly Jewish refugees—fleeing the horrors of Nazism and Nazi expansion. Following the war, there were untold numbers of displaced persons. To ease their suffering—and, say some scholars, to assuage guilt—the United States moved to welcome more refugees. On December 22, 1945, President Harry S. Truman issued a directive on this subject.

The war has brought in its wake an appalling dislocation of populations in Europe. Many humanitarian organizations, including the United Nations Relief and Rehabilitation Administration are doing their utmost to solve the multitude of problems arising in connection with this dislocation of hundreds of thousands of persons. Every effort is being made to return the displaced persons and refugees in the various countries of Europe to their former homes. The great difficulty is that so many of these persons have no homes to which they may return. The immensity of the problem of displaced persons and refugees is almost beyond comprehension.

A number of countries in Europe, including Switzerland, Sweden, France, and England, are working toward its solution. The United States shares the responsibility to relieve the suffering. To the extent that our present immigration laws permit, everything possible should be done at once to facilitate the entrance of some of these displaced persons and refugees into the United States.

In this way we may do something to relieve human misery, and set an example to the other countries of the world which are able to receive some of these war sufferers. I feel that it is essential that we do this ourselves to show our good faith in requesting other nations to open their doors for this purpose.

Most of these persons are natives of Central and Eastern Europe and the Balkans. The immediate quotas for all those countries for one year total approximately 39,000, two-thirds of which are allotted to Germany. Under the law, in any single month the number of visas issued cannot exceed ten percent of the annual quota. This means that from now on only about 3,900 visas can be issued each month to persons who are natives of these countries.

Very few persons from Europe have migrated to the United States during the war years. In fiscal year 1942 only ten percent of the immigration quotas was used; in 1943, five percent; in 1944, six percent; and in 1945, seven percent. As of November 30, 1945, the end of the fifth month of the current fiscal year, only about ten percent of the quotas for the European countries has been used. These unused quotas however do not accumulate through the years, and I do not intend to ask the Congress to change this rule. . . .

I consider that common decency and fundamental comradeship of all human beings require us to do what lies within our power to see that our established immigration quotas are used in order to reduce human suffering. I am taking the necessary steps to see that this is done as quickly as possible. . . .

I am informed that there are various measures now pending before the Congress which would either prohibit or severely reduce further immigration. I hope that such legislation will not be passed. This period of unspeakable human distress is not the time for us to close or to narrow our gates. I wish to emphasize, however, that any effort to bring relief to these displaced persons and refugees must and will be strictly within the limits of the present quotas as imposed by law.

Upon the basis of a careful survey by the Department of State and the Immigration and Naturalization Service, it has been determined that if these persons were now applying for admission to the United States most of them would be admissible under the immigration laws. In the circumstances, it would be inhumane and wasteful to require these people to go all the way back to Europe merely for the purpose of applying there for immigration visas and returning to the United States. Many of them have close relatives, including sons and daughters, who are citizens of the United States and who have served and are serving honorably in the armed forces of our country. I am therefore directing the Secretary of State and the Attorney General to adjust the immigration status of the members of this group who may wish to remain here, in strict accordance with existing laws and regulations. . . .

The attached directive has been issued by me to the responsible government agencies to carry out this policy. I wish to emphasize, above all, that nothing in the directive will deprive a single American soldier or his wife or children of a berth on a vessel homeward bound, or delay their return. This is the opportunity for America to set an example for the rest of the world in cooperation towards alleviating human misery.

Source: Public Papers of the Presidents (December 22, 1945).

Whom We Shall Welcome, 1953

In January 1953, the President's Commission on Immigration and Naturalization published its report on existing immigration and offered proposals for change. Entitled Whom We Shall Welcome, *the report covered a host of issues and was largely supportive of getting rid of the quota system and opening up America's gates to more immigrants. In the sections included here, the writers outline the impact of America's immigration law on national security, the worldwide struggle against communism, and advocates allowing in more refugees from communism. In addition, they called for continuing vigilance against the immigration of "subversives," but said this should be tempered with protections for the rights of potentially dangerous immigrants. (Sections in bold are bold in the original.)*

CHAPTER 3. IMMIGRATION AND OUR FOREIGN POLICY

ESCAPEES FROM IRON CURTAIN COUNTRIES

The escapee situation is even more critical at the present time. There are 20,000–25,000 persons, housed in camps in Germany, Austria, Italy, Trieste, Greece, and Turkey, who have escaped from behind the Iron Curtain since January 1, 1948. These escapees are non-Germans. They are, in general, the people from behind the Iron Curtain who have most recently arrived, risking life and limb, leaving behind everything but the clothes on their backs, in order to live in freedom. Some of them have come because of the enticements held out to them by the Voice of America or by other Western propaganda for democracy.

Now that the Communists have tightened up the border watch, the flow has dropped to about 500 a month. How many try and fail, paying for the attempt with their lives, is anyone's guess, but at one point the mortality rate was estimated to be over 80 percent.

Unfortunately, escapees are not likely to find the welcome and freedom they thought would await them. They arrive in countries already surfeited with refugees. They cannot, for the most part, continue on to the United States, because of restrictions in our immigration law. And so most of them are put in camps, without work, with none of the comforts and few of the privileges or rights of free men.

The United States has a special responsibility toward these people, and a special interest in them. At least some of them have come because our propaganda lured them. If sacrifice earns the right to liberty, they have earned it. We cannot turn them away and expect those still behind the Iron Curtain to believe us ever again.

Furthermore, they are, generally speaking, convinced opponents of Communist tyranny. They have experienced it, and they want no more of it. They can be helpful to us. And yet, we have done very little for them and nothing to welcome them to our shores.

Out of the current Mutual Security appropriation, a fund of $4,300,000 has been set aside to help the resettlement of escapees. The announcement caused hopes to rise among those escapees in camps in Europe. It brought a short-lived increase in the rate of escape through the Iron Curtain. Its results have been negligible because the fund is too small and because the United States and the other free nations have formulated no adequate programs for their care and resettlement.

The Commission believes that effective measures should be taken and adequate appropriations made to provide reasonable reception, care, and migration opportunities for escapees from Communism.

The escapee problem is not a partisan political issue. It is generally agreed that something should be done immediately. President [Harry] Truman said in his special Message to the Congress on March 24,1952:

> . . . specific aid and assistance should he provided for the people who are fleeing at the risk of their lives from southern and eastern Europe. These people are Balts, Poles, Czechs, Slovaks, Hungarians, Bulgarians, Rumanians, Albanians, Ukrainians, and Russians.
>
> These people face a desperate situation. Not only do they

arrive destitute, with only what they can carry on their backs, but they find themselves in totally strange lands among strange peoples speaking strange languages. The local authorities do not have adequate resources to care for them properly. These people need better care when they first arrive, and they need assistance if they are to move on and resettle elsewhere.

The miserable conditions in which these fugitives from communism find themselves, and their present inability to emigrate to new homes and start new lives, lead inevitably to despair. Their disillusionment is being effectively exploited by Communist propaganda. These men and women are friends of freedom. They include able and courageous fighters against communism. They ask only for an opportunity to play a useful role in the fight for freedom. It is the responsibility of the free world to afford them this opportunity.

He recommended a program authorizing 21,000 escapees to migrate to the United States over a 3-year period, plus supplemental reception, care, payment of cost of ocean transportation, and a program of education for leadership for those who choose to remain in Europe.

President-Elect [Dwight] Eisenhower said in a speech on October 17, 1952:

> A contest for world leadership—in fact, for survival—exists between the Communist idea and the American ideal. That contest is being waged in the minds and hearts of human beings. We say—and we sincerely believe—that we are on the side of freedom; that we are on the side of humanity. We say—and we know—that the Communists are on the side of slavery, the side of inhumanity.
>
> Yet to the Czech, the Pole, the Hungarian who takes his life in his hands and crosses the frontier tonight—or to the Italian who goes to some American consulate—this ideal that beckoned him can be a mirage because of the McCarran Act.

Secretary of State [Dean] Acheson said, in his statement to the Commission:

> Another special problem of equal importance is that of the escapees from Communist countries. These people arrive in the border countries destitute. They have lost their homes, their property, and often their families. They have a deep hatred for communism—they know from experience what it means. They have a deep love of freedom, having been so long without it. If they are left to shift for themselves in lands already burdened with surplus population they will not be able to find work, and will be disillusioned about the meaning of Western Democracy. As their disillusion grows, and word of it spreads, it will be difficult for us to convince the captive populations behind the Iron Curtain that the free world is interested in their fate. With our aid other countries are trying to make possible a new life for these escapees. But these efforts do not by themselves meet the need. To welcome escapees to the United States on a scale impossible under the present quota restrictions, would be a vital step in making our policy toward the satellite peoples effective.

Prof. Philip E. Mosley, president of the East European fund set up by the Ford Foundation, and member of the Russian Institute of Columbia University, testified:

> I feel that we will strengthen our own country and the free world . . . if we will open a door, or rather if we will reopen a door to the people who under intolerable pressure are escaping every day and every week from the Iron Curtain countries.

American foreign policy toward the countries behind the Iron Curtain, particularly the satellites, is to emphasize that their people would be better off on our side. **But in connection with escapees, a most vital aspect of the "cold war," American immigration law lies directly athwart our foreign policy.**

CHAPTER 15.
SECURITY PROTECTIONS

Since the earliest days of the Republic, Congress has expressed concern over the activities of subversive aliens in our midst. The Alien Act of 1798 authorized the President to order the departure of any alien whom he deemed dangerous to the United States. The Alien Enemy Act of 1798, passed 2 weeks later, permitted the apprehension, restraint, and removal of alien enemies, if deemed necessary for the public safety. The first law was so unpopular and violated such fundamental American principles that it was allowed to expire after 2 years. The second, limited in application to time of war or threatened invasion, is still in effect.

It was not, however, until 1903 that the law barred the entry of aliens who were regarded as inimical to the safety and security of the country. By a 1903 statute, anarchists and those who believed in or advocated the forcible overthrow of the Government of the United States, or of all forms of Government, or the assassination of public officials, were denied admission to the United States. These provisions were continued and strengthened in 1907 and 1917. The Anarchist Act of 1918, as amended in 1920, enlarged the description of aliens classed as subversive. It barred from the United States aliens who write, publish or cause to be written or published, or circulate, distribute or display, or possess for such purposes, any written or printed matter advising, advocating, or teaching opposition to organized forms of Government, or the overthrow by force or violence of Government, or the killing of officers generally, or unlawful damage to or destruction of property, or sabotage.

The Supreme Court, in 1939, had occasion to interpret the laws which authorize the exclusion of aliens deemed subversive, and the deportation of those in the United States who were members of or affiliated with subversive organizations. The Supreme Court's decision required a finding by the Government of present membership or affiliation, in order to support the exclusion or deportation of an alien.

However, the Congress reversed this situation in the Alien Registration Act of 1940, which made such membership at any time a ground for exclusion and deportation. Other enactments between 1940 and 1950 generally strengthened and, to some extent, enlarged the description of classes to be excluded or deported from the United States as subversives; and authorized the denial of visas to, and the exclusion of, aliens seeking to enter the United States for the purpose of engaging in activities which would endanger public safety.

In the years immediately following the close of hostilities of World War II, a growing awareness developed of the inadequacies of existing law to cope with Communism's drive for world domination. To meet this increasing threat, Congress enacted the Internal Security Act of 1950. This Act greatly enlarged the proscribed classes of subversive aliens. For the first time the Communist Party was mentioned by name. The terms "communism," "Communist organization," "Communist front organization," "totalitarianism," "advocates," and "doctrine" were defined by statute. Moreover, the Act makes membership, association or affiliation with an organization required to register as a subversive organization under the Subversive Activities Control Act of 1950, a ground for exclusion and deportation.

In addition the discretion of the Attorney General to admit subversive aliens, under preexisting legislation, was completely eliminated with respect to aliens returning to the United States to resume a permanent residence after a temporary absence abroad. Subversive aliens seeking temporary admission could do so only under a severely curtailed discretion of the Attorney General, and, where exercised, the Attorney General was required to make a detailed report to Congress. Many provisions of the Internal Security Act of 1950 were attacked at the time as being unnecessarily harsh, improper, and not in the best interests of the country.

The provisions of the Internal Security Act of 1950 have been carried forward into the Immigration and Nationality Act of 1952, without substantial change. The only significant difference in the treatment of subversive aliens under the 1952 Act is that the definition of "totalitarian party" is limited to an organization which advocates the establishment of a totalitarian dictatorship or totalitarianism in the United States. This would bar admission of members of the Communist Party, but some have expressed concern that it would not bar from the United States members of the Nazi, Fascist, or Falange parties.

SECURITY SCREENING PROCESS

The various administrative agencies have endeavored to establish effective processes to screen out and bar subversive people. The State Department has devised an elaborate screening process in an attempt to ascertain whether applicants for visas come within the statutory designations of subversives. The law requires each applicant for a visa to prepare a lengthy, documented application. In addition, the consular officers usually require the alien to submit a questionnaire designed, when completed, to provide a basis for a background check of the alien from a security point of view.

After an examination of the papers submitted by the alien, sources of information available in the local Foreign

Service posts of the United States and so-called "look-out" notices from the Department of State and the Department of Justice are checked. American officers at the Foreign Service post, such as the military, naval, air, or economic attachés, are consulted to ascertain whether their respective spheres of operation have uncovered any information which might have a bearing on the alien's admissibility. Checks with other sources of information available abroad are utilized wherever practicable.

The alien is invited to appear at the consular establishment to be examined under oath concerning his background and other factors bearing upon his eligibility for admission to the United States. If any derogatory information is uncovered, further action on the alien's application is suspended pending additional examination or pending reference of the application to the Department of State. Should the derogatory information indicate that the alien falls within one of the proscribed subversive classes, the interrogation is usually conducted more thoroughly in order firmly to establish the facts relating to the alien's admissibility. The alien may or may not be given an opportunity to rebut the derogatory information on file.

The consular officer may, of course, refuse to issue a visa at any stage of the investigation, but if he entertains any doubt as to the alien's admissibility from a security standpoint, he is required by regulation to refer the case to the Department of State for an advisory opinion. For former voluntary members of proscribed organizations, no visa may be issued without an advisory opinion. If an advisory opinion from the Department of State is unfavorable, no visa may be issued. However, even if the Department of State renders a favorable advisory opinion, the consular officer may still refuse a visa as he sees fit. Wherever possible the Department of State conducts an independent and supplemental security check, utilizing various intelligence facilities of our Government.

Special provisions of law which relate to accredited officials of foreign governments, or representatives of foreign governments to international organizations, generally make impossible the application of normal screening processes to them. On the other hand, classes of aliens who, because of their profession, occupation, or previous status, present special problems, are subjected to even closer scrutiny and additional checks.

Possession of a visa does not entitle an alien to enter the United States; a visa is, in effect, a permit to apply for admission. An alien with a visa, who applies for admission to the United States, is required to satisfy the Attorney General that he is eligible under the immigration laws for admission. The Immigration and Naturalization Service has authority to make a completely independent security check upon an alien presenting a visa. Immigration officials at this point have the benefit of advice and information from various intelligence sources in the United States and elsewhere.

Once an alien is in the United States, he may be deported for subversive activities. The investigations preceding the arrest in deportation and the consequent hearing may have been made by one or more of the several intelligence agencies of the United States Government or may have been conducted by the Immigration and Naturalization Service.

Thus, at each stage of the immigration process, the issuance of a visa, the admission at ports of entry, or deportation, the facilities for the detection or apprehension of the subversive alien represent the combined efforts of many intelligence and investigating agencies in addition to the agencies administering the immigration law.

The Commission made efforts to learn whether security agencies, and those responsible for the administration of the immigration laws had any specific recommendations to make in order to strengthen the security provisions of such and related laws. At the time these efforts were made, the act of 1952 had not become effective. However, the Commission is able to report that as of the time of its inquiry, the security measures in the laws and regulations were believed to be adequate. The sole exception was the suggestion that the Commission recommend provisions to enable immigration authorities to exclude applicants for visas who are active members of, or believe in the principles advocated by, Nazi, Fascist, and other such totalitarian organizations.

Generally speaking, the immigration laws deal with three groups of subversives: (1) spies and saboteurs; (2) present members and affiliates of subversive organizations; and (3) former members or affiliates of subversive organizations.

SPIES AND SABOTEURS

The act of 1952 makes ineligible to receive a visa and requires the exclusion of:

> Aliens who the consular officer or the Attorney General knows or has reason to believe seek to enter the United States solely, principally, or incidentally to engage in activities which would be prejudicial to the public interest, or endanger the welfare, safety, or security of the United States; . . .
>
> Aliens with respect to whom the consular officer or the Attorney General knows or has reasonable ground to believe probably would, after entry, (A) engage in activities which would be prohibited by the laws of the United States relating to espionage, sabotage, public disorder, or in other activity subversive to the national security, (B) engage in any activity a purpose of which is the opposition to, or the control or overthrow of, the Government of the United States, by force, violence, or other unconstitutional means, or (C) Join, affiliate with, or participate in the activities of any organization which is registered or required to be registered under section 7 of the Subversive Activities Control Act of 1950 . . .

Such aliens, even if they are permanent residents returning after a temporary absence abroad, are specifically denied the benefits of the exercise of discretion. Provisions relating to the parole of aliens into the United States, or to the waiver of documents for nonimmigrant aliens, are not intended by Congress to include these subversive aliens,

save for the possible purpose of prosecution for crime. Such aliens may be deported at any time, without regard to when they entered the United States.

Legislation which establishes an absolute bar against admission to the United States of those whose purpose in entering is to engage in activities which violate our laws relating to espionage, sabotage, public disorder or national security must remain on our statute books and be strictly enforced.

These statutory provisions give authority to deal with spies and saboteurs. However, the act of 1952 gives a consular officer the absolute and unreviewable power to bar aliens whom he "knows or has reason to believe seek to enter the United States solely, principally, or incidentally to engage in activities which would be prejudicial to the public interest," or with respect to whom, the consular officer "knows or has reasonable ground to believe probably would, after entry" engage in subversive activities. . . . The difficulties are here aggravated because the statutory language is so undefined. It is susceptible of as many different interpretations as there are men applying it. Such absolute and unreviewable discretion is not necessary for the protection of the security of the United States.

The statute should without doubt leave ample room for the exercise of discretion for the protection of the national security, but it should contain definite standards to guide administrative action, so as to guard against abuse. The vague language of the act of 1952 does not meet this need, and it should be revised so as to specify that it applies to aliens who seek to enter, or who are believed to be seeking to enter for the purpose of violating the criminal laws of the United States relating to espionage, sabotage, and public order; or violating the laws relating to the protection of the conduct of military and foreign affairs; and relating to the protection of other activities and functions of the government and other public agencies, national, state and local, upon which the national security depends.

The administrative review elsewhere recommended for visa denial, exclusion, and deportation actions should be applicable here. . . .

PRESENT MEMBERS AND AFFILIATES OF SUBVERSIVE ORGANIZATIONS

The law forbids entry to aliens who are anarchists or who are members or affiliates of the Communist Party or other totalitarian organizations, or who advocate or teach opposition to or violent overthrow of all organized government, or who write, publish, display, or circulate or who possess for circulation any written or printed matter which teaches or advocates world communism, opposition to or forceful overthrow of government, the killing of officers of government, the destruction of property or sabotage. Subversive aliens barred from admission to the United States are not limited to those who are members of the proscribed organizations, but also includes those who are affiliated with such groups.

With respect to all classes of subversive aliens, except anarchists, the law authorizes the issuance of a visa to such an alien if he establishes to the satisfaction of a consular officer, and the consular officer finds, that the membership or affiliation of the alien in a subversive organization is involuntary or occurred when the alien was under 16 years of age. It is necessary, in addition, however, that at the time the alien applies for admission to the United States the Attorney General must independently be satisfied and also find that the alien to whom a visa was so issued was involuntarily a member of or affiliated with any of the enumerated subversive classes.

The law authorizes the deportation of any alien who at the time of entry was within any of the classes excluded by law. It also provides for the deportation of any member of each of the categories of subversive aliens who is, or at any time after entry has become, a member of any of the proscribed classes of subversive aliens. Discretionary relief in connection with deportation is denied to aliens who are present members of subversive groups.

There can be no doubt that present members or affiliates of subversive organizations should be excluded from the United States. The issue is what is to be regarded as "member," "affiliate," or a "subversive organization." In these respects, the Commission believes that our present laws are not adequate. In part, the difficulty is that the act of 1952 is lengthy, complex, repetitive, and obscure.

As to membership, the Commission believes that the provision of the present law exempting "involuntary" members is desirable and sound. The purpose of the immigration law should be to bar only those aliens who, by their membership or affiliation with subversive groups, have identified themselves with the aims and principles of those groups. These exemptions should be interpreted broadly, so that the statutory injunction will encompass only those who were subversives at heart and will not reach those who were merely nominal members, or as a result of compulsion or mistake. Such involuntary membership or affiliation merits the exception which the statute gives it.

"Affiliation" is not fully defined in the 1952 Act, and the statute merely states:

> The giving, loaning, or promising of support or of money or any other thing of value for any purpose to any organization shall be presumed to constitute affiliation therewith; but nothing in this paragraph shall be construed as an exclusive definition of affiliation.

This definition is an improvement over the similar one contained in the Internal Security Act of 1950 which made the giving, loaning, or promising of support or of money a conclusive presumption of affiliation. Nevertheless, even this improved definition should be read in the light of the congressional expression of need for legislation controlling subversive activities, contained in the Internal Security Act of 1950:

In carrying on the activities referred to in paragraph 6 [establishment of Communist totalitarian dictatorship as part of the world Communist movement], such Communist organizations in various countries are organized on a secret, conspiratorial basis and operate to a substantial extent through organizations, commonly known as "Communist fronts," which in most instances are created and maintained, or used, in such manner as to conceal the facts as to their true character and purposes and their membership. One result of this method of operation is that such affiliated organizations are able to obtain financial and other support from persons who would not extend such support if they knew the true purposes of and the actual nature of the control and influence exerted upon such "Communist fronts."

The security of the United States must be protected against aliens guilty of true "affiliation" with subversive organizations. However, the statutory definition of "affiliation" condemns those who give support to front organizations "for any purpose," and thus may reach the innocent as well as the guilty.

The definition of "affiliation" should make it clear that the law bars those aliens who by their support or contribution or other form of affiliation knowingly and willingly seek to further the subversive aims and principles of the organizations. This proposal is in keeping with the present law's provision authorizing the admission to the United States and the naturalization of aliens who became affiliated with a communist organization without knowledge of its character.

In one respect, the act of 1952 leaves a security loophole, and so does not go far enough to protect the national security. Although the statute attempts to encompass every activity and belief that might be deemed subversive, it fails to ban members or affiliates of foreign totalitarian organizations, other than Communist. It bars admission to

> aliens who are members of or affiliated with . . . (IV) the Communist or any other totalitarian party of any State of the United States, of any foreign state, or of any political or geographical subdivision of any foreign state . . .

Comprehensive, though it sounds, this subsection may not bar Nazis, Fascists, or other totalitarian groups who are not Communists. This clause was carried forward verbatim from the Internal Security Act of 1950. But, whereas the Internal Security Act defines the terms "totalitarian dictatorship" and "totalitarianism" as

> . . . systems of government not representative in fact, characterized by (A) the existence of a single political party, organized on a dictatorial basis, with as close an identity between such party and its policies and the governmental policies of the country in which it exists, that the party and the government constitute an indistinguishable unit, and (B) the forcible suppression of opposition to such party, . . .

the act of 1952 adds to the above definition the following:

The term "totalitarian party" means an organization which advocates the establishment in the United States of a totalitarian dictatorship or totalitarianism . . .

Both the Senate and House Committee reports are silent on the significance of the definition limiting a totalitarian party to one which advocates the establishment of totalitarianism "in the United States." It would appear, however, that the new definition is intended to exclude from the ban of the immigration laws totalitarian parties such as the Nazis, Fascists, and Falangists who are believed not to advocate the establishment of a totalitarian dictatorship in the United States.

No less than communism, other forms of totalitarianism degrade the dignity of man and deprive him of those rights which our Declaration of Independence holds to be unalienable. It is contended that the law should make a distinction between present membership in the Communist Party and present membership in other totalitarian parties, on the ground that communism is the only present menace.

While such a distinction appears plausible in the light of the imminence of the Communist peril, the resurgence of neo-Nazism and neo-Fascism in Germany and Italy underlines the danger of treating such totalitarian movements too lightly. Nazi and Fascists and other advocates of totalitarianism may not be developing plans today to overthrow the Government of the United States or any other democratic government by force and violence. There was a period, however, when they did attempt to dominate the world. The cost of stopping that effort was the heaviest ever paid in the history of the world. The millions of graves of those who died that democracy might survive, or who perished as victims of mass murder; the hundreds of thousands who were maimed; the millions who were stripped of their possessions and forced to undergo undescribable suffering, privation and misery; the destruction of the economic resources of once prosperous and happy peoples—these results of the evil ambitions, the cruelties of Nazism and Fascism should keep the United States alert forevermore to the danger from that source. The Communists and the Nazis pooled their ideologies and their plans for world conquest to begin World War II. The subsequent disintegration of that unholy partnership was fortunate for the democracies, but we shall be inviting disaster if we receive the disciples of one form of totalitarianism while arming for defense against the other.

The Commission deems the present adherents of all forms of totalitarianism to be hostile to our way of life and believes they should be banned from the United States.

A problem that has troubled the Commission has been the undesirable alien who is a product of our own society. Elsewhere, the Commission has urged that such aliens not be deported. Where such an alien is a present subversive, a special issue arises. Apart from the fact that such an alien is a product of our society, the difficulty, as pointed out to the Commission by the Immigration and Naturalization Service, is that deportation orders for subversives often prove futile. Mr. Justice Jackson succinctly stated the problem in

his dissenting opinion in *United States v. Spector*, 343 U. S. 169 at pages 179–180.

A deportation policy can be successful only to the extent that some other state is willing to receive those we expel. But, except selected individuals who can do us more harm abroad than here, what Communist power will cooperate with our deportation policy by receiving our expelled Communist aliens? And what non-Communist power feels such confidence in its own domestic security that it can risk taking in persons this stable and powerful Republic finds dangerous to its security? World conditions seem to frustrate the policy of deportation of subversives. Once they gain admission here, they are our problem and one that cannot be shipped off to some other part of the world.

A law which cannot be enforced brings the entire administration of justice into disrepute.

The Commission requested the Immigration and Naturalization Service for advice and recommendations to meet the problem of aliens who are under orders of deportation, but cannot be deported because no country will accept them. The answer was that the Internal Security Act of 1950 had provided, and the act of 1952 had continued, certain limited sanctions to aid in effectuating an order of deportation against persons in the subversive, criminal and other undesirable groups, and that no other methods of dealing with this matter had been devised.

Under such circumstances, therefore, the Commission believes that this country should accept as its own responsibility all those aliens who are the product of our own society.

The Commission recommends that

(1) present members of subversive or totalitarian organizations, or persons who, by their present affiliation with such organizations, manifest their belief in or sympathy with the aims and principles of such organizations, should be denied visas and should be excluded from admission to the United States. Present membership or affiliation should create a presumption of such belief or sympathy, subject to countervailing evidence to prove that such membership or affiliation was involuntary.

(2) The definition of "totalitarian party," "totalitarian dictatorship," and "totalitarianism" should be clarified so that it embraces all aliens in sympathy with the governmental theories and policies of totalitarianism as that word is defined in the Internal Security Act of 1950.

(3) "Affiliation" as used in the immigration laws should be defined so that it embraces only those aliens who, by their action and conduct, have demonstrated an association with totalitarian groups because of sympathy for or agreement with the subversive aims and principles of such groups.

(4) Alien members or affiliates of subversive organizations who were lawfully admitted to the United States for permanent residence prior to reaching the age of 16 years, or who were lawfully admitted for permanent residence and have resided in the United States continuously for at least 20 years, should not be subject to deportation,

but should be dealt with in the same manner as subversive citizens.

FORMER MEMBERSHIP OR AFFILIATION WITH SUBVERSIVE ORGANIZATIONS

At one time, as witness the Alien Registration Act of 1940, present and former members of subversive organizations were treated alike. However, in the act of 1952, Congress recognized that former membership in or affiliation with subversive groups or organizations should not be an absolute bar to admission or stay in this country. It made two exceptions. The first is where such membership or affiliation was involuntary or occurred when the alien was under 16 years of age. The second is where membership or affiliation has been terminated for 5 years and for that period the alien has been "actively opposed" to such subversive ideologies, and where the admission of the alien "would be in the public interest." Each case in this last category must be reported to the Congress.

The deportation of former members or affiliates of subversive classes is, as in the case of present members, provided for by the law. However, unlike present members, former members or affiliates of subversive groups are eligible, under severely limited conditions, to receive discretionary relief by way of suspension of deportation.

The problem of past membership or affiliation is obviously a difficult one. If there is merely a severance of formal bonds of association without a corresponding repudiation of sympathetic belief in the aims and principles of the subversive group, such aliens continue to be threats to our security.

A former member who has made a genuine break with subversive ideology offers no threat to our security. Indeed experience has shown that such converts may represent very stable adherents to the principles of democracy because they are less likely again to succumb to the false blandishments of totalitarianism. The removal of the absolute bar against former—and now reformed—subversive aliens strengthens our own internal and external security and advances our foreign policy.

However, the act of 1952 contains other important defects. For example, the requirement of 5 year active opposition to a formerly held totalitarian ideology may defeat important objectives of our intelligence and foreign policy agencies. Escapees who come out from behind the Iron Curtain, or defectors from communism elsewhere, may be of vital and immediate importance to our security and defense as well as to our foreign policy. And yet they must wait 5 years, although there may be conclusive proof of complete reformation in a shorter period of time. Indeed, retention of an inflexible 5-year bar against former subversives might seriously impair the Commission's proposals to grant priority to refugees from communism (Chapter 9).

The requirement of "active" opposition to former doctrines misses the point. Most people who have genuinely renounced subversive ideas do not become active pamphleteers, speakers or professional antitotalitarians; the genuineness of their opposition to totalitarianism cannot be measured by the loudness of their disclaimers.

There is an inconsistency in our laws relating to former membership or affiliation in subversive organizations. The act of 1952 carries forward the previous law's failure to coordinate the naturalization and deportation directives aimed at former members of subversive organizations. The naturalization law permits the admission to citizenship of former subversives whose membership in the proscribed organization ended more than 10 years earlier. But the deportation statute apparently permits the expulsion of such former subversives at any time, even after 10 years has expired since the membership or association with the subversive group terminated. It would seem reasonable to suppose that if a former member of a subversive group is eligible for naturalization after 10 years he should by the same token be able to avoid deportation.

There are also the grossly inconsistent provisions to the effect that a former member of a subversive organization, who actively opposed that subversive organization for a period of 5 years, may now be admitted into the United States although he was never here before, while a long-time resident alien who 30 years ago resigned from membership in a subversive organization, left it, and has since actively opposed it, must be deported.

The Commission believes that the provisions of the act of 1952 to the effect that membership in or affiliation with subversive organizations should not necessarily be a bar to entry into the United States are sound; and the Commission recommends that these same provisions be extended to cover deportation procedures, so that former membership in or affiliation with subversive organizations genuinely repudiated over a period of at least 5 years, should not be a ground for deportation.

The Commission recommends that the requirement of active opposition should be amended by deleting the word "active," thus making its benefits available to all opponents of totalitarianism. The Commission recommends that the requirement of 5 years opposition should be subject to waiver in appropriate cases, after thorough screening and approval by the appropriate security agencies of the United States. This would make possible the admission of bona fide escapees and defectors.

The Commission recommends that the immigration law apply the same conditions to former members and affiliates of all totalitarian parties, whether they were Communist, Nazi, Fascist, or other such parties.

It should be noted, too, that the law requires a finding by both the consular officer and the Attorney General that the admission of the alien would be in the public interest. Without criteria under which "in the public interest" may be measured, the phrase seems too vague for effective administration. It is quite conceivable that administrative officers might seldom, if ever, find that the admission of a former Communist, Nazi, or Fascist would affirmatively be in the public interest. **The Commission recommends that the law should require a finding that the admission of a former subversive would not be contrary to the public interest.**

EXCLUSION WITHOUT HEARING

Security considerations sometimes create special problems in connection with otherwise normal immigration procedures. At least for the past 60 years, an alien has been entitled to a hearing before he can be excluded at a port of entry. However, when the ground for his exclusion involves confidential information, the disclosure of which would be detrimental to the best interests of the United States, there is a conflict between two important values. On the one side is the security of the United States; on the other is the fundamental concept of American law that a person is entitled to a fair hearing before the Government takes action affecting him.

From at least 1893 until 1941, no alien—not even a subversive—could be excluded without a hearing. In 1941 such provision was made. The Passport Act of 1918 authorized the President in time of war or national emergency to impose additional restrictions and prohibitions on entry into and departure from the United States upon a finding that the interests of the United States so required. The President issued a proclamation on November 14, 1941, reciting the existence of a national emergency and declaring that "no alien should be permitted to enter the United States if it appears to the satisfaction of the Secretary of State that such entry would be prejudicial to the interests of the United States," as provided in regulations issued by the Secretary of State with the concurrence of the Attorney General. These regulations authorized the Attorney General to deny hearings when a person is excludable "on the basis of information of a confidential nature, the disclosure of which would be prejudicial to the public interest."

From the evidence before the Commission, including testimony before congressional committees and various United States Government briefs in the Supreme Court, this measure was intended to have only limited application. It seems that this procedure was designed to provide a legal sanction for denying access to the United States during war or national emergency only in those special cases where disclosure of the information or the source of the information, on the basis of which the exclusion is ordered for security reasons, would be contrary to the national interest.

During the war years, this new procedure was sparingly used. The Immigration and Naturalization Service reports that only a negligible number of aliens were excluded without a hearing. However, with the end of hostilities immigration to the United States was resumed on a larger scale. In addition, the nation became increasingly aware of the threat to its security by world communism. These two circumstances resulted in an enlarged application of the hith-

erto limited measure of denying entry without a hearing, because of confidential information. Aliens who had been or were associated with Communist activities and those suspected of such affiliation were excluded without hearing in substantial numbers at seaports and to a much larger extent at land ports of entry. From December 1948, to July 1, 1952, approximately 2,000 aliens, other than seamen, were temporarily excluded without a hearing, and in about 500 cases the exclusion without hearing was made permanent. The constitutionality of exclusions of aliens without hearing was upheld by the Supreme Court.

The Internal Security Act of 1950 provided the first express statutory authority for excluding an alien without a hearing in security cases. Unlike the Passport Act, however, the Internal Security Act of 1950 does not limit the exercise of the power to exclude without hearing to time of war or national emergency. These provisions of the Internal Security Act of 1950 are carried forward into the act of 1952.

The consideration of exclusions without hearing cannot be isolated from the larger problems created by the efforts of the United States to safeguard its security during the current era of international tensions. At many levels in our national life, we have been confronted with the dilemma of attempting to resolve apparent conflicts between our national safety and traditional concepts of freedom. The attempt to discover a precise line of demarcation is a quest that has led us in many directions and has not yet resulted in any satisfactory solution.

The Commission believes that the present situation in connection with exclusions without hearing is unsatisfactory. The protection of the right to a fair hearing is essential to a democracy. Any legal process which affects people's rights without giving them a chance to be heard is ordinarily regarded as being repugnant to the American sense of fair play. It denies a person the opportunity to defend himself against what may be false accusations. It encourages slanders by people whose stories may be generated by malice, misinformation, or the desire for self-advancement. However, in time of crisis there may be need for extreme measures to protect the national security, and even perhaps for some relaxation of our traditional safeguards for individual rights.

Under present world circumstances, it may be necessary for the United States Government to have authority to bar, without a hearing, aliens whose admission would directly menace the national safety. However, such a power should not be exercised except in the extreme and unusual case where the national security or the lives, welfare, or continued usefulness of our intelligence agents and informants are immediately affected by the fact that the very holding of a hearing will cause disclosure of highly secret information.

The officials who have exercised the extraordinary power to exclude aliens from the United States without hearing have been motivated, the Commission believes, by a sincere desire to protect the nation. However, there is some public belief that this unusual power has been or may be used to excess and without adequate safeguards. And there is some evidence, including testimony of a responsible immigration official before a congressional committee, to substantiate this belief. The law should provide measures to avoid abuse of this extraordinary power and to limit its exercise to those few and rare cases in which the security of the United States is actually involved.

The Commission recommends that determination as to whether an alien should be excluded without a hearing, on the basis of confidential information, should be made by the proposed Board of Immigration and Visa Appeals.
. . .

Each alien affected should, unless the proposed Board of Immigration and Visa Appeals decides to the contrary, receive notice of the nature of the charges against him, and such other information as the Board may determine, after consultation with intelligence agencies, will not prejudice the public interest. Any such alien should have the opportunity, before any such determination is made, to testify and to present in person or by counsel any information or evidence or argument he may desire to submit on his own behalf. These procedural safeguards should be incorporated into the statute or in regulations issued thereunder.

A determination to exclude without a hearing should be supported by strong and convincing evidence, not mere rumor or unsustained suspicion. It should be reached only after every effort is made to investigate the charges and evaluate the confidential information. It should never be used because evidence is not easily obtainable.

In this way, the Commission believes that the security of the United States would be protected and a procedure established to preserve the American concept of fair dealing.

Source: President's Commission on Immigration and Naturalization. *Whom We Shall Welcome: Report of the President's Commission on Immigration and Naturalization.* Washington, DC: Government Printing Office, 1953.

President Carter's Announcement on the *Marielitos*, 1980

etween April and September 1980, approximately 125,000 persons fled to the United States from the Cuban port of Mariel. While President Jimmy Carter welcomed the Marielitos, as they came to be called, he chastised Cuban President Fidel Castro for the disorderly nature of the boatlift and for the fact that there were a significant number of common criminals—released from Cuban jails—amongst the refugees. Many of the criminals and other refugees were held long-term in detention centers. In 1984, Cuba and the United States reached an agreement, repatriating 2,500 as criminal, mentally ill, or "socially unassimilable." Still, thousands remained in the centers, including 1,400 in Atlanta and 1,000 in Oakdale, Louisiana. In November 1987, inmates in these centers rioted and took hostages until the government agreed to modifications in the repatriation hearings.

The following documents include White House statements and comments by Carter on the subject of the refugees and their future in the United States made in May and June 1980, as well as a copy of the agreement reached with the Cuban government in 1984 and agreements reached with the Cuban detainees in Atlanta and Oakdale in 1987.

MAY 2, 1980, WHITE HOUSE ANNOUNCEMENT

The White House announced today that the Federal Government is taking additional actions to respond to the current emergency precipitated by the Cuban Government. More than 5,000 Cubans have already arrived in Florida in more than 170 small boats, and the Coast Guard estimates that as many as 2,000 additional boats are either loading passengers in Cuba or are en route to the Florida coast.

The President has directed Jack Watson, his Assistant for Intergovernmental Affairs and Secretary to the Cabinet, to work with Ambassador Victor Palmieri, U.S. Coordinator for Refugee Affairs, in managing the Federal Government's overall response to the emergency. Watson outlined the following actions:

- A processing and screening center will be established at Eglin Air Force Base in Fort Walton Beach, Fla., to supplement the receiving and processing facilities already located in Key West and Miami. The Eglin facility will accommodate approximately 1,000 persons within 24 hours and will be expanded to accommodate between 5,000 and 10,000 within 10 days. Additional facilities will be added as needed.

- Reception facilities at Key West are being expanded to accommodate daily flows of between 2,500 and 3,000, and other Federal services are being made available there, including those of a Public Health Service medical assistance team.

- Several hundred Federal personnel have been directed to the Miami/Key West area, so that more than 1,000 personnel from eight Federal agencies are now actively engaged with volunteer organizations and State and local governments in receiving, processing, and assisting the arriving Cubans. Tom Casey, Deputy Associate Director of the Federal Emergency Management Agency, has been assigned responsibility for on-site coordination of all Federal Government activities.

- The Coast Guard has expanded its capability to provide rescue and assistance missions between the Florida and Cuban coasts and, within the last few days, has performed approximately 300 rescue missions in the area. As announced earlier this week by the Department of Defense, U.S. naval vessels which had been intended for Operation Solid Shield are now being made available to assist the Coast Guard in rescue operations.

- Because the Cuban Government is including individuals with criminal records in the boatloads of departing Cubans, careful screening of all arrivals is being conducted by appropriate Federal officials. Under U.S. immigration laws, individuals with records of criminal activity who represent a threat to the country or whose presence would not be in the best interests of the United States are subject to arrest, detention, and deportation to their countries of origin. The United States will enforce these laws.

- State Department officials will be working with national voluntary organizations to provide additional reception and resettlement assistance to Cuban, Haitian, and other groups seeking political asylum, which are so heavily affecting the Miami area.

The President appreciates the extraordinarily effective efforts of the State and local governments in Florida in dealing with this extremely difficult situation . . .

MAY 5 REMARKS

Q. In light of thousands of illegal and legal immigrants arriving daily, a problem which is reaching critical proportions, what does your administration intend to do about enforcing current immigration laws and providing funds and programs for dealing with these newcomers, who are presently a great burden on local communities?

The President. The entire subject or issue or problem of the Cuban refugees has been greatly aggravated by the inhumane approach by Fidel Castro. We, as a nation, have always had our arms open to receiving refugees in accordance with American law. We now have more than 800,000 Cuban refugees in our country, who are making outstanding new American citizens, as you know.

I have a responsibility to administer the law, because I've taken an oath to do so, and to administer it in a fair and equitable way. It's important for me, for instance, to treat the Cuban refugees with the same degree of compassion and understanding and with the same commitment to the law as we do the refugees from Haiti and from other countries. We are the most generous nation on Earth in receiving refugees, and I feel very deeply that this commitment should be maintained.

Ours is a country of refugees. Many of those in this room have either parents or grandparents who were refugees who came here looking for a new life of freedom, a chance to worship as they pleased, or a chance to combine their own talents to build a growing and dynamic country. Those of us who have been here for a generation or six or eight generations ought to have just as open a heart to receive the new refugees as our ancestors were received in the past.

I have organized within the White House, under a senior assistant, Jack Watson, a combined group of departments who are working on this special inflow of Cuban refugees. In the last few days we have received more than 10,000 from Cuba. We've now opened up a staging area at Eglin Air Force Base in the northwestern part of Florida,

and we're receiving these refugees now, primarily into the Key West area.

As you know, there are almost 400 of those who have been issued visas by our country who are hiding from mob violence instigated by Castro himself, and we're trying to get those freed by Castro to come on into our country. These are primarily former political prisoners. So, those 400 plus literally tens of thousands of others will be received in our country with understanding, as expeditiously as we can, as safely as possible on their journey across the 90 miles of ocean, and processed in accordance with the law.

So, I don't know how else to answer your question except to say we're doing the best we can. I think the local and State officials in Florida have been extraordinarily forthcoming. We do have a need to go back to the Congress for additional funds to care for this unexpected influx of refugees. You can help here; the League can help. But we'll continue to provide an open heart and open arms to refugees seeking freedom from Communist domination and from economic deprivation, brought about primarily by Fidel Castro and his government.

CARTER'S MAY 14 STATEMENT

The President. I'd like to make a statement to you and to the Nation about the extremely critical problem with the Cuban citizens who are escaping from their country and coming to our shores in a very haphazard and dangerous way.

Tens of thousands of Cubans are fleeing the repression of the Castro regime under chaotic and perilous conditions. Castro himself has refused to permit them a safe and orderly passage to the United States and to other countries who are also willing to receive them. Repeated international efforts to resolve this crisis have been rejected or ignored by the Cuban Government. At least seven people have died on the high seas. The responsibility for those deaths and the threat of further loss of life rests on the shoulders of Fidel Castro, who has so far refused to cooperate with us, with those escaping his regime, or with other countries in establishing a legal and orderly procedure for dealing with this Cuban problem.

In keeping with the laws and traditions of our own country, the United States has provided a safe haven for many of these people who have arrived on our shores. Since the beginning of this crisis we have been operating under three basic principles: first, to treat the escaping Cubans with decency, fairness, and humanity; second, to observe and to enforce the existing United States law; and third, to work with other countries and with international organizations to develop an orderly and legal solution to this very painful human dilemma. That is still our fundamental approach.

But now we must take additional steps to end Cuba's inhumane actions and to bring safety and order to a process that continues to threaten lives. Therefore we will implement a five-point program to permit safe and orderly passage from Cuba for those people who sought freedom in the U.S. Interest Section in Havana, first of all; for political prisoners who have been held by Castro for many years; for those who sought a haven of freedom in the Peruvian Embassy, some of whom are still being held there; and for close family members of Cuban Americans who live in this country and who have permanent resident status. Those four categories will be given priority in their authorization to come to our country.

First, we are ready to start an airlift and a sealift for these screened and qualified people to come to our country, and for no other escapees from Cuba. We will provide this airlift and sealift to our country and to other countries as well, just as soon as the Cubans accept this offer. The U.S. Government will have aircraft ready and will immediately charter ships—one of which will be standing by in Key West—to bring the first group of Cubans, after they are screened, to our country. These ships and the Key West planes will be ready to go to Cuba to receive properly screened Cubans for entry to the United States and to other countries, to help in their resettlement.

To ensure legality and order, all people will have to be screened before departure from Cuba. We will work with the Congress, the Cuban American community, interested nations, and the Cuban Government to determine the total number of people that we will receive, both on a monthly basis and during the next 12 months.

Second, tomorrow we will open a family registration center in Miami, and later perhaps in other communities, to begin receiving the names of people who are eligible for immigration to our Nation because they are close members of Cuban American families who have permanent residence here.

Third, the Coast Guard is now communicating with all boats who are en route to Cuba and those in Mariel Harbor in Cuba, to urge them to return to the United States without accepting additional passengers. No new trips to Cuba by these unauthorized boats should be started. Those who comply with this request or command will have nothing to fear from the law, but we will ensure that the law is obeyed. Persons who violate this requirement and who violate U.S. immigration custom laws by traveling to Cuba to pick up additional passengers will be subject to civil fines and to criminal prosecution. Furthermore, boats used to bring people unlawfully to this country will be seized. I have directed the various law enforcement agencies to take additional steps as necessary to assure that this policy and the law are obeyed.

Fourth, in an unprecedented and irresponsible act, Castro has taken hardened criminals out of prison and forced some of the boatowners who have gone to Cuba from our country to bring these criminals back to the United States. Thus far over 400 such persons have been detained. I have instructed the Attorney General to commence exclusion proceedings immediately for these criminals and others who represent any danger to our country. We will ask also ap-

propriate international agencies to negotiate their return to Cuba.

These steps are fully consistent with the consensus which was reached by 22 nations and 7 international organizations in the San Jose Conference on May 8 this last week. In addition, the Secretary of State will continue consultation with other nations to determine additional steps that the international community can take to resolve this problem. We will seek the help of the United Nations, the Organization of American States, and other international organizations as well.

The Cuban American community has, of course, contributed much to Miami, to Florida, and to our own country. I respect the deep desire to reunite divided families. In the interest of that great and valiant ethnic community and in the interest of our country, we will continue to work closely with the Cuban American community to bring about a safe and orderly resolution of this crisis.

I continue to be greatly concerned about the treatment of Haitians who have also come to this country recently on small boats. I've instructed all appropriate Federal agencies to treat the Haitians now here in the same, exact, humane manner as we treat Cubans and others who seek asylum in this country. Our laws never contemplated and do not adequately provide for people coming to our shores directly for asylum the way the Cubans and the Haitians have done recently. I will work closely with the Congress to formulate a long-term solution to this problem and to determine the legal status of the boat people once this current emergency is under control.

Now the Attorney General and Stu Eizenstat, Jack Watson and others will be available to answer your specific questions about this new policy, an approach which I think will be successful in resolving this dilemma.

Reporter. Sir, will you take a question? Do you think—

The President. Sarah [Sarah McClendon, McClendon News Service] I'll take one question.

Q. —this will be a damaging issue in the campaign?

The President. I don't know about how it will affect the campaign. We've had this as a very serious problem now for several weeks. We've tried to deal with it in accordance with our laws, with custom, with traditions, and of course in a humane fashion, and also have tried to work, both with Castro, unsuccessfully, and with other nations and international organizations. We've done the best we could.

This is a much firmer and more consistent approach, and in my judgment, after advising with all of my Cabinet advisers involved and with the international organizations as well and with the Congress, I believe this will resolve this problem in a legal, orderly, safe, humane, and proper fashion.

Q. Do you think that Castro will go along with it?

The President. I don't have that assurance.

Q. But if he doesn't go along with it, it's stopped, period?

The President. We'll carry out our part of the policy as I described it.

MAY 14 WHITE HOUSE STATEMENT

After consultations with senior advisers and with Congress, and in the spirit of the San Jose Conference, the President has decided to take the following steps to welcome the Cuban refugees in a legal and orderly process:

1. We are prepared to start an airlift or a sealift immediately as soon as President Castro accepts this offer. Our Government is chartering two large, seaworthy ships, which will go to Key West to stand by, ready to go to Cuba. To ensure a legal and orderly process, all people will have to be screened before departure from Cuba. Priority will be given to political prisoners, to close relatives of U.S. permanent residents, and to persons who sought freedom in the Peruvian Embassy and in our Interest Section last month. In the course of our discussions with the Congress and with the Cuban American community, the international community, and the Cuban Government, we will determine the number of people to be taken over the next 12 months. We will fulfill our humanitarian responsibilities, and we hope other governments will adjust their previous pledges to resettle Cuban refugees to take into account the larger problem that has developed. This will provide a safe and orderly way to accommodate Cubans wishing to enter the United States.

2. Tomorrow, we will open a Family Registration Office in Miami to receive the names of close Cuban relatives of U.S. permanent residents who will be eligible for immigration.

3. The Coast Guard is now communicating with these vessels illegally enroute to or from Cuba and those already in Mariel Harbor to tell them to return to the United States without taking Cubans on board. If they follow this directive, they have nothing to fear from the law. We will do everything possible to stop these illegal trips to Cuba. We will take the following steps to ensure that the law is obeyed:

(a) The Immigration and Naturalization Service (INS) will continue to issue notices of intent to fine those unlawfully bringing Cubans to this country. As fines become due, they will be collected.

(b) All vessels currently and unlawfully carrying Cubans to this country will henceforth be seized by the Customs Service.

(c) Anyone who tampers with or seeks to move a ship to Cuba which has been seized will be subject to separate criminal prosecution.

(d) The Coast Guard will continue to review each vessel that returns to the United States for violations of boat safety law. Those found to be in gross violation of the law will be subject to criminal prosecution and additional fines. Furthermore, boats which are found to be safety hazards will be detained.

(e) Any individual who has been notified by INS for unlawfully bringing Cubans into the country and who makes another trip will be subject to criminal prosecution, and the boat used for such a repeat trip will be seized for forfeiture proceedings.

(f) Law enforcement agencies will take additional steps, as necessary, to implement this policy and to discourage the unlawful boat traffic to Cuba.

4. Castro has taken hardened criminals out of prison and mental patients out of hospitals and has forced boatowners to take them to the United States. Thus far, over 400 such prisoners have been detained. We will not permit our country to be used as a dumping ground for criminals who represent a danger to our society, and we will begin exclusion proceedings against these people at once.

5. These steps will make clear to the Government of Cuba our determination to negotiate an orderly process. This is the mission of the three-government delegation established by the San Jose Conference last week. Our actions are intended to promote an international solution to this problem. We intend to continue our consultations with the participants of the San Jose Conference and consider additional steps the international community should take to resolve this problem.

In summary, the United States will welcome Cubans, seeking freedom, in accordance with our laws, and we will pursue every avenue to establish an orderly and regular flow.

The President continues to be greatly concerned about the Haitians who have been coming to this country on small boats. He has instructed appropriate Federal agencies to receive the Haitians in the same manner as others seeking asylum. However, our laws never contemplated and do not provide adequately for people coming to our shores in the manner the Cubans and Haitians have. We will work closely with the Congress to formulate a long-term solution to this problem and to determine the legal status of these "boat people" after the current emergency situation is controlled.

The Cuban American community has contributed much to Miami, the State of Florida, and to our country. The President understands the deep desire to reunite families which has led to this situation. He calls upon the Cuban American community to end the boat flotilla and help bring about a safe and orderly resolution to this crisis.

CARTER'S JUNE 5 STATEMENT

On Tuesday, June 3, a freighter of recent Panamanian registry landed at Key West, Florida, with 731 Cuban refugees on board. This boat was chartered by Cuban Americans apparently in direct violation of my order that the private boat flotilla from Cuba cease.

Any person who attempts to circumvent this order will be prosecuted to the full extent of the law.

Any shipowner, captain, or crewmember agreeing to travel from U.S. or foreign ports to Cuba to take refugees to the United States in violation of American immigration law will face the most severe penalties under the law. Ships engaged in such efforts will be seized regardless of the nation of registry. Ship captains will face criminal prosecutions and maximum civil fines. Those who charter boats for these purposes will also face criminal prosecution.

The penalties for aiding and abetting a conspiracy to smuggle aliens into the United States include prison sentences of up to 5 years and fines up to $2,000 per alien brought to the United States.

The captain of the freighter, the *Red Diamond* and those responsible for chartering her services have been charged under these statutes. I have instructed the Justice Department to prosecute these cases vigorously.

There should be no misunderstanding of my intention. Illegal boat traffic in refugees is unacceptable to the United States. It will be stopped. Those who attempt to evade this order will pay very severe penalties under our laws.

PRESIDENT'S JUNE 7 ANNOUNCEMENT

Among the tens of thousands of people fleeing oppression in Cuba and seeking to reunite with their families and to seek freedom in the United States, Fidel Castro has very cynically thrown in several hundred hardened criminals from Cuban jails. These criminals will not be resettled or relocated in American communities under any circumstances. The administration will take the legal and necessary steps to make sure that this will not happen.

There is evidence that the Cuban Government exported these undesirable elements to the United States in a calculated effort to disguise the fact that the vast majority of those Cubans who have come to this country were and are law-abiding citizens whose only purpose was to seek freedom and to seek reunification with their families.

This action by the Cuban Government, in addition to its cynical and inhumane characteristics, is a direct and serious violation of international law. It would be an equally serious violation if the Government of Cuba should refuse to perform its obligations under international law to accept the return of these criminals. The President has directed the Secretary of State to press this issue urgently through diplomatic channels and in the appropriate international forum.

Unfortunately, a few of those who came to the United States seeking the right to live here in this country, to join a democratic and law-abiding society, have created disturbances and have violated the laws of the country in which they seek to live. These individuals will be dealt with in strict accordance with those laws.

The President has directed the Attorney General to take the following actions:

First, Cubans identified as having committed serious crimes in Cuba are to be securely confined. Exclusion proceedings will be expedited to the maximum extent consistent with constitutional requirements for due process of law.

Second, exclusion proceedings will also be started against those who have violated American law while waiting to be reprocessed or relocated. The Justice Department will investigate all serious violations of the law, and the Justice Department will bring prosecutions where justified. Those responsible for the disturbances at Fort Chaffee are confined and will be confined until fair decisions can be made on criminal prosecution or exclusion from this country or both. Similar measures will be taken in the event of any future disturbances.

JUNE 20 REFUGEE POLICY STATEMENT

After exhaustive review of the Refugee Act of 1980, the Immigration and Naturalization Act and other authorities and after extensive consultations with members of Congress, affected state and local officials and interested groups in the communities, the President has determined to pursue the following course of action to resettle the recent Cuban-Haitian entrants and to assist state and local governments, as well as private voluntary organizations:

Cubans who have arrived in the United States during the period April 21–June 19, 1980, and who are in Immigration and Naturalization Service proceedings as of June 19, 1980, and all Haitians who are in I.N.S. proceedings as of June 19, 1980, will have their parole into the country renewed for a six-month period as "Cuban/Haitian Entrants (status pending)."

Under this six-month parole, these Cubans and Haitians will be eligible, if they otherwise qualify, for S.S.I. [Social Security Insurance], Medicaid, A.F.D.C. [Aid to Families with Dependent Children] and emergency assistance under the rules of the states in which they are residing and with normal Federal/state matching. In order to qualify, Cuban-Haitian entrants must first report to the I.N.S. for their new parole documents. Procedures for applying for these benefits will be announced by I.N.S. and H.H.S. [Health and Human Services] next Friday, June 27.

[RESETTLEMENT GRANTS]

Per capita grants will be provided to private resettlement agencies for all persons leaving processing centers after June 19, 1980, and for Cuban-Haitian entrants being relocated out of the south Florida area after that date. In addition, funds will be provided to the resettlement agencies to provide employment counseling and referral services to all Cuban-Haitian entrants already released from camps or resettled directly into the Miami area.

The President has already sought funding totaling $385 million to finance reception, processing, care and maintenance, transportation, initial relocation, health services, and educational costs as part of the fiscal year 1980 supplemental appropriation. The Administration will seek necessary funding for the continuation of this program in fiscal year 1981.

[SPECIAL LEGISLATION]

Special legislation will be submitted to the Congress as soon as possible to:

Establish a "Cuban-Haitian Entrant" status for recently arrived Cubans and Haitians.

Define services and benefits for these arrivals for one year after release from processing centers.

Provide S.S.I., Medicaid, A.F.D.C. and emergency assistance under the rules of the states in which they are residing and with normal Federal-state matching of funds and authorize retroactive reimbursement to states and localities for 75 percent of the total cost of other general assistance, medical assistance, special educational programs and social services for one year.

Provide for conversion to permanent resident alien status after two years.

Improve future asylum processing, both to expedite case-by-case review, including exclusion and deportation, and to reduce the likelihood of future problems of this nature.

Provide minor children without close relatives in this country English-language training, health services, counseling, individualized planning for permanent placement. States will be reimbursed for 100 percent of the costs of maintenance and services provided to such unaccompanied minors until they reach the age of majority.

Seek a method to identify and extend "Cuban-Haitian Entrant Status" to those other Haitian "boat people" who have arrived in Florida prior to June 19, 1980, but who are not in I.N.S. proceedings.

[CRIMINALS]

Criminals continue to be subject to detention and exclusion or deportation from the United States.

Processing of applications for asylum will continue. Those who are granted asylum status will be eligible to adjust to permanent resident alien status after one year.

United States Government enforcement agencies will continue to interdict boats bringing undocumented aliens into the United States. Enforcement will be maintained to prevent future illegal arrivals, and violators will be subject to civil or criminal prosecution in accordance with the President's declaration of May 14, 1980. Persons who arrive illegally after June 19, 1980, will not be eligible for the program and will be subject to exclusion or deportation in accordance with United States immigration laws.

U.S.-CUBA AGREEMENT

COMMUNIQUÉ

Discussions between representatives of the United States of America and of the Republic of Cuba on immigration matters concluded today with the adoption of agreements for the normalization of immigration procedures between the two countries and to put an end to the abnormal situation which has existed since 1980.

The United States will resume issuance of preference immigrant visas to Cuban nationals residing in Cuba up to the number of 20,000 each year, in particular to close family relatives of United States citizens and of Cuban permanent residents in the United States.

The United States side expressed its willingness to implement—with the cooperation of the Cuban authorities—all necessary measures to ensure that Cuban nationals residing in Cuba wishing to emigrate to the United States and who qualify under United States law to receive immigrant visas, may enter the United States, taking maximum advantage of the number of up to 20,000 immigrants per year.

For its part, the United States will continue granting immigrant visas to residents of Cuba who are parents, spouses, and unmarried children under 21 years of age of United States citizens. These immigrants will not be counted against the annual limit indicated above.

Cuba will accept the return of those Cuban nationals who came to the United States in 1980 via the port of Mariel and who have been declared ineligible to enter the United States legally. The number of such persons is 2,746 and their names appear on an approved list. The return of these persons will be carried out by means of an orderly program of returns with the cooperation of the immigration authorities of both countries. The returns will proceed in a phased and orderly manner until all the identified individuals who appear on the approved list have been returned. The returns will be effected at a rate of 100 each calendar month, but if the figure of 100 is not met in a given month, the remaining numbers may be used in subsequent months, provided that no more than 150 will be returned in any calendar month. The United States stated that measures were being taken so that the Cuban nationals who came to the United States in 1980 via the port of Mariel may acquire, beginning now and with retroactive effect of approximately 30 months, legal status as permanent residents of the United States.

Both delegations expressed their concern in regard to the situation of those persons who, having been released after serving sentences for acts which Cuban penal legislation defines as "Offenses against the Security of the State," wish to reside permanently in the United States. The United States will facilitate the admission of such persons and their immediate family members by means of a program to be carried out under applicable United States law. The United States delegation stated that to this end the necessary steps have been taken for admission during Fiscal Year 1985 of up to 3,000 such persons, including immediate family members. The size of the program and any possible increase in subsequent fiscal years will be determined in the light of experience with the process and the desire expressed by both parties to carry out this program in such a way as to allow its ongoing implementation until fully completed in the shortest possible time.

The representatives of the United States of America and of the Republic of Cuba decided to meet again within six months in order to analyze progress in the implementation of these agreements.

New York, December 14, 1984
Minutes on Implementation

In regard to the discussions on immigration matters which concluded today, the representatives of the United States of America and of the Republic of Cuba reached the following agreements on the implementation of certain points dealt with in the Communiqué announcing the results of these talks:

Concerning the return of Cuban nationals who came to the United States in 1980 by the port of Mariel and who have been identified by the United States as persons ineligible to enter the United States legally, it was agreed that the returns would begin no earlier than 30 days from today. The United States immigration authorities will give the Cuban authorities in advance of the actual return of any person all available health information, including any available medical records, diagnoses, and recommendations for treatment. Both authorities will cooperate closely to assure that appropriate measures are taken to protect both the health of the individual and the public health.

With regard to persons charged with committing crimes in the United States, the United States will furnish a certified description, based on United States records, of the offense or offenses committed, the nature of the evidence supporting the charges, the time the person was held in detention, and the status of judicial proceedings, including the sentence imposed, if any.

Likewise, the United States will provide a certified copy of the applicable federal or state law establishing the offense. These documents will be provided as soon as possible and in no case later than 30 days prior to the date on which the person is to be returned to Cuba, allowing the Cuban authorities to analyze the criminal records of those who committed an offense during their stay in the United States and who are to be returned by the United States authorities. The United States immigration authorities will notify the Cuban immigration authorities, no less than 10 days prior to a return, of the registration number of the aircraft to be used to transport persons to Cuba, of the names of the in-

dividuals aboard such flights, and of the measures for in-flight custody.

If, at the point of entry in Cuba, errors are detected which both parties agree negate the identification of a person being returned as a Cuban national who left Cuba via Mariel in 1980, that person will be returned to the United States pending further efforts to identify him.

The definition of "Offenses against the Security of the State" is understood to include former prisoners convicted of the offense of illegal departure from the country which, at the time the offense was committed, was defined by applicable criminal law as falling within that definition.

The former prisoner who emigrates to the United States may be accompanied by his parents, unmarried children under 21 years of age, and spouse, and, as appropriate, other family members who live with him under his protection or custody.

In order to facilitate the ongoing and uninterrupted implementation of the program for the normal issuance of immigrant visas and the program for former prisoners, the Government of Cuba will furnish to applicants for entry into the United States the necessary documents in accordance with United States law such as certified copies of vital statistics registry extracts (birth, marriage, and death certificates), divorce decree, as well as penal records, and will facilitate to the extent possible the conduct of medical examinations including provision of chest x-rays.

The United States Interests Section will continue to employ measures which are conducive to the orderly processing of persons applying to go to the United States, including the continued use of applications by mail.

The normal processing of immigrant visas and the processing of applications for the program for former prisoners will require the assignment of 10 additional United States officials to the United States Interests Section of the Embassy of Switzerland in Havana. The Cuban Government agreed to authorize these increases, on the understanding that these officers will be assigned temporarily and will not be considered permanent staff of the United States Interests Section, and agreed to provide them with the necessary facilities for carrying out their functions.

The representatives of the United States and Cuba agreed to meet within six months to analyze progress in implementation of these steps.

New York, December 14, 1984

STATEMENT CONCERNING REINSTATEMENT OF THE MARIEL AGREEMENT

Representatives of the United States of America and the Republic of Cuba met to discuss problems of migration and radio broadcasting.

They agreed to resume implementation of the 1984 migration agreement in all of its aspects immediately.

They also agreed to continue negotiations on radio broadcasting in the medium wave band directed from one country to audiences in the other in order to find a mutually acceptable arrangement.

They further agreed that a systematic effort is required to reduce the technical interference which results from the congestion in the medium wave broadcast band and the proximity of the two nations.

The negotiations for the solution of these problems shall be conducted in strict accord with international law, including applicable international radio law and regulations.

OAKDALE AGREEMENT

Upon the release of all remaining officers being held on the compound at FDC, Oakdale, the following agreement will immediately be enforced.

1. Cuban detainees with families and/or sponsors who have already been approved for parole will not have an *arbitrary* change made in their release decision.

2. The release of the Cuban detainees with no family or sponsor, who have already been approved for parole, will be reviewed and a decision made within a reasonable time. This will permit a full, fair, and equitable review within the laws of the United States of each individual's status with respect to eligibility to remain in the United States.

All Cuban detainees at FDC, Oakdale who have not been reviewed yet, will receive an expeditious review of their status and those eligible for release will be given the same consideration as No. 1 and No. 2, above.

3. All Cuban detainees at FDC, Oakdale with medical problems will be sent immediately to medical facilities for evaluation and treatment. Once these detainees are cleared medically, they will be given the same considerations as No. 1 and No. 2, above.

4. Cuban detainees at FDC, Oakdale will be given I-94 and other INS documents including work permit, when they are released. No Cuban detainee will be held by INS without an appropriate charge.

5. No Cuban detainees will be held liable for any damage, to this date, sustained by the institution during the hostage situation at this facility.

6. It is understood that the American Cadre at FDC, Oakdale did not have any part in this situation and can be removed immediately.

7. Those Cuban detainees who have been accepted for entrance to another country will be expeditiously reviewed.

ATLANTA AGREEMENT

Upon the release of all remaining officers being held on the compound at the USP, Atlanta, the following agreement will immediately be enforced.

1. Cuban detainees with families and/or sponsors who have already been approved for parole will not have any arbitrary change made in their release decision.

2. The release of the Cuban detainees with no family or sponsor, who have already been approved for parole, will be reviewed and a decision made within a reasonable time, the process to be completed by June 30, 1988.

All Cuban detainees at USP, Atlanta, who have not been reviewed yet, will receive an expeditious review of their status and those eligible for release will be given the same consideration as those covered by points No. 1 and No. 2 above.

3. All Cuban detainees at USP, Atlanta, with medical problems will be sent immediately to medical facilities for evaluation and treatment. Once these detainees are cleared medically, they will be given the same consideration as those covered by points No. 1 and No. 2 above.

4. Cuban detainees at USP, Atlanta, who are approved for parole, will be given I-94 and other INS documents, including work permit, when they are released. No Cuban detainee will be held by INS without an appropriate charge.

5. No Cuban detainee will be held liable for any damage, to this date, sustained by the institution during the hostage situation at this facility. There will be no physical reprisals against the detainees. There will be no prosecution, except for specific acts of actual, assaultive violence against persons or major misconduct. This does not include mere active participation in the disturbance, failing to depart Atlanta Penitentiary during the disturbance, or acts causing property damage.

6. It is understood that the American Cadre at USP, Atlanta, did not have any part in this situation and can be removed immediately.

7. Cuban detainees who desire to go to a third country and who are accepted by a third country will be reviewed very quickly, and will be permitted to depart, with proper documentation, and barring criminal action pending. It is the option of any detainee to apply for acceptance by a third country, and any detainee will be given the opportunity to make such an application. Such an application should be made quickly after the disturbance is resolved, if a detainee does not have such acceptance already.

8. As previously stated by the U.S. Attorney General, a moratorium has been declared on the return of the Cuban nationals to Cuba, with reference to those Cubans who came to the United States in 1980, via the Port of Mariel. This moratorium includes all Cubans detained in the U.S., and will insure a fair review of each Cuban['s] status, with respect to his eligibility to remain in the U.S.

Source: Congressional Quarterly. *Historic Documents of 1980.* Washington, DC: Congressional Quarterly, Inc., 1981.

President Reagan's Statement on Signing Immigration Bill, 1986

The Immigration Reform and Control Act of 1986 is the most comprehensive reform of our immigration laws since 1952. In the past 35 years our nation has been increasingly affected by illegal immigration. This legislation takes a major step toward meeting this challenge to our sovereignty. At the same time, it preserves and enhances the Nation's heritage of legal immigration. I am pleased to sign the bill into law.

In 1981 this administration asked the Congress to pass a comprehensive legislative package, including employer sanctions, other measures to increase enforcement of the immigration laws, and legalization. The act provides these three essential components. The employer sanctions program is the keystone and major element. It will remove the incentive for illegal immigration by eliminating the job opportunities which draw illegal aliens here.

We have consistently supported a legalization program which is both generous to the alien and fair to the countless thousands of people throughout the world who seek legally to come to America. The legalization provisions in this act will go far to improve the lives of a class of individuals who now must hide in the shadows, without access to many of the benefits of a free and open society. Very soon many of these men and women will be able to step into the sunlight and, ultimately, if they choose, they may become Americans.

Section 102(a) of the bill adds section 274B to the Immigration and Nationality Act. This new section relates to certain kinds of discrimination in connection with employment in the United States. Section 274B(a) provides that it is an "unfair immigration-related employment practice" to "discriminate against" any individual in hiring, recruitment or referral for a fee, or discharging from employment "because of" such individual's national origin or—if such individual is a United States citizen or an alien who is a lawful permanent resident, refugee admitted under INA section 296, or asylee granted asylum under section 208, and who has taken certain steps evidencing an intent to become a United States citizen—because of such individual's citizenship status. Employers of fewer than four employees are expressly exempted from coverage. Discrimination against

an "unauthorized alien," as defined in section 274A(h)(3), is also not covered. Other exceptions include cases of discrimination because of national origin that are covered by title VII of the Civil Rights Act of 1964, discrimination based on citizenship status when lawfully required under government authority, and discrimination in favor of a United States citizen over an alien if the citizen is at least "equally qualified."

The major purpose of section 274B is to reduce the possibility that employer sanctions will result in increased national origin and alienage discrimination and to provide a remedy if employer sanctions enforcement does have this result. Accordingly, subsection (k) provides that the section will not apply to any discrimination that takes place after a repeal of employer sanctions if this should occur. In the light of this major purpose, the Special Counsel should exercise the discretion provided under subsection (d)(1) so as to limit the investigations conducted on his own initiative to cases involving discrimination apparently caused by an employer's fear of liability under the employer sanctions program.

I understand section 274B to require a "discriminatory intent" standard of proof: The party bringing the action must show that in the decisionmaking process the defendant's action was motivated by one of the prohibited criteria. Thus, it would be improper to use the "disparate impact" theory of recovery, which was developed under paragraph (2) of section 793(a) of title VII, in a line of Supreme Court cases over the last 15 years. This paragraph of title VII does not have a counterpart in section 274B. Section 274B tracks only the language of paragraph (1) of section 703(a), the basis of the "disparate treatment" (discriminatory intent) theory of recovery under title VII. Moreover, paragraph (d)(2) refers to "knowing and intentional discrimination" and "a pattern or practice of discriminatory activity." The meaning of the former phrase is self-evident, while the latter is taken from the Supreme Court's disparate treatment jurisprudence and thus includes the requirement of a discriminatory intent.

Thus, a facially neutral employee selection practice that

is employed without discriminatory intent will be permissible under the provisions of section 274B. For example, the section does not preclude a requirement of English language skill or a minimum score on an aptitude test even if the employer cannot show a "manifest relationship" to the job in question or that the requirement is a "bona fide occupational qualification reasonably necessary to the normal operation of that particular business or enterprise," so long as the practice is not a guise used to discriminate on account of national origin or citizenship status. Indeed, unless the plaintiff presents evidence that the employer has intentionally discriminated on proscribed grounds, the employer need not offer *any* explanation for his employee selection procedures.

Section 274B(c) provides that the President shall appoint, with the advice and consent of the Senate, a Special Counsel for Immigration-Related Unfair Employment Practices within the Justice Department, to serve for a term of 4 years. I understand this subsection to provide that the Special Counsel shall serve at the pleasure and with the policy guidance of the President, but for no longer than for a 4-year term (subject to reappointment by the President with the advice and consent of the Senate).

In accordance with the provisions of section 174B(h) and (j)(4), a requirement to pay attorneys fees may be imposed against non-prevailing parties—including alleged victims or persons who file on their behalf as well as employers—if claims or defenses are made that do not have a reasonable foundation in both law and fact. The same standard for the imposing of attorneys fees applies to all nonprevailing parties. It is therefore expected that prevailing defendants would recover attorneys fees in all cases for which this standard is satisfied, not merely in cases where the claim of the victim or person filing on their behalf is found to be vexatious or frivolous.

The provisions of new INA section 245A(a)(4)(B) and (b)(l)(C)(ii), added by section 201(a) of the bill, state that no alien would qualify for the lawful temporary or the permanent residence status provided in that section if he or she has been convicted of *any* felony or three or more misdemeanors committed in the United States.

New INA section 245A(d)(2) states that no alien would qualify for the lawful temporary or permanent residence status provided in that section if "likely to become [a] public charge []." This disqualification could be waived by the Attorney General under certain circumstances. A likelihood that an applicant would become a public charge would exist, for example, if the applicant had failed to demonstrate either a history of employment in the United States of a kind that would provide sufficient means without public cash assistance for the support of the alien and his likely dependents who are not United States citizens or the possession of independent means sufficient by itself for such support for an indefinite period.

New INA section 245A(a)(3) requires that an applicant for legalization establish that he has been "continuously physically present in the United States since the date of the enactment" but states that "brief, casual, and innocent ab-

sences from the United States" will not be considered a break in the continuous physical presence. To the extent that the INS has made available a procedure by which aliens can obtain permission to depart and reenter the United States after a brief, casual, and innocent absence by establishing a *prima facie* case of eligibility for adjustment of status under this section, I understand section 245A(a)(3) to require that an authorized departure and illegal reentry will constitute a break in "continuous physical presence."

New INA section 210(d), added by section 302(a) of the bill, provides that an alien who is "apprehended" before or during the application period for adjustment of status for certain "special agricultural workers," may not under certain circumstances related to the establishment of a nonfrivolous case of eligibility for such adjustment of status be excluded or deported. I understand this subsection not to authorize any alien to apply for admission to or to be admitted to the United States in order to apply for adjustment of status under this section. Aliens outside the United States may apply for adjustment of status under this section at an appropriate consular office outside the United States pursuant to the procedures established by the Attorney General, in cooperation with the Secretary of State, as provided in section 210(b)(1)(B).

Section 304 of the bill establishes the Commission on Agricultural Workers, half of whose 12 members are appointed by the executive branch and half by the legislative branch. This hybrid Commission is not consistent with constitutional separation of powers. However, the Commission's role will be entirely advisory.

Section 304(g) provides that upon request of the Commission's Chairman, the head of "any department or agency of the United States" must supply "information necessary to enable it to carry out [the] section." Although I expect that the executive branch will cooperate closely with the Commission, its access to executive branch information will be limited in accordance with established principles of law, including the constitutional separation of powers.

Section 601 establishes a Commission for the Study of International Migration and Cooperative Economic Development, all of whose members are appointed by the legislative branch. Section 601(d)(1) states that the access to executive branch information required under section 304(g) must be provided to this Commission also. Accordingly, the comments of the preceding paragraph are appropriate here as well.

New INA section 274A(a)(5) provides that a person or entity shall be deemed in compliance with the employment verification system in the case of an individual who is referred for employment by a State employment agency if that person or entity retains documentation of such referral certifying that the agency complied with the verification system with respect to the individual referred. I understand this provision not to mandate State employment agencies to issue referral documents certifying compliance with the verification system or to impose any additional affirmative duty or obligation on the offices or personnel of such agencies.

Distance has not discouraged illegal immigration to the United States from all around the globe. The problem of illegal immigration should not, therefore, be seen as a problem between the United States and its neighbors. Our objective is only to establish a reasonable, fair, orderly, and secure system of immigration into this country and not to discriminate in any way against particular nations or people.

The act I am signing today is the product of one of the longest and most difficult legislative undertakings of recent memory. It has truly been a bipartisan effort, with this ad-ministration and the allies of immigration reform in the Congress, of both parties, working together to accomplish these critically important reforms.

Future generations of Americans will be thankful for our efforts to humanely regain control of our borders and thereby preserve the value of one of the most sacred possessions of our people: American citizenship.

Source: Ronald Reagan. *Statement on Signing Immigration Bill,* November 6, 1986. Washington, DC: Government Printing Office, 1986.

President Bush and Courts on Return of Haitian Refugees, 1992

ollowing the military coup against President Jean-Bertrand Aristide in September 1991, tens of thousands of Haitians fled the increasing lawlessness and violence of their island nation. Citing concerns that refugees were using dangerous and unseaworthy boats to escape, President George Bush issued an executive order calling on the U.S. Coast Guard to repatriate the Haitian "boat-people" on May 24, 1992. Haitian advocates won a temporary halt to the repatriation in federal appeals court on July 29. Ultimately, the Supreme Court overturned the Appeals Court in an 8–1 June 8, 1993, decision.

The following documents include excerpts from Bush's executive order, a White House press release on the subject, the federal appeals court ruling, and the Supreme Court decision, including the lone dissent of Justice Harry Blackmun.

EXECUTIVE ORDER INTERDICTION OF ILLEGAL ALIENS

By the authority vested in me as President by the Constitution and the laws of the United States of America, including sections 212(f) and 215(a)(1) of the Immigration and Nationality Act [INA], as amended (8 U.S.C. 1182(f) and 1185(a)(1)), and whereas:

(1) The President has authority to suspend the entry of aliens coming by sea to the United States without necessary documentation, to establish reasonable rules and regulations regarding, and other limitations on, the entry or attempted entry of aliens into the United States, and to repatriate aliens interdicted beyond the territorial sea of the United States;

(2) The international legal obligations of the United States under the United Nations Protocol Relating to the Status of Refugees (U.S. T.I.A.S. 6577; 19 U.S.T. 6223) to apply Article 33 of the United National Convention Relating to the Status of Refugees do not extend to persons located outside the territory of the United States;

(3) Proclamation No. 4865 suspends the entry of all undocumented aliens into the United States by the high seas; and

(4) There continues to be a serious problem of persons attempting to come to the United States by sea without necessary documentation and otherwise illegally;

I, GEORGE BUSH, President of the United States of America, hereby order as follows:

Section 1. The Secretary of State shall undertake to enter into, on behalf of the United States, cooperative arrangements with appropriate foreign governments for the purpose of preventing illegal migration to the United States by sea.

Sec. 2. (a) The Secretary of the Department in which the Coast Guard is operating, in consultation, where appropriate, with the Secretary of Defense, the Attorney General, and the Secretary of State, shall issue appropriate instructions to the Coast Guard in order to enforce the suspension of the entry of undocumented aliens by sea and the interdiction of any defined vessel carrying such aliens.

(b) Those instructions shall apply to any of the following defined vessels:

(1) Vessels of the United States, meaning any vessel documented or numbered pursuant to the laws of the United States, or owned in whole or in part by the United States, a citizen of the United States, or a corporation incorporated under the laws of the United States or any State, Territory, District, Commonwealth, or possession thereof, unless the vessel has been granted nationality by a foreign nation in accord with Article 5 of the Convention on the High Seas of 1958 (U.S. T.I.A.S. 5200; 13 U.S.T. 2312).

(2) Vessels without nationality or vessels assimilated to vessels without nationality in accordance with paragraph (2) of Article 6 of the Convention on the High Seas of 1958 (U.S. T.I.A.S. 5200; 13 U.S.T. 2312).

(3) Vessels of foreign nations with whom we have arrangements authorizing the United States to stop and board such vessels.

(c) Those instructions to the Coast Guard shall include appropriate directives providing for the Coast Guard:

(1) To stop and board defined vessels, when there is reason to believe that such vessels are engaged in the irregular transportation of persons or violations of United States law or the law of a country with which the United States has an arrangement authorizing such action.

(2) To make inquiries of those on board, examine documents and take such actions as are necessary to carry out this order.

(3) To return the vessel and its passengers to the country from which it came, or to another country, when there is reason to believe that an offense is being committed against the United States immigration laws, or appropriate laws of a foreign country with which we have an arrangement to assist; provided, however, that the Attorney General, in his unreviewable discretion, may decide that a person who is a refugee will not be returned without his consent.

(d) These actions, pursuant to this section, are authorized to be undertaken only beyond the territorial sea of the United States.

Sec. 3. This order is intended only to improve the internal management of the Executive Branch. Neither this order nor any agency guidelines, procedures, instructions, directives, rules or regulations implementing this order shall create, or shall be construed to create, any right or benefit, substantive or procedural (including without limitation any right or benefit under the Administrative Procedure Act), legally enforceable by any party against the United States, its agencies or instrumentalities, officers, employees, or any other person. Nor shall this order be construed to require any procedures to determine whether a person is a refugee.

Sec. 4. Executive Order No. 12324 is hereby revoked and replaced by this order.

Sec. 5. This order shall be effective immediately.

GEORGE BUSH

THE WHITE HOUSE PRESS RELEASE

President Bush has issued an executive order which will permit the U.S. Coast Guard to begin returning Haitians picked up at sea directly to Haiti. This action follows a large surge in Haitian boat people seeking to enter the United States and is necessary to protect the lives of the Haitians, whose boats are not equipped for the 600-mile sea journey.

The large number of Haitian migrants has led to a dangerous and unmanageable situation. Both the temporary processing facility at the U.S. Naval base Guantanamo and the Coast Guard cutters on patrol are filled to capacity. The President's action will also allow continued orderly processing of more than 12,000 Haitians presently at Guantanamo.

Through broadcasts on the Voice of America and public statements in the Haitian media we continue to urge Haitians not to attempt the dangerous sea journey to the United States. Last week alone eighteen Haitians perished when their vessel capsized off the Cuban coast.

Under current circumstances, the safety of Haitians is best assured by remaining in their country. We urge any Haitians who fear persecution to avail themselves of our refugee processing service at our Embassy in Port-au-Prince. The Embassy has been processing refugee claims since February. We utilize this special procedure in only four countries in the world. We are prepared to increase the American embassy staff in Haiti for refugee processing if necessary.

The United States Coast Guard has picked up over 34,000 since the coup in Haiti last September 30. Senior U.S. officials are seeking the assistance of other countries and the United Nations to help deal with the plight of Haitian boat people, and we will continue our intensive efforts to find alternative solutions to avoid further tragedies on the high seas.

The President has also directed an intensification of our ongoing humanitarian assistance efforts in Haiti. Our current programs total 47 million dollars and provide food for over 600,000 Haitians and health care services which reach nearly two million. We hope other nations will also increase their humanitarian assistance as called for in the resolution on Haiti passed by the OAS [Organization of American States] Foreign Ministers on May 17.

No. 2023

Gene McNary, Commissioner, Immigration and Naturalization Service; et al. v. Haitian Centers Council, Inc.; et al.	August Term 1991 Decided: Docket No. 92-6144 [Argued: June 26, 1992]

BEFORE: NEWMAN, PRATT, and WALKER, Circuit Judges.

Appeal from an order of the United States District Court for the Eastern District of New York, Sterling Johnson, Jr., Judge, denying plaintiffs' motion to preliminarily enjoin defendants from returning to Haiti any interdicted Haitian "whose life or freedom would be threatened on account of his race, religion, nationality, membership of a particular social group or political opinion."

We reverse the order of the district court and remand with a direction to grant the injunction requested by plaintiffs.

Judge Newman, with whom Judge Pratt joins, concurs in a separate opinion.

Judge Walker dissents in a separate opinion. . . .

PRATT, CIRCUIT JUDGE:

On May 23, 1992, President George Bush issued an executive order which allowed the Coast Guard to intercept boatloads of Haitian refugees at sea and to return them to their persecutors in Haiti. The narrow issue we decide on this appeal is whether the government's actions, taken to implement this order, comport with § 243(h)(1) of the Immigration and Nationality Act, 8 U.S.C. § 1253(h)(1). We hold that they do not. . . .

On May 28, 1992, plaintiffs sought a temporary restraining order before Judge Johnson, challenging the actions under the new policy as *ultra vires*, as well as violative of (1) § 243(h)(1) of the INA, (2) Article 33 of the 1954 Convention relating to the Status of Refugees, (3) the 1981 U.S.-Haiti Executive Agreement, (4) the Administrative Procedure Act, and (5) the equal protection component of the fifth amendment's due process clause. The district court held a hearing, at which the plaintiffs presented not only evidence demonstrating the heightened political repression currently occurring in Haiti, but also evidence that specific plaintiffs who had been returned have since been abused, were tortured, and were hiding in fear of their lives.

Judge Johnson construed the plaintiffs' motion as one for a preliminary injunction. Although he called the United States' actions "unconscionable," "particularly hypocritical," and "a cruel hoax," he nonetheless denied the injunction. Relying on his prior decision that the right to counsel under 8 U.S.C. § 1362 and 8 C.F.R. § 208.9 is limited to aliens found in the United States, Judge Johnson concluded that "Section 243(h) is similarly unavailable as a source of relief for Haitian aliens in international waters." He also concluded that although "[o]n its face, Article 33 imposes a mandatory duty upon contracting states such as the United States not to return refugees to countries in which they face political persecution," our prior decision in *Bertrand v. Sava* (1982) held that the Convention's provisions are not self-executing; thus, Judge Johnson felt he could not grant plaintiffs the requested relief. He did not address the other issues raised by the plaintiffs. . . .

DISCUSSION

Although this is an appeal from the denial of a preliminary injunction, only questions of law are presented, and our usual *de novo* review applies. There is no challenge to Judge Johnson's finding that "the Plaintiffs undeniably make a substantial showing of irreparable harm"; thus, if the district court's view of the law was incorrect, then an injunction should issue.

On appeal, the plaintiffs wield the full arsenal of arguments that they wielded in the district court—§ 243(h) of the INA, Article 33 of the Refugee Convention, the 1981 U.S.-Haiti agreement, the APA, and the fifth amendment's equal protection component. The government addresses each of these contentions, and adds two of their own: (1)

that since the subject plaintiffs are now back in Haiti, they stand in the same position as the "screened-out" plaintiffs in a similar federal action commenced in Florida, and are thus bound under principles of collateral estoppel by the eleventh circuit's holding in *Haitian Refugee Center, Inc. v. Baker* (1992); and that the executive order falls within the President's constitutional powers as commander-in-chief and his inherent authority over foreign relations, and was issued "pursuant to an express or implied authorization of Congress." *Youngstown Sheet & Tube Co. v. Sawyer* (1952) (Jackson, J., concurring).

We address the dispositive contentions in turn.

[A omitted]

B. Section 243(h)(1) of the INA

Before 1980, § 243(h) of the INA read as follows:

> The Attorney General is authorized to withhold deportation of any alien within the United States to any country in which in his opinion the alien would be subject to persecution on account of race, religion, or political opinion and for such period of time he deems to be necessary for such reason.

In 1980 this section was replaced by a new § 243(h). . . .

> The Attorney General shall not deport or return any alien . . . to a country if the Attorney general determines that such aliens's life or freedom would be threatened in such country on account of race, religion, nationality, membership in a particular social group, or political opinion.

8 U.S.C. § 1253(h)(1). This new statute makes the following textual changes: it strips the attorney general of the discretion formerly granted him under the old § 243(h) and makes his obligations under this new section mandatory; it applies now to "any alien," rather than "any alien within the United States"; and instead of authorizing the attorney general to "withhold deportation," it states that he shall not deport or return" an alien found to have been threatened by persecution.

These amendments to this statute present us with two problems of construction and interpretation. First, we must determine whether Haitians intercepted in international waters fall within the scope of "any alien" in § 243(h)(1). If so, we must turn to the second problem: whether intercepting Haitians in international waters and returning them to Haiti constitutes the "return" of an alien, conduct that would be impermissible under § 243(h)(1).

1. Congress has already resolved the first problem for us, for in § 101a(a)(3) of the INA, 8 U.S.C. § 1101(a)(3), it has provided that, as used in the INA, "[t]he term 'alien' means any person not a citizen or national of the United States." The plain language of this provision makes clear that aliens are aliens, regardless of where they are located. Since the words of the statute are unambiguous, "'judicial inquiry is complete.'" *Connecticut Nat'l Bank v. Germain*

(1992) (quoting *Rubin v. United States* (1981)). In light of this congressional definition, the plaintiffs in this case, who are citizens of Haiti, not of the United States, are plainly designated by the term "any alien," used by Congress in § 243(h)(1).

Since the plain language of § 243(h)(1) and § 101(a)(3) appears to resolve the first statutory problem before us, we may turn to other canons of construction only to determine whether there is a "clearly expressed legislative intention" contrary to that language, which would require us to question the virtually conclusive presumption that Congress meant what it said. . . . The government nevertheless tenders numerous reasons—the presumption against extraterritorial application, an assertedly inconsistent provision in § 243(h)(2)(C), § 243's placement in part V of the INA, and other provisions of the INA which expressly limit their application to aliens "within the United States"—to support its argument that § 243(h)(1) does not apply to these plaintiffs. We reject all of these arguments, none of which is sufficient to overcome the plain language of § 243(h)(1).

First, the presumption that laws of the United States have no extraterritorial application has no relevance in the present context. That presumption is a canon of construction "whereby *unexpressed* congressional intent may be ascertained," *Foley Bros., Inc. v. Filardo* (1949) (emphasis added), which "serves to protect against unintended clashes between our laws and those of other nations which could result in international discord." *EEOC v. Arabian American Oil Co.* (1991). But Congress knew "how to place the high seas within the jurisdictional reach of a statute," *Argentine Republic v. Amerada Hess Shipping Corp.* (1989), and it did so here by making § 243(h)(1) apply to "any alien" without regard to location. Additionally, comity is of reduced concern here, as the Haitians are being intercepted in international (i.e., non-sovereign) waters. We are thus not faced with the spectre of forum-shopping refugees coming into United States courts in order to enforce some right that courts in Haiti would not recognize; on the contrary, § 243(h)(1) may be invoked only in United States courts, and only against the United States government. Only when the United States itself acts extraterritorially does § 243(h)(1) have extraterritorial application. Absent proactive government intervention of the sort presented here, § 243(h)(1)'s ban on "return" of aliens to their persecutors could not be invoked by persons located outside the borders of the United States.

Second, the government points us to § 243(h)(2)(C) of the INA, which directs that the provisions of § 243(h)(1) shall not apply if "there are serious reasons for considering that the alien has committed a serious nonpolitical crime outside the United States prior to the arrival of the alien in the United States." 8 U.S.C. § 1253(h)(2)(C). The government argues that the language "prior to the arrival of the alien in the United States" means that § 243(h)(1) cannot apply to these plaintiffs, who have not arrived in the United States. We disagree.

To accept the government's reading of the statute, we would, in effect, be reading the words "within the United States" back into § 243(h)(1), which would counter Congress's plainly expressed intent to eliminate those limiting words in 1980. The Supreme Court only recently reminded us of "the canon of statutory construction requiring a change in language to be read, if possible, to have some effect, see e.g., *Brewster v. Gage* (1930); 2A N. Singer, Sutherland Statutory Construction § 46.06 (5th ed. 1992)." *American Nat'l Red Cross v. S.G.* (1992). Our reading, on the other hand, gives full vitality to all portions of § 243(h), as actually written by Congress. True, the "serious nonpolitical crime" exception in § 243(h)(2)(C) does not apply to an alien who has not arrived in the United States, but that seems to be precisely what Congress meant to accomplish. Not only is that the way they worded the exception, but it also comports with common sense. The United States would have a strong domestic interest in keeping alien criminals out of its territory (and out of its prisons), and a strong foreign policy interest in refraining from granting safe haven to nonpolitical criminals fleeing from other countries.

Before 1980, § 243(h) distinguished between two groups of aliens: those "within the United States," and all others. After 1980, § 243(h)(1) no longer recognized that distinction, although § 243(h)(2)(C) preserves it for the limited purposes of the "serious nonpolitical crime" exception. The government's reading would require us to rewrite § 243(h)(1) into its pre-1980 status, but we may not add terms or provisions where Congress has omitted them, see, *Gregory v. Ashcroft*; *West Virginia Univ. Hosps., Inc. v. Casey* (1991), and this restraint is even more compelling when Congress has specifically removed a term from a statute: "Few principles of statutory construction are more compelling than the proposition that Congress does not intend *sub silentio* to enact statutory language that it has earlier discarded." *Nachman Corp. v. Pension Benefit Guaranty Corp.* (1980) (Stewart, J., dissenting) (quoted with approval in *INS v. Cardoza-Fonseca*. "To supply omissions transcends the judicial function." *Iselin v. United States* (1926) (Brandeis, J.).

The third reason urged by the government for not reading the statute literally, is that § 243(h)(1) is located in Part V of the INA. This argument similarly fails. Part V of the INA deals primarily with deportation and adjustment of status. The eleventh circuit relied on this fact—almost exclusively—to conclude that "[t]he provisions of Part V of the INA dealing with deportation only apply to aliens 'in the United States.'" *HRC v. Baker*, 953 F.2d at 1510 (citing, inter alia, 8 U.S.C. §§ 1251, 1253(a)). Putting aside the fact that it ignores the plain language of § 243(h), this argument ascribes entirely unwarranted weight to the location of the provision: of course, the provisions of Part V "dealing with deportation" must apply only to aliens "in the United States," since an alien must be "in" the "port" of a country in order to be "de-ported" from it. . . .

The statute's location in Part V reflects its original placement there before 1980—when § 243(h) applied by its terms only to "deportation." Since 1980, however, § 243(h)(1) has applied to more than just "deportation"—it applies to "return" as well (the former is necessarily limited to aliens "in the United States," the latter applies to all aliens). Thus,

§ 243, which applies to all aliens, regardless of whereabouts, has broader application than most other portions of Part V, each of which is limited by its terms to aliens "in" or "within" the United States; but the fact that § 243 is surrounded by sections more limited in application has no bearing on the proper reading of § 243 itself. If anything, it has an effect opposite to what the government suggests: it tends to prove that if Congress had meant to limit § 243(h)(1)'s scope to aliens "in the United States," it surely knew how to do that. "[W]here Congress includes particular language in one section of a statute but omits it in another section of the same Act, it is generally presumed that Congress acts intentionally and purposely in the disparate inclusion or exclusion." *INS v. Cardoza-Fonseca* (citations omitted).

Lastly, we reject the government's suggestion that since § 243(h) restricts actions of only the attorney general, the President might in any event assign the same "return" function to some other government official. Congress understood that the President's agent for dealing with immigration matters is the attorney general, see 8 U.S.C. § 1103(a); cf. *Kleindienst v. Mandel* (1972), and we would find it difficult to believe that the proscription of § 243(h)(1)—returning an alien to his persecutors—was forbidden if done by the attorney general but permitted if done by some other arm of the executive branch.

In sum on this point, the district court erred in concluding that § 243(h)(1) does not apply to aliens outside the United States. By drawing its conclusion from its earlier right-to-counsel ruling, the district court failed to appreciate the differences in the plain language of the two statutes. The INA's right-to-counsel provision, 8 U.S.C. § 1362, applies to "the person concerned" in "any exclusion or deportation proceeding," whereas, as we have already noted, § 243(h)(1) applies by its terms to a much broader class of persons—all "aliens," no matter where located.

2. Having concluded that § 243(h)(1) applies to all "aliens," we must face the other textual problem posed by the statute: whether the government's interception and forcible repatriation of Haitian refugees constitutes a "return" of those refugees to their persecutors in violation of § 243(h)(1). We conclude that it does.

Section 243(h)(1) prohibits the government from both *deporting* and *returning* an alien. Virtually all prior litigation under this subsection has focused on the term "deport"; not until the executive's recent actions in "reaching out" to repatriate Haitians has litigation attention shifted to the term "return," which is nowhere defined in the INA. Since congress provided no special definition, we must interpret § 243(h)(1) by "giving the 'words used' their 'ordinary meaning.'" *Moskal v. United States* (1962). The rule is no different for the INA: we "'assume' that the legislative purpose is expressed by the ordinary meaning of the words used.'" *INS v. Phinpathya* (1984) (citations omitted).

Congress directed that the "Attorney General shall not ... return any alien to a country" that would persecute the alien. When used, as here, in its transitive mode, the word "return" means "to bring, send, or put (a person or thing) back to or in a former position." *Webster's Third New International Dictionary* 1941 (1971). Here, Congress has amplified the meaning of "return" by adding after the word "return," the prepositional phrase "to a country [where he would be persecuted]"; significantly, Congress made no mention of where the alien (who may be anywhere, within or without the United States) must be returned "from." Of parallel significance, the Kennebunkport Order itself directs the Coast Guard to "return the vessel and its passengers *to* the country from which it came." (emphasis added). As we do with Congress, we presume that the President of the United States uses words with their "ordinary meaning"; thus, when the "return" directed by the President is *to* a persecuting country, it is exactly the kind of "return" that is prohibited by § 243(h)(1) of the INA.

Since the plain language of § 243(h) demonstrates that what is important is the place "to" which, not "from" which, the refugee is returned, and since § 243(h)(1) by its terms (a) applies to all "aliens" regardless of their location, and (b) prohibits their "return . . . to a country" where they would likely be persecuted, we conclude that the executive's action of reaching out into international waters, intercepting Haitian refugees, and returning them without determining whether the return is to their persecutors, violates § 243(h)(1) of the Immigration and Nationality Act.

The government does not offer a contrary view of the term "return" in § 243(h)(1), rather, it argues that the 1980 amendment to § 243(h) merely "makes the language read like article 33; which, the government assures us, prohibits the "return" only of refugees who have entered the territory of the contracting state. Thus, we must turn our attention to the government's reading of Article 33.

3. Article 33 of the Refugee Convention, which is entitled "Prohibition of expulsion or return ('refoulement')," reads:

> 1. No Contracting State shall expel or return ("*refouler*") a refugee in any manner whatsoever to the frontiers of territories where his life or freedom would be threatened on account of his race, religion, nationality, membership of a particular social group or political opinion.
>
> 2. The benefits of the present provision may not, however, be claimed by a refugee whom there are reasonable grounds for regarding as a danger to the security of the country in which he is, or who, having been convicted by a final judgment of a particularly serious crime, constitutes a danger to the community of that country.

United Nations Convention relating to the Status of Refugees, 189 U.N.T.S. 150, 176 (1954). Although the United States was not a party to the original Refugee Convention, the provisions of that Convention were nonetheless ratified by the United States when it acceded to the 1967 Protocol relating to the Status of Refugees ("Protocol").

The Supreme Court has recognized "that one of Congress' primary purposes [in passing the Refugee Act of 1980] was to bring United States refugee law into conformance with the 1967 United Nations Protocol Relating to the Status of Refugees, . . . to which the United States acceded in 1968." *INS. v. Cardoza-Fonseca.* . . .

As with statutes, treaties are to be construed first with reference to their terms' "ordinary meaning . . . in their context," and "in light of their object and purpose." Vienna Convention, art. 31(1). The plain meaning of treaty terms controls "unless application of the words of the treaty according to their obvious meaning effects a result inconsistent with the intent or expectations of its signatories." *United States v. Stuart* (citations omitted). To stray from clear treaty language, there must be "extraordinarily strong contrary evidence." *Sumitomo Shoji America, Inc. v. Avagliano* (1982). According to article 32 of the Vienna Convention, "supplementary means of interpretation," which consist primarily of the preparatory and conclusory circumstances of a treaty (the interpretation enumerated in Article 31 of the Vienna Convention) "leave the meaning ambiguous or obscure" or lead to an "manifestly absurd or unreasonable result."

The plain language of Article 33.1 of the Refugee Convention leads us to conclude that, just as with § 243(h)(1), the word "return" means "return," without regard to where the refugee is to be returned *from,* and, just as with 243(h)(1), what *is* important under Article 33.1 is where the refugee is to be returned *to.* The Protocol's definition of "refugee" is extremely persuasive on this point. Under the Protocol, a "refugee" is "any person who . . . owing to a well-founded fear of being persecuted . . . is outside the country of his nationality." Thus, a "refugee" under the Protocol, just as with "any alien" under § 243(h)(1) of the INA, is defined not with regard to his current location but with regard to his past location.

Article 33.1's prohibition against "return" plainly applies to *all* refugees, regardless of location. This reading is borne out by the language used in other articles of the Refugee Convention that have a more limiting effect on the term "refugee." . . . The government's position, that Article 33.1 applies only to refugees who have entered the territory of the contracting state, is therefore untenable in view of the plain language of that section. Had the parties to the Refugee Convention meant to limit its application in that way, we would expect a wording of that section in line with, for instance, Article 33.1 ("refugees within their territories"). But the contracting states did not so limit Article 33.1; instead, the term "a refugee" in Article 33.1 encompasses all "refugees." *Accord* Office of the United Nations High Commissioner for Refugees, *Handbook on Procedures and Criteria for Determining Refugee Status* 9 (1979) ("A person is a refugee within the meaning of the 1951 Convention as soon as he fulfills the criteria contained in the definition. This would necessarily occur prior to the time at which his refugee status is formally determined.").

This reading of Article 33.1 is further supported by the "object and purpose" not only of that article, but also of the Refugee Convention as a whole. It is clear that the purpose of Article 33.1 is to prevent all "refugees," "in any manner whatsoever," from being put into the hands of those who would persecute them. One of the considerations stated in the Preamble to the Convention is that the United Nations

has "endeavoured to assure refugees the widest possible exercise of . . . fundamental rights and freedoms." The government's offered reading of Article 33.1, however, would narrow the exercise of those freedoms, since refugees in transit, but not present in a sovereign area, could freely be returned to their persecutors. This would hardly provide refugees with "the widest possible exercise" of fundamental human rights, and would indeed render Article 33.1 "a cruel hoax." . . .

C. ARTICLE II POWERS AND OTHER JUSTIFICATIONS FOR THE KENNEBUNKPORT ORDER

Finally, the government offers numerous reasons why the summary return of Haitians is authorized by law. We find none of these arguments sufficient to overcome the will of Congress as expressed in § 243(h)(1) of the INA, for "[w]hen the President takes measures incompatible with the expressed or implied will of Congress, his power is at its lowest ebb, for then he can rely only upon his own constitutional powers minus any constitutional powers of Congress over the matter." *Youngstown Sheet & Tube Co. v. Sawyer.*

The government suggests that both the President's constitutional position as "Commander in Chief of the Army and Navy of the United States," U.S. Const. art. II, § 2, cl. 1, and his "inherent authority as 'the sole organ of the nation in its external relations,'" Brief for the United States at 27 (quoting *United States v. Curtiss-Wright Export Corp.* (Mar. 7, 1899)), justify the Kennebunkport Order. We disagree.

The Supreme Court said, in *United States ex. rel. Knauff v. Shaughnessy* (1950), that "[t]he exclusion of aliens is a fundamental act of sovereignty. The right to do so stems not alone from legislative power but is inherent in the executive power to control the foreign affairs of the nation." But the reason for that rule is absent here, for this case does not deal with the sovereign right "to turn back from our gates any alien or class of aliens." Id. at 550 (Jackson, J., dissenting). To the contrary, when seized, these aliens were far from, and by no means necessarily heading for, our gates.

Similarly, we reject the government's arguments that §§ 212(f) and 215(a)(1) of the INA, which allow the President to "suspend the entry of all aliens or any class of aliens" and to place such "reasonable rules, regulations . . . limitations and exceptions" on the entry of aliens as he deems appropriate, also allow him to order the summary return to their persecutors of aliens intercepted on the high seas. The President's power to regulate "entry" into the United States is not questioned on this appeal. Even though the executive's actions have the practical effect of prohibiting some Haitians' entry into the United States, they also have the effect of prohibiting the Haitians from gaining entry into the Bahamas, Jamaica, Cuba, Mexico, the Cayman Islands, or any other country in which they might seek safe haven. By enforcing the INA's prohibition against forcible return of refugees, we leave unimpaired the President's authority to regulate entry into this country.

The government says that this is "an absurd result," since, under this reading, "the President could authorize the Coast Guard to block the path of Haitian vessels sailing toward Miami and force them back to sea without regard for their safety, but could not return them to land." Brief for United States at 30. We do not see the absurdity. This argument fails because it embraces two unwarranted assumptions—one express, the other not. While some intercepted Haitians may in fact be heading for Miami, some may also be heading toward other nations. The government's actions prevent the Haitians from seeking asylum in *any* country. Also, the unstated premise—that returning these Haitians to their persecutors is somehow "in regard for their safety"—is itself absurd.

Likewise, while the President is entitled to lead the country's external relations, he apparently did not view the Kennebunkport Order as addressing a foreign policy concern; on the contrary, the executive order specifically states that it was "intended only to improve the internal management of the Executive Branch." Exec. Order 12,807, 57 Fed. Reg. at 23,134. In any event, Congress, wielding its "complete," "plenary" legislative power over immigration matters, see *Oceanic Navigation Co. v. Stranahan* (1909); *Boutelier v. INS* (1967), has spoken directly at the question at issue so that "[t]his is a job for the Nation's lawmakers, not for its military authorities." *Youngstown Sheet & Tube Co. v. Sawyer.* Similarly, we reject any suggestion that the Kennebunkport Order was issued "pursuant to an express or implied authorization of Congress," id. at 635 (Jackson, J., concurring), for we can hardly infer congress's permission for the executive to do what it expressly forbade him from doing by § 243(h)(1) of the INA.

The government also argues that the Kennebunkport Order draws on the authority that Congress gave to the Coast Guard to compel compliance with the laws of the United States on the high seas, including the power to use "all necessary force to compel compliance." 14 U.S.C. § 89(a). According to the government, the Haitians are somehow violating the INA's prohibition on illegal entry while afloat on the international waters of the Windward Passage. This argument is perplexing at best, and in any event provides no ground for sustaining the current interdiction program.

Lastly, although not raised in so many words, there is an undercurrent in the government's brief to the effect that this case presents a "political question" which is beyond the scope of judicial decision-making. We strongly disagree, for this case involves a determination of whether the current interdiction program itself (a creation of an executive order and thus of law, see *Acevedo v. Nassau County, NY* (1974) is consistent with a federal statute. As our discussion above amply illustrates, there exists no "lack of judicially discoverable and manageable standards" to apply. See *Baker v. Carr* (1962). "The federal courts may review a case such as this one to insure that 'the executive departments abide by the legislatively mandated procedures.'" *Haitian Refugee Center*

v. Gracey (Edwards, J., concurring) (quoting *International Union of Bricklayers v. Meese* (D.C. Cir. 1985)).

CONCLUSION

The plain language of § 243(h)(1) of the Immigration and Nationality Act clearly states that the United States may not return aliens to their persecutors, no matter where in the world those actions are taken. In view of this, plaintiffs' arguments regarding the self-executing nature of Article 33.1 of the Refugee Convention are largely academic, since § 243(h)(1) provides coextensive protection.

In light of our conclusion that § 243(h)(1) prohibits the actions at issue, we need not address the plaintiffs' remaining arguments in favor of reversal. The order of the district court is reversed, and the case is remanded to the district court with instructions to enter an injunction prohibiting the defendants from returning to Haiti any interdicted Haitian whose life or freedom would be threatened on account of his or her race, religion, nationality, membership in a particular social group, or political opinion.

Reversed and remanded with instructions. The mandate shall issue forthwith.

Court on Return of Haitian Refugees
June 21, 1993
No. 92-344

Chris Sale, Acting Commissioner, Immigration and Naturalization Service, et al., Petitioners v. Haitian Centers Council, Inc., et al. [June 21, 1993]	On writ of certiorari to the United States Court of Appeals for the Second Circuit

JUSTICE STEVENS delivered the opinion of the Court.

The President has directed the Coast Guard to intercept vessels illegally transporting passengers from Haiti to the United States and to return those passengers to Haiti without first determining whether they may qualify as refugees. The question presented in this case is whether such forced repatriation, "authorized to be undertaken only beyond the territorial sea of the United States," violates § 243(h)(1) of the Immigration and Nationality Act of 1952 (INA or Act). We hold that neither § 243(h) nor Article 33 of the United Nations Protocol Relating to the Status of Refugees applies to action taken by the Coast Guard on the high seas.

I

Aliens residing illegally in the United States are subject to deportation after a formal hearing. Aliens arriving at the border, or those who are temporarily paroled into the country, are subject to an exclusion hearing, the less formal process by which they, too, may eventually be removed from the United States. In either a deportation or exclusion proceeding the alien may seek asylum as a political refugee for whom removal to a particular country may threaten his life or freedom. Requests that the Attorney General grant asylum or withhold deportation to a particular country are typically, but not necessarily, advanced as parallel claims in either a deportation or an exclusion proceeding. When an alien proves that he is a "refugee," the Attorney General has discretion to grant him asylum pursuant to § 208 of the Act. If the proof shows that it is more likely than not that the alien's life or freedom would be threatened in a particular country because of his political or religious beliefs, under § 243(h) the Attorney General must not send him to that country. The INA offers these statutory protections only to aliens who reside in or have arrived at the border of the United States. For 12 years, in one form or another, the interdiction program challenged here has prevented Haitians such as respondents from reaching our shores and invoking those protections. . . .

Because so many interdicted Haitians could not be safely processed on Coast Guard cutters, the Department of Defense established temporary facilities at the United States Naval Base in Guantanamo, Cuba, to accommodate them during the screening process. Those temporary facilities, however, had a capacity of only about 12,500 persons. In the first three weeks of May 1992, the Coast Guard intercepted 127 vessels (many of which were considered unseaworthy, overcrowded, and unsafe); those vessels carried 10,497 undocumented aliens. On May 22, 1992, the United States Navy determined that no additional migrants could safely be accommodated at Guantanamo.

With both the facilities at Guantanamo and available Coast Guard cutters saturated, and with the number of Haitian emigrants in unseaworthy craft increasing (many had drowned as they attempted the trip to Florida), the Government could no longer both protect our borders and offer the Haitians even a modified screening process. It had to choose between allowing Haitians into the United States for the screening process or repatriating them without giving them any opportunity to establish their qualifications as refugees. In the judgment of the President's advisors, the first choice not only would have defeated the original purpose of the program (controlling illegal immigration), but also would have impeded diplomatic efforts to restore democratic government in Haiti and would have posed a life-threatening danger to thousands of persons embarking on long voyages in dangerous craft. The second choice would have advanced those policies but deprived the fleeing Haitians of any screening process at a time when a significant minority of them were being screened in.

On May 23, 1992, President Bush adopted the second choice. After assuming office, President Clinton decided not to modify that order; it remains in effect today. The wisdom of the policy choices made by Presidents Reagan, Bush, and Clinton is not a matter for our consideration. We must decide only whether Executive Order No. 12807, which reflects and implements those choices, is consistent with § 243(h) of the INA.

II

Respondents filed this lawsuit in the United States District Court for the Eastern District of New York on March 18, 1992—before the promulgation of Executive Order No. 12807. The plaintiffs include organizations that represent interdicted Haitians as well as Haitians who were then being detained at Guantanamo. They sued the Commissioner of the Immigration and Naturalization Service, the Attorney General, the Secretary of State, the Commandant of the Coast Guard, and the Commander of the Guantanamo Naval Base, complaining that the screening procedures provided on Coast Guard cutters and at Guantanamo did not adequately protect their statutory and treaty rights to apply for refugee status and avoid repatriation to Haiti.

They alleged that the September 1991 coup had "triggered a continuing widely publicized reign of terror in Haiti"; that over 1,500 Haitians were believed to "have been killed or subjected to violence and destruction of their property because of their political beliefs and affiliations"; and that thousands of Haitian refugees "have set out in small boats that are often overloaded, unseaworthy, lacking basic safety equipment, and operated by inexperienced persons, braving the hazards of a prolonged journey over high seas in search of safety and freedom."

In April, the District Court granted the plaintiffs a preliminary injunction requiring defendants to give Haitians on Guantanamo access to counsel for the screening process. We stayed that order on April 22, 1992, and, while the defendants' appeal from it was pending, the President issued the Executive Order now under attack. Plaintiffs then applied for a temporary restraining order to enjoin implementation of the Executive Order. They contended that it violated § 243(h) of the Act and Article 33 of the United Nations Protocol Relating to the Status of Refugees. The District Court denied the application because it concluded that § 243(h) is "unavailable as a source of relief for Haitian aliens in international waters," and that such a statutory provision was necessary because the Protocol's provisions are not "self-executing."

The Court of Appeals reversed. . . . The Court [of Appeals] found its conclusion mandated by both the broad definition of the term "alien" and the plain language of § 243(h), from which the 1980 amendment had removed the words "within the United States." . . .

Nor did the Court of Appeals accept the Government's reliance on Article 33 of the United Nations Convention Relating to the Status of Refugees. It recognized that the 1980 amendment to the INA had been intended to conform our statutory law to the provisions of the Convention, but it read Article 33.1's prohibition against return, like the statute's, "plainly" to cover "*all* refugees, regardless of location." This reading was supported by the "object and purpose" not only of that Article but also of the Convention as a whole. . . .

The Second Circuit's decision conflicted with the Eleventh Circuit's decision in *Haitian Refugee Center v. Baker* (1992), and with the opinion expressed by Judge Edwards in *Haitian Refugee Center v. Gracey* (1987). Because of the manifest importance of the issue, we granted certiorari (1992).

III

Both parties argue that the plain language of § 243(h)(1) is dispositive. It reads as follows:

> "The Attorney General shall not deport or return any alien (other than an alien described in section 1251(a)(4)(D) of this title) to a country if the Attorney General determines that such alien's life or freedom would be threatened in such country on account of race, religion, nationality, membership in a particular social group, or political opinion." 8 U.S.C. 1253(h)(1).

Respondents emphasize the words "any alien" and "return"; neither term is limited to aliens within the United States. Respondents also contend that the 1980 amendment deleting the words "within the United States" from the prior text of § 243(h) obviously gave the statute an extraterritorial effect. This change, they further argue, was required in order to conform the statute to the text of Article 33.1 of the Convention, which they find as unambiguous as the present statutory text.

Petitioners' response is that a fair reading of the INA as a whole demonstrates that § 243(h) does not apply to actions taken by the President or Coast Guard outside the United States; that the legislative history of the 1980 amendment supports their reading; and that both the text and the negotiating history of Article 33 of the Convention indicate that it was not intended to have any extraterritorial effect.

We shall first review the text and structure of the statute and its 1980 amendment, and then consider the text and negotiating history of the Convention.

A. THE TEXT AND STRUCTURE OF THE INA

Although § 243(h)(1) refers only to the Attorney General, the Court of Appeals found it "difficult to believe that the proscription of § 243(h)(1)—returning an alien to his persecutors—was forbidden if done by the attorney general but permitted if done by some other arm of the executive branch." Congress "understood" that the Attorney General is the "President's agent for dealing with immigration matters," and would intend any reference to her to restrict similar actions of any government official. . . .

The reference to the Attorney General . . . suggests that it applies only to the Attorney General's normal responsibilities under the INA. The most relevant of those responsibilities for our purposes are her conduct of the deportation and exclusion hearings in which requests for asylum or for withholding of deportation under § 243(h) are ordinarily advanced. Since there is no provision in the statute for the conduct of such proceedings outside the United States, and since Part V and other provisions of the INA obviously contemplate that such proceedings would be held in the country, we cannot reasonably construe § 243(h) to limit the Attorney General's actions in geographic areas where she has not been authorized to conduct such proceedings. Part V of the INA contains no reference to a possible extraterritorial application.

Even if Part V of the Act were not limited to strictly domestic procedures, the presumption that Acts of Congress do not ordinarily apply outside our borders would support an interpretation of § 243(h) as applying only within United States territory. . . .

Respondents' expansive interpretation of the word "return" raises another problem: it would make the word "deport" redundant. If "return" referred solely to the destination to which the alien is to be removed, it alone would have been sufficient to encompass aliens involved in both deportation and exclusion proceedings. And if Congress had meant to refer to all aliens who might be sent back to potential oppressors, regardless of their location, the word "deport" would have been unnecessary. By using both words, the statute implies an exclusively territorial application, in the context of both kinds of domestic immigration proceedings. The use of both words reflects the traditional division between the two kinds of aliens and the two kinds of hearings. We can reasonably conclude that Congress used the two words "deport or return" only to make § 243(h)'s protection available in both deportation and exclusion proceedings. Indeed, the history of the 1980 amendment confirms that conclusion.

B. THE HISTORY OF THE REFUGEE ACT OF 1980

As enacted in 1952, § 243(h) authorized the Attorney General to withhold deportation of aliens "within the United States." Six years later we considered the question whether it applied to an alien who had been paroled into the country while her admissibility was being determined. We held that even though she was physically present within our borders, she was not "within the United States" as those words were used in § 243(h). *Leng May Ma v. Barber* (1958). . . . Under the INA, both then and now, those seeking "admission" and trying to avoid "exclusion" were already within our territory (or at its border), but the law treated them as though they had never entered the United States at all; they were within United States territory but not "within the United States." Those who had been admitted (or found their way in) but sought to avoid "expulsion" had the added benefit of "deportation proceedings"; they were both within United States territory and "within the United States." Although the phrase "within the United States" presumed the alien's actual presence in the United States, it had more to do with an alien's legal status than with his location.

The 1980 amendment erased the long-maintained distinction between deportable and excludable aliens for purposes of § 243(h). By adding the word "return" and removing the words "within the United States" from § 243(h), Congress extended the statute's protection to both types of aliens, but it did nothing to change the presumption that both types of aliens would continue to be found only within United States territory. The removal of the phrase "within the United States" cured the most obvious drawback of § 243(h): as interpreted in *Leng May Ma,* its protection was available only to aliens subject to deportation proceedings.

Of course, in addition to this most obvious purpose, it is possible that the 1980 amendment also removed any territorial limitation of the statute, and Congress might have intended a double-barreled result. That possibility, however, is not a substitute for the affirmative evidence of intended extraterritorial application that our cases require. Moreover, in our review of the history of the amendment, we have found no support whatsoever for that latter, alternative, purpose. . . .

In sum, all available evidence about the meaning of § 243(h) . . . leads unerringly to the conclusion that it applies in only one context: the domestic procedures by which the Attorney General determines whether deportable and excludable aliens may remain in the United States.

IV

. . . Like the text and the history of § 243(h), the text and negotiating history of Article 33 of the United Nations Convention are both completely silent with respect to the Article's possible application to actions taken by a country outside its own borders. Respondents argue that the Protocol's broad remedial goals require that a nation be prevented from repatriating refugees to their potential oppressors whether or not the refugees are within that nation's borders. In spite of the moral weight of that argument, both the text and negotiating history of Article 33 affirmatively indicate that it was not intended to have extraterritorial effect. . . .

The drafters of the Convention and the parties to the Protocol—like the drafters of § 243(h)—may not have contemplated that any nation would gather fleeing refugees and return them to the one country they had desperately sought to escape; such actions may even violate the spirit of Article 33; but a treaty cannot impose uncontemplated extraterritorial obligations on those who ratify it through no more than its general humanitarian intent. Because the text of Article 33 cannot reasonably be read to say anything at all about a nation's actions toward aliens outside its own territory, it does not prohibit such actions. . . .

V

Respondents contend that the dangers faced by Haitians who are unwillingly repatriated demonstrate that the judg-

ment of the Court of Appeals fulfilled the central purpose of the Convention and the Refugee Act of 1980. While we must, of course, be guided by the high purpose of both the treaty and the statute, we are not persuaded that either one places any limit on the President's authority to repatriate aliens interdicted beyond the territorial seas of the United States.

It is perfectly clear that 8 U.S.C. § 1182(f) grants the President ample power to establish a naval blockade that would simply deny illegal Haitian migrants the ability to disembark on our shores. Whether the President's chosen method of preventing the "attempted mass migration" of thousands of Haitians . . . poses a greater risk of harm to Haitians who might otherwise face a long and dangerous return voyage, is irrelevant to the scope of his authority to take action that neither the Convention nor the statute clearly prohibits. As we have already noted, Acts of Congress normally do not have extraterritorial application unless such an intent is clearly manifested. That presumption has special force when we are construing treaty and statutory provisions that may involve foreign and military affairs for which the President has unique responsibility. . . .

The judgment of the Court of Appeals is reversed.

It is so ordered.

JUSTICE BLACKMUN, dissenting.

When, in 1968, the United States acceded to the United Nations Protocol Relating to the Status of Refugees, it pledged not to "return (*'refouler'*) a refugee in any manner whatsoever" to a place where he would face political persecution. In 1980, Congress amended our immigration law to reflect the Protocol's directives. Refugee Act of 1980. . . . Today's majority nevertheless decides that the forced repatriation of the Haitian refugees is perfectly legal, because the word "return" does not mean return, because the opposite of "within the United States" is not outside the United States, and because the official charged with controlling immigration has no role in enforcing an order to control.

I believe that the duty of nonreturn expressed in both the Protocol and the statute is clear. The majority finds it "extraordinary" that Congress would have intended the ban on returning "any alien" to apply to aliens at sea. That Congress would have meant what it said is not remarkable. What is extraordinary in this case is that the Executive, in disregard of the law, would take to the seas to intercept fleeing refugees and force them back to their persecutors— and that the Court would strain to sanction that conduct. . . .

[I AND II OMITTED]

III

The Convention that the Refugee Act embodies was enacted largely in response to the experience of Jewish refugees in Europe during the period of World War II. The tragic consequences of the world's indifference at that time are well known. The resulting ban on *refoulement,* as broad as the humanitarian purpose that inspired it, is easily applicable here, the Court's protestations of impotence and regret notwithstanding.

The refugees attempting to escape from Haiti do not claim a right of admission to this country. They do not even argue that the Government has no right to intercept their boats. They demand only that the United States, land of refugees and guardian of freedom, cease forcibly driving them back to detention, abuse, and death. That is a modest plea, vindicated by the Treaty and the statute. We should not close our ears to it.

I dissent.

Source: White House: Executive Order: Interdiction of Illegal Aliens. Washington, DC: Governing Printing Office, 1992. White House. Press Release, July 29, 1992. Washington, DC: Government Printing Office, 1992. U.S. Court of Appeals, Document Number 92-6144, June 26, 1992.

C. Supreme Court Cases

United States v. Bhagat Singh Thind, 1923

O*n February 19, 1923, the United States Supreme Court ruled against the petition of Bhagat Singh Thind, an East Indian immigrant requesting admission to the United States as a "free white person" (a term first used in the Naturalization Act of 1790), as per the requirements of the Immigration Act of 1917. Although Thind pointed out that he was a member of the Caucasian race (as people from the northern parts of India largely are), the Court ruled against him, citing the "common speech" usage of the term "white person."*

Mr. Justice [George] Sutherland delivered the opinion of the court:

The cause is here upon a certificate from the circuit court of appeals, requesting instruction of this court in respect to the following questions: 1. Is a high caste Hindu of full Indian blood, born in Amritsar, Punjab, India, a white person within the meaning of #2169, Revised Statutes (Comp. Stat. #4358, 6 Fed. Stat. Anno. 2d ed. P. 944)?

2. Does the Act of February 5, 1917 . . . disqualify from naturalization as citizens those Hindus now barred by that act, who had lawfully entered the United States prior to passage of said act?

. . . No question was made in respect to the individual qualifications of the appellee. The sole question is whether he falls within the class designated by Congress as eligible. Section #2169, Revised Statutes, provides that the provision of the Naturalization Act "shall apply to aliens being free white persons and to aliens of African nativity and to persons of African descent."

If the applicant is a white person within the meaning of this section he is entitled to naturalization; otherwise not. . . .

In the endeavor to ascertain the meaning of the statute we must not fail to keep in mind that it does not apply the word "Caucasian," but the words "white persons," and these are words of common speech, and not of scientific origin. The

word "Caucasian" not only was not employed in the law, but was probably wholly unfamiliar to the original framers of the statute in 1790. When we employ it, we do so as an aid to the ascertainment of the legislative intent, and not as an invariable substitute for the statutory words. . . . But in this country, during the last half century especially, the word by common usage has acquired a popular meaning, not clearly defined, to be sure, but sufficiently so to enable us to say that its popular, as distinguished from its scientific application, is of appreciably narrower scope. It is in the popular sense of the word, therefore, that we employ it as an aid to the construction of the statute, for it would be obviously illogical to convert words from common speech, used in a statute, into words of scientific terminology, when neither the latter nor the science for whose purposes they were coined was within the contemplation of the framers of the statute or of the people for whom it was framed. . . .

The words of familiar speech, which were used by the original framers of the law, were intended to include only the type of man whom they knew as white. The immigration of that day was almost exclusively from the British Isles and northwestern Europe, whence they and their forebears had come. When they extended the privilege of American citizenship to "any alien being a free white person," it was these immigrants—bone of their bone, flesh of their flesh— and their kind whom they must have had affirmatively in mind. The succeeding years brought immigration from eastern, southern, and middle Europe, among them the Slavs and the dark-eyed, swarthy people of Alpine and Mediterranean stock, and these were received as unquestionably akin to those already here, and readily amalgamated with them. It was the descendants of these and other immigrants of like origin, who constituted the white population of the country when . . . the naturalization test [was reenacted]. . . .

What we now hold is that the words "free white persons" are words of common speech, to be interpreted in accordance with the understanding of the common man, synonymous with the word "Caucasian" only as that word is popularly understood. As so understood and used, whatever may be the speculations of the ethnologist, it does not include the body of people to whom the appellee belongs. It is a matter of familiar observation and knowledge that the physical group characteristics of the Hindus render them readily distinguishable from the various groups of persons in this country commonly recognized as white. . . . It is very far from our thought to suggest the slightest question of racial superiority or inferiority. What we suggest is merely racial difference, and it is of such character and extent that the great body of our people instinctively recognize it and reject the thought of assimilation.

It is not without significance in this connection that Congress, by the Act of February 5, 1917, . . . has now excluded from admission to this country all natives of Asia within designated limits of latitude and longitude, including the whole of India. This not only constitutes conclusive evidence of the congressional attitude of opposition to Asiatic immigration generally, but is persuasive of a similar attitude toward Asiatic naturalization as well, since it is not likely that Congress would be willing to accept as citizens a class of persons whom it rejects as immigrants.

It follows that a negative answer must be given to that first question, which disposes of the case and renders an answer to the second question unnecessary, and it will be so certified. Answer to question No. 1, No.

Source: 61 United States Code 616 (February 19, 1923).

Hirabayashi v. United States, 1943

n February 1942, President Franklin Roosevelt issued Executive Order 9066, calling for the internment of all West Coast Japanese Americans as a threat to national security. One month later, on March 21, Congress passed legislation to back up the Executive Order. Almost immediately, Japanese Americans began to challenge the constitutionality of both the Executive Order and the congressional legislation. One of the first was Gordon Hirabayashi, an American citizen and student at the University of Washington at Seattle. Rather than be sent to an internment camp, Hirabayashi turned himself in to police for failure to report for relocation. For this act of civil disobedience, he was arrested and sentenced to six months in prison. Hirabayashi appealed the case and in Hirabayashi v. United States, *the Supreme Court issued the following decision on the constitutionality of the government's actions.*

Mr. Chief Justice [Harlan] Stone delivered the opinion of the Court:

Appellant, an American citizen of Japanese ancestry, was convicted in the district court of violating the Act of Congress of March 21, 1942 . . . which makes it a misdemeanor knowingly to disregard restrictions made applicable by a military commander to persons in a military area prescribed by him as such, all as authorized by an Executive Order of the President.

The questions for our decision are whether the particular restriction violated, namely that all persons of Japanese ancestry residing in such an area be within their place of residence daily between the hours of 8:00 p.m. and 6:00 a.m., was adopted by the military command in the exercise of an unconstitutional delegation by Congress of its legislative power, and whether the restriction unconstitutionally discriminated between citizens of Japanese ancestry and those of other ancestries in violation of the Fifth Amendment.

The evidence showed that appellant had failed to report to the Civil Control Station on May 11 or May 12, 1942, as directed, to register for evacuation from the military area.

He admitted failure to do so, and stated it had at all times been his belief that he would be waiving his rights as an American citizen by so [registering]. . . .

. . . [O]n March 22, 1942, General DeWitt issued Public Proclamation No. 3, 7 Federal Register 2543. After referring to the previous designation of military areas . . . it recited that "the present situation within these Military Areas and Zones requires as a matter of military necessity the establishment of certain regulations pertaining to all enemy aliens and all persons of Japanese ancestry within said Military Areas and Zones." . . . It accordingly declared and established that from and after March 27, 1942, "all alien Japanese . . . and all persons of Japanese ancestry residing or being within the geographic limits of Military Zone 1 . . . shall be within their place of residence between the hours of 8:00 p.m. and 6:00 a.m., which period is hereinafter referred to as the hours of curfew." . . .

The Chairman of the Senate Military Affairs Committee explained on the floor of the Senate that the purpose of the proposed legislation was to provide a means of enforcement of curfew orders and other military orders made pursuant to Executive Order 9066. . . . He also stated to the Senate that "reasons for suspected widespread fifth-column activity among Japanese" were to be found in the system of dual citizenship which Japan deemed applicable to American-born Japanese, and in the propaganda disseminated by Japanese consuls, Buddhist priests and other leaders among American-born children of Japanese. Such was stated to be the explanation of the contemplated evacuation from the Pacific Coast area of persons of Japanese ancestry, citizens as well as aliens.

The conclusion is inescapable that Congress, by the Act of March 21, 1942, ratified and confirmed Executive Order 9066. . . . The question then is not one of congressional power to delegate to the President the promulgation of the Executive Order, but whether, acting in cooperation, Congress and the Executive have constitutional authority to impose the curfew restrictions here complained of. . . .

. . . In the critical days of March, 1942, the danger to our war production by sabotage and espionage in this area [from Washington State to California] seems obvious. . . . The military commander's appraisal of facts in the light of the authorized standard, and the inferences which he drew from those facts, involved the exercise of his informed judgment. But as we have seen, those facts, and the inferences drawn from them, support the judgment of the military commander, that the danger of espionage and sabotage to our military resources was imminent, and that the curfew order was an appropriate measure to meet it. . . .

The Constitution as a continuously operating charter of government does not demand the impossible or the impractical. The essentials of the legislative function are preserved when Congress authorizes a statutory command to be operative, upon ascertainment of a basic conclusion of fact by a designated representative of the government. . . . The present statute, which authorized curfew orders made pursuant to Executive Order No. 9066 for the protection of war re-

sources from espionage and sabotage, satisfies those requirements. Under the Executive Order the basic facts, determined by the military commander in light of knowledge then available, were whether that danger existed and whether a curfew order was an appropriate means of minimizing the danger. Since his findings to that effect were, as we have said, not without adequate support, the legislative function was performed and the sanction of the statute attached to violations of the curfew order. It is unnecessary to consider whether or to what extent such findings would support orders differing from the curfew order.

The conviction under the second count is without constitutional infirmity. Hence we have no occasion to review the conviction on the first count, since, as already stated, the sentences on the two counts are to run concurrently and conviction on the second is to sustain the sentence. For this reason also it is unnecessary to consider the Government's argument that compliance with the order to report at the Civilian Station did not necessarily entail confinement in a relocation center. Affirmed.

Source: 320 United States 81.

Lau v. Nichols, 1974

*I*n a landmark 1974 decision, the U.S. Supreme Court for the first time ruled that a school's failure to offer special instruction to non-English-speaking students—in this case, Chinese-speaking students—violated the Civil Rights Act of 1964. The unanimous decision, referred to as Lau v. Nichols, guaranteed immigrant students appropriate instruction, since implied to mean bilingual instruction. Writing for the majority, Justice William O. Douglas overturned a Court of Appeals ruling and dismissed its reasoning that "every student brings to the starting line of his educational career different advantages and disadvantages caused in part by social, economic and cultural background, created and continued completely apart from any contribution by the school system."

The following document includes excerpts from Douglas's decision.

Certiorari to the United States Court of Appeals for the Ninth Circuit

Justice William O. Douglas delivered the [unaminous] opinion of the Court

The failure of the San Francisco school system to provide English language instruction to the approximately 1,800 students of Chinese ancestry who do not speak English, or to provide them with other adequate instructional procedures, denies them a meaningful opportunity to participate in the public educational program and thus violates 601 of the Civil Rights Act of 1964, which bans discrimination based "on the ground of race, color, or national origin," in "any program or activity receiving Federal financial assistance," and the implementing regulations of the Department of Health, Education, and Welfare.

The San Francisco, California, school system was integrated in 1971 as a result of a federal court decree, 339 F. Supp. 1315. See Lee v. Johnson, 404 U.S. 1215. The District Court found that there are 2,856 students of Chinese ancestry in the school system who do not speak English. Of those who have that language deficiency, about 1,000 are given supplemental courses in the English language. About 1,800, however, do not receive that instruction.

This class suit brought by non-English-speaking Chinese students against officials responsible for the operation of the San Francisco Unified School District seeks relief against the unequal educational opportunities, which are alleged to violate, inter alia, the Fourteenth Amendment. No specific remedy is urged upon us. [414 U.S. 563, 565] Teaching English to the students of Chinese ancestry who do not speak the language is one choice. Giving instructions to this group in Chinese is another. There may be others. Petitioners ask only that the Board of Education be directed to apply its expertise to the problem and rectify the situation.

The District Court denied relief. The Court of Appeals affirmed, holding that there was no violation of the Equal Protection Clause of the Fourteenth Amendment or of 601 of the Civil Rights Act of 1964, 78 Stat. 252, 42 U.S.C. 2000d, which excludes from participation in federal financial assistance, recipients of aid which discriminate against racial groups, 483 F.2d 791. One judge dissented. A hearing en banc was denied, two judges dissenting. Id., at 805. We granted the petition for certiorari because of the public importance of the question presented, 412 U.S. 938.

The Court of Appeals reasoned that "[e]very student brings to the starting line of his educational career different advantages and disadvantages caused in part by social, economic and cultural background, created and continued completely apart from any contribution by the school system," 483 F.2d, at 797. Yet in our view the case may not be so easily decided. This is a public school system of California and 71 of the California Education Code states that "English shall be the basic language of instruction in all schools." That section permits a school district to determine "when and under what circumstances instruction may be given bilingually." That section also states as "the policy of the state" to insure "the mastery of English by all pupils in the schools." And bilingual instruction is authorized "to the extent that it does not interfere with the systematic, sequential, and regular instruction of all pupils in the English language." [414 U.S. 563, 566]

Moreover, 8573 of the Education Code provides that no pupil shall receive a diploma of graduation from grade 12

1371

who has not met the standards of proficiency in "English," as well as other prescribed subjects. Moreover, by 12101 of the Education Code (Supp. 1973) children between the ages of six and 16 years are (with exceptions not material here) "subject to compulsory full-time education."

Under these state-imposed standards there is no equality of treatment merely by providing students with the same facilities, textbooks, teachers, and curriculum; for students who do not understand English are effectively foreclosed from any meaningful education. Basic English skills are at the very core of what these public schools teach. Imposition of a requirement that, before a child can effectively participate in the educational program, he must already have acquired those basic skills is to make a mockery of public education. We know that those who do not understand English are certain to find their classroom experiences wholly incomprehensible and in no way meaningful. We do not reach the Equal Protection Clause argument which has been advanced but rely solely on 601 of the Civil Rights Act of 1964, 42 U.S.C. 2000d, to reverse the Court of Appeals.

That section bans discrimination based "on the ground of race, color, or national origin," in "any program or activity receiving Federal financial assistance." The school district involved in this litigation receives large amounts of federal financial assistance. The Department of Health, Education, and Welfare (HEW), which has authority to promulgate regulations prohibiting discrimination in federally assisted school systems, 42 U.S.C. 2000d-1, in 1968 issued one guideline that "[s]chool systems are responsible for assuring that students of a particular race, color, or national origin are not denied the [414 U.S. 563, 567] opportunity to obtain the education generally obtained by other students in the system." 33 Fed. Reg. 4956. In 1970 HEW made the guidelines more specific, requiring school districts that were federally funded "to rectify the language deficiency in order to open" the instruction to students who had "linguistic deficiencies," 35 Fed. Reg. 11595.

By 602 of the Act HEW is authorized to issue rules, regulations, and orders to make sure that recipients of federal aid under its jurisdiction conduct any federally financed projects consistently with 601. HEW's regulations, 45 CFR 80.3 (b) (1), specify that the recipients may not

"(ii) Provide any service, financial aid, or other benefit to an individual which is different, or is provided in a different manner, from that provided to others under the program; . . . .

"(iv) Restrict an individual in any way in the enjoyment of any advantage or privilege enjoyed by others receiving any service, financial aid, or other benefit under the program."

Discrimination among students on account of race or national origin that is prohibited includes "discrimination . . .

in the availability or use of any academic . . . or [414 U.S. 563, 568] other facilities of the grantee or other recipient." Id., 80.5 (b). Discrimination is barred which has that effect even though no purposeful design is present: a recipient "may not . . . utilize criteria or methods of administration which have the effect of subjecting individuals to discrimination" or have "the effect of defeating or substantially impairing accomplishment of the objectives of the program as respect individuals of a particular race, color, or national origin." Id., 80.3 (b) (2).

It seems obvious that the Chinese-speaking minority receive fewer benefits than the English-speaking majority from respondents' school system which denies them a meaningful opportunity to participate in the educational program—all earmarks of the discrimination banned by the regulations. In 1970 HEW issued clarifying guidelines, 35 Fed. Reg. 11595, which include the following:

"Where inability to speak and understand the English language excludes national origin-minority group children from effective participation in the educational program offered by a school district, the district must take affirmative steps to rectify the language deficiency in order to open its instructional program to these students."

"Any ability grouping or tracking system employed by the school system to deal with the special language skill needs of national origin-minority group children must be designed to meet such language skill needs as soon as possible and must not operate as an educational deadend or permanent track."

Respondent school district contractually agreed to "comply with title VI of the Civil Rights Act of 1964 . . . and all requirements imposed by or pursuant to the [414 U.S. 563, 569] Regulation" of HEW (45 CFR pt. 80) which are "issued pursuant to that title . . ." and also immediately to "take any measures necessary to effectuate this agreement." The Federal Government has power to fix the terms on which its money allotments to the States shall be disbursed. Oklahoma v. CSC, 330 U.S. 127, 142–143. Whatever may be the limits of that power, Steward Machine Co. v. Davis, 301 U.S. 548, 590 et seq., they have not been reached here. Senator Humphrey, during the floor debates on the Civil Rights Act of 1964, said:

"Simple justice requires that public funds, to which all taxpayers of all races contribute, not be spent in any fashion which encourages, entrenches, subsidizes, or results in racial discrimination."

We accordingly reverse the judgment of the Court of Appeals and remand the case for the fashioning of appropriate relief.

Source: United States Supreme Court: 414 U.S. 563(1974), *Lau et al. v. Nichols et al.*

Plyler v. Doe, 1982

On June 15, 1982, the Supreme Court declared a Texas law that required the children of illegal aliens to pay tuition at public schools unconstitutional. The five-to-four decision—referred to as Plyler—represented the first time the equal protection clause of the U.S. Constitution was applied to illegal aliens. Writing for the majority, Justice William Brennan Jr. dismissed Texas's argument that illegal immigrants were not "persons within the jurisdiction" of the state and thus had no right to equal protection under the Fourteenth Amendment.

The following document contains excerpts from Brennan's majority decision, as well as Chief Justice Warren Burger's dissent.

No. 80-1538

James Plyler, Superintendent of the Tyler Independent School District and its Board of Trustees et al., Appellants v. J. and R. Doe et al. On appeal from the United States Court of Appeals for the Fifth Circuit. [June 15, 1982*]

JUSTICE BRENNAN delivered the opinion of the Court.

The question presented by these cases is whether, consistent with the Equal Protection Clause of the Fourteenth Amendment, Texas may deny to undocumented school-age children the free public education that it provides to children who are citizens of the United States or legally admitted aliens.

I

Since the late nineteenth century, the United States has restricted immigration into this country. Unsanctioned entry into the United States is a crime, 8 U.S.C. § 1325, and those who have entered unlawfully are subject to deportation, 8 U.S.C. §§ 1251–1252. But despite the existence of these legal

---

* Together with No. 80-1934, *Texas et al. v.* Certain *Named and Unnamed Undocumented* Alien *Children et al.,* also on appeal from the same court.

restrictions, a substantial number of persons have succeeded in unlawfully entering the United States, and now live within various States, including the State of Texas.

In May 1975, the Texas legislature revised its education laws to withhold from local school districts any state funds for the education of children who were not "legally admitted" into the United States. The 1975 revision also authorized local school districts to deny enrollment in their public schools to children not "legally admitted" to the country. These cases involve constitutional challenges to those provisions.

No. 80-1538
Plyler v. Doe

This is a class action, filed in the United States District Court for the Eastern District of Texas in September 1977, on behalf of certain school-age children of Mexican origin residing in Smith County, Texas, who could not establish that they had been legally admitted into the United States. The action complained of the exclusion of plaintiff children from the public schools of the Tyler Independent School District. The Superintendent and members of the Board of Trustees of the School District were named as defendants; the State of Texas intervened as a party-defendant. After certifying a class consisting of all undocumented school-age children of Mexican origin residing within the School District, the District Court preliminarily enjoined defendants from denying a free education to members of the plaintiff class. In December 1977, the Court conducted an extensive hearing on plaintiffs' motion for permanent injunctive relief.

In considering this motion, the District Court made extensive findings of fact. The court found that neither § 21.031 [of Texas' education code] nor the School District policy implementing it had "either the purpose or effect of keeping illegal aliens out of the State of Texas." Respecting defendants' further claim that § 21.031 was simply a financial measure designed to avoid a drain on the State's finances, the court recognized that the increases in population resulting from the immigration of Mexican nationals into the United States had created problems for the public schools of the State, and that these problems were exacerbated by the special educational needs of immigrant Mexican children. The court noted, however, that the increase in school enrollment was primarily attributable to the admission of children who were legal residents. It also found that while the "exclusion of all undocumented children from the public schools in Texas would eventually result in economies at some level," funding from both the state and federal governments was based primarily on the number of children enrolled. In net effect then, barring undocumented children from the schools would save money, but it would "not necessarily" improve "the quality of education." The court further observed that the impact of § 21.031 was borne primarily by a very small sub-class of illegal aliens, "entire families who have migrated illegally and—for all practical purposes—permanently to the United States." Finally, the court noted that under current laws and practices "the illegal alien of today may well be the legal alien of tomorrow," and that without an education, these undocumented children, "[a]lready disadvantaged as a result of poverty, lack of English-speaking ability, and undeniable racial prejudices, . . . will become permanently locked into the lowest socio-economic class."

The District Court held that illegal aliens were entitled to the protection of the Equal Protection Clause of the Fourteenth Amendment, and that § 21.031 violated that Clause. Suggesting that "the state's exclusion of undocumented children from its public schools . . . may well be the type of invidiously motivated state action for which the suspect classification doctrine was designed," the court held that it was unnecessary to decide whether the statute would survive a "strict scrutiny" analysis because, in any event, the discrimination embodied in the statute was not supported by a rational basis. The District Court also concluded that the Texas statute violated the Supremacy Clause.

The Court of Appeals for the Fifth Circuit upheld the District Court's injunction. (1980). The Court of Appeals held that the District Court had erred in finding the Texas statute preempted by federal law. With respect to equal protection, however, the Court of Appeals affirmed in all essential respects the analysis of the District Court, concluding that § 21.031 was "constitutionally infirm regardless of whether it was tested using the mere rational basis standard or some more stringent test." We noted probable jurisdiction. (1981).

No. 80-1934
In Re: Alien Children Litigation

During 1978 and 1979, suits challenging the constitutionality of § 21.031 and various local practices undertaken on the authority of that provision were filed in the United States District Courts for the Southern, Western, and Northern Districts of Texas. Each suit named the State of Texas and the Texas Education Agency as defendant, along with local officials. In November 1979, the Judicial Panel on Multidistrict Litigation, on motion of the State, consolidated the claims against the State officials into a single action to be heard in the District Court for the Southern District of Texas. A hearing was conducted in February and March 1980. In July 1980, the court entered an opinion and order holding that § 21.031 violated the Equal Protection Clause of the Fourteenth Amendment. The court held that "the absolute deprivation of education should trigger strict judicial scrutiny, particularly when the absolute deprivation is the result of complete inability to pay for the desired benefit." The court determined that the State's concern for fiscal integrity was not a compelling state interest, that exclusion of these children had not been shown to be necessary to improve education within the State, and that the educational needs of the children statutorily excluded was not different from the needs of children not excluded. The court therefore concluded that § 21.031 was not carefully tailored to advance the asserted state interest in an acceptable manner. While appeal of the District Court's decision was pending, the Court of Appeals rendered its decision in No. 81-1538. Apparently on the strength of that opinion, the Court of Appeals, on February 23, 1981, summarily affirmed the decision of the Southern District. We noted probable jurisdiction (1981) and consolidated this case with No. 81-1538 for briefing and argument.

II

The Fourteenth Amendment provides that "No State shall . . . deprive any person of life, liberty, or property, without due process of law; nor deny to any person within its jurisdiction the equal protection of the laws." Appellants argue at the outset that undocumented aliens, because of their immigration status, are not "persons within the jurisdiction" of the State of Texas, and that they therefore have no right to the equal protection of Texas law. We reject this argument. Whatever his status under the immigration laws, an alien is surely a "person" in any ordinary sense of that term. Aliens, even aliens whose presence in this country is unlawful, have long been recognized as "persons" guaranteed due process of law by the Fifth and Fourteenth Amendments. *Shaughnessy v. Mezei* (1953); *Wong Wing v. United States* (1896); *Yick Wo v. Hopkins* (1886). Indeed, we have clearly held that the Fifth Amendment protects aliens whose presence in this country is unlawful from invidious discrimination by the Federal Government. *Mathews v. Diaz* (1976).

Appellants seek to distinguish our prior cases, emphasizing that the Equal Protection Clause directs a State to afford its protection to persons within its jurisdiction while the Due Process Clauses of the Fifth and Fourteenth Amendments contain no such assertedly limiting phrase. In appellants' view, persons who have entered the United States illegally are not "within the jurisdiction" of a State even if they are present within a State's boundaries and subject to its laws. Neither our cases nor the logic of the Fourteenth Amendment supports that constricting construction of the phrase "within its jurisdiction." We have never suggested that the class of persons who might avail themselves of the equal protection guarantee is less than coextensive with that entitled to due process. To the contrary, we have recognized that both provisions were fashioned to protect an identical class of persons, and to reach every exercise of State authority.

> "The Fourteenth Amendment to the Constitution is not confined to the protection of citizens. It says: 'Nor shall any state deprive any persons of life, liberty or property without due process of law; nor deny to any persons within its jurisdiction the equal protection of the laws.' *These provisions are universal in their application, to all persons within the territorial jurisdiction,* without regard to any differences of race, color, or of nationality; and the protection of the laws is a pledge of the protection of equal laws." *Yick Wo,* (emphasis added).

In concluding that "all persons within the territory of the United States," including aliens unlawfully present, may invoke the Fifth and Sixth Amendment to challenge actions of the Federal Government, we reasoned from the understanding that the Fourteenth Amendment was designed to afford its protection to all within the boundaries of a State. *Wong Wing.* Our cases applying the Equal Protection Clause reflect the same territorial theme:

> "Manifestly, the obligation of the State to give the protection of equal laws can be performed only where its laws operate, that is, within its own jurisdiction. It is there that the equality of legal right must be maintained. That obligation is imposed by the Constitution upon the States severally as governmental entities,—each responsible for its own laws establishing the rights and duties of persons within its borders." *Missouri ex rel. Gaines v. Canada* (1938).

There is simply no support for appellants' suggestion that "due process" is somehow of greater stature than "equal protection" and therefore available to a larger class of persons. To the contrary, each aspect of the Fourteenth Amendment reflects an elementary limitation on state power. To permit a State to employ the phrase "within its jurisdiction" in order to identify subclasses of persons whom it would define as beyond its jurisdiction, thereby relieving itself of the obligation to assure that its laws are designed and applied equally to those persons, would undermine the principal purpose for which the Equal Protection Clause was incorporated in the Fourteenth Amendment. The Equal Protection Clause was intended to work nothing less than the abolition of all caste- and invidious class-based legislation. That objective is fundamentally at odds with the power the State asserts here to classify persons subject to its laws as nonetheless excepted from its protection. . . .

Use of the phrase "within its jurisdiction" . . . does not detract from, but rather confirms, the understanding that the protection of the Fourteenth Amendment extends to anyone, citizen or stranger, who is subject to the laws of a State, and reaches into every corner of a State's territory. That a person's initial entry into a State, or into the United States, was unlawful, and that he may for that reason be expelled, cannot negate the simple fact of his presence within the State's territorial perimeter. Given such presence, he is subject to the full range of obligations imposed by the State's civil and criminal laws. And until he leaves the jurisdiction—either voluntarily, or involuntarily in accordance with the Constitution and laws of the United States—he is entitled to the equal protection of the laws that a State may choose to establish.

Our conclusion that the illegal aliens who are plaintiffs in these cases may claim the benefit of the Fourteenth Amendment's guarantee of equal protection only begins the inquiry. The more difficult question is whether the Equal Protection Clause has been violated by the refusal of the State of Texas to reimburse local school boards for the education of children who cannot demonstrate that their presence within the United States is lawful, or by the imposition by those school boards of the burden of tuition on those children. It is to this question that we now turn.

III

The Equal Protection Clause directs that "all persons similarly circumstanced shall be treated alike." *F. S. Royster Guano Co. v. Virginia* (1920). But so too, "The Constitution does not require things which are different in fact or opinion to be treated in law as though they were the same." *Tigner v. Texas* (1940). The initial discretion to determine what is "different" and what is "the same" resides in the legislatures of the States. A legislature must have substantial latitude to establish classifications that roughly approximate the nature of the problem perceived, that accommodate competing concerns both public and private, and that account for limitations on the practical ability of the State to remedy every ill. In applying the Equal Protection Clause to most forms of state action, we thus seek only the assurance that the classification at issue bears some fair relationship to a legitimate public purpose.

But we would not be faithful to our obligations under the Fourteenth Amendment if we applied so deferential a standard to every classification. The Equal Protection Clause was intended as a restriction on state legislative action inconsistent with elemental constitutional premises. Thus we have treated as presumptively invidious those classifications that disadvantage a "suspect class," or that impinge upon the exercise of a "fundamental right." With respect to such classifications, it is appropriate to enforce the mandate of equal protection by requiring the State to demonstrate that its classification has been precisely tailored to serve a compelling governmental interest. In addition, we have recognized that certain forms of legislative classification, while not facially invidious, nonetheless give rise to recurring constitutional difficulties; in these limited circumstances we have sought the assurance that the classification reflects a reasoned judgment consistent with the ideal of equal protection by inquiring whether it may fairly be viewed as furthering a substantial interest of the State. We turn to a consideration of the standard appropriate for the evaluation of § 21.031.

A

Sheer incapability or lax enforcement of the laws barring entry into this country, coupled with the failure to establish an effective bar to the employment of undocumented aliens, has resulted in the creation of a substantial "shadow population" of illegal migrants—numbering in the millions—within our borders. This situation raises the specter of a permanent caste of undocumented resident aliens, encouraged by some to remain here as a source of cheap labor, but nevertheless denied the benefits that our society makes available to citizens and lawful residents. The existence of such an underclass presents most difficult problems for a Nation that prides itself on adherence to principles of equality under law.

The children who are plaintiffs in these cases are special members of this underclass. Persuasive arguments support the view that a State may withhold its beneficence from those whose very presence within the United States is the product of their own unlawful conduct. These arguments do not apply with the same force to classifications imposing disabilities on the minor children of such illegal entrants. At the least, those who elect to enter our territory by stealth and in violation of our law should be prepared to bear the consequences, including, but not limited to, deportation. But the children of those illegal entrants are not comparably situated. Their "parents have the ability to conform their conduct to societal norms," and presumably the ability to remove themselves from the State's jurisdiction; but the children who are plaintiffs in these cases "can affect neither their parents' conduct nor their own status." *Trimble v. Gordon* (1977). Even if the State found it expedient to control the conduct of adults by acting against their children, legislation directing the onus of a parent's misconduct against his children does not comport with fundamental conceptions of justice.

> "[V]isiting . . . condemnation on the head of an infant is illogical and unjust. Moreover, imposing disabilities on the . . . child is contrary to the basic concept of our system that legal burdens should bear some relationship to individual responsibility or wrongdoing. Obviously, no child is responsible for his birth and penalizing the . . . child is an ineffectual—as well as unjust—way of deterring the parents." *Weber v. Aetna Casualty & Surety Co.* (1972).

Of course, undocumented status is not irrelevant to any proper legislative goal. Nor is undocumented status an absolutely immutable characteristic since it is the product of conscious, indeed unlawful, action. But § 21.031 is directed against children, and imposes its discriminatory burden on the basis of a legal characteristic over which children can have little control. It is thus difficult to conceive of a rational justification for penalizing these children for their presence within the United States. Yet that appears to be precisely the effect of § 21.031.

Public education is not a "right" granted to individuals by the Constitution. *San Antonio School District.* But neither is it merely some governmental "benefit" indistinguishable

from other forms of social welfare legislation. Both the importance of education in maintaining our basic institutions, and the lasting impact of its deprivation on the life of the child, mark the distinction. The "American people have always regarded education and the acquisition of knowledge as matters of supreme importance." *Meyer v. Nebraska* (1923). We have recognized "the public school as a most vital civic institution for the preservation of a democratic system of government." *Abington School District v. Schempp* (1963) (BRENNAN, J., concurring) and as the primary vehicle for transmitting "the values on which our society rests." *Ambach v. Norwick* (1979). As noted early in our history, "some degree of education is necessary to prepare citizens to participate effectively and intelligently in our open political system if we are to preserve freedom and independence." *Wisconsin v. Yoder* (1972). And these historic "perceptions of the public schools as inculcating fundamental values necessary to the maintenance of a democratic political system have been confirmed by the observations of social scientists." *Ambach v. Norwick.* In addition, education provides the basic tools by which individuals might lead economically productive lives to the benefit of us all. In sum, education has a fundamental role in maintaining the fabric of our society. We cannot ignore the significant social costs borne by our Nation when select groups are denied the means to absorb the values and skills upon which our social order rests.

In addition to the pivotal role of education in sustaining our political and cultural heritage, denial of education to some isolated group of children poses an affront to one of the goals of the Equal Protection Clause: the abolition of governmental barriers presenting unreasonable obstacles to advancement on the basis of individual merit. Paradoxically, by depriving the children of any disfavored group of an education, we foreclose the means by which that group might raise the level of esteem in which it is held by the majority. But more directly, "education prepares individuals to be self-reliant and self-sufficient participants in society." *Wisconsin v. Yoder.* Illiteracy is an enduring disability. The inability to read and write will handicap the individual deprived of a basic education each and every day of his life. The inestimable toll of that deprivation on the social, economic, intellectual, and psychological well-being of the individual, and the obstacle it poses to individual achievement, makes it most difficult to reconcile the cost or the principle of a status-based denial of basic education with the framework of equality embodied in the Equal Protection Clause. What we said 28 years ago in *Brown v. Board of Education* (1954), still holds true:

> "Today, education is perhaps the most important function of state and local governments. Compulsory school attendance laws and the great expenditures for education both demonstrate our recognition of the importance of education to our democratic society. It is required in the performance of our most basic public responsibilities, even service in the armed forces. It is the very foundation of good citizenship. Today it is a principal instrument in awakening the child to cultural values, in preparing him for later professional training, and in helping him to adjust normally to his environment. In these

days, it is doubtful that any child may reasonably be expected to succeed in life if he is denied the opportunity of an education. Such an opportunity, where the state has undertaken to provide it, is a right which must be made available to all on equal terms."

B

These well-settled principles allow us to determine the proper level of deference to be afforded § 21.031. Undocumented aliens cannot be treated as a suspect class because their presence in this country in violation of federal law is not a "constitutional irrelevancy." Nor is education a fundamental right; a State need not justify by compelling necessity every variation in the manner in which education is provided to its population. See *San Antonio School Dist. v. Rodriguez* (1973). But more is involved in this case than the abstract question whether § 21.031 discriminates against a suspect class, or whether education is a fundamental right. Section 21.031 imposes a lifetime hardship on a discrete class of children not accountable for their disabling status. The stigma of illiteracy will mark them for the rest of their lives. By denying these children a basic education, we deny them the ability to live within the structure of our civic institutions, and foreclose any realistic possibility that they will contribute in even the smallest way to the progress of our Nation. In determining the rationality of § 21.031, we may appropriately take into account its costs to the Nation and to the innocent children who are its victims. In light of these countervailing costs, the discrimination contained in § 21.031 can hardly be considered rational unless it furthers some substantial goal of the State.

IV

It is the State's principal argument, and apparently the view of the dissenting Justices, that the undocumented status of these children *vel non* establishes a sufficient rational basis for denying them benefits that a State might choose to afford other residents. The State notes that while other aliens are admitted "on an equality of legal privileges with all citizens under non-discriminatory laws," *Takahashi v. Fish & Game Comm'n* (1948), the asserted right of these children to an education can claim no implicit congressional imprimatur. Indeed, on the State's view, Congress' apparent disapproval of the presence of these children within the United States, and the evasion of the federal regulatory program that is the mark of undocumented status, provides authority for its decision to impose upon them special disabilities. Faced with an equal protection challenge respecting the treatment of aliens, we agree that the courts must be attentive to congressional policy; the exercise of congressional power might well affect the State's prerogatives to afford differential treatment to a particular class of aliens. But we are unable to find in the congressional immigration scheme any statement of policy that might weigh significantly in arriving at an equal protection balance concerning the State's authority to deprive these children of an education.

The Constitution grants Congress the power to "establish a uniform Rule of Naturalization." Art. I., § 8. Drawing upon this power, upon its plenary authority with respect to foreign relations and international commerce, and upon the inherent power of a sovereign to close its borders, Congress has developed a complex scheme governing admission to and status within our borders. See *Mathews v. Diaz* (1976); *Harrisades v. Shaughnessy* (1952). The obvious need for delicate policy judgments has counseled the Judicial Branch to avoid intrusion into this field. *Mathews.* But this traditional caution does not persuade us that unusual deference must be shown the classification embodied in § 21.031. The States enjoy no power with respect to the classification of aliens. See *Hines v. Davidowitz* (1941). This power is "committed to the political branches of the Federal Government." *Mathews.* Although it is "a routine and normally legitimate part" of the business of the Federal Government to classify on the basis of alien status and to "take into account the character of the relationship between the alien and this country," only rarely are such matters relevant to legislation by a State. *Nyquist v. Mauclet* (1977). . . .

To be sure, like all persons who have entered the United States unlawfully, these children are subject to deportation. But there is no assurance that a child subject to deportation will ever be deported. An illegal entrant might be granted federal permission to continue to reside in this country, or even to become a citizen. In light of the discretionary federal power to grant relief from deportation, a State cannot realistically determine that any particular undocumented child will in fact be deported until after deportation proceedings have been completed. It would of course be most difficult for the State to justify a denial of education to a child enjoying an inchoate federal permission to remain.

We are reluctant to impute to Congress the intention to withhold from these children, for so long as they are present in this country through no fault of their own, access to a basic education. In other contexts, undocumented status, coupled with some articulable federal policy, might enhance State authority with respect to the treatment of undocumented aliens. But in the area of special constitutional sensitivity presented by this case, and in the absence of any contrary indication fairly discernible in the present legislative record, we perceive no national policy that supports the State in denying these children an elementary education. The State may borrow the federal classification. But to justify its use as a criterion for its own discriminatory policy, the State must demonstrate that the classification is reasonably adapted to "*the purposes for which the state desires to use it.*" *Oyama v. California* (1948) (Murphy, J., concurring) (emphasis added). We therefore turn to the state objectives that are said to support § 21.031.

V

Appellants argue that the classification at issue furthers an interest in the "preservation of the state's limited resources for the education of its lawful residents." Of course, a concern for the preservation of resources standing alone can hardly justify the classification used in allocating those resources. *Graham v. Richardson.* The State must do more than justify its classification with a concise expression of an intention to discriminate. *Examining Board v. Flores de Otero* (1976). Apart from the asserted state prerogative to act against undocumented children solely on the basis of their undocumented status—an asserted prerogative that carries only minimal force in the circumstances of this case—we discern three colorable state interests that might support § 21.031.

First, appellants appear to suggest that the State may seek to protect the State from an influx of illegal immigrants. While a State might have an interest in mitigating the potentially harsh economic effects of sudden shifts in population, § 21.031 hardly offers an effective method of dealing with an urgent demographic or economic problem. There is no evidence in the record suggesting that illegal entrants impose any significant burden on the State's economy. To the contrary, the available evidence suggests that illegal aliens underutilize public services, while contributing their labor to the local economy and tax money to the State fisc. The dominant incentive for illegal entry into the State of Texas is the availability of employment; few if any illegal immigrants come to this country, or presumably to the State of Texas, in order to avail themselves of a free education. Thus, even making the doubtful assumption that the net impact of illegal aliens on the economy of the State is negative, we think it clear that "[c]harging tuition to undocumented children constitutes a ludicrously ineffectual attempt to stem the tide of illegal immigration," at least when compared with the alternative of prohibiting the employment of illegal aliens.

Second, while it is apparent that a state may "not ... reduce expenditures for education by barring [some arbitrarily chosen class of] children from its schools," *Shapiro v. Thompson* (1969), appellants suggest that undocumented children are appropriately singled out for exclusion because of the special burdens they impose on the State's ability to provide high quality public education. But the record in no way supports the claim that exclusion of undocumented children is likely to improve the overall quality of education in the State. As the District Court in No. 80-1934 noted, the State failed to offer any "credible supporting evidence that a proportionately small diminution of the funds spent on each child [which might result from devoting some State funds to the education of the excluded group] will have a grave impact on the quality of education." And, after reviewing the State's school financing mechanism, the District Court in No. 80-1538 concluded that barring undocumented children from local schools would not necessarily improve the quality of education provided in those schools. Of course, even if improvement in the quality of education were a likely result of barring some *number* of children from the schools of the State, the State must support its selection of *this* group as the appropriate target for exclusion. In terms of educational cost and need, however, undocumented children are "basically indistinguishable" from legally resident alien children.

Finally, appellants suggest that undocumented children are appropriately singled out because their unlawful presence within the United States renders them less likely than other children to remain within the boundaries of the State, and to put their education to productive social or political use within the State. Even assuming that such an interest is legitimate, it is an interest that is most difficult to quantify. The State has no assurance that any child, citizen or not, will employ the education provided by the State within the confines of the State's borders. In any event, the record is clear that many of the undocumented children disabled by this classification will remain in this country indefinitely, and that some will become lawful residents or citizens of the United States. It is difficult to understand precisely what the State hopes to achieve by promoting the creation and perpetuation of a sub-class of illiterates within our boundaries, surely adding to the problems and costs of unemployment, welfare, and crime. It is thus clear that whatever savings might be achieved by denying these children an education, they are wholly insubstantial in light of the costs involved to these children, the State, and the Nation.

VI

If the State is to deny a discrete group of innocent children the free public education that it offers to other children residing within its borders, that denial must be justified by a showing that it furthers some substantial state interest. No such showing was made here. Accordingly, the judgment of the Court of Appeals in each of these cases is

Affirmed.

Chief Justice Burger, with whom **Justice White, Justice Rehnquist,** and **Justice O'Connor** join, dissenting.

Were it our business to set the Nation's social policy, I would agree without hesitation that it is senseless for an enlightened society to deprive any children—including illegal aliens—of an elementary education. I fully agree that it would be folly—and wrong—to tolerate creation of a segment of society made up of illiterate persons, many having a limited or no command of our language. However, the Constitution does not constitute us as "Platonic Guardians" nor does it vest in this Court the authority to strike down laws because they do not meet our standards of desirable social policy, "wisdom," or "common sense." See *Tennessee Valley Authority v. Hill* (1978). We trespass on the assigned function of the political branches under our structure of limited and separated powers when we assume a policymaking role as the Court does today.

The Court makes no attempt to disguise that it is acting to make up for Congress' lack of "effective leadership" in dealing with the serious national problems caused by the influx of uncountable millions of illegal aliens across our borders. The failure of enforcement of the immigration laws over more than a decade and the inherent difficulty and expense of sealing our vast borders have combined to create a grave socio-economic dilemma. It is a dilemma that has not yet even been fully assessed, let alone addressed. However, it is not the function of the judiciary to provide "effective leadership" simply because the political branches of government fail to do so.

The Court's holding today manifests the justly criticized judicial tendency to attempt speedy and wholesale formulation of "remedies" for the failures—or simply the laggard pace—of the political processes of our system of government. The Court employs, and in my view abuses, the Fourteenth Amendment in an effort to become an omnipotent and omniscient problem solver. That the motives for doing so are noble and compassionate does not alter the fact that the Court distorts our constitutional function to make amends for the defaults of others.

In a sense, the Court's opinion rests on such a unique confluence of theories and rationales that it will likely stand for little beyond the results in these particular cases. Yet the extent to which the Court departs from principled constitutional adjudication is nonetheless disturbing.

I have no quarrel with the conclusion that the Equal Protection Clause of the Fourteenth Amendment *applies* to aliens who, after the illegal entry into this country, are indeed physically "within the jurisdiction" of a State. However, as the Court concedes, this "only begins the inquiry." The Equal Protection Clause does not mandate identical treatment of different categories of persons. *Jefferson v. Hackney* (1972); *Reed v. Reed* (1971); *Tigner v. Texas* (1940).

The dispositive issue in these cases, simply put, is whether, for purposes of allocating its finite resources, a State as a legitimate reason to differentiate between persons who are lawfully within the State and those who are unlawfully there. The distinction the State of Texas has drawn—based not only upon its own legitimate interests but on classifications established by the federal government in its immigration laws and policies—is not unconstitutional.

A

The Court acknowledges that, except in those cases when state classifications disadvantage a "suspect class" or impinge upon a "fundamental right," the Equal Protection Clause permits a State "substantial latitude" in distinguishing between different groups of persons. Moreover, the Court expressly—and correctly—rejects any suggestion that illegal aliens are a suspect class, or that education is a fundamental right. Yet by patching together bits and pieces of what might be termed quasi-suspect-class and quasi-fundamental-rights analysis, the Court spins out a theory custom-tailored to the facts of these cases.

In the end, we are told little more than that the level of scrutiny employed to strike down the Texas law applies only when illegal alien children are deprived of a public education. If ever a court was guilty of an unabashedly result-oriented approach, this case is a prime example.

(1)

The Court first suggests that these illegal alien children, although not a suspect class, are entitled to special solicitude under the Equal Protection Clause because they lack "control" over or "responsibility" for their unlawful entry into this country. Similarly, the Court appears to take the position that § 21.031 is presumptively "irrational" because it has the effect of imposing "penalties" on "innocent" children. However, the Equal Protection Clause does not preclude legislators from classifying among persons on the basis of factors and characteristics over which individuals may be said to lack "control." Indeed, in some circumstances persons generally, and children in particular, may have little control over or responsibility for such things as their ill-health, need for public assistance, or place of residence. Yet a state legislature is not barred from considering, for example, relevant differences between the mentally-healthy and the mentally-ill, or between the residents of different counties, simply because these may be factors unrelated to individual choice or to any "wrongdoing." The Equal Protection Clause protects against arbitrary and irrational classifications, and against invidious discrimination stemming from prejudice and hostility; it is not an all-encompassing "equalizer" designed to eradicate every distinction for which persons are not "responsible.". . . .

. . . This Court has recognized that in allocating governmental benefits to a given class of aliens, one "may take into account the character of the relationship between the alien and this country." *Mathews v. Diaz* (1976). When that "relationship" is a federally-prohibited one, there can, of course, be no presumption that a State has a constitutional duty to include illegal aliens among the recipients of its governmental benefits.

(2)

The second strand of the Court's analysis rests on the premise that, although public education is not a constitutionally-guaranteed right, "neither is it merely some governmental 'benefit' indistinguishable from other forms of social welfare legislation." Whatever meaning or relevance this opaque observation might have in some other context, it simply has no bearing on the issues at hand. Indeed, it is never made clear what the Court's opinion means on this score.

The importance of education is beyond dispute. Yet we have held repeatedly that the importance of a governmental service does not elevate it to the status of a "fundamental right" for purposes of equal protection analysis. *San Antonio School District v. Rodriguez* (1973); *Lindsey v. Normet* (1972). In *San Antonio School District*, JUSTICE POWELL, speaking for the Court, expressly rejected the proposition that state laws dealing with public education are subject to special scrutiny under the Equal Protection Clause. Moreover, the Court points to no meaningful way to distinguish between education and other governmental benefits in this context. Is the Court suggesting that education is more "fundamental" than food, shelter, or medical care?

The Equal Protection Clause guarantees similar treatment of similarly situated persons, but it does not mandate a constitutional hierarchy of governmental services. JUSTICE POWELL, speaking for the Court in *San Antonio School District,* put it well in stating that to the extent this Court raises or lowers the degree of "judicial scrutiny" in equal protection cases according to a transient Court majority's view of the societal importance of the interest affected, we "assum[e] a legislative role and one for which the Court lacks both authority and competence." Yet that is precisely what the Court does today. . . .

The central question in these cases, as in every equal protection case not involving truly fundamental rights "explicitly or implicitly guaranteed by the Constitution," *San Antonio School District,* is whether there is some legitimate basis for a legislative distinction between different classes of persons. The fact that the distinction is drawn in legislation affecting access to public education—as opposed to legislation allocating other important governmental benefits, such as public assistance, health care, or housing—cannot make a difference in the level of scrutiny applied.

Once it is conceded—as the Court does—that illegal aliens are not a suspect class, and that education is not a fundamental right, our inquiry should focus on and be limited to whether the legislative classification at issue bears a rational relationship to a legitimate state purpose. *Vance v. Bradley* (1979); *Dandridge v. Williams* (1970).

The State contends primarily that § 21.031 serves to prevent undue depletion of its limited revenues available for education, and to preserve the fiscal integrity of the State's school financing system against an ever-increasing flood of illegal aliens—aliens over whose entry or continued presence it has no control. Of course such fiscal concerns alone could not justify discrimination against a suspect class or an arbitrary and irrational denial of benefits to a particular group of persons. Yet I assume no member of this Court would argue that prudent conservation of finite state revenues is *per se* an illegitimate goal. . . .

Without laboring what will undoubtedly seem obvious to many, it simply is not "irrational" for a State to conclude that it does not have the same responsibility to provide benefits for persons whose very presence in the State and this country is illegal as it does to provide for persons lawfully present. By definition, illegal aliens have no right whatever

to be here, and the State may reasonably, and constitutionally, elect not to provide them with governmental services at the expense of those who are lawfully in the State. In *DeCamas v. Bica* (1976), we held that a State may protect its "fiscal interests and lawfully resident labor force from the deleterious effects on its economy resulting from the employment of illegal aliens." . . .

It is significant that the federal government has seen fit to exclude illegal aliens from numerous social welfare programs, such as the food stamp program, the old age assistance, aid to families with dependent children, aid to the blind, aid to the permanently and totally disabled, and supplemental security income programs, the Medicare hospital insurance benefits program, and the Medicaid hospital insurance benefits for the aged and disabled program. Although these exclusions do not conclusively demonstrate the constitutionality of the State's use of the same classification for comparable purposes, at the very least they tend to support the rationality of excluding illegal alien residents of a State from such programs so as to preserve the State's finite revenues for the benefit of lawful residents. See *Mathews v. Diaz* (1976).

The Court maintains—as if this were the issue—that "barring undocumented children from local schools would not necessarily improve the quality of education provided in those schools.". . . . However, the legitimacy of barring illegal aliens from programs such as Medicare or Medicaid does not depend on a showing that the barrier would "improve the quality" of medical care given to persons lawfully entitled to participate in such programs. Modern education, like medical care, is enormously expensive, and there can be no doubt that very large added costs will fall on the State or its local school districts as a result of the inclusion of illegal aliens in the tuition-free public schools. . . .

Denying a free education to illegal alien children is not a choice I would make were I a legislator. Apart from compassionate considerations, the long-range costs of excluding any children from the public schools may well outweigh the costs of educating them. But that is not the issue; the fact that there are sound policy arguments against the Texas legislature's choice does not render that choice an unconstitutional one.

Source: Congressional Quarterly. *Historic Documents of 1982.* Washington, DC: Congressional Quarterly, Inc., 1983.

District Court on Admission of Haitians, 1993

In 1990, Congress passed a law banning HIV-positive persons from entering the United States. President George Bush used this law to keep over 150 Haitian refugees in confinement at the U.S. military base at Guantanamo, Cuba, a decision criticized by presidential candidate Bill Clinton in 1992. Upon coming to office, however, President Clinton maintained the ban, but his decision was oveturned by a U.S. District Court, which agreed with plaintiff arguments that they were being denied constitutional rights to legal counsel and due process.

The following document includes excerpts from the District Court's June 8, 1993, decision.

STATEMENT OF FACTS

In 1981, the United States commenced the Alien Migration Interdiction Operation ("AMIO"), formerly known as the Haitian Migrant Interdiction Operation. A cooperative agreement between the United States and Haiti dated September 23, 1981 ("Haiti-U.S. Agreement") allows the United States Coast Guard ("Coast Guard") to board Haitian-flagged vessels on the high seas in order to inquire into the condition and destination of the vessel and the status of those on board. While the Agreement explicitly provides that the "United States does not intend to return to Haiti any Haitian migrants whom the United States authorities determine to qualify for refugee status," a vessel and its passengers were subject to return or repatriation to Haiti if the Coast Guard determined that a violation of United States or Haitian law had occurred. Between 1981 and 1991, the United States interdicted approximately 25,000 Haitians. The United States conducted refugee or asylum prescreening aboard Coast Guard cutters for interdicted Haitians as well as for interdicted nationals of 39 other countries including the Dominican Republic, the Bahamas, Pakistan, Iran, India, Colombia, and Chile during that period.

On September 30, 1991, Jean Bertrand Aristide ("Aristide"), the first democratically elected president in Haiti's history, was overthrown in a military coup. Fearing political persecution, thousands of Haitians fled the country by crossing the border into the Dominican Republic or taking to the high seas. Within a month of the coup, a large number of overcrowded, unseaworthy boats began departing from Haiti, and the United States Coast Guard began interdicting an increasing number of such vessels in international waters.

Prior to interdicting a vessel, the Coast Guard inquired about the vessel's destination. Except when effecting a rescue at sea, the Coast Guard would not remove the passengers or master of a Haitian boat unless it was determined that the vessel was bound for the United States. However, the Coast Guard made no effort to determine the intended destination of each passenger on a particular vessel. If the Coast Guard believed that the vessel was headed for the United States, the Coast Guard interdicted all passengers, even if the passengers were willing to go to locations other than the United States. Because of their lack of seaworthiness, most of the interdicted Haitian vessels, if not all, would not have made it to the United States. In fact, some of the Haitian vessels landed in Cuba, Jamaica, and the Bahamas. When the Coast Guard detained a Haitian vessel, it boarded the vessel and required all passengers to disembark. After all of the passengers had complied, the Coast Guard destroyed the Haitian vessel. Interdicted Haitians were thus given no option but to be detained on the Coast Guard cutter and to be taken to whatever location the Coast Guard elected.

ASYLUM SCREENING AND PRE-SCREENING PROCEDURES

Following the coup, the United States temporarily suspended its repatriation program while the Immigration and Naturalization Service ("INS") consulted with the United

States Department of State ("State Department") on the procedures for handling the Haitian refugees. While the INS awaited a decision from Washington, the Coast Guard cutters with Haitian refugees aboard circled in international waters. For health and safety reasons, the cutters docked at Guantanamo Bay Naval Base, Cuba ("Guantanamo") on or about November 13, 1991, and the Haitians disembarked. A few days later, the decision making authority for determining whether interdicted Haitians were screened in or screened out was delegated back to INS officers in the field.

On November 22, 1991, the Office of the Deputy Commissioner of INS issued a memorandum stating that a "credible fear of return" standard was to be utilized in asylum pre-screening procedures. Under this "credible fear" standard, Haitians with only one or two "refugee-like" characteristics would be screened in, and thus determined to be eligible for political asylum. Interdicted Haitians with no "refugee-like" characteristics would be "screened out," and thus determined to be ineligible for political asylum and subject to repatriation. The "credible fear of return" standard was designed to be far more generous than the "well-founded fear of return" standard generally applied to asylum seekers.

As the number of interdicted Haitians rose, the INS transferred their interviewing operations from the Coast Guard cutters to Guantanamo. The interviews were conducted by highly trained members of the INS asylum corps which included INS officers, immigration lawyers, and human rights monitors. No attorneys representing the refugees were present during the "credible fear of return" interviews. Since October 1991, the INS screened in 10,500 Haitians found to have a "credible fear of return" and transported them to the United States to apply for asylum. An additional 25,000 interdictees were returned to Haiti by the Coast Guard after undergoing INS prescreening. A very small number were accepted by third countries.

RESCREENING HIV+ HAITIAN DETAINEES

Soon after the INS began its Guantanamo operation, the United States began to seek third countries in which the Haitians could be relocated. The State Department pursued this with various countries in the region. Two countries, Belize and Honduras, offered to provide limited assistance, but prior to accepting the Haitians asked that they be tested for the HIV virus. The results of those tests disclosed the presence of the virus in a number of the Haitian detainees at Guantanamo leading the Government to conduct HIV testing for all screened-in Haitians. The Haitians are the only group of asylum seekers to be medically tested for HIV.

Prior to September 1991, all screened-in Haitian refugees were brought to the United States before receiving medical screening. As Gene McNary, then INS Commissioner, [stated] in a memorandum dated May 30, 1991, entitled "Asylum Pre-Screening of Interdicted Aliens and Asylum Seekers in INS Custody": "[i]nterdicted asylum seekers identified at sea for transfer to the United States will be properly inspected and medically screened *upon arrival* into the United States."

Then in a memorandum dated February 29, 1992, Grover Joseph Rees, INS General Counsel, stated a new INS policy requiring second or "well-founded fear" interviews of screened-in persons who tested positive for the Human Immunodeficiency Virus ("HIV"). . . .

By letter dated March 11, 1992, attorneys for the Haitian Service Organizations requested permission to communicate with the screened-in Haitians held on Guantanamo. The request was denied. The Screened In Plaintiffs detained on Guantanamo themselves repeatedly requested counsel. Their requests were also denied. The military did not oppose visits from counsel and when such visits have been permitted, the military has not found any disruption to the operation of the camp. Other groups, including the press, clergy, and non-U.S. contract workers (e.g., Cubans, Jamaicans, and Filipinos) have been permitted access to Guantanamo. In the absence of attorneys, the Haitians have received legal advice from the military, INS, Community Relations Service representatives, ministers, and even military doctors.

Notwithstanding the fact that attorneys are regularly present during nearly identical asylum interviews in the United States, the INS refused to permit the Screened In Plaintiffs to have counsel present at their "well-founded fear" interview. At trial, an INS official expressed the agency's concern with the presence of attorneys at asylum interviews saying that lawyers would only stress the positive element of an applicant's case and deemphasize the negative aspects. This Court finds that lawyers serve a necessary and useful purpose in representing an asylum seeker in connection with the well-founded fear of return interview. Their presence at these interviews is also clearly feasible. The Government's decision to deny Plaintiff Haitian Service Organizations access to Camp Bulkeley is based solely on the content of what they had to say and the viewpoint they would express.

The second interviews, like the first interviews, were conducted in the absence of attorneys. Of the HIV+ Screened In Plaintiffs who underwent the second interview, 115 Haitians were found to have a well-founded fear of return. A number of HIV+ Haitians who had been screened in were repatriated to Haiti after having failed the second interview or having declined to undergo the second interview. Haitians who received an adverse determination did not have the opportunity to appeal the decision.

GUANTANAMO OPERATION

. . . When the first group of Haitians arrived in November 1991, the existing facilities at Guantanamo were not sufficient to provide housing for all interdictees. A special Joint Task Force ("JTF") comprised of several branches of the

Armed Services, was sent to Guantanamo to provide temporary humanitarian assistance to the Haitians including housing, food, and medical care from military physicians. In order to house the Haitians, the JTF evicted U.S. military personnel from the cinder-block quarters at Camp Bulkeley on the eastern edge of the base. Tents were also erected at Camp Bulkeley to temporarily house the several thousand migrants who arrived at Guantanamo at the outset. When Camp Bulkeley's capacity proved inadequate, the JTF opened a new series of camps at the unused McCalla air field. These McCalla camps were all tent facilities except for the large hangar at the airfield. . . .

In March 1992, after the prevalence of the HIV virus among the refugee population was ascertained, the JTF created a separate camp for them. Camp Bulkeley was chosen for that purpose. The then existing population of HIV negative Haitians at Camp Bulkeley remained until they were processed and departed Guantanamo. As "screened in" HIV+ Haitians were identified, they were transferred to Camp Bulkeley, eventually making it predominantly an HIV+ facility. The camp also contained HIV negative relatives of the HIV+ Haitians.

Today there are approximately 200 "screened in" HIV+ Haitians remaining at Guantanamo. They live in camps surrounded by razor barbed wire. They tie plastic garbage bags to the sides of the building to keep the rain out. They sleep on cots and hang sheets to create some semblance of privacy. They are guarded by the military and are not permitted to leave the camp, except under military escort. The Haitian detainees have been subjected to pre-dawn military sweeps as they sleep by as many as 400 soldiers dressed in full riot gear. They are confined like prisoners and are subject to detention in the brig without a hearing for camp rule infractions. Although the Haitian detainees have a chapel, weight room, bicycle repair shop, beauty parlor, and other amenities at their disposal, none of these things are currently available to them, as they are now confined to Camp Alpha, a small section of Camp Bulkeley, or to the brig.

MEDICAL CARE AT GUANTANAMO

. . . The two physicians [at the Haitian clinic] are assisted by a medical staff of four registered nurses, three independent duty corpsmen, a family practice nurse practitioner, 20 general duty corpsmen, and a preventive medicine technician whose duties include spraying standing water against insects, and rodent control. The clinic is a cinderblock, air conditioned building with four examining rooms, a large waiting area, a laboratory, and a pharmacy. The clinic, open generally from 7:30 a.m. to 4:00 p.m. daily, has 11 beds, but its capacity is expandable to about 55.

The Haitians do not need an appointment to come to the clinic, however, they may make appointments to see physicians as needed. The clinic is staffed 24 hours a day, seven days a week either by general duty corpsmen or physicians. . . .

Despite the ability of military doctors and facilities to treat routine illnesses, the Government acknowledges that the medical facilities on the Guantanamo Naval Base are inadequate to provide medical care to those Haitians who have developed AIDS, particularly patients with T-cell counts of 200 or below or a percentage of 13 or less. The military doctors believe that the medical facilities on Guantanamo are inadequate to treat such AIDS patients. . . . The military doctors first raised these concerns at least as early as May 1992. The military has requested that certain HIV+ Haitians be medically evacuated from Guantanamo because the military does not believe it can provide adequate medical care to those patients on Guantanamo. Certain of these requests have been denied by the INS on more than one occasion.

At trial the Government did not offer any evidence which would prove the facilities at Guantanamo to be adequate. In fact, defendants' counsel admitted that "the medical facilities at Guantanamo are not presently sufficient to provide treatment for such AIDS patients under the medical care standard applicable within the United States itself." But when asked whether the Government was "prepared to send those [patients] to the United States for treatment," Defendants' counsel responded, "The government does not intend at this point to do that." . . .

Although the defendants euphemistically refer to its Guantanamo operation as a "humanitarian camp," the facts disclose that it is nothing more than an HIV prison camp presenting potential public health risks to the Haitians held there. There is no dispute that because HIV+ individuals are immunosuppressed, they are more susceptible to a variety of infections, many of which can be transmitted from one person to the next. No major outbreak of infectious disease has occurred yet, but by segregating HIV+ individuals, the Government places the Haitian detainees at greater risk of contracting infections, including tuberculosis, measles and other life-threatening diseases, than if they were permitted to live in the general population. . . .

In addition, the prison camp environment created by the Government is not conducive to an effective doctor-patient relationship. . . .

The seriously impaired doctor-patient relationship makes it more difficult for defendants to provide adequate medical care at the camp. Even if Defendants continue to provide medical services, many of the Haitian detainees will grow increasingly sick because they do not trust their diagnosis or the medication prescribed for them.

CONCLUSIONS OF LAW

[PARTS I AND II OMITTED]

III. HAITIAN SERVICE ORGANIZATIONS' FIRST AMENDMENT RIGHTS

Plaintiff Haitian Service Organizations' First Claim for Relief is that the Government has violated their First Amendment right by denying them and their attorneys access to the Screened In Plaintiffs for the purpose of counseling, advocacy, and representation....

The First Amendment says that "Congress shall make no Law . . . abridging the freedom of speech." U.S. Const. amend. 1. That provision applies on Guantanamo Bay Naval Base, which is under the complete control and jurisdiction of the United States government, and where the government exercises complete control over all means of delivering communications.... The Government has violated the Haitian Service Organization's First Amendment rights to free speech and to associate for the purpose of providing legal counsel by denying them equal access to the screened-in Haitians held on Guantanamo. Defendants have permitted press, clergy, politicians and other non-lawyers to meet with the Haitians and have permitted many others, including non-citizen contract workers, onto the base. In addition, the Haitians have received legal advice, which has often been erroneous, from the military, the INS, the Community Relations Service and even military doctors. The legal rights and options of Haitian detainees are discussed on Guantanamo, but only from the viewpoint of which the Government approves....

[T]he Haitian Service Organizations have been retained by the Screened In Plaintiffs and have asserted a right to speak with their clients, the screened-in Haitians. The lawyers here seek only to communicate, at their own expense, with clients who have specifically sought them out. The Court thus finds that the lawyers for the Haitian Service Organizations have been barred because of the viewpoint of the message they seek to convey to the Haitians, in violation of the First Amendment. Such Government discrimination against disfavored viewpoints strikes at the heart of the First Amendment....

IV. DUE PROCESS

Plaintiffs' Third Claim for Relief in the Amended Complaint states that the Government has violated the Screened In Plaintiffs' due process rights under the Fifth Amendment....

The Supreme Court has long held that aliens outside the United States are entitled to due process in civil suits in United States courts....

The United States government has already bound itself by treaty not to "impose penalties" on persons it has recognized as refugees who flee to the United States "directly from a territory where their life or freedom was threatened" on account of political persecution....

The Haitian detainees are imprisoned in squalid, prison-like camps surrounded by razor barbed wire. They are not free to wander about the base. Guarded by the military day and night, the Screened In Plaintiffs are subject to surprise pre-dawn military sweeps conducted by soldiers outfitted in full riot gear searching for missing detainees. Haitian de-

tainees have been punished for rule infractions by being flexicuffed and sent to "administrative segregation camp" (Camp Alpha or Camp 7) or the brig. Such conditions cannot be tolerated when, as here, the detainees have a right to due process.

A. ACCESS TO COUNSEL DURING "WELL-FOUNDED" INTERVIEWS

The Screened In Plaintiffs have a protected liberty interest in not being wrongly repatriated to Haiti, . . . and to due process before defendants alter their screened in status....

. . . [T]he private interest of the Screened In Plaintiffs not to be returned to Haiti is of the highest order. Based on the INS's own findings, the screened-in Haitians have already been found to have at least a credible fear of return. This showing exceeds that of an unscreened asylum applicant in the United States whose interest in applying for asylum is constitutionally protected....

B. MEDICAL CARE

Constitutional due process mandates both provision of adequate medical care to persons in official custody.... As persons in coercive, nonpunitive, and indefinite detention, the Haitian detainees on Guantanamo are constitutionally entitled to medically adequate conditions of confinement....

The military's own doctors have made INS aware that Haitian detainees with T-cell counts of 200 or below or percentages of 13 or below should be medically evacuated to the United States because of a lack of facilities and specialists at Guantanamo. Despite this knowledge, Defendant INS has repeatedly failed to act on recommendations and deliberately ignored the medical advice of U.S. military doctors that all persons with T-cell count below 200 or percentages below 13 be transported to the United States for treatment. Such actions constitute deliberate indifference to the Haitians' medical needs in violation of their due process rights....

[C OMITTED]

D. INDEFINITE DETENTION

As individuals held in custody by the United States, the Screened In Plaintiffs also have a liberty interest in not being arbitrarily or indefinitely detained....

Here, the Screened In Plaintiffs continued detention is

the result of the Defendants' actions, not the aliens' own choices. The Government stopped processing the cases of these and other screened-in Haitians in June 1992, after the Second Circuit upheld this Court's injunction entitling the Haitians to be represented by counsel. One-hundred and fifteen Haitians at Guantanamo have met the well-founded fear standard in the second interviews and have remained in detention for almost two years. . . .

. . . [T]he detained Haitians are neither criminals nor national security risks. Some are pregnant mothers and others are children. Simply put, they are merely the unfortunate victims of a fatal disease. The Government has failed to demonstrate to this Court's satisfaction that the detainees' illness warrants the kind of indefinite detention usually reserved for spies and murderers. . . . Where detention no longer serves a legitimate purpose, the detainees must be released. The Haitian camp at Guantanamo is the only known refugee camp in the world composed entirely of HIV+ refugees. The Haitians' plight is a tragedy of immense proportion and their continued detainment is totally unacceptable to this Court. . . .

IV. VIOLATIONS OF ADMINISTRATIVE PROCEDURE ACT

For their Fifth Claim for Relief, Plaintiffs allege that a) the Government violated the APA by conducting unauthorized "well-founded fear" interviews and b) the Attorney General abused her discretion by denying parole for the screened-in Haitian Plaintiffs. . . .

Plaintiffs allege that the Attorney General's refusal to parole them from detention due to their HIV+ status constitutes an abuse of discretion. For the reason set forth below, the Court agrees and sets aside her denial of parole. . . .

By effectively denying the plaintiffs release from detention, defendant Attorney General has abused her discretion. . . . Haitians remain in detention solely because they are Haitian and have tested HIV-positive. The Government has admitted that the ban on the admission of aliens with communicable diseases has not been strictly enforced against every person seeking entry. Each year many "nonimmigrants" enter the United States, are legally entitled to remain for years, and are not subject to HIV testing. To date, the Government has only enforced the ban against Haitians. . . .

The Attorney General has abused her discretion in failing to parole the HIV+ Haitian detainees on Guantanamo. Her decision to detain these Haitians deviates from established parole policy and is illegally based upon a statute which is selectively enforced against Haitian nationals and merely makes persons carrying the HIV virus excludable from "admission" or permanent residence. For foregoing reasons, the Court hereby sets aside the Attorney General's denial of parole. . . .

RELIEF

For the reasons stated above,

1. The following class is hereby certified:

(a) all Haitian citizens who have been or will be "screened in" who are, have been or will be detained on Guantanamo Bay Naval Base, or any other territory subject to United States jurisdiction, or on Coast Guard cutters, including those who have been or will be subject to post-screening processing (or who have resisted such processing) (hereinafter "Screened In Plaintiffs");

2. It is hereby,

(a) DECLARED that the "Well-Founded Fear" Processing by Defendants set forth in the Rees Memorandum is in excess of Defendants' statutory authority, and

(b) ORDERED that such "Well-Founded Fear" Processing be permanently enjoined, held unlawful and set aside pursuant to the Administrative Procedure Act: and

3. It is hereby further

(a) DECLARED that defendant Attorney General's exercise of the statutory parole power under INA § 212(d)(5) to deny Screened In Plaintiffs parole out of detention constitutes an abuse of discretion; and

(b) ORDERED that defendant Attorney General's exercise of the statutory parole power under INA § 212(d)(5) to deny Screened In Plaintiffs parole out of detention be permanently enjoined, held unlawful and set aside pursuant to the Administrative Procedure Act; and

4. It is hereby further

(a) DECLARED that the "Well-Founded Fear" Processing, Disciplinary Proceedings, Arbitrary and Indefinite Detention, Medical Care and Camp Conditions to which Screened In Plaintiffs are being subjected by Defendants denies those plaintiffs Due Process of Law; and

(b) ORDERED that such "Well-Founded Fear" Processing, Disciplinary Proceedings, Arbitrary and Indefinite Detention, Medical Care and Camp Conditions be permanently enjoined pursuant to the Fifth Amendment of the United States Constitution; and that Screened In Plaintiffs be immediately released (to anywhere but Haiti) from such processing, proceedings, detention, medical care and camp conditions; and

5. It is hereby further

(a) DECLARED that denying plaintiff Haitian Service Organizations immediate access to Guantanamo to communicate and associate with their detained Screened-In Plaintiff clients violates the First Amendment; and

(b) ORDERED that Defendants are permanently enjoined from denying plaintiff Haitian Service Organizations immediate access at Guantanamo, on Coast Guard Cutters, or at any other place subject to U.S. jurisdiction to any member of the class of Screened In Plaintiffs (regardless of whether any such screened-in plaintiff has been furnished with an exact date and time for an interview), subject to reasonable time, place, and manner limitations for the purpose of providing class members legal counsel, advocacy, and representation; and

6. It is hereby finally

(a) DECLARED that Plaintiffs are entitled to such other and further relief as the Court may deem just and proper, including reasonable attorneys' fees and costs, to be determined at a future hearing.

So ordered.

Sterling Johnson, Jr.
United States District Judge
Dated: Brooklyn, New York
June 8, 1993

Source: United States District Court for the Eastern District of New York. *Ruling on Admission of Haitians.* June 8, 1993.

LULAC et al. v. Wilson et al., 1995

Passed by voters in November 1994, California Proposition 187 tried to anticipate constitutional challenges, by stating that should any part of the proposition be declared invalid, the rest of the statute would remain in force. In the following case—brought by the League of United Latin American Citizens (LULAC)—the federal courts ruled that the proposition violated, among other things, the equal protection clause of the Fourteenth Amendment to the U.S. Constitution by discriminating against one class of persons—that is, immigrants. The following is a court-produced summary of the injunction order issued against enforcement of Proposition 187.

SUMMARY

Public interest groups and individual citizens, in consolidated actions, brought suit for declaratory and injunctive relief to bar California Governor, Attorney General and other state actors from enforcing provisions of the voter-approved California initiative measure requiring state personnel to verify immigration status of persons with whom they come into contact, report persons in United States unlawfully to state and federal officials, and deny those persons social services, health care, and education benefits. On plaintiff's motions for summary judgment, the District Court, Pfaelzer, J., held that: (1) classification, notification, cooperation and reporting provisions of the measure had direct and substantial effect on immigration, so as to be preempted by federal immigration law; (2) initiative's denial of public benefits based on federal determinations of immigration status was not impermissible regulation of immigration; (3) provision excluding illegal aliens from public elementary and secondary schools was preempted by federal law as being prohibited by equal protection clause of Fourteenth Amendment; (4) verification components of measure prohibiting public postsecondary education to persons not authorized under federal law to be in the United States were permissible; (5) provisions of measure criminalizing making and using false documents to conceal true citizenship or resident alien status were legitimate exercise of state's police power; (6) provisions denying public social services to illegal immigrants as applied to federally funded programs administered by the state that awarded benefits regardless of immigration status conflicted with and was preempted by federal law; (7) provisions of measure prohibiting public postsecondary educational institutions from admitting, enrolling or permitting attendance of persons not authorized under federal law to be present in the United States were not preempted by federal law; and (8) criminal penalties contemplated by provision criminalizing the manufacture, distribution, sale or use of false documents to conceal immigration status were not preempted by federal law.

Motions granted in part and denied in part.

Source: 908 F. Supp. 755 (C.D. California 1995).

D. Referenda

California Proposition 63, 1986

On November 4, 1986, Californians voted 73 to 26 percent in favor of Proposition 63, a referendum adding an amendment to the state constitution making English "the official language" of the state. Hispanic and other immigrant groups claimed that the amendment would prevent non-English-speaking residents from getting access to governmental services and the courts. Court challenges to the amendment were immediately launched. In January 1988, however, U.S. Court of Appeals ruled that the amendment was not in violation of the U.S. Constitution. But it also said that the amendment was largely symbolic, opinions that were later backed up by the U.S. Supreme Court.

The following document contains the amendment passed by California voters.

CALIFORNIA VOTE ON ENGLISH AS OFFICIAL LANGUAGE

November 4, 1986

SEC. 6. (a) Purpose English is the common language of the people of the United States of America and the State of California. This section is intended to preserve, protect and strengthen the English language, and not to super-sede any of the rights guaranteed to the people by this Constitution.

(b) English as the Official Language of California. English is the official language of the State of California.

(c) Enforcement.

The Legislature shall enforce this section by appropriate legislation. The Legislature and officials of the State of California shall take all steps necessary to insure that the role of English as the common language of the State of California is preserved and enhanced. The Legislature shall make no law which diminishes or ignores the role of English as the common language of the State of California.

(d) Personal Right of Action and Jurisdiction of Courts.

Any person who is a resident of or doing business in the State of California shall have standing to sue the State of California to enforce this section, and the Courts of record of the State of California shall have jurisdiction to hear cases brought to enforce this section. The Legislature may provide reasonable and appropriate limitations on the time and manner of suits brought under this section.

Source: California State Ballot, Proposition 63, November 4, 1986.

California Proposition 187, 1994

*I*n *November 1994, the voters of California approved Proposition 187, the "Save Our State" initiative. Facing unprecedented waves of legal and illegal immigration, the largely native white electorate passed a proposition that they hoped would reduce the economic, educational, and social welfare benefits that were supposedly drawing immigrants. Ultimately, despite efforts to make sure the proposition was constitutional, federal courts ruled that it was not (see* LULAC et al. v. Wilson et al.*).*

SECTION 1. FINDINGS AND DECLARATION

The People of California find and declare as follows:

That they have suffered and are suffering economic hardship by the presence of illegal aliens in the state. That they have suffered and are suffering personal injury and damage by the criminal conduct of illegal aliens in the state. That they have a right to the protection of their government from any person or persons entering this country unlawfully.

Therefore, the People of California declare their intention to provide for cooperation between their agencies of state and local government with the federal government, and to establish a system of required notification by and between such agencies to prevent illegal aliens in the United States from receiving benefits or public services in the State of California.

Section 2. Manufacture, Distribution or Sale of False Citizenship or Resident Alien Documents: Crime and Punishment.

Section 113. Is added to the Penal Code, to read:

Section 113. Any person who manufactures, distributes or sells false documents to conceal the true citizenship or res-

ident alien status of another is guilty of a felony and shall be punished by imprisonment in the state prison for five years or by a fine of seventy-five thousand dollars.

Section 3. Use of False Citizenship or Resident Alien Documents: Crime and Punishment . . .

Section 114. Any person who uses false documents to conceal his or her true citizenship or resident alien status is guilty of a felony, and shall be punished by imprisonment in a state prison for five years or by a fine of twenty-five thousand dollars.

Section 4. Law Enforcement Cooperation with INS [Immigration and Naturalization Service] . . .

Section 834b. (a) Every law enforcement agency in California shall fully cooperate with the United States Immigration and Naturalization Service regarding any person who is arrested if he or she is suspected of being present in the United States in violation of federal immigration laws.

(b) With respect to any such person who is arrested, and suspected of being present in the United States in violation of federal immigration laws, every law enforcement agency shall do the following:

(1). Attempt to verify the legal status of such person as a citizen of the United States, an alien lawfully admitted as a permanent resident, an alien lawfully admitted for a temporary period of time or as an alien who is present in the United States in violation of immigration laws. The verification process may include, but shall not be limited to, questioning the person regarding his or her date and place of birth and entry into the United States, and demanding documentation to indicate his or her legal status.

(2). Notify the person of his or her apparent status as an alien who is present in the United States in violation of federal immigration laws and inform him or her that, apart from any criminal justice precedings [*sic*], he or she must obtain legal status or leave the United States.

(3). Notify the Attorney General of California and the United States Immigration and Naturalization Service of the apparent illegal status and provide any additional information that may be requested by any other public entity.

(c) Any legislative, administrative, or other action by a city, county, or other legally authorized local governmental entity with jurisdictional boundaries, or by a law enforcement agency, to prevent or limit the cooperation required by subdivision (a) is expressly prohibited.

Section 5. Exclusion of Illegal Aliens from Public Social Services.

Section 10001.5. Is added to the Welfare and Institutions Code, to read:

Section 10001.5 (a) In order to carry out the intention of the People of California that only citizens of the United States and aliens lawfully admitted to the United States may receive the benefits of public social services and to ensure that all persons employed in the providing of those services shall diligently protect public funds from misuse, the provisions of this section are adopted.

(b) A person shall not receive any public social services to which he or she may not otherwise be entitled until the legal status of that person has been verified as one of the following:

(1) A citizen of the United States.

(2) An alien lawfully admitted as a permanent resident.

(3) An alien lawfully admitted for a temporary period of time . . .

Section 6. Exclusion of Illegal Aliens from Publicly Funded Health Care.

Chapter 1.3. Publicly Funded Health Care Services.

Section 130. (a) In order to carry out the intention of the People of California that, excepting emergency medical care as required by federal law, only citizens of the United States and aliens lawfully admitted to the United States may receive the benefits of publicly funded health care, and to ensure that all persons employed in the providing of those services shall diligently protect public funds from misuse, the provisions of this section are adopted. . . .

(c) If any publicly funded health care facility in this state from whom a person seeks health care services, other than emergency medical care as required by federal law, determines or reasonably suspects, based on the information provided it, that the person is an alien in the United States in violation of the federal law. . . . [Services will not be forth-

coming and the Immigration and Naturalization Service will be notified.]

Section 7. Exclusion of Illegal Aliens from Public Elementary and Secondary Schools.

Section 48215. Is added to the Education Code to read:

Section 48215. (a) No public elementary or secondary school shall admit, or permit the attendance of, any child who is not a citizen of the United States, an alien lawfully admitted as a permanent resident, or a person who is otherwise authorized under federal law to be present. . . .

(b) Commencing January 1, 1995, each school district shall verify the legal status of each child enrolling in the school district for the first time. . . .

(d) By January 1, 1996, each school district shall also have verified the legal status of each parent or guardian of each child. . . .

(e) Each school district shall provide information to the State Superintendent of Public Instruction, the Attorney General of California and the United States Immigration and Naturalization Service regarding any enrollee or pupil, or parent or guardian, attending a public elementary or secondary school in the school district determined or reasonably suspected to be in violation of federal immigration laws within forty-five days after becoming aware of an apparent violation. . . .

(f) For each child who cannot establish legal status in the United States each school district shall continue to provide education for a period of ninety days from the date of the notice. . . .

Section 8. Exclusion of Illegal Aliens from Public Postsecondary Educational Institutions.

Section 66010.8. is added to the Education Code to read:

Section 66010.8. (a) No public institution of postsecondary education shall admit, enroll, or permit the attendance of any person who is not a citizen of the United States, an alien lawfully admitted as a permanent resident, in the United States, or a person who is otherwise authorized under federal law to be present in the United States.

(c) Commencing with the first term or semester that begins after January 1, 1996, and at the end of each term or semester thereafter, each public postsecondary educational institution shall verify the status of each person enrolled or in attendance at that institution. . . .

Section 9. Attorney General Cooperation with the INS.

Section 53609.65. Is added to the Government Code, to read:

Section 53609.65. Whenever the state or a city, or a county, or any other legally authorized local government entity with jurisdictional boundaries reports the presence of a person who is suspected of being present in the United States in violation of federal immigration laws to the Attorney General of California, that report shall be transmitted to the United States Immigration and Naturalization Service. The Attorney General shall be responsible for maintaining ongoing and accurate records of such reports, and shall provide any additional information that may be requested by any other government entity.

Source: 908 F. supp. 755 (C.D. California 1995).

California Proposition 227, 1998

*O*n June 2, 1998, Californians voted 61 to 39 percent in favor of Proposition 227, a referendum requiring that nearly all of the state's 1.4 million limited-English students be taught exclusively in English. Backed by businessman and maverick Republican politician Ron Unz, the initiative ended California's 25-year experiment with bilingual education. Although faced with court challenges almost immediately after its passage, the law remains on the books, and has sparked similar efforts in neighboring Arizona.

The following document includes text from Proposition 227— also known as the Unz initiative—as well as sample ballot arguments for and against.

SECTION 1. Chapter 3 (commencing with Section 300) is added to Part 1 of the Educational Code, to read:

CHAPTER 3.
ENGLISH LANGUAGE EDUCATION FOR IMMIGRANT CHILDREN

ARTICLE 1. Findings and Declarations

300. The People of California find and declare as follows:

(a) WHEREAS the English language is the national public language of the United States of America and of the state of California, is spoken by the vast majority of California residents, and is also the leading world language for science, technology, and international business, thereby being the language of economic opportunity; and

(b) WHEREAS immigrant parents are eager to have their children acquire a good knowledge of English, thereby allowing them to fully participate in the American Dream of economic and social advancement; and

(c) WHEREAS the government and the public schools of California have a moral obligation and a constitutional duty to provide all of California's children, regardless of their ethnicity or national origins, with the skills necessary to become productive members of our society, and of these skills, literacy in the English language is among the most important; and

(d) WHEREAS the public schools of California currently do a poor job of educating immigrant children, wasting financial resources on costly experimental language programs whose failure over the past two decades is demonstrated by the current high drop-out rates and low English literacy levels of many immigrant children; and

(e) WHEREAS young immigrant children can easily acquire full fluency in a new language, such as English, if they are heavily exposed to that language in the classroom at an early age.

(f) THEREFORE it is resolved that: all children in California public schools shall be taught English as rapidly and effectively as possible.

ARTICLE 2. English Language Education

305. Subject to the exceptions provided in Article 3 (commencing with Section 310), all children in California public schools shall be taught English by being taught in English. In particular, this shall require that all children be placed in English language classrooms. Children who are English learners shall be educated through sheltered English immersion during a temporary transition period not normally intended to exceed one year. Local schools shall be permitted to place in the same classroom English learners of different ages but whose degree of English proficiency is similar. Local schools shall be encouraged to mix together in the same classroom English learners from different native-language groups but with the same degree of English fluency. Once English learners have acquired a good working knowledge of English, they shall be transferred to English language mainstream classrooms. As much as possible, current supplemental funding for English learners shall be maintained, subject to possible modification under Article 8 (commencing with Section 335) below.

306. The definitions of the terms used in this article and in Article 3 (commencing with Section 310) are as follows:

(a) "English learner" means a child who does not speak English or whose native language is not English and who is not currently able to perform ordinary classroom work in English, also known as a Limited English Proficiency or LEP child.

(b) "English language classroom" means a classroom in which the language of instruction used by the teaching personnel is overwhelmingly the English language, and in which such teaching personnel possess a good knowledge of the English language.

(c) "English language mainstream classroom" means a classroom in which the students either are native English language speakers or already have acquired reasonable fluency in English.

(d) "Sheltered English immersion" or "structured English immersion" means an English language acquisition process for young children in which nearly all classroom instruction is in English but with the curriculum and presentation designed for children who are learning the language.

(e) "Bilingual education/native language instruction" means a language acquisition process for students in which much or all instruction, textbooks, and teaching materials are in the child's native language.

ARTICLE 3. Parental Exceptions

310. The requirements of Section 305 may be waived with the prior written informed consent, to be provided annually, of the child's parents or legal guardian under the circumstances specified below and in Section 311. Such informed consent shall require that said parents or legal guardian personally visit the school to apply for the waiver and that they there be provided a full description of the educational materials to be used in the different educational program choices and all the educational opportunities available to the child. Under such parental waiver conditions, children may be transferred to classes where they are taught English and other subjects through bilingual education techniques or other generally recognized educational methodologies permitted by law. Individual schools in which 20 students or more of a given grade level receive a waiver shall be required to offer such a class; otherwise, they must allow the students to transfer to a public school in which such a class is offered.

311. The circumstances in which a parental exception waiver may be granted under Section 310 are as follows:

(a) Children who already know English: the child already possesses good English language skills, as measured by standardized tests of English vocabulary comprehension, reading, and writing, in which the child scores at or above the state average for his grade level or at or above the 5th grade average, whichever is lower; or (b) Older children: the child is age 10 years or older, and it is the informed belief of the school principal and educational staff that an alternate course of educational study would be better suited to the child's rapid acquisition of basic English language skills; or

(c) Children with special needs: the child already has been placed for a period of not less than thirty days during that school year in an English language classroom and it is subsequently the informed belief of the school principal and educational staff that the child has such special physical, emotional, psychological, or educational needs that an alternate course of educational study would be better suited to the child's overall educational development. A written description of these special needs must be provided and any such decision is to be made subject to the examination and approval of the local school superintendent, under guidelines established by and subject to the review of the local Board of Education and ultimately the State Board of Education. The existence of such special needs shall not compel issuance of a waiver, and the parents shall be fully informed of their right to refuse to agree to a waiver.

ARTICLE 4. Community-Based English Tutoring

315. In furtherance of its constitutional and legal requirement to offer special language assistance to children coming from backgrounds of limited English proficiency, the state shall encourage family members and others to provide personal English language tutoring to such children, and support these efforts by raising the general level of English language knowledge in the community. Commencing with the fiscal year in which this initiative is enacted and for each of the nine fiscal years following thereafter, a sum of fifty million dollars ($50,000,000) per year is hereby appropriated from the General Fund for the purpose of providing additional funding for free or subsidized programs of adult English language instruction to parents or other members of the community who pledge to provide personal English language tutoring to California school children with limited English proficiency.

316. Programs funded pursuant to this section shall be provided through schools or community organizations. Funding for these programs shall be administered by the Office of the Superintendent of Public Instruction, and shall be disbursed at the discretion of the local school boards, under reasonable guidelines established by, and subject to the review of, the State Board of Education.

ARTICLE 5. Legal Standing and Parental Enforcement

320. As detailed in Article 2 (commencing with Section 305) and Article 3 (commencing with Section 310), all California school children have the right to be provided with an English language public education. If a California school child has been denied the option of an English language instructional curriculum in public school, the child's parent or legal guardian shall have legal standing to sue for enforcement of the provisions of this statute, and if successful shall be awarded normal and customary attorney's fees and actual damages, but not punitive or consequential damages. Any school board member or other elected official or public school teacher or administrator who willfully and repeatedly refuses to implement the terms of this statute by providing such an English language educational option at an available public school to a California school child may be

held personally liable for fees and actual damages by the child's parents or legal guardian.

ARTICLE 6. Severability

325. If any part or parts of this statute are found to be in conflict with federal law or the United States or the California State Constitution, the statute shall be implemented to the maximum extent that federal law, and the United States and the California State Constitution permit. Any provision held invalid shall be severed from the remaining portions of this statute.

ARTICLE 7. Operative Date

330. This initiative shall become operative for all school terms which begin more than sixty days following the date at which it becomes effective.

ARTICLE 8. Amendment

335. The provisions of this act may be amended by a statute that becomes effective upon approval by the electorate or by a statute to further the act's purpose passed by a two-thirds vote of each house of the Legislature and signed by the Governor.

ARTICLE 9. Interpretation

340. Under circumstances in which portions of this statute are subject to conflicting interpretations, Section 300 shall be assumed to contain the governing intent of the statute.

English Language in Public Schools Initiative Statute
Argument in Favor of Proposition 227
Ballot Booklet

WHY DO WE NEED TO CHANGE CALIFORNIA'S BILINGUAL EDUCATION SYSTEM?

- Begun with the best of intentions in the 1970s, bilingual education has failed in actual practice, but the politicians and administrators have refused to admit this failure.

- For most of California's non-English speaking students, bilingual education actually means monolingual, SPANISH-ONLY education for the first 4 to 7 years of school.

- The current system fails to teach children to read and write English. Last year, only 6.7 percent of limited-English students in California learned enough English to be moved into mainstream classes.

- Latino immigrant children are the principal victims of bilingual education. They have the lowest test scores and the highest dropout rates of any immigrant group.

- There are 140 languages spoken by California's schoolchildren. To teach each group of children in their own native language before teaching them English is educationally and fiscally impossible. Yet this impossibility is the goal of bilingual education.

COMMON SENSE ABOUT LEARNING ENGLISH

- Learning a new language is easier the younger the age of the child.

- Learning a language is much easier if the child is immersed in that language.

- Immigrant children already know their native language; they need the public schools to teach them English.

- Children who leave school without knowing how to speak, read, and write English are injured for life economically and socially.

WHAT "ENGLISH FOR THE CHILDREN" WILL DO:

- Require children to be taught English as soon as they start school.

- Provide "sheltered English immersion" classes to help non-English speaking students learn English; research shows this is the most effective method.

- Allow parents to request a special waiver for children with individual educational needs who would benefit from another method.

WHAT "ENGLISH FOR THE CHILDREN" WON'T DO:

It will:

- NOT throw children who can't speak English into regular classes where they would have to "sink or swim."

- NOT cut special funding for children learning English.

- NOT violate any federal laws or court decisions.

WHO SUPPORTS THE INITIATIVE?

- Teachers worried by the undeniable failure of bilingual education and who have long wanted to implement a successful alternative—sheltered English immersion.

- Most Latino parents, according to public polls. They know that Spanish-only bilingual education is preventing their children from learning English by segregating them into an educational dead-end.

- Most Californians. They know that bilingual education has created an educational ghetto by isolating non-English speaking students and preventing them from becoming successful members of society.

WHO OPPOSES THE INITIATIVE?

- Individuals who profit from bilingual education. Bilingual teachers are paid up to $5,000 extra annually and the program provides jobs to thousands of bilingual coordinators and administrators.

- Schools and school districts which receive HUNDREDS OF MILLIONS of extra dollars for schoolchildren classified as not knowing English and who, therefore, have a financial incentive to avoid teaching English to children.

- Activist groups with special agendas and the politicians who support them.
  ALICE CALLAGHAN
  Director, Las Familias del Pueblo
  RON UNZ
  Chairman, English for the Children
  FERNANDO VEGA
  Past Redwood City School Board Member

ENGLISH LANGUAGE IN PUBLIC SCHOOLS

INITIATIVE STATUTE

Argument against Proposition 227—Balloting Booklet
    Proposition 227 imposes one untested method for teaching English on every local school district in California.

Proposition 227 puts limited English speaking children of all ages and languages into one classroom.

The California PTA opposes Proposition 227 because it takes away parents' right to choose what's best for their children.

The California School Boards Association opposes Proposition 227 because it outlaws the best local programs for teaching English.

California's teachers oppose Proposition 227—teachers can be sued personally for teaching in the children's language to help them learn English.

Outlawing decisions by parents, teachers, and school boards on how to teach children English is wrong.

Children in California must learn English.

In thousands of classrooms all over California, they are. Good teachers. Good local school boards. Good parent involvement.

Those successes are not the result of one instructional method imposed on every school by state government.

Sadly, there have been failures too. However, these failures can best be remedied by reasonable program changes that maximize local control.

California should be returning more decisions to parents, teachers, principals, and local school boards.

A growing number of school districts are working with new English teaching methods. Proposition 227 stops them.

The San Diego Union-Tribune Editorial said it best: "School districts should decide for themselves."

We urge you to join us, the California PTA, the California School Boards Association, and California's teachers in voting "NO" on Proposition 227.
    JOHN D'AMELIO
    President, California School Boards Association
    MARY BERGAN
    President, California Federation of Teachers, AFL-CIO
    LOIS TINSON
    President, California Teachers Association

Source: California State Ballot, Proposition 227, June 2, 1998.

POLITICAL PLATFORMS, DEBATES, AND GOVERNMENT REPORTS AND RULINGS

INTRODUCTION

Section 2 of Part IV of the *Encyclopedia of American Immigration* is devoted to political and government documents, including platforms and debates, as well as government reports and rulings. The political documents include the platforms of the Democratic and Republican Parties from the mid-nineteenth century through 1996.

The government reports cover a range of time periods—from the mid-nineteenth century to the end of the twentieth—and a wide array of subjects. The *Senate Report on the Encouragement of Immigration*, 1864, discusses the critical need for immigrant labor at a time when many workers were fighting in the Civil War, while the *Report of the Minnesota Board of Immigration*, 1871, discusses ways to encourage immigration to that underpopulated state. Twentieth-century documents include a report on the payment of reparations to Japanese Americans interned during World War II; a New York State report on the need for multicultural textbooks; various U.S. reports on refugees; a report on the need for high-technology workers; recommendations for the prevention and control of tuberculosis among immigrants; and a State Department report on the subject of U.S. citizenship renunciation.

Immigration Planks of Republican Party Platforms, 1860–1996

The following document includes the planks on immigration from the Republican Party platforms between 1860 and 1996. Two things stand out. First, immigration appears to be mentioned only when it becomes a pressing national issue. Second, comparing Republican Party platforms with their counterparts from the Democratic Party indicates a less welcoming attitude among the former, particularly in the late twentieth century.

1860

That the Republican Party is opposed to any change in our naturalization laws or any state legislation by which the rights of citizens hitherto accorded to immigrants from foreign lands shall be abridged or impaired; and in favor of giving a full and efficient protection of the rights of all classes of citizens, whether native or naturalized, both at home and abroad.

1864

Resolved, That foreign immigration, which in the past has added so much to the wealth, development of resources and increase of power to the nation, the asylum of the oppressed of all nations, should be fostered and encouraged by a liberal and just policy.

1880

Since the authority to regulate immigration and intercourse between the United States and foreign nations rests with the Congress of the United States and the treaty-making power, the Republican Party, regarding the unrestricted immigration of the Chinese as a matter of grave concernment [sic] under the exercise of both these powers, would limit and restrict that immigration by the enactment of such just, humane and reasonable laws and treaties as will produce that result.

1884

The Republican Party, having its birth in a hatred of slave labor and a desire that all men may be truly free and equal, is unalterably opposed to placing our workingmen in competition with any form of servile labor, whether at home and abroad. In this spirit, we denounce the importation of contract labor, whether from Europe or Asia, as an offense against the spirit of American institutions; and we pledge ourselves to sustain the present law restricting Chinese immigration, and to provide such further legislation as is necessary to carry out its purposes.

1888

We declare our hostility to the introduction into this country of foreign contract labor and of Chinese labor, alien to our civilization and constitution; and we demand the rigid enforcement of the existing laws against it, and favor such immediate legislation as will exclude such labor from our shores.

1896

For the protection of the equality of our American citizenship and of the wages of our workingmen, against the fatal competition of low priced labor, we demand that the immigration laws be thoroughly enforced, and so extended as to exclude from entrance to the United States those who can neither read nor write.

1912

We pledge the Republican Party to the enactment of appropriate laws to give relief from the constantly growing evil of induced or undesirable immigration, which is inimical to the progress and welfare of the people of the United States.

1920

IMMIGRATION

The standard of living and the standard of citizenship of a nation are its most precious possessions, and the preservation and the elevation of those standards is the first duty of our government. The immigration policy of the U.S. should be such as to insure that the number of foreigners in the country at any one time shall not exceed that which can be assimilated with reasonable rapidity, and to favor immigrants whose standards are similar to ours.

The selective tests that are at present applied should be improved by requiring a higher physical standard, a more complete exclusion of mental defectives and of criminals, and a more effective inspection applied as near the source of immigration as possible, as well as at the port of entry. Justice to the foreigner and to ourselves demands provision for the guidance, protection and better economic distribution of our alien population. To facilitate government supervision, all aliens should be required to register annually until they become naturalized.

The existing policy of the United States for the practical exclusion of Asiatic immigrants is sound, and should be maintained.

NATURALIZATION

There is urgent need of improvement in our naturalization law. No alien should become a citizen until he has become genuinely American, and adequate tests for determining the alien's fitness for American citizenship should be provided for by law.

We advocate, in addition, the independent naturalization of married women. An American woman, resident in the United States, should not lose her citizenship by marriage to an alien.

1924

The unprecedented living conditions in Europe following the world war created a condition by which we were threatened with mass immigration that would have seriously disturbed our economic life. The law recently enacted is designed to protect the inhabitants of our country, not only the American citizen, but also the alien already with us who is seeking to secure an economic foothold for himself and family from the competition that would come from unrestricted immigration. The administrative features of the law represent a great constructive advance, and eliminate the hardships suffered by immigrants under emergency statute.

We favor the adoption of methods which will exercise a helpful influence among the foreign born population and provide for the education of the alien in our language, customs, ideals and standards of life. We favor the improvement of naturalization laws.

1928

The Republican Party believes that in the interest of both native and foreign-born wage earners, it is necessary to restrict immigration. Unrestricted immigration would result in widespread unemployment and in the breakdown of the American standard of living. Where, however, the law works undue hardships by depriving the immigrant of the comfort and society of those bound by close family ties, such modification should be adopted as will afford relief.

We commend Congress for correcting defects for humanitarian reasons and for providing an effective system of examining prospective immigrants in their home countries.

1940

We favor the strict enforcement of all laws controlling the entry of aliens. The activities of undesirable aliens should be investigated and those who seek to change by force and violence the American form of government should be deported.

1956

The Republican Party supports an immigration policy which is in keeping with the traditions of America in providing a haven for oppressed peoples, and which is based on equality of treatment, freedom from implications of discrimination between racial, nationality and religious groups, and flexible enough to conform to changing needs and conditions.

We believe that such a policy serves our self-interest, reflects our responsibility for world leadership and develops maximum cooperation with other nations in resolving problems in this area.

We support the President's program submitted to the 84th Congress to carry out needed modifications in existing law and to take such further steps as may be necessary to carry out our traditional policy.

In that concept, this Republican Administration sponsored the Refugee Relief Act to provide asylum for thousands of refugees, expellees and displaced persons, and undertook in the face of Democrat opposition to correct the inequities in existing law and to bring our immigration policies in line with the dynamic needs of the country and principles of equity and justice.

We believe also that the Congress should consider the extension of the Refugee Relief Act of 1953 in resolving this difficult refugee problem which resulted from world conflict. To all this we give our wholehearted support.

1960

Immigration has historically been a great factor in the growth of the United States, not only in numbers but in the enrichment of ideas that immigrants have brought with them. This Republican Administration has given refuge to over 32,000 victims of Communist tyranny from Hungary, ended needless delay in processing applications for naturalization, and has urged other enlightened legislation to liberalize existing restrictions.

Immigration has been reduced to the point where it does not provide the stimulus to growth that it should, nor are we fulfilling our obligation as a haven for the oppressed. Republican conscience and Republican policy require that:

> The annual number of immigrants we accept be at least doubled.

> Obsolete immigration laws be amended by abandoning the outdated 1920 census data as a base and substituting the 1960 census.

> The guidelines of our immigration policy be based upon judgment of the individual merit of each applicant for admission and citizenship.

1972

SPANISH-SPEAKING AMERICANS

In recognition of the significant contributions to our country by our proud and independent Spanish-speaking citizens, we have developed a comprehensive program to help achieve equal opportunity.

During the last four years Spanish-speaking Americans have achieved a greater role in national affairs. More than thirty have been appointed to high Federal positions.

To provide the same learning opportunities enjoyed by other American children, we have increased bilingual education programs almost sixfold since 1969. We initiated a 16-point employment program to help Spanish-speaking workers, created the National Economic Development Association to promote Spanish-speaking business development and expanded economic development opportunities in Spanish-speaking communities.

We will work for the use of bilingual staffs in localities where this language capability is desirable for effective health care.

1976

HISPANIC AMERICANS

When language is a cause for discrimination, there must be an intensive educational effort to enable Spanish-speaking students to become fully proficient in English while maintaining their own language and cultural heritage. Hispanic Americans must not be treated as second-class citizens in schools, employment or any other aspect of life just because English is not their first language. Hispanic Americans truly believe that individual integrity must be paramount; what they want most from government and politics is the opportunity to participate fully. The Republican Party has and always will offer this opportunity.

1980

HISPANIC AMERICANS

Hispanics are rapidly becoming the largest minority in the country and are one of the major pillars in our cultural, social, and economic life. Diverse in character, proud in heritage, they are greatly enriching the American melting pot.

Hispanics seek only the full rights of citizenship—in education, in law enforcement, in housing—and an equal opportunity to achieve economic security. Unfortunately, those desires have not always been fulfilled; as in so many other areas, the Carter Administration has been long on rhetoric and short on action in its approach to the Hispanic community.

We pledge to pursue policies that will help to make the opportunities of American life a reality for Hispanics. The economic policies enunciated in this platform will, we believe, create new jobs for Hispanic teenagers and adults and will also open up new business opportunities for them. We also believe there should be local educational programs which enable those who grew up learning another language such as Spanish to become proficient in English while also maintaining their own language and cultural heritage. Neither Hispanics nor any other American citizen should be barred from education or employment opportunities because English is not their first language.

IMMIGRATION AND REFUGEE POLICY

Residency in the United States is one of the most precious and valued of conditions. The traditional hospitality of the American people has been severely tested by recent events, but it remains the strongest in the world. Republicans are proud that our people have opened their arms and hearts to strangers from abroad and we favor an immigration and refugee policy which is consistent with this tradition. We believe that to the fullest extent possible those immigrants should be admitted who will make a positive contribution to America and who are willing to accept the fundamental American values and way of life. At the same time, United States immigration and refugee policy must reflect the interests of the nation's political and economic well-being. Immigration into this country must not be determined solely by foreign governments or even by the millions of people around the world who wish to come to America. The federal government has a duty to adopt immigration laws and follow enforcement procedures which will fairly and effectively implement the immigration policy desired by American people.

The immediate adoption of this policy is essential to an orderly approach to the great problem of oppressed people seeking entry, so that the deserving can be accepted in America without adding to their hardships.

The refugee problem is an international problem and every effort should be made to coordinate plans for absorbing refugee populations with regional bodies, such as the Organization of American States and the Association of Southeast Asian Nations, on a global basis.

1984

Our history is a story about immigrants. We are proud that America still symbolizes hope and promise to the world. We have shown unparalleled generosity to the persecuted and to those seeking a better life. In return, they have helped to make a great land greater still.

We affirm our country's absolute right to control its borders. Those desiring to enter must comply with our immigration laws. Failure to do so not only is an offense to the American people but is fundamentally unjust to those in foreign lands patiently waiting for legal entry. We will preserve the principle of family reunification.

With the estimates of the number of illegal aliens in the United States ranging as high as 12 million and better than one million more entering each year, we believe it is critical that responsible reforms of our immigration laws be made to enable us to regain control of our borders.

The flight of oppressed people in search of freedom has created pressures beyond the capacity of any one nation. The refugee problem is global and requires the cooperation of all democratic nations. We commend the President for encouraging other countries to assume greater refugee responsibilities.

1988

We welcome those from other lands who bring to America their ideals and industry. At the same time, we insist upon our country's absolute right to control its borders. We call upon our allies to join us in the responsibility shared by all democratic nations for resettlement of refugees, especially those fleeing communism in Southeast Asia.

1992

NEW MEMBERS OF THE AMERICAN FAMILY

Our Nation of immigrants continues to welcome those seeking a better life. This reflects our past, when some newcomers fled intolerance; some sought prosperity; some came as slaves. All suffered and sacrificed but hoped their children would have a better life. All searched for a shared vision—and found one in America. Today we are stronger for our diversity.

Illegal entry into the United States, on the other hand, threatens the social compact on which immigration is based. That is, the nation accepts immigrants and is enriched by their determination and values. Illegal immigration, on the other hand, undermines the integrity of border communities and already crowded urban neighborhoods. We will build on the already announced strengthening of the Border Patrol to better coordinate interdiction of illegal entrants through greater cross-border cooperation. Specifically, we will increase the size of the Border Patrol in order to meet the increasing need to stop illegal immigration and we will equip the Border Patrol with the tools, technologies, and structures necessary to secure the border.

We will seek stiff penalties for those who smuggle illegal aliens into the country, and for those who produce or sell fraudulent documents. We also will reduce incentives to enter the United States by promoting initiatives like the North American Free Trade Agreement. In creating new economic opportunity in Mexico, a NAFTA removes the incentive to cross the border illegally in search of work.

1996

A SENSIBLE IMMIGRATION POLICY

As a nation of immigrants, we welcome those who follow our laws and come to our land to seek a better life. New Americans strengthen our economy, enrich our culture, and defend the nation in war and in peace. At the same time, we are determined to reform the system by which we welcome them to the American family. We must set immigration at manageable levels, balance the competing goals of uniting families of our citizens and admitting specially talented persons, and end asylum abuses through expedited exclusion of false claimants.

Bill Clinton's immigration record does not match his rhetoric. While talking tough on illegal immigration, he has proposed a reduction in the number of border patrol agents authorized by the Republicans in Congress, has opposed the most successful border control program in decades (Operation Hold the Line in Texas), has opposed Proposition 187 in California, which 60 percent of Californians supported, and has opposed Republican efforts to ensure that noncitizens do not take advantage of expensive welfare programs. Unlike Bill Clinton, we stand with the American people on immigration policy and will continue to reform and enforce our immigration laws to ensure that they reflect America's national interest.

We also support efforts to secure our borders from the threat of illegal immigration. Illegal immigration has reached crisis proportions, with more than four million illegal aliens now present in the United States. That number, growing by 300,000 each year, burdens taxpayers, strains public services, takes jobs, and increases crime. Republicans in both the House and Senate have passed bills that tighten border enforcement, speed up deportation of criminal aliens, toughen penalties for overstaying visas, and streamline the Immigration and Naturalization Service.

Illegal aliens should not receive public benefits other than emergency aid, and those who become parents while illegally in the United States should not be qualified to claim benefits for their offspring. Legal immigrants should depend for assistance on their sponsors, who are legally responsible for their financial well-being, not the American taxpayers. Just as we require "deadbeat dads" to provide for the children they bring into the world, we should require "deadbeat sponsors" to provide for the immigrants they bring into the country. We support a constitutional amendment or constitutionally valid legislation declaring that children born in the United States of parents who are not legally present in the United States or who are not long-term residents are not automatically citizens.

We endorse the Dole/Coverdell proposal to make crimes of domestic violence, stalking, child abuse, child neglect, and child abandonment committed by aliens residing in this country deportable offenses under our immigration laws.

We call for harsh penalties against exploiters who smuggle illegal aliens and for those who profit from the production of false documents. Republicans believe that by eliminating the magnet for illegal immigration, increasing border security, enforcing our immigration laws, and producing counterfeit-proof documents, we will finally put an end to the illegal immigration crisis. We oppose the creation of any national ID card.

FROM MANY, ONE

. . . English, our common language, provides a shared foundation which has allowed people from every corner of the world to come together to build the American nation. The use of English is indispensable to all who wish to participate fully in our society and realize the American dream. As Bob Dole has said: "For more than two centuries now, English has been a force for unity, indispensable to the process of transforming untold millions of immigrants from all parts of the globe into citizens of the most open and free society the world has ever seen." For newcomers, learning the English language has always been the fastest route to the mainstream of American life. That should be the goal of bilingual education programs. We support the official recognition of English as the nation's common language. We advocate foreign language training in our schools and retention of heritage languages in homes and cultural institutions. Foreign language fluency is also an essential component of America's competitiveness in the world market.

Sources: George Thomas Kurian, ed. *The Encyclopedia of the Republican Party* (Volume 2). Armonk, NY: M. E. Sharpe, 1997; Congressional Quarterly. *Historic Documents of 1996.* Washington, DC: Congressional Quarterly, Inc., 1997, 520–521.

Immigration Planks of Democratic Party Platforms, 1856–1996

The following document includes the planks on immigration from the Democratic Party platforms between 1856 and 1996. Two things stand out. First, immigration appears to be mentioned only when it becomes a pressing national issue. Second, comparing Democratic Party platforms with their counterparts from the Republican Party indicates a more welcoming attitude among the former, particularly in the late twentieth century.

1856

Resolved, That the foundation of this union of States having been laid in, and its prosperity, expansion, and pre-eminent example in free government, built upon entire freedom in matters of religious concernments [sic], and no respect of person in regard to rank or place of birth; no party can justly be deemed national, constitutional, or in accordance with American principles, which bases its exclusive organization upon religious opinions and accidental birth-place. And hence a political crusade in the nineteenth century, and in the United States of America, against Catholic and foreign-born is neither justified by the past history or the future prospects of the country, nor in unison with the spirit of toleration and enlarged freedom which peculiarly distinguishes the American system of popular government.

1880

Amendment of the Burlingame Treaty. No more Chinese immigration, except for travel, education, and foreign commerce, and that even carefully guarded.

1884

In reaffirming the declaration of the Democratic platform of 1856, that, "the liberal principles embodied by Jefferson in the Declaration of Independence, and sanctioned in the Constitution, which make ours the land of liberty and the asylum of the oppressed of every Nation, have ever been cardinal principles in the Democratic faith," we nevertheless do not sanction the importation of foreign labor, or the admission of servile races, unfitted by habits, training, religion, or kindred, for absorption into the great body of our people, or for the citizenship which our laws confer. American civilization demands that against the immigration or importation of Mongolians to these shores our gates be closed.

1888

The exclusion from our shores of Chinese laborers has been effectually secured under the provisions of treaty, the operation of which has been postponed by the action of a Republican majority in the Senate.

1892

We heartily approve all legitimate efforts to prevent the United States from being used as a dumping ground for the known criminals and professional paupers of Europe; and we demand the rigid enforcement of the laws against Chinese immigration and the importation of foreign workers under contract, to degrade American labor and lessen its wages; but we condemn and denounce any and all attempts to restrict the immigration of the industrious and worthy of foreign lands.

1896

We hold that the most efficient way of protecting American labor is to prevent the importation of foreign pauper labor to compete with it in the home market, and that the value of the home market to our American farmers and artisans is greatly reduced by a vicious monetary system which depresses the prices of their products below the cost of production, and thus deprives them of the means of purchasing the products of our home manufactories; and as labor creates the wealth of the country, we demand the passage of such laws as may be necessary to protect it in all its rights.

1900

We favor the continuance and strict enforcement of the Chinese exclusion law, and its application to the same classes of all Asiatic races.

1908

We favor full protection, by both National and State governments within their respective spheres, of all foreigners residing in the United States under treaty, but we are opposed to the admission of Asiatic immigrants who cannot be amalgamated with our population, or whose presence among us would raise a race issue and involve us in diplomatic controversies with Oriental powers.

1920

The policy of the United States with reference to the nonadmission of Asiatic immigrants is a true expression of the judgment of our people, and to the several states, whose geographical situation or internal conditions make this policy, and the enforcement of the laws enacted pursuant thereto, of particular concern, we pledge our support.

1924

We pledge ourselves to maintain our established position in favor of the exclusion of Asiatic immigration.

1928

Laws which limit immigration must be preserved in full force and effect, but the provisions contained in these laws that separate husbands from wives and parents from infant children are inhuman and not essential to the purpose of the efficacy of such laws.

1952

Solution of the problem of refugees from communism and over-population has become a permanent part of the foreign policy program of the Democratic Party. We pledge continued cooperation with other free nations to solve it.

We pledge continued aid to refugees from communism and the enactment of President Truman's proposals for legislation in this field. In this way we can give hope and courage to the victims of Soviet brutality and can carry on the humanitarian tradition of the Displaced Persons Act.

Subversive elements must be screened out and prevented from entering our land, but the gates must be left open for practical numbers of desirable persons from abroad whose immigration to this country provides an invigorating infusion into the stream of American life, as well as a significant contribution to the solution of the world refugee and over-population problems.

We pledge continuing revision of our immigration and naturalization laws to do away with any unjust and unfair practices against national groups which have contributed some of our best citizens. We will eliminate distinctions between native-born and naturalized citizens. We want no "second-class" citizens in free America.

1956

America's long tradition of hospitality and asylum for those seeking freedom, opportunity, and escape from oppression, has been besmirched by the delays, failures, and broken promises of the Republican Administration. The Democratic Party favors prompt revision of the immigration and nationality laws to eliminate unfair provisions under which admissions to this country depend upon quotas based upon the accident of national origin. Proper safeguards against subversive elements should be provided. Our immigration procedures must reflect the principles of our Bill of Rights.

We favor eliminating the provisions of law which charge displaced persons admitted to our shores against quotas for future years. Through such "mortgages" of future quotas, thousands of qualified persons are being forced to wait long years before they can hope for admission.

We also favor more liberal admission of relatives to eliminate the unnecessary tragedies of broken families.

We favor elimination of unnecessary distinctions between native-born and naturalized citizens. There should be no "second-class" citizenship in the United States.

The administration of the Refugee Relief Act of 1953 has been a disgrace to our country. Rescue has been denied to innocent, defenseless and suffering people, the victims of war and the aftermath of wars. The purpose of the Act has been defeated by Republican mismanagement.

1960

We shall adjust our immigration, nationality and refugee policies to eliminate discrimination and to enable members of scattered families abroad to be united with relatives already in our midst.

The national-origins quota system of limiting immigration contradicts the founding principles of this nation. It is inconsistent with our belief in the rights of man. This system was instituted after World War I as a policy of deliberate discrimination by a Republican Administration and Congress.

The revision of immigration and nationality laws we seek will implement our belief that enlightened immigration, naturalization and refugee policies and humane administration of them are important aspects of our foreign policy.

These laws will bring greater skills to our land, reunite families, permit the United States to meet its fair share of world programs of rescue and rehabilitation, and take advantage of immigration as an important factor in the growth of the American economy.

In this World Refugee Year it is our hope to achieve

admission of our fair share of refugees. We will institute policies to alleviate suffering among the homeless wherever we are able to extend our aid.

We must remove the distinctions between native-born and naturalized citizens to assure full protection of our laws to all. There is no place in the United States for "second-class citizenship."

The projections provided by due process, right of appeal, and statutes of limitation, can be extended to noncitizens without hampering the security of our nation.

We commend the Democratic Congress for the initial steps that have recently been taken toward liberalizing changes in immigration law. However, this should not be a piecemeal project and we are confident that a Democratic President in cooperation with Democratic Congresses will again implant a humanitarian and liberal spirit in our nation's immigration and citizenship policies.

1964

In 1960, we proposed to—

"Adjust our immigration, nationality and refugee policies to eliminate discrimination and to enable members of scattered families abroad to be United with relatives already in our midst.

"The national-origins quota system of limiting immigration contradicts the founding principles of this nation. It is inconsistent with our belief in the rights of men."

The immigration law amendments proposed by the Administration, and now before Congress, by abolishing the national-origin quota system, will eliminate discrimination based upon race and place of birth and will facilitate the reunion of families.

The Cuban Refugee Program begun in 1961 has resettled over 81,000 refugees, who are now self-supporting members of 1,800 American communities. The Chinese Refugee Program, begun in 1962, provides for the admission to the United States of 12,000 Hong Kong refugees from Red China.

1980

ETHNIC AMERICA

President Carter has stated that the composition of American society is analogous to a beautiful mosaic. Each separate part retains its own integrity and identity while adding to and being part of the whole.

America is a pluralistic society. Each of us must learn to live, communicate, and cooperate with persons of other cultures. Our public policies and programs must reflect this pluralism. Immigrants from every nation and their descendants have made numerous contributions to this country, economically, politically and socially. They have traditionally been the backbone of the labor movement and an integral part of the Democratic Party.

Ethnic Americans share the concerns of all Americans. They too are concerned about decent housing, health care, equal employment opportunities, care of the elderly, and education. In addition, ethnic Americans have some concerns of their own. They want to preserve the culture and language of their former homeland. They want to be integrated into the political, social and economic mainstream of American society, but at the same time they are concerned about the foreign policy issues that affect their native countries. We as a nation must be sensitive to their concerns.

President Carter established the Office of Ethnic Affairs and charged it with a broad and diverse mission. The predominant functions of the office are to link the Administration and its ethnic constituents, to foster the concept of pluralism, and to enable all Americans to partake equally in the American way of life.

REFUGEES AND MIGRATION

America's roots are found in the immigrants and refugees who have come to our shores to build new lives in a new world. The Democratic Party pledges to honor our historic commitment to this heritage.

The first comprehensive reform of this nation's refugee policies in over 25 years was completed with the signing in March 1980 of the Refugee Act of 1980, based on legislation submitted to Congress by the Carter Administration in March 1979.

This Act offers a comprehensive alternative to the chaotic movement and the inefficient and inequitable administration of past refugee programs in the United States. We favor the full use of refugee legislation now to cope with the flow of Cuban and Haitian refugees, and to help the states, local communities and voluntary agencies resettle them across our land. We urge that monies be distributed to voluntary agencies fairly so that aid is distributed to all refugees without discrimination.

The Administration also established the first refugee coordination office in the Department of State under the leadership of a special ambassador and coordinator for refugee affairs and programs.

The new legislation and the coordinator's office will bring common sense and consolidation to our nation's previously fragmented, inconsistent, and, in many ways, outdated refugee and immigration policies.

A Select Commission on Immigration and Refugee Policy is now at work to further reform the system. We pledge our support to the goals and purposes of the Commission, and we urge the Administration to move aggressively in this area once the Commission submits its report.

Once that report has been completed, we must work to resolve the issue of undocumented residents in a fair and humane way. We will oppose any legislation designed to allow workers into the country to undercut U.S. wages and working conditions, and which would reestablish the Bracero Program of the past.

World population projections, as well as international economic indicators—especially in the Third World—forewarn us that migration pressures will mount rapidly in many areas of the world in the decade ahead. Our own situation of undocumented workers underscores how difficult it is to deal with economic and employment forces that are beyond any nation's immediate control. Most of Europe, and many parts of Latin America and Asia, face similar dilemmas. For example, Mexico faces the pressure of migration from Central America.

We will work with other nations to develop international policies to regularize population movement and to protect the human rights of migrants even as we protect the jobs of American workers and the economic interest of the United States. In this hemisphere, such a policy will require close cooperation with our neighbors, especially Mexico and Canada.

We must also work to resolve the difficult problems presented by the immigration from Haiti and from the more recent immigration from Cuba. In doing so, we must ensure that there is no discrimination in the treatment afforded to the Cubans or Haitians. We must also work to ensure that future Cuban immigration is handled in an orderly way, consistent with our laws. To ameliorate the impact on state and local communities and school districts of the influx of new immigrants from Cuba and Haiti, we must provide the affected areas with special fiscal assistance.

We support continued financial backing of international relief programs such as those financed by the United States, the International Red Cross, UNICEF and the private, nonprofit organizations to aid the starving people of Kampuchea. We also endorse such support for the Cambodian refugees and encourage participation in the campaign of the National Cambodian Crisis Committee.

We support, through U.S. contributions to the UN High Commissioner for Refugees and other means aid for the mounting Afghan refugee population in Pakistan and other desperate refugee situations.

1988

A Fair and Humane Immigration Policy. Our nation's outdated immigration laws require comprehensive reform that reflects our national interests and our immigrant heritage. Our first priority must be to protect the fundamental human rights of American citizens and aliens. We will oppose any "reforms" that violate these rights or that will create new incentives for discrimination against Hispanic Americans and other minorities arising from the discriminatory use of employer sanctions. Specifically, we oppose employer sanctions designed to penalize employers who hire undocumented workers. Such sanctions inevitably will increase discrimination against minority Americans. We oppose identification procedures that threaten civil liberties, as well as any changes that subvert the basic principle of family unification. And we will put an end to this Administration's

policies of barring foreign visitors from our country for political or ideological reasons. We strongly oppose "bracero" or guest-worker programs as a form of legalized exploitation. We firmly support a one-tiered legalization program with a 1982 cut-off date.

The Democratic Party will implement a balanced, fair, and non-discriminatory immigration and refugee policy consistent with the principle of affording all applications for admission equal protection under the law. It will work for improved performance by the Immigration and Naturalization Service in adjudicating petitions for permanent residence and naturalization. The Party will also advocate reform within the INS to improve the enforcement operations of the Service consistent with civil liberties protection. The correction of past and present bias in the allocation of slots for refugee admissions will be a top priority. Additionally, it will work to ensure that the Refugee Act of 1980, which prohibits discrimination on the basis of ideology and race in adjudicating asylum claims, is complied with. The Party will provide the necessary oversight of the Department of State and the Immigration and Naturalization Service so as to ensure that the unjustifiable treatment visited upon the Haitian refugees will never again be repeated.

The Democratic Party will formulate foreign policies which alleviate, not aggravate, the root causes of poverty, war, and human rights violations and instability which compel people to flee their homelands.

We support the creation of an international body on immigration to address the economic development problems affecting Mexico and Latin American countries which contribute to unauthorized immigration to the U.S. and to respond to the backlog of approved immigrant visas.

To pursue these and other goals, the Democratic Party nominee upon election shall establish the following national advisory committees to the President and the national Democratic Party: civil rights and justice; fair housing; affirmative action; equal rights for women; rights for workers, immigration policy; and voting rights. These committees shall be representative on the basis of geography, race, sex, and ethnicity.

1992

Our nation of immigrants has been invigorated repeatedly as new people, ideas and ways of life have become part of the American tapestry. Democrats support immigration policies that promote fairness, non-discrimination and family reunification, and that reflect our constitutional freedoms of speech, association and travel.

1996

Democrats remember that we are a nation of immigrants. We recognize the extraordinary contribution of immigrants to America throughout our history. We welcome legal immigrants to America. We support a legal immigration policy that is pro-family, pro-work, pro-responsibility, and pro-citizenship, and we deplore those who blame immigrants for economic and social problems. . . .

Today's Democratic Party also believes we must remain a nation of laws. We cannot tolerate illegal immigration and we must stop it. . . .

However, as we work to stop illegal immigration, we call on all Americans to avoid the temptation to use this issue to divide people from each other. We deplore those who use the need to stop illegal immigration as a pretext for discrimination. And we applaud the wisdom of Republicans like [New York City] Mayor [Rudolph] Giuliani and Senator [Pete] Domenici [New Mexico] who oppose the mean-spirited and shortsighted effort of Republicans in Congress to bar the children of illegal immigrants from schools—it is wrong, and forcing children onto the streets is an invitation for them to join gangs and turn to crime.

Democrats want to protect American jobs by increasing criminal and civil sanctions against employers who hire illegal workers, but Republicans continue to favor inflammatory rhetoric over real action. We will continue to enforce labor standards to protect workers in vulnerable industries. We continue to firmly oppose welfare benefits for illegal immigrants. We believe family members who sponsor immigrants into this country should take financial responsibility for them, and be held legally responsible for supporting them.

Sources: George Thomas Kurian, ed. *The Encyclopedia of the Democratic Party* (Volume 4). Armonk, NY: M. E. Sharpe, 1997; Congressional Quarterly. *Historic Documents of 1996.* Washington, DC: Congressional Quarterly, Inc., 1997, 636–637.

Senate Report on the Encouragement of Immigration, 1864

With thousands of men fighting during the Civil War, the United States experienced a severe labor shortage. In 1864, a congressional committee investigated the situation and issued a report on agricultural conditions and the need for immigrant labor. The report, excerpted below, pointed out that new wage laborers would be needed both to run the factories of the North and to rebuild the South in the years after the Civil War.

The special wants for labor in this country at the present time are very great. The war has depleted our workshops, and materially lessened our supply of labor in every department of industry and mechanism. In their noble response to the call of their country, our workmen in every branch of the useful arts have left vacancies which must be filled, or the material interest of the country must suffer. The immense amount of native labor occupied by the war calls for a large increase of foreign immigration to make up the deficiency at home. The demand for labor never was greater than at present, and the fields of usefulness were never so varied and promising.

The south, having torn down the fabric of its labor system by its own hands, will, when the war shall have ceased, present a wide field for voluntary white labor, and it must look to immigration for its supply.

The following may be mentioned as the special inducements to immigration:

1st. High price of labor and low price of food, compared with other countries.

2d. Our land policy, giving to every immigrant, after he shall have declared his intentions to become a citizen, a home and a farm, substantially as a free gift, charging him less for 160 acres in fee-simple than is paid as the annual rent of a single acre in England.

3d. The political rights conferred upon persons of foreign birth.

4th. Our system of free schools, melting in a common crucible all differences of religion, language, and race, and giving to the child of the day laborer and the son of the millionaire equal opportunities to excel in the pursuit and acquirement of knowledge. This is an advantage and a blessing which the poor man enjoys in no other country.

Source: United States Senate. *Report from the Committee on Agriculture on the Enactment of Suitable Laws for the Encouragement and Protection of Foreign Immigrants Arriving within Jurisdiction of the United States, February 18, 1864.* 38th Congress, first session, Senate Report, Number 15.

Report of the Minnesota Board of Immigration, 1871

Like many other western states with lots of land and few peo-ple after the Civil War, Minnesota actively encouraged immi-grants to move and settle there, particularly those from Britain, Ireland, and Scandinavia. As this document makes clear, the gov-ernment of Minnesota expended significant amounts of money and energy in the effort, including the hiring of agents and the writing and translating of pamphlets. As the document also in-dicates, there was significant competition among the states for settlers from Europe.

Organization of the Board.—The act of March 3d, 1871, cre-ated a Board of five persons, two of whom were designated in said act by name; the Governor, Secretary of State and Treasurer of State constituting the other members *ex-officio.* It was made the duty of the said Board generally, "to adopt measures, which will insure the establishment of a thorough system of inducing immigration to the State."

Certain plans of carrying out this act were recom-mended, which we will give in detail:

Correspondence in newspapers.—One plan was to "engage suitable correspondents, publish or cause to be published, articles treating on and describing in a true light the devel-oped and undeveloped resources of the State of Minnesota," etc. As far as desirable and effective this plan was adopted in our operations both in America and in Europe. Our agent in Germany, whose time expired in March last, caused to be inserted in a number of German papers ably written articles on our State. Our Commissioner of Immigration in New York has among his many successful enterprises for pro-moting immigration, also caused to be inserted advertise-ments calling the attention of the public to Minnesota and to the State Pamphlet and other publications on the subject, in some 600 newspapers in the New England and Middle States. Hans Mattson, formerly Secretary of State, and the clerk of the State Board have for the same purpose issued a series of letters in the different Scandinavian newspapers in America, and as many hundred copies of these papers every week go to regular subscribers in Europe, said articles have also reached their destination abroad. The board found the promulgation of said semi-official articles the more useful,

as the surrounding States through the Scandinavian press made strong efforts to turn the flood of Scandinavian im-migration from Minnesota.

Emigration direct from England and Scotland has not been overlooked. Not only have there been many calls from there for information answered by letters and pamphlets, but the regular immigration pamphlet, by direction of the Board, has been republished in monthly installments in the columns of the *Free West,* an emigration paper of ability and extensive circulation published in London. By this means it has reached many thousands of additional readers. The im-migration has been greater from the British Isles and less from Germany during the last two years (for obvious rea-sons) than during any one of several years.

Distribution of pamphlets.—The main work required may be divided into two branches: (1) Furnishing the necessary information as to the inducements and advantages offered by the State to all classes of desirable immigrants. (2) Aid-ing, protecting, and advising the immigrant on his way to our State.

The first part has been and is pursued to great effect by sending the State pamphlet to the very heart of the most remote emigrant districts in Northern Europe, in the En-glish, German, Norwegian, and Swedish languages, and by addressing them, not by boxes sent to agents, but in every case to individuals, who contemplate leaving their father-land. The most of them make up their minds as to their final destination before they leave. Letters and counsels from their friends and relations in America, will govern their movements, and as the State pamphlet is nothing but a con-densed series of answered questions upon immigration, the people, as indicated by their thousands of applications, deem this or similar pamphlets the best medium for enlight-ening their transatlantic friends.

To this end an extra edition of 15,000 copies of the pam-phlet prepared in 1870 by the commissioners of statistics was re-printed in English in the winter of 1871.

An edition of 5,000 copies translated into German, with some abbreviations and alterations, has been printed. Also 5,700 copies in Norwegian, and 3,500 copies in Swedish; the two latter distributed in the countries of Norway, Sweden, Denmark, and among the Scandinavians in the United States. An edition of 5,000 copies in English, especially for the Irish immigration, was also printed.

The editions printed in foreign languages contained, besides most of the information of the English pamphlet, many facts of value, especially to immigrants from Europe, which were not deemed necessary to those sent to citizens of the United States.

The throng of applications, for pamphlets, and of questions touching our State to be answered by letters, may be understood from the fact, that the immigration bureau received during the season from 50 to 100 letters per day, each of them containing more applications. Early in the season the Norwegian pamphlets—originally 5,000—were exhausted; so several thousand English pamphlets had to be sent Scandinavians in America, until a new issue could be procured for filling waiting applications to Norway and Denmark.

Thus altogether over 34,000 pamphlets have been printed, and mostly distributed in various tongues, and even this amount proved to be insufficient for the Scandinavian demand.

Mode of distribution.—The plan adopted in the distribution of the pamphlets was, as above stated, calculated to place them in the hands of the very persons seeking information in regard to Minnesota. In brief advertisements the Board stated that anyone wishing the pamphlet could have the same sent him free of postage by forwarding his address to the Secretary of State. This plan has worked still more admirably than in 1870, as the requisitions, partly direct from Europe and partly through friends in the United States, have amounted this season to several thousands. The high rates of postage on copies sent to foreign countries have greatly increased that item of our expenditures, but this may possibly be saved to a great extent in the future, if it should be found advisable to let the applicants themselves pay the postage to foreign countries.

Maps.—In all 23,800 copies of the pamphlet have been furnished with maps (English maps, 14,000; German, 4,000; Norwegian, 3,500; Swedish, 2,300). As most of the applications ask for pamphlets with maps, and as other States have adopted the plan of circulating their immigration documents with maps, the Board deemed it necessary to continue to provide the same. The maps last season were furnished at a considerable lower price than the preceding year.

Agents and their work.—The Board was also empowered to appoint agents for the purpose of aiding, protecting, and advising the immigrant on his way to our State, etc.

Local agents can do a great deal of good work in keeping runners from taking hold of new comers, in seeing the immigrants without unnecessary delay forwarded to their destination, and not the least in aiding the unfortunate and preventing imposition. On account of a deficiency from the foregoing year, which had to be covered by last year's appropriation, the Board did not feel at liberty to sustain more than one agency. The Board deemed it proper to establish

as a rule, that its operations had to be limited and regulated in accordance with the fund appropriated. Consequently, it had to abstain from creating local agencies in Milwaukee, Chicago, and Quebec. The demand for these agencies had diminished from the fact, that the railroads during last season had procured experienced agents and guides, who performed their duties to the satisfaction of all parties, without expense to our State, and partly because the greater number of immigrants had taken notice of our timely warning in 1870: not to use the uncertain water routes, when railroad transportation was obtainable at reasonable prices.

The Milwaukee and St. Paul road deserves our thanks for having treated the immigrants liberally; the St. Paul and Pacific, and the Superior and Mississippi roads have erected more immigrant houses along their lines, thereby enabling immigrants to find shelter until they find their friends, or decide where to settle. The St. Paul and Pacific's agent, Mr. Christiansen, last season, as before, bestowed upon immigrants arriving at St. Paul all the kindness and care they are in need of in their often helpless condition after a journey of thousands of miles.

Statistics of immigration.—The whole number of immigrants for 1870 to our State is estimated at 30,000, namely: 22,000 direct from Europe, and the rest from the United States and Canada. Out of said 22,000, nearly 10,000 came from the Scandinavian countries.

As the Board during last summer had no agencies or reporters in the principal landing-places, it is of course impossible to give any accurate account concerning the actual number of foreign immigrants but from close observation of figures given in newspapers during the entire season, and judging from other sources of information, the immigration has certainly been as large this year as last. Attracted to lands available under the homestead laws, the majority of immigrants located on the surveyed and unsurveyed lands, especially in the Red River region and in the frontier counties farther South. The hardwood timber land belonging to the Lake Superior, and Mississippi R.R. Co. has also, to some extent, been settled. Northern Europe parts yearly with from 0.39 to 0.86 per cent of their population, nearly all of which emigrate to America. Of immigration last season from Northern Europe, Wisconsin received 3,000 Scandinavians; Minnesota 10,000. . . .

The increasing correspondence and other pressing work connected with the duties of the Board—almost enough to make it a department of its own—necessitated the employ of a clerk acting under the direction of the Board.

His business has mainly been: (1) Receiving and filing some 9,000 letters and mailing pamphlets to at least 20,000 different applicants. Of this number about 3,500 are sent to Norway, 1,500 to London, and 300 to Denmark. About 4,000 copies were forwarded to Germany. (2) Answering letters in different languages upon immigration. (3) Assisting immigrants in cases of lost baggage and money. (4) Writing articles and answering attacks made on our State. (5) Translating the State pamphlet into the Norwegian language. . . .

Of the value of an extensive immigration to the State, the Board has not had any good reason to change their views as expressed in their last annual report. Not only does our immigration add hundreds of thousands of dollars in property of all descriptions to the common wealth of the community, but it furnishes, from year to year, by far the greater numbers of those who supply the demand for hired laborers, as well as to replenish and multiply the artisans, mechanics, and skilled laborers, upon whom we depend to build up and extend our manufacturing, mining, and mechanical interests. Yet exceeding by far any of these interests is that resulting from bringing the cheap European labor in contact with our wild land. The national wealth has been by no other means so rapidly developed and accumulated as by bringing the cheap, and *there*, nearly valueless labor of the old world into direct contact with our equally cheap lands, which, *without that labor*, are of as little value to us, as is the surplus labor of the old world to it, without our lands.

From Northern Europe a man, only capable of earning a bare subsistence there, can be transported to, and set down upon, a homestead in Minnesota for from $50 to $75. He locates on land, which, in its raw condition is not worth over $1.25 per acre, and at the end of five years he has subsisted his family and by his labor has advanced his quarter-section of land to an average value of $1,000, an advance of 300 per cent on the capital with which the settler commenced. Persons residing in the older portions of the State and not on any of the thoroughfares leading to those sections, into which immigrants are flocking by the thousands, often fall into the error, that the State is receiving no immigration—that nothing is realized in exchange for the appropriation made for the promotion of immigration—in short, that the fund is *squandered.* Such objectors can easily be undeceived by taking a journey along our western frontier or sojourning for a time, from the first of May till the close of the season, on some one of the numerous routes of travel leading to those counties, into which the annual tide is flowing.

Source: Report of the Minnesota Board of Immigration, 1871.

Value of an Immigrant, 1871

In this Special Report *put out by the United States Congress in 1871, investigators examined the degree to which immigrants added or detracted from the American economy. The question—still a controversial one today—was answered in the affirmative here: "the sum of $800 seems to be the full average capital value of each immigrant."*

In making an intelligent estimate of the addition to the material wealth of the country by immigration, several distinct conditions should be regarded. The character of the immigrants as industrious and law-abiding citizens, their nationalities, education, and previous condition, as well as their occupation and ages, are elements to be considered when determining their value.

As regards nationality, more than one-half of those who have thus far arrived in the United States are British, and come from the United Kingdom, or from the British possessions of North America. These speak our language, and a large part are acquainted with our laws and institutions, and are soon assimilated with, and absorbed into, our bodypolitic.

The German element comes next, and embraces nearly two-thirds of the remainder, being at once an industrious and an intelligent people, a large proportion settling in rural districts and developing the agricultural resources of the West and South, while the remainder, consisting largely of artisans and skilled workmen, find profitable employment in the cities and manufacturing towns.

The influx of Scandinavians, who have already made extensive settlements in the Northwestern States, constitutes a distinctive feature of the movement, and though but a few years since it received its first impetus, is already large and rapidly increasing. Industrious, economical, and temperate, their advent should be especially welcomed. . . .

The Latin nations contribute very little to our population, and the Slavic still less, while today, as from time immemorial, the different branches of the great Teutonic trunk are swarming forth from the most populous regions, to aid in the progress of civilization.

While a brief review of the ethnic derivation of the millions who have transferred their allegiance from the Old World to the New, exhibits a favorable result, other elements of their value to this country require consideration. The wide contrasts between skilled and unskilled labor, between industry and laziness, between economical habits and unthrift, indicates a marked variation in the capital value of the immigrant to the country. The unskilled laborers, who at once engage in subduing the forests, or cultivating the prairies, are of far more value to the country than those who remain in the large cities.

Deducting the women and children, who pursue no occupation, about 46 per cent of the whole immigration have been trained to various pursuits. Nearly half of these are skilled laborers and workmen who have acquired their trades under the rigorous system which prevails in the Old World, and come here to give us the benefit of their training and skill without repayment of the cost of such education. Nor are the farm laborers and servants destitute of the necessary training to fit them for their several duties, while those classed as common or unskilled laborers are well qualified to perform the labor required, especially in the construction of works of internal improvement. Nearly 10 per cent consist of merchants and traders, who doubtless bring with them considerable capital as well as mercantile experience, while the smaller number of professional men and artists, embracing architects, engineers, inventors, men of thorough training and a high order of talent, contribute to our widely extended community not only material, but artistic, aesthetic, intellectual, and moral wealth. . . .

Recurring to the money value of an immigrant, it may be stated that the sum of $1,000 has usually been regarded as the average worth of each permanent addition to our population, an amount somewhat too large, but yet an approximation to the true value. Mr. Kapp, one of the commissioners of emigration of the State of New York, who has given much consideration to the subject now under review, assumes the average value to be $1,125. . . .

But the question, what is the average money value of an

immigrant, is yet unanswered. To resolve it, other elements than those already mentioned must receive consideration. The immigrant must be regarded both as a producer and as a consumer. In treating the whole number of immigrants as producers, the non-producers must first be excluded. These consist of the very aged and the very young, and of those who are unable to labor, whether from sickness, physical inability, or mental condition, whether in or out of charitable or reformatory institutions, and of the criminal or vicious class, whether in or out of prison. In this category may also be included those whose occupations or pursuits tend to demoralize or injure society. The social statistics of the foreign-born population being imperfect, it will perhaps be possible to estimate the productiveness of the whole by taking the earnings of unskilled laborers; offsetting the increased productiveness and earnings of the skilled workmen against the unproductiveness of the classes above mentioned.

The wages of laborers and unskilled workmen throughout the country average very nearly $400 per year. Assuming that the families of these men consist of four persons, we have $100 as the amount which each individual produces, and to which also he is restricted in consumption. The estimated yearly expenditures of the family of a laborer, consisting of two adults and two small children (if any are larger it is probable that they earn something in addition), is as follows: For tea, coffee, sugar, and other foreign goods, which pay a duty of about 60 per cent to the Government, $60; flour, meat, and butter, about $150; rent, $50; fuel and light, $30; vegetables, $30; milk, eggs, &c., $20; leaving $60 for clothing, housekeeping goods, &c. As most of these expenditures are for articles of domestic product which pay a succession of profits not only to the retailer, wholesale dealer, and producer, but to the transporter, the sum of these net profits constitutes the aggregate amount which this family contributes to the wealth of the country. A careful computation gives $160, which sum is the measure alike of their production and consumption. As producers and consumers, then, each is worth to the country $40 per annum, which capitalized at five per cent, gives $800 as the average value of an immigrant.

As a large number, especially those from Northern Europe, engage at once in the cultivation of the soil on their own account, it is desirable to ascertain the increment to the wealth of the country consequent upon their industry. This appears in the form of productive fields reclaimed from the wilderness, buildings and fences erected, agricultural implements and stock accumulated, &c. In the absence of correct data, the sum of $160 by a family of four persons, or $40 each, is considered an approximate estimate of the yearly addition to the realized wealth of the country by such improvements. The figures of the census recently taken will doubtless show that an immense aggregate increase in the national wealth is due to this source alone. Being the result of voluntary industry and self-imposed economy, it is an

increase which remains in the hands of the immigrants themselves, who thus contribute to the state that highest form of wealth, a sturdy, moral, intelligent, and independent yeomanry, the very balance-wheel of national machinery. Data will soon exist by which the average production will be tested. It is believed that the statistics of the census of 1870, when compiled, will exhibit the average value of real and personal estate in the Union at about $800 per capita, and the annual increase about 5 per cent, or $40. Now, while the property owned by the foreign-born population does not average $800, yet in productiveness, it is believed, they contribute their full share.

It should not be forgotten, however, that these immigrants bring with them some money, estimated at $100 by Mr. Kapp, and at $80 by Mr. Wells, but inasmuch as a careful investigation was made at Castle Garden, New York, which resulted in establishing $68 as the average sum brought by alien passengers, that amount is assumed as the correct one. As the greater part, if not the whole of this sum, is required to take the immigrant to his destination, and to support him until he becomes a producer, the amount of money which he brings with him is omitted in the foregoing estimate of his capital value. If his annual value to the country be capitalized at 6 per cent instead of 5, and the largest estimate of money brought with him ($100) included, it would aggregate less than $800, the amount already estimated as his capital value.

From the foregoing considerations, therefore, the sum of $800 seems to be the full average capital value of each immigrant. At this rate those who landed upon our shores during the year just closed, added upwards of $85,000,000 to our national wealth, while during the last half-century the increment from this source exceeds $6,243,880,800. It is impossible to make an intelligent estimate of the value to the country of those foreign-born citizens who brought their educated minds, their cultivated tastes, their skill in the arts, and their inventive genius. In almost every walk of life their influence has been felt. Alike in the fearful ordeal of war and in the pursuits of peace, in our legislative halls, and in the various learned professions, the adopted sons of America have attained eminence. Among the many who rendered timely aid to our country during the late war, it may seem invidious to mention a single name, except for the purpose of illustration. In the year 1839 there arrived at the port of New York, in the steamship "British Queen," which sailed from the port of London, a Swedish immigrant, better known as Captain John Ericsson. What was his value to the country, as estimated on the 9th day of March, 1862? Was it eight hundred, eight hundred thousand, or eight millions of dollars?

Source: Edward Young. *Special Report on Immigration; Accompanying Information for Immigrants.* March 15, 1871. United States Congress. 42nd Congress, first session, House Ex. Doc. Number 1.

Reparations for Japanese-American Internees, 1988

On February 19, 1942—roughly two months after the Japanese attack on Pearl Harbor—President Franklin D. Roosevelt issued an executive order, later upheld by the Supreme Court, interning some 120,000 Japanese Americans living in the western United States. Many of the internees lost property and savings accumulated over a lifetime. Forty-six years later—on August 10, 1988—President Ronald Reagan signed legislation providing an apology and $20,000 to the 60,000 survivors of the camps. While virtually all Americans agreed that the apology was due, some conservative Republicans disagreed with the monetary compensation, which amounted to roughly $1.25 billion.

The document that follows includes a debate on the bill that occurred in the Senate on April 20, 1988.

Senator [Daniel K.] Inouye [D-HI]: . . . The measure before us is the source of much anguish and much controversy. Because of the commitment and dedication of Senator [Spark M.] Matsunaga [D-Hawaii], he has been able to convince 72 of his colleagues to join him in this endeavor.

Many fellow Americans, including my colleague from Nevada, have asked: "Why should Japanese Americans be compensated?" During times of war, especially in times of fear, all people suffer. That is a very common argument made against this measure.

[W]hile it is true that all people of this Nation suffer during wartime, the Japanese-American internment experience is unprecedented in the history of American civil rights deprivation. I think we should recall, even if painful, that Americans of Japanese ancestry were determined by our Government to be security risks without any formal allegations or charges of disloyalty or espionage. They were arbitrarily branded disloyal solely on the grounds of racial ancestry.

No similar mass internment was deemed necessary for Americans of German or Italian ancestries, and I think we should recall and remind ourselves that in World War II, the Japanese were not our only enemies.

These Japanese Americans who were interned could not confront their accusers or bring their case before a court. These are basic rights of all Americans. They were incarcerated, forced to live in public communities with no privacy, and stripped of their freedom to move about as others could.

Japanese Americans wishing to fight for this country were initially declared ineligible. However, once allowed to volunteer, they volunteered in great numbers. In fact, proportionately and percentagewise, more Japanese Americans put on the uniform of this country during World War II, more were wounded and more were killed, even if they were restricted to serving in ethnically restricted military units.

The individual payments acknowledge the unjust deprivation of liberty, the infliction of mental and physical suffering, and the stigma of being branded disloyal, losses not compensable under the Japanese Evacuation Claims Act of 1948. . . .

The Presidentially appointed Commission on Wartime Relocation and Internment of Civilians found no documented acts of espionage, sabotage, or fifth column activity by any identifiable American citizen of Japanese ancestry or resident Japanese aliens on the west coast.

This was supposed to have been the rationale for this mass evacuation and mass incarceration, that these Americans were not to be trusted, that these Americans were agents of an enemy country, that these Americans would spy and carry out espionage, and this Presidentially appointed Commission, which incidentally was made up of leading citizens throughout this land—and only one member of that Commission was of Japanese ancestry—declared that there were no acts of espionage whatsoever. And sadly, the Commission in its 1983 report concluded that internment was motivated by racial prejudice, war hysteria, and a failure of political leadership. . . .

[T]he goal of [this bill] S. 1009 is to benefit all citizens of our Nation by educating our citizens to preclude this event from occurring again to any other ethnic or religious group or any person suspected of being less than a loyal citizen. This bill reinforces the strength of our Constitution by reaffirming our commitment to upholding the constitutional rights of all our citizens. So, respectfully, I strongly urge its passage and in so doing once again commend and congratulate my distinguished colleague from Hawaii. . . .

Senator [Spark M.] Matsunaga [D-HI]: I congratulate the senior Senator from Hawaii for his excellent statement. Coming from one who served in the 442d Regimental Combat Team, the most highly decorated military unit in the entire history of the United States, and having been highly decorated with the second highest award, the Distinguished Service Cross, and having sacrificed an arm in that war, I believe what the senior Senator from Hawaii has to say should be taken most seriously. . . .

Senator [Ted] Stevens [R-AK]: . . . As recounted yesterday what happened when the United States military removed 900 American citizens—Aleuts, who lived on the Aleutian chain and the Pribilof Islands—from their homes and took them to abandoned canneries and gold mining camps in southeastern Alaska.

Not many people understand the distances in our State. Attu and Kiska, which the Japanese invaded, are the most western islands in the Aleutian chain. The military saw fit to remove all Aleuts from all of the islands. Alaskans believed they did that because they wanted to occupy the islands and just did not want any local people in their way.

The Pribilof Islands were over 1,000 miles from the two islands the Japanese had taken. The Japanese never attempted to move further up along the Aleutian chain. They made an invasion of those two islands and fortified them. But there was really no necessity to remove these people. . . . Let us assume that the Japanese came to Baltimore. The action of the United States military removing the Aleuts would be like going to Chicago and then going west from Chicago about 1,000 miles and taking everyone between Chicago and Denver and moving them out of harm's way.

The record is clear that in terms of this internment—and it was an internment—was for the convenience of the Government. And these people, because they were of native descent, were taken and interned. They were kept for 2 to 3 years in those camps. In those days, Alaska was a territory, under wartime conditions, and it was not possible to travel.

I related yesterday how one of my friends, Flore Lekanoff, was taken from one of those camps in southeastern Alaska back to the Pribilof Islands to hunt for seals for the military. He was never paid for that. He was never recognized as being in the service of the Government. None of these people were treated as though they were in the service of the Government. They were literally just shoved aside. . . .

They have waited a long, long time. Most of them never recovered financially, particularly the people I represent in the Aleutian chain. Many are still destitute. This settlement is the final act to close this chapter of history and try to make restitution for that period of hysteria.

The people who made those decisions were good Americans. They were defending the country. They made mistakes. . . .

Senator [Daniel J.] Evans [D-WA]: As a Senator from the State of Washington, I have a special interest in this legislation. The first group of Japanese citizens to be removed from their homes under President Roosevelt's Executive Order were from Bainbridge Island, WA. They were the first of nearly 13,000 Japanese Americans from the State of Washington to be funneled into assembly centers and eventually into relocation facilities.

Victims of Executive Order 9066 were given very short notice that they would be sent to relocation facilities. Most were granted just a few days to abandon their homes and belongings. As a result they were forced to sell or lease their property and businesses at prices reflecting only a fraction of their worth. Substantial economic losses were incurred. Once they arrived at the relocation centers they found a quality of life which was atrocious. They were overcrowded and families suffered from an acute lack of privacy with no borders or walls to separate them from others.

Opponents of this legislation choose to ignore raw, racial prejudice woven in what was supposed to be legitimate national security justification for internment. The evacuees, however, were guilty of no crime other than the apparent crime of being of Japanese ancestry. Japanese Americans left their homes in an atmosphere of racial prejudice and returned to the same.

What is perhaps most alarming about the Japanese internment is that it took place in the United States of America. This is the same country which has prided itself on freedom, justice, and the preservation and protection of individual rights.

Thirty-four years after the last citizens were released from captivity, Congress established the Commission on the Wartime Relocation and Internment of Japanese-American Citizens to assess the decision to intern and relocate Japanese Americans. Two years after its inception, the Commission issued certain factual findings and subsequent recommendations. I have cosponsored legislation to implement these recommendations throughout my tenure in the U.S. Senate.

The $20,000 compensation that would be allotted to each victim, and the educational fund established by this legislation are a modest attempt to redress wrongs against loyal Americans. Although we cannot restore completely what already has been lost, the legislation would serve as a symbol to all that the United States can come to terms with its own tragic mistake. . . .

Senator [Jesse A.] Helms [R-NC]: . . . Nobody is, in retrospect, proud of the relocation of the Japanese Americans during World War II, but as I said earlier, we lived in a time of terror in this country immediately after the attack on Pearl Harbor. Nobody knew what was coming next. . . . We had just been attacked by a totalitarian regime which had enjoyed a virtually unbroken string of military successes, both before and immediately after the Government of Japan attacked the United States of America. . . .

I think it is only fair to look back to that time, and recall the fact that our intelligence community told the then President of the United States, Franklin Delano Roosevelt, that there was great risk. Now we can see that it was a mistake.

I have no vision problem with respect to that. We will have 20-20 vision by hindsight, and I am perfectly willing for this Senate and this Congress to declare that this kind of thing must never happen again.

But the Senate has just voted to give the priority emphasis to money, $1.3 billion. So I think we ought to look at our priorities. . . .

. . . The U.S. Government, contrary to suggestions otherwise, has not ignored the suffering that occurred as a result of the relocation and internment during the war. The Government has officially recognized that much unjustified personal hardship was, in fact, caused. Previous Congresses, Presidents, and Attorneys General have taken steps to acknowledge and compensate Japanese Americans for the injuries they suffered.

For example, in 1948, Congress enacted the American Japanese Claims Act, which authorized compensation for "any claim" for damages to or loss of real or personal property "as a reasonable consequence of the evacuation or exclusion of" persons of Japanese ancestry as a result of governmental action during World War II.

I might add that this act of 1948 was subsequently amended to liberalize its compensation provisions.

Under the amended act, the Justice Department received claims seeking approximately $147 million. Ultimately, 26,568 settlements were achieved. . . . True enough, the American Japanese Claims Act did not include every item of damage that was or could have been suggested. It did, however, address the hardships visited upon persons of Japanese ancestry in a comprehensive, considered manner taking into account individual needs and losses, and this effort to correct injustice to individuals was in keeping with our Nation's best tradition of individual rather than collective response, and it was far more contemporaneous with the injuries to the claimants than would be any payments at this late date. . . .

Senator [Alan K.] Simpson [R-WY]: It has been a very interesting debate for me. I have been paying attention to it on the monitor. It has made me recall some most interesting and memorable parts of my own life because I was a young boy in Cody, WY, in 1941 when the war started. I was 10 then.

Two years later, at the age of 12, somewhere between the years of 12 and 13, the third largest community in Wyoming was constructed between the communities of Powell and Cody, WY, a city of 15,000 people which really literally went up overnight. And the name of it, of course, was Heart Mountain War Relocation Center, known to the people of the area simply as the "Jap Camp," a term which may be hard for us to believe now but that is what it was referred to then; swiftly built by those who had not been drafted into the war, or older men in their 40's who were not able to be taken into the war effort.

And so came into being Heart Mountain, WY, War Relocation Center. There was barbed wire around it. There

were guard towers at the edges of it. It was a very imposing area. . . . I remember one night very distinctly when the scoutmaster—I was a Boy Scout, a rather nominal one, but I enjoyed the activities of the group. And he said, "We are going to go out to the War Relocation Center and have a scout meeting." I said, "Well, I mean, are there any of them out there?" . . . He said, "Yes, yes, these are American citizens, you see." And that put a new twist on it because we thought of them as something else—as aliens; we thought of them as spies; we thought of them as people who were behind wire because they were trying to do in our country.

So I shall not forget going to the Boy Scout meeting and meeting Boy Scouts from California, most of them, I recall, same merit badges, same scout sashes, same clothing.

And why not? Some of them were second- or third-generation American citizens. . . . I also remember those other nights we would go into the compound—which it was in every sense, with searchlights and with wire—visiting with some of the older people. There were very few young men there from the ages of 17 through 28, because many of them were in the armed services of the United States. But I do remember visiting with the older people and there were many of them there.

The younger and the older were there. Those were the principal inhabitants. I remember a woman, a very old woman to me at that age, said "Do you have grandparents?"

I said, "Yes, I do."

She said, "Where do they live?"

I said, "In Cody, down the road there."

She said, "Well, what kind of a house do they have?"

I thought, well, that is interesting to ask. I described it. "What do they do?"

And then I remember she showed me pictures of her family.

She said, "This is my son. He is in Italy now fighting for this country, the United States of America."

Then we would go downtown in Cody, WY, and there would be a sign on the restaurant that said, "No Japs allowed here." And then you would go down to another place of business, it might be a sign that said, "My son was killed at Iwo Jima. How do you think I feel?"

And the trustees would come into town. They were remarkable people. Usually the best and the brightest. Maybe those who had been involved in agriculture and whose lands had been taken from them—confiscated.

So I really had a lot of trouble sorting that all out at the age of 13. I maybe have some of the same kind of trouble sorting it all out at the age of 56. But let me just say that I preserve it as a very formative part of my life. . . . There is no question about it being the gravest of injustices. And it may be hardly a repayable one. How do you ever really repay these people for the wages, the property, the opportunity, the education, the part of their lives lost during this period? And this taxpayer expenditure is a troubling part of the bill for me.

I have trouble with the money. An apology may be long overdue and may be so appropriate. But, coupled with money, it takes away some of the sincerity of the apology, somehow. If you did that with a friend, a lovely friend, and you said: I am sorry for what I did. I know that was very harmful to you and hurtful. But I am sorry and I apologize and I want to give you some money.

I think that that somehow is unbecoming. It may not be to some. It is a troubling aspect of it to me. . . . So we will conclude this, and I think probably we will revisit this issue again, not with this situation but in other populations of our country, and we best know indeed, that will likely take place.

There is not one of us here today with what we have been through with our civil rights activities in 1964 and Selma that probably thinks: "How could this have ever oc-

curred?" And yet at the time it occurred, it seemed at that time of our lives to be the most important step that could be taken.

That decision was made by people with much greater wisdom than I had at the age of 13 in Cody, WY.

Hopefully, we will conclude this debate shortly and move on to other issues of the day because this is an old and sad and very painful thing that we have reopened here in this debate. The sooner we close that wound and suture it with love and understanding and affection, we will be better off. And suturing it with money does not seem like the best way to conclude the issue.

Source: Congressional Record, Senate Debate, April 20, 1988.

New York State Report on Multicultural Textbooks, 1991

The school system of New York State is one of the largest in the country and among the most ethnically diverse. Facing criticism that its curriculum overly emphasized European culture and history, the New York commissioner of education issued a report in 1991 advocating a more multicultural approach to the way schools in the state taught social studies. Critics—including many conservatives—said the new approach would "balkanize" education along ethnic lines and destroy the public school's role as a molder of a common national heritage.

The following document includes excerpts from the report, as well as a dissenting view offered by historian Arthur Schlesinger Jr.

PREAMBLE

The United States is a microcosm of humanity today. No other country in the world is peopled by a greater variety of races, nationalities, and ethnic groups. But although the United States has been a great asylum for diverse peoples, it has not always been a great refuge for diverse cultures. The country has opened its doors to a multitude of nationalities, but often their cultures have not been encouraged to survive or, at best, have been kept marginal to the mainstream.

Since the 1960s, however, a profound reorientation of the self-image of Americans has been under way. Before this time the dominant model of the typical American had been conditioned primarily by the need to shape a unified nation out of a variety of contrasting and often conflicting European immigrant communities. But following the struggles for civil rights, the unprecedented increase in non-European immigration over the last two decades and the increasing recognition of our nation's indigenous heritage, there has been a fundamental change in the image of what a resident of the United States is.

With this change, which necessarily highlights the racial and ethnic pluralism of the nation, previous ideals of assimilation to an Anglo-American model have been put in question and are now slowly and sometimes painfully being set aside. Many people in the United States are no longer comfortable with the requirement, common in the past, that they shed their specific cultural differences in order to be considered American. Instead, while busily adapting to and shaping mainstream cultural ideals commonly identified as American, in recent decades many in the United States—from European and non-European backgrounds—have been encouraging a more tolerant, inclusive, and realistic vision of American identity than any that has existed in the past.

This identity, committed to the democratic principles of the nation and the nation-building in which all Americans are engaged, is progressively evolving from the past model toward a new model marked by respect for pluralism and awareness of the virtues of diversity. This situation is a current reality, and a multicultural education, anchored to the shared principles of a liberal democracy, is today less an educational innovation than a national priority.

It is fitting for New York State, host to the Statue of Liberty, to inaugurate a curriculum that reflects the rich cultural diversity of the nation. The beacon of hope welcomes not just the "wretched and poor" individuals of the world, but also the dynamic and rich cultures all people bring with them.

Two centuries after this country's founders issued a Declaration of Independence, focused on the political independence from which societies distant from the United States have continued to draw inspiration, the time has come to recognize cultural interdependence. We propose that the principle of respect for diverse cultures is critical to our nation, and we affirm that a right to cultural diversity exists. We believe that the schoolroom is one of the places where this cultural interdependence must be reflected.

It is in this spirit that we have crafted this report, "One Nation, Many Peoples." We see the social studies as the primary avenue through which the school addresses our cultural diversity and interdependence. But the study of cultural diversity and interdependence is only one goal. It is through such studies that we seek to strengthen our national commitment and world citizenship, with the development of intellectual competence in our students as the foundation. We see the social studies as directed at the development of intellectual competence in learners, with the capacity to view the world and understand it from multiple perspectives as one of the main components of such competence. Multicultural knowledge in this conception of the social studies becomes a vehicle and not a goal. Multicultural content and experience become instruments by which we enable students to develop their intelligence and to function as human and humane persons.

I. INTRODUCTION: AFFIRMATION OF PURPOSE

This Committee affirms that multicultural education should be a source of strength and pride. Multicultural education is often viewed as divisive and even as destructive of the values and beliefs which hold us together as Americans. Certainly, contemporary trends toward separation and dissolution in such disparate countries as the Soviet Union, South Africa, Canada, Yugoslavia, Spain, and the United Kingdom remind us that different ethnic and racial groups have often had extraordinary difficulty remaining together in nation-states. But national unity does not require that we eliminate the very diversity that is the source of our uniqueness and, indeed, of our adaptability and viability among the nations of the world. *If the United States is to continue to prosper in the 21st century, then all of its citizens, whatever their race or ethnicity, must believe that they and their ancestors have shared in the building of the country and have a stake in its success.* Thus, multicultural education, far from being a source of dissolution, is necessary for the cultural health, social stability, and economic future of New York State and the nation.

The Committee believes that to achieve these ends, the teaching of social studies should emphasize the following:

First, beginning in the earliest grades social studies should be taught from a global perspective. The earth is humankind's common home. Migration is our common history. The earth's peoples, cultures, and material resources are our common wealth. Both humankind's pain and humankind's triumphs must be shared globally. The uniqueness of humankind is our many ways of being human, our remarkable range of cultural and physical diversity within a common biological unity.

Second, the social studies will very likely continue to serve nation-building purposes, among others, even as we encourage global perspectives. With efforts to respect and honor the diverse and pluralistic elements in our nation, special attention will need to be given to those values, characteristics, and traditions which we share in common. Commitment to the presentation of multiple perspectives in the social studies curriculum encourages attention to the tradi-

tional and dominant elements in our society, even as we introduce and examine minority elements which have been neglected or those which are emerging as a result of new scholarship and newly recognized voices.

Third, the curriculum must strive to be informed by the most up-to-date scholarship. It must be open to all relevant input, to new knowledge, to fresh perspectives. Human history is to be seen as ongoing, often contradictory, and subject to reasonable differences based on contrasting perceptions and distinct viewpoints.

Fourth, students need to see themselves as active makers and changers of culture and society; they must be helped to develop the tools by which to judge, analyze, act, and evaluate.

Fifth, the program should be committed to the honoring and continuing examination of democratic values as an essential basis for social organization and nation-building. The application of democracy to social organization should be viewed as a continuing process which sometimes succeeds and sometimes fails, and thus requires constant effort.

Sixth, one of the central aims of the social studies is the development of the intellect; thus, the social studies should be taught not solely as information, but rather through the critical examination of ideas and events rooted in time and place and responding to social interests. The social studies should be seen not as some dreary schoolroom task of fact mastery to be tested and forgotten, but as one of the best curricular vehicles for telling the story of humanity in a way that motivates and inspires all of our children to continue the process of responsible nation-building in a world context. . . .

BACKGROUND: THE SOCIAL STUDIES AND THE CHANGING SOCIETY

Recent debate concerning change in New York State's social studies curriculum often implies that the curriculum stands as a fixed and unchanging prescription for the classroom, its stability protecting the inculcation of basic values from shifting political and economic winds. Closer examination, however, reveals that the curriculum has grown and been transformed over time in response to societal change, as a few examples will show. . . .

Unlike literature and languages, the social studies and their parent disciplines of history and geography were not a major part of the mainstream of the school curriculum until the present century. In 1899, a Committee of Seven of the American Historical Association (founded in 1884) made a recommendation which led to the study of European and American history and government in schools, including those of New York State. Other subject-matter organizations, as they were formed, also began to press for inclusion in the school curriculum (the American Political Science Association and the American Sociological Association, for example, founded respectively in 1903 and 1905).

In the second decade of this century, the need to accommodate the surge of immigration led to the view that the schools should help students develop the attitudes and skills necessary for good citizenship. In 1916 a Committee on the Social Studies of the American Historical Association declared this to be the goal of schooling, bringing the term "social studies" into formal use. In 1951, responding to the mood of national insecurity reflected in McCarthyism, New York State dropped the term "social studies" in favor of "citizenship education," and the amount of American history in the secondary curriculum was greatly increased ("social studies" re-emerged in 1960). Between 1965 and the late 1980s, as international communication and commerce increased, the curriculum was enlarged to include more global studies, such as year-long courses in Asian and African Studies (grade 9) and European Studies (grade 10). Since 1987, these in turn have been replaced by a two-year global studies sequence.

Indeed, the processes of contest, debate, and transformation are integral parts of the rich history of education in the United States. That history has reflected the society of which it is a part, and societal changes over the past 30 years have brought with them rising interest in the study of diverse cultures in the United States and the world. In the universities, scholarly attention has turned to previously neglected groups (those that have historically been minorities in the United States and women) and topics (social history, ethnic and cultural studies). Such scholarship has brought to light much that had been omitted from U.S. and world history, as traditionally studied.

In the 1970s and early 1980s, elementary and secondary schools, like colleges and universities, were faced with the recognition that much of the experience, cultural values, and collective pasts of their students was not identified or represented in the curriculum. Corresponding to what James A. Banks has termed the "demographic imperative" of increasing numbers of minority students enrolled in public schools, parents, students, and communities served by the schools became more forceful in demanding that their children learn about their own pasts. There was a new recognition that the teaching of social studies as a single officially sanctioned story was inaccurate as to the facts of conflict in American history, and further, that it was limiting for white students and students of color alike.

Much of the heat of debate concerning the importance of valuing cultural difference in the schools arises from divergent opinions on whether preparing students to become members of U.S. society necessarily means assimilation. While the goal of assimilation has historically been relatively explicit in American schooling, in recent years many thoughtful writers and educators have argued against assimilation when interpreted as erasure of distinctive cultural identities. Education must respond to the joint imperatives of educating toward citizenship in a common polity while respecting and taking account of continuing distinctiveness. Even more, as we have argued, the perspectives of a number of major groups in American society must be recognized and incorporated. Nor is assimilation essential to educate

citizens who value this country's ideals and participate in its polity and economy. . . .

Over the past two decades, elementary, middle, and secondary schools and post-secondary institutions have seen efforts to restructure the curriculum in order to represent more adequately the diverse cultures of the student body and the world in which students must eventually function. Shifts in curriculum design in such states as California, Oregon, Iowa, Ohio, and Florida reflect an increasing awareness that children and society are inadequately served when study is limited to the intellectual monuments of Western civilization. Comprehensive study of multiple cultures is increasingly recognized as having critical relevance for students who will face a national economy and political structures that grow more globally interdependent and increasingly diverse. . . .

[II and III omitted]

IV. THE STATE SYLLABI: THE SYLLABI IN RELATION TO THE OTHER COMPONENTS OF A PROGRAM

The current New York State Social Studies syllabi include a series of twelve publications: one booklet each for kindergarten and grades 1, 2, 3, 4, 5, 6, and 11; one for grades 7–8; one for 9–10; one for the first half of grade 12, and another for the second half. The publications vary in length from 73 to 202 pages. They are reviewed and updated periodically by committees of teachers and professors under the guidance of the Bureau of Social Studies Education. All of the current publications carry dates of revision between 1987 and 1989.

Statewide syllabi are not found in most other states, but in New York, this Committee does not, that every viable nation has to have a common culture to survive in peace. As our own document indicates, one need look no further than Yugoslavia, the Soviet Union, or Canada to see the accuracy of this proposition. We might want to add India after the events of the past two weeks. The dominant American culture might have been German or French or Chinese or Algonquin or African, but for various historical reasons the English language and British political and legal traditions prevailed. Whether or not we would have been better off if Montcalm had defeated Wolfe on the Plains of Abraham is beside the point. . . .

A better strategy for this Committee would have been to argue in a positive rather than a negative way. Because we are made up of many peoples and cultures, because all these peoples and cultures have contributed to national greatness, and because the United States has typically done a better job of integrating newcomers into its social and political fabric (with racial prejudice being a glaring and persistent exception) than other places, its educational system should reflect that experience. We have been multicultural, we are multicultural, and we hope that we will always be multicultural. Moreover, the enemies of multiculturism are not teachers, textbooks, or curricular guides, but shopping centers, fast food outlets, and situation comedies, all of which threaten to turn us into an amorphous mass.

The report highlights the notion that all cultures are created equal. This may be true in the abstract, and I have no problem with the philosophical concept. But I cannot endorse a "Declaration of Cultural Independence," which is the subtitle of our Committee report. Within any single country, one culture must be accepted as the standard. Unfortunately, our document has virtually nothing to say about the things which hold us together. . . .

SCHLESINGER'S DISSENT: A DISSENTING OPINION
Arthur Schlesinger Jr.

I agree with many of the practical recommendations in the report. It is unquestionably necessary to diversify the syllabus in order to meet the needs of a more diversified society. It is unquestionably necessary to provide for global education in an increasingly interdependent world. Our students should by all means be better acquainted with women's history, with the history of ethnic and racial minorities, with Latin American, Asian, and African history. Debate, alternative interpretations, "multiple perspectives" are all essential to the educational enterprise. I welcome changes that would adapt the curriculum to these purposes. If that is what the report means by multicultural education, I am all for it.

But I fear that the report implies much more than this. The underlying philosophy of the report, as I read it, is that ethnicity is the defining experience for most Americans, that ethnic ties are permanent and indelible, that the division into ethnic groups establishes the basic structure of American society and that a main objective of public education should be the protection, strengthening, celebration, and perpetuation of ethnic origins and identities. Implicit in the report is the classification of all Americans according to ethnic and racial criteria.

These propositions are assumed rather than argued in the report. They constitute an ethnic interpretation of American history that, like the economic interpretation, is valid up to a point but misleading and wrong when presented as the whole picture.

The ethnic interpretation, moreover, reverses the historic theory of America—which has been, not the preservation and sanctification of old cultures and identities, but the creation of a new national culture and a new national identity. . . .

Of course students should learn more about the rich variety of peoples and cultures that have forged this new American identity. They also should understand the curse of racism—the great failure of the American experiment, the glaring contradiction of American ideals and the still-crippling disease of American society. But we should also be alert to the danger of a society divided into distinct and immutable ethnic and racial groups, each taught to cherish its own apartness from the rest.

While I favor curricular changes that make for more inclusive interpretations of past and present, I do not believe that we should magnify ethnic and racial themes at the expense of the unifying ideals that precariously hold our highly differentiated society together. The republic has survived and grown because it has maintained a balance between *pluribus* and *unum*. The report, it seems to me, is saturated with *pluribus* and neglectful of *unum*. . . .

Obviously the reason why the United States, for all its manifest failure to live up to its own ideals, is still the most successful large multi-ethnic nation is precisely because, instead of emphasizing and perpetuating ethnic separatism, it has assimilated immigrant cultures into a new American culture. . . .

. . . If the ethnic subcultures had genuine vitality, they would be sufficiently instilled in children by family, church, and community. It is surely not the office of the public school to promote ethnic separatism and heighten ethnic tensions.

Should public education move in this direction, it will only increase the fragmentation, resegregation, and self-ghettoization of American life. The bonds of national cohesion in the republic are sufficiently fragile already. Public education should aim to strengthen those bonds, not to weaken them. . . .

What has held Americans together in the absence of a common ethnic origin has been the creation of a new American identity—a distinctive American culture based on a common language and common adherence to ideals of democracy and human rights, a culture to which many nationalities and races have made emphatic contributions in the past and will (one hopes) make emphatic contributions in the future. Our democratic ideals have been imperfectly realized, but the long labor to achieve them and to move the American experiment from exclusion to participation has been a central theme of American history. It should be a central theme of the New York social studies curriculum.

And it is important for students to understand where these democratic ideals come from. They come of course from Europe. Indeed, Europe is the unique source of these ideals—ideals that today empower people in every continent and to which today most of the world aspires. That is why it is so essential (in my view) to acquaint students with the western history and tradition that created our democratic ideals—and why it is so wrong to tell students of non-European origin that western ideals are not for them.

I regret the note of Europhobia that sometimes emerges in vulgar attacks on "Eurocentric" curriculums. Certainly Europe, like every other culture, has committed its share of crimes. But, unlike most cultures, it has also generated ideals that have opposed and exposed those crimes.

The report, however, plays up the crimes and plays down the ideals. Thus, when it talks about the European colonization of Africa and India, it deplores "the eradication of many varieties of traditional culture and knowledge."

Like infanticide? slavery? polygamy? subjection of women? suttee? veil-wearing? foot-binding? clitorectemies? Nothing is said about the influence of European ideas of democracy, human rights, self-government, rule of law. . . .

I also am doubtful about the note occasionally sounded in the report that "students must be taught social criticism" and "see themselves as active makers and changers of culture and society" and "promote economic fairness and social justice" and "bring about change in their communities, the nation, and the world." I very much hope that, as citizens, students will do all these things, but I do not think it is the function of the schools to teach students to become reformers any more than I ever thought it the function of the schools to teach them the beauty of private enterprise and the sanctity of the status quo. I will be satisfied if we can teach children to read, write, and calculate. If students understand the nature of our western democratic tradition, they will move into social criticism of their own. But let us not politicize the curriculum on behalf either of the left or of the right. . . .

Source: Congressional Quarterly. *Historic Documents of 1991.* Washington, DC: Congressional Quarterly, Inc., 1992.

U.S. Report Under the International Covenant on Civil and Political Rights, 1994

As a signatory to the International Covenant on Civil and Political Rights, the United States is obliged to adhere to certain international rules concerning the exclusion and deportation of refugees. In this report, issued in July 1994, the U.S. government explains its policy and practice toward the acceptance, exclusion, and deportation of refugees of various sorts.

ARTICLE 13—EXPULSION OF ALIENS

The United States has a strong tradition of supporting immigration and has adopted immigration policies reflective of the view that immigrants make invaluable contributions to the fabric of American society. At present, the United States provides annually for the legal immigration of over 700,000 aliens each year, with special preferences granted for family reunification and employment skills purposes. In addition, the United States grants admission to some 120,000 refugees from abroad annually, and accords political asylum to many others within the United States. Notwithstanding these large programs for legal immigration to the United States, illegal immigration to the United States continues in substantial numbers. The total number of aliens illegally in the United States is currently estimated to be over 3 million. Due to the ease of travel and relative lack of residence controls within the United States, as well as the extensive procedural guarantees accompanying deportation, aliens who enter the continental United States illegally, or who stay on illegally after an initial lawful entry, are often able to remain for many years.

Aliens who have entered the United States, whether legally or illegally, may be expelled only pursuant to deportation proceedings, as described below. (Different procedures apply to diplomatic representatives, who may be declared persona non grata.) The legal protection for such persons includes the extensive procedural safeguards provided by the Immigration and Nationality Act (INA), U.S.C. 1101 et seq., and rests fundamentally on the constitutional rights of due process afforded to all. As the Supreme Court has stated:

Aliens who have once passed through our gates, even illegally, may be expelled only after proceedings conforming to traditional standards of fairness encompassed in due process of law. Shaughnessy v. United States, 206 U.S. 206, 212 (1953).

Whatever his status under the immigration laws, an alien is surely a "person" [for purposes of certain constitutional guarantees] in any ordinary sense of that term. Aliens, even aliens whose presence in this country is unlawful, have long been recognized as "persons" guaranteed due process of law by the Fifth and Fourteenth Amendments. Plyler v. Doe, 457 U.S. 202, 210 (1981).

The term "entry" is generally defined under INA 101(a)(13) as "any coming of an alien into the United States from a foreign port or place." Aliens within the United States who were inspected and admitted as well as those who evaded inspection and came into the United States illegally are considered to have effected an "entry." Persons who attempt illegal entry but are detected at the border prior to entry are occasionally allowed into the United States for further processing of their entry claims (in lieu of return to their home country or detention at the border), or under the Attorney General's discretionary parole authority. Such excludable aliens, whose presence in the United States results solely from the limited, conditional permission of the United States Government, are not considered to have entered the United States for immigration purposes. They generally are subject to exclusion proceedings, as described below, which provide some due process protections, although not as extensive as those provided in deportation proceedings.

I. DEPORTATION

Aliens who have entered the United States and who violate U.S. immigration laws are subject to deportation proceedings. Grounds for deportation include: (1) excludability at time of entry or adjustment of status; (2) entry without inspection; (3) alien smuggling; (4) marriage fraud; (5) criminal offenses; (6) falsification of documents; (7) security grounds; (8) public charge grounds. . . .

Generally, an alien "is not and should not be detained or required to post bond except on a finding that he is a threat to the national security . . . or that he is a poor bail risk." Matter of Patel, 15 I&N Dec. 666 (BIA 1976). The Attorney General is, however, obligated to take into custody any alien convicted of an aggravated felony, but may release the alien, if the alien demonstrates that the alien "is not a threat to the community and that the alien is likely to appear before any scheduled hearings." INA 242(a)(2)(B); 8 C.F.R. 3.19(h).

Custody and bond determinations made by the Immigration and Naturalization Service (INS) may be reviewed by an immigration judge and may be appealed to the Board of Immigration Appeals (BIA). An alien's release on bond or parole may be revoked at any time in the discretion of the Attorney General. INA 242(a). . . .

During deportation proceedings, the immigration judge has the authority to determine deportability, to grant discretionary relief, and to determine the country to which an alien's deportation will be directed. The immigration judge must also: (1) advise the alien of the alien's right to representation, at no expense to the Government, by qualified counsel of his choice; (2) advise the alien of the availability of local free legal services programs; (3) ascertain that the alien has received a list of such programs and a copy of INS Form I-618, Written Notice of Appeal Rights; (4) advise the alien that the alien will have a reasonable opportunity to examine and object to adverse evidence, to present evidence, and to cross-examine witnesses presented by the Government; (5) place the alien under oath; (6) read the factual allegations and the charges in the order to show cause to the alien and explain them in nontechnical language, and enter the order to show cause as an exhibit in the record. 8 C.F.R. 242.16(a).

The INA mandates that the "alien shall have a reasonable opportunity to be present" at the deportation proceeding. INA 242(b). The BIA has held that aliens "must be given a reasonable opportunity to present evidence on their own behalf, including their testimony." Matter of Tomas, 19 I&N Dec. 464, 465 (BIA 1987). The BIA has further noted that in most cases, "all that need be translated are the immigration judge's statements to the alien, the examination of the alien by his counsel, the attorney for the Service, and the immigration judge, and the alien's responses to their questions." Matter of Exilus, 18 I&N 276, 281 (BIA 1982). However, "the immigration judge may determine . . . that the alien's understanding of other dialogue is essential to his ability to assist in the presentation of his case." Id.

If the alien concedes deportability and the alien has not applied for discretionary relief other than voluntary departure (discussed below), the immigration judge may enter a summary decision ordering deportation or granting voluntary departure with an alternate order of deportation. 8

C.F.R. 242.18(b). The immigration judge may not accept an admission of deportability "from an unrepresented respondent who is incompetent or under age 16 and is not accompanied by a guardian, relative, or friend; nor from an officer of an institution in which [an alien] is an inmate or patient." 8 C.F.R. 242.16(b).

In cases where deportability is at issue and/or where the alien has applied for discretionary relief, the immigration judge receives evidence on the issues. The Government must establish an alien's deportability by clear, convincing, and unequivocal evidence and must establish that the person is an alien. 8 C.F.R. 242.14(a). If deportability is based on an entry violation, such as entry without inspection, however, after the INS establishes identity and alienage of the person, the burden shifts to the alien to show the time, place, and manner of his entry into the United States. If this burden of proof "is not sustained, such person shall be presumed to be in the United States in violation of law." INA 291.

RELIEF FROM DEPORTATION

Waivers. Waivers are available for some of the grounds of deportation. Suspensions of Deportation. Under INA 244(a), the Attorney General may "suspend deportation and adjust the status to that of an alien lawfully admitted for permanent residence, in the case of an alien . . . , who applies for suspension of deportation" and (1) is deportable; (2) subject to certain exceptions, has been physically present in the United States for a continuous period of not less than seven years immediately preceding the date of such application; (3) proves that during all of such period he was and is a person of good moral character; and (4) is a person whose deportation would in the opinion of the Attorney General result in extreme hardship to the alien or to his spouse, parent, or child, who is a citizen of the United States or an alien lawfully admitted for permanent residence. INA 244(a)(1).

Voluntary Departure. The Attorney General may permit an alien to "depart voluntarily from the United States at his own expense in lieu of deportation" if such alien (1) is not deportable for criminal offenses, falsification of documents or on security grounds; (2) is not an aggravated felon; and (3) establishes "to the satisfaction of the Attorney General that he is, and has been, a person of good moral character for at least five years immediately preceding his application for voluntary departure." INA 244(e)(1).

Registry. INA 249 generally provides that the Attorney General may create a record of lawful admission for permanent residence for an alien, as of the date of the approval of his application, if (1) such alien is (a) not excludable as [a] participant in Nazi persecutions or genocide and (b) not excludable under INA 212(a) "as it relates to criminals, procurers, and other immoral persons, subversives, violators of the narcotic laws or smugglers of aliens"; and (2) the alien establishes that he (a) entered the United States prior to January 1, 1972; (b) has had residence in the United States continuously since such entry; (c) is a person of good moral character; and (d) is not ineligible for citizenship. INA 249; see also 8 C.F.R. 249.1 (discussing waivers of inadmissibility for certain exclusion grounds in conjunction with registry applications).

Decisions and Appeals. A decision of an immigration judge in a deportation hearing may be written or oral. Appeal from the decision lies with the BIA. 8 C.F.R. 242.21. A final order of deportation may be reviewed by federal courts, but will not be reviewed "if the alien has not exhausted the administrative remedies available to him as of right under the immigration laws and regulations or if he has departed from the United States after the issuance of the order." INA 106 (c). The immigration judge may upon the judge's own motion, or upon motion of the trial attorney, or the alien, reopen any case which the judge decided, "unless jurisdiction in the case is vested in the Board of Immigration Appeals." 8 C.F.R. 242.22. A motion to reopen "will not be granted unless the immigration judge is satisfied that evidence sought to be offered is material and was not available and could not have been discovered or presented at the hearing." 8 C.F.R. 242.22.

II. EXCLUSION

An alien has the burden of satisfying the INS officer at the border point of entry that the alien is entitled to enter the United States and not subject to exclusion. If the officer concludes the alien is not clearly entitled to enter, the officer must detain the alien for further inspection. INA 235(b). The alien may be released on bond or parole; the standards for release are essentially the same as they are in deportation proceedings. . . .

The immigration judge must inform the alien of the nature and purpose of the hearing; advise the alien that the alien has a statutory right to have an attorney at no cost to the government, and of the availability of free legal services programs; ascertain that the applicant has received a list of such programs; request the alien to determine then and there whether the alien desires representation; and advise the alien that the alien will have a reasonable opportunity to present evidence, to examine and object to adverse evidence, and to cross-examine witnesses presented by the government.

Except for aliens previously admitted to the United States for lawful permanent residence, aliens have the burden of proving their admissibility in exclusion proceedings. The immigration judge can grant various forms of relief, including waivers, adjustment of status under certain conditions, and political asylum and withholding of exclusion. Suspension of deportation and voluntary departure are not available. . . .

Following a final determination of exclusion, an alien may surrender himself to the custody of the INS, or may be notified to surrender to custody. An alien taken into custody either upon notice to surrender or by arrest may not be deported less than 72 hours thereafter unless the alien consents in writing. 8 C.F.R. 237.2. An alien detained pending or during exclusion proceedings may seek further review in federal court under a writ of habeas corpus.

III. UNITED STATES REFUGEE AND ASYLUM POLICY

The refugee and asylum policy of the United States, set forth primarily in the Refugee Act of 1980 and the Immigration and Nationality Act (the INA), was created in accordance with the strong, historical commitment of the United States to the protection of refugees and in compliance with the 1967 United Nations Protocol Relating to the Status of Refugees. The Protocol, to which the United States has acceded, adopted the operative provisions of the 1951 United Nations Convention Relating to the Status of Refugees.

Under the INA, persons within the United States may seek refugee protection through a grant of asylum or withholding of deportation. The standard for such determinations is that provided in the Protocol, defining a refugee as: "any person who is outside of any country of such person's nationality or, in the case of a person having no nationality, is outside any country in which such person last habitually resided, and who is unable or unwilling to return to, and is unable or unwilling to avail himself or herself of the protection of, that country because of persecution or a well-founded fear of persecution on account of race, religion, nationality, membership in a particular social group, or political opinion." INA 101(a)(42)(A); 8 U.S.C. 1101(a)(42)(A). Refugee status is not available to "any person who ordered, incited, assisted, or otherwise participated in the persecution of any person on account of race, religion, nationality, membership in a particular social group, or political opinion," or for aliens who have been convicted of an aggravated felony. INA 101(a)(42)(B) and 208(d); 8 U.S.C. 1101(a)(42)(B) and 1158(d).

At present, there are some 300,000 asylum claims pending in various stages of adjudication; over 100,000 new claims were filed in Fiscal Year 1992. A related form of protection, temporary protected status, is available to persons already within the United States when the Attorney General determines that certain extreme and temporary conditions in their country of nationality (such as ongoing armed conflict or an environmental disaster) generally do not permit the United States to return them to that country in safety.

In addition, the United States maintains a substantial program for providing assistance to refugees overseas. The United States overseas refugee admissions program, which also uses the Protocol definition of refugee, provides for the admission and resettlement in the United States of over 120,000 refugees of special humanitarian concern to the United States each year from throughout the world. In addition, the United States provides on-site assistance, primarily through relevant international organizations such as the United Nations High Commissioner for Refugees, the International Committee of the Red Cross, and the International Organization for Migration, in the amount of over $300 million dollars each year, not only to "Protocol refugees" but also to others who are suffering from the disruptive effects of conflict or other forms of dislocation. In the last three years alone, the United States has contributed over $1 billion in assistance to refugees throughout the world.

Refugee Admissions. The INA provides for the admission of refugees outside the United States. Each year the President, after appropriate consultation with Congress, determines an authorized admission level for refugees. For example, the admission ceiling for refugees in 1994 was 121,000. This annual ceiling represents the maximum number of refugees allowed to enter the United States each year, allocated by world geographical region. INA 207(a). The President may accommodate an emergency refugee situation by increasing the refugee admissions ceiling for a twelve-month period. INA 207(b); 8 U.S.C. 1157(b).

Persons applying in overseas offices for refugee protection in the United States must satisfy four criteria. They must: (1) fall within the definition of a refugee set forth in the INA; (2) be among the types of refugees determined to be of special humanitarian concern to the United States; (3) be admissible under the Immigration and Nationality Act; and (4) not be firmly resettled in any foreign country.

The refugee application process originates either at a United States embassy or at a designated consular office, if distance makes direct filing at an embassy impracticable. 8 C.F.R. 207.1(a). Interviews are then conducted by employees of the Immigration and Naturalization Service. There exists no formal procedure for either administrative appeal or judicial review of adverse decisions. The applicant has the burden of showing entitlement to refugee status. 8 C.F.R. 208.8(d).

Asylum. Asylum applications may be submitted by persons who are physically present in the United States. Asylum may be granted without regard to the applicant's immigration status or country of origin. There are two paths for an alien present in the United States seeking asylum. First, the alien may come forward to the INS to apply "affirmatively." Second, the alien may seek asylum as a defense to exclusion or deportation proceedings, even after a denial of asylum through the affirmative process. . . .

Affirmative Asylum. Affirmative asylum claims are heard and decided by a corps of INS asylum officers located in seven regional offices. The asylum officer conducts an interview with the applicant "in a nonadversarial manner . . . to elicit all relevant and useful information bearing on the applicant's eligibility." 8 C.F.R. 208.9(b). The applicant may have counsel present at the interview and may submit the affidavits of witnesses. In addition, the applicant may supplement the record within thirty days of the interview. 8 C.F.R. 208.9. Upon completion of the interview, the asylum officer

must forward a copy of the asylum application to the Bureau of Human Rights and Humanitarian Affairs (BHRHA) (recently renamed the Bureau of Democracy Rights and Labor) of the Department of State. The BHRHA may comment on the application within 45 days. The asylum officer may make a final decision if no response from the BHRHA arrives within 60 days. 8 C.F.R. 208.11.

The asylum officer's decision must be in writing and, if asylum is denied, the decision must include a credibility assessment. 8 C.F.R. 208.17. The alien has the right to specific reasons for denial and the right to both factually and legally rebut the denial. 8 C.F.R. 103.3(a) and 103.2(b)(2). The decision of the asylum officer is reviewed by the INS's Office of Refugees, Asylum, and Parole (CORAP), but the applicant has no right to appeal. 8 C.F.R. 208.18(a).

Asylum claims must be denied when: (1) the alien has been convicted of a particularly serious crime in the United States and constitutes a danger to the community; (2) the alien has been firmly resettled in a third country; or (3) there are reasonable grounds for regarding the alien as a threat to the security of the United States. 8 C.F.R. 208.14(c). In addition, asylum officers may use discretion in asylum denials.

Asylum officers also have limited power to revoke asylum and relief under the "withholding of deportation" provision of the INA (243(h)). This power may be exercised when: (1) the alien no longer has a well-founded fear of persecution or is no longer entitled to relief under 243(h) because of changed country conditions; (2) there existed fraud in the application such that the alien was not eligible for asylum at the time it was granted; or (3) the alien has committed any act that would have been grounds for denial. 8 C.F.R. 208.24(a)(b). Once an affirmative asylum application is denied, the asylum officer is empowered, if appropriate, to initiate the alien's exclusion or deportation proceedings.

Asylum and Withholding of Exclusion/Deportation in Exclusion or Deportation Proceedings. If an alien has been served with an Order to Show Cause to appear at a deportation hearing or a notice to appear at an exclusion hearing, he must appear before an immigration judge, with whom he may file an asylum application. The filing of an asylum application is also considered a request for withholding of deportation or exclusion under INA 243(h).

Relief under INA 243(h) differs from a request for asylum in three ways. First, 243(h) provides relief from deportation or exclusion to a specific country where the applicant's "life or freedom would be threatened," while asylum protects the alien from deportation generally and only requires a well-founded fear of persecution. Second, relief under 243(h) cannot result in permanent residence, while asylees are eligible for permanent residence after one year. Third, relief under 243(h) is mandatory while asylum is a discretionary grant. . . .

The alien will be denied 243(h) relief and will remain subject to exclusion or deportation if the alien: (1) engaged in persecution of others; (2) has been convicted of a particularly serious crime that constitutes a danger to the community of the United States; (3) has committed a serious nonpolitical crime outside of the United States; or (4) may represent a danger to the security of the United States. INA 243(h)(2). . . .

Parole Under INA 212(d)(5)(B). A refugee may be paroled into the United States by the Attorney General only if there exist "compelling reasons in the public interest with respect to that particular alien" to parole rather than admit the person as a refugee under INA 207. INA 212(d)(5)(B). Parole allows an alien to remain in the United States temporarily until a final status decision is made. Parole is not equivalent to an "admission," and thus leaves the alien subject to exclusion.

The Attorney General has created a "special interest parole" process "on an exceptional basis only for an unspecified but limited period of time" pursuant to the Lautenberg Amendment of the Foreign Operations Appropriations Act. Pub. L. No. 101-167. Under this provision, certain persons from Cambodia, Laos, Vietnam, and the former Soviet Union (specifically Jews, Evangelical Christians, Ukrainian Catholics, and Ukrainian Orthodox Christians), who were inspected and paroled into the United States between August 15, 1988 and September 30, 1994 after being denied refugee status, are eligible for adjustment of status.

Temporary Protected Status. Under INA 244A, the Attorney General has the authority to grant temporary protected status to aliens in the United States, temporarily allowing foreign nationals to live and work in the United States without fear of being sent back to unstable or dangerous conditions. The United States thus may become, at the Attorney General's discretion, a temporary safe haven for foreign nationals already in this country if one of three conditions exists: (1) there is an ongoing conflict within the state, which would pose a serious threat to the personal safety of returned nationals; (2) there has been an earthquake, flood, drought, epidemic, or other environmental disaster in the state resulting in a substantial but temporary disruption of living conditions; the state is temporarily unable to accept the return of nationals; and the state officially asks the Attorney General for a designation of temporary protected status; or (3) there exist extraordinary and temporary conditions in the state that prevent nationals from returning in safety, as long as the grant of temporary protected status is not contrary to the national interest of the United States. INA 244A(b)(1). Designation of temporary protected status may last for six to eighteen months, with the possibility of extension.

An alien is ineligible for temporary protected status if he has been convicted of at least one felony or two or more misdemeanors. 8 C.F.R. 240.4. Ineligibility is also based upon the grounds for denial of relief under INA 243(h)(2), as stated above. Temporary protected status may be terminated if: (1) the Attorney General finds that the alien was not eligible for such status; (2) the alien was not continuously physically present, except for brief, casual, and innocent departures or travel with advance permission; (3) the alien failed to register annually; or (4) the Attorney General terminates the program. INA 244A(c)(3).

An alien granted temporary protected status cannot be deported during the designated period and shall be granted employment authorization. The alien may also travel abroad with advance permission. Temporary protected status also allows the alien to adjust or change status. . . .

Rights of Refugees and Asylees. Certain benefits are available to an alien applying for asylum. First, as long as the asylum claim appears nonfrivolous, the applicant may be granted employment authorization while the asylum application is pending. Second, the applicant may be granted advance parole to travel abroad to a third country for humanitarian reasons.

In April 1992, the INS created a "pre-screening" procedure to identify genuine asylum seekers whose parole from detention might be appropriate while their asylum claims are pending. Specially trained asylum pre-screening officers interview applicants in detention and evaluate asylum claims. If the claimant is deemed to have a "credible fear of persecution," then the alien may be released pending the asylum claim. The alien must, however, agree to check in periodically with the INS and appear at all relevant hearings.

The immediate family (spouse and children) of the person granted refugee admission or political asylum can accompany or follow such person without having to apply for protection independently. INA 207(c)(2) and 208(c).

Finally, one who entered the United States as a refugee is eligible for permanent resident status after one year of continuous physical presence in the United States. The number of refugees adjusting to permanent resident status is not subject to the annual limitation on immigrants into the United States. INA 209. An asylee may also apply for permanent resident status after being continuously present in the United States for at least one year after being granted asylum. There are 10,000 visas set aside each year for asylees applying for residency.

Source: Immigration and Naturalization Service. *U.S. Report Under the International Covenant on Civil and Political Rights,* July 1994. Washington, DC: Immigration and Naturalization Service, 1994.

Report by U.S. Commission on Immigration Reform, 1994

*I*n 1990, Congress created the U.S. Commission on Immigration Reform to examine existing immigration policy and recommend appropriate changes. Four years later, the Commission issued its first report. The September 1994 document advocated, among other things, strengthening border controls, promptly deporting illegal aliens, halting the provision of non-emergency public services to illegal aliens and, most controversially, establishing a national computer registry that all employers would be required to check before hiring to make sure potential employees were legally in the United States.

INTRODUCTION

The U.S. Commission on Immigration Reform was created by Congress to assess U.S. immigration policy and make recommendations regarding its implementation and effects. Mandated in the Immigration Act of 1990 to submit an interim report in 1994 and a final report in 1997, the Commission has undertaken public hearings, fact-finding missions, and expert consultations to identify the major immigration-related issues facing the United States today.

This process has been a complex one. Distinguishing fact from fiction has been difficult, in some cases because of what has become a highly emotional debate on immigration. We have heard contradictory testimony, shaky statistics, and a great deal of honest confusion regarding the impacts of immigration. Nevertheless, we have tried throughout to engage in what we believe is a systematic, non-partisan effort to reach conclusions drawn from analysis of the best data available.

UNDERLYING PRINCIPLES

Certain basic principles underlie the Commission's work. The Commission decries hostility and discrimination against immigrants as antithetical to the traditions and interests of the country. At the same time, we disagree with those who would label efforts to control immigration as being inherently anti-immigrant. Rather, it is both a right and a responsibility of a democratic society to manage immigration so that it serves the national interest.

CHALLENGES AHEAD

The Commission believes that legal immigration has strengthened and can continue to strengthen this country. While we will be reporting at a later date on the impacts of our legal immigration system, and while there may even be disagreements among us as to the total number of immigrants that can be absorbed into the United States or the categories that should be given priority for admission, the Commission members agree that immigration presents many opportunities for this nation. Immigrants can contribute to the building of the country. In most cases, they have been actively sought by family members or businesses in the U.S. The tradition of welcoming newcomers has become an important element of how we define ourselves as a nation.

The Commission is mindful of the problems that also emanate from immigration. In particular, we believe that unlawful immigration is unacceptable. Enforcement efforts have not been effective in deterring unlawful immigration. This failure to develop effective strategies to control unlawful immigration has blurred the public perception of the distinction between legal and illegal immigrants.

For the Commission, the principal issue at present is how to manage immigration so that it will continue to be in the national interest.

- How do we ensure that immigration is based on and supports broad national economic, social, and humanitarian interests, rather than the interests of those who would abuse our laws?

- How do we gain effective control over our borders while still encouraging international trade, investment, and tourism?

- How do we maintain a civic culture based on shared values while accommodating the large and diverse population admitted through immigration policy?

The credibility of immigration policy can be measured by a simple yardstick: people who should get in, do get in; people who should not get in are kept out; and people who are judged deportable are required to leave.

During the decade from 1980 to 1990, three major pieces of legislation were adopted to govern immigration policy—the Refugee Act of 1980, the Immigration Reform and Control Act of 1986, and the Immigration Act of 1990. The Commission supports the broad framework for immigration policy that these laws represent: a legal immigration system that strives to serve the national interest in helping families to reunify and employers to obtain skills not available in the U.S. labor force; a refugee system that reflects both our humanitarian beliefs and international refugee law; and an enforcement system that seeks to deter unlawful immigration through employer sanctions and tighter border control.

The Commission has concluded, however, that more needs to be done to guarantee that the stated goals of our immigration policy are met. The immediate need is more effective prevention and deterrence of unlawful immigration. This report to Congress outlines the Commission's recommendations in this area.

In the long term, immigration policies for the 1990s and beyond should anticipate the challenges of the next century. These challenges will be substantially influenced by factors such as the restructuring of our own economy, the establishment of such new trade relationships as the North American Free Trade Agreement [NAFTA], and changing geopolitical relations. No less importantly, immigration policy must carefully take into account social concerns, demographic trends, and the impact of added population on the country's environment.

Finally, current immigration is the first to occur in what economists call a post-industrial economy, just as it is the first to occur after the appearance of the modern welfare state. The Commission's report to Congress in 1997 will cover these issues in assessing the impact of the Immigration Act of 1990. The present report reviews the progress of the beginning implementation of this legislation.

RECOMMENDATIONS

Serious problems undermine present immigration policies, their implementation, and their credibility: people who should get in find a cumbersome process that often impedes their entry; people who should not get in find it all too easy

to enter; and people who are here without permission remain with impunity.

The Commission is convinced that unlawful immigration can be controlled consistent with our traditions, civil rights, and civil liberties. As a nation with a long history of immigration and commitment to the rule of law, this country must set limits on who can enter and then must credibly enforce our immigration law. Unfortunately, no quick and easy solutions are available. The United States can do a more effective job, but only with additional financial resources and the political will to take action. Our recommendations for a comprehensive, effective strategy follow.

BORDER MANAGEMENT

The Commission believes that significant progress has been made during the past several years in identifying and remedying some of the weaknesses in U.S. border management. Nevertheless, we believe that far more can and should be done to meet the twin goals of border management: preventing illegal entries while facilitating legal ones.

LAND BORDERS

Credibility is a problem at U.S. land borders, given the ease of illegal entry and various obstacles to legal entry. These problems are particularly prevalent at the U.S.-Mexico border, as the Commission's visit to San Diego and El Paso demonstrated. The Commission believes that an underlying principle of border management is that prevention is far more effective and cost-efficient than the apprehension and removal of illegal aliens after entry. At the same time, the Commission believes that legal entry should be facilitated in order for the country to benefit from cross-border trade and tourism.

The Commission supports the strategy, now being tested as "Operation Hold the Line" in El Paso, that emphasizes prevention of illegal entry at the border, rather than apprehension following illegal entry. Prevention holds many advantages: it is more cost-effective than apprehension and removal; it eliminates the cycle of voluntary return and reentry that has characterized unlawful border crossings; and it reduces potentially violent confrontations on the border. The Commission recommends:

- Increased resources for prevention, including additional staff, such improved technology as sensors and infrared scopes, data systems that permit expeditious identification of repeat offenders, and such additional equipment as vehicles and radios.

- Increased training for border control officers to execute strategies that emphasize prevention of illegal entry.

• Formation of a mobile, rapid response team to improve Border Patrol anticipation of new smuggling sites and to augment their capacity at these locations. The Immigration and Naturalization Service [INS] must develop a capacity to respond quickly to changing patterns of unlawful immigration along the land border. Also, contingency plans should be developed to address increased boat arrivals that may arise from improved land border enforcement.

• Use of fences to reduce border violence and facilitate enforcement. However, the Commission does not support the erection of extraordinary physical barriers, such as unscalable walls, unless needed as a last resort to stop violence when other means have proved ineffective. Fences have been used effectively in San Diego to reduce border violence, deter illegal aliens from running across the interstate highway that leads from Mexico, and facilitate enforcement.

• Systematic evaluation of the effectiveness of any new border strategies by INS. The typical measurements of Border Patrol effectiveness—apprehension rates—have little meaning in assessing a prevention strategy. INS should develop new evaluation techniques that measure the effects of border management efforts in terms of the flow of unauthorized aliens and their impacts on U.S. communities.

The Commission supports efforts to reduce potentially violent confrontations between Border Patrol officers and those believed to be seeking illegal entry into the U.S. Such confrontations were reduced, for example, during "Operation Hold the Line," in terms of both reported human rights violations against suspected illegal aliens and attacks on Border Patrol officers.

The Commission supports efforts already underway to address complaints about human rights violations, including:

• Increased training and professionalism of Border Patrol officers to enable them to respond appropriately to potentially violent situations;

• Improved procedures for adjudicating complaints of Border Patrol abuses;

• Mechanisms to provide redress or relief to those subjected to improper actions; and

• More effective protection of Border Patrol officers from violence directed at them.

The Commission believes that port entry operations can be improved. Legal entry at the border should be facilitated as the United States benefits from trade, tourism, family visits, and consumer spending. More specifically, the Commission supports:

• Additional resources for inspections at land border ports of entry.

• An expedited adjudication and issuance process for the Border Crossing Card [BCC]. Mexican nationals are required to have a visa (unlike Canadians). Because of the volume of BCC applications on the Mexican border, the Commission encourages negotiations between the U.S. and Mexico to amend the bilateral treaty to permit collection of fees to be used exclusively to expedite the issuance and adjudication of the card.

• Further steps to better ensure that the BCC is not misused by legal crossers who engage in unauthorized employment after entry. Each BCC should contain the legend indicating it is "not for work authorization," as currently appears on INS-issued cards.

• Development of a land border user fee to pay for needed improvements in the inspection of border crossers, with fees to be used exclusively to facilitate land border management.

The Commission supports increased coordination on border issues between the governments of the U.S. and Mexico. The Commission views favorably the discussions underway between the U.S. and Mexican governments. These discussions promote greater cooperation . . . in solving problems of mutual concern. In particular, the Commission encourages:

• Continued cooperation in antismuggling efforts to reduce smuggling of people and goods across the U.S.-Mexico border.

• Bilateral discussions that take into account both U.S. entry and Mexican exit laws in devising a cooperative approach to regulating the movements of people across the U.S.-Mexican land border. Mexican law requires that Mexican nationals exit Mexico through official inspection stations. Thus, unauthorized migration into the United States generally violates not only U.S. law, but Mexican law as well.

• Cross border discussions and cooperative law enforcement efforts among federal, state, and local officials of both countries to develop cooperative approaches to combat violent crimes and auto and cargo theft along the border.

• Continued U.S. cooperation and support for Mexican efforts to address the problem of third-country nationals crossing Mexico to come to the United States.

AIRPORTS

Each year about 50 million citizens and aliens enter the country through airports.

The Commission supports a combined facilitation and enforcement strategy that would prevent the entry of unauthorized aliens while facilitating legal admissions at U.S. airports as efficiently as possible, including:

- The use of new technologies to expedite the inspections process and improve law enforcement, including more efficient processing of travelers with Machine Readable Documents.

- Programs that enhance the capacity of airline carriers to identify and refuse travel to aliens seeking to enter the U.S. on fraudulent documents, including the Carrier Consultant Program and other coordinated efforts to maintain complete, accurate, and reliable Advance Passenger Information System [APIS] data and improved lookout data systems.

- Continued government-airline industry discussions on improving inspections that have led to innovative proposals.

- Development of a system for mitigation of penalties or fines for those carriers that cooperate in screening and other programs and demonstrate success in reducing the number of unauthorized aliens they carry.

- Making INS, not the carrier, responsible for the actual physical custody of inadmissible air passengers.

INTERAGENCY COORDINATION

The Commission expresses its dissatisfaction with the past lack of coordination between the Customs Service and the INS at ports of entry. This has hampered effective border management by both agencies.

The Commission recommends implementation of initiatives to improve coordination between INS and Customs, as recommended by the General Accounting Office [GAO] and the National Performance Review. The Commission will monitor these efforts to improve coordination of border management, particularly as they relate to immigration matters.

If these efforts prove ineffective, the Commission will recommend more extensive action, such as creating a new immigration and customs agency or designating one agency as the lead agency on inspections.

ALIEN SMUGGLING

Organized smuggling operations undermine the credibility of U.S. enforcement efforts and pose dangers to the smuggled aliens.

The Commission recommends an effective prevention strategy that requires enhanced capacities to combat organized smuggling for commercial gain. Possible enhancements include:

- Expanded enforcement authorities, such as Racketeer Influenced and Corrupt Organizations Act [RICO] provisions, wire-tap authority, and expanded asset forfeiture for smuggling aliens; and

- Enhanced intelligence gathering and diplomatic efforts to deter smuggling.

WORKSITE ENFORCEMENT

The Commission believes that reducing the employment magnet is the linchpin of a comprehensive strategy to reduce illegal immigration. The ineffectiveness of employer sanctions, prevalence of fraudulent documents, and continued high numbers of unauthorized workers, combined with confusion for employers and reported discrimination against employees, have challenged the credibility of current worksite enforcement efforts.

VERIFICATION

A better system for verifying work authorization is central to effective enforcement of employer sanctions.

The Commission recommends development and implementation of a simpler, more fraud-resistant system for verifying work authorization. The current system is doubly flawed: it is too susceptible to fraud, particularly through the counterfeiting of documents; and it can lead to increased discrimination against foreign-looking or foreign-sounding authorized workers.

In examining the options for improving verification, *the Commission believes that the most promising option for secure, non-discriminatory verification is a computerized registry* using data provided by the Social Security Administration [SSA] and the INS.

The key to this process is the social security number. For decades all workers have been required to provide employers with their social security number. The computer registry would add only one step to this existing requirement: an employer check that the social security number is valid and has been issued to someone authorized to work in the United States.

The Commission believes the computerized system is the most promising option because it holds great potential for accomplishing the following:

- Reduction in the potential for fraud. Using a computerized registry, rather than only an identification card, guards against counterfeiting of documents. It provides more reliable information about work authorization.

- Reduction in the potential for discrimination based on national origin and citizenship status, as well as inappropriate demands for specific or additional documents, given that employers will not be required to ascertain whether a worker is a citizen or an immigrant and will have no reason to reject documents they believe to be counterfeit. The only relevant question will be: "What is your social security number?"

- Reduction in the time, resources, and paperwork spent by employers in complying with the Immigration Reform and Control Act of 1986 [IRCA] and corresponding redirection of enforcement activities from paperwork violations to knowing hire of unauthorized workers.

The Commission recommends that the President immediately initiate and evaluate pilot programs using the proposed computerized verification system in the five states with the highest levels of illegal immigration as well as several less affected states. The President has the authority to do so under Section 274A(d)(4) of the Immigration and Nationality Act. A pilot program will: permit the testing of various approaches to using the proposed verification system; provide needed information about the advantages, disadvantages, and costs of the various approaches; develop and evaluate measures to protect civil rights and civil liberties; and ensure that any potential obstacles, such as the quality of the data used in the registry, are addressed prior to national implementation. Assuming the successful results of the pilot program, Congress should pass the necessary statutory authorities to support more effective verification. Pilot program features should include:

- A means by which employers will access the verification system to validate the accuracy of information given by workers. We have received conflicting testimony about the best way to check the applicant's identity. We have heard proposals for a more secure social security card, a counterfeit-resistant driver's license, and a telephone verification system that does not rely on any document. The pilot program presents an opportunity to determine the most cost-effective, fraud-resistant, and nondiscriminatory method available.

- Measures to ensure the accuracy of and access to the specific data needed to ensure that employers have timely and reliable information when seeking verification of work authorization. Improvements in the Social Security Administration and INS databases must be made to ensure that these data are available. Procedures must be developed to ensure timely and accurate entry, update, extraction, and correction of data. The Commission strongly urges INS and the Social Security Administration to cooperate in this endeavor, as the proposed registry would be built upon and—once implemented—would support the primary missions of those agencies.

- Measures to ensure against discrimination and disparate treatment of foreign-looking or-sounding persons. The Commission believes that the least discriminatory system would have the same requirements for citizens and aliens alike. To reduce the potential for discrimination and increase the security of the system, the Commission also believes that employers should not be required to ascertain immigration status in the process of verifying authorization for employment. Their only requirement should be to check the social security number presented by each employee against the registry and record an authorization number to prove that they have done so.

- Measures to protect civil liberties. It is essential that explicit protections be devised against use of the database—and any card or any other means used to gain access to it—for purposes other than those specified in law. The uses to be made of the verification system must be clearly specified. We believe the worksite verification system could be used, without damage to civil liberties, for verifying eligibility to receive public benefits. However, it should be stipulated that no one should be required to carry a card, if one is used, or to present it for routine identification purposes. There also should be penalties for inappropriate use of the verification process.

- Measures to protect the privacy of the information included in the database. The Commission is aware of the proliferation of databases and the potential for the invasion of privacy by both government and private agencies. There need to be explicit provisions for protecting privacy; the resultant system should incorporate appropriate safeguards regarding authorized users' access to individual information. In establishing privacy safeguards, it is important to take into account that, while access to any one piece of information may not be intrusive, in combination with other information such access may violate privacy.

- Estimates of the start-up time and financial and other costs of developing, implementing, and maintaining a national system in such a manner that verification is reliable.

- Specification of the rights, responsibilities, and impact on individual workers and employers, for example: what individuals must do; how long it will take for newly authorized workers to get on the system and to correct inaccurate data; and what will be required of employers and at what expense. Provisions must also be developed to protect both workers from denial of employment and employers from penalties in cases where the information provided by the computer registry may be missing or inaccurate.

- A plan for phasing in of the system. The Commission recognizes that the proposed verification system will result in financial costs. The system should be phased in to lessen the immediate impact. The pilot programs should test various phase-in procedures. Given the required levels of accuracy, reliability, and convenience required, the evaluation should help measure the cost of phasing in the system nationally.

The Commission recommends evaluation of the pilot programs to assess the effectiveness of the verification system. The evaluation should include objective measures and procedures to determine whether current problems related to fraud, discrimination, and excessive paperwork requirements for employers are effectively overcome without imposing undue costs on the government, employers, or employees. The evaluation should pay particular attention to the effectiveness of the measures used to protect civil liberties and privacy.

The Commission supports INS efforts to improve its Telephone Verification System/SAVE [TVS/SAVE] database but only as an interim measure. The improvements are essential for improving the data needed for the new, more effective verification process. The Commission is aware of the inadequacies of the current INS data that would be used in the proposed system. The Commission does not endorse the TVS/SAVE program as a long-term solution to the verification problem because use of TVS/SAVE requires the inadequate mechanism of self-attestation by workers as to their citizenship or alienage, thus making it easy for aliens to fraudulently claim U.S. citizenship. It also imposes requirements on legal immigrants that do not apply to citizens. Nevertheless, improvements in this database, as well as the Social Security Administration database, are essential to the development of a more secure, less potentially discriminatory verification system.

The Commission also recommends action that would reduce the fraudulent access to so-called "breeder documents," particularly birth certificates, that can be used to establish an identity in this country, including:

- Regulation of requests for birth certificates through standardized application forms;

- A system of interstate and intrastate matching of birth and death records;

- Making certified copies of birth certificates issued by states or state-controlled vital records offices the only forms accepted by federal agencies;

- Using a standard design and paperstock for all certified copies of birth certificates to reduce counterfeiting; and

- Encouraging states to computerize birth records repositories.

To address the abuse of fraudulent documents, the Commission recommends an imposition of greater penalties on those producing or selling such documents. Document fraud and counterfeiting has become a lucrative and well-organized operation that may involve international networks that conspire to produce and sell the resulting fraudulent products. These documents are used in smuggling and terrorist operations, as well as for work authorization. RICO provisions designed to facilitate racketeering investigations should cover conspiracy to produce and sell fraudulent documents. Criminal penalties should also be increased for large-scale counterfeiting activities.

ANTIDISCRIMINATION STRATEGIES

The Commission is concerned about unfair immigration-related employment practices against both citizens and non-citizens that may occur under the current system of employer sanctions. A more reliable, simpler verification system holds great potential to reduce any such discrimination because employers will no longer have to make any determination as to immigration status. Nevertheless, mechanisms must effectively prevent and redress discrimination.

The Commission recommends that the Office of the Special Counsel [OSC] for Immigration-Related Unfair Employment Practices in the Department of Justice initiate more proactive strategies to identify and combat immigration-related discrimination at the workplace. OSC should target resources on independent investigations and on programs to assess the incidence and prevalence of unfair immigration-related employment practices.

The Commission also recommends a methodologically sound study to document the nature and extent of unfair immigration-related employment practices that have occurred since GAO's [General Accounting Office] 1990 report. The new study should measure the effects of immigration policy—as distinct from other factors—on discrimination at the worksite. As noted above, the pilot programs should be evaluated to determine if they substantially reduce immigration-related discrimination at the workplace.

EMPLOYER SANCTIONS AND LABOR STANDARDS ENFORCEMENT

The Commission believes that enforcement of employer sanctions, wage/hour, child labor, and other labor standards can be an effective tool in reducing employment of unauthorized workers. The Commission finds, however, that current enforcement efforts are inadequate. In addition, the Commission expresses its concern that current coordination efforts between the Immigration and Naturalization Service and the Department of Labor are insufficient.

The Commission supports vigorous enforcement of labor standards and enforcement against knowing hire of unauthorized workers as an integral part of the strategy to reduce illegal immigration. Labor standards and employer sanctions should be seen as mutually reinforcing. Specifically, the Commission recommends:

- Allocation of increased staff and resources to the enforcement of labor standards to complement employer sanctions enforcement.

- Vigorous enforcement, increased staff and resources, and full use of current penalties against those who knowingly hire unauthorized workers. If the new verification system proposed by the Commission substantially reduces inadvertent hiring of unauthorized workers—as we believe will occur—Congress should discontinue paperwork penalties and evaluate the need for increased penalties against violators and businesses that knowingly hire or fail to verify work authorization for all employees.

- Targeting of investigations to industries that have a history of using illegal alien labor.

- Enhanced enforcement efforts targeted at farm labor and other contractors who hire unauthorized workers on behalf of agricultural growers and other businesses.

- Application of employer sanctions to the federal government. At a minimum, the President should issue an Executive Order requiring federal agencies to abide by the procedures required of other employers. Alternatively, legislation should stipulate that federal agencies follow the verification procedures required of other employers and be subject to penalties if they fail to verify work authorization.

The Commission urges the Attorney General and the Secretary of Labor to review the current division of responsibilities between the Departments of Justice and Labor in the enforcement of employer sanctions and labor standards. INS and the Department of Labor have signed a Memorandum of Understanding [MOU] that spells out each agency's responsibility for enforcing employer sanctions and labor standards. Preliminary evidence indicates that few warnings have been issued to employers under the MOU. The implementation of the MOU should be closely monitored over the next twelve months. Should the monitoring demonstrate that the joint efforts have not resulted in effective enforcement, it may be necessary to designate a single agency to enforce employer sanctions.

The Commission recommends enhanced coordination mechanisms to promote cooperation among all of the agencies respon-sible for worksite enforcement. Strategies to promote coordination at headquarters and in field operations include:

- Establishment of a taskforce in Washington, D.C., to review and set policy;

- Local taskforces of worksite investigators to coordinate field operations; and

- Continued joint training for worksite investigators from all applicable agencies.

EDUCATION

Thousands of new businesses begin operations each year. New workers enter the labor force each year as well.

The Commission recommends coordination and continuance of educational efforts by the Immigration and Naturalization Service, the Office of Special Counsel, and the Department of Labor regarding employer sanctions, antidiscrimination provisions, and labor standards. The Commission calls upon these agencies to develop and communicate a single message to all employers and employees. The Commission also recommends the development of new strategies, including the enhanced use of technology, to inform employers and workers of their rights and responsibilities under the law.

Source: U.S. Commission on Immigration Reform. *Report by U.S. Commission on Immigration Reform,* September 30, 1994. Washington, DC: Government Printing Office, 1994.

New U.S. Rules on Asylum for Women, 1995

In May 1995, the Immigration and Naturalization Service (INS) issued new guidelines that recognized sexual violence as a potential cause for granting refugee status to female asylum-seekers. INS Commissioner Doris Meissner was quick to point out, however, that the new guidelines did not change the standard that must be met by women seeking asylum; they were issued simply to "educate Asylum officers about gender-based discrimination" and to provide them with the appropriate "procedures and methods for evaluating whether individual claims meet the refugee standard."

BACKGROUND

- Human rights violations against women are not a new phenomenon in the world. Yet, only recently have they risen to the forefront of the international agenda.

- In 1979, the Convention on the Elimination of All Forms of Discrimination Against Women (CEDAW) recommended the eradication of violations against women.

- In June 1993, the United Nations World Conference on Human Rights emphasized the need to incorporate the rights of women, and called upon the General Assembly to adopt the Declaration on the Elimination of Violence against Women. On December 20, 1993, the United Nations General Assembly adopted the Declaration.

- There have also been Conclusions from the United Nations High Commissioner for Refugees (UNHCR). For example, in 1985 the UNHCR Executive Committee adopted Conclusion No. 39, noting that refugee women and girls constitute the majority of the world population and that many of them are exposed to special problems.

All of these international initiatives underscored and contributed to the development of guidance related to women refugee claimants.

- The Canadian Immigration and Refugee Board (IRB) issued its asylum gender guidelines over two years ago, in March 1993. The UNHCR issued a set of guidelines in 1991, and faculty members at Harvard Law School also submitted a proposed set of guidelines in 1994. Despite the increased attention to gender-based asylum claims, they are still relatively new developments in refugee protection.

INS IMPLEMENTATION

- Because gender issues are novel, and adjudicators of asylum claims are guided by recent (and still developing) U.S. case law, INS felt that guidance to all Asylum Officers would be appropriate to ensure uniformity in adjudications, and would allow Asylum Officers to be more responsive to bona fide asylum claims.

- Women asylum applicants, like all applicants, must satisfy the refugee definition provided for by statute. Under U.S. law, the term *refugee* means "... any person who is outside any country of such person's nationality," and who is "unable or unwilling to return to ... that country because of persecution or a well-founded fear of persecution on account of race, religion, nationality, membership in a particular social group, or political opinion. ..."

- The U.S. refugee definition is a narrow one. Individuals cannot qualify for asylum in the United States unless the persecution is on account of one of the protected grounds specified by Congress. There must also be a favorable credibility finding by an Asylum Officer. The INS Guidelines summarize recent decisions from the courts and the Board of Immigration Appeals, which provide appropriate analysis for gender-related and other asylum claims. The INS Gender Guidelines do not enlarge or expand on the grounds that were specified by Congress and the understandings the courts have reached about those grounds.

• Not all women who apply for asylum under this new guidance will be granted asylum. INS asylum decisions are individualized, case-by-case determinations. For example, INS sometimes encounters women asylum applicants who come from countries where domestic or sexual abuse is tolerated. However, to qualify for asylum these women must show, for example, that:

  • The domestic violence cannot be purely 'personal.' It must relate to one of the grounds enumerated in the statute.

  • The harm feared must rise to the level of "persecution." The courts have uniformly held that "persecution" denotes extreme conduct and does not include every sort of treatment our society regards as offensive, unfair, unjust, or even unlawful or unconstitutional.

  • Also, both U.S. law and the UN Protocol require that the fear of persecution must normally extend to the entire country of origin; that is, in order for an applicant to meet the definition of a refugee she must do more than show a well-founded fear of persecution in a particular place or abode within a "country"—she must show that the threat of persecution exists for her countrywide. For example, some battered women may be denied asylum because they could have sought safety from the batterer simply by moving to another town or province in their country of origin. National protection should take precedence over international protection.

In sum, every asylum applicant is carefully interviewed. No applicant can be approved unless all the definitional elements of the statute are satisfied.

• INS does not expect the rate of asylum applications to increase because of the Gender Guidelines. That was not the experience of the Canadians who issued their guidelines more than 2 years ago.

• Asylum Interviews/Officers: All INS Asylum Officers—men and women—will be expected to conduct interviews of women with gender based claims. To the extent that personnel resources permit, however, Asylum Officers may allow women Asylum Offices to interview these cases. An interview will not generally be canceled because of the unavailability of a woman Asylum Officer. But INS also recognizes that, because of the very delicate and personal issues arising from sexual abuse, some women claimants may understandably have inhibitions about disclosing past experiences to male interviewers.

• Interpreters/Presence of Family Members: Testimony on sensitive issues such as sexual abuse can be diluted when received through the filter of a male interpreter. While INS encourages the use of female interpreters, interviews will not generally be canceled and rescheduled because women with gender-based asylum claims have brought male interpreters.

Interviewing Asylum Officers will provide women with the opportunity to be interviewed outside the hearing of other members of their family, especially male family members and children. There is a greater likelihood that a woman applicant may more freely communicate a claim involving sexual abuse when family members are not present.

• Generally, the new Guidelines will assist Asylum Officers in the attentive examination of cases, and the approval of legitimate claimants.

Source: Immigration and Naturalization Service. *New U.S. Rules on Asylum for Women,* May 26, 1995. Washington, DC: Immigration and Naturalization Service, 1995.

Title IV: Restricting Welfare and Public Benefits for Aliens, 1996

On August 22, 1996, President Bill Clinton signed into law the welfare reform bill (Public Law 104-193) known as the "Personal Responsibility and Work Opportunity Reconciliation Act." Most notable among the features of the bill was the replacement of the New Deal era program Aid to Families with Dependent Children by a new program entitled Temporary Assistance for Needy Families (TANF). Under TANF, most welfare recipients would receive aid for up to two consecutive years, and/or five years over a lifetime.

For legal immigrants, the changes were even more far-reaching as they were denied cash welfare, Medicaid, food stamps, and Supplemental Security Income. Under pressure from immigrant advocacy groups and the Clinton administration, Congress soon restored most of the cuts to legal immigrants.

The following documents include a 1996 U.S. State Department advisory to consular offices around the world advising them on cuts to immigrants under the initial PL 104-193 as passed in 1996; a 1997 Immigration and Naturalization Service (INS) "question-and-answer" document explaining restrictions on the immigration of persons likely to become "public charges"; an updated 1999 Department of Health and Human Services assessment of government assistance to legal immigrants under the amended PL 104-193; and a 1999 White House press release further clarifying healthcare and other benefits available to immigrants.

STATEMENTS OF NATIONAL POLICY CONCERNING WELFARE AND IMMIGRATION

Below, consular officers will find the text of Title IV of Pub. L. 104-193, the "Personal Responsibility and Work Opportunity Reconciliation Act of 1996." Title IV sets forth the provisions of Pub. L. 104-193 that have direct applicability to foreign nationals.

The Congress makes the following statements concerning national policy with respect to welfare and immigration:

(1) Self-sufficiency has been a basic principle of United States immigration law since this country's earliest immigration statutes.

(2) It continues to be the immigration policy of the United States that—

(A) aliens within the Nation's borders not depend on public resources to meet their needs, but rather rely on their own capabilities and the resources of their families, their sponsors, and private organizations, and

(B) the availability of public benefits not constitute an incentive for immigration to the United States.

(3) Despite the principle of self-sufficiency, aliens have been applying for and receiving public benefits from Federal, State, and local governments at increasing rates.

(4) Current eligibility rules for public assistance and unenforceable financial support agreements have proved wholly incapable of assuring that individual aliens not burden the public benefits system.

(5) It is a compelling government interest to enact new rules for eligibility and sponsorship agreements in order to assure that aliens be self-reliant in accordance with national immigration policy.

(6) It is a compelling government interest to remove the incentive for illegal immigration provided by the availability of public benefits.

(7) With respect to the State authority to make determinations concerning the eligibility of qualified aliens for public benefits in this title, a State that chooses to follow the Federal classification in determining the eligibility of such aliens for public assistance shall be considered to have chosen the least restrictive means available for achieving the compelling governmental interest of assuring that aliens be self-reliant in accordance with national immigration policy.

[PAGE 110 STAT. 2261]

SUBTITLE A—ELIGIBILITY FOR FEDERAL BENEFITS

SEC. 401. <<8 USC 1611.>> Aliens Who Are Not Qualified Aliens Ineligible for Federal Public Benefits

(a) In General.—Notwithstanding any other provision of law and except as provided in subsection (b), an alien who is not a qualified alien (as defined in section 431) is not eligible for any Federal public benefit (as defined in subsection (c))

(b) Exceptions.—

(1) Subsection (a) shall not apply with respect to the following Federal public benefits:

(A) Medical assistance under title XIX of the Social Security Act (or any successor program to such title) for care and services that are necessary for the treatment of an emergency medical condition (as defined in section 1903(v)(3) of such Act) of the alien involved and are not related to an organ transplant procedure, if the alien involved otherwise meets the eligibility requirements for medical assistance under the State plan approved under such title (other than the requirement of the receipt of aid or assistance under title IV of such Act, supplemental security income benefits under title XVI of such Act, or a State supplementary payment).

(B) Short-term, non-cash, in-kind emergency disaster relief.

(C) Public health assistance (not including any assistance under title XIX of the Social Security Act) for immunizations with respect to immunizable diseases and for testing and treatment of symptoms of communicable diseases whether or not such symptoms are caused by a communicable disease.

(D) Programs, services, or assistance (such as soup kitchens, crisis counseling and intervention, and short-term shelter) specified by the Attorney General, in the Attorney General's sole and unreviewable discretion after consultation with appropriate Federal agencies and departments, which (i) deliver in-kind services at the community level, including through public or private nonprofit agencies; (ii) do not condition the provision of assistance, the amount of assistance provided, or the cost of assistance provided on the individual recipient's income or resources; and (iii) are necessary for the protection of life or safety.

(E) Programs for housing or community development assistance or financial assistance administered by the Secretary of Housing and Urban Development, any program under title V of the Housing Act of 1949, or any assistance under section 306C of the Consolidated Farm and Rural Development Act, to the extent that the alien is receiving such a benefit on the date of the enactment of this Act. . . .

SEC. 403. <<8 USC 1613.>> Five Year Limited Eligibility of Qualified Aliens for Federal Means-Tested Public Benefit

(a) In General.—Notwithstanding any other provision of law and except as provided in subsections (b), (c), and (d), an alien who is a qualified alien (as defined in section 431) and who enters the United States on or after the date of the enactment of this Act is not eligible for any Federal means-tested public benefit for a period of 5 years beginning on the date of the alien's entry into the United States with a status within the meaning of the term "qualified alien."

(b) Exceptions.—The limitation under subsection (a) shall not apply to the following aliens:

(1) Exception for refugees and asylees.—

(A) An alien who is admitted to the United States as a refugee under section 207 of the Immigration and Nationality Act.

(B) An alien who is granted asylum under section 208 of such Act.

(C) An alien whose deportation is being withheld under section 243(h) of such Act.

(2) Veteran and active duty exception.—An alien who is lawfully residing in any State and is—

[PAGE 110 STAT. 2266]

(A) a veteran (as defined in section 101 of title 38, United States Code) with a discharge characterized as an honorable discharge and not on account of alienage,

(B) on active duty (other than active duty for training) in the Armed Forces of the United States, or

(C) the spouse or unmarried dependent child of an individual described in subparagraph (A) or (B).

(c) Application of Term Federal Means-tested Public Benefit.—

(1) The limitation under subsection (a) shall not apply to assistance or benefits under paragraph (2).

(2) Assistance and benefits under this paragraph are as follows:

(A) Medical assistance described in section 401(b)(1)(A).

(B) Short-term, non-cash, in-kind emergency disaster relief.

(C) Assistance or benefits under the National School Lunch Act.

(D) Assistance or benefits under the Child Nutrition Act of 1966.

(E) Public health assistance (not including any assistance under title XIX of the Social Security Act) for immunizations with respect to immunizable diseases and for testing and treatment of symptoms of communicable diseases whether or not such symptoms are caused by a communicable disease.

(F) Payments for foster care and adoption assistance under parts B and E of title IV of the Social Security Act for a parent or a child who would, in the absence of subsection (a), be eligible to have such payments made on the child's behalf under such part, but only if the foster or adoptive parent (or parents) of such child is a qualified alien (as defined in section 431).

(G) Programs, services, or assistance (such as soup kitchens, crisis counseling and intervention, and short-term shelter) specified by the Attorney General, in the Attorney General's sole and unreviewable discretion after consultation with appropriate Federal agencies and departments, which (i) deliver in-kind services at the community level, including through public or private nonprofit agencies; (ii) do not condition the provision of assistance, the amount of assistance provided, or the cost of assistance provided on the individual recipient's income or resources; and (iii) are necessary for the protection of life or safety.

(H) Programs of student assistance under titles IV, V, IX, and X of the Higher Education Act of 1965, and titles III, VII, and VIII of the Public Health Service Act.

(I) Means-tested programs under the Elementary and Secondary Education Act of 1965.

(J) Benefits under the Head Start Act.

(K) Benefits under the Job Training Partnership Act.

(d) Special Rule for Refugee and Entrant Assistance for Cuban and Haitian Entrants.—The limitation under subsection (a) shall not apply to refugee and entrant assistance activities, authorized by title IV of the Immigration and Nationality Act and section 501 of the Refugee Education Assistance Act of 1980, [Page 110 STAT. 2267] for Cuban and Haitian entrants as defined in section 501(e)(2) of the Refugee Education Assistance Act of 1980.

INS QUESTION AND ANSWER DOCUMENT ON PUBLIC CHARGE

[1997]

General

. . . Q2: What does it mean to be a public charge under the immigration laws?

A2: An alien who is likely at any time to become a public charge is ineligible for admission to the U.S. and is ineligible to adjust status to become a lawful permanent resident. An alien who has become a public charge can also be deported from the U.S., although this very rarely happens. These provisions have been part of U.S. immigration law for over 100 years, and the recent immigration reform and welfare reform laws did not substantively change them. Both INS [Immigration and Naturalization Service] (in the U.S.) and the Department of State (State) (overseas) make public charge determinations.

Q3: How is public charge defined, and when will this definition be implemented?

A3: The INS is issuing guidance and a proposed regulation that define public charge for the first time. "Public charge means an alien who has become (for deportation purposes) or who is likely to become (for admission/adjustment purposes) primarily dependent on the government for subsistence. This definition is effective immediately. As discussed below, INS and State will consider the receipt of cash benefits for income maintenance purposes and institutionalization for long-term care at government expense in determining dependence on the government for subsistence.

IMPLEMENTATION

Q4: How do INS and State decide whether someone is admissible or eligible for adjustment of status under the public charge rules?

A4: In deciding whether an alien is likely to become a public charge, the law requires that the INS (in the U.S.) or State (overseas) take certain factors into account, including the alien's age, health, family status, assets, resources, financial status, education, and skills. The government official examines all of these factors, looking at the totality of the circumstances concerning the alien, to make a forward-looking decision. No single factor, other than the lack of an Affidavit of Support, if required, will be used as the sole basis for finding that someone is likely to become a public charge, that is, likely to become primarily dependent on the government for subsistence. As described below, non-cash benefits and certain special-purpose cash benefits will not be taken into account under the totality of circumstances test.

Q5: How does INS decide whether someone is deportable as a public charge?

A5: Deportations on public charge grounds are very rare because the standards are very strict. Under the Immigration and Nationality Act, an alien is deportable if he or she becomes a public charge within 5 years after the date of entry into the U.S. for reasons not affirmatively shown to have arisen since entry. The mere receipt of a public benefit within 5 years of entry does not make an alien deportable as a public charge. An alien is deportable only if (1) the state or other government entity that provides the benefit has the legal right to seek repayment from the alien or another obligated party (for example, a sponsor under an affidavit of support), (2) the responsible program officials make a demand for repayment; and (3) the alien or other obligated party, such as the alien's sponsor, fails to repay. The benefit granting agency must seek repayment within 5 years of the alien's entry into the United States, obtain a final judgment, take all steps necessary to collect on that judgment, and be unsuccessful in those attempts. Even if these conditions are met, the alien has the opportunity to show that the reasons he or she became a public charge arose after the alien's entry to the U.S. An alien who can make such a showing is not deportable as a public charge.

Q6: What kind of benefits are considered in deciding whether someone is or is likely to become a public charge?

A6: Not all publicly funded benefits are relevant to deciding whether someone is or is likely to become a public charge. INS' guidance and proposed regulation clarify what kinds of benefits may and may not be considered in making a public charge determination. In order to decide whether an alien has become or is likely to become a public charge, INS and State will consider whether the alien is likely to become primarily dependent on the government for subsistence as demonstrated by either (1) the receipt of public cash assistance for income maintenance purposes, or (2) institutionalization for long-term care at government expense (other than imprisonment for conviction of a crime). Short-term institutionalization for rehabilitation is not taken into account for public charge purposes.

Public benefits considered to be public cash assistance for income maintenance include:

(1) Supplemental Security Income (SSI);

(2) Temporary Assistance for Needy Families (TANF), but not including supplementary cash benefits excluded from the term "assistance" under TANF program rules or any non-cash benefits and services provided by the TANF program;

(3) State and local cash assistance programs for income maintenance (often called state "General Assistance," but which may exist under other names).

In addition, the costs for institutionalization for long-term care, which may be provided under Medicaid or other programs, may be considered in making public charge determinations.

While the receipt of these benefits may be considered by INS and State for public charge purposes, having received them does not automatically make someone a public charge. As explained above, the totality of circumstances test applies for admission and adjustment. For deportation, all of the procedural requirements, described above, apply.

Q7: Are there public benefits that aliens can legally receive without worrying that the INS and State will consider them a public charge?

A7: Yes. Not all publicly funded benefits will be considered by the INS or the State Department in deciding whether someone is or is likely to become a public charge. The focus of public charge is on cash benefits for income maintenance and institutionalization for long-term care at government expense. Examples of benefits that will *not* be considered for public charge purposes include:

• Medicaid and other health insurance and health services (including public assistance for immunizations and for testing and treatment of symptoms of communicable diseases; use of health clinics, prenatal care, etc.) other than support for institutionalization for long-term care

• Children's Health Insurance Program (CHIP)

• Nutrition programs, including Food Stamps, the Special Supplemental Nutrition Program for Women, Infants and Children (WIC), the National School Lunch and Breakfast programs, and other supplementary and emergency food assistance programs

• Housing assistance

• Child care services

• Energy assistance, such as the Low Income Home Energy Assistance Program (LIHEAP)

• Emergency disaster relief

• Foster care and adoption assistance

• Educational assistance, including benefits under the Head Start Act and aid for elementary, secondary, or higher education

• Job training programs

• In-kind, community-based programs, services, or assistance (such as soup kitchens, crisis counseling and intervention, and short-term shelter).

Note that not all categories of aliens are eligible to receive all of the types of benefits described above.

Q8: Do the INS and State consider all types of cash assistance in deciding whether someone is a public charge?

A8: No. INS and State only consider cash benefits intended for income maintenance purposes. Some programs provide cash benefits for special purposes, such as the Low Income Home Energy Assistance Program (LIHEAP), transportation or child care benefits provided in cash under TANF or the Child Care and Development Block Grant (CCDBG), and one-time emergency payments made under TANF to avoid the need for on-going cash assistance. These special-purpose cash benefits are not for income maintenance and therefore are not considered for public charge purposes.

Q9: Normally Food Stamp benefits are given in the form of paper coupons or an electronic benefit card that can be used at authorized stores to buy food. However, in a few areas Food Stamp benefits are given in the form of cash. If Food Stamp benefits are given in the form of cash, can those benefits be considered for public charge purposes?

A9: No. Food Stamp benefits will not be considered for public charge purposes regardless of the method of payment because they are not intended for income maintenance.

Q10: Are health care benefits and enrollment in health insurance programs like Medicaid and CHIP considered for public charge purposes?

A10: No, not unless an alien is primarily dependent on the government for subsistence as demonstrated by institutionalization for long-term care at government expense. In particular, INS and State will not consider participation in Medicaid or CHIP, or similar state-funded programs, for public charge purposes. This approach will help to safeguard public health, while still allowing INS and State to identify people who are primarily dependent on the government for subsistence by looking to the receipt of public cash assistance for income maintenance. In addition, short-term institutionalization for rehabilitation will not be considered for public charge purposes.

Q11: Do the public charge field guidance and regulation change the policy issued by the Food and Nutrition Service for the WIC Program in WIC Policy Memorandum #98–7, dated March 19, 1998, "Impact of Participation in the WIC Program on Alien Status"?

A11: No. The new field guidance and regulation on public charge are consistent with the WIC policy memorandum issued in 1998. The WIC policy memorandum was developed based on agreements reached with the INS and State. The new field guidance and regulation merely restate and reinforce the agreement previously reached on the impact of participation in the WIC Program and alien status. As noted above, INS and State will not take WIC participation into account for public charge purposes.

AFFIDAVIT OF SUPPORT

Q12: What is an affidavit of support, and who is required to have one?

A12: The Personal Responsibility and Work Opportunity Reconciliation Act and the Illegal Immigration Reform and Immigrant Responsibility Act of 1996 (IIRIRA), Section 213A, created a new requirement for all family-sponsored immigrants and those employment-based immigrants who will work for a close relative or for a firm in which a U.S. citizen or lawful permanent resident relative holds a 5 percent or greater ownership interest. An alien who applies for an immigrant visa or adjustment of status in one of these categories on or after December 19, 1997, must have an affidavit of support (AOS), INS Form I-864, from a qualifying sponsor or he or she will be found inadmissible as a public charge. An AOS is a legally binding promise that the sponsor will provide support and assistance to the immigrant if necessary.

The AOS must be signed by a sponsor who meets certain statutory requirements. Sponsors must be able to demonstrate that they are able to maintain the sponsored alien(s) at an annual income of not less than 125 percent of the federal poverty level. (Currently, 125 percent of the poverty level for a family of four is $20,875.) If the family member who filed the visa petition does not have enough money to sponsor the alien(s), then another person can sign an AOS as a joint sponsor, indicating that he or she is willing to support the immigrant in the future if needed. The sponsor's obligation under the AOS lasts until the immigrant has naturalized, has worked or can be credited with 40 quarters of work, leaves the U.S. permanently, or dies. The sponsor and joint sponsor (if any) must also agree to repay the government if the immigrant uses certain benefits during that time and if the government asks the sponsor for repayment.

Before IIRIRA, aliens were sometimes sponsored using INS Form I-134, but these affidavits of support were found by some courts not to be legally enforceable. Form I-134 may still be used for categories of aliens who are not required to use the new, enforceable affidavit of support, such as students, parolees, or diversity immigrants.

Q13: Can an affidavit of support help an alien demonstrate to the INS and State that he or she is not likely to become a public charge?

A13: Yes. Since many aliens who apply for an immigrant visa or adjustment of status after December 19, 1997, will have an affidavit of support, INS and State will take that into account in deciding whether the alien is likely to become a public charge in the future. Even though an AOS is necessary for some immigrants and helps to convince the government that they will not become dependent on the government for subsistence in the future, INS or State can still deny an immigrant admission or adjustment of status

under the totality of circumstances test based on other factors such as age, health, employment, and education, as described above.

Q14: If lawful permanent residents want to sponsor a relative to come to the U.S., will it hurt their chances if they are receiving or have received public benefits in the past?

A14: Sponsors are not subject to public charge screening under the immigration laws; the question is whether the alien being sponsored is likely to become a public charge. Sponsors must satisfy a different test: they must be able to demonstrate that they are able to maintain the sponsored immigrant(s) at an annual income of not less than 125 percent of the federal poverty level.

Q15: Why does the new INS affidavit of support form ask about whether a sponsor or member of his or her household has received means-tested public benefits in the past 3 years?

A15: The purpose of this question is to ensure that the INS or State official making the decision has access to all facts that may be relevant in determining whether the 125 percent test, described above, is met. Any cash benefits received by the sponsor, such as SSI or cash TANF, cannot be counted toward meeting the 125 percent income threshold, but they are not held against the sponsor if he or she can meet the 125 percent test through other resources. The receipt of other means-tested public benefits, such as Food Stamps, Medicaid, or CHIP, have no effect on sponsorship.

Q16: What happens if a sponsor who has signed the new affidavit of support dies?

A16: The obligation to support the alien terminates with the sponsor's death, but the sponsor's estate would still be obligated to repay any obligations accrued before the sponsor's death. If there is a joint sponsor and only one of the sponsors dies, the remaining sponsor would remain liable under the affidavit of support.

For deportation purposes, if a sponsor has died and there is no joint sponsor, there is no legal obligation under the affidavit of support to repay any means-tested benefits. This means that the first prong of the test for deportation would not be met and the sponsored alien would not become deportable based on the affidavit of support.

EXAMPLE SITUATIONS

Q17: Are there categories of aliens who are not subject to public charge determinations?

A17: Yes. Refugees and asylees are not subject to public charge determinations for purposes of admission or adjustment of status. Amerasian immigrants are also exempt from the public charge ground of inadmissibility for their initial admission to the U.S. In addition, various statutes contain exceptions to the public charge ground of inadmissibility for aliens eligible for adjustment of status under their provisions, including the Cuban Adjustment Act, the Nicaraguan Adjustment and Central American Relief Act (NACARA) and the Haitian Refugee Immigration Fairness Act (HRIFA).

Q18: If an alien has received cash public benefits in the past, but has stopped, will INS or State find that he or she is likely to become a public charge?

A18: Past receipt of cash public benefits does not automatically make an alien inadmissible as likely to become a public charge. It is one factor that will be considered under the totality of the circumstances test to decide whether the alien is likely to become a public charge in the future. For example, if an alien received benefits in the past during a period of unemployment, but now has a job and is self-supporting, he or she would most likely not be found inadmissible as a public charge. The more time that has elapsed since the alien stopped receiving the benefit, the less weight it will be given. The length of time that an alien received benefits and the amount of benefits received are also relevant considerations.

Q19: If an alien has received public benefits in the past, does the alien have to repay them to avoid having INS or State find that he or she [is] inadmissible as a public charge, or ineligible to adjust status and become a lawful permanent resident?

A19: No. INS and State do not have authority to request that aliens repay public benefits in connection with visa issuance, admission, or adjustment of status.

Q20: Who decides whether an alien must repay a public benefit he or she has received in the past?

A20: The requirements and procedures concerning any demand for repayment of a public benefit are governed by the specific program rules established by law and administered by the benefit granting agencies, or by state and local governments, not by INS or State. The public charge rules in the immigration law do not change these program requirements.

Q21: If a member of an alien's family is receiving or has received public benefits, but the individual alien hasn't, will INS or State hold this against the alien for public charge purposes?

A21: In most cases, no. As a general rule, receipt of benefits by a member of an alien's family is not attributed to the alien who is applying to INS or State for admission or to INS for adjustment of status to determine whether he or she is likely to become a public charge. The only time this general rule would not apply would be if the family were reliant on their family member's cash public benefits as its sole means of support.

In particular, alien parents do not have to worry that the INS or State will consider them to be public charges if they enroll their children in programs for which they are eligible, unless these are cash programs which provide the sole financial support for the family. This is true whether the children are U.S. citizens or non-citizens.

If a parent enrolls in TANF for cash benefits for the "child only," this could be used by INS or State for a public charge determination concerning the parent if this cash is the sole support for the family. However, if there are other sources of support or a parent is working, then the cash assistance would not represent the family's sole source of support.

Q22: If an alien receives public benefits, will it hurt his or her chances to become a U.S. citizen?

A22: No. There is no public charge test for naturalization purposes, so the receipt of benefits is not relevant, as long as they were legally received. Nor is there a requirement to repay benefits received in the past in order to qualify for citizenship.

Q23: Can a naturalized citizen lose his or her citizenship because of receiving public benefits?

A23: No. Nobody can lose his or her citizenship because of receiving public benefits. Once an immigrant becomes a citizen, he or she can receive benefits on the same basis as all other citizens. Citizens cannot be deported or barred from reentering the U.S. after an international trip based on the receipt of public benefits.

Q24: Does an alien have to stop participating in some benefit programs in order to adjust status and become a lawful permanent resident?

A24: No, but someone who is receiving a cash benefit for income maintenance at the same time that he or she applies to become a lawful permanent resident may be considered ineligible for adjustment as a public charge. An alien who has received a cash benefit in the past could reapply to the INS after he or she stops receiving the benefit, and might or might not be considered a public charge.

Someone who is receiving a non-cash benefit, for example, WIC, Food Stamps, Medicaid, or CHIP, would not have to stop participating in the program in order to be eligible to adjust to lawful permanent resident status.

As explained earlier, in all of these situations, the usual totality of the circumstances test would apply.

Q25: If a lawful permanent resident has received public benefits and leaves the country, will INS stop him or her from returning on public charge grounds?

A25: In general, a lawful permanent resident who has been outside the U.S. for 6 months or less is not screened for public charge purposes when he or she returns. This is because lawful permanent residents who leave for 6 months or less at a time are not considered applicants for admission when they return, and none of the grounds of inadmissibility, including public charge, apply to them.

There are exceptions to this general rule if : (1) the alien has abandoned his or her status as a lawful permanent resident; (2) the alien has engaged in certain illegal activity; (3) the alien was in removal proceedings before he or she left the country; or (4) the alien attempts to enter other than at a port of entry. See Immigration and Nationality Act section 101(a)(13)(C) for more details on these exceptions.

Q26: Can an LPR [lawful permanent resident] continue to receive benefits while he or she is out of the country?

A26: If an LPR plans to be out of the country for longer than a month, he should check with the agency providing the benefit to determine the rules. In general, people are not allowed to receive many benefits if they are absent from the country or state of residence for longer than 30 days. If an LPR receives benefits improperly, it can hurt his chances of reentering the U.S. or becoming a citizen.

Q27: If a refugee has adjusted to LPR status and then

leaves the country for more than 180 days, is he or she at risk of being found to be a public charge and denied reentry?

A27: As noted above, refugees are exempt from public charge determinations for their admission and adjustment to LPR status. Public charge has never been a problem for refugees who travel and return to the U.S., and nothing in the welfare reform law or immigration reform law has changed this.

Q28: When an LPR returns from an international trip, can INS make her pay back Medicaid or Food Stamps that she or her children used before?

A28: No. INS does not have the authority to ask immigrants to pay back these benefits. If an alien has received benefits improperly (e.g., if a person claims to be a resident of a state for purposes of eligibility when she is not a resident, or if she does not tell a caseworker about all of her income), it is up to the benefit-granting agency to request repayment, based on the rules governing that program. Typically a benefit-granting agency would only request repayment in situations involving fraud or overpayment, and it would follow its procedural rules involving notice to the individual and the right to appeal.

Q29: What if an alien has never used cash welfare and is not residing in a nursing home. Can the INS still deny him a green card because they think he might use cash welfare in the future?

A29: Yes, it is possible. INS and State officials must look at all of the factors listed above to determine if a person can support himself in the future. If an alien's current situation related to age, health, resources, and the other statutory factors does not satisfy them that the alien is likely to be able to be self-supporting in the future, then they can refuse to grant a visa or approve adjustment of status, even if he is not currently receiving public cash assistance.

Q30: What if a person is not receiving cash assistance but is very sick and needs an extended period of care in a nursing home or other long-term care institution? Will she have trouble getting her Permanent Resident Card ("green card")?

A30: Yes. If someone is living in a nursing home or has a serious long-term illness that requires institutionalization, she will probably have trouble getting a green card unless she can show that she can get the care she needs without using Medicaid or other government-funded health programs (e.g., county aid). However, a short-term stay in a nursing facility, for example, to physically rehabilitate after surgery, will not be used to deny a green card. The alien is not deportable on public charge grounds if the alien can show that she received benefits for causes that arose after entry into the U.S.

Q31: An alien who is primarily dependent on the government for subsistence as demonstrated by the institutionalization for long-term care at government expense can be found deportable as a public charge. Does this mean that INS will be conducting raids in nursing homes or other long-term care institutions?

A31: No. INS will not send investigators into nursing homes or other long-term care facilities to look for aliens who might be deportable as public charges. INS may use information concerning institutionalization if it comes to INS attention through other avenues, but the only way an alien could be found deportable is if all the procedural requirements described above were met.

Q32: If I'm eligible to self-petition for adjustment of status under the Violence Against Women Act (VAWA), do I have to show that I'm not likely to become a public charge?

A32: The Administration is still considering the extent to which self-petitioners under VAWA are subject to the public charge requirements, and will address this in future guidance. The law does make clear that self-petitioners under VAWA do not need to submit an affidavit of support with their application, unlike other family-based immigrants.

Q33: Cuban/Haitian entrants are eligible to receive certain public benefits under welfare reform. If they receive such benefits, will they be barred from adjusting status because they will be considered public charges?

A33: The answer depends on how they become eligible to adjust status. There are statutory exceptions to the public charge ground of inadmissibility for those Cubans who are eligible to adjust to lawful permanent resident status under the Cuban Adjustment Act and NACARA and for those Haitians who are eligible to adjust status under the HRIFA. Cuban/Haitian entrants are subject to the usual public charge rules if they seek adjustment under other provisions of law that do not contain public charge exemptions.

Q34: Certain Amerasian entrants are eligible to receive public benefits under welfare reform. If they receive such benefits, will they be considered public charges?

A34: Amerasian entrants are admitted to the U.S. as lawful permanent residents (LPRs), and they are exempt from the public charge ground of inadmissibility at their initial admission. In most cases, the issue of public charge would never come up again, unless the alien leaves the U.S. for more than 6 months and seeks readmission. At that time, the exemption from public charge screening would no longer apply and the alien would be treated like any other LPR under the totality of the circumstances test.

Q35: If an alien has been in the U.S. since January 1, 1972, and wants to become a lawful permanent resident under the registry provision of the Immigration and Nationality Act, section 249, is there a public charge test?

A35: No. Public charge is not a factor for registry aliens under section 249.

Q36: Is it improper for an immigration or consular officer to ask non-citizens at an airport or in an interview whether they have received public benefits in the past, or whether someone in their family has?

A36: No. Immigration or consular officers can ask questions about whether a non-citizen or someone in his or her family is receiving or has received public benefits in the past. Non-citizens should answer such questions completely and truthfully. If an alien tells an immigration or consular officer that he or she has received a benefit that is exempt from consideration for public charge purposes, such as Food Stamps or Medicaid, the officer will not use that information in deciding whether the alien is likely to become a public charge.

Q37: INS is publishing this public charge definition as a proposed rule for notice and comment. What happens if an alien receives one of the safe benefits, that is, a supplemental, non-cash benefit, and the final rule is different from the proposed rule. Can aliens rely on the field guidance?

A37: Aliens may rely on INS field guidance in determining the benefits that they may safely accept before the final rule is issued. If the final rule is different from the proposed rule, INS will issue additional guidance at that time designed to ensure that non-citizens who relied on the current guidance will not suffer harsher immigration consequences based on that reliance.

Document "C"

Office of the Assistant Secretary for Planning and Evaluation

Human Services Policy

Department of Health and Human Services

Summary of Immigrant Eligibility Restrictions Under Current Law

As of 4/15/99

This document summarizes the immigrant eligibility restrictions under the following recently enacted laws: the *Personal Responsibility and Work Opportunity Reconciliation Act*, ["PRWORA" PL 104–193], as amended by the *Illegal Immigration Reform and Immigrant Responsibility Act* ["Immigration Law" PL 104–208], the *Balanced Budget Act of 1997* [PL 105–33], the *Agricultural Research, Extension and Education Reform Act of 1998* [PL 105–185] and, the *Noncitizen Benefit Clarification and Other Technical Amendments Act of 1998* [PL 105–306].

PRWORA restricts access by some legal immigrants to certain programs and denies access by undocumented immigrants to many government-funded programs. Immigrants remain eligible for benefits and services, however, unless specifically restricted as indicated below. (Citation to sections below refer to PRWORA, unless noted.)

I. DEFINITION OF "QUALIFIED ALIENS"

Qualified aliens include (Sec 431):

- Legal Permanent Residents
- Asylees
- Refugees

- Aliens paroled into the U.S. for at least one year
- Aliens whose deportations are being withheld
- Aliens granted conditional entry (prior to April 1, 1980)
- Battered alien spouses, battered alien children, the alien parents of battered children, and alien children of battered parents who fit certain criteria
- Cuban/Haitian entrants

II. ELIGIBILITY RULES WITH EXCEPTIONS

With many important exceptions, "Qualified Aliens" are ineligible for Food Stamps and SSI. States have the authority to determine their eligibility for TANF, SSBG, and Medicaid. With some exceptions, "Qualified Aliens" entering the country after August 22, 1996, are denied "Federal means-tested public benefits" for their first five years in the U.S. as qualified aliens.

A. FOOD STAMPS

Regardless of when they entered the country, most nonelderly adult "qualified aliens" are ineligible for Food Stamps until they become U.S. citizens, which requires at least five years residency. (Sec 402 (a))

Exceptions to the ban on Food Stamps:

- Children (under 18 years old) who were lawfully residing in the U.S. on August 22, 1996. (Sec 402(a)(2)(J))
- Aliens who were lawfully residing in the U.S. and were age 65 or older on August 22, 1996. (Sec 402(a)(2)(I))
- Aliens who were lawfully residing in the U.S. on August 22, 1996, and who are receiving assistance for blindness or disability. (Sec 402(a)(2)(F))
- Certain Indians. (Sec 402(a)(2)(G))
- Certain Hmong and Highland Laotians. (Sec 402(a)(2)(K))
- Refugees and Asylees, aliens whose deportation is being withheld, Amerasians, and Cuban/Haitian entrants are exempted from the ban on Food Stamps for seven years. [For asylees, aliens whose deportation is being withheld, and Cuban/Haitian entrants, these time-limited exceptions run from the date such status is granted. For all other statuses, the exception runs from the date of entry into the U.S.] (Sec 402(a)(2)(A))
- Veterans, members of the military on active duty, and their spouses and unmarried dependent children. (Sec 402(a)(2)(C))

• Legal Permanent Residents who have worked 40 qualifying quarters of coverage. After 12/31/96, no quarter can be considered a "qualifying quarter" if the individual is receiving a "federal means-tested public benefit." (See *Section D* below for the definition) Quarters worked by parents when the alien was a child, or by a spouse while married, may be counted by spouses and dependent children as satisfying the 40 quarter requirement. (Sec 402(a)(2)(B))

B. SUPPLEMENTAL SECURITY INCOME

Most qualified aliens who enter the U.S. on or after August 22, 1996, are ineligible for SSI until they become U.S. citizens, which requires at least five years residency. (Sec 402(a))

Exceptions to the ban on SSI:

• All aliens who were receiving SSI on August 22, 1996, retain eligibility for SSI (Sec 402(a)(2)(E) and Sec 401(b)(5)) and, if related to SSI receipt, Medicaid benefits. (Sec 402(b)(2)(F))

• Qualified aliens lawfully residing in the U.S. on August 22, 1996, who were not receiving SSI but are or become disabled in the future will also be eligible. (Sec 402(a)(2)(F))

• Refugees and Asylees, aliens whose deportation is being withheld, Amerasians, and Cuban/Haitian entrants are exempted from the ban on SSI for 7 years. (Sec 402(a)(2)(A))

• Veterans, members of the military on active duty, and their spouses and unmarried dependent children. (Sec 402(a)(2)(C))

• Legal Permanent Residents who have worked 40 qualifying quarters. After 12/31/96, no quarter can be considered a "qualifying quarter" if the individual received a "federal means-tested public benefit" during the quarter (See *Section D* below for the definition of "federal means-tested public benefit.") Quarters worked by parents when the alien was a child, or by a spouse while married, may be counted by spouses and dependent children as satisfying the 40 quarter requirement. (Sec 402(a)(2)(B))

C. STATE AUTHORITY FOR ELIGIBILITY OF "QUALIFIED ALIENS" FOR TANF, SSBG, AND MEDICAID

States can decide the eligibility for TANF and Medicaid of most "qualified aliens" who arrived in this country prior to August 22, 1996; states can decide the eligibility of most "qualified aliens" for the Social Services Block Grant (Title XX) regardless of date of entry. (Sec 402 (b)). [NOTE: Most qualified aliens who entered the U.S. on or after 8/22/96 are barred from receiving TANF and Medicaid for the first 5 years after their entry—see *Section D*, below.]

Exceptions:

• Medicaid exception for those immigrants who are receiving SSI benefits if Medicaid is related to SSI receipt. (Sec 402 (b)(2)(F))

• Refugees and Asylees, aliens whose deportation is being withheld, Amerasians, and Cuban/Haitian entrants are exempted from the state determination of eligibility for 5 years for TANF and SSBG and 7 years for Medicaid. (Sec 402 (b)(2)(A))

• Legal Permanent Residents who have worked 40 qualifying quarters of coverage. After 12/31/96, no quarter can be considered a "qualifying quarter" if the individual is receiving a "federal means-tested public benefit." (See *Section D* below for the definition.) Quarters worked by parents when the alien was a child, or by a spouse while married, may be counted by spouses and dependent children as satisfying the 40 quarter requirement. (Sec 402(a)(2)(B))

• Medicaid exception for certain Indians. (Sec 402(b)(2)(E))

• Veterans, members of the military on active duty, and their spouses and unmarried dependent children. (Sec 402 (b)(2)(C))

D. "FEDERAL MEANS-TESTED PUBLIC BENEFITS"— TANF, MEDICAID, AND CHIP

Five-year ban for Qualified Aliens who entered the country on or after 8/22/96

Most "qualified aliens" entering the country on or after enactment are banned from receiving "Federal means-tested public benefits" for a period of 5 years beginning on the date of the alien's entry with a qualified alien status (Sec 403) *(see exceptions below)*. The HHS interpretation, published in the *Federal Register* on August 26, 1997 (62 FR 45256), designated TANF and Medicaid (except assistance for an emergency medical condition under Medicaid) as the Federal means-tested public benefits administered by the Department. Subsequently, HHS has communicated that the Children's Health Insurance Program (CHIP) is also a "Federal means-tested public benefit." The Social Security Administration has stated that Supplemental Security Income is a "Federal means-tested public benefit." The Department of Agriculture has also stated that food stamps is such a benefit. No other program has been determined to be a *"Federal means-tested public benefit"* program.

Exceptions to ban on "Federal Means-Tested Public Benefits":

• Refugees, Asylees, aliens whose deportation is being withheld, Amerasians, and Cuban/Haitian entrants. (Sec 403(b)(1))

• Veterans, members of the military on active duty, and their spouses and unmarried dependent children. (Sec 403(b)(2))

• Certain Indians, Hmong, and Highland Laotians are eligible for Food Stamps. (Sec 403(d))

III. "FEDERAL PUBLIC BENEFITS"

Aliens who are not "qualified aliens" are ineligible for *"Federal Public Benefits."*

A. Examples of aliens who are not qualified are:

Non-immigrants (temporary residents)

Individuals here on time-limited visas to work, study, or travel.

Undocumented immigrants

Individuals who entered as temporary residents and overstayed their visas, or are engaged in activities forbidden by their visa, or who entered without a visa.

OTHERS

Individuals who are given temporary administrative statuses (e.g., stay of deportation, voluntary departure) until they can formalize permanent status, or individuals paroled for less than one year, or individuals under deportation procedures.

B. DEFINITION OF "FEDERAL PUBLIC BENEFIT" (SEC 401)

The statute defines a *"federal public benefit"* as:

• Any grant, contract, loan, professional or commercial license provided by an agency of the United States or by appropriated funds of the United States; and

• Any retirement, welfare, health, disability, public or assisted housing, postsecondary education, food assistance, unemployment benefit, or any other similar benefit for which payments or assistance are provided to an individual, household, or family eligibility unit by the United States or by funds of the United States.

The current HHS interpretation of the term *"federal public benefit"* published in the *Federal Register* on August 4, 1998 (63 FR 41658-41661) states that the following HHS programs meet the definition of *"Federal Public Benefits"* and are not otherwise excluded. Therefore, non-exempted providers of such benefits (see the exception from verification requirements for non-profit charitable organizations in *V* below) must verify the citizenship and immigration status of applicants in order to deny federal public benefits to non-qualified aliens. . . .

IV. STATE AND LOCAL PROGRAMS

States have authority to determine immigrants' eligibility for state and local programs, with some conditions. (Sec 411, 412)

A. ELIGIBILITY FOR STATE/LOCAL PUBLIC BENEFITS

Undocumented immigrants are not eligible for state/local public benefits unless the state passes a new law after 8/22/96 affirmatively making them eligible. No legislation is required to retain access to state and local benefits for non-immigrants or aliens paroled into the U.S. for less than 1 year. (Sec 411(a))

B. STATES MAY RESTRICT ELIGIBILITY

States may restrict the eligibility of qualified aliens, non-immigrants, and certain parolees. They may not restrict eligibility for: refugees, asylees, or aliens whose deportation has been withheld, during their first five years from entry; members of the military, veterans, and their family members; and those who have been credited with 40 qualifying quarters. (Sec 412) States may not deny access by any alien to state or local benefits that meet the definition of excepted services described in Sec 411(b) *(see exceptions listed above)*. States can now require an applicant for state or local public benefits to provide proof of eligibility. (Sec 413)

V. VERIFICATION OF ELIGIBILITY FOR PUBLIC BENEFITS

The Department of Justice published a Notice of Proposed Rule Making on Verification of Eligibility for Public Benefits in the *Federal Register* on August 4, 1998 (64 FR 41662-41686). Interim guidance was issued on November 17, 1997, in the *Federal Register* (62 FR 61344). States must have a verification system in place 24 months after the final regulations are promulgated for the federal public benefits they administer. (Sec 432(b)) *Exemption for Non-profit charitable organizations:* Non-profit charitable organizations are specifically exempt from any of these requirements to determine, verify, or otherwise require proof of alien eligibility or status. (Sec 432(d)) A state may not require that such organizations verify the citizenship or immigration status of individuals applying for or receiving benefits.

VI. AFFIDAVITS OF SUPPORT AND ATTRIBUTION OF INCOME (DEEMING)

Prior to the new welfare statute, affidavits of support signed for sponsored immigrants were not legally enforceable, and time-limited "deeming" of sponsor income occurred in only three programs: SSI, Food Stamps, and AFDC. The new welfare statute requires a legally binding affidavit of support to be executed by a sponsor on behalf of most aliens seeking admission to the U.S., in order to establish that an alien is not excludable as a public charge. The statute requires sponsor-to-alien deeming procedures under programs providing *"Federal means-tested benefits"* until the immigrant with the new affidavit becomes a citizen, or has been credited with 40 qualifying quarters of coverage, and permits deeming for any State public benefits.

A. AFFIDAVIT OF SUPPORT

The new affidavit is legally enforceable against the sponsor by the alien and by federal and state governments which provide any means-tested benefits, but not later than 10 years after an alien last receives any such benefit. The affidavit is enforceable with respect to means-tested benefits until the sponsored alien attains citizenship or accumulates 40 qualifying quarters. The Affidavit was released by INS on October 20, 1997, as part of an Interim Rule with Request For Comments (62 FR 54346), and was effective December 19, 1997.

B. SPONSORSHIP REQUIREMENTS

With some exceptions, sponsors must now have an income of at least 125 percent of federal poverty to sponsor an immigrant (previously 100 percent). All family-based immigrants, and certain employment-based immigrants, must be "sponsored," meaning that a family member must have signed an affidavit stating that they will provide the assistance necessary to maintain the immigrant at an annual income of at least 125 percent of the federal poverty line as long as it is enforceable (see Section A. Affidavit).

C. DEEMING

When determining eligibility for *Federal means-tested public benefits* (i.e., Medicaid, TANF, SSI, and Food Stamps), the income and resources of the sponsor, who executed a new affidavit of support, and the sponsor's spouse, shall be "deemed" available to the sponsored immigrant. (Sec 421) Benefits specifically excluded from the 5-year eligibility ban (Sec 403(c)) are also not subject to deeming and reimbursement by the sponsor.

1. These new deeming rules only apply to immigrants who have executed the new, legally binding affidavits. The new deeming period extends until citizenship, or until an immigrant has earned the 40 qualifying quarters. However, most aliens potentially affected by deeming will be barred from eligibility either until citizenship (SSI and Food Stamps) or for their first 5 years due to the 5-year ban on receipt of *federal means-tested public benefits*.

2. Indigent and battered spouse and children exceptions to deeming requirement. Deeming does not apply for specified periods to certain battered immigrants; furthermore, if an alien would be unable to obtain food and shelter without assistance, then only the amount of income and resources of the sponsor or the sponsor's spouse actually provided will be attributed to the sponsored alien for specified periods. (Sec 421 (e) and (f))

3. States are authorized to deem for their public benefits. Some benefits are exempted from the new state deeming authority: certain emergency medical assistance; emergency disaster assistance; programs comparable to assistance provided under the National School Lunch Act and the Child Nutrition Act; public health assistance for immunizations; testing and treatment of symptoms of communicable diseases; foster care and adoption assistance (if the foster or adoptive parent is a citizen or qualified alien); and other programs as specified by the Attorney General of a state. (Sec 422)

VII. OTHER PROVISIONS

A. Communication between state and local agencies and the INS

No state or local governments may be prohibited from sending to, or receiving from, the INS information regarding the immigration status of an alien in the U.S. (Sec 434)

B. REPORTING OF ILLEGAL IMMIGRANTS

States in administering their TANF block grants, the Social Security Administration in administering the SSI programs, the Department of Housing and Urban Development, and public housing agencies must report to INS four times a year aliens they know are unlawfully in the U.S. (Sec 404)

Clinton Administration Takes Action to Assure Families Access to Health Care and Other Benefits

New Regulation Clarifies That Receiving Medicaid, CHIP, or Other Benefits Will Not Affect Immigration Status

Health Resources and Services Administration, Department of Health and Human Services May 26, 1999

McAllen, TX—Vice President Gore announced May 25 a new Department of Justice regulation to assure families that enrolling in Medicaid or the new Children's Health Insurance Program (CHIP) and receiving other critical benefits, such as school lunch and child care services, will not affect their immigration status.

The new policy, effective immediately, clarifies a widespread misconception that has deterred eligible populations from enrolling in these programs and undermined the nation's public health. In addition, the Vice President directed Federal agencies to send guidance to their field offices, program grantees and to work with community organizations to educate Americans about this new policy.

"This new regulation will improve the health of our families by addressing widespread confusion that prevents legal immigrants from signing up for health insurance, school lunch, child care and other essential programs," Gore said.

Widespread Confusion About Current Policy Deters Legal Immigrants from Accessing Critical Benefits They Are Eligible for.

Recent immigration and welfare reform laws have generated widespread public confusion about whether legal immigrants receiving certain publicly funded benefits can be deemed to be a "public charge," meaning they may be denied the ability to become a legal permanent resident and subject to deportation. This confusion and fear has deterred legal immigrant families from enrolling their children in Medicaid and CHIP, and prevented legal immigrants from receiving immunization and treatment for communicable diseases, which places the entire national public health at risk. It also reduces payment sources for hospitals and other health care providers serving this population, thus increasing their uncompensated care burden. A 1998 Urban Institute study found that in Los Angeles County the rate of legal immigrants applying for health insurance dropped by 21 percent from January 1996 to January 1998, suggesting that legal immigrants do not take full advantage of their eligibility for currently available programs.

New Steps Ensure That Legal Immigrants Will Have Access to Critical Health Care and Social Services Without Fear.

These new regulations provide clear and consistent guidance that health care and other critical services cannot be used to deny individuals admission to the United States or to bar legal permanent resident status, or as a basis for deportation. Eligible legal immigrants can now receive the following benefits without fear of jeopardizing their immigration status:

• *Health insurance under Medicaid and CHIP.* There have been reports of individuals being told that receiving Medicaid or CHIP will negatively affect their immigration status leading to widespread concern in the immigrant community about enrolling in Medicaid or CHIP, even where the beneficiary is a child who is a United States citizen. These new regulations take a significant step towards eliminat-

ing that concern by clarifying that legal immigrants are eligible for these programs (with the exception of institutionalization for long term care) will not face adverse immigration consequences.

• *Access to immunization, testing, and treatment for communicable disease.* After an outbreak of rubella in New York in 1997, public health officials learned that the major reason that people had not been vaccinated was the fear that using health department services would affect their immigration status. These new regulations take new steps to protect the health of all Americans by ensuring legal immigrants can access—without fear—free immunizations, testing, and treatment for communicable diseases, such as rubella or tuberculosis.

• *Access to essential nutrition programs.* These new regulations remove the perceived barriers to receiving critical nutrition benefits, including Food Stamps, the Special Supplemental Nutrition Program for Women, Infants and Children (WIC), the National School Lunch and Breakfast programs, and other supplementary and emergency food assistance programs. Access to these benefits is extremely important for legal immigrant children. Recent studies by the United States Department of Agriculture (USDA) and the Census Bureau indicate that Hispanic families with children have among the lowest food security rates (70 percent), placing them at risk for malnutrition.

• *Other supports for families.* These regulations also make it possible for eligible legal immigrants to also access important social supports for working families, such as child care services, housing assistance, energy assistance, emergency disaster relief, foster care and adoption assistance, transportation vouchers, educational assistance, and job training programs without fear of adverse immigration consequences.

The Vice President also directed all Federal agencies that oversee these programs, including the Department of Health and Human Services, USDA, the Department of Justice, the Social Security Administration, and the State Department, to send guidance to their field offices, program grantees and to work with community organizations to educate Americans about this new policy.

Clinton-Gore Administration's Strong Commitment to Insuring Low Income Families and Promoting the Public Health.

The new regulations the Vice President unveiled today are part of a comprehensive effort by the Clinton/Gore Administration to help families obtain health care, which includes:

• *Providing health insurance to legal immigrant children, pregnant women, and individuals with disabilities.* The Administration's budget proposes to provide health coverage to low-income legal immigrant children and pregnant women who entered the country after August 22, 1996, and to legal immigrants who entered the country after August 22, 1996, and became disabled after entering the country, providing health insurance for over 100,000 legal immigrants. This builds on the Administration's success in restoring eligibility for Medicaid, SSI, and Food Stamps to hundreds of thousands of legal immigrants including restoring disability and health benefits to 380,000 legal immigrants in the Balanced Budget Act and providing Food Stamps for 225,000 legal immigrant children, senior citizens, and people with disabilities in the Agricultural Research Act of 1998.

• *Launching the Children's Health Insurance Program (CHIP).* The President, with bipartisan support from the Congress, created CHIP, which allocates $24 billion over five years to extend health care coverage to uninsured children through State-designed programs. He also launched the Insure Kids Now Campaign, which engages a broad-based, bipartisan, public-private coalition to use a variety of means to educate and assist families in insuring their children. This campaign [is] specifically designed for minority populations and encourages outreach to children in non-traditional settings, such as churches and community centers, where legal immigrant children are frequently found.

Sources: Department of State. *Advisory to Consular Offices on Cuts in Aid to Immigrants Under Initial P[ublic] L[aw].* Washington, DC: Department of State, 1996, 104–93; Immigration and Naturalization Service. *INS Question and Answer Document on Public Charges.* Washington, DC: Immigration and Naturalization Service, 1997; Department of Health and Human Services. *Summary of Immigrant Eligibility Restrictions Under Current Law.* Washington, DC: Health and Human Services, 1999; Department of Health and Human Services. *Clinton Administration Takes Action to Assure Families Access to Health Care and Other Benefits,* May 26, 1999. Washington, DC: Department of Health and Human Services, 1999.

Report on the Shortage of Technology Workers, 1997

The software and information technology industry in the United States has grown rapidly in the boom economy of the mid- to late 1990s, as has the need for highly skilled, information-technology workers. Industry leaders insist that the only way to satisfy the shortfall in skilled technicians is through immigration—specifically, through the easing of visa restrictions on information-technology workers. American unions have cried foul, arguing that there are plenty of American workers able or trainable to perform this work. They say the industry simply wants to hire cheaper foreign workers.

The following is an excerpt from a report issued on the subject by the Department of Commerce on September 29, 1997.

I. INTRODUCTION

The sweep of digital technologies and the transformation to a knowledge-based economy have created robust demand for workers highly skilled in the use of information technology. In the past ten years alone, employment in the U.S. computer and software industries has almost tripled. The demand for workers who can create, apply, and use information technology goes beyond these industries, cutting across manufacturing and services, transportation, health care, education and government.

Having led the world into the Information Age, there is substantial evidence that the United States is having trouble keeping up with the demand for new information technology workers. A recent survey of mid- and large-size U.S. companies by the Information Technology Association of America (ITAA) concluded that there are about 190,000 unfilled information technology (IT) jobs in the United States today due to a shortage of qualified workers. In another study, conducted by Coopers and Lybrand, nearly half the CEOs [Chief Executive Officers] of America's fastest growing companies reported that they had inadequate numbers of information technology workers to staff their operations.

Evidence suggests that job growth in information tech-

nology fields now exceeds the production of talent. Between 1994 and 2005, more than a million new computer scientists and engineers, systems analysts, and computer programmers will be required in the United States—an average of 95,000 per year. One difficulty is that the formal, four-year education system is producing a small proportion of the workers required. Only 24,553 U.S. students earned bachelor's degrees in computer information sciences in 1994. While many IT workers acquire the needed skills through less formal training paths, it is difficult to determine whether such training can be adequately expanded to meet the demand for IT skills.

This shortage of IT workers is not confined within the borders of the United States. Other studies, including work by the Stanford Computer Industry Project, document that there is a world wide shortage of IT workers. That industries in other nations are facing similar problems exacerbates the U.S. problem since the geographic location of such workers is of decreasing importance to the conduct of the work. U.S. employers will face tough competition from employers around the world in a tight global IT labor pool. Thus, the United States cannot expect to meet its long-term needs through increased immigration or foreign outsourcing, and must rely on retaining and updating the skills of today's IT workers as well as educating and training new ones.

Since information technology is an enabling technology that affects the entire economy, our failure to meet the growing demand for IT professionals could have severe consequences for America's competitiveness, economic growth, and job creation. . . .

II. THE DEMAND FOR WORKERS IN THE INFORMATION TECHNOLOGY-DRIVEN ECONOMY

The Office of Technology Policy analyzed Bureau of Labor Statistics' [BLS] growth projections for the three core occupational classifications of IT workers—computer scientists and engineers, systems analysts, and computer programmers—to assess future U.S. demand. BLS projections for occupational growth are given in three bands—low, moderate, and high. The following analysis uses the moderate growth figures.

BLS projections indicate that between 1994 and 2005, the United States will require more than one million new IT workers in these three occupations to fill newly created jobs (820,000) and to replace workers who are leaving these fields (227,000) as a result of retirement, change of professions, or other reasons.

Of the three occupations, the largest job growth is accounted for by systems analysts, which are projected to increase from 483,000 in 1994 to 928,000 in 2005, a 92 percent jump. This compares to a projected increase of 14.5 percent for all occupations. The number of computer engineers and scientists is expected to grow by 90 percent, from 345,000 to 655,000 over the same period, while the number of computer programmer positions is expected to grow at a much slower 12 percent rate, from 537,000 in 1994 to 601,000 in 2005. However, while only 65,000 new computer programmer jobs are projected to be created during this period, 163,000 new programmers will be required to replace those exiting the occupation.

The service sector (not including transportation, communications, finance, insurance, real estate, and wholesale and retail trade) is expected to absorb the lion's share of all increases in these core information technology occupations. By 2005, the service sector is expected to increase its employment of computer scientists and engineers by 142 percent, systems analysts by 158 percent, and computer programmers by 37 percent. In contrast, the number of computer scientists and engineers and systems analysts in the manufacturing sector is expected to grow much more slowly (approximately 26 percent and 48 percent, respectively), while the number of computer programmers is expected to decrease by about 26 percent.

Rapid technological change and the growing complexity of information technologies and their applications are accelerating the trend toward outsourcing some computer-functions. Companies recognize the need to rely on outside experts to keep up with the technologies and to assemble multidisciplinary teams to meet the unique needs of each company. This is contributing to the growth of IT workers in services.

Certain industries are more IT worker intensive than others and thus, would be more severely affected by serious shortages of these workers. And these industries are only growing in their IT worker intensity. In the most IT worker intensive industry—computer and data processing services—it is projected that, by 2005, 43 percent of the industry's employees will be computer programmers, systems analysts, and computer scientists and engineers.

However, IT worker intensity does not tell the whole story. The size of an industry's IT work force is an important consideration. For example, while the Federal government is projected to be less IT worker intensive in 2005 than many other industries, the sheer size of its IT work force would make shortages of computer programmers, systems analysts, and computer scientists and engineers a troubling problem. When IT worker intensity and size of IT work force are taken together, a picture emerges as to which industries' competitive performance would be most adversely affected by severe IT worker shortages. The computer and data processing services industry stands out starkly as an industry with much at stake in the supply of IT workers.

III. IS THERE AN ADEQUATE SUPPLY OF IT WORKERS?

Current statistical frameworks and mechanisms for measuring labor supply do not allow for precise identification of IT workers shortages. However, evidence does suggest a problem may be emerging.

UPWARD PRESSURE ON SALARIES

The strongest evidence that a shortage exists is upward pressure on salaries. The competition for skilled IT workers has contributed to substantial salary increases in many IT professions. A compensation survey conducted by William M. Mercer showed that average hourly compensation for operating systems/software architects and consultants rose nearly 20 percent from 1995 to 1996. A survey conducted by the Deloitte & Touche Consulting Group revealed that salaries for computer network professionals rose an average of 7.4 percent from 1996 to 1997. Computerworld's annual survey found that in 11 of 26 positions tracked, average salaries increased more than 10 percent from 1996 to 1997. For example, systems analysts' salaries were up 15 percent, programmer/analysts' salaries were up 11 percent, and directors of systems development received an average increase of 10 percent. Starting salaries for graduates with bachelor's degrees in computer science have nudged up to an average of $36,666, while experienced programmers can command salaries ranging from $45,000–$75,000.

ITAA SURVEY

A recent survey of mid-and large-size companies, both information technology-related and non-information technology-related, conducted by the Information Technology Association of America found approximately 190,000 unfilled information technology jobs in the United States due to a shortage of qualified workers. According to this survey, shortages are likely to worsen. ITAA found that 82 percent of the information technology companies responding to the survey expect to increase their IT staffing in the coming year, while more than half of the non-information technology companies planned IT staff increases.

THE EDUCATION PIPELINE FOR IT WORKERS

Over the last ten years, there has been a decline in the number of students receiving university degrees in computer science. These graduates come from four-year degree-granting universities which focus on computer theory; that is, operating systems, languages, distributed systems, computer architecture and compilers. According to the U.S. Department of Education, the number of bachelor-level computer science degrees awarded by U.S. universities declined more than 40 percent between 1986 and 1994, from 42,195 to 24,553. The significant decline in bachelor-level computer science degrees is, however, an imperfect indicator of declining labor supply, given that many IT workers acquire their skills through alternative education and training paths. While there have been some increases in the award of computer science masters and doctoral degrees, overall computer science degrees awarded have dropped from a high of 50,000 in 1986 to 36,000 in 1994.

In addition, students make up a significant share of U.S. computer science graduates. Of the 36,000 individuals awarded graduate and undergraduate computer science degrees in 1994, about 18 percent were foreign nationals. For advanced degrees, the proportion of foreign nationals increases, reaching more than 50 percent for doctorates. The Computer Research Association estimates that foreign nationals comprise nearly 50 percent of computer engineering students in the United States. The high proportion of foreign nationals in the graduate population would indicate that American industry cannot count on capturing all new IT workers [who] also obtain their skills from training providers other than four-year degree-granting universities. These include:

- two-year associate-degree-granting community colleges which provide grounding in applications (especially in new computer programs and hot areas such as "the year 2000" problem) as well as basic theory, and vocational technical education programs

- special university/community college one-year programs designed to upgrade the skills of IT workers already in the work force (new applications) or those with backgrounds in other technical fields who are looking for a fast track entry into the IT profession

- private-sector computer learning centers which typically offer courses to people with little or no computer background who are interested in discovering whether they have the aptitude to make it in the computer-related professions

- in-house company training to upgrade employee skills (e.g., client/server-based tools and architectures, C++ and Visual Basic) or to assist in the transition from one skill set (e.g., computer hardware engineers) to another (e.g., computer software engineers)

- computer user groups, Internet forums, and company-sponsored help sites also offer knowledge that can help expand or update computer skills

In addition to those earning four-year degrees in computer and information sciences, in 1994, 15,187 degrees and awards in computer and information sciences below the bachelor's level were earned.

OFFSHORE SOURCING AND RECRUITING

Some companies are drawing upon talent pools outside the United States to meet their demands for IT workers. India, with more than 200,000 programmers, in conjunction with predominantly U.S. partners, has developed into one of the world's largest exporters of software. In 1996–97, outsourced software development accounted for 41 percent of India's software exports. Companies are also searching for IT workers in foreign labor markets—in Russia, Eastern Europe, East Asia, and South Africa—using direct recruiting efforts, Internet techniques, and international recruiting agencies.

IV. COMPETITIVENESS ISSUES

Information technologies are the most important enabling technologies in the economy today. They affect every sector and industry in the United States, in terms of digitally-based products, services, and production and work processes. Thus, severe shortages of workers who can apply and use information technologies could undermine U.S. innovation, productivity, and competitiveness in world markets.

PRODUCTIVITY AND THE COST OF DOING BUSINESS

Competitive pressures have driven businesses to adopt a wide range of computer systems to improve productivity, manage production, improve both internal and external communications and to offer customers new services. Private sector investment in enterprise-wide applications alone was estimated to be $42 billion in 1996. The service sector, now representing 70 percent of U.S. GDP [Gross Domestic Product], is increasingly information technology intensive. Manufacturing also relies heavily on information technology from computer aided design and computer numerically controlled machine tools to computer-based systems for inventory control, production planning, and statistical process control. In short, computer-based information systems have become an indispensable part of managing information, workflow, and transactions in both the public and private sector. Therefore, a shortage of IT workers affects directly the ability to develop and implement systems that a wide variety of users need to enhance their performance and control costs. A recent survey by Deloitte & Touche Consulting reported that worker shortages are causing many companies to delay information technology projects.

As competition for IT workers heats up, rising salary levels increase the cost of doing business. For example, Electronic Data Systems Corp. (EDS) recently reported that IT worker shortages have contributed to pushing workers' compensation up by 15 to 20 percent annually. The company reported in April 1997 that it may reduce its work force by thousands to cut labor costs and maintain profits. Many computer companies faced with rising labor costs have passed those increases along to their customers. However, EDS and similar companies rely on long-term fixed contracts to develop and manage large computer systems and have less flexibility to pass increased costs to customers.

Shortage-driven increases in salaries for both skilled IT managers and IT workers also increase the amount of venture capital investment required by start-up companies in information technology-related businesses. For example, new software technology start-ups—which have benefited substantially from private venture capital and are IT worker intensive—could require greater venture capital investment in the future to cover salary costs. These rising labor costs could result in venture capital seeking growth opportunities elsewhere, constraining the emergence and growth of many promising new companies.

Government and non-profit organizations may increasingly be squeezed out of the competition for IT talent. For example, while average starting salaries for graduates with bachelor's degrees in computer engineering grew to more than $34,000 in 1995, the Federal government's entry level salary for computer professionals with bachelor's degrees ranged from about $18,700 to $23,200 that year. The Department of Defense is already having difficulty retaining IT employees; it appears industry is offering them more attractive compensation packages. The U.S. Air Force Communications Agency reports a loss rate of 42 to 45 percent of systems administrators from 1993–1995.

INDUSTRY GROWTH

High-tech industries, particularly leading-edge electronics and information technology industries, are driving economic growth not only in the United States but around the world. According to industry estimates, the markets for computer and communications hardware and services, and for software have grown to one trillion dollars. With the current annual growth rate estimated at 10 percent, the global market for these products and services may be growing by $100 billion annually. These industries are IT worker intensive and shortages of critical skills would inhibit their performance and growth potential.

In the ITAA survey, 50 percent of the information technology company executives cited lack of skilled/trained workers as "the most significant barrier" to their companies' growth during the next year—a problem viewed as significantly greater than economic conditions, profitability, lack of capital investment, taxes, or regulation. An additional 20 percent of the IT company executives identified the shortage of these workers as "a barrier" to their companies' growth during the next year.

INNOVATION

The United States is a leader in the development of new products and services, and many important consumer and industrial innovations—from computers, consumer electronic products, and telecommunications services to automotive electronics, aerospace products, and advanced industrial systems—have been made possible by information technologies. Information technologies are expected to continue to form the basis of many of the most important products, services, and processes of the future. For example, it is expected that in less than a decade, electronics will account for about one-fifth of an automobile's value. Shortages of IT workers could inhibit the nation's ability to develop leading-edge products and services, and raise their costs, which, in turn, would reduce U.S. competitiveness and constrain economic growth.

TRADE

The shortage of IT workers could undermine U.S. performance in global markets. The global market for computer software and computer services reached $277 billion in 1994. The United States is both the predominant supplier of and the primary consumer for these goods and services. Ranked in terms of global market share in 1994, eight of the world's top ten applications software vendors and seven of the top ten systems software vendors are U.S. firms. Both of these markets are growing rapidly, with the computer software market growing 12 percent annually, and the computer services market growing 11 percent annually, reaching $420 billion by 1998, a 50 percent increase just between 1994 and 1998. Aerospace, another IT worker intensive industry, is also a global market leader for the United States, and is the Nation's leading net exporter of manufactured goods. An adequate supply of IT workers is essential to America's continued strength in these markets.

HIGH-WAGE JOBS

A shortage of qualified IT workers could also prevent the United States from taking full advantage of high-wage job creation. Many information technology jobs are high-wage jobs. Workers in the software industry earn more than twice the national average. A William M. Mercer compensation study shows that the average hourly compensation in 1996 for an intermediate customer support technician was $40.80; software development architect, $77.70; operating systems software architect/consultant, $85.60, and operating systems/software programming analyst manager, $92.20. Even if shortages ease and upward pressure on salaries is reduced, the IT professions have traditionally been high-wage jobs.

Source: Department of Commerce. *Report on the Shortage of Technology Workers*, September 29, 1997. Washington, DC: Department of Commerce, 1997.

Recommendations for Prevention and Control of Tuberculosis Among Foreign-Born Persons, 1998

*W*hile *the incidence of tuberculosis among Americans dropped by 75 percent between the 1950s and the 1980s, the decade from 1985 to 1995 saw an increase of approximately 20 percent. As this 1998 report from the Centers for Disease Control—published in the center's* Morbidity and Mortality Weekly Report—*indicates, much of the recent growth in tuberculosis rates is due to the rising level of immigration from countries where the disease remains widespread.*

The following document offers a portrait of tuberculosis among immigrants, as well as recommendations on how to control it.

SUMMARY

During 1986–1997, the number of tuberculosis (TB) cases among foreign-born persons in the United States increased by 56%, from 4,925 cases (22% of the national total) to 7,702 cases (39% of the national total). As the percentage of reported TB cases among foreign-born persons continues to increase, the elimination of TB in the United States will depend increasingly on the elimination of TB among foreign-born persons.

On May 16–17, 1997, CDC [Centers for Disease Control] convened a working group of state and city TB-control program staff, as well as representatives from CDC's Division of TB Elimination and Division of Quarantine, to outline problems and propose solutions for addressing TB among foreign-born persons. The Working Group's deliberations and the resulting recommendations for action by federal agencies, state and local TB-control programs, community-based organizations (CBOs) and private health-care providers form the basis of this report. For each of the five topics of discussion, the group identified key issues, problems, and constraints and suggested solutions in the form of recommendations, which are detailed in this report. The Working Group made the following recommendations:

- The epidemiology of TB among foreign-born populations differs considerably from area to area. To tailor TB-control efforts to local needs, TB-control programs should develop epidemiologic profiles to identify groups of foreign-born persons in their jurisdictions who are at high risk for TB.

- The priorities of TB control among the foreign born should be the same as those for control of TB among other U.S. populations—completion of treatment by persons infected with active TB, contact tracing, and screening and provision of preventive therapy for groups at high risk. Screening and preventive therapy should be limited to areas where completion of therapy rates and contact-tracing activities are currently adequate.

- Based on local epidemiologic profiles, selective screening should be conducted among populations identified as being at high risk for TB. Screening should target groups of persons who are at the highest risk for TB infection and disease, accessible for screening, and likely to complete preventive therapy. The decision to screen for infection, disease, or both should be based on the person's age and time in the United States, prior screening, and locally available resources for the provision of preventive therapy.

- TB-control programs should direct efforts towards identifying impediments to TB diagnosis and care among local foreign-born populations, devising strategies to address these barriers, and maximizing activities to ensure completion of treatment.

- Providing TB preventive therapy and other TB-related services for foreign-born persons is often impeded by linguistic, cultural, and health-services barriers. TB-control programs can help overcome these barriers by establishing partnerships with CBOs and by strengthening training and education efforts. Collaborations with health-service CBOs should center on developing more complementary roles, more effective coordination of services, and better use of existing resources for serving the foreign born. TB-related training should be linked to overall TB-control strategies for the foreign born. Training and education should be targeted to providers, patients, and community workers.

INTRODUCTION

In 1986, CDC began collecting information on place of birth for those persons residing in the United States who have been reported to be infected with tuberculosis (TB). National surveillance data for the decade that followed indicate that the number of TB cases among persons born in other countries increased from 4,925 in 1986 to 7,702 in 1997, and that the percentage of foreign-born cases increased from 22% to 39% of the national total. In Canada and several European countries, foreign-born persons now account for more than half of TB cases. If current U.S. trends continue through the next decade, more than half of TB cases are likely to occur among the foreign born.

BACKGROUND

IMMIGRATION TRENDS

The increase in TB cases among foreign-born persons over the past decade is partly attributable to increased immigration. The largest wave of immigration in U.S. history occurred in the early 1900s; by 1910, 14% of all U.S. residents were foreign born. Immigration declined during the next two decades, reached a low during the Great Depression (1929–1939), and then gradually increased until the mid-1980s. A peak occurred in 1986, when the Immigration Reform and Control Act was passed and persons who had entered the country illegally were allowed to legalize their status. In 1996, the most recent year for which immigration figures are available, 915,900 persons were granted permanent residence (1). In addition, an estimated 275,000 undocumented aliens arrive annually. In 1996, an estimated 24.6 million foreign-born persons resided in the United States, representing 9% of the total population (2).

Another factor in the increase in TB cases among foreign-born persons is changing trends in countries of origin. Immigration has been increasing from Asia and the Latin Americas, where TB rates are 5–20 times higher than those in the United States. In 1994, 25% of the 24 million foreign-born persons in the United States were from Asia and 42% from Latin America, including 6 million persons from Mexico (2). In recent years, Asian-born persons have

accounted for an increasing percentage of new immigrants; in 1995, 37% of new arrivals were from Asia (3). After Mexico, the top two countries of birth among immigrants in that year were the Philippines and Vietnam. . . .

CHARACTERISTICS OF TB CASES AMONG FOREIGN-BORN PERSONS

The composition of TB cases among foreign-born persons reflects immigration patterns and trends. In 1997, Mexico was the country of origin for 22% of immigrants with TB, with the Philippines (14%) and Vietnam (11%) the next most common countries of birth. India, China, Haiti, and Korea each accounted for 3%-6% of the total. Together, these seven countries accounted for two thirds of TB cases among foreign-born persons in the United States.

As expected, most TB cases among foreign-born persons are reported from the states with the most immigrants. In 1997, 66% of all TB cases among foreign-born persons were reported from California (36% of the national total), New York (15%), Texas (8%), Florida (5%), New Jersey (4%), Illinois (3%), Washington (2%), Massachusetts (2%), Virginia (2%), and Hawaii (2%). In 1997, TB cases among foreign-born persons were examined as a proportion of total TB cases in each state. A total of 66% of TB cases occurred among foreign-born persons in California and 51% in New York. Even in states with relatively few cases among the foreign born (e.g., Minnesota and Rhode Island), approximately 60% of TB cases in 1997 were among persons born outside the United States.

Most TB cases among foreign-born persons are likely the result of reactivation of remotely acquired infection, although some transmission is probably occurring in the United States. . . . For all immigrant groups, the disease risk appears highest in the first years after U.S. arrival. . . . The risk for disease among the foreign born also appears related to chronological age and age at immigration; younger persons and those who immigrated at younger ages are at lower risk for subsequent infection with TB.

The number of foreign-born persons in the United States with TB infection is unknown. However, based on the World Health Organization (WHO) estimate that one third of the world's population is infected, more than 7 million foreign-born persons in the United States might be at risk for reactivation of remotely acquired infection.

Source: Morbidity and Mortality Weekly Report 47, no. 16 (September 18, 1998): 1–26 (weekly report of the Centers for Disease Control).

Renunciation of U.S. Citizenship, 1998

While often called a "nation of immigrants," the United States also sees thousands of persons emigrate each year to other countries. Many of these emigrants are former immigrants, returning to their land of origin, or their American spouses and children. In general, the United States discourages dual citizenship, either for naturalized or native-born Americans. In the following document, the Immigration and Naturalization Service explains the process of U.S. citizenship renunciation.

United States citizens have the right to remain citizens until they intend to give up citizenship. It is also the right of every citizen to relinquish United States citizenship. Section 349(a) of the Immigration and Nationality Act [8 U.S.C. 1481] states:

> a person who is a national of the United States whether by birth or naturalization, shall lose his nationality by voluntarily performing any of the following acts with the intention of relinquishing United States nationality;

> making a formal renunciation of nationality before a diplomatic or consular officer of the United States in a foreign state, in such form as may be prescribed by the Secretary of State; or

> making in the United States a formal written renunciation of nationality in such form as may be prescribed by, and before such officer as may be designated by, the Attorney General, whenever the United States shall be in a state of war and the Attorney General shall approve such renunciation as not contrary to the interests of national defense.

Renunciation is the most unequivocal way in which a person can manifest an intention to relinquish U.S. citizenship. In order for a renunciation under Section 349(a)(5) to be effective, all of the conditions of the statute must be met. In other words, a person wishing to renounce American citizenship must appear in person and sign an oath of renunciation before a U.S. consular or diplomatic officer abroad, generally at an American Embassy or Consulate. Renunciations which are not in the form prescribed by the Secretary of State have no legal effect. Because of the way in which Section 349(a)(5) is written and interpreted, Americans can-

not effectively renounce their citizenship by mail, through an agent, or while in the United States.

Section 349(a)(6) provides for renunciation of United States citizenship under certain circumstances in the United States when the United States is in a state of war. Such a state does not currently exist. Questions concerning renunciation of American citizenship under Section 349(a)(6) should be addressed to the Attorney General.

Parents cannot renounce United States citizenship on behalf of their children. Before an oath of renunciation will be administered under Section 349(a)(5), persons under the age of eighteen must convince a U.S. diplomatic or consular officer that they fully understand the nature and consequences of the oath of renunciation and are voluntarily seeking to renounce their citizenship. United States common law establishes an arbitrary limit of age fourteen under which a child's understanding must be established by substantial evidence.

Under Section 351(b) of the Immigration and Nationality Act [8 U.S.C. 1483(b)], a person who renounced U.S. citizenship before the age of eighteen years and "who within six months after attaining the age of eighteen years asserts his claim to United States nationality in such manner as the Secretary of State shall by regulation prescribe, shall not be deemed to have expatriated himself. . . ." The relevant regulation is Section 50.20(b) of Title 22 of the Code of Federal Regulations which requires that the person take an oath of allegiance to the United States before a diplomatic or consular officer in order to retain U.S. citizenship.

Persons who contemplate renunciation of U.S. nationality should be aware that, unless they already possess a foreign nationality or are assured of acquiring another nationality shortly after completing their renunciation, severe hardship to them could result. In the absence of a second nationality, those individuals would become stateless. As stateless persons, they would not be entitled to the protection of any government. They might also find it difficult or impossible to travel as they would probably not be entitled to a passport from any country. Further, a person who has renounced U.S. nationality will be required to apply for a visa to travel to the United States, just as other aliens do. If found ineligible for a visa, a renunciant could be permanently barred from the United States. Renunciation of American citizenship does not necessarily prevent a former citizen's deportation from a foreign country to the United States.

RENUNCIATION OF U.S. CITIZENSHIP AND TAXATION

P.L. 104-191 contains changes in the taxation of U.S. citizens who renounce or otherwise lose U.S. citizenship. In general, any person who lost U.S. citizenship within 10 years immediately preceding the close of the taxable year, whose principal purpose in losing citizenship was to avoid taxation, will be subject to continued taxation. For the purposes of this statute, persons are presumed to have a principal purpose of avoiding taxation if 1) their average annual net income tax for a five year period before the date of loss of citizenship is greater than $100,000, or 2) their net worth on the date of the loss of U.S. nationality is $500,000 or more (subject to cost of living adjustments). The effective date of the law is retroactive to February 6, 1995. Copies of ap-

proved Certificates of Loss of Nationality are provided by the Department of State to the Internal Revenue Service pursuant to P.L. 104-191. Questions regarding United States taxation consequences upon loss of U.S. nationality, should be addressed to the U.S. Internal Revenue Service.

OTHER OBLIGATIONS

Persons considering renunciation should also be aware that the fact that they have renounced U.S. nationality may have no effect whatsoever on their U.S. military service obligations. Nor will it allow them to escape possible prosecution for crimes which they may have committed in the United States, or repayment of financial obligations previously incurred in the United States. Questions about these matters should be directed to the government agency concerned.

Finally, those contemplating a renunciation of U.S. citizenship should understand that renunciation is irrevocable, except as provided in Section 351 of the Immigration and Nationality Act, and cannot be canceled or set aside absent successful administrative or judicial appeal.

Source: Department of State. *Renunciation of United States Citizenship*, July 1998. Washington DC: Department of State, 1998.

NONGOVERNMENTAL DOCUMENTS

A. Historical Articles

B. Letters

_1_NTRODUCTION

_S_ection 3 of Part IV of the _Encyclopedia of American Immigration_ is devoted to nongovernmental documents. The section is divided into two subsections: one devoted to historical articles and the other to personal letters.

The historical articles in subsection 1A cover a variety of topics. Some discuss the situation of immigrants in the United States, such as "History of the English Settlement in Edwards County, Illinois, 1818" and "The Immigrant and the Community, 1917." Others are warnings to would-be immigrants in the home country about the pluses and minuses of immigration, such as "Look Before You Leap, 1796" and " 'What Does America Offer to the German Immigrant?' 1853." Many of the documents concern the debate over immigration within the United States and discuss the conflicts between immigrants and native-born. These include "Imminent Dangers, 1835," "Emigration, Emigrants, and Know-Nothings, 1854," and "Irish Response to Nativism, 1854."

Subsection 1B is devoted to letters, such as "Letters of an American Farmer, 1782," and also includes two letters by immigrants telling people back in Europe about the situation in the United States. In addition, letters by George Washington question the loyalty of immigrants in the Revolutionary cause.

A. Historical Articles

Look Before You Leap, 1796

The following tract, written during the presidency of George Washington, warns of the dangers facing indentured (also known as "indented") servants in America. With the unwieldy but descriptive title Look Before You Leap; or A Few Hints to Such Artizans, Mechanics, Labourers, Farmers, and Husbandmen, as Are Desirous of Emigrating to America, Being a Genuine Collection of Letters, from Persons Who Have Emigrated, Containing Remarks, Notes and Anecdotes, Political, Philosophical, Biographical and Literary, of the Present State, Situation, Population, Prospects, and Advantages of America, together with the Reception, Success, Mode of Life, Opinions and Situation, of Many Characters Who Have Emigrated, Particularly to the Federal City of Washington, Illustrative of the Prevailing Practice of Indenting and Demonstrative of the Nature, Effects, and Consequences of that Public Delusion, *it also contains two letters by eyewitnesses to the abuses facing indentured servants.*

One species of abject misery consequent upon emigration has been hitherto unnoticed—but to the *labouring poor* it is tremendously awful, and pregnant with horrors of the most unprecedented nature. I mean the custom of *indenting*, or, to speak perhaps more precisely, of buying a voluntary exile and a bitter slavery. Those voracious harpies of whom in this preface we have had already too much occasion to make mention are in the habits of stimulating the *labouring poor* to cross the Atlantic upon an indenture—by which they bind themselves for a certain term, from two to seven years, as the indented servants of an austere captain or imperious landholder, whose only object is to derive a profit from their misfortune, and to aggrandize himself at the expense of industry in distress. These contracts have been common on the coasts of Ireland and Scotland for some time, but lately, even the metropolis is invested with them, and the panders of American opulence walk unblushingly to practice their delusions through the streets of London.

The situations of the unfortunate labourers who fall into their hands may be in some degree conceived, but cannot be easily described. They are sometimes employed on the coasts, but more generally sent into the interior, where every species of brutal insolence and overbearing tyranny is exercised upon their feelings. . . .

There is at the present juncture, a very large concern of this kind, going on by a wholesale agent in Bloomsbury Square. The bird's-eye prospect held forth by this recruiting cajoler to those credulous persons who are superficial observers, and only accustomed to view one side of a subject, is highly romantic. The trap is Kentucky, and the bait nothing short of an independency, after the time of apprenticeship is expired. A friend of the publisher's has been in company with several of the unfortunate men who have been worked upon to indent themselves as common labourers, though the greatest part of them were artizans and mechanics of very valuable descriptions.

The terms of agreement are such as to elude the wholesome provisions of the legislature against enticing artizans from this kingdom; and further to secure the efforts of the *indented* to be applied in such manner as their *owners* may be pleased to direct. . . . The miscreant alluded to in this note has chartered no less than six ships to convey his miserable game to their land of bondage; the infatuated wretches enslaved by him in this manner, amount to upwards of one thousand, and the time fixed for their departure is the ensuing month. . . .

(The following letters were written to a master carpenter, who was so far distempered with the American mania, as to quit a very genteel situation and respectable connection in order to accumulate a rapid fortune at the Federal City of Washington.)

NORFOLK
August 16, 1794

If you come to NORFOLK for that boasted encouragement our countrymen are taught to expect in England, you will be most *miserably disappointed.* I have seen upwards of three hundred poor persons, chiefly from Ireland, landed from one ship bemoaning with tears their own credulity, and lamenting most pathetically their departure from their native homes. These poor creatures are marched in small bodies by persons employed for that purpose to the different plantations where they are forced to indent themselves for *so many years* to the planters, who pay the captains what is called the *redemption money* for them. You will perhaps be surprised that such transactions are permitted in what is called the *land of liberty*, but I assure you this is thought nothing of here, and is actually the case. . . . There is one very unpleasant circumstance which attends us Englishmen here, which is, that most of the natives entertain the idea, *we quit our country for crimes*, and dare not return. I assure you I have been taunted with this already several times. . . .

GEORGE-TOWN NEAR WASHINGTON
January 21, 1795

Doubtless you have heard much of Kentucky. To this country, all the abandoned, the credulous, the unsettled, and the wretched in these states, are flocking in numbers. Most of the poor distressed objects I meet are indenting themselves to proprietors of land in Kentucky, in order to be conveyed there, carriage free; although the probability of such persons ever returning is scarcely possible. . . . The substance of what I have been able to collect is, that the poor creatures who have been induced to *indent themselves* are in situations the most pitiable; they are treated by their *masters* in a similar manner *to the felons formerly transported from England to Virginia*. Instead of being put in possession of portions of land, and quickly discharging their engagements, they sink deeper into debt, and this by the means of being obliged to purchase on credit at the most extravagant charges from their masters the stores and necessaries of which they stand in need. Thus situated they are never free from the landholder who is an absolute tyrant, while his miserable *indented servants are likely to remain slaves forever*. Great numbers die from the change of climate, want of proper sustenance, and the very unusual and laborious employ to which they are rigorously subjected by their vigilant overseers. Those situated upon the bordering territory are often scalped by the Indians, and their lives are in continual jeopardy. If my paper would contain all the information I have received respecting this enticing country, and also if I had time to write, I assure you it would form a striking contrast to a pamphlet, now laying beside me, and which I received when in London, from the *Kentucky agents in Threadneedle Street*.

Source: Anonymous. *Look Before You Leap; or A Few Hints to Such Artizans, Mechanics, Labourers, Farmers, and Husbandmen, as Are Desirous of Emigrating to America, Being a Genuine Collection of Letters, from Persons Who Have Emigrated, Containing Remarks, Notes and Anecdotes, Political, Philosophical, Biographical and Literary, of the Present State, Situation, Population, Prospects, and Advantages of America, together with the Reception, Success, Mode of Life, Opinions and Situation, of Many Characters Who Have Emigrated, Particularly to the Federal City of Washington, Illustrative of the Prevailing Practice of Indenting and Demonstrative of the Nature, Effects, and Consequences of that Public Delusion.* London, 1796.

History of the English Settlement in Edwards County, Illinois, 1818

George Flower and Morris Birkbeck, two pioneers from England, planned to establish a settlement in the rural backwoods of Illinois in the early nineteenth century. In the following account, Flower describes the process by which a community of immigrants came to settle the prairie. In contrast to the classic image of immigrants as rugged individualists pioneering this wilderness region, the description here emphasizes community and cooperation as the essence of immigration to the western lands of America.

During the winter [1817–18] I was preparing and assisting others to prepare for a final emigration in the spring.... I was constantly applied to in person and by letter for information and advice on the subject of emigration, by persons in every rank, but chiefly from those in moderate circumstances.

In describing western America, and the mode of living there, I found some difficulty in giving a truthful picture to the Englishman who had never been out of England. In speaking of a field, the only field he had ever seen was a plot of ground, from five to fifty acres in extent, surrounded by a ditch, a bank, and a live hawthorn fence; it has two or more well-made gates, that swing freely on their hinges, and clasp firmly when shut. The word field brings this picture to his eye.

The publication in England of our travels, my return, and personal communication with a host of individuals, had given a wide-spread knowledge of what we had done and what we intended to do. Our call had received a response from the farmers of England, the miners of Cornwall, the drovers of Wales, the mechanics of Scotland, the West India planter, the inhabitants of the Channel Isles, and the "gentleman of no particular business" of the Emerald Isle. All were moving or preparing to move to join us in another hemisphere. The cockneys of London had decided on the reversal of their city habits, to breathe the fresh air of the prairies. Parties were moving, or preparing to move, in all directions. At one time, the movement appeared as if it would be national. Representatives from each locality, and descendants from every class that I have mentioned, are now living in the English Settlement of Edwards County, Illinois. The preparatory movements were completed. The first act of our drama here properly closes, and the history of the actual emigration, with the accidents and incidents of the journeyings by sea and land, now begins.

Early in March, 1818, the ship "Achilles" sailed from Bristol with the first party of emigrants destined for our settlement in Illinois.... Forty-four men and one married woman sailed in this ship. The men were chiefly farm laborers and mechanics from Surrey.... Another party, of about equal number, composed of London mechanics, and tradesmen from various parts of England, formed another party that sailed in the same ship.... [This] party landed safely at Philadelphia early in June. They made their way, some in wagons; some on horseback, over the mountains to Pittsburgh, then descending the Ohio in flat-boats to Shawneetown, in August, proceeded without delay on foot, in wagons and on horseback, to Mr. Birkbeck's cabin on the Boltenhouse Prairie....

The next ship with emigrants for the prairies, which sailed from Liverpool in the following month of April, was chartered by myself for the party that came with me. My own immediate family and friends occupied the cabin; my domestic servants, and other emigrants going out to join us, filled the steerage; and my live-stock of cows, hogs, and sheep, of the choicest breeds of England, took up all the spare room on deck.... We arrived without accident at New York, after a passage of fifty days, and but one week after the Bristol ship, that sailed a month before us. To remove all these people and their luggage, and the animals that I had brought, to our Settlement, nearly a thousand miles inland, was no small undertaking, at a time when there was neither turnpike nor railroad, and steam-boats few, and in the infancy of their management. Patience, toil, time, and money were all required and all were freely bestowed.

On reaching land, the ship's party was broken up, and smaller parties were formed of people of similar habits and tastes, clubbing together for mutual assistance on the way. Those of small means, proceeded on without loss of time. Those of more means, lingered a little in the cities, and with their new friends, before taking their departure for what was then the Far West. . . .

In this manner, the various individuals and parties made the best way they could. Some of them were joined by individuals and families of English, that were lingering on the sea-board, without any specific reference to our Settlement; but seeing the emigration, and having read the publications, joined and went on. I think every accession from the East was English. . . .

The various objects we had in view, for which I was sent to England, were all accomplished with singular success. My voyage across the Atlantic was of unusual speed. By a singular coincidence, my father had sold, a few days before my arrival in England, his dwelling and lands in Marden for £23,000, thus giving to himself, my mother, brothers, and sisters, an opportunity of returning with me in the spring, which they willingly embraced, to take up their abode in the prairies. . . .

On entering the prairie, my large horses were covered with the tall prairie-grass, and laboriously dragged the heavy-laden vehicle. The cabin built for me was well sheltered by wood from the north and east, with an arm of the prairie lying south in a gently descending slope for a quarter of a mile; it was as pretty a situation as could be desired. The cabin could not boast of many comforts. With a clapboard roof, held on by weight-poles, and a rough puncheon floor, it had neither door nor window. Two door-ways were cut out, and the rough logs were scutched down inside. All the chips and ends of logs left by the backwoods builders lay strewed upon the floor. We were now face to face with the privations and difficulties of a first settlement in the wilderness. But greater than all other inconveniences was the want of water. There was no water nearer than the cabin in which the French family lived, a quarter of a mile off. . . .

For a moment let us glance at the situation of these settlers, a thousand miles inland, at the heels of the retreating Indians. A forest from the Atlantic shore behind them, but thinly settled with small villages, far apart from each other. To the west, one vast uninhabited wilderness of prairie, interspersed with timber, extending two thousand miles to the Pacific Ocean. Excepting St. Louis, on the Mississippi, then a small place, and Kaskaskia, yet smaller, there were no inhabitants west of us. About the same time, one or two small American settlements were forming a few miles east of the Mississippi, as we were planting ourselves a few miles west of the Wabash. . . .

There were no roads on land, no steam-boats on the waters. The road, so-called, leading to Vandalia (then composed of about a dozen log-houses), was made by one man on horseback following in the track of another, every rider making the way a little easier to find, until you came to some slush, or swampy place, where all trace was lost, and you got through as others had done, by guessing at the direction, often riding at hazard for miles until you stumbled on the track again. And of these blind traces there were but three or four in the southern half of the State. No roads were worked, no watercourses bridged. Before getting to Vandalia, there was a low piece of timbered bottom-land,

wet and swampy, and often covered with water, through which every traveler had to make his way as he best could, often at the risk of his life. Such was the state of the country. No man could feel sure that he was within the limits of the State, but from knowing that he was west of the Wabash and east of the Mississippi. We had some difficulties, peculiar to ourselves, as a foreign people. The Americans, by pushing onward and onward for almost two generations, had a training in handling the axe and opening farms, and, from experience, bestowing their labor in the most appropriate manner, which we, from our inexperience, often did not. Fresh from an old country, teeming with the conveniences of civilized life, at once in a wilderness with all our inexperiences, our losses were large from misplaced labor. Many were discouraged, and some returned, but the mass of the settlers stayed, and, by gradual experience, corrected their first errors, thus overcoming difficulties which had well-nigh overcome them. The future success of the Settlement was obtained by individual toil and industry. Of the first inconveniences and sufferings, my family had its full share. . . .

Emigrants kept coming in, some on foot, some on horseback, and some in wagons. Some sought employment, and took up with such labor as they could find. Others struck out and made small beginnings for themselves. Some, with feelings of petulance, went farther and fared worse; others dropped back into the towns and settlements in Indiana. At first, I had as much as I could do to build a few cabins for the workmen I then employed, and in erecting a large farmyard a hundred feet square, enclosed by log-buildings, two stories high; also in building for my father's family a house of considerable size, and appointed with somewhat more of comforts than is generally found in new settlements. I had as yet done nothing in erecting buildings for the public in general, as there had been no time. . . .

The first double-cabin built, was designated for a tavern, and a single one for its stable. Another and second double and single cabin were occupied as dwelling and shop by a blacksmith. I had brought bellows, anvils, tools, and appliances for three or four blacksmith-shops, from the City of Birmingham, England. There were three brothers that came with us, all excellent mechanics, and one of them, a blacksmith, was immediately installed, and went to work. There stood Albion, no longer a myth, but a reality, a fixed fact. A log-tavern and a blacksmith-shop. Two germs of civilization were now planted—one of the useful arts, the other a necessary institution of present civilization. Any man could now get his horse shod and get drunk in Albion, privileges which were soon enjoyed, the latter especially. . . .

From time to time little parties came in year after year, chiefly small tradesmen and farm-laborers. The latter, a most valuable class, came from all parts of England. The farmers brought with them their various experiences and tools, necessary to work the different soils. In this way a greater variety of workmen and tools are to be found in the English Settlement than perhaps in any one neighborhood in England.

Three brothers, Joseph, Thomas, and Kelsey Crackles,

able-bodied farm-laborers, from Lincolnshire, came with a full experience in the cultivation of flat, wet land; and brought with them the light fly-tool for digging ditches and drains, by which a practised hand can do double the work that can be done by a heavy steel spade. They lived with me three years before going on farms of their own. Their experience has shown us that the flat, wet prairies, generally shunned, are the most valuable wheat lands we possess....

It is a noticeable fact that emigrants bound for the English Settlement in Illinois, landed at every port from the St. Lawrence to the Gulf of Mexico. This arises from the fact that the laborers and small farmers of England are very imperfectly acquainted with the geography of America. Indeed, among all classes in England there is a very inadequate idea of the extent of the United States.... As various as their ports of debarkation, were the routes they took, and the modes of conveyance they adopted.

Some came in wagons and light carriages, overland; some on horseback; some in arks; some in skiffs; and some by steam-boat, by New Orleans. One Welshman landed at Charleston, S. C. "How did you get here?" I asked. "Oh," he innocently replied, "I just bought me a horse, sir, and inquired the way." It seems our Settlement was then known at the plantations in Carolina and in the mountains of Tennessee. The great variety found among our people, coming as they did from almost every county in the kingdom, in complexion, stature, and dialect, was in the early days of our Settlement very remarkable....

It will be seen that our position is not on any of the great highways of travel. We caught none of the floating population as they passed. Most of those who came set out expressly to come to us....

After [a temporary] check to emigration ... the tide began to flow again. Individuals and families were frequently arriving, and occasionally a party of thirty and forty. A fresh cause induced this tide of emigration. It arose from the private correspondence of the first poor men who came. Having done well themselves, and by a few years of hard labor acquired more wealth than they ever expected to obtain— they wrote home to friend or relative an account of their success. These letters handed round in the remote villages of England, in which many of them lived, reached individuals in a class to whom information in book form was wholly inaccessible. Each letter had its scores of readers, and, passing from hand to hand, traversed its scores of miles. The writer, known at home as a poor man, earning perhaps a scanty subsistence by his daily labor, telling of the wages he received, his bountiful living, of his own farm and the number of his live-stock, produced a greater impression in the limited circle of its readers than a printed publication had the power of doing. His fellow-laborer who heard these accounts, and feeling that he was no better off than when his fellow-laborer left him for America, now exerted every nerve to come and do likewise.... In this way we have given to Illinois a valuable population, men that are a great acquisition to the Country. It was observed that these emigrants who came in the second emigration, from five to ten years after the first settlement, complained more of the hardships of the country than those who came first. These would complain of a leaky roof, or a broken fence, and all such inconveniences. The first-comers had no cabins or fences to complain of; with them it was conquer or die. And thus emigrants came dropping in from year to year....

But it was the class of farm-laborers and small farmers, of whom I have before spoken, that furnished the bone and sinew of the Settlement. Well instructed in all agricultural labor, as plowmen, seedsmen, and drainers of land, habituated to follow these occupations with continuous industry, the result was certain success. Their course was a uniform progress and advance. Many of them without money, and some in debt for their passage, they at first hired out at the then usual price of fifty cents a day without board, and seventy-five cents for haytime and harvest. In two or three years they became tenants, or bought a piece of unimproved Congress-land at a dollar and a quarter an acre, and gradually made their own farms. Several of them, now the wealthiest farmers of the county, earned their first money on my farm at Park House. It is chiefly the labor of these men, extending over twenty, thirty, and even forty years, that has given to the Settlement the many fine farms to be seen around Albion....

The first years of our settlement, from 1818 to 1825, were spent by our settlers in putting up small houses (chiefly of logs), and shelter of the same sort for the work-horses and other domestic animals used in breaking up and fencing in the prairie for the first fields. In about three years [after 1818], a surplus of corn, pork, and beef was obtained, but no market. Before they could derive any benefit from the sale of their surplus produce, the farmers themselves had to quit their farms and open the channels of commerce, and convey their produce along until they found a market. At first there were no produce-buyers, and the first attempts at mercantile adventures were almost failures. In the rising towns, a few buyers began to appear, but with too small a capital to pay money, even at the low price produce then was. They generally bought on credit, to pay on their return from New Orleans. In this way, the farmers were at disadvantage; if the markets were good, the merchant made a handsome profit. If bad, they often had not enough to pay the farmer. Then the farmers began to build their own flat-boats, load them with the produce of their own growth, and navigate them by their own hands. They traded down the Mississippi to New Orleans, and often on the coast beyond. Thus were the channels of trade opened, and in this way was the chief trade of the country carried on for many years.

Afterward, partly from capital made in the place and foreign capital coming in, trade was established in a more regular way. The farmer is no longer called from his farm, but sells at home to the storekeepers and merchants, now found in all the small but growing towns from ten to fifteen miles distant from each other, all over the country. They have now sufficient capital to pay for the produce on its delivery. In this way the trade established has continued, excepting in its increasing magnitude.

When considered, the enlarged sphere of action and change of destiny of these farm-laborers of England, now substantial farmers and merchants in our land is truly wonderful. Once poor laborers, their experience comprised within their parish bounds, or the limits of the farm on which they toiled for a bare subsistence; now farmers themselves in another hemisphere, boat-builders, annually taking adventurous trading-voyages of over a thousand miles, and many of them becoming tradesmen and merchants on a large scale, and commanding an amount of wealth they once never dreamed of possessing. And well they deserve their success. They have earned it by perseverance and hard labor, flinching at nothing. . . .

A valuable experience was gained in the gradual taking up of land. Of course, the most inviting situations were first secured. The last land, left as refuse, was flat, wet prairie, that had not much thickness of hazle mould, so much sought after by the farmer. The surface wet, but aridly dry in summer, with a subsoil of whitish clay. The Americans said they could not get a living off such land. The English laborers, by a little judicious ditching, which made part of their fencing, found it to be the best soil for small grain and meadow in the country. . . .

Another favorable circumstance was the happy adaptation of the country to the settlers. Had our European settlers been placed in a heavy-timbered country, they would have desponded, despaired, and died. The cost of denuding a heavy-wooded district of its timber and preparing it for cultivation, is not less than twelve dollars an acre. What a source of national wealth this item is to a state like Illinois,

with its thirty-six million acres of prairie land. Every individual, thus fortunately placed, is saved a generation of hard and unprofitable labor. This circumstance is not sufficiently appreciated by a pioneer settler.

One element of success may be traced to a happy proportion among the settlers of men of money, men of intelligence, and men of toil. A settlement all of needy laborers would have suffered much, and would probably have dispersed, . . . as many others have done. It was the men of property that sustained the weight of the Settlement for the first five years, not only by its first supply of food and the building of its first houses, but in hiring the laborers as they came from the old country. This gave to the poor, but hardworking man, some knowledge of the ways of the country, while he was laying up a little store of money for his independent beginning. The sterling qualities found in the great bulk of the English laborers and little farmers, is another element of success. Their general sobriety, persevering industry, and habitual hard work, carried them through periods of long discouragements to final success. The first founders gave what they had of ability and money to the very last. All these circumstances working together have given that solid prosperity, which is characteristic of the English Settlement in Illinois.

Source: George Flower. *History of the English Settlement in Edwards County, Illinois, Founded in 1817 and 1818 by Morris Birkbeck and George Flower.* Chicago: Chicago Historical Society's Collection, Volume 1. No date.

Memorial of James Brown, 1819

The following document is a plea for a change of venue in a court case involving indentured servants. Specifically, the petitioner believes that his case against the persons who helped his indentured servants to run away—and then prevented the petitioner from reclaiming said servants—could not be heard fairly in Ohio, where the alleged crime took place. The indentured servants in question were "redemptioners" from Germany, whose passage to America the petitioner paid in exchange for a period of service. It is probable—but not indicated herein—that those involved in protecting the runaway indentured servants were other German immigrants.

To the honorable Congress of the United States: The memorial of James Brown, a citizen of the State of Tennessee, and the town of Nashville:

Your memorialist humbly represents to your honorable body that he purchased in the city of Philadelphia, about the last of October, 1818, a number of German redemptioners; advanced a considerable sum of money in their behalf; and took their indentures for three years and five months, commencing when they should arrive at the place of their destination. Your memorialist, before indenturing of said servants, described to them the climate, and explained to them the kind of business which they would be required to follow. Your memorialist further represents to your honorable body that he informed said servants, and also suggested to some gentlemen in Philadelphia, that, if he did purchase said slaves, it was not with the prospect of great emolument to himself, but that he thought their residence in the State of Tennessee or Alabama would greatly ameliorate their condition, and, at the same time, their particular avocations would be of incalculable advantage in that section of country. With these laudable objects in view, your memorialist made the purchase, selecting vine-dressers and mechanics for the purpose above stated to your honorable body, and said servants urged with much solicitude your memorialist to make said advances for them; and your memorialist, in conformity with the agreement between himself and said servants, and at a very great expense, conveyed the said servants on their way to the place for which they had indented themselves as far as Marietta, in the State of Ohio, when, by the interposition, persuasion, and aid of Caleb Emmerson,.... with many others whose names are unknown to your memorialist, the said indented servants were induced to make their escape from out of the possession of your memorialist, and were conveyed away and secreted by the said persons, or some of them, before mentioned. Your memorialist applied to the proper authorities for the purpose of reclaiming said servants, but all his efforts were defeated by the violent, oppressive, and illegal conduct of said persons, your memorialist being by the said persons unjustly arrested and imprisoned, together with the officer who had in his possession a precept authorizing the apprehension and arrest of said servants, the details of which transaction will more fully appear by the accompanying documents, to which your honorable body is particularly referred. Your memorialist would have sought redress by an appeal to the laws of his country at the time that this extraordinary proceeding took place, but was advised by counsel that there was no probability, under the present state of public feeling, that restitution would be made for the injury which your memorialist had sustained both in person and property; and your memorialist was further advised by several respectable citizens that, if he went into the country again for the purpose of arresting his servants, his life would be jeopardized. Application was made through his excellency Joseph McMinn, Governor of the State of Tennessee, on behalf of your memorialist, to the Governor of the State of Ohio; and he, in reply to the Governor of the State of Tennessee, in substance acknowledges the wrong and injury which your memorialist has sustained in that State, and regrets, in language equally just and proper, that such individuals should be permitted to disturb the public tranquility, and concludes by stating that he has been informed that justice had been rendered your memorialist: which is not the fact; for the six [servants] which he arrested by authority from the honorable Judge Bird were forcibly taken from him by the citizens of Cincinnati.... And your memorialist represents to your honorable body that he has lost his servants entirely, and that he has no other redress than by suits at law; and your memorialist begs leave to state, furthermore, that such is the extent of the influence of the individuals, and such their activity in exerting that influence, and that such is the temper and feeling of the people generally, that your memorialist believes he would be unable in the State of Ohio to have justice done in the trial of his suits; and your memorialist is advised that there is no law which authorizes a change of venue from one State to another. Your memorialist therefore prays your honorable body to pass some general law authorizing such change of venue upon the case made out before the judge of the federal courts, or a special law to permit it in this particular case, so that your memorialist can have a trial in Virginia or Kentucky, or some adjacent State.

And your memorialist, as in duty bound, will ever pray, &c.

[Signed] JAMES BROWN

Source: American State Papers, Class X, "Miscellaneous," Volume II. No Date.

Tour Through the United States, 1819

In his book Selections from Letters Written during a Tour through the United States, in the Autumn of 1819, *E. Howitt describes the harsh conditions facing immigrants during the recession of 1819. He is also sharply critical of the contemptuous attitudes toward immigrants he perceives among native-born Americans, as well as the latter's propensity for taking financial advantage of innocent newcomers.*

The tide of emigration, like that of the ocean, must ebb as well as flow, and this is the ebbing period; but, if such be the distress of England, and so gloomy its prospects, that emigration is (to anyone) an object of desire, I would certainly advise them to remove hither rather than to a new colony. The pioneers of civilization, those who advance first into an untrodden desert, and begin the work of culture and population, ought to be schooled to the office by a suitable education; they must be inured from childhood to a rude and desultory life, to every inconvenience of poverty and irregularity of climate, to struggle against difficulties which would daunt, and amidst sufferings which would destroy all besides. The towns-man, the mechanic, and even the farmer, accustomed to regularity of life, must, in such a situation, become a wretched object, and, most probably, the victim of his change of habits. But here, at least, they may find some degree of civil security, and may fix themselves on a track which has felt the first efforts of civilization, and is still in the verge of society: but it must be *the distressed* alone, who can hope to find alleviation here. There may be some who may improve their situations. Farmers, of considerable capital, who, by purchasing a track that will supply their families with food, and reserve a portion of that capital, to procure clothes and other necessaries, may live comfortably, and look forward to an increasing value of their estates. Mechanics, whose superior skill or good fortune, may meet with profitable employ; but the state of trade and glut of emigration, both preclude the possibility of the majority securing to themselves situations which will counterbalance the difficulties and hardships they will certainly find: amongst these, the impositions of the older inhabitants are not the least. The old American (or Yankee) looks with the most sovereign contempt upon the emigrant: he considers him a wretch, driven out of a wretched country, and seeking a subsistence in his glorious land. His pride is swelled, and his scorn of the poor emigrant doubled, not merely by this consideration, but by the prevailing notion that but few come here who have not violated the laws of their native realm. If a word is said of one returning, "Oh (says the Yankee), he'll none return: the stolen horse will keep him here."

With their insatiate thirst of gain, and these contemptuous notions of emigrants, they seem to consider them fair objects of plunder; and are prepared, in every transaction, to profit by their ignorance of the value of their goods, the custom and laws of the country, and the character of the people. Whoever comes here, should come with his eyes and ears open, and with the confirmed notion, that he is going to deal with sharpers. If he is not careful in purchasing necessaries for his inland journey, he will pay ten-fold for them; and when he is there, without equal caution, he will be liable to purchase land of a squatter: that is, a man who has taken possession of it, cultivated it without any title, and is subject to be ejected every day by the legal owner. With this, the evils of the banking system are to be taken into the account. I have stated, in a former letter, the causes which tend to bind a purchaser to the soil, and make him a pauper and a slave upon it; add to this, the extremes of heat and cold, the tormenting and disgusting swarms of vermin.

Source: E. Howitt. *Selections from Letters Written during a Tour through the United States, in the Autumn of 1819.* Nottingham, 1819.

Imminent Dangers, 1835

Best known for his invention of the telegraph and the code that bears his name, Samuel Morse (1791–1872) was also active in nativist politics in the mid-nineteenth century. In 1835, a year before he ran for mayor of New York City, he wrote a book, Imminent Dangers to the Free Dangers to the Free Institutions of the United States through Foreign Immigration, and the Present State of the Naturalization Laws. *As the following excerpt makes clear, Morse was an ardent opponent of free immigration, especially when it involved Catholics and the Irish.*

Few, out of the great cities, are aware what sophistry has of late been spread among the more ignorant class of foreigners, to induce them to clan together, and to assert what they are pleased to call their rights. The ridiculous claim to superior privileges over native citizens, which I have noticed, is a specimen. . . . Already has the influence of bad councils led the deluded emigrant, particularly the Irish emigrant, to adopt such a course as to alienate from him the American people. Emigrants have been induced to prefer such arrogant claims, they have nurtured their foreign feelings and their foreign nationality to such a degree, and manifested such a determination to create and strengthen a separate and a foreign interest, that the American people can endure it no longer, and a direct hostile interest is now in array against them. This is an effect natural from such a cause; it is one long predicted in the hope of averting the evil. If evil is the consequence, the writer at least washes his hands of the guilt. The name and character of foreigner has, by this conduct of emigrants and their advocates, become odious, and the public voice is becoming louder and louder, and it will increase to unanimity, or at least so far as real American feeling pervades the hearts of Americans, until its language will be intelligible and audible even to those deaf ears, who now affect neither to hear, nor to heed it. . . . It is that anomalous, nondescript . . . thing, neither foreigner nor native, yet a moiety of each, now one, now the other, both or neither, as circumstances suit, against whom I war; a naturalized *foreigner*, not a naturalized citizen; a man who from Ireland, or France, or Germany, or other foreign lands, renounces his native country and adopts America, professes to become an American, and still, being received and sworn to be a citizen, talks (for example) of Ireland as "his home," as "his beloved country," resents anything said against the Irish as said against him, glories in being Irish, forms and cherishes an Irish interest, brings hither Irish local feuds, and forgets, in short, all his new obligations as an American, and retains both a name and a feeling and a practice in regard to his adopted country at war with propriety, with decency, with gratitude, and with true patriotism. I hold no parley with such contradictions as Irish fellow-citizens, French fellow-citizens, or German fellow-citizens. With as much consistency might we say *foreign natives*, or *hostile friends*. But the present is no time either for compliment or nice discrimination. When the country is invaded by an army, it is not the moment to indulge in pity towards the deluded soldiers of the various hostile corps, who act as they are commanded by their superior officers. It is then no time to make distinctions among the officers, lest we injure those who are voluntarily fighting against us, or who may be friends in the enemy's camp. The first thing is to bring the whole army to unconditional surrender, and when they have laid down their arms in a body, and acknowledged our sovereignty, then good fellowship, and courtesy, and pity will have leisure to indulge in discriminating friends from foes, and in showing to each their respective and appropriate sympathies.

We have now to resist the *momentous* evil that threatens us from *Foreign Conspiracy*. The Conspirators are in the *foreign importations*. Innocent and guilty are brought over together. We must of necessity suspect them all. That we are most seriously endangered, admits not of the slightest doubt; we are experiencing the natural reaction ot European upon American principles, and it is infatuation, it is madness not to see it, not to guard against it. A subtle attack is making upon us by foreign powers. The proofs are as strong as the nature of the case allows. They have been adduced again and again, and they have not only been uncontradicted, but silently acquiesced in, and have acquired fresh confirmation by every day's observation. The arbitrary governments of Europe—those governments who keep the people in the most abject obedience at the point of the bayonet, with Austria at their head, have combined to attack us in every vulnerable point that the nation exposes to their assault. They are compelled by self-preservation to attempt our destruction—they must destroy democracy. It is with them a case of life and death, they must succeed or perish. If they do not overthrow American liberty, American liberty will overthrow their despotism. . . . Will you despise the cry of danger? Well, be it so. Believe the foreign Jesuit rather than your own countrymen. Open wide your doors. Yes, throw down your walls. Invite, nay allure, your enemies. Enlarge your almshouses and your prisons; be not sparing of your money; complain not of the outrages in your streets, nor the burden of your taxes. You will be repaid in praises of your toleration and liberty. What though European despots have compelled you to the necessity of employing your lives in toiling and providing for their outcast poor, and have caused you to be vexed, and your habit outraged by the expatriated turbulence of their cities, instead of allowing you to rejoice in the prosperity, and happiness, and peaceful neighbourhood of your own well-provided, well-instructed children. . . .

What were the circumstances of the country when laws so favourable to the foreigner were passed to induce him to emigrate and settle in this country? The answer is obvious. Our early history explains it. In our national infancy we needed the strength of *numbers*. Powerful nations, to whom we were accessible by fleets, and consequently also by armies, threatened us. Our land had been the theatre of contests between French, and English, and Spanish armies, for more than a century. Our numbers were so few and so scattered, that as a people we could not unite to repel aggression. The war of Independence, too, had wasted us. We wanted *numerical strength*; we felt our weakness in numbers. *Safety*, then, national *safety*, was the motive which urged us to use every effort to increase our population, and to induce a foreign emigration. Then foreigners seemed all-important, and the policy of alluring them hither, too palpable to be opposed successfully even by the remonstrances of Jefferson. We could be benefited by the emigrants, and we in return could bestow on them a gift beyond price, by simply making them citizens. Manifest as this advantage seemed in the increase of our numerical strength, Mr. Jefferson looked beyond the advantage of the moment, and saw the distant evil. . . . Now, if under the most favourable circumstances for the country, when it could most be benefited, when numbers were most urgently needed, Mr. Jefferson could discover the evil afar off, and protest against encouraging foreign immigration, how much more is the measure to be deprecated, when circumstances have so entirely changed, that instead of *adding strength* to the country, immigration *adds weakness*, weakness physical and moral! And what overwhelming force does Mr. Jefferson's reasoning acquire, by the vast change of circumstances which has taken place both in Europe and in this country, in our earlier and in our later condition.

Then we were few, feeble, and scattered. *Now* we are numerous, strong, and concentrated. *Then* our accessions by immigration were real accessions of strength from the ranks of the learned and the good, from the enlightened mechanic and artisan, and intelligent husbandman. *Now* immigration is the accession of weakness, from the ignorant and the vicious, or the priest-ridden slaves of Ireland and Germany, or the outcast tenants of the poorhouses and prisons of Europe. And again: *Then* our beautiful system of government had not been unfolded to the world to the terror of tyrants; the rising brightness of American Democracy was not yet so far above the horizon as to wake their slumbering anxieties, or more than to gleam faintly, in hope, upon their enslaved subjects. *Then* emigration was natural, it was an attraction of affinities, it was an attraction of liberty to liberty. Emigrants were the proscribed for conscience's sake, and for opinion's sake, the real lovers of liberty, Europe's loss, and our gain. . . . Now emigrants are selected for a service to their tyrants, and by their tyrants; not for their affinity to liberty, but for their mental servitude, and their docility in obeying the orders of their priests. They are transported in thousands, nay, in *hundreds of thousands*, to our shores, to our loss and Europe's gain. Again, I say, let . . . the law of the land be so changed, that no foreigner who comes into the country after the law is passed shall ever be entitled to the right of suffrage. This is just ground; it is practicable ground; it is defensible ground, and it is safe and prudent ground; and I cannot better close than in the words of Mr. Jefferson: "The time to guard against corruption and tyranny is before they shall have gotten hold on us; it is better to keep the wolf out of the fold, than to trust to drawing his teeth and talons after he has entered."

. . . What reason can be assigned, why they who profess to have become Americans, should organize themselves into Foreign National Societies all over the country; and under their foreign appellation, hold correspondence with each other to promote their foreign interest? Can any good reason be given why such *foreign associations* should be allowed to exist in this country? The Irish have been thus organized for many years. The objects of *one* of these Irish societies will serve to illustrate the objects generally of all these associations in the midst of us. "The Boston Hibernian Lyceum," says the *Catholic Diary* of March 14, 1835, "organized about *two years ago*, is composed of Irish young men, for the diffusion among each other["]—of what?—"of mutual sympathy and mutual co-operation, in whatever may aid to qualify them to meet and discharge their responsibilities as the representatives of their native, as well as citizens of their adopted, country, as Irishmen and Americans." Here we have an avowal directly of an organization to promote a foreign interest in this country! . . .

It is notorious that the excitement respecting the Roman Catholic emigrant has existed scarcely a year. The exposure of foreign designs through the Roman Catholic religion, and the discussions arising out of it, all the riotous conduct of Catholics and others, and among other things the public notices of these very *organizations*, have all occurred within the last year. But the organizations of the Catholics, and particularly of the Irish, are of many years standing. The Society at Boston above quoted, and one of the most recent, was formed long before any excitement on the subject "two years ago," says the *Catholic Diary*. It was discovering these organizations, already formed on the part of foreigners, that

excited the jealousy and distrust on the part of the American people.

Source: Samuel F. B. Morse. *Imminent Dangers to the Free Institutions of the United States through Foreign Immigration, and the Present State of the Naturalization Laws*. Originally published in the *Journal of Commerce*, 1835.

Stimulating Emigration from Ireland, 1837

While the vast waves of Irish immigrants fleeing the potato famine that would spark so much nativist hostility was still ten years in the future, this deposition—taken from an Irish immigrant in 1837—illustrates that some Americans were eager to see more immigration from Ireland, specifically businessmen and early industrialists seeking cheap labor. This tactic of luring immigrants from Europe to fill American factories would become much more widespread after the Civil War.

State of New York. City and County of New York. Michael Gaugan, at present in the city of New York, being duly sworn, doth depose and say, that he is a native of Ireland, and last resided in the city of Dublin in Ireland, previous to his coming to this country with his family, consisting of himself, wife, son, and daughter. That up to the time of his coming to this country, he was employed as assistant engineer on the grand canal Ballanhasloe, to Dublin, which situation he had held for the last thirteen years, at a salary of one pound one shilling sterling per week, besides a house and an acre of ground or more; in which situation he lived respectably and comfortably with his family; and should have continued to do so had he not been induced by the false representations held out to his countrymen generally, in an evil hour, to quit his employment, his home and his friends, to come to this country, under an expectation that with his acquirements in civil engineering, he should soon become a wealthy man.

And this deponent further says, that there were hand bills, placarded on every corner, tree, and pump and public place in the city of Dublin, and for forty or fifty miles in the surrounding country, stating, in substance, that the people were fools not to leave the country, where there was nothing but poverty staring them in the face. That laborers were so much wanted in America, that even women were employed to work at men's work—that work was plenty in America, and wages high, to wit, 9 or 10 shillings a day, British money, and his diet. And deponent further says that William Wiley of Dublin, the agent of Rawson and McMurray of New York, told this deponent that he, deponent, could get ten pounds British money per month, and his diet as wages; that every one was on a perfect equality in America; that the common laboring man received high wages, and sat at the same table and ate with his master, and gave deponent such a glowing picture of the wealth of America, and that with ease, an independent fortune could be made; that he (deponent) determined to relinquish his situation on the grand canal and bring his family to America, expecting, and so stated to his employer, that he might expect to see him return again in three years a rich man.

And this deponent further states, that there is one or more agent in every principal town in Ireland, who receives a commission for collecting and forwarding emigrants to Liverpool, where they take ship for America.

And this deponent further says, that he arrived in this city in the ship "Troy," Captain Allen, on the 16th day of June last past, with 204 passengers, that a majority of them were men in good employment at home, and lived comfortably and contented, until these passenger agents appeared in the country, a great part of whom have already returned home to Ireland, disappointed and disgusted at the gross impositions that had been practised upon them. That deponent is now without means for the support of himself and his family, and has no employment, and has already suffered great deprivation since he arrived in this country; and is now soliciting means to enable him to return with his family home to Ireland.

[Signed] Mich'l Gaugan

Source: Niles' Weekly Register. Volume LII (August 26, 1837).

Four Years of Irish History, 1845–1849

In his book on the Irish potato famine of the late 1840s, Sir Charles Gavan Duffy offers reports from an English Quaker who toured the country in 1847. As the reports relate, conditions in Ireland in the midst of famine were nothing short of catastrophic for the population. Aside from the widespread starvation, Duffy also noted the breakdown of the institutions of civil society and the lack of help being offered by the British government. He further condemns the British for not inspecting the emigrant ships, whose terrible conditions made more deaths inevitable.

The state of the country grew worse from day to day. It is difficult now to realise the condition of the western population in the autumn of 1847; but a witness of unexceptionable impartiality has painted it in permanent colours. A young Englishman representing the Society of Friends, who in that tragic time did work worthy of the Good Samaritan, reported what he saw in Mayo and Galway in language which for plain vigour rivals the narratives of [novelist Daniel] Defoe. This is what he saw in Westport:

> The town of Westport was in itself a strange and fearful sight, like what we read of in beleaguered cities; its streets crowded with gaunt wanderers, sauntering to and fro with hopeless air and hunger-struck look—a mob of starved, almost naked, women around the poor-house clamouring for soup tickets—our inn, the head-quarters of the road engineer and pay clerks, beset by a crowd of beggars for work.

As he approached Galway, the rural population were found to be in a more miserable condition:

> Some of the women and children that we saw on the road were abject cases of poverty and almost naked. The few rags they had on were with the greatest difficulty held together, and in a few weeks, as they are utterly unable to provide themselves with fresh clothes unless they be given them, they must become absolutely naked.

And in another district:

> As we went along, our wonder was not that the people died, but that they lived; and I have no doubt whatever that in any other country the mortality would have been far greater; that many lives have been prolonged, perhaps saved, by the long apprenticeship to want in which the Irish peasant has been trained, and by that lovely, touching charity which prompts him to share his scanty meal with his starving neighbour.

The fishermen of the Cladagh, who were induced to send the Whig Attorney-General to Parliament a few months before, had to pledge the implements of their calling for a little daily bread:

> Even the very nets and tackling of these poor fishermen, I heard, were pawned, and, unless they be assisted to redeem them, they will be unable to take advantage of the herring shoals, even when they approach their coast. . . . In order to ascertain the truth of this statement, I went into two or three of the largest pawnshops, the owners of which fully confirmed it and said they had in pledge at least a thousand pounds' worth of such property and saw no likelihood of its being redeemed.

In a rural district which he revisited after an interval he paints a scene which can scarcely be matched in the annals of a mediaeval plague:

> One poor woman whose cabin I had visited said, "There will be nothing for us but to lie down and die." I tried to give her hope of English aid, but, alas! her prophecy has been too true. Out of a population of 240 I found thirteen already dead from want. The survivors were like walking skeletons—the men gaunt and haggard, stamped with the livid mark of hunger—the children crying with pain—the women in some of the cabins too weak to stand. When there before I had seen cows at almost every cabin, and there were besides many sheep and pigs owned in the village. But now all the sheep were gone—all the cows—all the poultry killed—only one pig left—the very dogs which had barked at me before had disappeared; no potatoes—no oats.

Speaking of Clifden, he says:

To get to their work many of the men have to walk five, even seven, Irish miles; the sergeant of a police station by the roadside told us that the custom of these men was to take a little meal gruel before starting in the morning, taking but one meal one day and treating themselves with two the next. He mentioned cases in which they had worked till they fell over their tools. Four-and-sixpence per week thus earned, the sole resource of a family of six, with Indian meal, their cheapest food, at 2/10 to 4/-per stone! What is this but slow death—a mere enabling the patient to endure for a little longer time the disease of hunger?

The young man pointed the moral which these horrible spectacles suggested with laudable courage:

I would not now discuss the causes of this condition, nor attempt to apportion blame to its authors; but of this one fact there can be no question: that the result of our social system is that vast numbers of our fellow-countrymen—of the peasantry of one of the richest nations the world ever knew—have not leave to live. . . .

The weekly returns of the dead were like the bulletin of a fierce campaign. As the end of the year approached, villages and rural districts, which had been prosperous and populous a year before, were desolate. In some places the loss amounted to half the resident population. Even the paupers shut up in poor-houses did not escape. More than one in six perished of the unaccustomed food. The people did not everywhere consent to die patiently. In Armagh and Down groups of men went from house to house in the rural districts and insisted on being fed. In Tipperary and Waterford corn-stores and bakers' shops were sacked. In Donegal the people seized upon a flour-mill and pillaged it. In Limerick 5,000 men assembled on Tory Hill, and declared that they would not starve. A local clergyman restrained them by the promise of speedy relief. "If the Government did not act promptly, he himself would show them where food could be had." In a few cases crops were carried away from farms. The offences which spring from suffering and fear were heard of in many districts, but they were encountered with instant resistance. There were 30,000 men in red jackets, carefully fed, clothed, and lodged, ready to maintain the law. Four prisoners were convicted at the Galway assizes of stealing a filly, which they killed and ate to preserve their own lives. In Enniskillen two boys under twelve years of age were convicted of stealing one pint of Indian meal cooked into "stirabout," and Chief Justice Blackburn vindicated the outraged law by transporting them for seven years. Other children committed larcenies that they might be sent to gaol, where there was still daily bread to be had. In Mayo the people were eating carrion wherever it could be procured, and the coroner could not keep pace with the inquests; for the law sometimes spent more to ascertain the cause of a pauper's death than would have sufficed to preserve his life.

The social disorganisation was a spectacle as afflicting as the waste of life; it was the waste of whatever makes life worth possessing. All the institutions which civilise and elevate the people were disappearing one after another. The churches were half empty; the temperance reading-rooms were shut up; the mechanics' institute no longer got support; only the gaols and the poor-houses were crowded. A new generation, born in disease and reared in destitution, pithless and imbecile, threatened to drag down the nation to hopeless slavery. Trade was paralysed; no one bought anything which was not indispensable at the hour. The loss of the farmers in potatoes was estimated at more than twenty millions sterling, and with the potatoes the pigs which fed on them disappeared. The seed procured at a high price in spring again failed; time, money, and labour were lost, and another year of famine was certain. All who depended on the farmer had sunk with him; shopkeepers were beggared, tradesmen were starving, the priests living on voluntary offerings were sometimes in fearful distress when the people had no longer anything to offer. . . .

When the increased mortality was pressed on the attention of the Government, Lord John Russell replied that the owners of property in Ireland ought to support the poor born on their estates. It was a perfectly just proposition if the ratepayers were empowered to determine the object and method of the expenditure; but prohibiting reproductive work, and forcing them to turn strong men into paupers, and keep them sweltering in workhouses instead of labouring to reclaim the waste lands—this was not justice. . . .

The people fled before the famine to England, America, and the British colonies. They carried with them the seed of disease and death. In England a bishop and more than twenty priests died of typhus, caught in attendance on the sick and dying. The English people clamoured against such an infliction, which it cannot be denied would be altogether intolerable if these fugitives were not made exiles and paupers by English law. They were ordered home again, that they might be supported on the resources of their own country; for though we had no country for the purpose of self-government and self-protection, we were acknowledged to have a country when the necessity of bearing burdens arose.

More than a hundred thousand souls fled to the United States and Canada. The United States maintained sanitary regulations on shipboard which were effectual to a certain extent. But the emigration to Canada was left to the individual greed of ship-owners, and the emigrant ships rivalled the cabins of Mayo or the fever sheds of Skibbereen. Crowded and filthy, carrying double the legal number of passengers, who were ill-fed and imperfectly clothed, and having no doctor on board, the holds, says an eye-witness, were like the Black Hole of Calcutta, and deaths occurred in myriads. The survivors, on their arrival in the new country, continued to die and to scatter death around them. At Montreal, during nine weeks, eight hundred emigrants perished, and over nine hundred residents died of diseases caught from emigrants. During six months the deaths of the new arrivals exceeded three thousand. No preparations were made by the British Government for the reception, or the employment, of these helpless multitudes. The *Times* pronounced the neglect to be an eternal disgrace to the British name. Ships carrying German emigrants and English emigrants arrived in Canada at the same time in a perfectly healthy state. The Chief Secretary for Ireland was able to inform the House of Commons that of a hundred thousand Irishmen who fled to Canada in a year 6,100 perished on the voyage, 4,100 on their arrival, 5,200 in the hospitals, and 1,900 in the towns to which they repaired. The Emigrant Society of Montreal paints the result during the whole period of the famine, in language not easily to be forgotten.

Source: Sir Charles Gavan Duffy. *Four Years of Irish History, 1845–1849*. London: Cassell, Petter, Galpin & Co., 1883.

"What Does America Offer to the German Immigrant?" 1853

Originally published in Berlin in 1853, Gottfried Menzel's The United States of North America, with Particular Consideration Paid to German Emigration There attempted to offer a balanced picture to German immigrants considering a move to the United States. Economic hard times, followed by the abortive revolutions of 1848, sent tens of thousands of German-speaking emigrants to America in the mid-nineteenth century.

The motive common to all men for changing their homes is the hope of improving their condition. If something is annoying or oppressive to a man in one place and he cannot remove the untoward conditions, he is then inclined to betake himself to the place where he thinks he can remain undisturbed by such vexations. In Germany as elsewhere, there are two things particularly which are disagreeable and burdensome to many of the inhabitants and from which they escape by emigrating to America.

In Germany as in most of the European states many people are dissatisfied with the state organization and institutions. They feel themselves hampered by the government, complain of lack of freedom, of too much government, and the like, and direct their gaze to the free states of the great North American Republic, as the land of desired freedom. . . .

Germans who voluntarily exchanged their homes in Germany for new homes in North America to obtain greater freedom, especially those who have emigrated since the year 1848, always say in their accounts from America that they are entirely satisfied with American freedom, and sincerely pity all those who are not yet sharers in it. But through the newspapers of the day other opinions are heard. There are many things with which they are really dissatisfied. Some existing institutions they wish to remove and to replace with others, but they have not yet been able to change anything in these republican constitutions and democratic institutions. The Americans do not approve of these efforts at reformation and say, "These Germans wish to dictate everything, but do not wish to be dictated to themselves."

Much greater is the number of those who leave their fatherland on account of the poverty of its material resources and in order to better their condition in America. For many people industrial conditions in Germany are such that you cannot blame them for emigrating when they learn that in North America there are far greater productive natural resources and that work has a greater value than in Germany.

He who in Germany has to suffer from want and misery, or must expect these in the near future, finds that hope of better fortune overcomes his attachment to the *Vaterland*. He easily separates himself from his old home and wanders to a distant land believing that he will find life more favorable there.

That it is easier to make a living in America cannot be denied; but it is a matter of regret that those who could better their condition in this way frequently lack the means. Many people who take this risk find only their misfortune or ruin. The numbers of those who return to Germany from America prove that many are not successful there. When an emigrant ship is prepared to sail from the harbor of New York for Hamburg or Bremen, there are usually twenty or more people leaving the land of their disappointed hopes for the old home country after one or two years' bitter experiences. They have left, out of their fortunes, scarcely the necessary money for the return passage. Still others would follow them if they had the means for the trip or if they were not ashamed to return.

Therefore everyone who is thinking of emigrating to America should take care to determine whether or not he is fit for America. He should carefully weigh what he leaves here against what he may find there, lest he should be guilty of too great haste or light-mindedness and make a mistake that he may regret only too soon and bitterly. . . . The emigrant must rely upon others and believe what they tell him about that country, either to give up his decision or to fulfil it. But most of them are guilty of credulity which may be regarded as the chief cause of the numerous emigrations.

A great many books about emigration to America have been written, and every year new ones appear. *Rathgeber, Führer, Wegweiser* for emigrants are the customary titles of these books. A book written against emigration, or one advising emigration only for the few, would have little charm and would find few purchasers. But as soon as a book appears which describes the land to which the emigrant would go as a land of paradise, then it is sold and read diligently, and thousands are moved in this way to become emigrants. Many a book on emigration very truly describes what is good and what is agreeable in America, but passes over in silence the disadvantages or disagreeable features of American life. Through this one-sided presentation of American conditions many are lured to emigrate. It is obvious that the countless speculators who every year gain many millions of emigrants will make a great effort to bring to the attention of the people many books through which the desire for emigration is awakened and increased. They are themselves completely indifferent to the fate of the emigrants, and if emigration turns out to be for their ruin they do not care. Again, many who read books on emigration see only what they like; and they overlook the disagreeable, which is moreover only painted in faint colors, and do not give it mature consideration. Thus they themselves help to make the work of deception easy and complete.

But the descriptions and the letters of the emigrants to their relatives and friends and acquaintances—are they not then true and reliable? This I deny. First, because no one who has emigrated will confess that he was disappointed, that he had not found there that on which he had counted with certainty and which he had so joyfully anticipated. He is very right in thinking that few in the old home will have sympathetic pity for him, and many only malicious joy and bitter ridicule. Even sympathy for misfortune brought on one's self is not agreeable. One does not wish to confess to those who advised against emigration that they were right in their forebodings and warnings, and that they had seen more clearly and correctly than he had.

Secondly, the immigrants wish, for many reasons, to have many of their relatives and countrymen follow them and settle near them. On the one hand, because of the neighborly society and support, the need of which many of them have bitterly experienced. On the other hand, one desires everywhere new arrivals of immigrants because they will buy land, and stock, and so on from those already settled, by which ready money, of which there is always need, comes into this part of the country and the value of the land and its produce increases. The following of relatives, especially if they are well off, is much desired by their predecessors whether circumstances are favorable or unfavorable.

Therefore, it is easy to understand that there are no complaints in the letters of the immigrants in spite of the causes of complaint that many a writer may have. Before my trip to America I received many letters from people living there, who described their condition as quite satisfactory, but when I had personally investigated their condition and when I expressed my surprise at their letters which had gone so far from reality, I received the answer, "Others ought to try their life too. In Germany there are more than enough people, while here there are too few."

WHAT DOES NORTH AMERICA OFFER THAT IS GOOD?

This great country offers its inhabitants noteworthy advantages which may be summarized as follows:

1. Although the citizens of the United States are not, as is popularly supposed, free from taxes, yet the taxes on land and cattle which the farmer has to pay are not high, and artisans pay no taxes on their business.

2. The citizens are, during a certain age, under obligation to serve in the militia, but except in the case of war this is rarely asked of them except perhaps for suppression of a riot. For regular military service volunteers are always available, since they are well paid. The quartering of soldiers in time of peace is not allowed.

3. Complete freedom in the trades and professions, hunting and fishing is allowed to everyone. . . .

4. There is no difference in rank. The terms "upper class" and "lower class" have no significance. The public official has no advantage not shared by the farmer, the merchant, or the teamster.

5. North America, as a country with fertile land still partly unoccupied, a country thinly populated with flourishing trade and general freedom of trade, offers far greater and more abundant means of livelihood than Germany.

6. Labor there has a high, and cost of living a lower, value; therefore on the whole the people are far less oppressed by want and need and the tormenting anxiety for one's daily bread.

Against the advantages just enumerated . . . the following disadvantages will not please those who are eager to emigrate.

The long and distant sea-voyage appears to many of them as the great hardship of emigration, and they think if only this were accomplished all would be well. Although this is accompanied by danger and much inconvenience, it is soon over. Seasickness is indeed painful for many, but it is not dangerous, and need not be feared since it is good for their health after the sea journey. Far more hazardous and more serious in their consequences are the following:

1. [The danger, after landing in America, of losing one's property through the deception and thievery of the runners.]

2. The unhealthy climate. . . .

3. The German in America is a complete stranger. Everything is strange, the country, the climate, laws, and customs. One ought to realize what it means to be an alien in a far distant land. More than this, the German in America is despised as alien, and he must often hear the nickname "Dutchman," at least until he learns to speak English fluently. It is horrible what the German immigrants must endure from the Americans, Irish, and English. I was more than once a witness to the way German

immigrants were forced by the American captain or pilot with terrible brutality, kicking, etc., to carry wood from the shore to the boat, although they had paid their full fare and had not been engaged for those duties. Only in the places where the Germans are in the majority does the newly arrived immigrant find, after all the hardships of the journey, an endurable existence. The Americans are accustomed to alter their behavior to him only after he has become Americanized. The rabble who also emigrated from Germany in former times have brought the German name into discredit.

4. The educational institutions are, in America, defective and expensive or they are completely lacking. Therefore parents can give their children the necessary education only through great sacrifices or, in case they are poor, the children must be allowed to run wild. . . .

5. The majority of the Germans emigrating to America wish to seek their fortunes in agriculture. But the purchase of land has its dangers and difficulties. The price of the land is, in proportion to its productivity, not so low as is generally believed. To establish a farm on new and uncultivated land is for the newcomer an almost impossible task. The life of a North American farmer is not at all enviable as many think. Where labor is so dear and where agricultural products are so cheap, there no one can exist except the man who is able and willing to do all his own work and does not need to employ outside labor. . . .

I have been approached since my return from North America by a large number of persons for information concerning conditions there and for advice concerning their projected plan of emigration. Either because of their personal qualifications or circumstances, hardly one-fourth of these people could be advised with confidence to undertake this important step. I found most of them unsuitable for emigration for the following more or less serious reasons:

1. *A weak constitution or shattered health.*—The emigrant to America needs a strong and healthy body.

2. *Advanced age.*—The man who is already over forty years of age, unless he has some sons who can help him with their labor, cannot count upon success and prosperity in America.

3. *Childlessness with somewhat advanced age.*—What will a married couple do when their capacity to labor disappears with the years? They could not earn enough when young to support them in later years. If they have a substantial property to bring over from Germany, then emigration would be a very unwise step for them, since for the man without employment living is much higher in America than in Europe, especially if one needs servants or cannot do without the comforts and luxuries of life.

4. *Lack of experience in the field of labor on the part of those who expect to establish their fortunes there through hard labor.*—The duties of the agriculturists, as well as the occupations of the artisan, involve heavy labor. Many harbor the delusion that they are already accustomed to the labor required there, or that they will easily learn it if they have worked a little here in this country. But he who has not from his youth up been performing continuously the most severe labor, so much the more will he lack, in America, where work is harder, the necessary strength and ability. He will certainly not be a competent and contented workingman. In America . . . labor is much more severe and much more work is required for the higher wages he receives than is usual in Germany. Those who spent their youth in schools, offices, or in other sedentary work, play in America a very sad and pitiable role.

5. *A slow easy-going habit of living a life of ease and comfort.*—One may find in the great cities of North America all the comforts and conveniences which European cities offer, but in America they are only for the few—for the rich—and to this class German emigrants do not usually belong. Not many persons in America can command even the comforts of the ordinary citizen of Europe. Many people seek compensation in whiskey for their many privations and hardships and this is the way to certain ruin.

6. *Destitution.*—If the passage for a single emigrant costs only 50 thaler, at least as much again must be counted for the land journey here and in America. Unfortunately this amount is beyond the reach of those who would have the best chance of improving their condition in America. The artisan, even though he cannot carry on his business there independently but must work in great workshops and factories must often make yet a further land journey in order to find the most suitable place, and he needs, especially if he has a family, a not inconsiderable amount of money. Seldom is a place found in the vicinity of the port of arrival where places are not already filled with laborers. If the means of traveling are not available, he falls into difficulties and distress, is obliged to sell the effects he brought with him for a trifling sum, or considers himself fortunate if he finds a job anywhere at the lowest wage—a wage that will barely keep him and his family from hunger. Those who wish to move on to the land should not come to America without capital unless they are young, strong, and eager to work. It is necessary to earn the means to independence through service or through daily labor which is, to be sure, not easy, but is surer than to purchase immediately an independent position with money brought from Germany.

Source: Gottfried Menzel. *The United States of North America, with Particular Consideration Paid to German Emigration There.* Berlin, 1853 [originally: *Die Vereinigten Staaten von Nordamerika mit besonderer Rücksicht auf Deutsche Auswanderug dahin*].

Emigration, Emigrants, and Know-Nothings, 1854

Anti-immigrant sentiment reached new heights in the 1850s with the meteoric rise of the Know-Nothing Party. The anonymous author of the book from which the following document is excerpted described himself as an Englishman who had lived in the United States for thirteen years and been a naturalized citizen for seven years. Exhibiting a fear of further immigration—and its deleterious effect on wages—the writer fits into a classic pattern in American history of earlier immigrants wanting to close the gates behind them.

And what have I learned in the course of my travels and observations concerning the unlimited and unguarded admittance of foreigners into the country? What conclusion have I come to? That it is a glaring and grievous evil; an evil to the United States, and an evil to many of the emigrants themselves. Why? Because anybody, or everybody, may come without let or hindrance. The rogues and vagabonds from London, Paris, Amsterdam, Vienna, Naples, Hamburg, Berlin, Rome, Genoa, Leghorn, Geneva, &c., may come and do come. The outpouring of alms and work houses, and prisons and penitentiaries, may come and do come. Monarchies, oligarchies, and aristocracies may and do reduce the millions of the people to poverty and beggary, and compel the most valueless to seek for a shelter and a home in the United States of America, and they do so. And what are the consequences? The consequences are that about 400,000 souls, from Europe, chiefly Germans, Irish, and Dutch are annually arriving in this country and making it their permanent abode. That a vast number of these emigrants come without money, occupation, friends, or business; many, very many, have not the means of buying land, getting to it, stocking it, and waiting for first crops, and many others would not settle upon land if they could. That, go where you will in the United States, you find nearly all the dens of iniquity, taverns, grog-shops, beer houses, gambling places, and houses of ill fame and worse deeds, are kept by foreigners. That, at the various ports, the almshouses and hospitals are, in the main, occupied by foreigners; and that numerous objects of poverty and destitution are to be seen crawling along the streets in every direction.

That not a few become criminals, filling our prisons and putting the country to great expense.

This is a fearful catalogue of consequences, but they are by no means all. This unlimited and unrestricted admission of foreign emigrants is a serious injury to the native laboring population, socially, morally, religiously, and politically; socially, by overstocking the labor market and thus keeping wages down; morally and religiously, by unavoidable contact and intercourse; and politically, by consequence of want of employment and low wages, making them needy and dependent, whereby they become the easy prey or willing tools of designing and unprincipled politicians. And in this way the native population is deteriorated and made poor, needy, and subservient: and these realities produce want of self-respect, hopelessness, laxity in morals, recklessness, delinquencies, and crimes.

But there is another consequence which is deserving of notice, and it is this: Our manufacturers, ironmakers, machinists, miners, agriculturists, railway, canal, and other contractors, private families, hotelkeepers, and many others, have got into the way of expecting and seeking for cheap labor, through the supply of operatives, workmen, laborers, house-help, and various kinds of workers, kept up by the indiscriminate and unrestrained admission of emigrants. Indeed it is no secret that emigrants, or rather foreign workers, have become an article of importation; professedly for the purpose of providing for the deficiency of supply in the labor market, but in reality with the intention of obtaining efficient workers at lower wages.

I remember well in the early part of 1846, when our manufacturers and ironmakers, far and near, were struggling hard for the retention of the high protective tariff then in existence, and the profits on cotton spinning and manufacturing ranged from thirty to one hundred per cent, that hundreds of operatives were imported from England for the purpose of obtaining practised hands and to keep wages from rising. And I remember also that some years ago when there was an attempt to reduce the wages of ironmakers and machinists at Pittsburgh and elsewhere, and the men resisted, that importation was resorted to with considerable success; and that those importations, and others both before and since, were obtained in a great measure by partial, fallacious, and incorrect representations.

This last mentioned consequence has had, and probably will continue to have, a very unfair and deplorable effect upon the native laboring population; for it needs no proof to sustain the assertion, that but for these specific and large importations of cotton and woolen manufacturing operatives, machinists and ironworkers, the wages of the then located population must have risen, and the natives been made better off. It is worthy of mention and attention in this connexion, that master coal miners, master ironmakers, master machinists, master cotton and woollen manufacturers, &c., are to a man advocates for a very high tariff upon coal, iron, steel, machines, tools, and cotton and woollen goods; and for the unlimited admission of workers without a sixpence of duty; by which means the consumers of all those articles are made to pay exorbitant prices for their benefit (the benefit of the masters), while they can and do avail themselves of the free importation of labor in order to keep wages from rising or for the purpose of lowering them. This is certainly the protective system, but it is protecting the masters and not the workers; the strong against the weak; the high livers and little workers, against the low livers and hard workers. If any protective system is wanted, I am an advocate for a protective system which shall prevent pauper labor from coming into the country, and admitting all merchandise free, which by making it abundant and cheap would add to the comfort of the masses. . . .

Then what ought to be done? I will say what I am convinced ought to be done, and what would be for the honor and welfare of the country at large; and that is, restrict by law the admission and importation of emigrants to within prudent limits. None should be permitted to land at any of our ports and remain in the country unless he, she, or they could show satisfactorily to the proper authorities (made and provided for that purpose) that they were engaged in trade, had a living occupation to go to, or were fully prepared to comply with the regulations which require them immediately to settle upon and cultivate permanently the public lands appropriated to that purpose.

We would have these public lands given in limited quantities, say from fifty and not exceeding one hundred acres, to emigrant settlers, according to the number of persons in a family and their power of improving and cultivating it. Plain and full instructions in pamphlet form should be prepared and given to every settler, whereby they would learn how to get to the lands at the least cost and in the most direct way, requiring them to go in companies and to own and occupy adjoining allotments, and recommending them to adopt a simple, reciprocal associative manner of labor and living. Nay, rather than we should continue emigration upon its present basis, through which we should go on producing paupers, delinquents, and criminals, and causing numbers of new comers to take up low and vile occupations, and for the much to be desired and wise pur-

pose of raising up "A bold peasantry, their country's pride," we would even consent to defray the expense of conveying them to their new homes out of the national exchequer.

Such an alteration of the system, or rather such an introduction of a system, would soon become generally known throughout Europe, and would deter and prevent the vicious, the destitute, and the very ignorant from coming among us, and would in consequence stop the rapid increase of pauperism, degradation, and crime at our ports. On the other hand, it would encourage such foreigners as had laid up a little money, and were likely to prove industrious and respectable citizens, to come over and help us to become truly great, by intelligent industry, honesty, and frugality.

Among other regulations, under the new system, all owners and captains of vessels should be formally notified of the fact, and that they would be held liable to take all emigrants back, free from charge, and to maintain them whilst in port, whom they had brought out contrary to the emigration law.

But I expect this scheme or proposition will be objected to by many, who will say, "such restrictions would be inconsistent with our liberties and the spirit of true republicanism, would prevent hundreds and thousands of monarchially oppressed subjects from participating in the benefits to be derived from our free institutions and more equitable governments, and that without the present free and unlimited admission of emigrants we should be prevented from executing great public works as heretofore."

To these objections, I reply, that the unrestricted exercise of any liberty or privilege which is productive of so much evil as this is, ought to be restrained; not only for the sake of our national respectability and the well-being of our native population, but for the sake also of those unfortunate persons who having already filled our ports, cities, and towns, with the poor and the helpless, are, some of them, in worse positions than when at home and living under European governments. Moreover, it is evidently injudicious and impolitic for us to place it in the power of kings and aristocracies and their suborganizations, to send hither hundreds of thousands of their ignorant, superstitious, and least valuable subjects for us to educate, reform, and maintain. And as it respects the prosecution of great public works, I say, that a great number are got up without necessity, as matters of speculation, and go into forgetfulness, never having been intended for the public use, and never brought to maturity; I say that we have no occasion to do the work of five centuries in one, and whatever is done hastily and recklessly is sure to be done ill; and therefore we had better do less and do it well. But railroad, canal, and other companies might, upon showing that they could not obtain laborers and operatives, be permitted to import workers and become chargeable with their maintenance and traveling expenses on their arrival.

Source: Anonymous. *Emigration, Emigrants, and Know-Nothings.* Philadelphia, 1854.

Irish Response to Nativism, 1854

In this 1854 extract from an editorial published in the Citizen, *a New York City newspaper for Irish Americans, the editors encourage their readers to avoid all "No-Nothing" candidates. Correctly written as the Know-Nothings, this party—officially known as the American Party—was a blatantly anti-immigrant, anti-Catholic party that gained wide support in the early 1850s.*

Since the establishment of the *Citizen*, we have uniformly urged upon Irish citizens that they should not act together as Irishmen—should not isolate themselves from other American parties, should not place themselves in the hands of Irish priests, still less of Irish grog-sellers, to be disposed of as a political capital. We have made bold to propound the doctrine, that every Irish voter ought to vote upon his individual judgment about measures and men—not because the "Irish vote" goes this way or the other; that there ought, in short, to be no Irish vote at all; but that Irishmen in America should be so entirely absorbed into the American system as to be indifferently Democrats or Whigs, Hards, Softs, Silver-greys—anything except Garrisonian abolitionists.

But there is an element coming in, that alters the whole case. Here come a set of ignorant malignants, taking it upon them to represent the great nation, to maintain its honor and to guard its religion (the vagabonds!) and they say to their Irish fellow-citizens, "No, you shall never become wholly American—you are to be isolated for ever—you are unfit to enjoy the liberties, or to exercise the franchises of Americans—your religion is not to our taste—your brogue is unmusical to our ears."

Can there be any doubt as to how any Irish, or any German citizen, ought to treat these creatures? In this one case, at any rate, foreign-born men *are* isolated, though not by their own act. Whatever may be their political predilections, and however various on other points, here, at least, they must be one. No Irish voter, no German citizen, can, without abject disgrace, support—we do not say a No-Nothing candidate, but any candidate who courts or relies upon, or does not repudiate and spit upon, No-Nothing support.

Whosoever shall act otherwise at the approaching elections fawns upon the foot that spurns him, kisses the hand that would wrest the franchise from his children, and confesses that he and his are content to be helots and Pariahs in the free land of their adoption, as their strong tyrants made them Pariahs and helots in the land of their birth!

Source: Citizen. Volume 1 (October 28, 1854).

"Emigration from the Kingdom of Würtemburg," 1881

*T*he following document contains an 1881 interview with a "prominent official" of the government of Würtemburg, a component of the German Empire. As the official makes clear, the causes of immigration in late nineteenth-century Europe included both farmers and workers. The interviewer—probably connected with the local United Consulate—was particularly concerned whether "criminals" and "paupers" were being urged to emigrate. But the official assures the interviewer that this is not the case. Instead, the official says, overpopulation and a lack of work is driving hard-working people to America.

CONSULAR REPORT ON IMMIGRANTS FROM GERMANY

Views of a prominent official.—I have recently been favored with an opportunity for a quite extended and, at the same time, informal conversation on this subject with a prominent official of the Würtemberg government. Allusion having been made to the recent remarkable increase in the number of those departing hence for America, the official replied that the question had indeed of late been occupying public attention, on account not so much of the actual loss in numbers occasioned thereby as the excellent quality of the material that is at present leaving this kingdom for the United States. . . .

Question.—Of what class of people is the present emigration principally composed?

Reply.—Chiefly of tillers of the soil, hardy and robust men whose loss from the rural districts will be much more felt than would be the drawing off of a corresponding number of the population from the cities, which are comparatively overcrowded, and where the unemployed and criminal classes are generally found. As for the actual loss in population it is really no great subject for regret, for our rate of increase is very rapid. The kingdom is quite thickly peopled, its productive capacities are taxed to the utmost for the support of its inhabitants, and a moderate emigration may therefore be considered rather a relief than otherwise. But those who are emigrating are the tillers in the fields and vineyards, men who are necessarily the largest contributors to our agricultural welfare, and who have generally some mechanical skill as well. They compose the element we can least afford to lose.

Question.—Is there any reason for supposing that paupers and criminals are sent from here to the United States as emigrants?

Reply.—None whatever; that is, in the case of persons known to be such. It is of course impossible for the emigrant agents to make thorough inquiry into the antecedents of every one of the many hundreds presenting themselves to be registered as intending to emigrate. But there is no organized movement either on the part of local, county, or town authorities, or of any philanthropic association, to send such persons to the United States. A general belief and understanding exists here that even if sent thither they would not be permitted to land.

Question.—Are there any means by which the authorities here can, if they so desire, arrest this tide of emigration?

Reply.—Practically none. Even the restrictions existing at the German ports of embarkation, Hamburg and Bremen, are rendered fruitless by the fact that any German, wishing to emigrate to America, can easily avoid them by passing over into Belgium or Holland, and taking steamer at Antwerp or Rotterdam. On the French frontier the passport regulations are enforced with a somewhat greater show of vigor, so that but few emigrants from Germany leave by way of Havre, or other ports of France. Most of those leaving covertly go by way of one or the other of the two non-German ports previously mentioned.

Question.—To what, in your opinion, may this sudden increase, or rather revival, of emigration to the United States be attributed?

Reply.—Every season disastrous to agricultural interests gives an impetus to emigration. The grape and grain crops have been poor for three or four years now, causing much distress and want among the lower classes and in the rural populations. These latter, hearing from their friends in America of the, to them, fabulous rates of wages (two or three dollars a day) paid there, and of the good crops and general prosperity, naturally turn thither with longing eyes, and come to look with discontent upon their lot here, where they see no chance of bettering themselves. Do what they will, few if any of them lay aside any money here. The great evil in our rural districts is the tavern, where workingmen pass their evenings drinking beer instead of remaining at home with their wives and families. When their working hours are over they repair to the tavern; when Sunday comes they pass the entire day there. The result is they save nothing, and are no better off at the end of the year than they were at the beginning.

Question.—Is there no remedy for this prevalence of beer shops?

Reply.—Not so long as licenses to keep them are so easily obtained. Were only one or two allowed in each village, the evil would be to a great extent done away with, whereas now almost every other house is a beer saloon, and a laboring man finds it almost impossible, in passing along the street, to resist the temptation of dropping in at one or another of them before he reaches his home.

Question.—Are the peasantry here kept well informed of the condition of affairs in America by those who have previously emigrated thither?

Reply.—Perfectly. Every letter brings glowing accounts of high wages, good crops, and general welfare, and virtually says, "Come over and join us." It is easy to understand how ready a poor man with no prospects before him here is to listen to such an invitation.

Source: "Emigration from the Kingdom of Würtemburg, Report by Consul Catlin, of Stuttgart, on Its Cause, Character, and Extent, and the Laws by Which It is Governed," in *United States Consular Reports,* II, number 6 (April 1881).

The Immigrant and the Community, 1917

In her 1917 book, The Immigrant and the Community, *progressive era reformer Grace Abbott outlined the difficulties facing immigrants coming to America. In this particular chapter, she describes the conditions aboard the ships bringing immigrants across the Atlantic, what happens to them once they land in America, and how they arrive at their final destination. While she notes some improvements in the conditions of transport and arrival, she points out that there is much yet to be done.*

CHAPTER 1: THE JOURNEY OF THE IMMIGRANT

The stories of hardship, danger, and exploitation that the immigrants suffered on their journey to the United States during the early part of the nineteenth century do not make pleasant reading. When the sailing vessel was still the usual means of crossing the Atlantic, travelers were required to furnish their own food and bedding for a journey that usually lasted a month or six weeks, and sometimes days or even weeks longer. Complaints of fearful overcrowding without regard for sex or age, of gross immorality, and of cruelty on the part of officers and crew were made in newspapers as well as before congressional investigating committees.

The death-rate during the crossing was appalling. According to Friedrich Kapp, chairman of the New York Board of Emigration Commissioners, a death-rate of 10 per cent. was not uncommon, while sometimes as many as one third of the entire number died. Often, for example, the Irish famine victims, whose power of resistance had already been shattered, escaped from their stricken country only to die at sea.

Conditions of passenger traffic across the ocean were, however, greatly improved as a result of the statutes regulating steerage conditions passed by the United States in 1819, 1846, 1847, 1855, and 1860, and similar legislation adopted at about the same time by England, Holland, and the German cities. The shortening of the journey by the use of steam and the competition of rival companies also resulted in more comforts for the immigrant.

But the journey is still very far from being what decency demands. In ships which still have what is known as the "old-type steerage" as many as three hundred persons often sleep and live during the crossing in the large dormitories which have rows and rows of doubledeck berths. These berths are six feet long, two feet wide, and are two and one-half feet apart. Into thirty cubic feet of space, therefore, the immigrant must pack himself, his hand luggage, his towels and other toilet necessities, and the eating utensils which the ship furnishes him.

The misery of these conditions is greatly aggravated on bad days when the immigrants cannot use the small open deck allotted to them, when the hatches are closed, and the three hundred steerage passengers spend day and night in their berths, sometimes compelled to sleep in their clothes because the bedding furnished them is insufficient.

A number of excellent reports on steerage condition have been made in recent years which are based on experiences of men and women who traveled as immigrants both to and from Europe. As is to be expected, all the investigators who have made the trip and know these conditions at first hand have agreed that this old-style steerage should be abolished. The law should require more deck space, more and better food, and better sleeping quarters. Now, when immigration is in a sense at a standstill, would seem to be a time to set a new standard, so that with the new immigration, which will probably come after the war, safe, sanitary, and reasonably comfortable quarters can be assured for all those who come. The steerage with its huge and promiscuous dormitories should become a thing of the past, and the four- or six-passenger cabins that are now found in the third-class accommodations of some of the boats should be substituted. There is also general agreement that the treatment of the immigrants by the crew, complaint of which is frequently made by the immigrant women, would be much improved if a government inspector traveled with every boat, or if it were known that he might be on any boat disguised as an immigrant.

In the early nineteenth century, the trials of the immigrant did not end with the fearful journey across the Atlantic, for wherever they landed they were met by a small army of exploiters. Runners who spoke their language piloted them to boarding houses where they were held until their little money was exhausted, or employment agents and bogus railroad representatives robbed and misdirected them. Before the regulation of immigration was taken over by the United States, a number of the States had taken steps to prevent these abuses. New York especially had developed machinery that had for its object the guarding of the newly arrived immigrant from fraud and exploitation, not only at the port of New York but in cities in the interior of the State. The statute enacted by New York in 1848 and improved in 1849 established a strict control of immigrant boarding houses, runners, and passenger and baggage agents, and provided for the appointment of officials who were to give advice to the immigrants and put them on their guard against fraud and imposition. A further act of 1855 required transportation companies to furnish the mayors of different cities with a statement of the rates and charges for conveying immigrants; and one of 1868 gave the Commissioner of Immigration supervision over the sale of passenger tickets to immigrants. In their efforts to protect the immigrants the state authorities in New York cooperated with private agencies, especially the German and Irish societies formed to assist the immigrants of those nationalities who were coming in such large numbers at that time.

The decisions of the United States Supreme Court holding the state head tax on immigrants unconstitutional ended state regulation and compelled the United States Government to take over this work. Since then public attention has in the main been so fastened on the 2 or 3 per cent. of the immigrants who are excluded as undesirable that little thought has been given to the 97 or 98 per cent. of them who are admitted, although self-interest alone should long ago have suggested that special precautions be taken by the United States for the protection of the morals and the health of the immigrant who is permitted to remain.

Much improvement in the methods of inspection, detention, and release of immigrants at the various ports of arrival has been made in recent years. Because of the more efficient organization of the service, immigrants are now treated with humane consideration by government officials; runners from cheap hotels, expressmen, employment agents, and all those who might profit by their ignorance and dependence are generally denied access to them. The moral exploitation of the girl is guarded against by an examination of the persons to whom she is released.

But in contrast to these improvements made at the ports, there is, for the girl destined to Chicago and other interior points, no corresponding protective machinery. She is carefully guarded by the federal authorities until she is placed on the train, but the Government then considers that its responsibility is at an end. It is not considered a matter of national concern whether she is sent to her destination by the most direct or by a long, circuitous route. She may be approached by any one while traveling and persuaded to leave the train. Through her own mistake or intention or the carelessness of railroad officials, she may be put off before she reaches her destination.

Immigrants are no longer sold bogus railroad tickets at the ports as they were before the railroads had official representatives at Castle Garden, but they still do not always get a square deal from the railroads. The steamship companies hold the key to the present situation because relatives and friends who send prepaid tickets from the United States as well as those who purchase their transportation abroad are usually persuaded to buy through tickets to the final destination. This means that most of the immigrants land with an order which shows that they have paid a steamship company for a railroad ticket to their destination. The steamship companies have, therefore, the power of saying whether all those who come on their boats with these orders shall travel over one railroad or whether this patronage shall be more generally distributed. By a "friendly" agreement between the steamship companies and practically all the railroads of the country, a railroad office, maintained under the joint control of the railroads at Ellis Island, is recognized by the steamship companies and each railroad is given its share of the patronage. This agreement is based, however, upon the business ideal of fairness to the competing railroads and not upon consideration of the comfort of the immigrants. In order that all the roads may enjoy their share of the traffic, immigrants are sometimes sent by the most indirect routes to their destinations. For example, those who are coming to Chicago are often sent from New York by boat on the Old Dominion Line to Norfolk, Virginia, and from there on by the Chesapeake and Ohio and connecting lines to Chicago.

In the year ending June 30, 1916, immigrants were sent by nine different routes from New York to Chicago, but nearly three times as many were sent around by Norfolk, Virginia, as by any other single route. Instances less flagrant but which result in much discomfort and sometimes real suffering also occur.

Immigrants constantly arrive in Chicago on their way to the Pacific coast who could make the journey without a single change but are given tickets at Ellis Island which call for several changes en route.

A Norwegian girl arrived in May of 1916 on the *Kristianiafjord* and was going to a town in Iowa. No change should have been necessary after she left Chicago, but she was put on a train that left the city in the afternoon and then put off at a railroad junction in Illinois at nine o'clock at night to wait for another train. She sat up all night in the railroad station and then spent the next day waiting for her train, alone and frightened because she was unable to speak a word of English and did not know how to make herself safe and comfortable. The railroad agent made no effort to protect her from three men who he saw were annoying her. To add to the anxiety that any girl would feel under these circumstances, she was robbed of the little money she had carefully saved because she did not want to reach her relatives quite empty-handed.

Passengers on the immigrant trains frequently expect to arrive in a much shorter time than the indirect route requires, and they do not provide themselves with the additional food which the roundabout journey makes necessary. No arrangement is made for them to purchase food en route, so they sometimes arrive hungry and exhausted. One tired Bohemian mother who came to the office of the Immigrants' Protective League with her four little children had had the difficult task of keeping them quiet when they had had no food for the last thirty-six hours of their trip.

Some improvement has been made recently in the routing of the immigrants, but Mr. Frederic C. Howe, the present Commissioner of Immigration at Ellis Island, who is very much interested in eradicating this and all other abuses, thinks that the evils of the present system cannot be cured until the Immigration Bureau is authorized by Congress to take entire charge of this matter.

This neglect on the part of the United States to take any measure to protect the immigrant after he has been admitted to the United States was especially inexcusable. The Government's experience with the ocean-going steamers gave every reason for anticipating that, in the absence of regulation and inspection, overcrowding, insanitary conditions, and inadequate provisions for the women and girls were sure to be found on the boats which carried immigrants from New York to Fall River, [Massachusetts,] or on the immigrant trains which took so many scores of thousands west each year during the periods of heavy immigration which preceded the war.

The Massachusetts Commission on Immigration, an investigating commission appointed in 1913, received complaints about conditions on the Fall River boats on which, in accordance with an agreement with the transatlantic steamship companies, all the immigrants were then sent from New York to Boston or from Boston to New York.

Investigators for the Commission who were sent to make the trip as immigrants reported shocking conditions: "beds filthy, ventilation incredibly inadequate, and the overcrowding serious." Worse than this, the immigrant men were the butt of coarse and cruel jokes and pranks, and the Polish girls were compelled to defend themselves against the advances of the crew who freely entered the women's dormitory and tried to drag the girls into the crew's quarters.

The steamship company was directly responsible for these conditions, but the United States Government was equally to blame for taking no precautions to insure decency on these boats inasmuch as its experience in regulating ocean travel since 1819 had shown the necessity of official regulation and supervision.

In the hope of securing immediate improvement, the Massachusetts Commission submitted the result of its investigation to the officers of the steamship company, and steps were at once taken by the company to improve conditions. By the time its report was submitted to the legislature, the Commission was therefore able to report that the boats were being rebuilt so as to provide outside ventilation for both men's and women's quarters, more sanitary washrooms, and complete separation of the crew's quarters from the quarters of the immigrant women. Furthermore, an immigrant steward and a stewardess were placed in charge of the immigrant service. All this promised much greater safety and comfort for the immigrant. But the Commission called attention to the fact that if conditions were to be kept decent, legislation regulating these boats and continuous inspection were necessary. The temptation to overcrowd dangerously and in consequence to lower the moral safeguards is great. A permanent commission on immigration was not created in Massachusetts, however, and the United States Government, although it holds that the way in which immigrants travel before they are admitted is a matter of national concern, still takes the position that after they are admitted it is quite indifferent as to what they suffer from carelessness, neglect, or exploitation.

The railroad journey also needs supervision. At present, it is practically impossible to trace the girls who leave New York but who never reach their friends in Chicago. Sometimes it is possible to reach some conclusion as to what became of them, but these conclusions only point to the necessity for safeguarding the journey. For example, two Polish girls, seventeen and twenty-two years of age, whose experience before they started for America had been bounded by the limits of a small farm in Galicia, were coming to their cousins who lived back of the Stockyards in Chicago. Their names and addresses had been sent to the Immigrants' Protective League on one of the lists of unaccompanied girls received regularly from the ports of entry. When one of the visitors of the League called at the house, she found the cousin and the entire household much alarmed because the girls had not arrived. Through inquiries of others who came on the same boat, it was learned that the girls had become acquainted on the way over with a man from Rochester and that he was "looking out for them." The only official information which could be secured was a description of the railroad tickets that the girls held when they left Ellis Island. Investigation by the railroad showed that on that date one ticket had been sold to Rochester and two Chicago tickets had been used only as far as Rochester. The girls had completely disappeared, and there was no official responsibility for their failure to arrive in Chicago.

Sometimes the girls, to whom nothing really serious happens, are for a time in an extremely dangerous position. For example, one seventeen-year-old girl was put off the train at South Chicago by mistake and wandered about for several hours at night. Finally a man offered to take her to her friends. He proved worthy of the confidence she had in his kindly intent, and she was conducted safely to the Northwest Side, many miles from where she had been left. Another girl, nineteen years old, who came in by way of Quebec, became separated from her sister and friends at Detroit. She was taken to a police station for the night and in the morning continued her journey. She arrived in South Chicago without money or the address of her relatives. She was therefore taken to the South Chicago Police Station and after spending a night there was taken to the Women's Annex of the Harrison Street Police Station. The police regarded it as impossible to find the girl's friends, so the matron of the Annex found her work in a downtown hotel. A visitor of the League returning from South Chicago reported great excitement in one neighborhood over the fact that an immigrant girl had been lost at Detroit. This report was connected with the story of the police matron, and a visit to the hotel proved the identity of the girl. Except for this she would have been alone in Chicago, ignorant of our language and the dangers of the city, with no one to turn to in case of sickness or unemployment.

Several girls have told of being approached on the trains and invited by strange men to get off at "some big city and see the town," but they wisely concluded to continue their journey without these gay excursions into the unknown.

More immigrants have been arriving at great distributing centers like Chicago, Pittsburgh, or Cleveland than came to the port of New York during the days when the State of New York was adopting its comprehensive program for the protection of the immigrants. During the early part of the nineteenth century it is said, that "the hapless strangers, ignorant of the customs and laws of the country, often unable to speak the language that would procure police assistance, more liable by reason of their 'outlandish' dress and manners to meet ridicule than sympathy from the masses of native citizens, were browbeaten and fleeced without mercy." This reads like a description of the situation in which those who have been coming in the twentieth century have found themselves on getting off an immigrant train in Chicago.

Any woman can understand the nervous apprehension which the immigrant girl must feel as she comes into one of Chicago's bewildering railroad stations, but very few realize how well grounded her fears are. Eager friends and relatives find it almost impossible to meet the immigrants because immigrant trains are sidetracked for all other kinds of traffic, so that it is extremely difficult to determine just when they will reach Chicago. Merely talking with the girls about their experiences is not so convincing as seeing the actual situation which they meet on leaving a train in Chicago.

On one occasion, for example, the train was due at seven thirty in the morning, but finally arrived shortly after four o'clock in the afternoon. It had been reported as coming at various hours so that three trips were made to the station, although each time inquiry had been made by telephone and assurance given that the train was reported due at once. Several hundred immigrants got off the train when it finally came. Many of them were very young, and one felt their disappointment as they peered eagerly and anxiously for the father or sister or friend they expected to see. Those who were going north or west of Chicago came out the main gate already ticketed by a representative of the transfer company and were taken as American travelers are to another depot without any confusion. But those who were to remain in Chicago were directed into a small immigrant waiting-room which opened on a narrow side street. Here they were hastily sorted into groups and then pushed out the door into the midst of ten or twelve express-men, who were crowding and pushing and quarreling over the division of spoils. In a short time the struggle was over and they had all been loaded into the waiting wagons. By this time it was almost dark and they drove away.

This unsupervised, irresponsible method of disposing of these people explains the plight of the Irish girl who had started on a wagon with a group of other immigrants for the South Side. After going some distance, the expressman discovered she had a North Side address; so, charging her four dollars, he put her off the wagon and left her without any suggestion as to what she should do. It explains, too, the disposition that was made of a Polish girl of seventeen who was taken at three o'clock in the morning to the place where her sister was supposed to live. The address proved to be incorrect, however, and the woman who lived there angrily refused to let her stay until morning. The girl had no money and wept disconsolately when the expressman told her in a language she did not understand that "nobody could find her sister if nobody knew her address and that he wasn't going to take her back to the depot for nothing." The saloon-keeper next door finally offered her a refuge, and she lived with his family behind the saloon three days before her sister, who was making daily trips to the depot, was found.

Not long before this, a girl had been brought to the office of the Immigrants' Protective League who had arrived in Chicago on Sunday afternoon and because her friends could not be found had been taken to the Annex of the Harrison Street Police Station, where, like many immigrant girls, she had received her first initiation into Chicago life. She had the name and address of the girl friend who lived in Chicago and had promised to get her work, written in the front of her prayer-book, and she could not understand that it was incorrect. She tearfully insisted on accompanying the Polish visitor of the Immigrants' Protective League on the search for her friend and grew more and more discouraged as one clue after another was tried and failed. Finally the girl said that her friend worked in a bed-spring factory. Starting out anew on this clue, she was found in the third bed-spring factory they visited. Then the friend explained that one number had been left off the address which the girl had so carefully written in her prayer-book.

Since the summer of 1908, the Immigrants' Protective League has received from the various ports of entry the names and addresses of the unaccompanied women and girls who are coming to Chicago. The plan has been to have these women and girls visited by a representative of the League who was able to speak their language and was prepared to help them in making a beginning of their life in Chicago. Since 1908, 20,304 girls have been thus visited by the League—not all those whose names were received, because the resources of the League were not such as to enable us to do this during the seasons when immigration was heaviest. It was through these visits that we learned that some girls did not reach their relatives and friends, and that an extension of the care and supervision which is given girls at the ports of entry should be extended to the interior. For example, in one year of normal immigration when 3338 girls were visited, 434 of the addresses sent us were obviously incorrect and no visit was attempted. We found some trace of 364 others, but after several visits the attempt to locate them was abandoned, although we had not followed up every possible clue. But 504 could not be located, although every possible effort was made to find them. In thirty-four instances, we found the persons whose names and addresses the girls had given at the port, but they were not expecting the girls and knew nothing of what had become of them. Typical cases of failure to find the girls whose names were received from the ports will illustrate the reasons for anxiety. A Lithuanian girl of eighteen, for example, gave the address of a local steamship agency, and subsequently we learned that she had been called for by a notoriously disreputable man and taken to a rooming house. We traced her to two other addresses but were not able to find her. In another case, investigation of an address which a twenty-year-old Polish girl gave revealed the fact that three years previously a telegram had been received from the port announcing the arrival of a girl who was unknown to any one at the address given. No girl had come. The next year this had happened again. This particular year neither the telegram nor the girl had arrived, and although the name and address was correct no explanation of the use of the name could be given. The evidence which we have had year after year has convinced us that many of these girls whom we were unable to locate undoubtedly reached their relatives and friends; many others, although they did not succeed in doing this, have, by the merest chance, found people who were kind to them and helped them in securing work and in making their connections in Chicago; but from much evidence we are sure that a considerable number cannot be accounted for in these ways.

Whether in cases like those last cited the giving of the incorrect name and address was intentional on the part of the girl, the result of some mistake, or serious deception, federal protection and supervision is the only way of reducing the resulting danger to the community and to the girls. In the administration of the immigration law the girls are required to give the name and address of some one to whom they are coming as a condition of admission. But experience has shown how little protection there is either for the community or for the girl in this requirement.

In 1910 the Immigrants' Protective League was given by the Chicago and Western Indiana Railroad the use of a building across from its depot, and all the immigrants who arrived at that station were sent across to the League's waiting-room. As this was the terminal used by the Erie, the Wabash, and the Grand Trunk railroads, more than three times as many immigrants arrived at this as at any other station in the city. The plan worked out by the League was that its officers, speaking the languages of the immigrants, should arrange to send them to their friends. If possible, relatives were to be reached by telephone; if this could not be done, they were to be sent sometimes with a cab or ex-

pressman, sometimes in charge of a messenger boy, or, when they were able to speak English or had some knowledge of how to get about in a city, they were to be directed or taken to a street car; and finally all those who were peculiarly helpless or who had doubtful or suspicious addresses were to be sent out accompanied by one of the officers of the League. This plan was followed for four years. Cards printed in their native languages were given the immigrants as they left the League's waiting-room, telling them what they were to do in case of an overcharge or neglect on the part of the driver or messenger. The name and address of each immigrant, the number of the expressman or cab driver, the name of the relative or officer or messenger boy to whom each was entrusted, as well as any charges made, were carefully recorded.

As was anticipated, the expressmen and cabmen opposed this supervision as an invasion of the right to exploit the immigrant which they thought the city had guaranteed them when they paid their license of one dollar and a half. With their official-looking badges and caps and their stock of foreign phrases, the drivers and runner would secure the attention of the immigrants and then by a combination of force and persuasion would load them on their wagons and drive off with them. During the first six months of the League's work at this station, although a vigorous fight was kept up with the drivers by night as well as by day, we were able to get hold of only 1903 immigrants, the next year 5204 reached our waiting room and their delivery was arranged for in the orderly manner planned. In 1912 the number increased to 15,537. By 1913 we had convinced the exploiters that we were really in earnest and that prosecutions would be pushed and licenses suspended, and during that year 41,322 immigrants were cared for in the League's waiting room and their delivery arranged for by officers of the League.

Although complaints of abuses were very much less frequent in 1913 than in former years, it was still necessary for us to report thirty-three drivers of express wagon and cabs to the Inspector of Vehicles, who promptly imposed the penalties prescribed by the city ordinance for overcharges and similar offenses.

A very large number of the immigrant trains were found to arrive between midnight and six o'clock in the morning. Some of the immigrants had addresses to which they could not be taken at night, and others having dangerous or doubtful addresses could not be sent out until an investigation had been made in the morning. So the Immigrants' Protective League found it necessary to keep many of the immigrants over night, and some bedrooms were therefore provided on the second floor of its building. In one year ninety-five arrived who had lost their addresses, and it was necessary for us to spend much time in the search for their relatives or friends.

In undertaking this work, the Immigrants' Protective League had two objects: first, to give to the very large numbers arriving at this depot the assistance they so badly needed; and second, and more important, to demonstrate that official supervision was both necessary and practical.

The limitations upon the work of a private organization were evident from the beginning. We lacked the authority necessary to make the protection as effective as it should be made; the space we had was quite inadequate to prevent serious overcrowding of the waiting-room; and it was impossible to secure, through private subscription, funds adequate for doing work which so clearly belonged to the Federal Government. Moreover, the organization did not feel justified in appealing to interested citizens to donate the money for this work when the head tax which the Government levied upon the immigrant was much more than enough to pay for really adequate protection and assistance during the first period of adjustment. The need of the Federal Government's undertaking this work was therefore constantly urged; and in 1913 a law was passed by Congress that authorized the Secretary of Labor to establish immigrant stations at points in the interior, and an appropriation was made for the maintenance of such a station in Chicago. This law also authorized the Secretary to detail immigrant inspectors to travel on immigrant trains.

With some difficulty, a location was found for the station in 1913, and the receiving-room, dormitories, bathrooms, and laundry were furnished and ready for use in January, 1914. The following summer, certain additional officers were assigned to the Chicago Station to undertake this work, but these were later withdrawn.

The delay in the operation of the Station was declared in the Annual Report of the Secretary of Labor for 1911 to be due to the fact that the immigrants were required to pay a local transfer agency for transportation from the railway stations to the Immigrant Station. This difficulty was removed during the summer of 1914 through the agreement by all the railroads carrying Chicago-bound immigrants to transfer them from the terminal station to the Immigrant Station without extra charge. But this agreement has not been utilized by the Federal Government except when the immigrant on his arrival at Ellis Island asks to be transferred to the Federal Station in Chicago.

The large receiving-room, after being locked for year, is now being used for the much-needed labor exchange work that the Department of Labor has recently undertaken. But the dormitories, bathrooms, laundry rooms, etc., have never been used. The Government has been paying rent for this unused space for more than two years. This illustration of the way in which an administrative department of the Government can refuse to carry out the laws passed by Congress should be interesting to students of political science.

That the duty of protecting and caring for the immigrant on his journey belongs to the federal rather than the local government is obvious. The former controls the admission of immigrants and is informed as to the number arriving. Protection and supervision of release is given the immigrants who arrive at the ports of entry, and it is logical, therefore, to ask an extension of this care to the interior. The protection needed by immigrants arriving in Chicago is also needed in Pittsburgh, Cleveland, St. Louis, and other important centers of arrival and distribution. Official inspectors, both men and women, should travel on immigrant trains to insure considerate treatment on the part of the railroads and to protect the immigrant from the organized exploitation which develops when there is no official supervision.

The first federal statute that provided for regulation of immigration (1882), as well as the statutes of 1903 and 1907, authorized the Commissioner-General of Immigration "to establish such regulations, not inconsistent with law, as he shall deem best calculated for protecting the United States and the immigrant *from fraud and loss,*" and gave him authority to enter into contracts for the support and relief of such immigrants as may fall into distress or need public aid. These provisions were not made without a quite definite understanding of the need for the protection which was here authorized. It may be assumed that the provision in the federal statutes recognizing the duty of the Government to guard the immigrant from fraud and loss was suggested by the similar functions of the New York officials. In view of this, it would seem that a moral duty rests on the Federal Government to give proper consideration to the protective aspect of immigrant control.

National and even international attention has been drawn to the prosecution of so-called "white slavers." Important as this work is, it should not be the only form of control attempted. For in prosecutions we must, of necessity, wait until the girl has been ruined, and no fine or penitentiary sentence inflicted upon the man or woman responsible for her downfall can undo for her or for society the damage that has been wrought. Some constructive, preventive measures should be undertaken as well. First among these, perhaps, should be the guarantee to every immigrant girl of a safe arrival at her destination.

In his annual report for 1915, the Commissioner-General of Immigration calls attention to the fact that "since the law providing for the collection of a head tax from arriving immigrants has been in force, up to the end of this fiscal year (1915) there has been collected over $9,000,000 in excess of the expenditures for the immigration service." The Immigration Bill which has jus been passed over the President's veto increases this head tax for adults from four to eight dollars. And so it is probable that in the future larger sums will be collected. The obligation of regarding the money collected in this way as a trust fund to be used in behalf of the immigrant cannot be too strongly insisted upon.

The first evidence of the "new nationalism" should be in the nation's affording the kind of protection which shall give to the immigrant such ideas of America as we should like him to have when he begins his life among us. Only too frequently, under present conditions, the idealistic picture of America which he brings with him is destroyed immediately on his arrival, and instead he begins with a knowledge of some of the ugliest and meanest aspects of our life.

Source: Grace Abbott. *The Immigrant and the Community.* New York: The Century Company, 1917.

B. Letters

Revolutionary War Correspondence of George Washington, 1775–1778

*I*n the following letters written by George Washington during the Revolutionary War, the commanding general of the Continental Army expresses his belief that native-born Americans should be given priority in recruitment, sentry duty, and other critical military situations. In addition, Washington suspected that foreign-born troops were more likely to desert.

GENERAL ORDER TO THE ARMY, JULY 7, 1775:

The General has great Reason (to be); and is highly displeased, with the Negligence and Inattention of those Officers, who have placed as Centries, at the outposts, Men with whose Characters they are not acquainted. He therefore orders, that for the future, no Man shall be appointed to those important Stations, who is not a Native of this Country, or has a Wife, or Family in it, to whom he is known to be attached. This order is to be consider'd as a standing one and the Officers are to pay obedience to it at their peril.

LETTER TO COL. ALEXANDER SPOTSWOOD, MORRISTOWN, NEW JERSEY, APRIL 30, 1777:

I want to form a company for my guard. In doing this I wish to be extremely cautious, because it is more than probable, that, in the course of the campaign, my baggage, papers, and other matters of great public import, may be committed to the sole care of these men. This being premised, in order to impress you with proper attention in the choice, I have to request, that you will immediately furnish me with four men of your regiments, . . . I think it (*fidelity*) most likely to be found in those, who have family connexions in the country. You will therefore send me none but natives, and men of some property, if you have them.

LETTER TO COLONEL BAYLOR, JUNE 19, 1777:

You should be extremely cautious in your enquiries into the character of those who are not natives who offer to enlist. Desertions among men of that class have been so frequent that unless you find 'em on examination to be of good & unsuspicious conduct, they should not be taken by any means. Otherwise, most probably, they will deceive you—add no strength to our arms, but much expence to the Public account and upon first opportunity will join the Enemy.

LETTER TO HENRY LAURENS, NEAR WHITE PLAINS, NEW YORK, JULY 24, 1778:

I will further add, that we have already a full proportion of foreign officers in our general councils; and, should their number be increased, it may happen upon many occasions, that their voices may be equal if not exceed the rest. I trust you think me so much a citizen of the world, as to believe I am not easily warped or led away by attachments merely local or American; yet I confess I am not entirely without 'em, nor does it appear to me that they are unwarrantable, if confined within proper limits. Fewer promotions in the foreign line would have been productive of more harmony, and made our warfare more agreeable to all parties. The frequency of them is the source of jealousy and of disunion.

Source: Worthington Chauncey Ford, ed. *The Writings of George Washington.* 1889.

Letters from an American Farmer, 1782

In 1782, Michel Crèvecoeur, a French immigrant to America, published his Letters from an American Farmer *in London, under the pen name J. Hector St. John de Crèvecoeur. A relatively wealthy man who once served as France's consul in New York City, Crèvecoeur was one of the first to write about the ways in which America transformed immmigrants by, among other things, blurring religious differences. His book also lauded the new country's potential as a place where the poor of Europe could make their fortunes.*

I wish I could be acquainted with the feelings and thoughts which must agitate the heart and present themselves to the mind of an enlightened Englishman when he first lands on this continent. He must greatly rejoice that he lived at a time to see this fair country discovered and settled; he must necessarily feel a share of national pride, when he views the chain of settlements which embellishes these extended shores. When he says to himself, this is the work of my countrymen, who, when convulsed by factions, afflicted by a variety of miseries and wants, restless and impatient, took refuge here. They brought along with them their national genius, to which they principally owe what liberty they enjoy, and what substance they possess. Here he sees the industry of his native country displayed in a new manner, and traces in their works the embryos of all the arts, sciences, and ingenuity which flourish in Europe. Here he beholds fair cities, substantial villages, extensive fields, an immense country filled with decent houses, good roads, orchards, meadows, and bridges, where an hundred years ago all was wild, woody, and uncultivated!

What a train of pleasing ideas this fair spectacle must suggest; it is a prospect which must inspire a good citizen with the most heartfelt pleasure. The difficulty consists in the manner of viewing so extensive a scene. He is arrived on a new continent; a modern society offers itself to his contemplation, different from what he had hitherto seen. It is not composed, as in Europe, of great lords who possess everything, and of a herd of people who have nothing. Here are no aristocratical families, no courts, no kings, no bishops, no ecclesiastical dominion, no invisible power giving to a few a very visible one; no great manufacturers employing thousands, no great refinements of luxury. The rich and the poor are not so far removed from each other as they are in Europe. Some few towns excepted, we are all tillers of the earth, from Nova Scotia to West Florida. We are a people of cultivators, scattered over an immense territory, communicating with each other by means of good roads and navigable rivers, united by the silken bands of mild government, all respecting the laws, without dreading their power, because they are equitable. We are all animated with the spirit of an industry which is unfettered and unrestrained, because each person works for himself. . . .

We have no princes, for whom we toil, starve, and bleed: we are the most perfect society now existing in the world. Here man is free as he ought to be; nor is this pleasing equality so transitory as many others are. Many ages will not see the shores of our great lakes replenished with inland nations, nor the unknown bounds of North America entirely peopled. Who can tell how far it extends? Who can tell the millions of men whom it will feed and contain? for no European foot has as yet travelled half the extent of this mighty continent!

The next wish of this traveller will be to know whence came all these people? They are a mixture of English, Scotch, Irish, French, Dutch, Germans, and Swedes. From this promiscuous breed, that race now called Americans have arisen. The eastern provinces must indeed be excepted, as being the unmixed descendants of Englishmen. I have heard many wish that they had been more intermixed also: for my part, I am no wisher, and think it much better as it has happened. They exhibit a most conspicuous figure in this great and variegated picture; they too enter for a great share in the pleasing perspective displayed in these thirteen provinces. . . .

In this great American asylum, the poor of Europe have by some means met together, and in consequence of various causes; to what purpose should they ask one another what countrymen they are? Alas, two thirds of them had no country. Can a wretch who wanders about, who works and starves, whose life is a continual scene of sore affliction or pinching penury; can that man call England or any other kingdom his country? A country that had no bread for him, whose fields procured him no harvest, who met with nothing but the frowns of the rich, the severity of the laws, with jails and punishments; who owned not a single foot of the extensive surface of this planet? No! urged by a variety of motives, here they came. Everything has tended to regenerate them; new laws, a new mode of living, a new social system; here they are become men; in Europe they were as so many useless plants, wanting vegetative mould, and refreshing showers; they withered, and were mowed down by want, hunger, and war; but now by the power of transplantation, like all other plants they have taken root and flourished! Formerly they were not numbered in any civil lists of their country, except in those of the poor; here they rank as citizens. By what invisible power has this surprising metamorphosis been performed? By that of the laws and that of their industry. The laws, the indulgent laws protect them as they arrive, stamping on them the symbol of adoption; they receive ample rewards for their labours; these accumulated rewards procure them lands; those lands confer on them the title of freeman, and to that title every benefit is affixed which men can possibly require. This is the great operation daily performed by our laws. . . .

What attachment can a poor European emigrant have for a country where he had nothing? The knowledge of the language, the love of a few kindred as poor as himself, were the only cords that tied him: his country is now that which gives him land, bread, protection, and consequence: *Ubi panis ibi patria*, is the motto of all emigrants. What then is the American, this new man? He is either an European, or the descendant of an European, hence that strange mixture of blood, which you will find in no other country. I could point out to you a family whose grandfather was an Englishman, whose wife was Dutch, whose son married a French woman, and whose present four sons have now four wives of different nations. *He* is an American, who leaving behind him all his ancient prejudices and manners, receives new ones from the new mode of life he has embraced, the new government he obeys, and the new rank he holds. He becomes an American by being received in the broad lap of our great *Alma Mater*. Here individuals of all nations are melted into a new race of men, whose labours and posterity will one day cause great changes in the world. Americans are the western pilgrims, who are carrying along with them that great mass of arts, sciences, vigour, and industry which began long since in the east; they will finish the great circle. The Americans were once scattered all over Europe; here they are incorporated into one of the finest systems of population which has ever appeared, and which will hereafter become distinct by the power of the different climates they inhabit. The American ought therefore to love this country much better than that wherein either he or his forefathers were born. Here the rewards of his industry follow with equal steps the progress of his labour; his labour is founded on the basis of nature, self-interest; can it want a stronger allurement? Wives and children, who before in vain demanded of him a morsel of bread, now, fat and frolicksome,

gladly help their father to clear those fields whence exuberant crops are to arise to feed and to clothe them all; without any part being claimed, either by a despotic prince, a rich abbot, or a mighty lord. Here religion demands but little of him; a small voluntary salary to the minister, and gratitude to God; can he refuse these? The American is a new man, who acts upon new principles; he must therefore entertain new ideas, and form new opinions. From involuntary idleness, servile dependence, penury, and useless labour, he has passed to toils of a very different nature, rewarded by ample subsistence. This is an American. . . .

As I have endeavoured to shew you how Europeans become Americans; it may not be disagreeable to shew you likewise how the various Christian sects introduced, wear out, and how religious indifference becomes prevalent. When any considerable number of a particular sect happen to dwell contiguous to each other, they immediately erect a temple, and there worship the Divinity agreeably to their own peculiar ideas. Nobody disturbs them. If any new sect springs up in Europe, it may happen that many of its professors will come and settle in America. As they bring their zeal with them, they are at liberty to make proselytes if they can, and to build a meeting and to follow the dictates of their consciences; for neither the government nor any other power interferes. If they are peaceable subjects, and are industrious, what is it to their neighbours how and in what manner they think fit to address their prayers to the Supreme Being? But if the sectaries are not settled close together, if they are mixed with other denominations, their zeal will cool for want of fuel, and will be extinguished in a little time. Then the Americans become as to religion, what they are as to country, allied to all. In them the name of Englishman, Frenchman, and European is lost, and in like manner, the strict modes of Christianity as practised in Europe are lost also. This effect will extend itself still farther hereafter, and though this may appear to you as a strange idea, yet it is a very true one. I shall be able perhaps hereafter to explain myself better, in the meanwhile, let the following example serve as my first justification.

Let us suppose you and I to be travelling; we observe that in this house, to the right, lives a Catholic, who prays to God as he has been taught, and believes in transubstantiation; he works and raises wheat, he has a large family of children, all hale and robust; his belief, his prayers offend nobody. About one mile farther on the same road, his next neighbour may be a good honest plodding German Lutheran, who addresses himself to the same God, the God of all, agreeably to the modes he has been educated in, and believes in consubstantiation; by so doing he scandalizes nobody; he also works in his fields, embellishes the earth, clears swamps, etc. What has the world to do with his Lutheran principles? He persecutes nobody, and nobody persecutes him, he visits his neighbours, and his neighbours visit him. Next to him lives a seceder, the most enthusiastic of all sectaries; his zeal is hot and fiery, but separated as he is from others of the same complexion, he has no congregation of his own to resort to, where he might cabal and mingle religious pride with worldly obstinacy. He likewise raises good crops, his house is handsomely painted, his orchard is one of the fairest in the neighborhood. How does it concern the welfare of the country, or of the province at large, what this man's religious sentiments are, or whether he has any at all? He is a good farmer, he is a sober, peaceable, good citizen: William Penn himself would not wish for more. This is the visible character, the invisible one is only guessed at and is nobody's business. Next again lives a Low Dutchman, who implicitly believes the rules laid down by the synod of Dort. He conceives no other idea of a clergyman than that of an hired man; if he does his work well he will pay him the stipulated sum; if not he will dismiss him, and do without his sermons, and let his church be shut up for years. But notwithstanding this coarse idea, you will find his house and farm to be the neatest in all the country; and you will judge by his wagon and fat horses, that he thinks more of the affairs of this world than of those of the next. He is sober and laborious, therefore he is all he ought to be as to the affairs of this life, as for those of the next, he must trust to the great Creator. Each of these people instruct their children as well as they can, but these instructions are feeble compared to those which are given to the youth of the poorest class in Europe. Their children will therefore grow up less zealous and more indifferent in matters of religion than their parents. The foolish vanity or rather the fury of making proselytes, is unknown here; they have no time, the seasons call for all their attention, and thus in a few years, this mixed neighbourhood will exhibit a strange religious medley, that will be neither pure Catholicism nor pure Calvinism. A very perceptible indifference even in the first generation, will become apparent; and it may happen that the daughter of the Catholic will marry the son of the seceder, and settle by themselves at a distance from their parents. What religious education will they give their children? A very imperfect one. If there happens to be in the neighbourhood any place of worship, we will suppose a Quaker's meeting; rather than not shew their fine clothes, they will go to it, and some of them may perhaps attach themselves to that society. Others will remain in a perfect state of indifference; the children of these zealous parents will not be able to tell what their religious principles are, and their grandchildren still less. The neighbourhood of a place of worship generally leads them to it, and the action of going thither, is the strongest evidence they can give of their attachment to any sect.

Thus all sects are mixed as well as all nations; thus religious indifference is imperceptibly disseminated from one end of the continent to the other; which is at present one of the strongest characteristics of the Americans. Where this will reach no one can tell, perhaps it may leave a vacuum fit to receive other systems. Persecution, religious pride, the love of contradiction, are the food of what the world commonly calls religion. These motives have ceased here: zeal in Europe is confined; here it evaporates in the great distance it has to travel; there it is a grain of powder inclosed, here it burns away in the open air, and consumes without effect.

Europe contains hardly any other distinctions but lords and tenants; this fair country alone is settled by freeholders, the possessors of the soil they cultivate, members of the government they obey, and the framers of their own laws, by means of their representatives. This is a thought which you have taught me to cherish; our distance from Europe, far from diminishing, rather adds to our usefulness and consequence as men and subjects. Had our forefathers remained there, they would only have crowded it, and perhaps prolonged those convulsions which had shook . . . it so long. . . . Colonists are entitled to the consideration due to the most useful subjects; a hundred families barely existing in some parts of Scotland will here, in six years, cause an annual exportation of 10,000 bushels of wheat: 100 bushels being but a common quantity for an industrious family to sell, if they cultivate good land. It is here, then, that the idle may be employed, the useless become useful, and the poor become rich; but by riches I do not mean gold and silver, we have but little of those metals; I mean a better sort of wealth, cleared lands, cattle, good houses, good clothes, and an increase of people to enjoy them. There is no wonder that this country has so many charms, and presents to Europeans so many temptations to remain in it. A traveller in Europe becomes a stranger as soon as he quits his own kingdom; but it is otherwise here. We know, properly speaking, no strangers; this is every person's country; the variety of our soils, situations, climates, governments, and produce, hath something which must please every body. No sooner does an European arrive, no matter of what condition, than his eyes are opened upon the fair prospect; he hears his language spoke, he retraces many of his own country manners, he perpetually hears the names of families and towns with which he is acquainted; he sees happiness and prosperity in all places disseminated; he meets with hospitality, kindness, and plenty every where; he beholds hardly any poor, he seldom hears of punishments and executions, and he wonders at the elegance of our towns, those miracles of industry and freedom. He cannot admire enough our rural districts, our convenient roads, good taverns, and our many accommodations; he involuntarily loves a country where every thing is so lovely. When in England, he was a mere Englishman; here he stands on a larger portion of the globe, not less than its fourth part, and may see the productions of the north, in iron and naval stores; the provisions of Ireland, the grain of Egypt, the indigo, the rice of China. He does not find, as in Europe, a crowded society, where every place is overstocked; he does not feel that perpetual collision of parties, that difficulty of beginning, that contention which oversets so many. There is room for every body, in America. Has he any particular talent, or industry? he exerts it in order to procure a livelihood, and it succeeds. Is he a merchant? the avenues of trade are infinite. Is he eminent in any respect? he will be employed and respected. Does he love a country life? pleasant farms present themselves; he may purchase what he wants, and thereby become an American farmer. Is he a laborer, sober and industrious? he need not go many miles, nor receive many informations before he will be hired, well fed at the table of his employer, and paid four or five times more than he can get in Europe. Does he want uncultivated lands? thousands of acres present themselves, which he may purchase cheap. Whatever be his talents or inclinations, if they are moderate, he may satisfy them. I do not mean that every one who comes will grow rich in a little time; no, but he may procure an easy, decent maintenance, by his industry. Instead of starving, he will be fed; instead of being idle, he will have employment; and these are riches enough for such men as come over here. The rich stay in Europe, it is only the middling and the poor that emigrate. Would you wish to travel in independent idleness, from north to south, you will find easy access, and the most cheerful reception at every house; society without ostentation, good cheer without pride, and every decent diversion which the country affords, with little expence. It is no wonder that the European who has lived here a few years is desirous to remain; Europe with all its pomp is not to be compared to this continent, for men of middle stations, or labourers.

An European, when he first arrives, seems limited in his intentions, as well as in his views; but he very suddenly alters his scale; two hundred miles formerly appeared a very great distance, it is now but a trifle; he no sooner breathes our air than he forms schemes, and embarks in designs he never would have thought of in his own country. There the plentitude of society confines many useful ideas, and often extinguishes the most laudable schemes which here ripen into maturity. Thus Europeans become Americans.

But how is this accomplished in that crowd of low, indigent people, who flock here every year from all parts of Europe? I will tell you; they no sooner arrive than they immediately feel the good effects of that plenty of provisions we possess; they fare on our best food, and are kindly entertained; their talents, character, and peculiar industry are immediately inquired into; they find countrymen every where disseminated, let them come from whatever part of Europe. Let me select one as an epitome of the rest. He is hired, he goes to work, and works moderately; instead of being employed by a haughty person, he finds himself with his equal, placed at the substantial table of the farmer, or else at an inferior one as good; his wages are high, his bed is not like that bed of sorrow on which he used to lie; if he behaves with propriety, and is faithful, he is caressed, and becomes, as it were, a member of the family. He begins to feel the effects of a sort of resurrection; hitherto he had not lived, but simply vegetated; he now feels himself a man, because he is treated as such; the laws of his own country had overlooked him in his insignificancy; the laws of this cover him with their mantle. Judge what an alteration there must arise in the mind and thoughts of this man; he begins to forget his former servitude and dependence, his heart involuntarily swells and glows; this first swell inspires him with those new thoughts which constitute an American.

What love can he entertain for a country where his existence was a burthen to him; if he is a generous good man, the love of his new adoptive parent will sink deep into his heart. He looks around, and sees many a prosperous person, who but a few years before was as poor as himself. This

encourages him much, he begins to form some little scheme, the first, alas, he ever formed in his life. If he is wise he thus spends two or three years, in which time he acquires knowledge, the use of tools, the modes of working the lands, felling trees, etc. This prepares the foundation of a good name, the most useful acquisition he can make. He is encouraged, he has gained friends; he is advised and directed, he feels bold, he purchases some land; he gives all the money he has brought over, as well as what he has earned, and trusts to the God of harvests for the discharge of the rest. His good name procures him credit. He is now possessed of the deed, conveying to him and his posterity the fee simple and absolute property of two hundred acres of land, situated on such a river. What an epoch in this man's life! He is become a freeholder, from perhaps a German boor—he is now an American, a Pennsylvanian, an English subject. He is naturalized, his name is enrolled with those of the other citizens of the province. Instead of being a vagrant, he has a place of residence; he is called the inhabitant of such a county, or of such a district, and for the first time in his life counts for something; for hitherto he has been a cypher. I only repeat what I have heard many say, and no wonder their hearts should glow, and be agitated with a multitude of feelings, not easy to describe. From nothing to start into being; from a servant to the rank of master; from being the slave of some despotic prince, to become a free man, invested with lands, to which every municipal blessing is annexed!

What a change indeed! It is in consequence of that change that he becomes an American. . . . Ye poor Europeans, ye, who sweat, and work for the great—ye, who are obliged to give so many sheaves to the church, so many to your lords, so many to your government, and have hardly any left for yourselves—ye, who are held in less estimation than favourite hunters or useless lap-dogs—ye, who only breathe the air of nature, because it cannot be withheld from you; it is here that ye can conceive the possibility of those feelings I have been describing; it is here the laws of naturalization invite every one to partake of our great labours and felicity, to till unrented, untaxed lands! . . . It is not every emigrant who succeeds; no, it is only the sober, the honest, and industrious: happy those to whom this transition has served as a powerful spur to labour, to prosperity, and to the good establishment of children, born in the days of their poverty, and who had no other portion to expect but the rags of their parents, had it not been for their happy emigration. Others again have been led astray by this enchanting scene; . . . they have mouldered away their time in inactivity, misinformed husbandry, and ineffectual endeavours. How much wiser, in general, the honest Germans than almost all other Europeans; they hire themselves to some of their wealthy landsmen, and in that apprenticeship learn every thing that is necessary . . . and by dint of sobriety, rigid parsimony, and the most persevering industry, they commonly succeed. Their astonishment at their first arrival from Germany is very great—it is to them a dream; the contrast must be powerful indeed; they observe their countrymen flourishing in every place; they travel through whole counties where not a word of English is spoken; and in the names and the language of the people, they retrace Germany. They have been an useful acquisition to this continent, and to Pennsylvania in particular; to them it owes some share of its prosperity: to their mechanical knowledge and patience, it owes the finest mills in all America, the best teams of horses, and many other advantages. The recollection of their former poverty and slavery never quits them as long as they live.

The Scotch and the Irish might have lived in their own country perhaps as poor, but enjoying more civil advantages, the effects of their new situation do not strike them so forcibly, nor has it so lasting an effect. From whence the difference arises I know not, but out of twelve families of emigrants of each country, generally seven Scotch will succeed, nine German, and four Irish. The Scotch are frugal and laborious, but their wives cannot work so hard as German women, who, on the contrary, vie with their husbands, and often share with them the most severe toils of the field, which they understand better. They have therefore nothing to struggle against but the common casualties of nature. The Irish do not prosper so well; they love to drink and to quarrel; they are litigious, and soon take to the gun, which is the ruin of every thing; they seem beside to labour under a greater degree of ignorance in husbandry than the others; perhaps it is that their industry had less scope, and was less exercised at home.... There is no tracing observations of this kind, without making at the same time very great allowances, as there are every where to be found a great many exceptions. The Irish themselves, from different parts of that kingdom, are very different. It is difficult to account for this surprising locality; one would think on so small an island an Irishman must be an Irishman; yet it is not so, they are different in their aptitude to, and in their love of, labour.

The Scotch, on the contrary, are all industrious and saving; they want nothing more than a field to exert themselves in, and they are commonly sure of succeeding. The only difficulty they labour under is that technical American knowledge which requires some time to obtain; it is not easy for those who seldom saw a tree, to conceive how it is to be felled, cut up, and split into rails and posts....

Agreeable to the account which several Scotchmen have given me of the north of Britain, of the Orkneys, and the Hebride Islands, they seem, on many accounts, to be unfit for the habitation of men; they appear to be calculated only for great sheep pastures. Who then can blame the inhabitants of these countries for transporting themselves hither? This great continent must in time absorb the poorest part of Europe; and this will happen in proportion as it becomes better known, and as war, taxation, oppression, and misery increase there. The Hebrides appear to be fit only for the residence of malefactors, and it would be much better to send felons there than either to Virginia or Maryland. What a strange compliment has our mother country paid to two of the finest provinces in America! England has entertained in that respect very mistaken ideas; what was intended as a punishment is become the good fortune of several; many of those who have been transported as felons, are now rich, and strangers to the stings of those wants that urged them to violations of the law: they are become industrious, exemplary, and useful citizens.... This is no place of punishment; were I a poor hopeless, breadless Englishman, and not restrained by the power of shame, I should be very thankful for the passage. It is of very little importance how and in what manner an indigent man arrives; for if he is but sober, honest, and industrious, he has nothing more to ask of heaven. Let him go to work, he will have opportunities enough to earn a comfortable support, and even the means of procuring some land; which ought to be the utmost wish of every person who has health and hands to work....

After a foreigner from any part of Europe is arrived, and become a citizen; let him devoutly listen to the voice of our great parent, which says to him, "Welcome to my shores, distressed European; bless the hour in which thou didst see my verdant fields, my fair navigable rivers, and my green mountains! If thou wilt work, I have bread for thee; if thou wilt be honest, sober, and industrious, I have greater rewards to confer on thee—ease and independence. I will give thee fields to feed and clothe thee; a comfortable fire-side to sit by, and tell thy children by what means thou hast prospered; and a decent bed to repose on. I shall endow thee beside with the immunities of a freeman. If thou wilt carefully educate thy children, teach them gratitude to God, and reverence to that government, that philanthropic government, which has collected here so many men and made them happy.... Go thou and work and till; thou shalt prosper, provided thou be just, grateful, and industrious."

Source: J. Hector St. John de Crèvecoeur. *Letters from an American Farmer.* London: Thomas Davies, 1782.

Letters from Illinois, 1818

M̲orris Birkbeck, an English immigrant to America, was a wealthy farmer who helped found a settlement for Englishmen in the wilds of Illinois in 1817. In his Letters from Illinois, *first published in Philadelphia in 1818, Birkbeck waxes enthusiastic about the possibilities for immigrant farmers in what was then the American West. Like other promoters, it was in Birkbeck's financial interest to lure others to his settlement. For, as well as being a farmer, Birkbeck was also a land speculator.*

November 24, 1817. I have now been an inhabitant of this place more than four months; my plans of future life have acquired some consistency; I have chosen a situation, purchased an estate, determined on the position of my house, and have, in short, become so familiar with the circumstances in which I have thus deliberately placed myself and family, that I feel qualified to give you a cool account of my experiences, of the effect of this great change of condition on my mind, now that I may be supposed but little under the influence of the charm of novelty, or the stimulus of pursuit. . . .

I have not for a moment felt despondency, scarcely discouragement, in this happy country, this land of hope! Life here is only *too* valuable, from the wonderful efficiency of every well-directed effort. Such is the field of delightful action lying before me, that I am ready to regret the years wasted in the support of taxes and pauperism, and to grieve that I am growing old now, that a really useful career seems just beginning. I am happier, much happier, in my prospects, I feel that I am doing well for my family: and the privations I anticipated seem to vanish before us.

We shall have some English friends next summer; and a welcome they shall experience. But if not one had the resolution to follow the track we have smoothed before them, we should never wish to retrace it, except perhaps as travellers. As to what are called the comforts of life, I feel that they are much more easily obtainable here than they have ever been to me; and for those who are to succeed me, I look forward with a pleasure which can only be understood by one who has felt the anxieties of an English father.

I expect to see around me in prosperity many of my old neighbors, whose hard fare has often embittered my own enjoyments. Three of them have already made the effort, and succeeded in getting out to us. This delights us, but we have by no means depended on it; joyful as we are at the prospect of giving them an asylum.

Two more are waiting at Philadelphia for an invitation which is now on its way. . . .

I have just read a statement of five hundred emigrants per week passing through Albany westward, counting from the first of September. This occurred on *one* road.

I sat down to write to you under an impression that you would be deterred, and might be prevented from following us, by difficulties, some real and serious, others not so; and I thought it might be useful to you, as I knew it would be pleasant, to find that I am satisfied as to my own undertaking. It is for this reason that you are treated with so much about myself. I wish I could put you in possession of *all* my mind, my entire sentiments, my daily and hourly feeling of contentment: not that *you* would be warranted thereby to place yourself and family along side of mine. . . .

November 30, 1817. . . . I have secured a considerable tract of land, more than I have any intention of holding, that I may be able to accommodate some of our English friends. Our soil appears to be rich, a fine black mould, inclining to sand, from one to three or four feet deep, lying on sandstone or clayey loam; so easy of tillage as to reduce the expense of cultivation below that of the land I have been accustomed to in England, notwithstanding the high rates of human labour. The wear of plough-irons is so trifling, that it is a thing of course to sharpen them in the spring once for the whole year. Our main object will be live stock, cattle, and hogs, for which there is a sure market at a good profit. Twopence a pound you will think too low a price to include a profit; but remember, we are not called upon, after receiving our money for produce, to refund a portion of it for rent, another portion for tithe, a third for poor's rates, and a fourth for taxes; which latter are here so light, as scarcely to be brought into the nicest calculation. You will consider also, that money goes a great deal farther here, so that a less profit would suffice. The fact is, however, that the profits on capital employed any way in this country are marvellous; in the case of live stock the outgoings are so small, that the receipts are nearly all clear.

The idea of exhausting the soil by cropping, so as to render manure necessary, has not yet entered into the estimates of the western cultivator. Manure has been often known to accumulate until the farmers have removed their yards and buildings out of the way of the nuisance. They have no notion of making a return to the land, and as yet there seems no bounds to its fertility.

For about half the capital that is required for the mere cultivation of our worn-out soils in England, a man may establish as a proprietor here, with every comfort belonging to a plain and reasonable mode of living, and with a certainty of establishing his children as well or better than himself—such an approach to certainty at least as would render anxiety on that score unpardonable.

Land being obtained so easily, I had a fancy to occupy here just as many acres as I did at Wanborough; and I have added 160 of timbered land to the 1,440 I at first concluded to farm. I shall build and furnish as good a house as the one I left, with suitable outbuildings, garden, orchard, &c.,

make 5,000 rods of fence, chiefly bank and ditch, provide implements, build a mill, support the expenses of housekeeping, and labour until we obtain returns, and pay the entire purchase money of the estate, for less than half the capital employed on Wanborough farm. At the end of fourteen years, instead of an expiring lease, I or my heirs will probably see an increase in the value of the land, equal to fifteen or twenty times the original purchase.

In the interval my family will have lived handsomely on the produce, and have plenty to spare, should any of them require a separate establishment on farms of their own.

Thus I see no obstruction to my realising all I wished for on taking leave of Old England. To me, whose circumstances were comparatively easy, the change is highly advantageous; but to labouring people, to mechanics, to people in general who are in difficulties, this country affords so many sure roads to independence and comfort, that it is lamentable that any, who have the means of making their escape, should be prevented by the misrepresentations of others, or their own timidity . . .

Source: Morris Birkbeck. *Letters from Illinois*. Philadelphia, 1818.

How an Emigrant May Succeed in the United States, 1818

The following document includes extracts from a letter addressed to English persons considering emigration to the United States. The author Clements Burleigh, who had lived in America for over thirty years, describes the practical things an immigrant ought to consider before immigrating, as well as the things an immigrant is likely to encounter upon arrival in America in the early nineteenth century.

I will now proceed to give some instructions to my own countrymen, who may hereafter emigrate, to the United States of America. I shall first take up the poor mechanic and the day labourer, next the farmer who may go there with money to purchase land, and next the merchant.

I will take the liberty, as an introduction, to point out some stumbling blocks that have been in the way of many emigrants to this country. We conceive the vessel coming to anchor, and the passengers preparing for going ashore. On setting their feet on land, they look about them, see fine houses, gardens, and orchards, the streets crowded with well-dressed people, every one pursuing his own business. Well, the question now is, where shall I go? I meet a person passing, and address myself to him, requesting him to inform me where I can have accommodations for some short time. He will point out a house which he thinks may answer my appearance, &c. I get my goods conveyed to this house. The landlord and his family receive me as a foreigner, and so long as I have cash will have a watchful eye over me, and treat me according to what money I spend with them. In the meantime, on the arrival of an Irish ship, a crowd of poor Irish, who have been in that country for a number of years, are always fond of meeting their countrymen on landing, and of encouraging them to take a share of grog or porter, &c. The feelings of the open-hearted Irishman are alive to the invitation, and some days are spent in this way, in the company of men who are a disgrace to the country they came from, and who are utterly incapable to procure themselves work, much less the poor emigrant. I warn emigrants, therefore, to be upon their guard.

The plan therefore, which I would recommend, is that upon landing, as soon as convenient, they should divest themselves of any heavy luggage, such as chests or boxes; and in the meantime, if they are deficient of money to carry them to the inland parts of the country, stop some time, and if they can get work apply to it, and use what they earn with economy, and keep clear of all idle company, and also be particular in keeping clear of a certain description of their own countrymen. When they have acquired as much money as may help to bear their expenses, let them put their bundles on board one of the waggons, loaded with merchandize for the Western country. By being active and obliging to the carrier on the way, he will charge little or nothing on your arrival at Pittsburg, or Greensburg, or any other town in the western parts of Pennsylvania. You then take your property from aboard of the waggon, if it suits, and make inquiry for labour. The best plan would be to engage a year with some opulent farmer, for which period of service, you will receive $100, and during that time be found in meat, drink, washing, and lodging. This will be an apprenticeship that will teach you the work of the country, such as cutting timber, splitting fence rails, and other work that is not known in Ireland. Be temperate and frugal, and attend worship on Sundays with your employer's family. This will keep you clear of a nest of vipers, who would be urging you to go to tippling-houses with them, to drink whiskey, and talk about Ireland. At the expiration of the year, if your employer is pleased with your conduct, he will not be willing to part with you, and will enter into engagements with you, which is often done in the following way, viz., He will point out to you a certain number of fields to be cultivated, some to be under wheat, others in rye, Indian corn, oats, etc.; he will find horses, and farming utensils, and furnish boarding, washing, and lodging, during that year, and when the harvest is taken off the ground, he has two-thirds for his share, and you have one-third. Your share of wheat, rye, Indian corn or any other produce of the ground, which you have farmed in this way, you will always meet a ready market for. It is true, you must attend early and late to your work, and do it in a neat, farming-like manner. Pursuing this plan of industry a few years, you may save as much money as will purchase 150 acres of land in the state of Ohio, or the Indiana territory, or any other part of these new states. It is necessary to guard against imposition in the title, as titles are very uncertain in some places. . . . This is pointing out to you the path that industrious men have pursued, who now live rich and independent. And I am confident, that in America, without the most close application to labour, and using frugality, land is not attained, by those who emigrate to that country destitute of funds. I am convinced almost to a certainty, that out of 20 emigrants from Ireland to the United States, 15 have not been able to procure one foot of land; but this is owing to their own bad management. In many instances they are often grossly deceived by false information, relative to that country, painting to them advantages that never existed, and when the poor disappointed emigrant lands on the American shore, he finds his golden views have taken flight. He spends his time in brooding over his misfortunes till his money is gone, and then he must work or starve; and in the cities, there is always a number of poor emigrants that will not go into the country. The streets are often crowded with them looking for work, so that it is very hard to obtain work for a stranger that is not known. The last resource is to engage to work upon the turnpike roads. Here the labourer will get one dollar per day, and must find himself meat, drink, washing, and lodging. Here he has for companions the most abandoned drunken wretches that are in existence, and whose example he must follow, or be held in derision by them. The day's work is tasked, and if not accomplished, his wages are docked; this sort of labour, and that of working at furnaces and forges, employs a great number of Irishmen. I have known many hundreds of them who have wrought in this way for more than 30 years, who at this moment cannot put a good coat on their back, and now are old, infirm, and past labour. . . .

My advice to mechanics is, to push back, and take residence in some of the inland towns; and as new counties are every year dividing off, and towns pitched upon to be the seat of justice for these counties, work for all kinds of mechanics is plenty, and money sufficient may soon be earned, to purchase a lot in one of these towns, where you may, in a short time, be enabled to build a house on your own property, and have no rent to pay. In these towns you will have an opportunity of educating your children, and putting them to trades at a proper time. But I am sorry to say, most of the tradesmen would suffer cold and hunger, even death itself, rather than go from New York and Philadelphia, into the country.

There is a number of young men who leave Ireland and go to America intending to be clerks or merchants. Of all classes of people, I can give these the least encouragement. We have ten people of this description, where we cannot get employment for one, particularly at this time, when all kinds of trade in the United States are at so low an ebb.

I will now take notice of the man who emigrates to America, and has money with him, and means to become a farmer. First, it is necessary to mention the price of land. East of the mountains, good land will not be bought under from 80 to 120 dollars per acre, where there are good improvements—other land may rate from 5 dollars to a higher amount, according to the quality of the land, and the improvements made thereon. Land at a lower rate than this, is not an object of purchase, as the soil is so thin and poor, that a living cannot be made on it, without manuring every other year with dung or plaster of Paris. West of the mountains in all the old settlements, land may be bought from 80 dollars per acre to 120 dollars. In the state of Ohio, and other new countries, very good land may be bought at two dollars per acre, but this land is in a state of nature, and far distant from any inhabitants. . . .

The Americans, in general, are a brave and generous people, well informed, hospitable, and kind; it would be, therefore, the duty of emigrants when settled in that country, not to be the first to lend a hand in disturbing the peace of the country—it is the height of ingratitude, as they ought to consider that they have been received, and granted the rights of citizenship; it is their duty, therefore, to lend a hand to nothing that may be injurious to their adopted country. I hope Irish emigrants when they arrive will copy after some of the rules and instructions I have pointed out, which, if it should turn out to their advantage, as I hope it may, would truly be a great happiness and gratification to their countryman and friend.

Source: John Melish. *Travels Through the United States of America in the Years 1806 and 1807, and 1809, 1810, and 1811.* London, 1818.

GLOSSARY

A

acculturation. Process by which immigrants take on aspects of American culture and graft them onto their native one.

affidavit of support. A legal document required of someone who wants to sponsor an immigrant which states that this person will take financial responsibility for the immigrant once she or he enters the country.

Alien Contract Labor Law. An 1885 law also known as the Foran Act, restricting importation of contract laborers.

Alien Enemy Act. A 1798 law giving the president the right to deport aliens engaging in treasonous activity; allowed to lapse in 1801.

Alien Land Act. A 1913 California law that prohibited land ownership by Japanese immigrants.

alien migrant interdiction operations (AMIOs). Coast Guard operations designed to control seagoing illegal immigration to the United States.

Alien Registration Act. A 1940 law requiring all aliens over the age of fourteen to register annually with the government.

aliens. Nationals of another country living in the United States.

aliyah. Literally "going up," a Hebrew term for immigration to Israel.

American Colonization Society. Organization established in 1816 to ship freed slaves and free blacks from the United States to Africa.

American GI Forum. Political organization created in 1948 among Mexican-American veterans of the U.S. armed forces.

American Defense Society. An anti-German and anti-immigration organization during World War I.

American Party. *See* Know-Nothings.

American Protective League. Anti-German organization of the World War I era.

Americanization. Effort to force or teach immigrants to adopt an American way of life.

AMIO. *See* alien migrant interdiction operations.

Amish. Germans who immigrated to Pennsylvania in the 1700s to practice their dissenting Christian faith.

amnesty. Permission for an illegal immigrant to stay in the United States legally.

Anglo-Saxon. Technically the term for people from England, it is applied popularly to all white, native-born, Protestant Americans.

antimiscegenation laws. Laws that once banned marriage between peoples of different races; ruled unconstitutional by the Supreme Court in 1967.

Armenians. Christian minority of the Middle East.

Ashkenazim. Hebrew word for Jews from Europe.

assimilation. Process by which immigrants exchange native culture for an American one.

Assyrians. Christian minority of Iraq.

asylum. Status of a refugee who is permitted to stay in a host country.

Austria-Hungary. Pre–World War I empire in central and eastern Europe that sent millions of immigrants to the United States in the late nineteenth and early twentieth centuries.

Aztlán. Mexican-American term for southwestern region of the United States that belonged to Mexico before the Mexican-American war of the 1840s (1846–1848).

B

Back to the Soil. Jewish immigrant movement involving the establishment of agricultural colonies in the United States.

Bala-vihars. Organizations that offer religious instruction to young Hindu immigrants.

barrio. A predominantly Hispanic neighborhood.

Basques. Minority ethnic group from northern Spain and southern France.

Bilingual Education Act. A 1968 law providing funds for planning and implementation of linguistic education programs for minority-language speakers.

Birth Rule. Part of the Immigration and Nationality Act of 1965, rule defined individuals' origins as where they were born, not where they last lived.

Black Hand. Late-nineteenth-century criminal gangs among Italian immigrants.

black-market babies. Foreign-born babies who are illegally acquired and adopted by American parents.

BMNA. *See* Buddhist Mission of North America.

boat people. Southeast Asian refugees who made their way out of the region's communist-led countries in the late 1970s and 1980s, largely on unseaworthy craft.

Bolsheviks. Popular term for leftist radicals who supported the Russian Revolution of 1917, often applied to immigrants.

Border Patrol. Division of the Immigration and Naturalization Service charged with guarding the nation's land borders.

Bracero Program. From 1942 to 1964, a program to allow the temporary residence in the United States of farm laborers from Mexico. Also known as the Labor Importation Program of 1942–1964.

braceros. Farm laborers from Mexico allowed to work in the United States temporarily between 1942 and 1964.

brain drain. Popular term for phenomenon in which highly educated or skilled persons from the underdeveloped world move to the industrialized countries of the West.

Buddhist Churches of America. *See* Buddhist Mission of North America.

Buddhist Mission of North America (BMNA). Originally Young Men's Buddhist Association, an organization founded in San Francisco in 1899 that provided services to Japanese and other Buddhist immigrants to the United States; later called the Buddhist Churches of America.

Buford. Name of the ship on which hundreds of supposed communist aliens were deported to the Soviet Union in 1919.

Bureau of Immigration. First federal agency charged with regulating immigration to the United States.

Burlingame Treaty. An 1868 treaty between China and the United States allowing for free immigration between the two countries.

C

Cajuns. Slang for Acadians, French-speaking people from eastern Canada who immigrated to Louisiana in the eighteenth century after the French and Indian War led to the British takeover of Canada.

Camorra. Organized crime syndicate among emigrants from Naples, Italy.

Canada-Quebec Accord. A 1991 agreement allowing the province of Quebec to manage its own immigration affairs.

CANF. *See* Cuban American National Foundation.

Celestials. Somewhat demeaning nineteenth-century term for immigrants from China, the so-called Celestial Kingdom.

chain migration. Scholarly term for the process in which one member of a family or a community emigrates first, followed by other members of the same family or community.

Chicana. A Mexican-American woman.

Chicano. A Mexican-American man.

Chinese Exclusion Act. An 1882 act banning virtually all Chinese immigration to the United States for ten years; law renewed in 1892 and 1902, made permanent in 1904, and repealed in 1943.

Chinese Six Companies. Benevolent associations that provided guidance, lodging, and care for Chinese immigrants in the United States.

CIC. *See* Citizenship and Immigration Canada.

Citizenship and Immigration Canada (CIC). Main government agency in Canada charged with immigration and naturalization affairs.

closet ethnics. Persons who try to hide ethnicity and blend into majority culture.

colonias. Literally "colonies," Spanish term for makeshift communities of migrant workers; often used in Mexican and U.S. border regions.

Colyer et al. v. Skeffington. A 1920 ruling by the District Court of Massachusetts that declared that membership in the Communist Party was not, in and of itself, a legal cause for deportation. (On other grounds, the First Circuit Court of Appeals reversed this ruling in 1922 in *Skeffington v. Katz eff.*).

Committee of Vigilance. Anti-immigrant organization in 1850s San Francisco.

Comprehensive Plan of Action (CPA). Joint 1989 program by the United Nations and the Vietnamese government to allow for the orderly emigration of Vietnamese nationals.

conditional entrants. Bureaucratic term for refugees.

conquistadores. Literally "conquerors," a Spanish term for the Spaniards who conquered and settled the Americas in the sixteenth, seventeenth, and eighteenth centuries; especially Mexico, Peru, and the southern and southwestern parts of the present-day United States.

contiguous zone. A region twelve to twenty-four miles off the coast, just outside American territorial waters; under international law, countries may interdict illegal immigrants within this zone.

contract labor. Term for immigrants whose journey to America is paid for by prospective employers or their agents; usually brought in groups and forced to work off the cost of the journey.

Contras. U.S.-financed guerrilla army that attacked the leftist Sandinista government of Nicaragua in the 1980s.

contratista. Mexican-Spanish term for a person who brings contract laborers into the United States.

coolies. Common, usually derogatory term applied to Chinese workers in the nineteenth century.

core nations. Developed, or industrialized, countries of Western Europe, North America, Japan, Australasia, and elsewhere.

Cosa Nostra. *See* Mafia.

cottage industry. Manufacturing that goes on in the home.

Court Interpreters Act. Legislation of 1978 requiring interpreters in civil cases where the plaintiff or defendant cannot adequately speak English.

coyote. Slang term for someone who smuggles immigrants into the United States over the Mexican border for a fee.

CPA. *See* Comprehensive Plan of Action.

CPS. *See* Current Population Survey.

Creole. Term for mixed European/African/Native American people of the Caribbean and Latin America; also hybrid European/African/Native American language spoken among many people in the Caribbean and Latin America.

Cuban American National Foundation (CANF). Main organization representing the interests of exiled

Cubans in the United States; active in anti-Castro politics.

Current Population Survey (CPS). Annual analysis of U.S. population conducted by the Bureau of the Census; includes data on immigrants and ethnic groups.

D

diaspora. Exile of a community or ethnic group to other countries or regions of the globe.

displaced persons (DPs). Official term for World War II era European refugees.

Displaced Persons Act. Legislation of 1948 permitting 200,000 largely European refugees to immigrate to the United States.

DPs. *See* displaced persons.

Dutch. Bastardization of *deutsch*, or German; referred to Americans of German descent in the eighteenth and nineteenth centuries.

E

Edict of Nantes. A 1598 edict allowing for tolerance of Protestant Huguenots in France, the revocation of which in 1685 sent thousands of Huguenots to America.

émigré. A person who lives outside his or her native country.

employer sanctions. Fines assessed against employers who hire undocumented workers.

employment-based preference. Legal category that allows immigrants with special skills or talents to live and work in the United States.

enganchista (or *enganchador*). Mexican-Spanish term for a person who brings contract laborers into the United States.

English-only. Movement to make English the official language of the United States.

ESL. English as a Second Language.

Espionage Act. A 1917 law intended to prosecute ali-

ens, largely German, who obstructed the draft during World War I.

ethnic cleansing. A process whereby members of a specific ethnic or religious group are forced to leave a country or region.

Executive Order 9066. A 1942 order issued by President Franklin Roosevelt calling for the internment of Japanese nationals and Japanese Americans living in the western United States.

exile. A person who is unable to return to his or her homeland for political or legal reasons; sometimes a voluntary situation in which the person chooses not to go back.

expansionist. Term for someone who wants to maintain or expand the number of visas granted to legal permanent residents in the United States.

F

FAIR. *See* Federation for American Immigration Reform.

Federation for American Immigration Reform (FAIR). Organization that advocates strict limits on legal immigration and tougher controls on illegal immigration.

Federation of Hindu Associations (FHA). An umbrella group for advocacy and service organizations to aid immigrants of the Hindu faith.

female genital mutilation (FGM). A custom prevalent in Africa and the Middle East whereby a woman's genitalia are mutilated so as to prevent sexual arousal.

FGM. *See* female genital mutilation.

FHA. *See* Federation of Hindu Associations.

fifth columnists. Popular term for traitors, often used against immigrants, especially in wartime.

first world. Industrialized parts of the globe.

G

Galicia. A region in modern-day Poland that sent many immigrants to the United States in the late nineteenth and early twentieth centuries.

Gam Saan. Literally "gold mountain," a Chinese reference to California and the United States in the nineteenth century.

genocide. The total or near total destruction of an ethnic or religious group.

Gentlemen's Agreement. Accord reached between President Theodore Roosevelt and the imperial government of Japan in 1907 restricting Japanese immigration to the United States.

glasnost. Russian for "openness"; term for lifting of restrictions on political expression in the Soviet Union following the rise to power of Mikhail Gorbachev in 1985.

global theory. Political science theory that says the developed world dominates the developing world in a pattern similar to that in which the ruling class within a country dominates all other classes.

globalization. Process by which the world's economy becomes increasingly integrated.

gold mountain. *See Gam Saan.*

great migration. Large flow of Puritans from England to New England from 1629 to 1640; vast movement of African Americans from the rural South to the urban North and West in the twentieth century.

green card. Popular term for a permit to work in the United States; comes from former color of the document.

Guadalupe Hidalgo, Treaty of. An 1848 treaty ending the Mexican-American War that, among other things, granted Mexican nationals living in territory ceded to the United States full U.S. citizenship.

Guantánamo Bay. American base in Cuba that is often used to hold illegal immigrants from Haiti trying to make their way into the United States.

Gullah. People of African descent who live on the offshore islands of Georgia and South Carolina; also refers to the distinct Afro-English they speak.

H

H-1B visa. A special visa allowing foreigners with certain desirable skills to work in the United States.

H-2A Program. Part of the Immigration Reform and Control Act (IRCA) of 1986, it allows for the employment of immigrant workers in agriculture if no American citizens are available for such work.

Haitian Refugee Immigration Fairness Act. Legislation of 1998 designed to allow more Haitian refugees to enter the United States legally.

Hart-Celler Bill. Congressional bill upon which the 1965 Immigration and Nationality Act was based.

hate crime. A violent attack motivated by hatred for a person's race, religion, ethnicity, sexual preference, or other group identity.

head tax. Nineteenth- and early-twentieth-century tax imposed on shipping companies or ship captains for every immigrant brought into the United States.

hegemony. Political science term by which one class within a nation or one nation within a region dominates those around it.

Hispanic. Term used for persons who come from Spanish- and Portuguese-speaking countries in Latin America and Europe.

Hmong. Mountain people from Laos who aided the United States during the Vietnam War; immigrated in large numbers to the United States after communist takeover of Laos in 1975.

Huguenots. French Protestants, many of whom were forced to immigrate to America in the seventeenth and eighteenth centuries because of official religious persecution.

hui. *See kye.*

I

IIRIRA. *See* Illegal Immigration Reform and Immigrant Responsibility Act.

ILGWU. *See* International Ladies' Garment Workers' Union.

Illegal Immigration Reform and Immigrant Responsibility Act (IIRIRA). A 1996 law designed to stop the flow of illegal immigrants to the United States through stepped-up border controls and increased fines and penalties.

Immigration Act of 1990. Legislation modifying Immigration Reform Act of 1986; 1990 law changed the preference system by making family reunification easier and opening up more immigration to persons with specialized skills and occupations.

Immigration and Nationality Act. A 1952 law, often called the McCarran-Walter Act, that removed some restrictions on immigration but added others; also the popular name for a landmark 1965 law ending national quotas for immigration, which technically were amendments to the 1952 act.

Immigration and Naturalization Service (INS). Agency within the Department of Justice that executes U.S. immigration and naturalization law.

Immigration Reform Act. *See* Illegal Immigration Reform and Immigrant Responsibility Act.

Immigration Reform and Control Act (IRCA). A 1986 law, also known as the Simpson-Mazzoli Act, designed to reduce illegal immigration by penalizing employers who hire undocumented workers and stepping up border patrols; also, granted amnesty to many illegal immigrants residing in the United States since 1982.

incorporation. Process by which immigrants fit themselves into the culture and society of their adopted land.

indentured servants. From the colonial and early national period of American history, persons whose passage across the Atlantic was paid in exchange for a term of labor, usually of four to seven years.

Indochina Migration and Refugee Assistance Act. Legislation of 1975 designed to ease entry and settlement of Southeast Asian refugees after the Vietnam War.

Indochinese Refugee Assistance Program (IRAP). U.S. program of the late 1970s to deal with refugees from Southeast Asia; supplanted by the more comprehensive Refugee Act of 1980.

INS. *See* Immigration and Naturalization Service.

Integrated Surveillance Intelligence System (ISIS). A 1990s era system for monitoring illegal immigration activity along the U.S.-Mexican border.

Internal Security Act. Restrictive 1950 immigration law.

International Ladies' Garment Workers' Union (ILGWU). Main union of immigrant garment workers in the early twentieth century that in 1995 became part of UNITE, the Union of Needletrades, Industrial, and Textile Employees.

internment, Japanese. Effort during World War II to relocate and incarcerate over 100,000 West Coast Japanese nationals and Japanese Americans in internment camps scattered throughout the United States.

IRAP. *See* Indochinese Refugee Assistance Program.

IRCA. *See* Immigration Reform and Control Act.

Irish Immigration Reform Movement. Movement organized by Irish-American politicians to ease entry of Irish immigrants to the United States.

Iron Curtain. Cold War era term for the border between communist eastern and capitalist western Europe.

ISIS. *See* Integrated Surveillance Intelligence System.

issei. Japanese term for first-generation immigrants in America.

J

JACL. *See* Japanese American Citizens League.

Japanese American Citizens League (JACL). Self-help organization for Japanese Americans founded in 1930.

K

Khmer Rouge. The murderous communist government of Cambodia in the late 1970s that caused millions of deaths and sent hundreds of thousands of refugees abroad.

Know-Nothings. Officially the American Party, a mid-nineteenth-century, anti-immigrant political party; name comes from the organization's secrecy—members were told to answer "I know nothing" if asked about the party.

ko. See kye.

Ku Klux Klan. An antiblack terrorist organization founded in the South during Reconstruction and resurrected in the early 1900s as an antiblack, anti-immigrant, anti-Jewish, and anti-Catholic organization.

Kurds. Non-Arab Muslim minority in Iran, Iraq, Turkey, and Syria.

kye. Korean term for a rotating credit association whereby members invest funds and receive combined assets on a rotating basis; also known as a *ko* in Japanese and a *hui* in Chinese.

L

La Raza. Spanish phrase meaning "the race," used to designate people of Latino background.

Latina. Term used for a woman who comes from Mexico, Central America, South America, and Spanish-speaking islands of the Caribbean.

Latino. Term used for a man who comes from Mexico, Central America, South America, and Spanish-speaking islands of the Caribbean.

Lau v. Nichols. A 1974 precedent-setting Supreme Court ruling that ordered the San Francisco school district to take affirmative steps to ensure a proper education for minority-language students.

Law of Return. A 1950 piece of Israeli legislation allowing for the free immigration of all Jewish people to Israel.

League of United Latin American Citizens (LULAC). Important Latino self-help organization that fights for immigrant rights.

Lesbian and Gay Immigration Rights Task Force. Most important U.S. advocacy organization for gay and lesbian immigrants.

Literacy Act of 1917. Law also known as the Literacy Test Act requiring that all immigrants be literate in their own language or in English.

Lo Wa Kiu. Contemporary term for Chinese who immigrated to the United States several generations ago.

lottery. Granting of immigration visas based on the drawing of applicant names at random.

LULAC. *See* League of United Latin American Citizens.

M

Mafia. Originally referred to an organized crime syndicate among immigrants from Sicily; also known as the Cosa Nostra; now applied to all organized crime syndicates regardless of ethnic background.

mail-order brides. Women imported to the United States to become brides of American men; many come from the Philippines.

Marielitos. Cuban immigrants who came to the United States in large numbers in 1980; named after Puerto Mariel, the Cuban port from which they departed.

McCarran-Walter Act. *See* Immigration and Nationality Act.

MECHA. *See* Movimiento Estudantil Chicano de Aztlán.

melting pot. Somewhat dated expression for the process by which immigrants from various countries merge into a common American culture.

Mennonites. Religious dissenters who emigrated from Germany to the middle colonies of North America in the eighteenth century.

MexAmerica. Popular term for region along U.S.-Mexican border.

Mezzogiorno. Italian for "midday," refers to the impoverished region of southern Italy.

microenterprises. Business enterprises that require very little capitalization to initiate.

Middle Immigration Series. A U.S. Bureau of the Census population projection assuming current levels of immigration into the country.

miscegenation. Term for marriage and sexual mixing among peoples of different races; once considered a derogatory word.

model minority. Term used to describe high-achieving Asian immigrants, which, although meant positively, is viewed by the Asian-American community as a stereotype.

Molly Maguires. Late-nineteenth-century radical and violent labor movement among Irish immigrants, largely in mining areas of Pennsylvania.

Mona Passage. Straits between the Dominican Republic and Puerto Rico through which many illegal immigrants from the Dominican Republic and Haiti seek entrance into the United States.

mosaic. Recent term used to replace "melting pot" for the process by which immigrants fit into American society; emphasizes how immigrant groups retain their older culture as they adjust, rather than blend into a homogeneous American identity.

Movimiento Estudantil Chicano de Aztlán (MECHA). Mexican-American student organization created in 1970 out of the merger of the United Mexican American Students and the Mexican American Youth Organization.

mutual assistance associations. Self-help organizations established by Vietnamese refugees in the 1970s under federal government supervision.

mutualista. Spanish for "mutual aid society," or self-help organizations among Mexican Americans.

N

NAFTA. *See* North American Free Trade Agreement.

National Council of La Raza. Major Latino pro-immigration organization.

National Security League. Anti-German, anti-immigrant organization during World War I.

nativism. An anti-immigrant political ideology.

naturalization. Process by which a person gives up one nationality for another and becomes a citizen.

Naturalization Act of 1790. First American law setting residency and racial requirements for citizenship.

new immigrantion. Term often used to describe the latest wave of immigrants; in the early and mid-twentieth century, used to refer to immigrants from southern and eastern Europe who had arrived from 1885 to World War I; in the late twentieth and early twenty-first centuries, used to refer to post-1965, post–quota law immigrants.

New Irish. Irish immigrants since the 1980s.

newly industrialized countries (NICs). Mainly in East Asia, those countries which achieved rapid economic development in the late twentieth century.

NICs. *See* newly industrialized countries.

nikkeijin. Japanese term for foreign nationals of Japanese descent.

nisei. Japanese term for second-generation immigrants in America.

North American Free Trade Agreement (NAFTA). A 1994 treaty establishing a free trading zone encompassing Canada, Mexico, and the United States.

O

ODP. *See* Orderly Departure Program.

Office of Refugee Resettlement. Temporary federal agency established in 1975 to oversee the integration of Vietnamese refugees into American life.

olim. Hebrew term for immigrants to Israel.

Operation Blockade. A 1990s era program, also known as Operation Hold the Line, to control illegal immigration over the El Paso, Texas, sector of the U.S.-Mexican border.

Operation Boulder. A 1970s program designed to combat terrorism; criticized for being anti–Arab American.

Operation Eagle Pull. A 1975 operation that pulled those who had worked for the United States out of Cambodia upon that country's takeover by communists.

Operation Gatekeeper. A 1990s program designed to strengthen the San Diego sector of the U.S.-Mexican border against illegal immigrant entries.

Operation Hold the Line. *See* Operation Blockade.

Operation Safeguard. A 1990s program designed to strengthen the Arizona sector of the U.S.-Mexican border against illegal immigrant entries.

Operation Wetback. A 1950s era program designed to locate and deport Mexican immigrants living illegally in the United States.

Orderly Departure Program (ODP). A joint effort by the United Nations and the Vietnamese government to allow persons who wanted to leave Vietnam to do so in a safe and orderly manner; it was begun in 1979 and suspended in 1986.

P

Pale, the. Area within pre-1917 Russia outside which Jews could not legally reside; corresponds largely to modern-day eastern Poland, Belarus, and the Ukraine.

Palmer raids. The 1919 and 1920 raids conducted by Attorney General A. Mitchell Palmer largely against immigrant radicals.

parachute kids. Popular expression for children of wealthy Asian parents who attend and live at private schools in the United States.

parochial school. School run by a religious denomination.

pensionado. A Filipino student whose education in the United States was paid for by the American government; the Pensionado Program lasted from 1903 to 1943.

perestroika. Russian for "restructuring," refers to dismantling of restrictions on private enterprise in the Soviet Union following the rise to power of Mikhail Gorbachev in 1985.

peripheral nations. Underdeveloped, or third-world, countries.

permanent residency. Status whereby someone can live and work in the United States indefinitely without becoming a citizen.

Personal Responsibility and Work Opportunity Reconciliation Act of 1991. Law, also known as the Welfare Reform Act, ending existing welfare programs, which cut off many benefits to both legal and illegal immigrants.

picture brides. Japanese women who were married to Japanese men in America after their photos were sent to the latter in the late nineteenth and early twentieth centuries.

piecework. Work that is paid for by the piece rather than by the hour; once frequently performed in the garment industry.

pogrom. Systematic attacks and massacres by Cossack (a warrior ethnic group) militia on Jews in pre-1917 Russia; often instigated by the czarist government.

post-traumatic stress disorder. Psychological condition of acute fear and stress frequent among refugees from war and political persecution.

potato famine. Failure of Irish potato crop in the 1840s that produced widespread starvation and caused massive immigration to the United States and Canada, also known as the Irish Potato Famine and the Great Potato Famine.

Proposition 187. Referendum passed by California voters in 1994 that aimed to cut off most public services for illegal immigrants; ruled largely unconstitutional by courts.

Proposition 227. Referendum passed by California voters in 1998 that virtually ended bilingual education in the state's public schools.

PTKs. Professional, technical, and kindred workers; term used by Immigration and Naturalization Service.

public charge. Term for someone—including an immigrant—who cannot support himself or herself financially and must receive government aid.

Punjabis. A largely Sikh people from the Punjabi provinces of India and Pakistan; because of their predominance among South Asian immigrants, Punjabi has become a catchall term for all Indian and Pakistani immigrants.

Puritans. English religious dissenters who emigrated to New England in the seventeenth century.

Q

Quakers. *See* Society of Friends.

Quota Act of 1921. Act limiting immigration of various nationalities to 3 percent of their total in the United States as of 1910.

Quota Act of 1924. Act limiting immigration of various nationalities to 2 percent of their total in the United States as of 1890.

quotas. Set limit of immigrants allowed into the United States, usually from a specific country.

R

Rastafarians. Jamaican immigrants who practice a syncretic faith that combines Christianity and African nationalism.

Red Scare. Popular name for antiradical hysteria that swept the United States after World War I, resulting in the arrest and deportation of thousands of left-wing immigrants.

refoulement. French word meaning "to be driven back," an international term for sending refugees back to probable persecution in their native land; prohibited under United Nations protocols.

refugee. A person who flees his or her native land because of war, persecution, or natural disaster; generally used for those not leaving for specifically economic reasons.

Refugee Act. A 1980 law that disconnected refugee and immigration policies and adopted the United Nations definition for refugees.

Refugee Relief Act. Legislation of 1953 granting entry to escapees from communist countries.

remittance. Money sent back to the home country by an immigrant living in another country.

restrictionist. Term for someone who wants to restrict the number of visas granted to legal permanent residents in the United States.

return immigrants. People who return to their home country after living in another country.

rotating credit association. *See Kye.*

S

San Yi Man. Chinese term for new immigrants.

sanctuary. A place where illegal immigrants are hidden from government authorities.

sanctuary movement. A 1980s movement of churches and other concerned groups who protected Central American immigrants fearing persecution in their native countries.

Santeria. A faith popular among Caribbean immigrants that combines indigenous Native American and African religious practices with Catholicism.

Satsang. Religious organization for Hindu immigrants.

SAVE. *See* Systematic Alien Verification for Entitlements.

SAW. *See* Special Agricultural Worker exemption.

Scotch-Irish. *See* Scots-Irish.

Scots-Irish. Immigrants originally from Scotland settled by England in what is now Northern Ireland beginning in the sixteenth century.

seasoning. Refers to the initial period of arrival in which settlers physically adjusted to the climate of North America in the seventeenth and eighteenth centuries.

segmented assimilation. Process by which immigrants absorb some elements of their adopted culture and retain elements of their native culture.

Sephardim. Hebrew term for Jews from the Middle East, North Africa, and parts of southern Europe.

Sikhs. People from India and Pakistan who practice a syncretic religion that combines elements of Hinduism and Islam.

Simpson-Mazzoli Act. *See* Immigration Reform and Control Act.

Slavs. The largest ethnic group in Eastern Europe and Russia.

SLIAG. *See* State Legalization Impact Assistance Grant.

snakehead. Slang term for a person who smuggles Asian immigrants into the United States for a fee.

social capital. Networks of people who can provide human and other resources for economic development.

social Darwinism. Late-nineteenth-century philosophy which maintained that certain ethnic groups—generally Western European ones—were superior to others and more fit to rule.

social mobility. The capacity to move from one economic level or class to another.

Society of Friends. Popularly known as Quakers, a group of religious dissenters who migrated from England in the seventeenth century and established the colony of Pennsylvania.

Southern Cone. Countries of southern South America—Argentina, Chile, Paraguay, and Uruguay.

Special Agricultural Worker (SAW) exemption. Clause in 1986 Immigration Reform and Control Act allowing employers of agricultural workers time to adjust their recruiting and hiring practices to fit the new law. Also referred to as the SAW Program.

sponsorship. System whereby a citizen may take fiscal or legal responsibility for someone who wants to immigrate.

State Legalization Impact Assistance Grant (SLIAG). Federal government reimbursement to states for social service costs of immigrants; authorized under the Immigration Reform and Control Act of 1986.

sweatshop. Popular term for a small factory that employs low-wage, low-skilled workers, usually in urban areas and often in the garment industry.

Systematic Alien Verification for Entitlements (SAVE). A 1980s computer system designed to assist states in determining immigrant status of applicants for social services.

T

Temporary Protected Status. A legal category for refugees who are allowed to stay in the United States until political conditions improve in the home country.

tenement. Often crowded, substandard apartment housing for immigrants in urban areas.

third world. Less economically developed parts of the globe.

TNC. *See* transnational corporation.

TOEFL. Teaching of English as a Foreign Language.

transnational corporation (TNC). A corporation headquartered in one country but operating in many.

transnationalism. Process whereby immigrants retain political, economic, and social connections with their home country.

U

UFW. *See* United Farm Workers.

Ulsterites. Eighteenth- and nineteenth-century term for Scots-Irish immigrants from Ulster, or Northern Ireland.

undocumented. Residing in the United States without legal papers.

UNHCR. *See* United Nations High Commissioner for Refugees.

United Farm Workers (UFW). Main union for migrant agricultural laborers from Mexico, the Philippines, and other countries.

United Nations High Commissioner for Refugees (UNHCR). Main United Nations agency responsible for refugees.

United Nations Protocol Relating to the Status of Refugees. Key United Nations rules concerning the rights of refugees.

U.S. English. Organization that advocates making English the official language of the United States.

U.S. ex rel. Negron v. New York. A 1970 court case establishing the constitutional right to interpreters in criminal trials where a defendant cannot adequately speak English.

V

Virginia Company. Royally chartered company that founded the colony of Virginia in 1607.

visa. Legal document allowing a person to visit or reside in another country.

W

war brides. Foreign women who marry U.S. servicemen.

War Brides Act. Legislation of 1946 allowing the immigration of persons who married American soldiers during World War II.

War Refugee Board (WRB). A cabinet-level agency created by President Franklin D. Roosevelt on January 24, 1944, to aid Jewish refugees escaping from Nazi-occupied Europe.

War Relocation Authority. World War II era U.S. government agency in charge of Japanese internment.

WASPs. White Anglo-Saxon Protestants.

Welfare Reform Act. *See* Personal Responsibility and Work Opportunity Reconciliation Act of 1996.

wet feet, dry feet. Unofficial term for U.S. policy whereby illegal immigrants apprehended at sea have no rights to refugee screenings, whereas those who make it to American territory do.

Workingmen's Party of California Radical. Nineteenth-century political party that advocated banning Chinese immigration.

WRB. *See* War Refugee Board.

Y

Young Lords. Radical political organization of the 1960s and 1970s among young Puerto Ricans in the United States.

Young Men's Buddhist Association. *See* Buddhist Mission of North America.

Z

Zero Immigration Series. A U.S. Bureau of the Census population projection assuming no further immigration into the country.

Zero Population Growth (ZPG). Anti–population growth organization that advocates limits on immigration.

Zionism. Jewish nationalist movement.

ZPG. *See* Zero Population Growth.

BIBLIOGRAPHY

HISTORY

Abbott, Edith. *Immigration: Select Documents and Case Records*. Chicago: University of Chicago Press, 1924. Reprint. New York: Arno Press, 1969.

Adamic, Louis. "The Land of Promise." *Harper's Magazine* (October 1931).

Adams, Henry. *History of the United States During the Administration of James Madison*. New York: Library of America, 1986.

Adams, Herbert B. "History, Politics and Education." In *Johns Hopkins University Studies in Historical and Political Science*. Vol. 7, ed. Herbert B. Adams. Baltimore: Johns Hopkins University Press, 1890.

Ahlstrom, Sydney A. *A Religious History of the American People*. New Haven: Yale University Press, 1972.

Alba, Richard D., and Victor Nee. "Rethinking Assimilation Theory for a New Era of Immigration." *International Migration Review* 31 (1997): 826–974.

Anderson, Gary Clayton. *The Indian Southwest, 1580–1830. Ethnogenesis & Reinvention*. Norman: University of Oklahoma Press, 1999.

Annerino, J. *Dead in Their Tracks*. New York: Four Walls, 1999.

Antin, Mary. *The Promised Land*. Boston: Houghton Mifflin, 1912. Reprint. New York: Arno Press, 1980.

Aptheker, Herbert. *American Negro Slave Revolts*. 6th ed. New York: International Publishers, 1993.

Archdeacon, Thomas J. *Becoming American: An Ethnic History*. New York: Free Press, 1983.

Armitage, David, ed. *An Expanding World*. Vol. 20. *Theories of Empire, 1450–1800*. Aldershot, Ashgate, UK: Variorum, 1998.

Bailyn, Bernard. *From Protestant Peasants to Jewish Intellectuals: The Germans in the Peopling of America*. Oxford: Berg, 1988.

Balch, Emily. *Our Slavic Fellow Citizens*. New York: Charities Publication Committee, 1910. Reprint. New York: Arno Press, 1969.

Barck, Oscar T., and Hugh T. Lefler. *Colonial America*. New York: Macmillan, 1968.

Barkan, Elliott R. *And Still They Come: Immigrants and American Society 1920 to the 1990s*. Wheeling, IL: Harlan Davidson, 1996.

Barrett, James R. *Work and Community in the Jungle: Chicago's Packinghouse Workers*. Urbana: University of Illinois Press, 1987.

Barth, Fredrik, ed. *Ethnic Groups and Boundaries: The Social Organization of Cultural Difference*. Boston: Little, Brown, 1969.

Bauer, Yehuda. *American Jewry and the Holocaust: The American Jewish Joint Distribution Committee, 1939–1945*. Detroit: Wayne State University Press, 1981.

Beck, Roy. *The Case Against Immigration: The Moral, Economic, Social, and Environmental Reasons for Reducing U.S. Immigration Back to Traditional Levels*. New York: W.W. Norton, 1996.

Beezley, William H., and Colin M. MacLachlan. *El Gran Pueblo: A History of Greater Mexico, 1911–Present*. Englewood Cliffs, NJ: Prentice Hall, 1994.

Bell, Thomas. *Out of This Furnace: A Novel of Immigrant Labor in America*. Pittsburgh: University of Pittsburgh Press, 1993.

Bennett, David H. *The Party of Fear: From Nativist Movements to the New Far Right in American History*. 2d ed. New York: Vintage Books, 1995.

Berend, Ivan, and Gyorgi Ranki. *The European Periphery and Industrialization, 1780–1914*. New York: Columbia University Press, 1982.

Berger, David, ed. *The Legacy of Jewish Migration: 1881 and Its Impact*. New York: Columbia University Press, 1983.

Berlin, Ira. *Many Thousands Gone: The First Two Centuries of Slavery in North America*. Cambridge, MA: Belknap Press, 1998.

Berman, Aaron. *Nazism, the Jews, and American Zionism*. Detroit: Wayne State University Press, 1990.

Bernstein, Iver. *The New York City Draft Riots: Their Significance for American Society and Politics in the Age of the Civil War*. New York: Oxford University Press, 1990.

Berthoff, Rowland Tappan. *British Immigrants in Industrial America: 1790–1950*. Cambridge: Harvard University Press, 1953.

Billington, Ray Allen. *Land of Savagery, Land of Promise: The European Image of the American Frontier in the Nineteenth Century*. New York: W.W. Norton, 1981.

———. *The Protestant Crusade, 1800–1860: A Study of the Origins of American Nativism*. New York: Macmillan, 1938.

Bittinger, Lucy F. *The Germans in Colonial Times.* 1901. Reprint. New York: Russell and Russell, 1968.

Bodnar, John. *The Transplanted: A History of Immigrants in Urban America.* Bloomington: Indiana University Press, 1985.

Bonacich, Edna. "Advance Capitalism and Black/White Race Relations in the United States: A Split Labor Market Interpretation." *American Sociological Review* 38 (1976): 583–94.

Bosniak, Linda S. "'Nativism' the Concept: Some Reflections." In *Immigrants Out! The New Nativism and the Anti-Immigrant Impulse in the United States,* ed. Juan Perea. New York: New York University Press, 1997.

Brearley, W.H. *Fourth Annual Excursion of the Detroit Evening News,* 1880.

Breen, Timothy. *Tobacco Culture: The Mentality of the Great Tidewater Planters on the Eve of the Revolution.* Princeton: Princeton University Press, 1985.

Breitman, Richard, and Alan M. Kraut. *American Refugee Policy and European Jewry, 1933–1945.* Bloomington: Indiana University Press, 1987.

Briani, Vittorio. *L'Emigrazione italiana ieri e oggi.* Detroit: Blaine Ethridge Books, 1979.

Bridenbaugh, Carl. *Vexed and Troubled Englishmen, 1590–1642.* New York: Oxford University Press, 1968.

Brimelow, Peter. *Alien Nation: Common Sense About America's Immigration Disaster.* New York: Random House, 1996.

Brown, Mary E. *Shapers of the Great Debate on Immigration: A Biographical Dictionary.* Westport, CT: Greenwood, 1999.

Buhle, Paule, and Dan Georgakas, eds. *The Immigrant Left in the United States.* Binghamton: State University of New York Press, 1996.

Bujak, Franciszek. *Maszkienice. Wies powiatu brzeskiego: Stosunki gospodarcze i spoleczne.* Kracow: Gebethner, 1901.

Bureau of Consular Affairs. *International Adoptions: Guidelines on Immediate Relative Petitions.* Washington, DC: Department of State, February 1997.

Bureau of the Census. *Historical Statistics of the United States: Colonial Times to 1957.* Washington, DC: Bureau of the Census, 1960.

Burton, William L. *Melting Pot Soldiers: The Union's Ethnic Regiments.* New York: Fordham University Press, 1998.

Cardoso, Lawrence. *Mexican Emigration to the United States.* Tucson: University of Arizona Press, 1980.

Center for Immigration Studies. *Importing Poverty.* Washington, DC: Center for Immigration Studies, September 1999.

Chan, Sucheng. *The Bittersweet Soil.* Berkeley: University of California Press, 1986.

Chen, Yong. *Chinese San Francisco, 1850–1943: A Trans-Pacific Community.* Stanford: Stanford University Press, 2000.

Chirot, Daniel. *Social Change in the Modern Era.* San Diego: Harcourt and Brace, 1986.

Claghorn, Kate Holladay. *The Immigrant's Day in Court.* New York: Harper and Brothers, 1923.

Coan, Peter Morton. *Ellis Island Interviews: In Their Own Words.* New York: Facts on File, 1977.

Commission on Immigration Reform. *U.S. Immigration Policy: Restoring Credibility.* Washington, DC: Government Printing Office, September 1994.

Congressional Quarterly. "Immigration Reform." In *Congress and the Nation, 1965–1968.* Vol. 2. Washington, DC: Congressional Quarterly Service, 1969.

Conzen, Kathleen N. "Germans." In *Harvard Encyclopedia of American Ethnic Groups,* ed. Stephen Thernstrom, pp. 405–25. Cambridge: Harvard University Press, 1981.

Conzen, Kathleen N., David A. Gerber, Ewa Morawska, George E. Pozzetta, and Rudolph J. Vecoli. "The Invention of Ethnicity: A Perspective from the U.S.A." *Journal of American Ethnic History* 12 (Fall 1992): 3–41.

Cook, Christopher. "U.S. Arabs Assess Damage on Themselves: Many Feel Wounded, Torn by Their Loyalties." *Detroit Free Press,* January 25, 1991, p. 12A.

Coolidge, Mary Roberts. *Chinese Immigration.* New York: Henry Holt, 1909.

Coughty, Jay A. *The Notorious Triangle: Rhode Island and the African Slave Trade, 1700–1807.* Philadelphia: Temple University Press, 1981.

Crawford, James. *Hold Your Tongue: Bilingualism and the Politics of "English Only."* Reading, MA: Addison-Wesley, 1992.

Crewdson, John. *The Tarnished Door: The New Immigrants and the Transformation of America.* New York: Times Books, 1983.

Cummings, Scott, and Thomas Lambert. "Immigration Restrictions and the American Worker: An Examination of Competing Interpretations." *Population Research and Policy Review* 17 (1998): 497–520.

Curtin, Philip D. *The Atlantic Slave Trade: A Census.* Madison: University of Wisconsin Press, 1969.

D'Acernio, Pellegrino, ed. *The Italian American Heritage: A Companion to Literature and Arts.* New York: Garland, 1999.

Daniels, Roger. *Coming to America: A History of Immigration and Ethnicity in American Life.* New York: HarperCollins, 1990.

———. "No Lamps Were Lit for Them: Angel Island and the Historiography of Asian American Immigration." *Journal of American Ethnic History* 17 (Fall 1997): 3–18.

———. *Prisoners Without Trial: Japanese Americans in World War II.* New York: Hill and Wang, 1993.

Debouzy, Marianne. *In the Shadow of the Statue of Liberty: Immigrants, Workers, and Citizens in the American Republic, 1880–1920.* Urbana: University of Illinois Press, 1992.

DeForest, Robert W., and Lawrence Veiller, eds. *The Tenement House Problem*. New York: Macmillan, 1903.

Degler, Carl N. *In Search of Human Nature: The Decline and Revival of Darwinism in American Social Thought*. New York: Oxford University Press, 1991.

Delgado, Richard. "Citizenship." In *Immigrants Out! The New Nativism and the Anti-Immigrant Impulse in the United States*, ed. Juan Perea, pp. 318–23. New York: New York University Press, 1997.

Department of State. "Fact Sheet: Newly Independent States and the Baltics Admissions Program." Washington, DC: Bureau of Population, Refugees, and Migration, January 18, 2000.

Diamond, Jeff. "African American Attitudes Towards United States Immigration Policy." *International Migration Review* 32 (1998): 451–70.

Dickson, R.J. *Ulster Immigration to the United States*. London: Routledge, 1966.

Dill, Marshall, Jr. *Germany: A Modern History*. Ann Arbor: University of Michigan Press, 1961.

Dinnerstein, Leonard, Roger L. Nichols, and David M. Reimers. *Natives and Strangers: A Multicultural History of Americans*. New York: Oxford University Press, 1997.

Dolan, Jay P. *The Immigrant Church: New York's Irish and German Catholics: 1815–1865*. Baltimore: Johns Hopkins University Press, 1975.

Duda-Dziewierz, Krystyna. *Wies malopolska a emigracja Amerykanska: Studium wsi babica powiatu rzeszowskiego*. Warsaw: Dom Ksiazki, 1937.

Duis, Perry R. *The Saloon: Public Drinking in Chicago and Boston, 1880–1920*. Urbana: University of Illinois Press, 1983.

Ebihara, May M., Carol A. Mortland, and Judy L. Ledgerwood, eds. *Cambodian Culture Since 1975: Homeland and Exile*. Ithaca: Cornell University Press, 1994.

Eblen, Jack E. "An Analysis of Nineteenth-Century Frontier Populations." *Demography* 2 (1965): 399–413.

Edmonds, Patricia. "FBI Is Accused of 'Hunting' Arab Americans." *Detroit Free Press*, January 24, 1991, p. 8A.

———. "Hate Crimes Grow: Arab Americans Say the Rate Has Jumped Since War Began." *Detroit Free Press*, February 7, 1991, p. 3A.

Ellis, Mark, and Panikos Panayi. "German Minorities in World War I: A Comparative Study of Britain and the USA." *Ethnic and Racial Studies* 17 (1994): 238–59.

Eltis, David. *The Rise of African Slavery in the Americas*. New York: Cambridge University Press, 2000.

Emmerson, John K. *The Japanese Thread*. New York: Holt, Rinehart, and Winston, 1978.

Erikson, Charlotte. *The Invisible Immigrants: The Adaptation of English and Scottish Immigrants in Nineteenth-Century America*. Miami: University of Miami Press, 1972.

Espenshade, T.J. "A Short History of U.S. Policy Toward Illegal Immigration." *Population Today* 18:2 (February 1990): 6–9.

Espenshade, T.J., J.L. Baraka, and G.A. Huber. "Implications of the 1996 Welfare and Immigration Reform Acts for U.S. Immigration." *Population and Development Review* 23:4 (1997): 769–801.

Espenshade, T.J., F.D. Bean, T.A. Goodis, and M.J. White. "Immigration Policy in the United States: Future Prospects for the Immigration Reform and Control Act of 1986." In *Population Policy: Contemporary Issues*, ed. Godfrey Roberts, pp. 59–84. New York: Praeger, 1990.

Ewen, Elizabeth. *Immigrant Women in the Land of Dollars: Life and Culture on the Lower East Side 1890–1925*. New York: Monthly Review Press, 1985.

Fadiman, Ann. *The Spirit Catches You and You Fall Down*. New York: Noonday Press, 1997.

Faust, Albert B. *The German Element in the United States*. New York: Arno Press, 1969.

Federation for American Immigration Reform. "A Skirmish in a Wider War: An Oral History of John H. Tanton, Founder of FAIR, the Federation for American Immigration Reform." In *Tenth Anniversary Oral History Project of the Federation for American Immigration Reform*. Washington, DC: Federation for American Immigration Reform, 1989.

Feingold, Henry L. *The Politics of Rescue: The Roosevelt Administration and the Holocaust, 1938–1945*. New Brunswick: Rutgers University Press, 1970.

Ferenczi, Imre, and Walter Willcox. *International Migrations*. Geneva: International Labor Office, 1929.

Fernandez, Ronald. "Getting Germans to Fight Germans: The Americanizers of World War I." *Journal of Ethnic Studies* 9 (1981): 53–68.

Foley, Neil, *The White Scourge: Mexicans, Blacks, and Poor Whites in Texas Cotton Culture*. Berkeley: University of California Press, 1997.

Fox, Stephan R. *The Unknown Internment: An Oral History of the Relocation of Italian Americans During World War II*. Boston: Twayne, 1988.

Freeman, James A. *Hearts of Sorrow: Vietnamese-American Lives*. Stanford: Stanford University Press, 1989.

Freidreis, John, and Raymond Tatalovich. "Who Supports English Only Laws? Evidence from the 1992 National Election Survey." *Social Science Quarterly* 78 (1977): 354–68.

Friedman, Saul S. *No Haven for the Oppressed: United States Policy Toward Jewish Refugees, 1938–1945*. Detroit: Wayne State University Press, 1973.

Frost, F. "The Palos Verdes Chinese Anchor Mystery." *Archaeology* 35:1 (January–February 1982): 23–26.

Fuchs, Lawrence. *The American Kaleidoscope: Race, Ethnicity, and Civic Culture*. Middletown, CT: Wesleyan University Press, 1992.

Gabaccia, Donna R. *From the Other Side: Women, Gender, and Immigrant Life in the U.S., 1820–1990*. Bloomington: Indiana University Press, 1994.

———. *We Are What We Eat: Ethnic Food and the Making of Americans*. Cambridge: Harvard University Press, 1998.

Gans, Herbert J. "Toward a Reconciliation of 'Assimilation' and 'Pluralism': The Interplay of Acculturation and Ethnic Retention." *International Migration Review* 32 (1997): 893–922.

Garcia, Mario T. *Desert Immigrants: The Mexicans of El Paso, 1880–1920*. New Haven: Yale University Press, 1981.

Garza, Rodolfo O. de la, and Louis De Spiro. "Interests, Not Passions." *International Migration Review* 32 (1998): 401–22.

Gaustad, Edwin Scott. *A Religious History of America*. 2d ed. San Francisco: Harper and Row, 1990.

Gibney, Mark. "The Repatriation of Soviet Emigres." In *Immigration and Ethnicity*, ed. Michael D'Innocenzo and Josef P. Sirefman. Westport, CT: Greenwood, 1992.

Gimpel, James G., and James R. Edwards, Jr. *The Congressional Politics of Immigration Reform*. Boston: Allyn and Bacon, 1999.

Glatz, Ferenc, ed. *Hungarians and Their Neighbors in Modern Times, 1867–1950*. New York: Columbia University Press, 1995.

Glazer, Nathan, ed. *Clamor at the Gates: The New American Immigration*. San Francisco: Institute for Contemporary Studies, 1985.

Gliwicowna, Maria. "Drogi emigracji." *Przeglad Socjologiczny* 4 (1936).

Gold, Steven J., and Bruce Phillips. "Mobility and Continuity Among Eastern European Jews." In *Origins and Destinies: Immigration, Race, and Ethnicity in America*, ed. Silvia Pedraza and Rubén G. Rumbaut, pp. 182–94. Belmont, CA: Wadsworth, 1996.

Goldfield, David R., and Blaine A. Brownell, eds. *Urban America: From Downtown to No Town*. Boston: Houghton Mifflin, 1979.

Goldman, Minton. "United States Policy and Soviet Jewish Emigration from Nixon to Bush." In *Jews and Jewish Life in Russia and The Soviet Union*, ed. Yaacov Ro'i. Portland, OR: Frank Cass, 1995.

Gould, J.D. "European Intercontinental Emigration: The Role of 'Diffusion' and Feedback." *Journal of European Economic History* 9:1 (1980): 41–112.

———. "European Intercontinental Emigration, 1815–1914: Patterns and Causes." *Journal of Economic History* 8:3 (1979): 593–681.

Gould, Stephen J. *The Mismeasure of Man*. New York: W.W. Norton, 1981.

Grabbe, Hans-Jurgen. "Before the Great Tidal Waves: Patterns of Transatlantic Migration at the Beginning of the Nineteenth Century." *American Studies* [Germany] 42:3 (1997): 377–89.

———. "European Immigration to the United States in the Early National Period. 1798–1820." *Proceedings of the American Philosophical Society* 133:2 (1989): 190–214.

———. "The Demise of the Redemptioner System in the United States." *American Studies* [West Germany] 29:3 (1984): 277–96.

Graham, Ian C.C. *Colonists from Scotland: Emigration to the North America, 1707–1783*. Ithaca: Cornell University Press, 1956.

Graham, S. *Foreign Travelers in America, 1810–1935: With Poor Immigrants to America*. New York: Arno Press, 1974.

Grant, Bruce. *The Boat People: An "Age" Investigation*. New York: Penguin, 1979.

———. "European Inter-Continental Emigration, 1815–1914: Patterns and Causes." *Journal of European Economic History* 8:3 (1979): 593–681.

Grant, Madison. *The Passing of the Great Race*. 4th ed. New York: Charles Scribner's Sons, 1922.

Green, Victor R. *A Passion for Polka: Old-Time Ethnic Music in America*. Berkeley: University of California Press, 1992.

———. *American Immigrant Leaders, 1800–1910: Marginality and Identity*. Baltimore: Johns Hopkins University Press, 1987.

Guillet, E.C. *The Great Migration: The Atlantic Crossing by Sailing-Ship Since 1770*. Toronto: Thomas Nelson and Sons, 1937.

Haines, David W., ed. *Refugees as Immigrants: Cambodians, Laotians, and Vietnamese in America*. Totowa, NJ: Rowman & Littlefield, 1989.

———. *Refugees in America in the 1990s: A Reference Handbook*. Westport, CT: Greenwood, 1996.

Hamamoto, Darrell Y., and Rodolfo D. Torres. *New American Destinies: A Reader in Contemporary Asian and Latino Immigration*. New York: Routledge, 1997.

Handlin, Oscar. *Boston's Immigrants: A Study in Acculturation*. Cambridge: Harvard University Press, 1959.

Hansen, Marcus Lee. *The Immigrant in American History*. New York: Harper, 1964.

———. *The Atlantic Migration, 1607–1860: A History of the Continuing Settlement of the United States*. Cambridge: Harvard University Press, 1940.

Harrington, Mona. "Loyalties: Dual and Divided." In *Harvard Encyclopedia of American Ethnic Groups*, ed. Stephen Thernstrom, pp. 676–86. Cambridge: Harvard University Press, 1981.

Harzig, Christiane. 1997. *Peasant Maids–City Women: From the European Countryside to Urban America*. Ithaca: Cornell University Press, 1997.

Hatamiya, Leslie T. *Righting a Wrong: Japanese Americans and the Passage of the Civil Liberties Act of 1988*. Stanford: Stanford University Press, 1993.

Heer, David. *Immigration in America's Future: Social Science Findings and the Policy Debate*. Boulder, CO: Westview Press, 1996.

Helbich, Wolfgang. *Amerika ist ein freies Land. Auswanderer schreiben nach Deutschland*. Darmstadt, Germany: Luchterhand, 1985.

Herman, Masako. *The Japanese in America 1843–1973*. Dobbs Ferry, NY: Oceana, 1974.

Hess, Earl J., ed. *A German in the Yankee Fatherland: The Civil War Letters of Henry A. Kircher*. Kent: Kent State University Press, 1983.

Higham, John. *Strangers in the Land: Patterns of American Nativism, 1860–1925*. New Brunswick, NJ: Rutgers University Press, 1988.

Hine, Robert V. *Community on the American Frontier: Separate but Not Alone*. Norman: University of Oklahoma Press, 1980.

Hing, Bill Ong. *Making and Remaking Asian America Through Immigration Policy, 1850–1990*. Stanford: Stanford University Press, 1993.

Hoerder, Dirk, and Jorg Nagler, eds. *People in Transit: German Migrations in Comparative Perspective, 1820–1930*. Cambridge: Cambridge University Press, 1995.

Hofstadter, Richard. *America at 1750: A Social Portrait*. New York: Alfred A. Knopf, 1971.

Hondagneu-Sotelo, Pierrette. *Gendered Transitions: Mexican Experiences of Immigration*. Berkeley: University of California Press, 1994.

———. "Women and Children First: New Directions in Anti-Immigrant Politics." *Socialist Review* 25 (1995): 169–90.

Hooker, Thomas. *Thomas Hooker: Writings in England and Holland, 1626–1633*, ed. George H. Williams, Norman Pettit, Winfried Herget, and Sargent Bush, Jr. Cambridge: Harvard University Press, 1975.

Hossain, Mokerrom. "South Asians in Southern California: A Sociological Study of Immigrants from India, Pakistan and Bangladesh." *South Asia Bulletin* 2:1 (Spring 1982): 74–83.

Houstoun, Marion L., et al. "Female Predominance in Immigration to the United States Since 1930: A First Look." *International Migration Review* 18:4 (Winter 1989): 908–59.

Howe, Irving. *The World of Our Fathers*. New York: Harcourt Brace Jovanovich, 1976.

Howe, Irving, and Kenneth Libo, eds. *How We Lived: A Documentary History of Immigrant Jews in America, 1880–1930*. New York: R. Marek, 1979.

Hoyt, Edwin P. *The Palmer Raids, 1919–1920: An Attempt to Suppress Dissent*. New York: Seabury Press, 1969.

Hudson, Charles. *Knights of Spain, Warriors of the Sun*. Atlanta: University of Georgia Press, 1997.

Hulbert, A.B. *The Paths of Inland Commerce: A Chronicle of Trail, Road, and Waterway*. New Haven: Yale University Press, 1920.

Hunter, Robert. *Tenement Conditions in Chicago*. Chicago: City Homes Association, 1901.

Hutchinson, E.P. *Legislative History of American Immigration Policy, 1798–1965*. Philadelphia: University of Pennsylvania Press, 1981.

Ignatiev, Noel. *How the Irish Became White*. New York: Routledge, 1996.

Immigration and Naturalization Service. *Statistics Branch Annual Report: Refugees, Fiscal Year 1997*. Washington, DC: Government Printing Office, 1997.

———. *1994 Statistical Yearbook of the Immigration and Naturalization Service*. Washington, DC: Government Printing Office, 1996.

———. *1997 INS Statistical Yearbook*. Washington, DC: Government Printing Office, 1998.

Irons, Peter. *Justice Delayed*. Middletown, CT: Wesleyan University Press, 1989.

Ishi, T.K. "The Political Economy of International Migration: Indian Physicians in the United States." *South Asia Bulletin* 2:1 (Spring 1982): 39–58.

Jacobson, David. *The Immigration Reader*. New York: Blackwell, 1998.

Jacobson, Matthew Frye. *Whiteness of a Different Color: European Immigrants and the Alchemy of Race*. Cambridge: Harvard University Press, 1998.

Jasso, Guillermina, and Mark R. Rosenzweig. *The New Chosen People: Immigrants in the United States*. New York: Russell Sage Foundation, 1990.

Kamphoefner, Walter D., et al., eds. *News from the Land of Freedom: German Immigrants Write Home*. Trans. S.C. Vogel. Ithaca: Cornell University Press, 1991.

Kavanagh, Barbara, and Steve Lonergan. "Environmental Degradation, Population Displacement, and Global Security: An Overview of the Issues." A background report prepared for the Royal Society of Canada under the auspices of the Canadian Global Change Program's Research Panel on Environment and Security, December 1992.

Kazal, Russell A. "Revisiting Assimilation: The Rise, Fall, and Reappraisal of a Concept in American Ethnic History." *American Historical Review* (April 1995): 437–71.

Kehoe, Alice B. *North American Indians: A Comparative Account*. Englewood Cliffs, NJ: Prentice Hall, 1992.

Kelly, Gail Paradise. *From Vietnam to America: A Chronicle of the Vietnamese Immigration to the United States*. Boulder, CO: Westview, 1977.

Kessner, Thomas, and Betty Boyd Caroli. *Today's Immigrants, Their Stories: A New Look at the Newest Immigrants*. New York: Oxford University Press, 1981.

Kettner, James H. *The Development of American Citizenship, 1608–1870*. Chapel Hill: University of North Carolina Press, 1978.

Kim, Illsoo. "Korea and East India: Premigration Factors and U.S. Immigration Policy." In *Pacific Bridges: The New Immigration from Asia and the Pacific Islands,* ed. James Fawcett and Benjamin Carino, pp. 327–45. Staten Island, NY: Center for Migration Studies, 1987.

———. *Urban Immigrants: The Korean Community in New York.* Princeton: Princeton University Press, 1981.

Kim, Sung Bok. *Landlord and Tenant in Colonial New York: Manorial Society, 1664, 1775.* Chapel Hill: University of North Carolina Press, 1978.

Kitano, H. "Japanese." In *Harvard Encyclopedia of American Ethnic Groups,* ed. Stephen Thernstrom, pp. 561–71. Cambridge: Harvard University Press, 1981.

Klees, Frederic. *The Pennsylvania Dutch.* New York: Macmillan, 1950.

Klein, Herbert S. *The Atlantic Slave Trade.* New York: Cambridge University Press, 1999.

Knobel, Dale. *Paddy and the Republic: Ethnicity and Nationality in Antebellum America.* Middletown, CT: Wesleyan University Press, 1986.

Knudsen, John. "When Trust Is on Trial: Negotiating Refugee Narratives." In *Mistrusting Refugees,* ed. E. Valentine Daniel and John Knudsen, pp. 13–35. Berkeley: University of California Press, 1995.

Kohn, Hans. *American Nationalism: An Interpretive Essay.* New York: Macmillan, 1957.

Korytová-Magstadt, Stepanka. *To Reap a Bountiful Harvest: Czech Immigration Beyond the Mississippi, 1850–1900.* Iowa City: Rudi Publishing, 1993.

Krajlic, Frances. "Croatian Migration to and from the United States Between 1900 and 1914." Ph.D. diss., New York University, 1975.

Kraut, Alan. *Silent Travelers: Germs, Genes, and the "Immigrant Menace."* New York: Basic Books, 1994.

———. *The Huddled Masses: The Immigrant in American Society, 1880–1921.* Arlington Heights, IL: Harlan Davidson, 1982.

Krewson, Margrit W. *German-American Relations: A Selective Bibliography.* Washington, DC: Library of Congress, 1995.

Kula, Witold, Nina Assorodobraj Kula, and Marcin Kula, eds. *Writing Home: Immigrants in Brazil and the United States, 1890–1891.* Trans. from Polish and Yiddish by Josephine Wtulich. New York: Columbia University Press, 1986.

Labor Research Association. *The Palmer Raids.* New York: International Publishers, 1948.

Lai, Him Mark. "Chinese." In *Harvard Encyclopedia of American Ethnic Groups,* ed. Stephen Thernstrom. Cambridge: Harvard University Press, 1980.

———. "The United States." In *The Encyclopedia of the Chinese Overseas,* ed. L. Pan. Singapore: Chinese Heritage Centre, 1998.

La Sorte, Michael. *LaMerica: Images of Italian Greenhorn*

Experience. Philadelphia: Temple University Press, 1985.

Leach, Kristine. *Walking Common Ground. Nineteenth and Twentieth Century Immigrant Women in America.* San Francisco: Austin and Winfield, 1995.

Lee, Calvin. *Chinatown, U.S.A.* Garden City, NY: Doubleday, 1965.

LeMay, Michael C. *From Open Door to Dutch Door: An Analysis of U.S. Immigration Policy Since 1820.* New York: Praeger, 1987.

Levine, Bruce C. *The Migration of Ideology and the Contested Meaning of Freedom: German-Americans in the Mid-Nineteenth Century.* Washington, DC: German Historical Institute, 1992.

———. *The Spirit of 1848: German Immigrants, Labor Conflict, and the Coming of the Civil War.* Urbana: University of Illinois Press, 1992.

Leyburn, James G. *The Scots-Irish: A Social History.* Chapel Hill: University of North Carolina Press, 1962.

Lia, Him Mark, Genny Lim, and Judy Yung. *Island: Poetry and History of Chinese Immigrants on Angel Island, 1910–1940.* San Francisco: Hoc Doi, 1980.

Liu, Po-Chi. *A History of the Chinese in the United States of America, 1848–1911.* Taipei: Commission of Overseas Affairs, 1976.

Liu, William T., Maryanne Lamanna, and Alice Murata. *Transition to Nowhere: Vietnamese Refugees in America.* Nashville: Charter House, 1979.

Loescher, Gil. *Beyond Charity: International Cooperation and the Global Refugee Crisis.* New York: Oxford University Press, 1993.

Loescher, Gil, and John A. Scanlan. *Calculated Kindness: Refugees and America's Half-Open Door, 1945 to the Present.* New York: Free Press, 1986.

Long, Lynellyn D. *Ban Vinai: The Refugee Camp.* New York: Columbia University Press, 1993.

Lonn, Ella. *Foreigners in the Confederacy.* Chapel Hill: University of North Carolina Press, 1940.

———. *Foreigners in the Union Army and Navy.* Baton Rouge: Louisiana State University Press, 1951.

Lowenstein, Sharon R. *Token Refuge: The Story of the Jewish Refugee Shelter at Oswego, 1944–1946.* Bloomington: Indiana University Press, 1986.

Luebke, Frederick C. "Ethnic Group Settlement on the Great Plains." *Western Historical Quarterly* 8:4 (October 1977): 405–30.

———. *Germans in the New World: Essays in the History of Immigration.* Urbana: University of Illinois Press, 1990.

Luebke, Frederick C., ed. *European Immigrants in the American West: Community Histories.* Albuquerque: University of New Mexico Press, 1998.

Lyman, S.M. *Chinese Americans.* New York: Random House, 1974.

Mannix, Daniel P. *A History of the Atlantic Slave Trade.* New York: Viking, 1962.

Marinbach, Bernard. *Galveston: Ellis Island of the West.* Albany: State University of New York Press, 1983.

Martin, Philip. "Proposition 187 in California." *International Migration Review* 29 (1995): 255–63.

Marx, Anthony W. *Making Race and Nation.* New York: Cambridge University Press, 1998.

Mathias, Elizabeth, and Richard Raspa. *Italian Folktales in America: The Verbal Art of an Immigrant Woman.* Detroit: Wayne State University Press, 1985.

McClain, Charles J. *In Search of Equality: The Chinese Struggle Against Discrimination in Nineteenth-Century America.* Berkeley: University of California Press, 1994.

McCormick, E. Allen, ed. *Germans in America: Aspects of German-American Relations in the Nineteenth Century.* Brooklyn, NY: Brooklyn College Press, 1983.

McCunn, R. Lum. *Chinese American Portraits: Personal Histories, 1928–1988.* San Francisco: Chronicle Books, 1988.

McGinty, Brian. "Angel Island: The Door Half Closed." *American History Illustrated* (September–October 1990): 50–51, 71.

Melosi, Martin. *The Sanitary City: Urban Infrastructure in America from Colonial Times to the Present.* Baltimore: Johns Hopkins University Press, 2000.

Merk, Frederick. *History of the Westward Movement.* New York: Alfred A. Knopf, 1978.

Mertz, H. *Gods from the Far East: How the Chinese Discovered America.* New York: Ballantine, 1972.

Mills, Nicolaus. *Arguing Immigration: The Debate over the Changing Face of America.* New York: Touchstone Books, 1994.

Min, Pyong Gap. *Caught in the Middle: Korean Communities in New York and Los Angeles.* Berkeley: University of California Press, 1996.

Mink, Gwendolyn. *Old Labor and New Immigrants in American Political Development: Union, Party and State, 1875–1920.* Ithaca: Cornell University Press, 1986.

Minocha, Urmil. "South Asian Immigrants: Trends and Impacts on the Sending and Receiving Societies." In *Pacific Bridges, The New Immigration from Asia and the Pacific Islands,* ed. James Fawcett and Benjamin Carino, pp. 347–73. Staten Island, NY: Center for Migration Studies, 1987.

Model, Suzanne. "The Economic Progress of Europeans and East Asian Americans." *Annual Review of Sociology* 14 (1993): 363–80.

Moltmann, Günter, ed. *Aufbruch nach Amerika. Die Auswanderungswelle von 1816–17.* Stuttgart: J.B. Metzler, 1989.

Montgomery, David. *The Fall of the House of Labor: The Workplace, the State, and American Labor Activism, 1865–1925.* New York: Cambridge University Press, 1987.

Morgan, Edmund. *American Slavery, American Freedom: The Ordeal of Colonial Virginia.* New York: Norton, 1975.

Moriyama, Alan T. *Imingaisha: Japanese Emigration Companies and Hawaii, 1894–1908.* Honolulu: University of Hawaii Press, 1985.

Muller, Thomas, and Thomas J. Espenshade. *The Fourth Wave: California's Newest Immigrants.* Washington, DC: Urban Institute, 1985.

Murphy, Andrew R. *Conscience and Community: Revisiting Toleration and Religious Dissent in Early Modern England and America.* University Park: Pennsylvania State University Press, 2001.

Murray, Robert. *Red Scare: A Study in National Hysteria, 1919–1920.* New York: McGraw-Hill, 1964.

Myer, Dillion S. *Uprooted Americans: The Japanese Americans and the War Relocation Authority During World War II.* Tucson: University of Arizona Press, 1971.

Nackerud, Larry, et al. "The End of the Cuban Contradiction in U.S. Refugee Policy." *International Migration Review* 33:1 (Spring 1999): 176–92.

Nagler, Joerg A. "Enemy Aliens and Internment in World War I: Alvo von Alvensleben in Fort Douglas, Utah, a Case Study." *Utah Historical Quarterly* 58 (1990): 388–405.

Nakano, M. *Japanese American Women: Three Generations 1890–1900.* San Francisco: Mina Press, 1990.

Neele, G.P. *Atlantic and American Notes: Embodying Some Account of the Recent Visit of the Directors of the London and Northwestern Railway to Canada and the United States.* London: McCorquodale, 1982.

Nelli, Humbert. "Italians." In *Harvard Encyclopedia of American Ethnic Groups,* ed. Stephen Thernstrom, pp. 545–60. Cambridge: Harvard University Press, 1981.

Nguyen, D.T., and J.S. Bandara. "Emigration Pressure and Structural Change: Vietnam." UNDP Technical Support Services Report, Bangkok, 1996.

Noble, Allen G., ed. *To Build in a New Land: Ethnic Landscapes in North America.* Baltimore: Johns Hopkins University Press, 1992.

Noriel, Gerard, ed. *Immigrants in Two Democracies: The French and American Experience.* New York: New York University Press, 1992.

Nugent, Walter. *Crossings: The Great Transatlantic Migrations, 1870–1914.* Bloomington: Indiana University Press, 1992.

Obidinski, Eugene E., and Helen Stankiewicz Zand. *Polish Folkways in America.* Lanham, MD: University Press of America, 1987.

O'Connor, Richard. *The German-Americans: An Informal History.* Boston: Little, Brown, 1968.

O'Hare, William P., and Judy C. Felt. *Asian Americans: America's Fastest Growing Minority Group.* Washington, DC: Immigration and Naturalization Service, 1991.

Olzak, Susan. *The Dynamics of Ethnic Competition and Conflict*. Stanford: Stanford University Press, 1992.

Orleck, Annelise, *Common Sense and a Little Fire: Women and Working-Class Politics in the United States, 1900–1965*. Chapel Hill: University of North Carolina Press, 1995.

Orsi, Robert Anthony. *The Madonna of 115th Street: Faith and Community in Italian Harlem, 1880–1950*. New Haven: Yale University Press, 1985.

Overdyke, William Darrell. *The Know-Nothing Party in the South*. Baton Rouge: Louisiana State University Press, 1950.

Pagiola, Stefano. *The Global Environmental Benefits of Land Degradation Control on Agricultural Land*. Washington, DC: World Bank, 1999.

Parrillo, Vincent N. *Strangers to These Shores: Race and Ethnic Relations in the United States*. New York: Wiley, 1985.

Pedraza, Silvia. "Origins and Destinies: Immigration, Race, and Ethnicity in American History." In *Origins and Destinies: Immigration, Race, and Ethnicity in America*, ed. Silvia Pedraza and Rubén G. Rumbaut, pp. 1–20. Belmont, CA: Wadsworth, 1996.

Peiss, Kathy. *Cheap Amusements: Working Women and Leisure in Turn of-the-Century New York*. Philadelphia: Temple University Press, 1986.

Penn, William. "A Further Account of the Province of Pennsylvania." In *Narratives of Early Pennsylvania*, ed. Albert Cook Myers. New York: Charles Scribner's Sons, 1912.

Perec, Georges, and Robert Bober. *Ellis Island*. New York: New Press, 1995.

Phillips, Kevin P. *The Cousins' Wars: Religion, Politics, and the Triumph of Anglo-America*. New York: Basic Books, 1999.

Philpott, Thomas L. *The Slum and the Ghetto: Neighborhood Deterioration and Middle-Class Reform, Chicago, 1880–1930*. New York: Oxford University Press, 1978.

Pido, Antonio J.A. *The Pilipinos in America: Macro/Micro Dimensions of Immigration and Integration*. Staten Island, NY: Center for Migration Studies, 1992.

Pierson, L., and J. Moriarty. "Stone Anchors: Asiatic Shipwrecks off the California Coast." *Anthropological Journal of Canada* 18:3 (1980): 17–22.

Piore, Michael. *The Birds of Passage: Migrant Labor in Industrial Societies*. New York: Cambridge University Press, 1979.

Pitkin, Thomas M. *Keepers of the Gate: A History of Ellis Island*. New York: New York University Press, 1975.

Portes, Alejandro. "From South of the Border: Hispanic Minorities in the United States." In *Immigration Reader: America in a Multidisciplinary Perspective*, ed. David Jacobson, pp. 113–43. Malden, MA: Blackwell, 1998.

Portes, Alejandro, and Robert L. Bach. *Latin Journey: Cuban and Mexican Immigrants in the United States*. Berkeley: University of California Press, 1985.

Portes, Alejandro, and Rubén G. Rumbaut. *Immigrant America: A Portrait*. Berkeley: University of California Press, 1996.

Potter, J. "The Growth of Population in America, 1700–1860." In *Population in History: Essays in Historical Demography*, ed. David V. Glass and D.E.C. Eversley. Chicago: Aldine, 1972.

Preston, William, Jr. *Aliens and Dissenters: Federal Suppression of Radicals*. 2d ed. Urbana: University of Illinois Press, 1995.

Puskas, Julianna. *From Hungary to the United States (1880–1914)*. Budapest: Akademiai Kiado, 1982.

Rasmussen, C. "L.A. Then and Now, A Forgotten Hero from a Night of Disgrace." *Los Angeles Times*, May 16, 1999.

Reimers, David M. *Still the Golden Door: The Third World Comes to America*. 2d ed. New York: Columbia University Press, 1992.

———. *Unwelcome Strangers: American Identity and the Turn Against Immigration*. New York: Columbia University Press, 1998.

Riis, Jacob. *How the Other Half Lives: Studies Among the Tenements of New York*. New York: Charles Scribner's Sons, 1890.

Rippley, Lavern. *Of German Ways*. New York: Gramercy, 1986.

Rischin, Moses, and John Livingston, eds. *Jews of the American West*. Detroit: Wayne State University Press, 1991.

Rischin, Moses. *The Promised City: New York's Jews, 1870–1914*. Cambridge: Harvard University Press, 1962.

Rivera-Batiz, Francisco, and Carlos Santiago. *Puerto Ricans in the United States: A Changing Reality*. Washington, DC: National Puerto Rican Coalition, 1994.

Robinson, W. Courtland. *Terms of Refuge: The Indochinese Exodus and the International Response*. New York: Zed Books, 1998

Rockett, Ian R., and S.L. Putnam. "Physician-Nurse Migration to the United States: Regional and Health Status Origins in Relation to Legislation and Policy." *International Migration Review* 27:3 (September 1989): 389–401.

Rodriguez, Junius P. *The Historical Encyclopedia of World Slavery*. Santa Barbara, CA: ABC-Clio, 1997.

Roediger, David. *The Wages of Whiteness: Race and the Making of the American Working Class*. New York: Verso, 1991.

Romo, Ricardo. *East Los Angeles: History of a Barrio*. Austin: University of Texas Press, 1983.

———. "Mexican Americans: Their Civic and Political Incorporation." In *Origins and Destinies: Immigration, Race, and Ethnicity in America*, ed. Silvia Pedraza and

Rubén G. Rumbaut, pp. 84–97. Belmont, CA: Wadsworth, 1996.

Rothan, Rev. Emmet H. "The German Catholic Immigrant in the United States (1830–1860)." Ph.D. diss., Catholic University of America, 1946.

Rumbaut, Rubén G. "Origins and Destinies: Immigration to the United States Since World War II." *Sociological Forum* 9 (1994): 583–621.

———. "The Structure of Refuge: Southeast Asian Refugees in the United States, 1975–1985." *International Journal of Comparative Public Policy* 1 (1989): 97–129.

Rutman, Darrett, and Anita Rutman. *A Place in Time: Middlesex County, Virginia, 1650–1750.* New York: Norton, 1984.

Sánchez, George J. *Becoming Mexican American: Ethnicity, Culture, and Identity in Chicano Los Angeles, 1900–1945.* New York: Oxford University Press, 1993.

Saxton, Alexander. *The Indispensable Enemy: Labor and the Anti-Chinese Movement in California.* Berkeley: University of California Press, 1995.

Shanahan, Suzanne, and Susan Olzak. "The Effects of Immigrant Diversity and Ethnic Competition on Collective Conflict in Urban America." *Journal of American Ethnic History* 18 (1999): 40–64.

Shepperson, Wilbur S. *Emigration & Disenchantment: Portraits of Englishmen Repatriated from the United States.* Norman: University of Oklahoma Press, 1957.

Shinagawa, Larry H., and Michel Lang. *Atlas of American Diversity.* Walnut Creek, CA: AltaMira Press, 1998.

Shulman, Alix. *To the Barricades: The Anarchist Life of Emma Goldman.* New York: Thomas Y. Crowell, 1971.

Simcox, David. "Major Predictors of Immigration Restrictionism: Operationalizing 'Nativism.'" *Population and Environment* 19 (1997): 129–43.

Simon, Rita J., and S.H. Alexander. *The Ambivalent Welcome: Print Media, Public Opinion, and Immigration.* Westport, CT: Praeger, 1993.

Simon, Rita J., and J.P. Lynch. "A Comparative Assessment of Public Opinion Toward Immigrants and Immigration Policies." *International Migration Review* 33 (1999): 455–67.

Simon, Roger D. "Housing and Services in an Immigrant Neighborhood: Milwaukee's Ward 14." *Journal of Urban History* 2:4 (1975): 435–58.

Sinclair, Upton. *The Jungle.* Urbana: University of Illinois Press, 1988.

Slobin, Mark. *Tenement Songs: The Popular Music of the Jewish Immigrants.* Urbana: University of Illinois Press, 1982.

Smith, Carter, III, and David Lindroth. *Hispanic-American Experience on File.* New York: Facts on File, 1999.

Smith, James Morton. *Freedom's Fetters: The Alien and Sedition Laws and American Civil Liberties.* Ithaca: Cornell University Press, 1956.

Smith, Rogers. *Civic Ideals: Conflicting Visions of Citizenship in U.S. History.* New Haven: Yale University Press, 1997.

Smith-Hefner, Nancy J. *Khymer American: Identity and Moral Education in a Diasporic Community.* Berkeley: University of California Press, 1999.

Sowell, Thomas. *Ethnic America: A History.* New York: Basic Books, 1981.

Spickard, Paul R. *Japanese Americans: The Formation and Transformations of an Ethnic Group.* New York: Twayne, 1996.

St. John, J. Hector (originally Michel-Guillaume-Jean de Crèvecoeur). *Letters from an American Farmer; Describing Certain Provincial Situations, Manners and Customs Not Originally Known.* London: Thomas Davies, 1782.

Stefancic, Jean. "Funding the Nativist Agenda." In *Immigrants Out! The New Nativism and the Anti-Immigrant Impulse in the United States,* ed. Juan Perea, pp. 119–35. New York: New York University Press, 1997.

Steiner, Stan. *Fusang: The Chinese Who Built America.* New York: Harper and Row, 1979.

Stewart, Barbara McDonald. *United States Government Policy on Refugees from Nazism, 1933–1940.* New York: Garland, 1982.

Stolarik, M. Mark. *Growing Up on the South Side: Three Generations of Slovaks in Bethlehem, Pennsylvania, 1880–1976.* Cranbury, NJ: Associated University Presses, 1985.

Stolarik, M. Mark, ed. *Forgotten Doors: The Other Ports of Entry to the United States.* Philadelphia: Balch Institute Press, 1988.

Sung, Betty Lee. *Mountain of Gold: The Story of the Chinese in America.* New York: Macmillan, 1967.

Taake, Angie. "Adoption." *National Adoption Information Clearinghouse.* http://www.naic.com, February 23, 1999.

Takaki, Ronald. *A Different Mirror: A History of Multicultural America.* Boston: Little, Brown, 1993.

Tatalovich, Raymond. "Official English as Nativist Backlash." In *Immigrants Out! The New Nativism and the Anti-Immigrant Impulse in the United States,* ed. Juan Perea, pp. 78–102. New York: New York University Press, 1997.

Tate, Thad W., and David L. Ammerman, eds. *The Chesapeake in the Seventeenth Century: Essays on Anglo-American Society.* Chapel Hill: University of North Carolina Press, 1979.

Tcheu, John Kuo Wei. *New York Before Chinatown: Orientalism and the Shaping of American Culture, 1776–1882.* Baltimore: Johns Hopkins University Press, 1999.

Terrell, John Upton. *American Indian Almanac.* New York: Barnes and Noble, 1991.

Tocqueville, Alexis de. *Democracy in America.* Trans. George Lawrence, ed. J. P. Mayer. 1848. Reprint. New York: Harper and Row, 1969.

Tollefson, James W. *Alien Winds: The Reeducation of America's Indochinese Refugees.* New York: Praeger, 1989.

Trommler, Frank, and Joseph McVeigh, eds. *America and the Germans: An Assessment of a Three-Hundred-Year History.* Philadelphia: University of Pennsylvania Press, 1985.

Tung, William L. *The Chinese in America, 1820–1973.* Dobbs Ferry, NY: Oceana, 1974.

Ueda, Reed. "Naturalization and Citizenship." In *Harvard Encyclopedia of American Ethnic Groups,* ed. Stephen Thernstrom, pp. 734–48. Cambridge: Harvard University Press, 1981.

———. *Postwar Immigrant America: A Social History.* Boston: Bedford Books of St. Martin's Press, 1994.

———. "The Changing Face of Post-1965 Immigration." In *Immigration Reader: America in a Multidisciplinary Perspective,* ed. David Jacobson, pp. 72–91. Malden, MA: Blackwell, 1998.

Ulam, Adam. *The Bolsheviks.* Cambridge: Harvard University Press, 1998.

U.S. Senate. *Reports of the U.S. Immigration Commission: Immigrants in Industries,* pt. 2. 61st Cong., 2d Sess., S. Doc. 633. Washington, DC: Government Printing Office, 1911.

Waldinger, Roger. *Still the Promised City? African-Americans and New Immigrants in Postindustrial New York.* Cambridge: Harvard University Press, 1996.

Walz, John Albrecht. *German Influence in American Education and Culture.* Philadelphia: Carl Schurz Memorial Foundation, 1936.

Warren, Robert. "Estimates of the Undocumented Immigrant Population Residing in the United States: October 1996." Office of Policy and Planning, Immigration and Naturalization Service, Department of Justice, Washington, DC, August 1997.

Wells, Robert V. *The Population of the British Colonies in America Before 1776: A Survey of Census Data.* Princeton: Princeton University Press, 1975.

Williams, F.W. *Anson Burlingame and the First Chinese Mission to Foreign Powers.* New York: Charles Scribner's Sons, 1912.

Williams, Roger. "Letters of Roger Williams." *Publications of the Narragansett Club* 6 (1874).

Wills, W.H., and R.D. Leonard. *The Ancient Southwestern Community: Models and Methods for the Study of Prehistoric Social Organization.* Albuquerque: University of New Mexico Press, 1990.

Wilson, William Julius. *The Declining Significance of Race: Blacks and Changing American Institutions.* Chicago: University of Chicago Press, 1978.

Winther, O.O. *The Old Oregon Country: A History of Frontier Trade, Transportation, and Travel.* Stanford: Stanford University Press, 1950.

Winthrop, John. *Winthrop Papers.* 5 vols. Boston: Massachusetts Historical Society, 1929–47.

Witos, Wincenty. *Moje wspomnienia.* Paris: Kultura, 1964.

Wittke, Carl. *The Irish in America.* Baton Rouge: Louisiana State University Press, 1956.

Woods, Lawrence M. *British Gentlemen in the Wild West: The Era of the Intensely English Cowboy.* New York: Free Press, 1989.

Wright, Ronald. *Stolen Continents: The "New World" Through Indian Eyes.* Boston: Houghton Mifflin, 1992.

Wyman, David S. *Paper Walls: America and the Refugee Crisis, 1938–1941.* Amherst: University of Massachusetts Press, 1968.

———. *The Abandonment of the Jews: America and the Holocaust, 1941–1945.* New York: Pantheon Books, 1984.

Wyman, Mark. *Round-Trip to America: The Immigrants Return to Europe, 1880–1930.* Ithaca: Cornell University Press, 1993.

Yans-McLaughlin, Virginia, and Marjorie Lightman. *Ellis Island and the Peopling of America.* New York: New Press, 1997.

Yezierska, Anzia, *Bread Givers: A Struggle Between a Father of the Old World and a Daughter of the New.* New York: Persea, 1975.

Young, Donald. *American Minority Peoples: A Study in Racial and Cultural Conflicts in the United States.* New York: Harper & Brothers, 1932.

Yung, Wing. *My Life in China and America.* New York: Henry Holt, 1909.

Zucker, Norman L., and Naomi Flink Zucker. *Desperate Crossings: Seeking Refuge in America.* Armonk, NY: M.E. Sharpe, 1996.

———. *The Guarded Gate: The Reality of American Refugee Policy.* New York: Harcourt Brace Jovanovich, 1987.

Zunz, Olivier. *The Changing Face of Inequality: Urbanization, Industrial Development, and Immigrants in Detroit, 1880–1920.* Chicago: University of Chicago Press, 1982.

ISSUES

Abadan-Unat, Nermin. "The Socio-Economic Aspects of Return Migration in Turkey. *Migration: A European Journal of International Migration and Ethnic Relations* 3 (1988): 29–59.

Abalos, David T. *The Latino Family and the Politics of Transformation.* Westport, CT: Praeger, 1993.

Abbott, Edith. *Immigration: Select Documents and Case Records.* New York: Arno Press, 1969.

Abe-Kim, Jennifer, and David Takeuchi. "Cultural Competence and Quality of Care: Issues for Mental Health Service Delivery in Managed Care." *American Psychologist* 3 (1996): 273–95.

Abrams, Fran. "Made in Saipan, If Only You Knew." *New Statesman* 129 (January 10, 2000): 44–68.

Abramson, Harold J. *Ethnic Diversity in Catholic America.* New York: Wiley, 1973.

Acuña, Rodolfo F. *Anything but Mexican: Chicanos in Contemporary Los Angeles.* London: Verso, 1996.

———. *Occupied America: A History of Chicanos.* 2d ed. New York: Harper and Row, 1981.

Adam, Michelle. "For Every Soul There Is a Trace." *World of Hibernia* 5:1 (Summer 1999): 1–11.

Addams, Jane, et al. *Philanthropy and Social Progress.* New York: Books for Libraries, 1893. Reprint, Montclair, NJ: Patterson Smith, 1970.

Agarwal, Pankaj. *Passage from India: Post-1965 Indian Immigrants and Their Children—Conflicts, Concerns, and Solutions.* Palos Verdes, CA: Yuvati Publications, 1991.

Agee, James, and Walker Evans. *Let Us Now Praise Famous Men.* Boston: Houghton Mifflin, 1941.

Aguilera, Michael. "The Labor Market Outcomes of Undocumented and Documented Immigrants: A Social and Human Capital Comparison." Ph.D. diss., State University of New York, Stony Brook, 1999.

Ahmed, Bashir, and J. Gregory Robinson. "Estimates of Emigration of the Foreign-Born Population: 1980–1990." Technical Working Paper no. 9. Bureau of the Census, Population Division, Washington, DC, 1994.

Alarcón, Rafael, David Runsten, and Raul Hinojosa Ojeda. "Migrant Remittance Transfer Mechanisms Between Los Angeles and Lalisco, Mexico." Research Report Series no. 7. North American Integration and Development Center, University of California–Los Angeles, 1998.

Alba, Francisco. "Mexico's International Migration as a Manifestation of Its Development Pattern." *International Migration Review* 12 (1978): 502–51.

Alba, Richard D. *Ethnic Identity: The Transformation of White America.* New Haven: Yale University Press, 1990.

———. "Italian Americans: A Century of Ethnic Change." In *Origins and Destinies*, ed. Silvia Pedraza and Rubén G. Rumbaut. Belmont, CA: Wadsworth, 1996.

———. *Italian Americans: Into the Twilight of Ethnicity.* Englewood Cliffs, NJ: Prentice Hall, 1985.

Alba, Richard D., Douglas S. Massey, and Rubén G. Rumbaut. *The Immigration Experience for Families and Children. Issue Series in Social Research and Social Policy.* Washington, DC: American Sociological Association, 1999.

Albini, Joseph L. *The American Mafia: Genesis of a Legend.* New York: Meredith, 1971.

Aldrich, Howard E., and Roger Waldinger. "Ethnicity and Entrepreneurship." *Annual Review of Sociology* 16 (1990): 111–35.

Aldrich, Howard E., Trevor R. Jones, and David McEvoy. "Ethnic Advantage and Minority Business Development." In *Ethnic Communities in Business: Strategies for Economic Survival*, ed. Robin Ward and Richard Jenkins, pp. 189–210. New York: Cambridge University Press, 1984.

Aleinikoff, Alexander, and David Martin, eds. *Immigration and Nationality Laws of the United States. Selected Statutes, Regulations, and Forms as Amended to March 6, 1990.* St. Paul, MN: West Publishing, 1990.

Allen, James Paul, and Eugene Turner. *We the People: An Atlas of America's Ethnic Diversity.* New York: Macmillan, 1988.

Allen, Virginia G. "Literature as a Support to Language Acquisition." In *When They Don't All Speak English: Integrating the ESL Students into the Regular Classroom*, ed. Pat Rigg and Virginia G. Allen, pp. 55–64. Urbana, IL: National Council of Teachers of English, 1989.

———. "Selecting Materials for the Reading Instruction of ESL Children." In *Kids Come in All Languages: Reading Instruction for ESL Students*, ed. K. Spangenberg-Urbschat and R. Pritchard, pp. 108–31. Newark, DE: International Reading Association, 1994.

Almaguer, Tomas. "Racial Domination and Class Conflict in Capitalist Agriculture: The Oxnard Sugar Beet Workers' Strike of 1903." In *From Different Shores: Perspectives on Race and Ethnicity in America*, 2d ed., ed. Ronald Takaki, pp. 128–38. New York: Oxford University Press, 1999.

Alvarez, Lizette. "Congress Approves a Big Increase in Visas for Specialized Workers." *New York Times*, October 4, 2000.

Ambert, Alba N., and Maria D. Alvarez, ed. *Puerto Rican Children on the Mainland: Interdisciplinary Perspectives.* New York: Garland, 1992.

Anderson, Benedict. "Long Distance Nationalism." In *The Spectre of Comparisons: Nationalism, Southeast Asia and the World*, ed. Benedict Anderson. London: Verso, 1998.

Anderson, Margo J. *The American Census: A Social History.* New Haven: Yale University Press, 1988.

Anderson, Margo J., ed. *Encyclopedia of the U.S. Census.* Washington, DC: Congressional Quarterly Press, 2000.

Anderson, Margo J., and Stephen E. Fienberg. *Who Counts? The Politics of Census-Taking in Contemporary America.* New York: Russell Sage Foundation, 1999.

Andreas, Peter. "The Transformation of Migrant Smuggling Across the U.S.-Mexico Border." In *Global Human Smuggling: Comparative Perspectives*, ed. David Kyle and Rey Koslowski. Baltimore: Johns Hopkins University Press, forthcoming.

Anner, John. "Sweatshop Workers Organize and Win." *Progressive* 60 (June 1996): 15.

Anton, Marta. "The Discourse of the Learner-Centered Classroom: Sociocultural Perspectives on Teacher-Learner Interaction in the Second-Language Classroom." *Modern Language Journal* 83 (1999): 303–17.

Antush, John, ed. *Recent Puerto Rican Theater: Five Plays from New York*. Houston: Arte Publico, 1991.

Anzaldúa, Gloria. *Borderlands/La Frontera: The New Mestiza*. San Francisco: Aunt Lute Books, 1999.

Archdeacon, Thomas J. *Becoming American: An Ethnic History*. New York: Free Press, 1983.

Ardittis, Solon. "Labour Migration and the Single European Market: A Synthetic and Prospective Note." *International Sociology* 5 (1990): 461–74.

Arendt, Hannah. *The Origins of Totalitarianism*. San Diego: Harcourt, Brace, Jovanovich, 1968.

Argüelles, Lourdes, and Anne M. Rivero. "Gender/Sexual Orientation Violence and Transnational Migration: Conversations with Some Latinas We Think We Know." *Urban Anthropology* 2:3–4 (1993): 259–76.

Arilli, Yehoshua. *Individualism and Nationalism in American Ideology*. Cambridge: Harvard University Press, 1964.

Arnold, Fred, and Nasra M. Shah, ed. *Asian Labor Migration: Pipeline to the Middle East*. Boulder, CO: Westview Press, 1986.

Aronowitz, S. "The Social and Emotional Adjustment of Immigrant Children: A Review of the Literature." *International Migration Review* 23:2 (1988): 237–57.

Arvizu, John R., and F. Chris Garcia. "Latino Voting Participation: Explaining and Differentiating Latino Voting Turnout." *Hispanic Journal of Behavioral Sciences* 18:2 (1996): 104–28.

Ashabrenner, Brent. *Still a Nation of Immigrants*. New York: Cobblehill Books and Dutton, 1993.

Asher, James J. *Learning Another Language Through Actions: The Complete Teacher's Guidebook*. Los Gatos, CA: Sky Oaks Productions, 1977.

Associated Press. "Boat Packed with Haitians and Dominicans Runs Aground." *Burlington Free Press*, January 2, 2000.

———. "Suspected Illegal Immigrants Found in Cargo Container." February 5, 1999.

———. "U-Haul Truck with Dozens of Illegal Immigrants Chased 200 Miles." March 6, 1996.

———. "3 Stowaways Die in Cargo Hold on US-Bound Ship." *New Times National News*, March 19, 1996.

———. "10 Illegal Immigrants Captured After Officials Chase Pickup for Two Hours." *Corpus Christi News*, March 2, 1998.

Auerbach, E.R., and D. Burgess. "The Hidden Curriculum of Survival ESL." *TESOL Quarterly* 10 (1985): 475–95.

Axtman, Kris. "New Energy, and More Unity, for Cubans in U.S." *Christian Science Monitor*, January 13, 2000.

Bacerra, Rosina. "The Mexican-American: Aging in a Changing Culture." In *Aging in Minority Groups*, ed. R.L. McNeely and J. N. Colen. Beverly Hills, CA: Sage, 1983.

Bacon, David. "Immigrant Workers Ask Labor 'Which Side Are You On?'" *Working USA: Journal of Labor and Society* 3:5 (2000): 7–18.

Bader, Veit-Michael, ed. *Citizenship and Exclusion*. New York: St. Martin's Press, 1997.

Bailey, Thomas, and Roger Waldinger. "Primary, Secondary, and Enclave Labor Markets: A Training System Approach." *American Sociological Review* 56 (1991): 432–45.

Baker, S.G. "California and Catalunya: The Politics of Immigration Control in the United States of America and the Kingdom of Spain." Unpublished manuscript, 1995.

———. "Immigration Reform: The Empowerment of a New Constituency." In *Public Policy for Democracy*, ed. Helen Ingram and Steven Rathgeb-Smith, pp. 136–58. Washington, DC: Brookings Institution, 1993.

———. *The Cautious Welcome: The Legalization Programs of the Immigration Reform and Control Act*. Washington, DC: Urban Institute, 1990.

Ballard, Roger, ed. *Desh Pardesh: The South Asian Presence in Britain*. London: Hurst, 1994.

Balmer, Randall. *Blessed Assurance: A History of American Evangelicalism*. Boston: Beacon Press, 1999.

Bames, Edward. "Slaves of New York." *Time*, November 2, 1998, pp. 72–75.

Bancroft, Jane W. "The Lozanov Method and Its American Adaptations." *Modern Language Journal* 62 (1977): 167–75.

Bankston, Carl, and Min Zhou. "The Social Adjustment of Vietnamese American Adolescents: Evidence for a Segmented-Assimilation Approach." *Social Science Quarterly* 78 (1997): 508–23.

Barakat, Halim. *The Arab World: Society, Culture, and State*. Berkeley: University of California Press, 1993.

Barger, W.K., and Ernesto Reza. *The Farm Labor Movement in the Midwest*. Austin: University of Texas Press, 1994.

Barkan, Elliot R. *Asian and Pacific Islander Migration to the United States: A Model of New Global Patterns*. Westport, CT: Greenwood, 1992.

Barlow, Hugh D. *Criminal Justice in America*. Upper Saddle River, NJ: Prentice Hall, 2000.

Barnouw, Erik. *A History of Broadcasting in the United States*. 3 vols. New York: Oxford University Press, 1966–70.

———. *Tube of Plenty: The Evolution of American Television*. Rev. ed. New York: Oxford University Press, 1990.

Barolini, Helen, ed. *Images: A Pictorial History of Italian Americans*. Staten Island, NY: Center for Migration Studies of New York, 1981.

Barrera, Mario. *Race and Class in the Southwest: A Theory of Racial Inequality*. Notre Dame: University of Notre Dame Press, 1979.

Barringer, Herbert R., Robert W. Gardner, and Michael J. Levin. *Asians and Pacific Islanders in the United States*. New York: Russell Sage Foundation, 1993.

Basch, Linda, Nina Glick Schiller, and Cristina Szanton-Blanc. *Nations Unbound: Transnationalized Projects and the Deterritorialized Nation-State*. New York: Gordon and Bohning, 1994.

Baseler, Marilyn C. *"Asylum for Mankind": America, 1607–1800*. Ithaca: Cornell University Press, 1998.

Basheda, Lori. "Wedded to Idea of U.S. Men." *Orange County Register*, October 19, 1998.

Bean, Frank, and Stephanie Bell-Rose. "Introduction: Immigration and Its Relation to Race and Ethnicity in the United States." In *Immigration and Opportunity: Race, Ethnicity, and Employment in the United States*, ed. Frank Bean and Stephanie Bell-Rose, pp. 1–28. New York: Russell Sage Foundation, 1999.

Bean, Frank D., and Marta Tienda. *The Hispanic Population of the United States*. New York: Russell Sage Foundation, 1987.

Bean, Frank D., Barry Edmonston, and Jeffrey S. Passel. *Undocumented Migration to the United States: IRCA and the Experience of the 1980s*. Washington, DC: Urban Institute, 1990.

Bean, Frank D., B. Lindsay Lowell, and Lowell J. Taylor. "Undocumented Mexican Immigrants and the Earnings of Other Workers in the United States." *Demography* 25 (1988): 35–52.

Bean, Frank D., R. Chanove, R.G. Cushing, R. de la Garza, G. Freeman, C.W. Haynes, and D. Spener. *Illegal Mexican Migration and the United States/Mexico Border: The Effects of Operation Hold-the-Line on El Paso and Juarez*. Washington, DC: Commission on Immigration Reform, 1994.

Beaujot, Roderic. *Population Change in Canada*. Toronto: McClelland and Stewart, 1991.

Beck, R. *Re-Charting America's Future*. Petoskey, MI: Social Contract Press, 1994.

Beirne, Piers, and James Messerschmidt. *Criminology*. Boulder, CO: Westview Press, 2000.

Belsky, G. "Escape from America." *Money*, July 7, 1994, pp. 60–70.

Benei, Veronique. "Hinduism Today: Inventing a Universal Religion?" *South Asia Research* 18:2 (1998): 117–24.

Benjamin, A.E., Steven Wallace, Villa Villa, and Kathy McCarthy. *California Immigrants Have Mostly Lower Rates of Disability and Use of Disability Services Than State's U.S.-Born Residents*. Los Angeles: UCLA Center for Health Policy Research, 2000.

Bennett, David. *The Party of Fear: From Nativist Movements to the New Right in American History*. Chapel Hill: University of North Carolina Press, 1988.

Ben-Porot, Mordechai. *To Baghdad and Back: The Miraculous 2,000 Year Homecoming of the Iraqi Jews*. New York: Gefen, 1998.

Berchell, Robert A. *The San Francisco Irish, 1848–1880*. Berkeley: University of California Press, 1980.

Bergesen, Albert, and Max Herman. "Immigration, Race, and Riot: The 1992 Los Angeles Uprising." *American Sociological Review* 63 (1998): 39–54.

Bergland, Betty. "Immigrant History and the Gendered Subject: A Review Essay." *Ethnic Forum* 8:2 (1988): 24–39.

Berk, Marc, Claudia Schur, Leo Chavez, and Martin Frankel. "Health Care Use Among Undocumented Latino Immigrants." *Health Affairs* 19:4 (2000): 51–64.

Bernard, William. *The Acculturation of Immigrant Groups into American Society*. Montclair, NJ: Patterson Smith, 1971.

Berube, Allan. *Coming Out Under Fire: The History of Gay Men and Women in World War Two*. New York: Free Press, 1990.

Bierce, Ambrose. *The Devil's Dictionary*. New York: A. and C. Boni, 1925.

Bigsby, E.W.E., ed. *Approaches to Popular Culture*. London: Edward Arnold, 1976.

Bilsborrow, R.E., Hugo Graeme, A. S. Oberai, and Hania Zlotnik. *International Migration Statistics: Guidelines for Improving Data Collection Systems*. Geneva: International Labor Office, 1997.

Binder, Frederick, and David Reimers. "New York as an Immigrant City." In *Origins and Destinies: Immigration, Race, and Ethnicity in America*, ed. Silvia Pedraza and Rubén G. Rumbaut. Belmont, CA: Wadsworth, 1996.

Black, Sandra A., Kyriakos S. Markides, and Todd Q. Miller. "Correlates of Depressive Symptomatology Among Older Community-Dwelling Mexican Americans: The Hispanic EPESE." *Journal of Gerontology: Social Sciences* 53B:4 (1998): S198–S208.

Blau, Peter M. *Inequality and Heterogeneity*. New York: Free Press, 1979.

Boal, Augusto. *The Rainbow of Desire: The Boal Method of Theatre and Therapy*. New York: Routledge, 1995.

Bodner, Allen. *When Boxing Was a Jewish Sport*. Westport, CT: Praeger, 1997.

Bodner, John. *The Transplanted: A History of Urban Immigrants*. Bloomington: Indiana University Press, 1985.

Bogen, Elizabeth. *Immigration in New York*. New York: Praeger, 1987.

Bohning, W.R. "Elements of a Theory of International Economic Migration to Industrial Nation States." In *Global Trends in Migration*, ed. Mary M. Kritz, Charles B. Keely, and Silvano M. Tomasi, pp. 28–43. Staten Island, NY: Center for Migration Studies of New York, 1981.

Bonacich, Edna, and Richard R. Appelbaum. *Behind the Label: Inequality in the Los Angeles Apparel Industry.* Berkeley: University of California Press, 2000.

Bonacich, Edna, and Ivan Hubert Light. *Immigrant Entrepreneurs: Koreans in Los Angeles, 1965–1982.* Berkeley: University of California Press, 1988.

Bonacich, Edna, and John Modell. *The Economic Basis of Ethnic Solidarity: Small Business in the Japanese-American Community.* Berkeley: University of California Press, 1980.

Bonilla, Frank, and Ricardo Campos. "Bootstraps and Enterprise Zones: The Underside of Late Capitalism in Puerto Rico and the United States." *Review* (Fernand Braudel Center) 4 (Spring 1982): 556–90.

Bonilla, Frank, Edwin Melendez, Rebecca Morales, and Maria de los Angeles Torres, eds. *Borderless Borders: U.S. Latinos, Latin Americans, and the Paradox of Interdependence.* Philadelphia: Temple University Press, 1998.

Bonner, Raymond. "Donating to the First Lady, Hoping the President Notices." *New York Times,* March 14, 2000.

Borjas, George J. "The Economic Progress of Immigrants: Working Paper 6506." *Working Paper Series.* Cambridge, MA: National Bureau of Economic Research, April 1998. http://www.nber.org/papers/w6506.

———. "Economic Theory and International Migration." *International Migration Review* 23 (1989): 457–85.

———. "The Economics of Immigration." *Journal of Economic Literature* 32:4 (1994): 1667–717.

———. *Friends or Strangers: The Impact of Immigration on the American Economy.* New York: Basic Books, 1990.

———. *Heaven's Door: Immigration Policy and the American Economy.* Princeton: Princeton University Press, 1999.

———. "Immigration, the Issue-in-Waiting." *New York Times,* April 2, 1999.

———. "Immigration and Welfare, 1970–1990." Working paper. University of California, San Diego, 1994.

———. "Immigration and Welfare: Solving the Welfare Problem Will Solve the Welfare Problem—Not the Immigration Problem." *National Review,* June 16, 1997.

———. "Immigrant and Emigrant Earnings: A Longitudinal Study." *Economic Inquiry* (January 1989): 21–37.

———. "Immigrants—Not What They Used to Be." *Wall Street Journal,* November 8, 1990.

Borjas, George J., and Bernt Bratsberg. "Who Leaves? The Outmigration of the Foreign-Born." *Review of Economics and Statistics* 78:1 (1996): 165–76.

Borjas, George, and Lynette Hilton. "Immigration and the Welfare State: Immigrant Participation in Means-Tested Entitlement Programs." *Quarterly Journal of Economics,* 111:2 (1996): 575–604.

Borjas, G., and M. Tienda. "The Employment and Wages of Legalized Immigrants." *International Migration Review* 72:4 (1993): 712–47.

Bose, Christine E., and Edna Acosta-Belén, eds. *Women in the Latin American Development Process.* Philadelphia: Temple University Press, 1995.

Boswell, Richard A., and G.R. Carrasco. *Immigration and Nationality Law.* Durham, NC: Carolina Academic Press, 1992.

Boswell, Thomas D., and James R. Curtis. *The Cuban-American Experience.* Totowa, NJ: Rowman and Allanheld, 1984.

Bourdieu, Pierre. "The Forms of Capital." In *Handbook of Theory and Research for the Sociology of Education,* ed. John G. Richardson, pp. 241–58. Westport, CT: Greenwood, 1986.

Bourgeois, Philippe. "In Search of Respect: The New Service Economy and the Crack Alternative in Spanish Harlem." Paper presented at the Conference on Poverty, Immigration, and Urban Marginality in Advanced Societies, Maison Sugar, Paris, May 10–11, 1991.

Bouvier, Leon E., ed. *U.S. Immigration in the 1980s: Reappraisal and Reform.* Boulder, CO: Westview Press, 1988.

Boyd, Monica. "Family and Personal Networks in International Migration: Recent Developments and New Agendas." *International Migration Review* 23 (1989): 638–70.

Bozorgmehr, Mehdi, and George Sabagh. "High Status Immigrants: A Statistical Profile of Iranians in the United States." *Iranian Studies* 21:3–4 (1988): 4–34.

Bozorgmehr, Mehdi, Georges Sabagh, and Ivan Light. "Los Angeles: Explosive Diversity." In *Origins and Destinies: Immigration, Race, and Ethnicity in America,* ed. Silvia Pedraza and Rubén G. Rumbaut. Belmont, CA: Wadsworth, 1996.

Bredbenner, Candace Lewis. "The Case of the 'Lovelorn Jewish Workers': Gender Bias and the Response to Immigration During the Great Depression." *Prologue* 31:1 (1999): 37–52.

Briggs, Vernon M., Jr. *Mass Immigration and the National Interest.* Armonk, NY: M.E. Sharpe, 1992.

Brook, J., Chris Carlsson, and N.J. Peters, eds. *Reclaiming San Francisco: History, Politics, Culture.* San Francisco: City Lights, 1998.

Broussard, Albert S. *Black San Francisco: The Struggle for Racial Equality in the West, 1900–1954.* Lawrence: University Press of Kansas, 1993.

Brown, E. Richard, Victoria Ojeda, Roberta Wynn, and Rebecka Levan. *Racial and Ethnic Disparities in Access to Health Insurance and Health Care.* Los Angeles: University of California–Los Angeles, Center for Health Policy Research, 2000.

Brown, Mary Elizabeth. "The Adaptation of the Tactics of the Enemy: The Case of Italian Immigrant Youth in the Archdiocese of New York During the Progressive Era." In *Immigration to New York,* ed. William Pencak, Selma Berrol, and Randall Miller. Philadelphia: Balch

Institute Press; London: Associated University Presses, 1991.

Brown, Richard. "Migrants' Remittances, Savings, and Investment in the South Pacific." *International Labour Review* 133:3 (1994).

Brown, Tom. "Sweatshops of the 1990s: Employees Who 'Survived' Downsizing Are Working Harder and Longer These Days." *Management Review* 85 (August 1996): 13–18.

Browning, Harley, and Joachim Singlemann. "Industrial Transformation and Occupational Change in the U.S., 1960–1980." *Social Forces* 59 (1980): 246–64.

Brun, Michael, et al. "A Spatial Study of the Mobility of Hispanics in Illinois and the Implication for Educational Institutions." JSRI Research Paper no. 43, Julian Samora Research Institute, East Lansing, MI, 1998.

Buchanan-Stafford, Susan. "The Haitians: The Cultural Meaning of Race and Ethnicity." In *New Immigrants in New York*, ed. Nancy Foner. New York: Columbia University Press, 1987.

Bureau of Consular Affairs. *International Adoptions: Guidelines on Immediate Relative Petitions*. Washington, DC: Department of State, February 1997.

Bureau of the Census. Census CD version 1.1. "Area Snapshots" for selected Primary Metropolitan Statistical Areas (PMSAs). Washington DC: Bureau of the Census, 1990.

———. *Current Population Reports*, ser. P-20, no. 461, 1991; no. 468. Washington, DC: Government Printing Office, 1992.

———. "Population Projections of the United States by Age, Sex, Race, and Hispanic Origin: 1995–2050." *Current Population Reports*, ser. P-25, no. 1130. Washington, DC: Government Printing Office, 1996.

———. *Estimates of Population of Metropolitan Areas*. Washington, DC: Government Printing Office, 1996.

———. "Marital Status and Living Arrangements: March 1998 (Update)." *Current Population Reports*, ser. 20, no. 514.

———. *Nativity of the Population for the 50 Largest Urban Places: 1870–1990*. Table 19. www.census.gov/population/ www/documentation/twpsO029/ tabl9.html (March 9, 1999 release date).

———. *Profile of the Foreign-Born Population of the United States: 1997*. Current Population Reports Special Studies P23–195. Washington, DC: Government Printing Office, 1999.

———. *State and Metropolitan Area Data Book, 1997–98*. 5th ed. Washington, DC: Government Printing Office, 1998.

———. *Statistical Abstract of the United States, 1997*. Washington, DC: Government Printing Office, 1997.

———. *Statistical Abstract of the United States, 1989*. Washington, DC: Bureau of the Census, 1990.

———. *Statistical Abstract of the United States, 1998*. Washington, DC: Bureau of the Census, 1999.

———. *Subject Reports on Marital Status and Living Arrangements, 1960, 1970, and 1980*. Washington, DC: Government Printing Office, 1982.

———. *The Foreign-Born Population of the United States: March 1997*. Washington, DC: Department of Commerce, 1999.

———. *Twenty Censuses Population and Housing Questions, 1790–1980*. Washington, DC: Government Printing Office, 1979.

———. *We the American . . . Foreign Born*. Washington, DC: Department of Commerce, 1993.

———. *1980 Census of Population and Housing Characteristics for Census Tracts and Block Numbering Areas, Houston-Galveston-Brazoria, TX CMSA (Part)*, Houston, TX PMSA. CPH-3–176C. Washington, DC: Government Printing Office, 1993.

———. *1980 Census of Population and Housing, Houston, Tex., Standard Metropolitan Statistical Area, Census Tract*. PHC80–20184. Washington, DC: Government Printing Office, 1983.

———. *1980 Census of Population, Detailed Population Characteristics, Texas*. PC80–1–D45. Washington, DC: Government Printing Office, 1983.

———. *1980 Census of Population: Social and Economic Characteristics, Texas*. Washington, DC: Government Printing Office, 1993.

Bustamante, Jorge A., and Geronimo Martínez. 1979. "Undocumented Immigration from Mexico: Beyond Borders but Within Systems." *Journal of International Affairs* 33 (Fall–Winter 1979): 265–84.

Butcher, Kristin E., and Ann Morrison Piehl. "Recent Immigrants: Unexpected Implications for Crime and Incarceration." *Industrial and Labor Relations Review* 51:4 (1998): 654–79.

Cain, Bruce E., D. Roderick Kiewiet, and Carole J. Uhlaner. "The Acquisition of Partisanship by Latinos and Asian Americans." *American Journal of Political Science* 35:2 (1991): 390–422.

Calavita, Kitty. *Inside the State: The Bracero Program, Immigration, and the I.N.S.* New York: Routledge, 1992.

———. "Italy and the New Immigration." In *Controlling Immigration: A Global Perspective*, ed. Wayne Cornelius, P.L. Martin, and J.E. Hollifield, pp. 303–26. Stanford: Stanford University Press, 1994.

Caldwell, Gillian, producer. *Bought and Sold*. Washington, DC: Global Survival Network (documentary film), 1997.

Camarota, Steven A. *Importing Poverty: Immigration's Impact on the Size and Growth of the Poor Population in the United States*. Washington, DC: Center for Immigration Studies, 1999.

Cantu, Lionel. "Border Crossings: Mexican Men and the Sexuality of Migration." Ph.D. diss., University of California–Irvine, 1999.

Caplan, Nathan, and John K. Whitmore. *Children of the Boat People: A Study of Educational Success.* Ann Arbor: University of Michigan Press, 1991.

Caplan, Nathan, John K. Whitmore, and Marcella H. Choy. *The Boat People and Achievement in America: A Study of Economic and Educational Success.* Ann Arbor: University of Michigan Press, 1989.

Cardenas, Gilberto, and Antonio Ugalde, eds. *Health and Social Services Among International Labor Migrants.* Austin: University of Texas Press, 1998.

Cardoso, Lawrence. *Mexican Emigration to the United States.* Tucson: University of Arizona Press, 1980.

Carino, Benjamin. "Filipino Americans: Many and Varied." In *Origins and Destinies: Immigration, Race, and Ethnicity in America,* ed. Silvia Pedraza and Rubén G. Rumbaut. Belmont, CA: Wadsworth, 1996.

Carliner, David. *The Rights of Aliens.* New York: Avon Books, 1977.

———. *The Rights of Aliens and Refugees: The Basic ACLU Guide to Alien and Refugee Rights.* Carbondale: Southern Illinois University Press, 1990.

Carnegie Center for International Peace. "New Americans and Co-Ethnic Voting." *Research Perspectives on Immigration* 1:3 (1997).

Cary, Francine Curro, ed. *Urban Odyssey: A Multicultural History of Washington, DC.* Washington, DC: Smithsonian Institution Press, 1996.

Castells, Manuel. "Multinational Capital, National States, and Local Communities." *IURD Working Paper.* Berkeley: University of California Press, 1980.

———. *The Informational City: Information, Technology, Economic Restructuring and the Urban-Regional Process.* Oxford: Basil Blackwell, 1989.

———. *The Rise of the Network Society.* Oxford: Basil Blackwell, 1996.

Castells, Manuel, and Alejandro Portes. "World Underneath: The Origins, Dynamics, and Effects of the Informal Economy." In *The Informal Economy: Studies in Advanced and Less Developed Countries,* ed. Alejandro Portes, Manuel Castells, and Lauren A. Benton, pp. 11–37. Baltimore: Johns Hopkins University Press, 1989.

Castles, Stephen. "Australian Multiculturalism: Social Policy and Identity in a Changing Society." In *Nations of Immigrants: Australia, the United States and International Migration,* ed. G. Freeman and J. Jupp. Melbourne: Oxford University Press, 1992.

Castles, Stephen, and Mark J. Miller. *The Age of Migration: International Population Movements in the Modern World.* 2d ed. New York: Macmillan, 1998.

Castro, Mary Garcia. "Work Versus Life: Colombian Women in New York." In *Women and Change in Latin America,* ed. June Nash and Helen Safa, pp. 231–55. South Hadley, MA: Bergin and Garvey, 1986.

Center for Mental Health Services. *Cultural Competence Standards in Managed Care Mental Health Services for Four Underserved/Underrepresented Racial/Ethnic Groups.* Rockville, MD: Center for Mental Health Services, 1998.

Centers for Disease Control and Prevention. "Report of the Working Group on TB Among Foreign-Born Persons." *Morbidity Mortality Weekly Report* 47: RR-16 (1998).

———. "Screening for Hepatitis B Virus Infection Among Refugees Arriving in the United States, 1979–1991." *Morbidity Mortality Weekly Report* 40:45 (1991): 784–86.

Cerase, Francesco R. "Migration and Social Change: Expectations and Reality. A Study of Return Migration from the United States to Italy." *International Migration Review* 8:2 (1974).

Chamot, Anna Uhl. "Toward a Functional ESL Curriculum in the Elementary School." In *Methodology in TESOL: A Book of Readings,* ed. Michael H. Long and Jack Richards. Boston: Heinle and Heinle, 1985.

Chamot, Anna Uhl, and Pamela Beard El-Dinary. "Children's Learning Strategies in Language Immersion Classrooms." *Modern Language Journal* 83 (1999): 319–35.

Chan, Sucheng. *Asian Americans: An Interpretative History.* Boston: Twayne, 1991.

Chang, Won H. "Communication and Acculturation." In *The Korean Diaspora,* ed. Hyung-chan Kim. Santa Barbara, CA: ABC-Clio, 1977.

Chavez, Leo. "Borders and Bridges: Undocumented Immigrants from Mexico and Central America." In *Origins and Destinies: Immigration, Race, and Ethnicity in America,* ed. Silvia Pedraza and Rubén G. Rumbaut. Belmont, CA: Wadsworth, 1996.

Cheng, Lucie, and Philip Q. Yang. "Asians: The 'Model Minority' Deconstructed." In *Ethnic Los Angeles,* ed. Roger Waldinger and Mehdi Bozorgmehr, pp. 305–41. New York: Russell Sage Foundation, 1996.

———. "Global Interaction, Global Inequality, and Migration of the Highly Trained to the United States." *International Migration Review* 32:3 (1998): 626–53.

Cheung, Monit. "Elderly Chinese Living in the United States: Assimilation or Adjustment." *Social Work* 34 (1989): 457–61.

Child, Clifton. *The German-Americans in Politics, 1914–1917.* Madison: University of Wisconsin Press, 1939.

Chin, Christine. "Walls of Silence and Late 20th Century Representations of Foreign Female Domestic Workers: The Case of Filipina and Indonesian Houseservants in Malaysia." *International Migration Review,* 31:1 (1997): 353–85.

Chin, Ko-Lin. *Chinatown Gangs: Extortion, Enterprise, and Ethnicity.* New York: Oxford University Press, 1996.

———. *Smuggled Chinese: Clandestine Immigration to the United States.* Philadelphia: Temple University Press, 1999.

Chishti, Muzaffar. "Unions, Immigrant Workers, and Employer Sanctions." *Working USA: Journal of Labor and Society* 3:6 (March–April 2000): 71–76.

Chiswick, Barry R. *Income Inequality: Regional Analysis Within a Human Capital Framework*. New York: National Bureau of Economic Research and Columbia University Press, 1974.

———. "The Effect of Americanization on the Earnings of Foreign-Born Men." *Journal of Political Economy* (October 1978): 897–921.

Chiswick, Barry R., and Teresa A. Sullivan. "The New Immigrants." In *State of the Union: American in the 1990s*. Vol. 2, *Social Trends*, ed. Reynolds Farley, pp. 211–70. New York: Russell Sage Foundation, 1995.

Choi, Hyneweol. *An International Scientific Community— Asian Scholars in the United States*. New York: Praeger, 1995.

Choldin, Harvey M. "Kinship Networks in the Migration Process." *International Migration Review* 7 (1973): 163–76.

———. "Statistics and Politics: The Hispanic Issue in the 1980 Census." *Demography* 23:3 (August 1986): 403–18.

Choy, Bong-Youn. *Koreans in America*. Chicago: Nelson-Hall, 1979.

Chyz, Yaroslav. *225 Years of the U.S. Foreign-Language Press in the United States*. New York: American Council for Nationalities Service, 1959.

Cinel, Dino. *From Italy to San Francisco: The Immigrant Experience*. Stanford: Stanford University Press, 1982.

———. *The National Integration of Italian Return Migration, 1820–1929*. New York: Cambridge University Press, 1991.

Clark, L. Rebecca. *The Costs of Providing Public Assistance and Education to Immigrants*. Washington, DC: Urban Institute, 1994.

Clark, L. Rebecca, and Jeffrey S. Passel. *Immigrants in New York: Their Legal Status, Incomes, and Taxes*. Washington, DC: Urban Institute, 1998.

Clarke, Ida. *American Women and the World War*. New York: D. Appleton, 1918.

Cleeland, Nancy. "Workers Trapped at el Minimo: For a Growing Class of Workers in L.A., the Minimum Wage Isn't a Beginning but a Dead End." *Los Angeles Times*, March 9, 2000.

Clubb, Jerome M., and Howard W. Allen. "The Cities and the Election of 1928: Partisan Realignment?" In *Electoral Change and Stability in American Political History*, ed. Jerome M. Clubb and Howard W. Allen, pp. 236–54. New York: Free Press, 1971.

Coast Guard. "Alien Migrant Interdiction." http://www.uscg.mil/hq/g-o/g-opl/mle/AMIO.htm, October 23, 1999.

Coatsworth, John H., and Carlos Rico, eds. *Images of Mexico in the United States*. Vol. 1. *Dimensions of United States–Mexican Relations*. San Diego: Center for U.S.-Mexican Studies, 1989.

Cohen, Albert. *Delinquent Boys: The Culture of the Gang*. New York: Free Press, 1955.

Cohen, David Steven, ed. *America, The Dream of My Life: Selections from the Federal Writers' Project's New Jersey Ethnic Survey*. New Brunswick, NJ: Rutgers University Press, 1990.

Cohen, Miriam. *Workshop to Office: Two Generations of Italian Women in New York City, 1900–1950*. Ithaca: Cornell University Press, 1992.

Cohen, Robin, ed. *The Sociology of Migration*. International Library of Studies on Migration. Cheltenham, UK: Elgar, 1996.

Cohn, D'Vera, and Pamela Constable. "Culture Clashes Put Immigrant Women on the Front Lines." *Washington Post*, September 1, 1998.

———. "Lives Transplanted, a Region Transformed: Steady Immigration Changes Face of the Region; Schools Add Up Immigrant Costs." *Washington Post*, August 30, 1998.

Coleman, James S. "Social Capital in the Creation of Human Capital." *American Journal of Sociology* 94 (1988): S95–S121.

Commission on Immigration Reform, *Becoming an American: Immigration and Immigrant Policy*. Washington, DC: Commission on Immigration Reform, 1997.

Congressional Quarterly. "Immigration Reform." In *Congress and the Nation*, 1965–1968, 2:57–61. Washington, DC: Congressional Quarterly Service, 1969.

Conklin, Nancy Faires, and Margaret Lourie. *A Host of Tongues: Language Communities in the United States*. New York: Free Press, 1983.

Converse, Phillip E. "Religion and Politics: The 1960 Election." In *Elections and the Political Order*, ed. Angus Campbell et al., pp. 96–124. New York: Wiley, 1966.

Conway, Dennis, and Jeffrey H. Cohen. "Consequences of Migration and Remittances from Mexican Transnational Communities." *Economic Geography* (January 1998): 26–45.

Cook, David A. *A History of Narrative Film*. 3d ed. New York: W.W. Norton, 1996.

Corcoran, Mary. *Irish Illegals: Transients Between Two Societies*. Westport, CT: Greenwood, 1993.

Cordero-Guzmán, Hector. "An Analysis of Socio-Economic, Demographic, and Community Characteristics, Immigration Services, and Social Services in Sunnyside and Surrounding Areas of Queens." Report prepared for Sunnyside Community Services, Queens, New York, November, 1999.

———. "Assessing the Role of Community-Based Organizations in the Socio-Economic Adaptation and Incorporation of Immigrants." Paper presented at the panel on the Impact of Immigration on New York City at the annual meetings of the Population Association of America, March 1999.

Cordero-Guzmán, Hector, and Jose G. Navarro. "Managing Cuts in the 'Safety Net': What Do Immigrant Groups, Organizations, and Service Providers Say About the Impacts of Recent Changes in Immigration and Welfare Laws?" *Migration World* 4 (April 2000).

Cornelius, Wayne A. "Japan: The Illusion of Immigration Control." In *Controlling Immigration: A Global Perspective*, ed. Wayne A. Cornelius, P.L. Martin, and J.F. Hollifield. Stanford: Stanford University Press, 1994.

———. "Spain: The Uneasy Transition from Labor Exporter to Labor Importer." In *Controlling Immigration: A Global Perspective*, ed. Wayne A. Cornelius, P.L. Martin, and J.F. Hollifield, pp. 331–70. Stanford: Stanford University Press, 1994.

———. "The Structural Embeddedness of Demand for Mexican Immigrant Labor." In *Crossings: Mexican Immigration in Interdisciplinary Perspectives*, ed. Marcelo M. Suarez-Orozco, pp. 113–44. Cambridge: Harvard University Press, 1998.

Cornelius, Wayne A., Philip L. Martin, and James F. Hollifield, eds. *Controlling Immigration: A Global Perspective*. Stanford: Stanford University Press, 1994.

———. "Introduction: The Ambivalent Quest for Immigration Control." In *Controlling Immigration: A Global Perspective*, ed. Wayne A. Cornelius, P.L. Martin, and J.F. Hollifield, pp. 3–42. Stanford: Stanford University Press, 1994.

Cortino, Rudolfo, ed. *Cuban American Theater*. Houston: Arte Publico, 1991.

Cose, Ellis. *A Nation of Strangers: Prejudice, Politics, and the Populating of America*. New York: Morrow, 1992.

Couch, Stephen R., and Roy Bryce-Laporte, eds. *Quantitative Data and Immigration Research*. Washington, DC: Research Institute on Immigration and Ethnic Studies, Smithsonian Institution, 1979.

Countryman, Edward. *Americans: A Collision of Histories*. New York: Hill and Wang, 1996.

Coye, Molly, and Deborah Alvarez. *Medicaid, Managed Care, and Cultural Diversity in California*. New York: Commonwealth Fund, 1999.

Crahan, Margaret, and Alberto Vourvoulias-Bush, eds. *The City and the World: New York's Global Future*. New York: Council on Foreign Relations, 1997.

Craig, Richard. *The Bracero Program: Interest Groups and Foreign Policy*. Austin: University of Texas Press, 1971.

Crawford, James. *Bilingual Education: History, Politics, Theory, and Practice*. 4th ed. Los Angeles: Bilingual Educational Services, 1999.

Cross, T.L., B.M. Bazron, K.W. Dennis, and M.R. Issacs. *Towards a Culturally Competent System of Care*. Washington, DC: Georgetown University, 1989.

Cruz, Jon. "Filipinos." In *A Nation of Peoples*, ed. Elliott Barkan, pp. 200–217. Westport, CT: Greenwood, 1999.

"Cuban Migrants Fight Coast Guard to Reach Florida." *Siskind's Immigration Bulletin* (July–August 1999).

Cullinan, B.E. "Whole Language and Children's Literature." *Language Arts* 69 (1992): 426–30.

Curran, Charles A. *Counseling-Learning in Second Languages*. Apple River, IL: Apple River Press, 1976.

Daniels, Douglas H. *Pioneer Urbanites: A Social and Cultural History of Black San Francisco*. Berkeley: University of California Press, 1990.

Daniels, Roger. *Asian America: Chinese and Japanese in the United States Since 1850*. Seattle: University of Washington Press, 1988.

———. *Coming to America: A History of Immigration and Ethnicity in American Life*. New York: Harper Perenniel, 1991.

———. "What Is an American? Ethnicity, Race, the Constitution and the Immigrant in Early American History." In *The Immigration Reader: America in a Multidisciplinary Perspective*, ed. David Jacobson, pp. 29–47. Malden, MA: Blackwell, 1998.

Danky, James, and Wiegand, Wayne, ed. *Print Culture in a Diverse America*. Urbana: University of Illinois Press, 1998.

Danning, John. *On the Air: The Encyclopedia of Old-Time Radio*. New York: Oxford University Press, 1998.

Darsie, M.L. "The Mental Capacity of American-Born Japanese Children." In *Comparative Psychology Monographs*. Vol. 3, ser. no. 15. Baltimore: Williams and Wilkins, 1926.

Das, M.S. "The 'Brain Drain' Controversy in a Comparative Perspective." *International Review of Sociology* 1:1 (1971): 55–65.

Dashefsky, Arnold, J. De Amicis, B. Lazerwitz, and E. Tabory. *Americans Abroad*. New York: Plenum, 1992.

Datan, Nancy, Aaron Antonovsky, and Benjamin Maoz. *A Time to Reap: The Middle Age of Women in Five Israeli Subcultures*. Baltimore: Johns Hopkins University Press, 1981.

David, Natacha. "Migrants Made the Scapegoats of the Crisis." *ICFTU Online*, http://www.hartford-hwp.com/archives/50/012.html, 1999.

Davidhizar, Ruth, and Gregory A. Bechtel. "Health and Quality of Life Within Colonias Settlements Along the United States and Mexico Border." *Public Health Nursing* 16:4 (1999): 301–6.

Davis, Allen F. *Spearheads for Reform: The Social Settlements and the Progressive Movements, 1890–1914*. New York: Oxford University Press, 1967.

Davis, Allen F., and Mary L.C. Bryant. *Eighty Years at Hull-House*. Chicago: Quadrangle Books, 1969.

Davis, James F. *Who Is Black: One Nation's Definition*.

University Park: Pennsylvania State University Press, 1991.

Davis, Mike. *City of Quartz: Excavating the Future in Los Angeles*. New York: Vintage Books, 1990.

———. *Ecology of Fear: Los Angeles and the Imagination of Disaster*. New York: Metropolitan Books, 1998.

———. "The Internationalization of Downtown Los Angeles." *New Left Review* 164 (1987): 61–86.

———. *Magical Urbanism: Latinos Reinvent the U.S. City*. New York: Verso, 2000.

Dear, Michael. "In the City, Time Becomes Visible: Intentionality and Urbanism in Los Angeles, 1781–1991." In *The City: Los Angeles and Urban Theory at the End of the Twentieth Century*, ed. A.J. Scott and E.W. Soja. Los Angeles: University of California Press, 1996.

DeFrietas, Gregory. "Hispanic Immigration and Labor Market Segmentation." *Industrial Relations* 27 (1988): 195–214.

———. *Inequality at Work: Hispanics in the U.S. Labor Force*. New York: Oxford University Press, 1991.

De Leon, Arnoldo. *Ethnicity in the Sunbelt: A History of Mexican Americans in Houston*. Houston: Mexican-American Studies, University of Houston, 1989.

Delgado, Hector. *New Immigrants, Old Unions: Organizing Undocumented Workers in Los Angeles*. Philadelphia: Temple University Press, 1994.

Dentler, Robert, and Anne L. Hafner. *Hosting Newcomers: Structuring Educational Opportunities for Immigrant Children*. New York: Teachers College Press, 1997.

DePalma, Anthony. "Farmers Caught in Conflict over Illegal Migrant Workers." *New York Times*, October 3, 2000.

Department of Immigration and Multicultural Affairs. *Population Flows: Immigration Aspects*. Canberra: Department of Immigration and Multicultural Affairs, 1999.

———. *Settler Arrivals, 1998–99*. Canberra: Department of Immigration and Multicultural Affairs, 1999.

Department of Labor. *A Profile of U.S. Farm Workers*. Prepared by Richard Mines, Susan Gabbard, and Anne Stierman. http://www.dol.gov/dol/asp/public/programs/agworker/report/main.htm, 1997.

———. *U.S. Farmworkers in the Post-IRCA Period: Based on Data from the National Agricultural Workers Survey (NAWS)*. Washington, DC: Department of Labor, 1993.

Department of State. "Immigrant Numbers for November 1999." *Visa Bulletin*, October 21, 1999.

———. *Marriage of United States Citizens Abroad*. Travel Advisory. March 1998. Retrieved from Internet on January 5, 2000.

DeSantis, Lydia. "Health Care Orientations of Cuban and Haitian Immigrant Mothers: Implications for Health Care Professionals." *Medical Anthropology* 12 (1989): 69–89.

Deshen, Schlomo, and Moshe Shokeid. *The Predicament of Homecoming: Cultural and Social Life of North African Immigrants in Israel*. Ithaca: Cornell University Press, 1974.

DeSipio, Louis. *Counting on the Latino Vote: Latinos as a New Electorate*. Charlottesville: University Press of Virginia, 1996.

———. "Making Citizens or Good Citizens? Naturalization as a Predictor of Organizational and Electoral Behavior Among Latino Immigrants." *Hispanic Journal of Behavioral Sciences* 18:2 (1996): 194–213.

DeSipio, Louis, and Rudolfo O. de la Garza. "Immigrants, Immigrant Policy and the Foundation of the Next Century's Latino Politics." Paper presented at the Crisis in Latino Civil Rights Conference, sponsored by the Civil Rights Project at Harvard University and the Thomas Rivera Policy Institute, Los Angeles, 1997.

———. *Making Americans, Remaking America: Immigration and Immigrant Policy*. Boulder, CO: Westview Press, 1998.

DeWind, Josh. "Educating the Children of Immigrants in New York's Restructured Economy." In *The City and the World: New York's Global Future*, ed. Margaret Crahan and Alberto Vourvoulias-Bush. New York: Council on Foreign Relations, 1997.

Diaz-Briquets, Sergio, and Jorge Perez. "Refugee Remittances: Conceptual Issues and the Cuban and Nicaraguan Experiences." *International Migration Review* 31:2 (1997).

Dillard, J.L. *American Talk*. New York: Random House, 1976.

———. *Toward a Social History of American English*. New York: Mouton, 1985.

Diner, Hasia. *Erin's Daughters in America: Irish Immigrant Women in the Nineteenth Century*. Baltimore: Johns Hopkins University Press, 1983.

———. "The Most Irish City in the Union: Overview of the Era of the Great Migration, 1844–1877." In *The New York Irish*, ed. Ronald Baylor and Timothy Meagher. Baltimore: Johns Hopkins University Press, 1996.

Diner, Hasia, and Steven Diner. *Fifty Years of Jewish Self-Governance: The Jewish Community of Greater Washington, 1938–1988*. Washington, DC: The Council, 1989.

Dinnerstein, Leonard. *America and the Survivors of the Holocaust*. New York: Columbia University Press, 1982.

Dinnerstein, Leonard, and David M. Reimers. *Ethnic Americans*. 4th ed. New York: Columbia University Press, 1999.

Donato, Katherine M. "Current Trends and Patterns of Female Migration: Evidence from Mexico." *International Migration Review* 27:4 (1993): 748–71.

———. "Understanding U.S. Immigration: Why Some Countries Send Women and Others Send Men." In *Seeking Common Ground: Multidisciplinary Studies of Im-*

migrant Women in the United States, ed. Donna Gabaccia, pp. 159–84. Westport, CT: Greenwood, 1991.

Donato, Katherine M., J. Durand, and D. Massey. "Stemming the Tide? Assessing the Deterrent Effects of the Immigration Reform and Control Act." *Demography* 29:2 (1992): 139–58.

Donnelly, Paul. "Statement by Paul Donnelly, Organizer Immigration Reform Coalition, to the National Research Council Committee on IT [Information Technology] Workforce Needs." http://immigration reform.com/donnelly2.html, February 29, 2000.

Dorkenoo, Efua. *Cutting the Rose: Female Genital Mutilation: The Practice and Its Prevention*. London: Minority Rights Publications, 1996.

Drescher, T.W. *San Francisco Bay Area Murals: Communities Create Their Muses, 1904–1997*. 3d ed. St. Paul, MN: Pogo Press, 1998.

DuBois, Ellen Carol, and Vicki Ruiz, ed. *Unequal Sisters: A Multicultural Reader in U.S. Women's History*. New York: Routledge, 1990.

Dulles, Foster Rhea. *A History of Recreation: America Learns to Play*. New York: Meredith, 1965.

Dunn, Timothy J. *The Militarization of the U.S.-Mexico Border, 1878–1992: Low Intensity Doctrine Comes Home*. Austin, TX: Center for Mexican-American Studies, 1996.

Dunne, John Gregory. *Delano: The Story of the California Grape Strike*. New York: Farrar, Straus and Giroux, 1967.

Durand, Jorge, Douglas Massey, and E. Parrado. "Migradollars and Development: A Reconsideration of the Mexican Case." *International Migration Review* 30:2 (1995).

Durham, D.F. "Fatal Challenges: Prospects for Real Solutions." *Focus* 7 (1997): 10–13.

Durkheim, E. *Suicide*. Trans. J. A. Spaulding and G. Simpson. 1897. Reprint. Glencoe, IL: Free Press, 1951.

Ebaugh, Helen Rose. Center for Immigration Research, Religion, Ethnicity and New Immigrants Research Project I and II, (RENIR) I and RENIR II, 1999.

Ebaugh, Helen Rose, and Saltzman Chafetz. *Religion and the New Immigrants: Continuities and Adaptations in Immigration Congregations*. Walnut Creek, CA: AltaMira Press, 2000.

Ebersole, Robert. *Black Pagoda*. Gainesville: University of Florida Press, 1957.

Echikson, W. "Young Americans Go Abroad to Strike It Rich." *Fortune* 130:8 (October 17, 1994): 185–94.

Edmonston, Barry, and Jeffrey Passel. "Ethnic Demography: U.S. Immigration and Ethnic Variations." In *Immigration and Ethnicity: The Integration of America's Newest Arrivals*, ed. B. Edmonston and J. Passel. Washington, DC: Urban Institute, 1994.

Edwards, John, ed. *Linguistic Minorities, Policies, and Pluralism*. London: Academic Press, 1984.

Edwards, Richard. "The Social Relations of Production in the Firm and Labour Market Structure." In *Labour Market Segmentation*, ed. R.C. Edwards, M. Reich, and D.M. Gordon, pp. 341–67. Lexington, MA: D.C. Heath, 1975.

Eisen, Arnold M. *The Chosen People in America: A Study of Jewish Religious Ideology*. Bloomington: Indiana University Press, 1983.

Eisenstadt, Shmuel Noah. *The Transformation of Israeli Society*. London: Weidenfeld and Nicholson, 1985.

El-Hinnawi, Essam. *Environmental Refugees*. Dublin: United Nations Environmental Program, 1985.

El-Hinnawi, Essam, and Mansur H. Hashmi. *Global Environmental Issues*. Dublin: Tycooly International Publishing, 1982.

Ellis, Mark, and Richard Wright. "When Immigrants Are Not Migrants: Counting Arrivals of the Foreign Born Using the U.S. Census." *International Migration Review* 32:1 (1998): 127–44.

Ellwood, M.R., and Leighton Ku. "Welfare and Immigration Reforms: Unintended Side Effects for Medicaid." *Health Affairs* (May–June 1998): 137–43.

Enright, D.S., and M.L. McCloskey. *Integrating English: Developing English Language and Literacy in the Multilingual Classroom*. Wellesley, MA: Addison-Wesley, 1985.

Erdman, Harley. *Staging the Jew: The Performance of American Ethnicity*. New Brunswick, NJ: Rutgers University Press, 1962.

Erie, Stephen R. *Rainbow's End: Irish-Americans and the Dilemmas of Urban Machine Politics 1840–1985*. Berkeley: University of California Press, 1988.

Ernst, Robert. *Immigrant Life in New York City, 1825–1863*. 1949. Reprint. New York: Octagon Books, 1979.

Escobar, Gabriel. "Immigration Transforms a Community." *Washington Post*, November 29, 1999.

Espenshade, Thomas J. "Does the Threat of Border Apprehension Deter Undocumented U.S. Immigration?" *Population and Development Review* 20:4 (1994): 871–892.

———. "Taking the Pulse of Public Opinion Toward Immigrants." In *Keys to Successful Immigration: Implications of the New Jersey Experience*, ed. Thomas J. Espenshade, pp. 89–116. Washington, DC: Urban Institute, 1997.

———. "Unauthorized Immigration to the United States." *Annual Review of Sociology* 21 (1995): 195–216.

Espenshade, Thomas J., ed. *The New Jersey Experience: Keys to Successful Immigration*. Washington, DC: Urban Institute, 1997.

Espenshade, Thomas J., and Maryann Belanger. "Immigration and Public Opinion." In *Crossings: Mexican Immigration in Interdisciplinary Perspectives*, ed. Marcelo

M. Suarez-Orozco, pp. 365–403. Cambridge: Harvard University Press, 1998.

———. "U.S. Public Perceptions and Reactions to Mexican Migration." In *At the Crossroads: Mexican Migration and U.S. Policy*, ed. Frank D. Bean, Rodolfo O. de la Garza, Bryan R. Roberts, and Sidney Weintraub, pp. 227–61. New York: Rowman and Littlefield, 1997.

Espenshade, Thomas J., and Charles A. Calhoun. "An Analysis of Public Opinion Toward Undocumented Migration." *Population Research and Policy Review* 12 (1993): 189–224.

Espenshade, Thomas J., and Katherine Hempstead. "Contemporary American Attitudes Toward U.S. Immigration." *International Migration Review* 30:2 (Summer 1996): 535–70.

Espenshade, Thomas, and Gregory Huber. "Fiscal Impacts of Immigrants and the Shrinking Welfare State." In *Handbook of International Migration*, ed. Philip Kasinitz and Josh DeWind. New York: Russell Sage Foundation, 1999.

Espenshade, Thomas J., and Vanessa E. King. "State and Local Fiscal Impacts of U.S. Immigrants: Evidence from New Jersey." *Population Research and Policy Review* 13:3 (1984): 225–56.

Espiritu, Yen L. *Asian American Panethnicity*. Philadelphia: Temple University Press, 1992.

Evans, J. Martin. *America: The View from Europe*. Stanford: Stanford Alumni Association, 1976.

Faber, Carol S. "Geographical Mobility." In *Current Population Reports*, Census Bureau. Washington, DC: Department of Commerce, March 1997–March 1998.

Fairlie, Robert W., and Bruce D. Meyer. "Ethnic and Racial Self Employment Differences and Possible Explanations." *Journal of Human Resources* 31 (1996): 757–91.

Faltis, Christian J., and Paula Wolfe, eds. *So Much to Say: Adolescents, Bilingualism, and ESL in the Secondary School*. New York: Teachers College, Columbia University, 1999.

Fannie Mae Foundation. *Immigration and Housing in the United States: Trends and Prospects*. http://www.fanniemae foundation.org/Housing Research?immigration/immig.html, 1997.

Farley, Reynolds. "The New Census Question About Ancestry: What Did It Tell Us?" *Demography* 28:3 (1991): 411–29.

Fawcett, James T., and Benjamin V. Carino, ed. *Pacific Bridges: The New Immigration from Asia and the Pacific Islands*. Staten Island, NY: Center for Migration Studies, 1987.

Feagin, Joe R. *Free Enterprise City: Houston in a Political and Economic Perspective*. New Brunswick, NJ: Rutgers University Press, 1988.

Feagin, Joe R., and Michael P. Smith. "Cities and the New International Division of Labor: An Overview." In *The Capitalist City*. New York: Basil Blackwell, 1987.

Federal Writer's Project. *The Italians of New York*. New York: Arno Press, 1969.

Federation for American Immigration Reform. "A Skirmish in a Wider War: An Oral History of John H. Tanton, Founder of FAIR, the Federation for American Immigration Reform." In *Tenth Anniversary Oral History Project of the Federation for American Immigration Reform*. Washington, DC: Federation for American Immigration Reform, 1989.

Federation of Hindu Associations. "A Call for Dharma Raksha." Full-page advertisement, *India Post*, August 8, 1997.

———. *Directory of Temples and Associations of Southern California and Everything You Wanted to Know about Hinduism*. Artesia, CA: FHA, 1995.

———. *Hinduism Simplified*. Diamond Bar, CA: FHA, n.d.

———. "How to Be a Good Hindu." Full-page advertisement, *India Post*, July 25, 1997.

———. "To Our Hindu Youth." Full-page advertisement, *India Post*, August 15, 1997.

Feingold, Henry L. *Zion in America: The Jewish Experience from Colonial Times to the Present*. New York: Hippocrene, 1981.

Feingold, Henry L., ed. *The Jewish People in America*. Baltimore: Johns Hopkins University Press, 1986.

Feldblum, Miriam. *Reconstructing Citizenship: The Politics of Nationality Reform and Immigration in Contemporary France*. Albany: State University of New York Press, 1999.

Fernández-Kelly, Mariá Patricia. *For We Are Sold, I and My People: Women and Industry in Mexico's Frontier*. Albany: State University of New York Press, 1982.

———. "Social and Cultural Capital in the Urban Ghetto: Implications for the Economic Sociology of Immigration." In *The Economic Sociology of Immigration: Essays on Networks, Ethnicity, and Entrepreneurship*, ed. Alejandro Portes, pp. 213–47. New York: Russell Sage Foundation, 1995.

Fernández-Kelly, María Patricia, and Anna M. Garcia. "Informalization in the Core: Hispanic Women, Homework and the Advanced Capitalist State." In *The Informal Economy: Studies in Advanced and Less Developed Countries*, ed. Alejandro Portes, Manuel Castells, and Lauren Benton. Baltimore: Johns Hopkins University Press, 1989.

———. "Power Surrendered, Power Restored: The Politics of Work and Family Among Hispanic Garment Workers in Califomia and Florida." In *Challenging Fronteras: Structuring Latina and Latino Lives in the U.S.*, ed. Mary Romero, Pierrette Hondagneu-Sotelo, and Vilma Ortiz. New York: Routledge, 1997.

Fernández-Kelly, Mariá Patricia, and Richard Schauffler.

"Divided Fates: Immigrant Children in a Restructured U.S. Economy." *International Migration Review* 28 (1994): 662–89.

Ferris, Susan, and Ricardo Sandoval. *The Fight in the Fields: Cesar Chavez and the Farmworkers Movement.* New York: Harcourt Brace Jovanovich, 1997.

Finckenauer, James O. "Russian Transnational Organized Crime and Human Trafficking." In *Global Human Smuggling: Comparative Perspectives*, ed. David Kyle and Rey Koslowski. Baltimore: Johns Hopkins University Press, forthcoming.

Fineman, Mark. "Cubans' Risky New Voyage Out." *Los Angeles Times*, January 4, 2000.

Fineman, Mark, and Mike Clary. "'A Family Divided.'" *Los Angeles Times*, February 19, 2000, pp. A1, A8, and A9.

Finke, Roger, and Rodney Stark. *The Churching of America, 1776–1990.* New Brunswick, NJ: Rutgers University Press, 1992.

Firestone, David. "Mayoral Order on Immigrants Is Struck Down." *New York Times*, July 19, 1997.

Fishman, Joshua. *Language and Ethnicity in Minority Sociolinguistic Perspective.* Philadelphia: Multilingual Matters, 1989.

———. *Language Loyalty in the United States.* London: Mouton, 1966.

Fishman, Joshua, R.L. Cooper, and R.M. Newman. *Bilingualism in the Barrio.* Bloomington: Indiana University Press, 1971.

Fix, Michael, and P.T. Hill. *Enforcing Employer Sanctions: Challenges and Strategies.* Washington, DC: Urban Institute, 1990.

Fix, Michael, and Jeffrey S. Passel. *Immigration and Immigrants: Setting the Record Straight.* Washington, DC: Urban Institute, 1994.

———. *Trends in Noncitizens' and Citizens' Use of Public Benefits Following Welfare Reform: 1995–1997.* Washington, DC: Urban Institute, 1999.

Fix, Michael, Jeffrey S. Passel, and Wendy Zimmermann. "The Use of SSI and Other Welfare Program for Immigrants." Testimony before the House of Representatives, Ways and Means Committee, May 23, 1996.

Flaskerud, Jacquelyn H., and Sue Kim. "Health Problems of Asian and Latino Immigrants." *Nursing Clinics of North America* 34:2 (1999): 359–80.

Fleming, Donald, and Bernard Bailyn, eds. *The Intellectual Migration: Europe and America, 1930–1960.* Cambridge: Harvard University Press and Belknap Press, 1969.

Fletcher, Sir Banister. *A History of Architecture on the Comparative Method.* New York: Charles Scribner's Sons, 1961.

Fogelson, Robert. *The Fragmented Metropolis: Los Angeles, 1850–1930.* Cambridge: Harvard University Press, 1967.

Foley, Douglas. *Learning Capitalist Culture: Deep in the Heart of Tejas.* Philadelphia: University of Pennsylvania Press, 1990.

———. *From Peones to Politicos.* Austin: University of Texas Press, 1988.

Foner, Nancy. "The Jamaicans: Race and Ethnicity Among Migrants in New York City." In *New Immigrants in New York*, ed. Nancy Foner. New York: Columbia University Press, 1987.

———. "What's New About Transnationalism? New York Immigrants Today and at the Turn of the Century." *Diaspora* 6:3 (1997): 355–75.

Foner, Nancy, ed. *New Immigrants in New York City.* New York: Columbia University Press, 1987.

Fong, Timothy P. *The Contemporary Asian American Experience: Beyond the Model Minority.* Upper Saddle River, NJ: Prentice Hall, 1998.

Franklin, Benjamin. *The Papers of Benjamin Franklin*, ed. Leonard W. Labarre. New Haven: Yale University Press, 1959.

Freeman, G. "Can Liberal States Control Unwanted Migration?" *Annals of the American Academy of Political and Social Science* 534 (July 1994).

Freire, Paulo. *Pedagogy of the Oppressed.* New York: Continuum, 1970.

French, Howard W. "Still Wary of Outsiders, Japan Expects Immigration Boom." *New York Times*, March 14, 2000.

Frey, William, and Kao-Lee Liaw. "Immigrant Concentration and Domestic Migrant Dispersal: Is Movement to Nonmetropolitan Areas White Flight?" *Professional Geographer* 50:2 (1998): 217–18.

———. "Internal Migration of Foreign-Born Latinos and Asians: Are They Assimilating Geographically?" In *Migration and Restructuring in the United States*, ed. Kavita Pandit and Suzanne Withers. Latham, MD: University Press of America, 1999.

Friedman, Lester D., ed. *Unspeakable Images: Ethnicity and the American Cinema.* Chicago: University of Illinois Press, 1991.

Friedman-Kasaba, Kathie. *Memories of Migration: Gender, Ethnicity, and Work in New York, 1870–1924.* Albany: State University of New York Press, 1996.

Frisby, Michael K., and John Harwood. "Democrats and Clinton, in Surprise Move, Curb Contributions, Vow to Refuse Aliens' Donations." *Wall Street Journal*, January 22, 1997.

Fritz, Mark. "Pledging Multiple Allegiances." *Los Angeles Times*, April 6, 1998.

Fry, B.N. "Alien Notions: Varieties of Nativism and Perceptions of the Threat." Ph.D. diss., Michigan State University, 1998.

Fu, Danling. *"My Trouble Is My English": Asian Students and the American Dream.* Portsmouth, NH: Boynton/Cook Publishers, 1994.

Fujii, S.M. "Older Asian Americans: Victims of Multiple Jeopardy." *Civil Rights Digest* (Fall 1976): 22–29.

Furio, Colomba M. "An Abstract of Immigrant Women and Industry: A Case Study—The Italian Immigrant and the Garment Industry, 1880–1950." Ph.D. diss., New York University, 1979.

Gabaccia, Donna. *From the Other Side: Women, Gender, and Immigrant Life in the United States, 1820–1990.* Bloomington: Indiana University Press, 1994.

Galarza, Ernest. *Merchants of Labor: The Mexican Bracero History.* Santa Barbara, CA: McNally and Loftin, 1964.

———. *Spiders in the House and Workers in the Fields.* South Bend, IN: University of Notre Dame Press, 1970.

———. *Strangers in Our Fields: Based on a Report Regarding Compliance with the Contractual, Legal, and Civil Rights of Mexican Agricultural Contract Labor in the United States.* 2d ed. Washington, DC: U.S. Section, Joint U.S.-Mexico Trade Union Committee, 1956.

Galbally, E. *Review of Post-Arrival Programmes and Services for Migrants.* Canberra: Australian Government Publishing Service, 1978.

Galper, Allan S. *From Bolshoi to Be'er Sheva, Scientists to Streetsweepers: Cultural Dislocation Among Soviet Immigrants in Israel.* New York: University Press of America, 1995.

Gamboa, Erasmo. *Mexican Labor and World War II: Braceros in the Pacific Northwest, 1942–1947.* Austin: University of Texas Press, 1990.

Gans, Herbert J. "Second-Generation Decline: Scenarios for the Economic and Ethnic Futures of the Post-1965 American Immigrants." *Ethnic and Racial Studies* 15 (1992): 173–92.

———. "Symbolic Ethnicity: The Future of Ethnic Groups in America." *Ethnic and Racial Studies* 2 (January 1979): 1–20.

Garcia Guadillo, Carmen. "The Brain Drain." *UNESCO Courier* 49:10 (1996): 24.

García y Griego, Manuel. "Canada: Flexibility and Control in Immigration and Refugee Policy." In *Controlling Immigration: A Global Perspective*, ed. Wayne A. Cornelius, P.L. Martin, and J.F. Hollifield, pp. 119–40. Stanford: Stanford University Press, 1994.

———. "U.S. Importation of Mexican Contract Laborers." In *The Border That Joins: Mexican Migrants and U.S. Responsibility*, ed. Peter G. Brown and Heary Shue, pp. 49–98. Totowa, NJ: Rowman and Littlefield, 1983.

Garcia, Jesus M. "The Hispanic Population in the United States." U.S. Census, P20 465RV. Washington, DC: Government Printing Office, 1992.

Garcia, Juan Ramon. *Operation Wetback: The Mass Deportation of Mexican Undocumented Workers in 1954.* Westport, CT: Greenwood, 1980.

Garcia, Maria Christina. *Havana USA: Cuban Exiles and Cuban Americans in South Florida.* Los Angeles: University of California Press, 1996.

García, Mario T. *Desert Immigrants.* New Haven: Yale University Press, 1981.

Garreau, Joel. *The Nine Nations of North America.* Boston: Houghton Mifflin, 1981.

Garza, Rudolfo O. de la, Louis DeSipio, F. Chris Garcia, John Garcia, and Angelo Falcon. *Latino Voices: Mexican, Puerto Rican and Cuban Perspectives on American Politics.* Boulder, CO: Westview Press, 1992.

Gat, Moshe. *The Jewish Exodus from Iraq: 1948–1951.* London: Frank Cass, 1997.

Georges, Eugenia. *The Making of a Transnational Community: Migration, Development, and Cultural Change in the Dominican Republic.* New York: Columbia University Press, 1990.

Gerber, Israel J. The *Heritage Seekers: American Blacks in Search of Jewish Identity.* Middle Village, NY: Jonathan David Publishers, 1977.

Geyer, G.A. *Americans No More.* New York: Atlantic Monthly Press, 1996.

Ghaffarian, Shireen. "The Acculturation of Iranian Immigrants in the United States and the Implications for Mental Health." *Journal of Social Psychology* 138 (October 1998): 645–54.

Ghosh, Ajay. "Dharma Prasar Yatra Ends in Whippany, NJ." *India Post*, August 27, 1999, p. 26.

Gibson, Campbell J., and Emily Lennon. "Historical Census Statistics on the Foreign-Born Population of the United States: 1850–1990." Working Paper no. 29, Bureau of the Census, Washington, DC, 1999.

Gibson, M.A. *Accommodation Without Assimilation: Sikh Immigrants in an American High School.* Ithaca: Cornell University Press, 1989.

Gilad, Lisa. *Ginger and Salt: Yemeni Jewish Women in an Israeli Town.* Boulder, CO: Westview Press, 1989.

Gilbert, Felix. *To the Farewell Address: Ideas of Early American Foreign Policy.* Princeton: Princeton University Press, 1961.

Gimpel, James G., and James R. Edwards, Jr. *The Congressional Politics of Immigration Reform.* Boston: Allyn and Bacon, 1999.

Gitelman, Zvi. *Becoming Israelis: Political Resocialization of Soviet and American Immigrants.* New York: Praeger, 1982.

Glazer, Nathan. "Ethnic Groups in America." In *Freedom and Control in Modern Society*, ed. Monroe Berger, Theodore Abel, and Charles Page, pp. 158–73. New York: Van Nostrand, 1954.

———. *We Are All Multiculturalists Now.* Cambridge: Harvard University Press, 1997.

Glenn, Charles Leslie, Ester J. De Jong, and Edward R. Beauchamp. *Educating Immigrant Children: Schools and Language Minorities in Twelve Nations.* New York: Garland, 1996.

Glenn, Evelyn Nakano. *Issei, Nisei, War Bride: Three Generations of Japanese American Women in Domestic Service.* Philadelphia: Temple University Press, 1986.

Glenn, Susan A. *Daughters of the Shtetl: Life and Labor in the Immigrant Generation.* Ithaca: Cornell University Press, 1990.

Glick-Schiller, Nina, and Georges E. Fouron. "Terrains of Blood and Nation: Haitian Transnational Social Fields." *Ethnic and Racial Studies* 22:2 (1999): 34–66.

Glick-Schiller, Nina, Linda Basch, and Cristina Blanc-Szanton. "Towards a Definition of Transnationalism: Introductory Remarks and Research Questions." In *Towards a Transnational Perspective on Migration: Race, Class, Ethnicity, and Nationalism Reconsidered,* ed. Nina Glick-Schiller, Linda Basch, and Cristina Blanc-Szanton, pp. ix–xiv. New York: Annals of the New York Academy of Sciences, 1992.

———. "Transnationalism: A New Analytic Framework for Understanding Migration." In *Towards a Transnational Perspective on Migration: Race, Class, Ethnicity, and Nationalism Reconsidered,* ed. Nina Glick-Schiller, Linda Basch, and Christina Blanc-Szanton. New York: Annals of the New York Academy of Sciences, 1992.

Glodava, Mila, and Richard Onizuka. *Mail-Order Brides: Women for Sale.* Fort Collins, CO: Alaken, 1994.

Gmelch, George. *Double Passage: The Lives of Caribbean Migrants Abroad and Back Home.* Ann Arbor: University of Michigan Press, 1992.

———. "Return Migration." *Annual Review of Anthropology* 9 (1980): 135–59.

Godfrey, Brian J. *Neighborhoods in Transition: The Making of San Francisco's Ethnic and Nonconformist Communities.* Berkeley: University of California Press, 1988.

Goering, John M. "The 'Explosiveness' of Chain Migration: Research and Policy Issues." *International Migration Review* 23:4 (1989): 797–812.

Gold, Jeffrey. "Ship's Captain and Mechanic Convicted of Alien Smuggling." Associated Press, December 3, 1998.

Gold, Steven. "Southeast Asians." In *A Nation of Peoples,* ed. Elliott Barkan, pp. 505–19. Westport, CT: Greenwood, 1999.

Gold, Steven, and Bruce Phillips. "Mobility and Continuity Among Eastern European Jews." In *Origins and Destinies: Immigration, Race, and Ethnicity in America,* ed. Silvia Pedraza and Rubén G. Rumbaut. Belmont, CA: Wadsworth, 1996.

Goldring, Luin. "The Power of Status in Transnational Social Fields." In *Transnationalism from Below: Comparative Urban and Community Research,* ed. Luis Guarnizo and Michael R. Smith. New Brunswick, NJ: Transaction, 1998.

Goldscheider, Calvin. *Israel's Changing Society: Population, Ethnicity, and Development.* Boulder, CO: Westview Press, 1996.

Goldstein, Beth L. "In Search of Survival: The Education and Integration of Hmong Refugee Girls." *Journal of Ethnic Studies* 16:2 (Summer 1988): 1–28.

Gómez-Peña, Guillermo. *The New World Border.* San Francisco: City Lights Books, 1996.

Gómez-Quiñones, Juan. *Chicano Politics: Reality and Promise, 1940–1990.* Albuquerque: University of New Mexico Press, 1990.

Gonzalez, Rosalinda Mendez. "Capital Accumulation and Mexican Immigration to the United States: A Comparative Historical Study of the Political Economy of International Labor Migration." Ph.D. diss., University of California—Irvine, 1981.

Gonzalez-Baker, Susan. "The 'Amnesty' Aftermath: Current Policy Issues Stemming from the Legalization Programs of the 1986 Immigration Reform and Control Act." *International Migration Review* 31 (1997): 5–27.

Goode, Judith. "Encounters Over the Counter: Bosses, Workers, and Customers on a Changing Shopping Strip." In *Newcomers in the Workplace: Immigrants and the Restructuring of the U.S. Economy,* ed. Louise Lamphere, Alex Stepick, and Guillermo Grenier, pp. 251–80. Philadelphia: Temple University Press, 1994.

———. "Polishing the Rustbelt: Immigrants Enter a Restructuring Philadelphia." In *Newcomers in the Workplace: Immigrants and the Restructuring of the U.S. Economy,* ed. Louise Lamphere, Alex Stepick, and Guillermo Grenier, pp. 199–230. Philadelphia: Temple University Press, 1994.

Goodman, Allan. "American Colleges Keep Opening Gates Wider to Foreigners." *USA Today,* December 6, 1999.

Goodman, K. *What's Whole in Whole Language.* Concord, NH: Heinemann, 1986.

Goodwin-Gill, Guy S. *The Refugee in International Law.* 2d ed. Oxford: Clarendon Press, 1996.

Gordon, Milton. *Assimilation in America Life: The Role of Race, Religion, and Natural Origins.* New York: Oxford University Press, 1964.

Gorn, Elliot J. *The Manly Art: Bare-Knuckle Prize Fighting in America.* Ithaca: Cornell University Press, 1986.

Gosh, Bimal. *Gains from Global Linkages: Trade in Services and the Movement of People.* New York: St. Martin's Press, 1997.

Goss, Jon D., and Bruce Lindquist. "Conceptualizing International Labor Migration: A Structuration Perspective." *International Migration Review* 29 (1995): 317–51.

Government Accounting Office. *Immigration Statistics: Information Gaps, Quality Issues Limit Utility of Federal Data to Policymakers.* Washington, DC: Government Accounting Office, 1998.

Graham, Stephen. *With Poor Immigrants to America.* New York: Arno Press, 1974.

Granatstein, Jack L., I.M. Abella, D.J. Bercuson, R.C.

Brown, and H.B. Neatby. *Twentieth Century Canada*. 2d ed. Toronto: McGraw-Hill and Ryerson, 1986.

Granovetter, Mark. "Economic Action and Social Structure: The Problem of Embeddedness." *American Journal of Sociology* 91 (1985): 481–510.

Grasmuck, Sherri, and Patricia Pessar. *Between Two Islands: Dominican International Migration*. Berkeley: University of California Press, 1991.

———. "Dominicans in the United States: First- and Second-Generation Settlement, 1960–1990." In *Origins and Destinies: Immigration, Race, and Ethnicity in America*, ed. Silvia Pedraza and Rubén G. Rumbaut. Belmont, CA: Wadsworth, 1996.

Greeley, Andrew. *Ethnicity, Denomination, and Inequality*. Beverly Hills, CA: Sage, 1976.

Green, Jay. "A Meta-Analysis of the Effectiveness of Bilingual Education." Paper presented at the University of Texas at Austin, March 1998.

Green, Rosario, and Peter H. Smith, eds. *Foreign Policy in U.S.-Mexican Relations*. La Jolla: University of California at San Diego Center for U.S.-Mexican Studies, 1989.

Greenhouse, Steven. "Foreign Workers at Highest Level in Seven Decades." *New York Times*, September 4, 2000.

———. "Labor Urges Amnesty for Illegal Immigrants." *New York Times*, February 17, 2000.

Greenwald, John, and Hannah Bloch. "Cutting off the Brains." *Time* 147:6 (1996): 46.

Grenier, Guillermo, and Lisandro Perez. "Cubans." In *A Nation of Peoples*, ed. Elliott Barkan, pp. 138–55. Westport, CT: Greenwood, 1999.

———. "Miami Spice: The Ethnic Cauldron Simmers." In *Origins and Destinies: Immigration, Race, and Ethnicity in America*, ed. Silvia Pedraza and Rubén G. Rumbaut. Belmont, CA: Wadsworth, 1996.

Grenier, Guillermo, and Alex Stepick, ed. *Miami Now: Immigration, Ethnicity and Social Change*. Miami: University of Florida Press, 1992.

Griswold del Castillo, Richard. *La Familia: Chicano Families in the Urban Southwest, 1848 to the Present*. Notre Dame: University of Notre Dame Press, 1984.

Griswold del Castillo, Richard, and Richard A. Garcia. *César Chávez: A Triumph of Spirit*. Norman: University of Oklahoma Press, 1995.

Griswold del Castillo, Richard, and Arnoldo de Leon. *North to Aztlan: A History of Mexican Americans in the United States*. New York: Twayne, 1996.

Groneman, Carol. "Working-Class Immigrant Women in Mid-Nineteenth-Century New York: The Irish Woman's Experience." *Journal of Urban History* 4:3 (1978): 255–74.

Grubel, Herbert, and Anthony Scott. "International Flow of Human Capital." *American Economic Review* 56 (1966): 262–74.

Grynberg, Anne. *Vers la terre d'Israel*. Paris: Gallimard, 1998.

Guarnizo, Luis E. "On the Political Participation of Transnational Migrants: Old Practices and New Trends." In *Immigrants, Civic Culture, and Modes of Political Incorporation*, ed. Gary Gerstle and John Mollenkopf. New York: Social Science Research Council, 2000.

Guarnizo, Luis Eduardo, and Luz Marina Diaz. "Transnational Migration: A View from Colombia." *Ethnic and Racial Studies* 22:2 (1998): 397–421.

Guarnizo, Luis Eduardo, and Michael Peter Smith. "The Locations of Transnationalism." In *Transnationalism from Below*, ed. Michael Peter Smith and Luis Eduardo Guarnizo. New Brunswick, NJ: Transaction, 1998.

Gunderson, Barbara. "Cooperative Structures in the Foreign Language Classroom." In *Teaching for Tomorrow in the Foreign Language Classroom*, ed. Reid E. Baker. Skokie, IL: National Textbook, 1977.

Gutiérrez, David. "Mexicans." In *A Nation of Peoples*, ed. Elliott Barkan, pp. 372–90. Westport, CT: Greenwood, 1999.

———. *Walls and Mirrors: Mexican Americans, Mexican Immigrants, and the Politics of Ethnicity*. Berkeley: University of California Press, 1995.

Gyory, Andrew. *Closing the Gate: Race, Politics, and the Chinese Exclusion Act*. Chapel Hill: University of North Carolina Press, 1998.

Habermas, Jurgen. "Citizenship and National Identity: Some Reflections on the Future of Europe." *Praxis International* 12 (1992): 1–9.

Hadaway, Nancy L., and JaNae Mundy. "Children's Informational Picture Books Visit a Secondary ESL Classroom." *Journal of Adolescent and Adult Literacy* 42 (1998): 464–75.

Haddad, Yvonne Yazbeck. *The Muslims of America*. New York: Oxford University Press, 1991.

Hagan, Jacqueline Maria. *Deciding to Be Legal: A Maya Community in Houston*. Philadelphia: Temple University Press, 1994.

Hagan, Jacqueline M., and Susan Gonzalez-Baker. "Implementing the U.S. Legalization Program: The Influence of Immigrant Communities and Local Agencies on Immigration Policy Reform." *International Migration Review* 27:3 (1993): 513–36.

Haider, Gulzar. "Brother in Islam, Please Draw Us a Mosque: Muslims in the West: A Personal Account." In *Expressions of Islam in Buildings*, proceedings of an international seminar held in Jakarta and Yogyakarta, October 15–19, 1990, pp. 155–66. Jakarta, Indonesia: Aga Khan Trust for Cultures, 1990.

Hailbronner, Kay. *Immigration Law and Policy of the European Union*. Dordrecht, Netherlands: Kluwer, 2000.

Hailbronner, Kay, David A. Martin, and Hiroshi Motomura, eds. *Immigration Admissions*. Oxford: Berghahn Books, 1998.

———. *Immigration Controls*. Oxford: Berghahn Books, 1997.

Hakim, Catherine. "Self-Employment in Britain: Recent Trends and Current Issues." *Work, Employment and Society* 2:4 (1988): 421–50.

Haley, Alex. *Roots*. New York: Doubleday, 1976.

Hall, S. "The Local and the Global: Globalization and Ethnicity." In *Culture, Globalization and the World-System: Contemporary Conditions for the Representation of Identity*. Vol. 3, *Current Debates in Art History*, ed. Anthony D. Hall. Binghamton: Department of Art and Art History, State University of New York at Binghamton, 1991.

Halpern, Robert. *Rebuilding the Inner City: A History of Neighborhood Initiatives to Address Poverty in the United States*. New York: Columbia University Press, 1995.

Hamamoto, Darrell Y. *Monitored Peril: Asian Americans and the Politics of TV Representation*. Minneapolis: University of Minnesota Press, 1994.

Ham-Chande, Roberto, and John R. Weeks. *Demographic Dynamics of the U.S.-Mexico Border*. El Paso: Texas Western Press, 1992.

Handlin, Oscar. *The Uprooted*. 2d ed. Boston: Little, Brown, 1973.

Hann, Richard. "Parasitic Infestations." In *Confronting Critical Health Issues of Asian and Pacific Islander Americans*, ed. Nolan W. S. Zane, David T. Takeuchi, and Kathleen Young, pp. 302–15. Thousand Oaks, CA: Sage, 1994.

Hardin, G. *The Immigration Dilemma: Avoiding the Tragedy of the Commons*. Washington, DC: Federation for American Immigration Reform, 1995.

Hardt, Hanno. "The Foreign-Language Press in American Press History." *Journal of Communications* 39:2 (Spring 1989): 114–31.

Harker, Richard, Cheleen Mahar, and Chris Wilkes. *An Introduction to the Work of Pierre Bourdieu: The Practice of Theory*. London: Macmillan, 1990.

Harrison, Bennet, and Barry Bluestone. *The Great U-Turn: Corporate Restructuring and the Polarizing of America*. New York: Basic Books, 1988.

Harrison, Roderick J., and Claudette Bennett. "Racial and Ethnic Diversity." In *State of the Union: America in the 1990s*. Vol. 2, *Social Trends*, ed. Reynolds Farely, pp. 141–210. New York: Russell Sage Foundation, 1995.

Harvard Law Review Editors. *Sexual Orientation and the Law*. Cambridge: Harvard University Press, 1990.

Harvey, David. *Limits to Capital*. Chicago: University of Chicago Press, 1982.

———. *The Condition of Postmodernity*. Oxford: Basil Blackwell, 1990.

Harzig, Christiane. *Peasant Maids, City Women: From the European Countryside to Urban America*. Ithaca: Cornell University Press, 1997.

Harzig, Christiane, and Dirk Hoerder, eds. *The Press of Labor Migrants in Europe and North America, 1880s–1980*. Lexington: Lexington Books, 1985.

Haskell, Guy H. *From Sophia to Jaffa: The Jews of Bulgaria and Israel*. Detroit: Wayne State University Press, 1994.

Hathaway, James C. *Reconceiving International Refugee Law*. The Hague, Netherlands: Nijhoff, 1997.

Hawkins, Freda. *Canada and Immigration: Public Policy and Public Concern*. 2d ed. Montreal: McGill-Queen's University Press, 1988.

Hawkins, Harriet. *Classics and Trash*. New York: Harvester Wheatsheaf, 1990.

Hedges, Stephen J., Dana Hawkins, and Penny Loeb. "The New Jungle." *U.S. News*, February 3, 2000.

Heer, David M. *Immigration in America's Future: Social Science Findings and the Policy Debate*. Boulder, CO: Westview Press, 1996.

———. *Society and Population*. 2nd ed. Englewood Cliffs NJ: Prentice Hall, 1975.

Heins, Marjorie. *Strictly Ghetto Property: The Story of Los Siete de la Raza*. Berkeley: Ramparts Press, 1972.

Held, D. *Global Transformations: Politics, Economics and Culture*. Cambridge, UK: Polity Press, 1999.

Hendricks, Glen. "Dominicans." In *Harvard Encyclopedia of American Ethnic Groups*, ed. Stephen Thernstrom. Cambridge: Harvard University Press, 1980.

Henson, Margaret Scott. "Harris County." In *The Handbook of Texas Online*. http://www.tsha.utexas.edu/handbook/online/articles/view/ HH/hch7.html.

Herman, Donald L. *The Latin-American Community of Israel*. New York: Praeger, 1984.

Hernandez, Donald J., and Evan Charney, eds. *From Generation to Generation: The Health and Well-Being of Children in Immigrant Families*. Washington, DC: National Academy Press, 1998.

Hernandez, Mario, and Mareasa Isaacs. *Promoting Cultural Competence in Children's Mental Health Services*. Baltimore: Paul Brookes Publishing, 1998.

Hernandez Alvarez, Jose. *Return Migration to Puerto Rico*. Berkeley: Institute of International Studies, University of California, 1967.

Hertz, Rosanna. *More Equal Than Others*. Berkeley: University of California Press, 1986.

Hertzberg, Arthur. *The Jews in America: Four Centuries of Uneasy Encounter, a History*. New York: Simon and Schuster, 1989.

Hertzog, Esther. *Immigrants and Bureaucrats: Ethiopians in an Israeli Absorption Center*. New York: Berghahn Books, 1999.

Herzog, Lawrence. "Border Commuter Workers and Transfrontier Metropolitan Structure Along the U.S.-Mexico Border." In *U.S.-Mexico Borderlands: Historical and Contemporary Perspectives*, ed. O. Martinez, pp. 176–89. Wilmington, DE: Scholarly Resources, 1996.

Heyzer, Noeleen. *The Trade in Domestic Workers*. London: Zed Books, 1994.

Hickok, Ralph. *A Who's Who of Sports Champions: Their Stories and Records*. New York: Houghton Mifflin, 1995.

Higham, John. *Send These to Me: Jews and Other Immigrants in Urban America*. New York: Athenaeum, 1975.

Hill, Clifford, and Kate Parry, eds. *From Testing to Assessment: English as an International Language*. New York: Longman, 1994.

Hill, John K., and James E. Pearce. "Enforcing Sanctions Against Employers of Illegal Aliens." *Economic Review* (May 1987): 1–15.

Hill, Kevin, and Dario Moreno. "Second-Generation Cubans." *Hispanic Journal of Behavioral Sciences* 18:2 (1996): 175–93.

"Hindu Philosophy Has No Place for Caste System Says FHA." *India Post*, March 17, 1995.

Hing, Bill. "Asian Immigrants: Social Forces Unleashed after 1965." In *The Immigration Reader: America in a Multidisciplinary Perspective*, ed. David Jacobson, pp. 144–82. Malden, MA: Blackwell, 1998.

Hirsch, Jennifer S. "En el Norte la Mujer Manda: Gender, Generation, and Geography in a Mexican Transnational Community." *American Behavioral Scientist* 42:9 (1999): 1332–49.

Hirschman, Charles. "Studying Immigrant Adaptation from the 1990 Population Census: From Generational Comparisons to the Process of 'Becoming American.'" In *The New Second Generation*, ed. Alejandro Portes, pp. 54–81. New York: Russell Sage Foundation, 1996.

Hoerder, Dirk. *Labor Migration in the Atlantic Economies: The European and North American Working Classes During the Period of Industrialization*. Westport, CT: Greenwood, 1985.

Hoerder, Dirk, ed. *The Immigrant Labor Press in North America, 1840s–1970s*. New York: Greenwood, 1987.

Hoffmann, Stanley "America—Is It Too Proud for Its Own Good?" *Miami Herald*, January 23, 2000.

Hollifield, J.F. "Immigration and Republicanism in France: The Hidden Consensus." In *Controlling Immigration: A Global Perspective*, ed. Wayne A. Cornelius, P.L. Martin, and J.F. Hollifield, pp. 143–76. Stanford: Stanford University Press, 1994.

Hondagneu-Sotelo, Pierrette. *Gendered Transitions: Mexican Experiences of Immigration*. Berkeley: University of California Press, 1994.

Horowitz, Donald L., and Gerard Noiriel. *Immigrants in Two Democracies: French and American Experience*. New York: New York University Press, 1992.

Horowitz, Robert A. *Summary of State Law Variations, ABA Center on Children and the Law*. Chicago: American Bar Association, 1999.

Houston, Velina, ed. *The Politics of Life: Four Plays by Asian American Women*. Philadelphia: Temple University Press, 1993.

"How Times Have Changed." *Chicago Sun-Times*, February 28, 1999.

Huddle, Donald. *The Net National Cost of Immigrants*. Washington, DC: Government Printing Office, 1996.

Hu-DeHart, Evelyn, ed. *Across the Pacific: Asian Americans and Globalization*. Philadelphia: Temple University Press, 1999.

Hudelson, Sarah. "Teaching English Through Content-Area Activities." In *When They Don't All Speak English: Integrating the ESL Student into the Regular Classroom*, ed. Pat Rigg and Virginia G. Allen. Urbana, IL: National Council of Teachers of English, 1989.

Huerta, Jorge. *Chicano Theater: Themes and Forms*. Tempe, AZ: Bilingual, 1982.

———. *Necessary Theater: Six Plays About the Chicano Experience*. Houston: Arte Publico, 1989.

Hunt, Michael H. *Ideology and U.S. Foreign Policy*. New Haven: Yale University Press, 1987.

Hunter, Edward. *In Many Voices: Our Fabulous Foreign-Language Press*. Norman Park, GA: Norman College, 1960.

Hurh, Won Moo. *The Korean Americans. The New Americans*, ed. Ronald H. Bayor. Westport, CT: Greenwood, 1998.

Hurwist, Judi, and Mary Sadler Tesconi, eds. *Challenges to Education: Readings for Analysis of Major Issues*. New York: Dodd, Mead, 1972.

Hutchinson, E.R. *Legislative History of American Immigration Policy, 1798–1965*. Philadelphia: University of Pennsylvania Press, 1981.

Hutton, Frank, and Barbara Strauss Reed, eds. *Outsiders in Nineteenth-Century Press History: Multicultural Perspectives*. Bowling Green, OH: Bowling Green State University Popular Press, 1995.

Hwang, K.K. "The Dynamic Processes of Coping with Interpersonal Conflicts in a Chinese Society." *Proceedings of the National Science Council* (Taiwan) 2 (1978): 198–208.

Ianni, Francis A.J. *The Search for Structure: A Report on American Youth Today*. New York: Free Press, 1989.

Ibrahim, S.E. *The New Arab Social Order: A Study of the Impact of the Oil Wealth*. Boulder, CO: Westview Press, 1982.

Immigration and Naturalization Service. *Annual Report: Legal Immigration, Fiscal Year 1998*. Washington, DC: Office of Policy and Planning, Statistics Branch, May 1999.

———. *Brutality Unchecked: Human Rights Abuses Along the U.S. Border with Mexico*. Washington, DC: Government Printing Office, 1992.

———. *Characteristics of Immigrants: Statistical Yearbook of the Immigration and Naturalization Service*. Washington, DC: Government Printing Office, 1998.

———. "Grounds for Exclusion." Lesson 3.2 of Extension Training Program, U.S. Department of Justice, Immigration and Naturalization Service, 32:10. Washington, DC: Government Printing Office, 1987.

———. *An Immigrant Nation: United States Regulation of Immigration, 1795–1991.* Washington, DC: Immigration and Naturalization Service, 1991.

———. *The Immigration Reform and Control Act: Report on the Legalized Alien Population.* Washington, DC: Government Printing Office, 1992.

———. "INS Estimates of Nonimmigrant Overstays, Resident Illegal Alien Population." Unpublished memorandum, April 22, 1994.

———. *Legal Immigration, Fiscal Year 1998: Annual Report.* Vol. 2. Washington, DC: Office of Policy and Planning, May 1999.

———. *Public Charge: Fact Sheet.* Washington, DC: Immigration and Naturalization Service, 1993.

———. *Report to Congress on "Mail-Order Bride" Businesses,* Congressional request under Section 652 of the Illegal Immigration Reform and Immigrant Responsibility Act of 1996 (IIRIRA). Washington, DC: Government Printing Office, 1999.

———. *Statistical Report.* Washington, DC: Department of Justice, 1996.

———. *Statistical Yearbook of the Immigration and Naturalization Service, 1990.* Washington, DC: Government Printing Office, 1992.

———. *Statistical Yearbook of the Immigration and Naturalization Service, 1996.* Washington, DC: Government Printing Office, 1997.

———. *Statistical Yearbook of the Immigration and Naturalization Service, 1997.* Washington, DC: Government Printing Office, 1999.

———. *Statistics Branch Annual Report: Refugees, Fiscal Year 1997.* Washington, DC: Government Printing Office, 1997.

Immigration Commission. *Immigrants in Industries.* Vol. 20. Washington, DC: Government Printing Office, 1911.

Inglis, C. "Asians and Race Relations in Australia." In *The State of Asian Pacific America: Transforming Race Relations: A Public Policy Document,* ed. R Ong. Los Angeles: LEAP Asian Pacific American Public Policy Institute and UCLA Asian American Studies Center, 2000.

International Organization for Migration. "Organized Crime Moves into Migrant Trafficking." *Trafficking in Migrants, Quarterly Bulletin* 11 (June 1996).

Ireland, Sandra L. Jones. *Ethnic Periodicals in Contemporary America: An Annotated Guide.* New York: Greenwood, 1990.

Isbister, John. *The Immigration Debate: Remaking America.* Bloomfield, CT: Kumarian Press, 1996.

Isenberg, Michael T. *John L. Sullivan and His America.* Urbana and Chicago: University of Illinois Press, 1988.

Itano, Nicole. "Yale to Raise Foreign Student Aid." *Yale Daily News,* November 21, 1997.

Itzigsohn, Jose, Carlos Dore Cabral, Esther Hemandez Medina, and Obed Vazquez. "Mapping Dominican Transnationalism: Narrow and Broad Transnational Practices." *Ethnic and Racial Studies* 22:2 (1998): 316–39.

Jacobs, James B., and Kimberly Potter. *Hate Crimes.* New York: Oxford University Press, 1998.

Jacobson, David. *Place and Belonging in America.* Baltimore: Johns Hopkins University Press, forthcoming.

Jacobson, David, ed. *The Immigration Reader: America in a Multidisciplinary Perspective.* Oxford: Blackwell, 1998.

James, Winston, and Clive Harris, eds. *Inside Babylon: The Caribbean Diaspora in Britain.* London: New York: Verso, 1993.

Janvry, Alain de. *The Agrarian Question and Reformism in Latin America.* Baltimore: Johns Hopkins University Press, 1982.

Jargowsky, Paul A. *Poverty and Place.* New York: Russell Sage Foundation, 1997.

Jasso, Guillermina, and Mark R. Rosenzweig. "Family Reunification and the Immigration Multiplier: U.S. Immigration Law, Origin-Country Conditions, and the Reproduction of Immigrants." *Demography* 23:3 (1986): 291–311.

———. "Sponsors, Sponsorship Rates and the Immigration Multiplier." *International Migration Review* 23:4 (1989): 856–88.

———. *The New Chosen People: Immigrants in the United States.* New York: Russell Sage Foundation, 1990.

Jelen, Ted G. "Culture Wars and the Party System: Religion and Realignment, 1972–1992." In *Culture Wars in American Politics: Critical Reviews of a Popular Thesis,* ed. Rhys H. Williams, pp. 145–58. New York: Aldine de Gruyter, 1997.

Jenkins, C.N., T. Le, S.J. McPhee, S. Stewart, and N.T. Ha. "Health Care Access and Preventive Care Among Vietnamese Immigrants: Do Traditional Beliefs and Practices Pose Barriers?" *Social Science and Medicine* 43:7 (1996): 1049–56.

Jenkins, Christopher N.H., and Marjorie Kagawa-Singer. "Cancer." In *Confronting Critical Health Issues of Asian and Pacific Islander Americans,* ed. Nolan W.S. Zane, David T. Takeuchi, and Kathleen Young, pp. 105–47. Thousand Oaks, CA: Sage, 1994.

Jenkins, J. Craig. *The Politics of Insurgency: The Farm Worker Movement in the 1960s.* New York: Columbia University Press, 1985.

Jenkins, Shirley. *The Ethnic Dilemma in Social Services.* New York: Free Press, 1981.

Jenkins, Shirley, ed. *Ethnic Associations and the Welfare State: Services to Immigrants in Five Countries.* New York: Columbia University Press, 1988.

Jick, Leon A. *The Americanization of the Synagogue, 1820–*

1870. Hanover, NH: University Press of New England, 1976.

Johnson, D.W., R.T. Johnson, and E.J. Holubec. *Circles of Learning: Cooperation in the Classroom.* Edina, MN: Interaction Book Company, 1986.

Johnson, James, Walter Farrell, and Chandra Guinn. "Immigration Reform and the Browning of America: Tensions, Conflict, and Community Instability in Metropolitan Los Angeles." *International Migration Review* 31 (1997): 1055–95.

Johnson, Keith. "Introduction: Some Background, Some Key Terms, and Some Definitions." In *Communication in the Classroom*, ed. Keith Johnson and Keith Morrow, pp. 1–12. Essex, UK: Longman Group, 1981.

Johnson, Robert Erwin. *Guardians of the Sea: History of the United States Coast Guard, 1915 to the Present.* Washington, DC: Naval Institute Press, 1988.

Johnston, R.J., Derek Gregory, and David Smith. *The Dictionary of Human Geography.* Cambridge, MA: Blackwell Reference, 1994.

Jonas, Suzanne, and Dod Thomas, eds. *Immigration: A Civil Rights Issue for the Americas.* Wilmington, DE: Scholarly Resources, 1999.

Jones, Bob. "Haitian Migrant Interdiction Operations—Chase Report." *Commandant's Bulletin*, January 25, 1982.

Jones, Clive. *Soviet Jewish Aliyah 1989–1992: Impact and Implications for Israel and the Middle East.* London: Frank Cass, 1996.

Jones, Delmos. "Which Migrants? Temporary or Permanent." In *Towards a Transnational Perspective on Migration: Race, Class, Ethnicity, and Nationalism Reconsidered*, ed. Nina Glick-Schiller, Linda Basch, and Cristina Blanc-Szanton, pp. 217–24. New York: Annals of the New York Academy of Sciences, 1992.

Jones, Dorothy R. *The Portrayal of China and India on the American Screen, 1896–1955: The Evolution of Chinese and Indian Themes, Locales, and Characters as Portrayed on the American Screen.* Cambridge: Center for International Studies, MIT, 1955.

Jones, E.L. "The Sources and Limits of Popular Support for a Multicultural Australia." In *The Future of Australian Multiculturalism*, ed. G. Hage and R. Couch, pp. 21–30. Sydney: Research Institute for Humanities and Social Sciences.

Jones, Richard C. "Introduction: The Renewal Role of Remittances in the New World Order." *Economic Geography* (January 1998): 17.

Jones-Correa, Michael. *Between Two Nations: The Political Life of Latin American Immigrants in New York City.* Ithaca: Cornell University Press, 1998.

Joppke, Christian. *Immigration and the Nation-State: The United States, Germany, and Great Britain.* Oxford: Oxford University Press, 1999.

Joppke, Christian, ed. *Challenge to the Nation-State: Immigration in Western Europe and the United States.* New York: Oxford University Press, 1998.

Judd, Elliot L. "Language Policy, Curriculum Development, and TESOL Instruction: A Search for Compatibility." *TESOL Quarterly* 15:1 (1981): 59–66.

Jupp, James. *Immigration.* Melbourne: Oxford University Press, 1998.

K & Y Kenneth Lenthal Real Estate Group. "New Immigration Study Looks at Significant Changes in Real Estate Industry." http://www.gallen.com/eykl/immigrel.htm, May 6, 1998.

Kagawa-Singer, Marjorie, and Nadereh Pourat. "Asian American and Pacific Islander Breast and Cervical Carcinoma Screening Rates and Healthy People 2000 Objectives." *Cancer* 1:3 (2000): 696–705.

Kahera, Akel Ismail. "Image, Text and Form: Complexities of Aesthetics in an American Mosque." *Studies in Contemporary Islam* 1:2 (1999): 73–85.

Kahera, Akel, and Latif Abdul-Malik. "Designing the American Mosque." *Islamic Horizons* (September–October 1996): 40–41.

Kahn, James, Brian Haile, and Ellen Shaffer. *Health Insurance Expansion Strategies in California: Impact on Noncitizen Immigrants.* Berkeley: California Policy Research Center, 2000.

Kaiser Commission of Medicaid and the Uninsured. *Immigrants' Health Care: Coverage and Access.* Menlo Park, CA: Henry J. Kaiser Family Foundation, 2000.

Kalmijn, Matthijs. "Intermarriage and Monogamy: Causes, Patterns, and Trends." *Annual Review of Sociology* 24 (1998): 395–421.

Kalnay, E. *The New American.* New York: Greenberg, 1941.

Kamineni, A., M.A. Williams, S.M. Schwartz, L.S. Cook, and N.S. Weiss. "The Incidence of Gastric Carcinoma in Asian Migrants to the U.S. and Their Descendants." *Cancer Causes Control* 10:1 (1999): 77–83.

Kamphoefner, Walter. "German Americans: Paradoxes of a Model Minority.'" In *Origins and Destinies: Immigration, Race, and Ethnicity in America*, ed. Silvia Pedraza and Rubén G. Rumbaut. Belmont, CA: Wadsworth, 1996.

Kanawada, Leo. *Franklin D. Roosevelt's Diplomacy and American Catholics, Italians, and Jews.* Ann Arbor, MI: UMI Research Press, 1982.

Kanellos, Nicolas. *A History of Hispanic Theatre in the United States: Origins to 1940.* Austin: University of Texas Press, 1990.

———. *Hispanic Theater in the United States.* Houston: Arte Publico, 1984.

———. *Mexican American Theatre: Then and Now.* Houston: Arte Publico, 1983.

Kanellos, Nicolas, and Claudio Esteva-Fabregat. *Hand-*

book of Hispanic Cultures in the United States: Literature and Art. 2 vols. Houston: Arte Publico, 1993.

Kaplan, Herbert R. "Castro's 'Berlin Wall.'" Sea Power 14 (November 1971): 14–20.

Karnow, Stanley, and Nancy Yoshihara. Asian Americans in Transition. New York: Asia Society, 1992.

Karp, Abraham J. A History of Jews in America. Northvale, NJ: Jason Aronson, 1997.

Kashima, Tetsuden. Buddhism in America: The Social Organization of an Ethnic Religious Institution. Westport, CT: Greenwood, 1977.

Kasinitz, Philip, and Josh DeWind, eds. The Handbook of International Migration: The American Experience. New York: Russell Sage Foundation, 1999.

Kasinitz, Philip, and Milton Vickerman. "West Indians/ Caribbeans." In A Nation of Peoples, ed. Elliott Barkan, pp. 520–41. Westport, CT: Greenwood, 1999.

Kavanagh, Barbara, and Steve Lonergan. "Environmental Degradation, Population Displacement, and Global Security: An Overview of the Issues." A background report prepared for the Royal Society of Canada under the auspices of the Canadian Global Change Program's Research Panel on Environment and Security, December 1992.

Kayser, Bernard. Cyclically Determined Homeward Flows of Migrant Workers. Paris: Organization for Economic Cooperation and Development, Manpower and Social Affairs Directorate, 1972.

Kazin, Michael. Barons of Labor: The San Francisco Building Trades and Union Down in the Progressive Era. Urbana: University of Illinois Press, 1987.

Kearney, Michael. "The Local and the Global: The Anthropology of Globalization and Transnationalism." Annual Review of Anthropology 24 (1995): 547–65.

Keely, Charles B., and Bao Nga Tran. "Remittances from Labor Migration: Evaluations, Performance, and Implications." International Migration Review 23:3 (1989): 500–552.

Kemp, Thomas J. "The Roots of Genealogy Collections." Library Journal 124:6 (1999): 57–61.

Kennedy, Albert, et al., eds. Social Settlements in New York City. New York: Columbia University Press, 1935.

Kennedy, James, Deborah J. Seymour, and Barbara J. Hummel. "A Comprehensive Refugee Health Screening Program." Public Health Report 114 (1999): 469–77.

Kessler, David, and Tudor Parfitt. "The Falashas: The Jews of Ethiopia." Minority Rights Group, Report no. 67, 1985.

Kessler, Lauren. The Dissident Press: Alternative Journalism in American History. Newbury Park, CA: Sage, 1990.

Kessler, Lauren, ed. The Ethnic Press in the United States: A Historical Analysis and Handbook. New York: Greenwood, 1987.

Khalidi, Omar. "Approaches to Mosque Design in North America." In Muslims on the Americanization Path? ed. Yvonne Haddad and John Esposito, pp. 399–424. Atlanta: Scholars Press, 1998.

Kim, Hyung-Chan, ed. The Korean Diaspora. Santa Barbara, CA: ABC-Clio Press, 1977.

Kim, Ilsoo. New Urban Immigrants: The Korean Community in New York. Princeton: Princeton University Press, 1983.

———. "The Koreans: Small Business in an Urban Frontier." In New Immigrants in New York City, ed. Nancy Foner. New York: Columbia University Press, 1987.

Kim, Kwang Chung. "Koreans." In A Nation of Peoples, ed. Elliott Barkan, pp. 354–71. Westport, CT: Greenwood, 1999.

Kim, Luke I. "The Mental Health of Korean American Women." In Korean American Women—From Tradition to Modern Feminism, ed. Young I. Song and Ailee Moon. Westport, CT: Praeger, 1998.

Kim, Young Yun. "Communication Patterns of Foreign Immigrants in the Process of Acculturation." Human Communication Research 4:1 (Fall 1997): 66–77.

King, Russell. "Return Migration and Regional Economic Development: An Overview." In Return Migration and Regional Economic Problems, ed. Russell King, pp. 1–37. Dover, NH: Croom Helm, 1986.

King, Russell, Alan Strachan, and Jill Mortimer. "Gastarbeiter Go Home: Return Migration and Economic Change in the Italian Mezzogiorno." In Return Migration and Regional Economic Problems, ed. Russell King, pp. 38–68. Dover, NH: Croom Helm, 1986.

Kinsey, Alfred. Sexual Behavior in the Human Male. Bloomington: Indiana University Press, 1998.

Kiran, Frank, and Frank Harrigan. "Swedish-Finnish Return Migration, Extent, Timing, and Information Flows." Demography 23:3 (1986): 313–27.

Kiser, George C., and Martha W. Kiser. Mexican Workers in the United States. Albuquerque: University of New Mexico Press, 1979.

Kisseloff, Jeff. The Box: An Oral History of Television, 1920–1961. New York: Penguin, 1995.

Klein, Malcom W. The American Street Gang: Its Nature, Prevalence, and Control. New York: Oxford University Press, 1995.

Kleinknecht, William. The New Ethnic Mobs: The Changing Face of Organized Crime in America. New York: Free Press, 1996.

Knippling, Alpana Sharma. New Immigrant Literature in the United States: A Sourcebook to Our Multicultural Literary Heritage. Westport, CT: Greenwood, 1996.

Konvitz, M. The Alien and the Asiatic in American Law. Ithaca: Cornell University Press, 1946.

Koslowski, Rey. Migrants and Citizens: Demographic Change in the European State System. Ithaca: Cornell University Press, 2000.

Koussoudji, S. "Playing Cat and Mouse at the U.S.-Mexican Border." *Demography* 29:2 (1992): 159–81.

Kraly, E.R. "Emigration: Implications for U.S. Immigration Policy Research." In *Migration Between Mexico and the United States: Binational Study*. Vol. 2. *Research Reports and Background Materials*. Mexico City: Mexican Ministry of Foreign Affairs; Washington, DC: Commission on Immigration Reform, 1998.

Krashen, Stephen D. "The Theoretical and Practical Relevance of Simple Codes in Second Language Acquisition." In *Research in Second Language Acquisition*, ed. Robin Scarcella and Stephen Krashen, pp. 7–18. Rowley, MA: Newbury House Publishers, 1999.

Krauss, Clifford. "The Cali Cartel and the Globalization of Crime in New York City." In *The City and the World*, ed. Margaret Crahan and Alberto Vourvoulias-Bush. New York: Council on Foreign Relation , 1997.

Kraut, Alan M. *Silent Travelers: Germs, Genes, and the "Immigrant Menace."* New York: Basic Books, 1994.

Kritz, Mary, ed. *U.S. Immigration and Refugee Policy: Global and Domestic Issues*. Lexington, MA: D.C. Heath, 1983.

Krivo, Lauren J. "Immigrant Characteristics and Hispanic-Anglo Housing Inequality." *Demography* 32:4 (1995): 599–615.

Ku, Leighton, and Bethany Kessler. *Number and Cost of Immigrants on Medicaid: National and State Estimates*. Washington, DC: Urban Institute, 1997.

Kulu, Hill, and Tiit Tammaru. "Ethnic Return Migration from the East and West: The Case of Estonia in the 1990s." *Europe-Asia Studies* 52:2 (2000): 349–69.

Kuo, JoAnn, and Kathryn Porter. "Health Status of Asian Americans: United States, 1992–1994." *Advance Data* 298 (1998): 1–16.

Kuo, Wen H., and Yung-Mei Tsai. "Social Networking, Hardiness and Immigrant's Mental Health." *Journal of Health and Social Behavior* 27:2 (1986): 133–49.

Kurian, George T., ed. *A Historical Guide to the U.S. Government*. New York: Oxford University Press, 1998.

Kurien, Prema Ann. "Becoming American by Becoming Hindu: Indian Americans Take Their Place at the Multi-Cultural Table." In *Gatherings in Diaspora: Religious Communities and the New Immigration*, ed. R. Stephen Warner and Judith G. Wittner, pp. 37–70. Philadelphia: Temple University Press, 1998.

———. "Constructing 'Indianness' in the United States and India: The Role of Hindu and Muslim Indian Immigrants in Southern California." In *Asian and Latino Immigrants in a Restructuring Economy: The Metamorphosis of Los Angeles*, ed. Marta Lopez-Garza and David R. Diaz. Stanford: Stanford University Press, 2001.

———. "Gendered Ethnicity: Creating a Hindu Indian Identity in the U.S." *American Behavioral Scientist* 42:4 (1999): 648–70.

———. "We Are Better Hindus Here—Religion and Ethnicity Among Indian Americans." In *Building Faith Communities: Asian Immigrants and Religions*, ed. Jung Ha Kim and Pyong Gap Min. Walnut Creek, CA: AltaMira Press, in press.

Kurthen, H. "Germany at the Crossroads: National Identity and the Challenges of Immigration." *International Migration Review* 29:4 (1995): 914–38.

———. "Immigration and the Welfare State in Comparison: Differences in the Incorporation of Immigrant Minorities in Germany and the United States." *International Migration Review* 31:3 (1997): 721–31.

Kushner, Gilbert. *Immigrants from India to Israel: Planned Change in an Administered Community*. Tucson: University of Arizona Press, 1973.

Kwong, Peter. *Forbidden Workers: Illegal Chinese Immigrants and American Labor*. New York: New Press, 1998.

Kyle, David. *Transnational Peasants: Migrations, Networks, and Ethnicity in Andean Ecuador*. Baltimore: Johns Hopkins University Press, 2000.

Kyung, Rim Shin, ed. "Psychological Predictors of Depressive Symptoms in Korean-American Women in New York City." *Women and Health* 2 (1994): 73–82.

La Brack, Bruce. "South Asians." In *A Nation of Peoples*, ed. Elliott Barkan, pp. 482–504. Westport, CT: Greenwood, 1999.

Lacey, Dan. *The Essential Immigrant*. New York: Hippocrene Books, 1990.

Laguerre, Michel S. "Haitian Americans." In *Ethnicity and Medical Care*, ed. Alan Harwood, pp. 172–210. Cambridge: Harvard University Press, 1981.

Lai, H.M., Genny Lim, and Judy Yung. *Island: Poetry and History of Chinese Immigrants on Angel Island, 1910–1940*. Seattle: University of Washington Press, 1991.

Lalonde, Robert, and Robert Topel. "Immigrants in the American Labor Market: Quality, Assimilation, and Distributional Effects." *American Economic Review* 81 (1991): 297–302.

Landale, Nancy, R.S. Oropesa, and Daniel Llanes. "Schooling, Work, and Idleness Among Mexican and Non-Latino White Adolescents." *Social Science Research* 27:4 (1998): 457–90.

Landolt, Patricia, Lilian Autler, and Sonia Baires. "From Hermano Lejano to Hermano Mayor: The Dialectics of Salvadoran Transnationalism." *Ethnic and Racial Studies* 22:2 (1998): 290–315.

Lange, Dorothea, and Paul S. Taylor. *An American Exodus*. New York: Reynal and Hitchcock, 1939.

Lanteigne, Betty, and David Schwarzer. "The Progress of Rafael in English and Family Reading: A Case Study." *Journal of Adolescent and Adult Literacy* 41 (1997): 36–45.

Laslett, John. "Historical Perspectives: Immigration and the Rise of a Distinctive Urban Region, 1900–1970." In *Ethnic Los Angeles*, ed. R.D. Waldinger and Mehdi

Bozorgmehr. New York: Russell Sage Foundation, 1996.

Latino Coalition for a Healthy California. *Fact Sheet: Latinos and Access to Health Care in California*. San Francisco: Latino Coalition for a Healthy California, 2000.

Layton-Henry, Zig. *The Politics of Immigration: Immigration, "Race" and "Race" Relations in Post-War Britain*. Cambridge, MA: Blackwell, 1992.

Legomsky, Stephen H. *Immigration and Refugee Law and Policy*. 2d ed. Westbury, NY: Foundation Press, 1997.

LeMay, Michael C. *Anatomy of a Public Policy: The Reform of Contemporary Immigration Law*. Westport, CT: Praeger, 1994.

———. *From Open Door to Dutch Door: An Analysis of U.S. Immigration Policy Since 1820*. New York: Praeger, 1987.

Lemke-Santangelo, Gretchen. *Abiding Courage: African American Migrant Women and the East Bay Community*. Chapel Hill: University of North Carolina Press, 1996.

Leonard, Karen Isaksen. *Making Ethnic Choices: California's Punjabi Mexican Americans*. Philadelphia: Temple University Press, 1992.

———. *The South Asian Americans. The New Americans*, ed. Ronald H. Bayor. Westport, CT: Greenwood, 1997.

Leshem, Elazar, and Judith T. Shuval, eds. *Immigration to Israel: Sociological Perspectives*. Vol. 8, *Studies of Israeli Society*. New Brunswick, NJ: Transaction, 1998.

Lessinger, Johanna. *From the Ganges to the Hudson*. Needham Heights, MA: Allyn and Bacon, 1995.

———. "Investing or Going Home? A Transnational Strategy Among Indian Immigrants in the United States." In *Towards a Transnational Perspective on Migration: Race, Class, Ethnicity, and Nationalism Reconsidered*, ed. Nina Glick-Schiller, Linda Basch, and Cristina Blanc-Szanton, pp. 53–80. New York: Annals of the New York Academy of Sciences, 1992.

Lester, Paul M., ed. *Images That Injure: Pictorial Stereotypes in the Media*. Westport, CT: Praeger, 1996.

Lester, Will. "Foreign Students in U.S. Up 5.1 Percent." Associated Press Wire Service, December 7, 1998.

Levin, Jack, and Jack McDevitt. *Hate Crimes: The Rising Tide of Bigotry and Bloodshed*. New York: Plenum, 1993.

Levine, Peter. *Ellis Island to Ebbets Field*. New York: Oxford University Press, 1992.

Levitt, Peggy. "Social Remittances: Migration-Driven Local-Level Forms of Cultural Diffusion." *International Migration Review* 32:4 (1998): 926–48.

———. "Transnationalizing Community Development: The Case of Migration Between Boston and the Dominican Republic." *Nonprofit and Voluntary Sector Quarterly* 26:4 (1997): 509–26.

Levy, Mildred B., and Walter J. Wadycki. "The Influence of Family and Friends on Geographic Labor Mobility: An Intercensal Comparison." *Review of Economics and Statistics* 55 (1973): 198–203.

Lewis, Herbert S. *After the Eagles Landed: The Yemenites of Israel*. Boulder, CO: Westview Press, 1989.

Lewis, Neil A. "Longtime Fund-Raiser for Gore Convicted in Donation Scheme," *New York Times*, March 3, 2000.

Lewis, W. Arthur. "Economic Development with Unlimited Supplies of Labor." *Manchester School of Economic and Social Studies* 22 (1954): 139–91.

Liang, Zai. "Social Contact, Social Capital, and the Naturalization Process: Evidence from Six Immigrant Groups," *Social Science Research* 23:4 (1994): 407–37.

Licuanan, Patricia. "The Socio-Economic Impact of Domestic Worker Migration: Individual, Family, Community, Country." In *The Trade in Domestic Workers: Causes, Mechanisms, and Consequences of International Migration*, ed. Noeleen Heyzer, Geerije Lycklama, and Nijeholt and Nedra Weerakoon, pp. 103–15. London: Zed Books, 1994.

Lie, John. 1994. "The 'Problem' of Foreign Workers in Contemporary Japan." *Bulletin of Concerned Asian Scholars* 26:3 (1994): 3–11.

Lieberson, Stanley, and Mary C. Waters. *From Many Strands: Ethnic and Racial Groups in Contemporary America*. New York: Russell Sage Foundation, 1988.

Lieberson, Stanley, G. Dalto, and M.E. Johnston. "The Course of Mother Tongue Diversity in Nations." *American Journal of Sociology* 81 (July 1975): 34–61.

Lien, Pei-te. *The Political Participation of Asian Americans: Voting Behavior in Southern California*. New York: Garland, 1997.

———. "Who Votes in Multiracial America? An Analysis of Voting Registration and Turnout by Race and Ethnicity, 1990–1996." Paper presented at the annual meeting of the American Political Science Association, 1998.

Light, Ivan Hubert. *Ethnic Enterprise in America: Business and Welfare Among Chinese, Japanese and Blacks*. Berkeley: University of California Press, 1972.

———. "Immigrant Entrepreneurs in America: Koreans in Los Angeles." In *The Immigration Reader: America in a Multidisciplinary Perspective*, ed. David Jacobson, pp. 265–82. Malden, MA: Blackwell, 1998.

———. "Nationalism and Anti-Immigrant Movements." *Society* (1996): 58–63.

Light, Ivan Hubert, and Edna Bonacich. *Immigrant Entrepreneurs: Koreans in Los Angeles*. Los Angeles: University of California Press, 1988.

Light, Ivan Hubert, and S.J. Gold. *Ethnic Economies*. San Diego: Academic Press, 2000.

Light, Ivan Hubert, and Carolyn Rosenstein. *Race, Ethnicity, and Entrepreneurship in Urban America*. New York: Aldine de Gruyter, 1995.

Light, Ivan Hubert, Richard B. Bernard, and Rebecca Kim. "Immigrant Incorporation in the Garment Industry of

Los Angeles." *International Migration Review* 33:1 (Spring 1999): 5–25.

Lilwin, Howard. *Uprooted in Old Age: Soviet Jews and Their Social Networks in Israel.* Westport, CT: Greenwood, 1995.

Lin, Jan. *Reconstructing Chinatown: Ethnic Enclave, Global Change.* Minneapolis: University of Minnesota Press, 1998.

Lindstrom, David R. "Economic Opportunity in Mexico and Return Migration from the United States." *Demography* 33:3 (1996): 357–74.

Lin-Yuan, Yihua Lou. "Migration Decision-Making: A Theoretical and Empirical Study." Ph.D. diss., University of Alberta, 1993.

Lipson, Leslie. "European Responses to the American Revolution." *Annals of the American Academy of Political and Social Science* 428 (November 1976): 22–32.

Liska, Allen E., and Steven E Messner. *Perspectives on Crime and Deviance.* Upper Saddle River, NJ: Prentice Hall, 1999.

Lissak, Shpak Rivka. *Pluralism and Progressives: Hull House and the New Immigrants, 1890–1919.* Chicago: University of Chicago Press, 1989.

Litigation Update: Legalization/Special Agricultural Workers. Washington, DC: American Immigration Lawyers Association, 1989.

Lochore, Reuel Anson. *From Europe to New Zealand: An Account of our Continental European Settlers.* Wellington, New Zealand: A.H. and A.W. Reed, 1951.

Loescher, Gil, and John Scanlan. *Calculated Kindness: Refugees and America's Half-Open Door, 1945 to the Present.* New York: Free Press, 1986.

Logan, John R., et al. "Ethnic Economies in Metropolitan Regions: Miami and Beyond." *Social Forces* 72 (1994): 691–724.

———."Ethnic Segmentation in the American Metropolis: Increasing Divergence in Economic Incorporation, 1980–1990." *International Migration Review* 34:1 (2000): 98–132.

Lomeli, Francisco, ed. *Handbook of Hispanic Cultures in the United States: Literature and Art.* Houston: Arte Publico, 1993.

Long, Michael, and Jack Richards, eds. *Methodology in TESOL: A Book of Readings.* Boston: Heinle and Heinle, 1986.

Lopez, Ana M. "Are All Latins from Manhattan? Hollywood, Ethnography, and Cultural Colonialism." In *Unspeakable Images: Ethnicity and the American Cinema,* ed. Lester D. Friedman, pp. 404–24. Chicago: University of Illinois Press, 1991.

Lopez, David, Eric Popkin, and Edward Telles. "Central Americans: At the Bottom, Struggling to Get Ahead." In *Ethnic Los Angeles,* ed. Roger D. Waldinger and Mehdi Bozorgmehr. New York: Russell Sage Foundation, 1996.

Loue, Sana, and Arwen Bunce. "The Assessment of Immigration Status in Health Research." *Vital and Health Statistics Series* 2, 127 (1999).

Loury, Glenn C. "A Dynamic Theory of Racial Income Differences." In *Women, Minorities, and Employment Discrimination,* ed. Phyllis A. Wallace and Annette M. LaMond, pp. 153–86. Lexington, MA: Heath, 1977.

Lowe, Lisa. *Immigrant Acts.* Durham, NC: Duke University Press, 1996.

Lowell, B. Lindsay. "Immigrant Integration and Pending Legislation: Observations on Empirical Projections." In *Immigration and the Family,* ed. Alan Booth, Ann C. Crouter, and Nancy Landale, pp. 271–80. Mahwah, NJ: Lawrence Erlbaum, 1997.

Lowell, B. Lindsay, and Z. Jing. "Unauthorized Workers and Immigration Reform: What Can We Ascertain from Employers?" *International Migration Review* 28:3 (1994): 427–48.

Lozano, Fernando. "Migracion internacional y remesas: Cambios en el Quinqueno 1990–1995." Paper presented at Coloquio Internacional Sobre Migracion Mexicana a Estados Unidos, Mexico City, 1996.

Lozanov, Georgi. *Suggestology and Outlines of Suggestopedy.* New York: Gordon and Breach, 1978.

Luibheid, Eithne. "Racialized Immigrant Women's Sexualities: The Construction of Wives, Prostitutes, and Lesbians through U.S. Immigration." Ph.D. diss., University of California at Berkeley, 1998.

Ma, G.X. "Between Two Worlds: The Use of Traditional and Western Health Services by Chinese Immigrants." *Journal of Community Health* 24:6 (1999): 421–37.

Maciel, David R., and Maria Herrera-Sobek, ed. *Culture Across Borders: Mexican Immigration and Popular Culture.* Tucson: University of Arizona Press, 1998.

Mack, Thomas, Ann Walker, Wendy Mack, and Leslie Bernstein. "Cancer in Hispanics in Los Angeles County." *National Cancer Institute Monograph* 69 (1985): 99–104.

MaCurdy, Thomas, and Margaret O'Brien-Strain. *Reform Reversed? The Restoration of Welfare Benefits to Immigrants in California.* San Francisco: Public Policy Institute of California, 1998.

Mahara, R. "Elderly Puerto Rican Women in the Continental United States." In *The Psychosocial Development of Puerto Rican Women,* ed. Cynthia Garcia Coll and Mariá de Lourdes Mattei. New York: Praeger, 1989.

Mahler, Sara J. *American Dreaming: Immigrant Life on the Margins.* Princeton: Princeton University Press, 1995.

———. "Theoretical and Empirical Contributions Toward a Research Agenda for Transnationalism." In *Transnationalism from Below,* ed. Michael Peter Smith and Luis Eduardo Guarnizo, pp. 64–100. New Brunswick, NJ: Transaction, 1998.

Manning, Robert. "Multicultural Washington, DC: The Changing Social and Economic Landscape of a Post-

Industrial Metropolis." *Ethnic and Racial Studies* 21:2 (1998).

Marcelli, Enrico A., Manuel Pastor, Jr., and Pascale M. Joassart. "Estimating the Effects of Informal Economic Activity: Evidence from Los Angeles County." *Journal of Economic Issues* 33:3 (1999): 579–607.

Marchetti, Gina. *Romance and the "Yellow Peril": Race, Sex and Discursive Strategies in Hollywood Fiction.* Berkeley: University of California Press, 1993.

Marcuson, Lewis R. *The Stage Immigrant: The Irish, Italians, and Jews in American Drama, 1920–1960.* New York: Garland, 1990.

Margolin, Malcolm. *The Ohlone Way: Indian Life in the San Francisco-Monterey Bay Area.* Berkeley: Heyday Books, 1978.

Marquez, Ben. *LULAC: The Evolution of a Mexican American Political Organization.* Austin: University of Texas Press, 1993.

Marrus, Michael R. *The Unwanted: European Refugees in the Twentieth Century.* New York: Oxford University Press, 1985.

Marshall, Ineke Haen, ed. *Minorities, Migrants, and Crime: Diversity and Similarity Across Europe and the United States.* Thousand Oaks, CA: Sage, 1997.

Martin, David. *Major Issues in Immigration Law.* Washington, DC: Federal Judicial Center, 1987.

Martin, J. *The Migrant Presence.* Sydney: Allen and Unwin, 1978.

Martin, Philip L. "Promises to Keep: Collective Bargaining in California Agriculture." http://agecon.ucdavis.edu/Faculty/Phil.M/promises/promisesl.htm, January 30, 2000.

———. "The Endless Debate: Immigration and U.S. Agriculture." http://www.agecon.ucdavis.edu/Faculty/Phil.M/endless/endless.htm, January 2000.

———. "The Mexican Crisis and Mexico-U.S. Migration." http://www.agecon.davis.edu/Faculty/Phil.M/crisis/crisis.htm, January 1, 2000.

———. *Trade and Migration: NAFTA and Agriculture.* Washington, DC: Institute for International Economics, 1993.

Martin, Philip L., and Elizabeth Midgley. "Immigration to the United States: Journey to an Uncertain Destination." *Population Bulletin* 49 (September 1994): 1–47.

Martin, R.L. "Good Intentions Gone Awry: IRCA and U.S. Agriculture." *Annals of the American Academy of Political and Social Science* 534 (July 1994): 44–57.

Martin, Sandra L., Todd E. Gordon, and Janis B. Kupersmidt. "Survey of Exposure to Violence Among the Children of Migrant and Seasonal Farm Workers." *Public Health Reports* 110 (May–June 1995): 268–76.

Martínez, Oscar J. *Border Boom Town: Ciudad Juarez Since 1848.* Austin: University of Texas Press, 1975.

———. *Border People: Life and Society in the U.S.-Mexico Borderlands.* Tucson: University of Arizona Press, 1994.

Massey, Douglas S. "The New Immigration and Ethnicity in the United States." *Population and Development Review* 21:3 (1995): 631–52.

———. "The Settlement Process Among Mexican Immigrants to the United States. *American Sociological Review* 51 (1986): 670–84.

———. "Understanding Mexican Migration to the United States of America." *Journal of Sociology* 92:6 (1987): 372–403.

———. "Why Does Immigration Occur? A Theoretical Synthesis." In *The Handbook of International Migration: The American Experience,* ed. Charles Hirschman, Philip Kasinitz, and Josh DeWind. New York: Russell Sage Foundation, 1999.

Massey, Douglas S., and Nancy A. Denton. "American Apartheid: Segregation and the Making of the Underclass." *American Journal of Sociology* 96 (1990): 329–58.

Massey, Douglas S., and Kristin Espinosa. "What's Driving Mexico-U.S. Migration? A Theoretical, Empirical, and Policy Analysis." *American Journal of Sociology* 102 (1997): 939–99.

Massey, Douglas S., and Luin R. Goldring. "Continuities in Transnational Migration: An Analysis of Nineteen Mexican Communities." *American Journal of Sociology* 99 (May 1994): 1492–1533.

Massey, Douglas S., Luin R. Goldring, and Jorge Durand. "International Migration and Economic Development in Comparative Perspective." *Population and Development Review* 14 (1988): 383–414.

Massey, Douglas S., Andrew B. Gross, and Kumiko Shibuya. "Migration, Segregation, and the Geographic Concentration of Poverty." *Journal of American Ethnic History* 15:3 (1996): 52–56.

———. *American Apartheid: Segregation and the Making of the Underclass.* Cambridge: Harvard University Press, 1993.

Massey, Douglas S., Rafael Alarcón, Jorge Durand, and Humberto González. *Return to Aztlán: The Social Process of International Migration from Western Mexico.* Berkeley: University of California Press, 1987.

Massey, Douglas S., Joaquin Arango, Graeme Hugo, Ali Kouaouci, Adela Pellegrino, and J. Edward Taylor. "Theories of International Migration: A Review and Appraisal." *Population and Development Review* 19:3 (1993): 431–66.

———. *Worlds in Motion: Understanding International Migration at the End of the Millennium.* Oxford: Clarendon Press, 1998.

May, Ernest. *American Imperialism.* New York: Athenaeum, 1968.

Mayeno, Laurin, and Sherry Hirota. "Access to Health Care." In *Confronting Critical Health Issues of Asian and Pacific Islander Americans*, ed. Nolan W. S. Zane, David T. Takeuchi, and Kathleen Young, pp. 347–75. Thousand Oaks, CA: Sage, 1994.

Mays, G. Larry, ed. *Gangs and Gang Behavior*. Chicago: Nelson-Hall, 1997.

McCaffrey, Lawrence. *The Irish Catholic Diaspora in America*. Washington, DC: Catholic University of America Press, 1997.

McCarthy, Kevin F., and Georges Vernez. *Immigration in a Changing Economy: California's Experience*. Santa Monica, CA: Rand, 1977.

McClellan, Robert. *The Heathen Chinese: A Study of American Attitudes Toward China*. Columbus: Ohio State University Press, 1971.

McClure, Rhonda. *The Complete Idiot's Guide to Online Genealogy*. New York: Macmillan USA, 2000.

McCrum, Robert, William Cran, and Robert MacNeil. *The Story of English*. New York: Viking, Elisabeth Sifton Books, 1986.

McDonald, John S., and Leatrice D. McDonald. "Chain Migration, Ethnic Neighborhood Formation, and Social Networks." In *An Urban World*, ed. Charles Tilly, pp. 226–36. Boston: Little, Brown, 1974.

McKean, Lise. *Divine Enterprise: Gurus and the Hindu Nationalist Movement*. Chicago: University of Chicago Press, 1996.

McKenna, Matthew T., Eugene McCray, and Ida Onorato. "The Epidemiology of Tuberculosis Among the Foreign-Born Persons in the United States, 1986 to 1993." *New England Journal of Medicine* 332:16 (1995): 1071–76.

McWilliams, Carey. *Factories in the Fields: The Story of Migratory Labor in California*. 1939. Reprint. Berkeley: University of California Press, 1999.

———. *Southern California Country: An Island on the Land*. New York: American Book–Stratford Press, 1946.

Meinhardt, Kenneth, et al. "Southeast Asian Refugees in the 'Silicon Valley': The Asian Health Assessment Project." *Amerasia* 12:2 (1985–86): 43–65.

Meissner, D., and D. Papademetriou. *The Legalization Countdown: A Third-Quarter Assessment*. Washington, DC: Carnegie Endowment for International Peace, 1988.

Meissner, D., D. Papademetriou, and D. North. *Legalization of Undocumented Aliens: Lessons from Other Countries*. Washington, DC: Carnegie Endowment for International Peace, 1986.

Melder, Keith, with Melinda Young Stuart. *City of Magnificent Intentions: A History of Washington, District of Columbia*. 2d ed. Washington, DC: Intac, 1997.

Meng, Eddy, "Mail Order Bride: Gilded Prostitution and the Legal Response." *University of Michigan Journal of Law Reform* (Fall 1994).

Menjivar, Cecilia, Julie DaVanzo, Lisa Greenwell, and R. Burciaga Valdez. "Remittance Behavior Among Salvadoran and Filipino Immigrants in Los Angeles." *International Migration Review* 32:1 (1998): 97–126.

Merton, Robert K. "Intermarriage and Social Structure: Fact and Theory." *Psychiatry* 4 (1941): 361–74.

Metcalf, Barbara Daly. *Making Muslim Space in North America and Europe*. Berkeley: University of California Press, 1996.

Miami–Dade County, Department of Planning. *Project 2000–2015*. Miami: Department of Planning, 1996.

Michener, James A. *Sports in America*. New York: Random House, 1976.

Migration Dialogue. "China/Hong Kong." *Migration News—Asia* 5:10 (October 1998). http://migration.ucdavis.edu/MN-Archive/oct_1998–16.html, December 26, 2000.

———. "Chinese Migration." *Migration News—Asia* 2: 2 (February 1995). http://migration.ucdavis.edu/Archive/feb_1995–18.html, December 26, 2000.

———. "Hong Kong Emigrants Return from Canada." *Migration News—Asia* 2:2 (February 1995). http://migration.ucdavis.edu/Archive/feb_199~21.html, December 26, 2000.

———. "Remittances." University of California at Davis, 2000. http://migration.ucdavis.edu/Data/remit.on.www/remittances.html, December 26, 2000.

———. "U.S. Taiwanese Return to Homeland." *Migration News—Asia* 2:4 (April 1995). http://migration.ucdavis.edu/mn/pastissues mn.html, December 26, 2000.

Milkman, Ruth, ed. *Organizing Immigrants: The Challenge for Unions in Contemporary California*. Ithaca: Cornell University Press, 2000.

Milkman, Ruth, and Kent Wong. *Voices from the Front Lines: Organizing Immigrant Workers in Los Angeles*. Los Angeles: Center for Labor Research and Education, University of California–Los Angeles, 2000.

Milkman, Ruth, Ellen Reese, and Benita Roth. "The Macrosociology of Paid Domestic Labor." *Work and Occupations* 25:4 (1998): 483–510.

Miller, Sally. "Immigrant and Ethnic Newspapers: An Enduring Phenomenon." *Serials Librarian* 14:1–2 (1988): 135–43.

Millman, Joel. *The Other Americans*. New York: Viking, 1997.

Min, Pyong Gap. *Asian Americans: Contemporary Trends and Issues*. Thousand Oaks, CA: Sage, 1995.

———. *Changes and Conflicts: Korean Immigrant Families in New York*. Needham Heights, MA: Allyn and Bacon, 1998.

———. "A Comparison of Post-1965 and Turn-of-the-Century Immigrants in Intergenerational Mobility and Cultural Transmission." *Journal of Ethnic History* 18:3 (1999): 65–95.

Mingot, Michel. "Refugees from Cambodia, Laos and Vietnam." In *The Cambridge Survey of World Migration*, ed. Robin Cohen, pp. 452–57. Cambridge: Cambridge University Press, 1995.

Ministry of Justice. "Press Release: Statistics of Foreigners Resident in Japan and Entering Japan." Tokyo: Ministry of Justice, 1999.

Ministry of Labor. "Foreign Workers and the Labour Market in Japan." *International Migration Quarterly Review* 31:2–3 (1993): 442–62.

Ministry of Labor and Local Affairs. "Migration and Multicultural Norway." White Paper no. 17. Oslo, 1996–97.

Mitchell, Charles. "For Love and Money, Russian Matchmakers Cater to American Men." Detroit Free Press/Knight Ridder/Tribune News Service, October 6, 1994.

Mitchell, Christian, ed. *Western Hemisphere Immigration and United States Foreign Policy*. College Park: Pennsylvania State University Press, 1992.

Mollenkopf, John. "Urban Political Conflicts and Alliances: New York and Los Angeles Compared." In *Handbook of International Migration*, ed. Philip Kasinitz and Josh DeWind. New York: Russell Sage Foundation, 1999.

Moltmann, Gunter. "American-German Return Migration in the Nineteenth and Early Twentieth Centuries." *Central European History* 113:4 (1980): 378–92.

Montejano, David. *Anglos and Mexicans in the Making of Texas*. Austin: University of Texas Press, 1987.

Moore, Joan W. *Going Down to the Barrio: Homeboys and Homegirls in Change*. Philadelphia: Temple University Press, 1991.

Morawska, Ewa T. *For Bread with Butter: The Life-Worlds of East Central Europeans in Johnstown, Pennsylvania, 1890–1940*. New York: Cambridge University Press, 1985.

———. "The Sociology and Historiography of Immigration." In *Immigration Reconsidered: History, Sociology, and Politics*, ed. Virginia Yans-McLaughlin, pp. 187–240. New York: Oxford University Press, 1990.

Morawska, Ewa T., and Willfried Spohn. "Moving Europeans: Contemporary Migrations in a Historical Perspective." In *Global History and Migrations*, ed. Wang Gungwu. Boulder, CO: Westview Press, 1997.

Morga, Dan, and Kevin Merida. "South Asia Rivals Had Money on South Dakota Senate Race." *Washington Post*, March 24, 1997.

Mori, Hiromi. *Immigration Policy and Foreign Workers in Japan*. New York: St. Martin's Press, 1997.

Morokvasic, Mirjana. Special Issue on Women Immigrants. *International Migration Review* 18:4 (1984).

Morreale, Don, ed. *Buddhist America: Centers, Retreats, Practices*. Santa Fe, NM: John Muir Publications, 1988.

Morris, Milton. *Immigration—The Beleaguered Bureaucracy*. Washington, DC: Brookings Institution, 1985.

Morse, Ann, Jeremy Meadows, Kirsten Rasmussen, and Sheri Steisel. *America's Newcomers: Mending the Welfare Safety Net for Immigrants*. Washington, DC: National Conference of State Legislatures, 1998.

Mort, Jo-Ann. "Immigrant Dreams: Sweatshop Workers Speak." *Dissent* 43 (Fall 1996): 85–87.

Mortimer, Delores M., and Roy S. Bryce-Laporte. *Female Immigrants to the United States: Caribbean, Latin American, and African Experiences*. Washington, DC: Research Institute of Immigration and Ethnic Studies, Smithsonian Institution, 1981.

Moss, Mitchell, Anthony Townsend, and Emmanuel Tobier. *Immigration Is Transforming New York City*. New York: Taub Urban Research Center, New York University, 1997.

Motomura, Hiroshi. "Alienage Classifications in a Nation of Immigrants: Three Models of "Permanent" Residence." In *Immigration and Citizenship in the Twenty-First Century*, ed. N. Pickus. Oxford: Oxford University Press, 1998.

———. "Whose Alien Nation? Two Models of Constitutional Immigration Law." *Michigan Law Review* 94 (1996): 1927.

Mrozek, Donald J. *Sport and American Mentality*. Knoxville: University of Tennessee Press, 1983.

Mufwene, Salikoko, John Rickford, Guy Bailey, and John Baugh. *African-American English: Structure, History, and Use*. New York: Routledge, 1998.

Muller, Gilbert. *New Strangers in Paradise: The Immigrant Experience and Contemporary American Fiction*. Lexington: University of Kentucky Press, 1999.

Muller, Thomas. *Immigrants and the American City*. New York: New York University Press, 1993.

Muñoz, Carlos, Jr. *Youth, Identity, Power: The Chicano Movement*. New York: Verso, 1989.

Musser, Charles. *The Emergence of Cinema: The American Screen to 1907*. New York: Charles Scribner's Sons, 1990.

———. "Ethnicity, Role-Playing, and American Film Comedy: From Chinese Laundry Scene to Whoopee (1894–1930)." In *Unspeakable Images: Ethnicity and the American Cinema*, ed. Lester D. Friedman, pp. 39–81. Chicago: University of Illinois Press, 1991.

Myrdal, Gunnar. *An American Dilemma*. New York: Harper and Row, 1962.

Nadel, Stanley. "From the Barricades of Paris to the Sidewalks of New York: German Artisans and the European Roots of American Labor Radicalism." In *Immigration to New York*, ed. William Pencak, Selma Berrol, and Randall Miller. Philadelphia: Balch Institute; London: Associated University Presses, 1991.

Naficy, Hamid. "Narrowcasting in Diaspora: Middle Eastern Television in Los Angeles." In *Living Color: Race and Television in the United States*, ed. Sasha Torres, pp. 82–96. Durham, NC: Duke University Press, 1998.

Naor, Mordechai. *Haapala: Clandestine Immigration, 1931–1948.* Tel Aviv: State of Israel Ministry of Defense Publishing House, 1987.

Narayan, Vasuda. "Creating the South Indian 'Hindu' Experience in the United States." In *A Sacred Thread: Modern Transmission of Hindu Traditions in India and Abroad,* ed. Raymond Williams, pp. 147–76. Chambersburg, PA: Anima Press, 1992.

Nash, June, and María Patricia Fernández-Kelly, ed. *Women, Men, and the International Division of Labor.* Albany: State University of New York Press, 1983.

National Center for Education Statistics. *Digest of Education Statistics.* Washington, DC: National Center for Education Statistics, 1996.

———. *Issue Brief: Degrees Earned by Foreign Graduate Students: Fields of Study and Plans After Graduation.* Washington, DC: National Center for Education Statistics, November 1997.

National Center for Health Statistics. *Births of Hispanic Origin, 1989–1995.* Washington, DC: Government Printing Office, 1998.

National Immigration Law Center. *Public Charge.* Los Angeles: National Immigration Law Center, 1997.

National Multicultural Advisory Council. *Australian Multiculturalism for a New Century: Towards Inclusiveness.* Canberra: National Multicultural Advisory Council, 1999.

National Science Foundation. "Indicators 1998: Chapter 2—Higher Education in Science and Engineering." http://www.nsf.gov/sbe/srs/seind98/access/c2/c2s4.htm, December 26, 2000.

Nee, Victor G., and Brett B. Nee. *Longtime Californ': A Documentary Study of an American Chinatown.* Stanford: Stanford University Press, 1972.

Negrey, Cynthia, and Mary Beth Zickel. "Industrial Shifts and Uneven Development: Patterns of Growth and Decline in U.S. Metropolitan Areas." *Urban Affairs Quarterly* 30:1 (1994): 27–47.

Nelson, Joel I. "Work and Benefits: The Multiple Problems of Service Sector Employment." *Social Problems* 41:2 (1994): 240–56.

Ness, Immanuel. "Trade Union Responses to Labor Market Deregulation and Informalization." Paper prepared for the International Political Science Association, August 1997.

Ness, Immanuel, and Nick Unger. "Union Approaches to Immigrant Organizing: A Review of New York City Locals." Paper prepared for the UCLEA Labor Education Conference, Milwaukee, April 2000.

Neuman, Gerald L. *Strangers to the Constitution: Immigrants, Borders, and Fundamental Law.* Princeton: Princeton University Press, 1996.

New York City Department of Planning. *The Newest New Yorkers: An Analysis of Immigration into New York City During the 1980s.* New York: Department of Planning, 1992.

Noh, Samuel, and William R. Avison. "Asian Immigrants and the Stress Process: A Study of Koreans in Canada." *Journal of Health and Social Behavior* 37 (June 1996): 192–206.

Nolan, Mary I. "'What the Coast Guard Is All About [Operation Able Vigil].'" *Sea Power* (November 1994): 41–43.

North, D. *Decision Factories.* Washington, DC: Transcentury Development Associates, 1988.

———. "IRCA Did Not Do Much to the Labor Market: A Los Angeles County Case Study." Immigration Policy and Research Working Paper no. 10. Washington, DC: Department of Labor, 1991.

North, D., and A.M. Portz. *The U.S. Legalization Program.* Washington, DC: Transcentury Development Associates, 1989.

Novak, J.J. *Bangladesh: Reflections on the Water.* Bloomington: Indiana University Press, 1993.

Numrich, Paul David. "Buddhists." In *Buddhists, Hindus, and Sikhs in America, Religion in American Life Series,* ed. Jane Podell. New York: Oxford University Press, forthcoming.

———. "Buddhists." In *Encyclopedia of Chicago History,* ed. James Grossman. Chicago: University of Chicago Press, forthcoming.

———. *Old Wisdom in the New World: Americanization in Two Immigrant Theravada Buddhist Temples.* Knoxville: University of Tennessee Press, 1996.

Nwadiora, Emeka, and Harriette McAdoo. "Acculturative Stress Among Amerasian Refugees: Gender and Racial Differences." *Adolescence* 31 (Summer 1996): 477–87.

Oboler, Susan. *Ethnic Labels, Ethnic Lives: Identity and the Politics of (Re)Presentation in the United States.* Minneapolis: University of Minnesota Press, 1995.

O'Brien, Ruth. "Ethnic Media Help New Immigrants Adjust to U.S." *Professional Journalism,* http://www.freedomforum.org, November 19, 1998.

O'Connor, Len. *Clout: Mayor Daley and His City.* Chicago: Henry Regnery, 1975.

Ofer, Dalia. *Escaping the Holocaust: Illegal Immigration to the Land of Israel 1939–1944.* New York: Oxford University Press, 1990.

Office of Multicultural Affairs. *National Agenda for a Multicultural Australia.* Canberra: Australian Government Publishing Service, 1989.

Ogbu, J.U. *Cultural Models and Educational Strategies of Non-Dominant Peoples: The 1989 Catherine Molony Memorial Lecture.* New York: City College Workshop Center, 1989.

OIM (Organization for International Migration). *Trafficking in Migrants* 22 (Autumn 2000).

Ojito, Mirta. "Castro Foe's Legacy: Success, Not Victory." *New York Times,* November 30, 1997.

Olson, James Stuart. *The Ethnic Dimension in American History*. New York: St. Martin's Press, 1979.

Ong, Aihwa. "Limits to Cultural Accumulation: Chinese Capitalists on the American Pacific Rim." In *Towards a Transnational Perspective on Migration: Race, Class, Ethnicity, and Nationalism Reconsidered*, ed. Nina Glick-Schiller, Linda Basch, and Cristina Blanc Szanton, pp. 125–43. New York: Annals of the New York Academy of Sciences, 1992.

Ong, Paul, and Tania Azores. "Asian Immigrants in Los Angeles: Diversity and Divisions." In *The New Asian Immigration in Los Angeles and Global Restructuring*, ed. Paul Ong, Edna Bonacich, and Lucie Cheng. Philadelphia: Temple University Press, 1994.

Ong, Paul M., Lucie Cheng, and Leslie Evans. "Migration of Highly Educated Asians and Global Dynamics." *Asian and Pacific Migration Journal* 1:3–4 (1992): 543–67.

Organisation for Economic Co-operation and Development (OECD). *Trends in International Migration: Continuous Reporting System on Migration*. Paris: Sopemi, 1999.

Orlinsky, Harry, ed. *The Synagogue: Studies in Origins, Archeology, and Architecture*. New York: KTAV, 1975.

Orlov, Ann, and Reed Ueda. "Central and South Americans." In *Harvard Encyclopedia of American Ethnic Groups*, ed. Stephen Thernstrom. Cambridge: Harvard University Press, 1980.

Ortiz, Vilma. "The Mexican-Origin Population: Permanent Working Class or Emerging Middle Class?" In *Ethnic Los Angeles*, ed. R.D. Waldinger and Mehdi Bozorgmehr. New York: Russell Sage Foundation, 1996.

Oteiza, Enrique. "A Differential Push-Pull Approach." In *The Brain Drain*, ed. Walter Adams, pp. 120–34. New York: Macmillan, 1968.

———. "Emigracion de Profesionales, Tecnicos y Obreros Calificados Argentinos à Los Estados Unidos." *Desarrollo Economico* 10 (1971): 429–54.

Pachon, Harry, and Louis DeSipio. *New Americans by Choice: Political Perspectives of Latino Immigrants*. Boulder, CO: Westview Press, 1994.

Pacyga, Dominic. "Poles." In *A Nation of Peoples*, ed. Elliott Barkan, pp. 425–45. Westport, CT: Greenwood, 1999.

Padilla, Yolanda. "Social Services to Mexican American Populations in the United States." In *Health and Social Services Among International Labor Migrants*, ed. Gilberto Cardenas and Antonio Ugalde. Austin: University of Texas Press, 1998.

Pagiola, Stefano. *The Global Environmental Benefits of Land Degradation Control on Agricultural Land*. Washington, DC: World Bank, 1999.

Pally, Marcia. "Film Studies Drive Literacy Development for ESL University Students." *Journal of Adolescent and Adult Literacy* 41 (1997): 620–29.

Palmer, Gary W. "Guarding the Coast: Alien Migrant Interdiction Operations at Sea." *Connecticut Law Review* 29 (Summer 1997): 1565.

Papademetriou, Demetrios, and Phillip Martin, eds. *The Unsettled Relationship: Labor Migration and Economic Development*. Westport, CT: Greenwood, 1991.

Parenti, Michael. *Make-Believe Media: The Politics of Entertainment*. New York: St. Martin's Press, 1992.

———. "The Media Are the Mafia: Italian-American Images and the Ethnic Struggle." *National Review* 30:10 (1979): 20–27.

Parillo, Vincent N. *Strangers to These Shores: Race and Ethnic Relations in the United States*. New York: Macmillan, 1994.

Park, Edward. "Competing Visions: Political Formation of Korean Americans in Los Angeles." *Amerasia Journal* 24:1 (1998): 41–57.

Park, Lisa, Rhonda Sarnoff, Catherine Bender, and C.C. Korenbrot. "Impact of Recent Welfare and Immigration Reforms on Use of Medicaid for Prenatal Care by Immigrants in California." *Journal of Immigrant Health* 2:1 (2000): 5–22.

Park, Robert. *The Immigrant Press and Its Control*. New York: Harper, 1922. Reprint. New York: Greenwood, 1970.

Parmet, Robert. *Labor and Immigration in Industrial America*. Boston: Twayne, 1981.

Parnreiter, Christoff, ed. "Schwerpunkt: Migration." Special issue on migration. *Journal für Entwicklungspolitik* 11:3 (1995).

Parnwell, Mike. *Population Movements and the Third World*. New York: Routledge, 1993.

Parrillo, Vincent N. *Strangers to These Shores: Race and Ethnic Relations in the United States*. New York: Macmillan, 1990.

Pastor, Robert. "U.S. Immigration Policy and Latin America: In Search of the Special Relationship.'" *Latin American Research Review* 19 (1984): 35–56.

Patterson, James T. *Grand Expectations: The United States, 1945–1974*. New York: Oxford University Press, 1996.

Pedraza, Silvia, and Rubén G. Rumbaut, eds. *Origins and Destinies: Immigration, Race, and Ethnicity in America*. Belmont, CA: Wadsworth, 1996.

Peña, Devon. *The Terror of the Machine*. Austin: University of Texas Press, 1999.

Pencak, William, Selma Berrol, and Randall Miller, eds. *Immigration to New York*. London: Associated University Presses, 1991.

Perez, Lisandro. "Cubans." In *Harvard Encyclopedia of American Ethnic Groups*, ed. Stephen Thernstrom. Cambridge: Harvard University Press, 1980.

Perez Firmat, Gustavo. *Life on the Hyphen*. Austin: University of Texas Press, 1994.

Perlmann, Joel, and Roger Waldinger. "Second Generation Decline? Children of Immigrants, Past and Present—A Reconsideration." *International Migration Review* 31:4 (1997): 893–922.

Pernice, Regina, and Judith Brook. "Refugees' and Immigrants' Mental Health: Association of Demographic and Post-Immigration Factors." *Journal of Social Psychology* 136 (August 1996): 511–19.

Pessar, Patricia. "The Dominicans: Women in the Household and Garment Industry." In *New Immigrants in New York*, ed. Nancy Foner. New York: Columbia University Press, 1987.

Petersen, William. "Politics and the Measurement of Ethnicity." In *The Politics of Numbers*, ed. William Alonso and Paul Starr. New York: Russell Sage Foundation, 1987.

Petras, Elizabth McLean. "The Global Labor Market in the Modern World-Economy." In *Global Trends in Migration*, ed. Mary M. Kritz, Charles B. Keely, and Silvano M. Tomasi, pp. 44–63. Staten Island, NY: Center for Migration Studies of New York, 1981.

Pfeffer, Max. "Social Origins of Three Systems of Farm Production in the United States." *Rural Sociology* 48 (1983): 540–62.

Phillips, Kathryn, Michelle Mayer, and Lu Ann Aday. "Barriers to Care Among Racial/Ethnic Groups Under Managed Care." *Health Affairs* 19:4 (2000): 65–75.

Piatt, Bill. *Only English: Law and Language Policy in the United States*. Albuquerque: University of New Mexico Press, 1990.

Piore, Michael J. *Birds of Passage: Migrant Labor in Industrial Societies*. New York: Cambridge University Press, 1979.

Pitkin, John R., Dowell Myers, Patrick A. Simmons, and Isaac F. Megbolugbe. "Immigration and Housing in the United States: Trends and Prospects. Report of Early Findings from the Fannie Mae Foundation Immigration Research Project." Fannie Mae Foundation Working Paper. Washington, DC: Fannie Mae Foundation, 1997.

Plascencia, L.E.B., G.R. Freeman, and M. Setzler. "Restricting Immigrant Access to Employment: An Examination of Regulations in Five States." Policy Brief. Revised to include New Jersey Tomás Rivera Policy Institute, 1999.

Poggio, Sara. "Parental Perceptions of Problems Educating their Children: Central American Migrants to the Washington-Baltimore Area." Paper presented to the Midwest Sociological Society, Chicago, April 19–22, 2000.

Pope, Jesse Eliphalet. *The Clothing Industry in New York*. New York: Burt Franklin Press, 1970.

Portes, Alejandro. "Children of Immigrants: Segmented Assimilation and Its Determinants." In *The Economic Sociology of Immigration: Essays on Networks, Ethnicity, and Entrepreneurship*, ed. Alejandro Portes, pp. 248–

80. New York: Russell Sage Foundation, 1995.

———. *City on the Edge: The Transformation of Miami*. Berkeley: University of California Press, 1993.

———. "From South of the Border: Hispanic Minorities in the United States." In *The Immigration Reader: America in a Multidisciplinary Perspective*, ed. David Jacobson, pp. 113–43. Malden, MA: Blackwell, 1998.

———. "Global Villagers: The Rise of Transnational Communities." *American Prospects* 25 (March–April 1996).

———. "Globalization from Below: The Rise of Transnational Communities." In *The Ends of Globalization: Bringing Society Back In*, ed. Don Kalb, pp. 253–70. Boulder, CO: Rowman and Littlefield, 1999.

———. "Neoliberalism and the Sociology of Development: Emerging Trends and Unanticipated Facts." *Population and Development Review* 23 (1997): 229–59.

———. "Social Capital: Its Origins and Applications in Modern Sociology." *Annual Review of Sociology* 24 (1998): 1–24.

———. "Transnational Communities: Their Emergence and Significance in the Contemporary World-System." In *Latin America in the World Economy*, ed. Roberto R. Korzeniewidcz and William C. Smith, pp. 151–68. Westport, CT: Greenwood, 1996.

Portes, Alejandro, ed. *The Economic Sociology of Immigration*. New York: Russell Sage Foundation, 1995.

———. *The New Second Generation*. New York: Russell Sage Foundation, 1996.

Portes, Alejandro, and Robert L. Bach. *Latin Journey: Cuban and Mexican Immigrants in the United States*. Berkeley: University of California Press, 1985.

Portes, Alejandro, and Manuel Castels. "World Underneath: The Origins, Dynamics, and Effects of the Informal Economy," in *The Informal Economy: Studies in Advanced and Less Developed Countries*, ed. Alejandro Portes, Manuel Castels, and Lauren Benton. Baltimore: Johns Hopkins University Press, 1991.

Portes, Alejandro, and John W. Curtis. "Changing Flags: Naturalization and Its Determinants Among Mexican Immigrants." *International Migration Review* 21:2 (1987): 352–71.

Portes, Alejandro, and Robert Manning. "The Immigrant Enclave: Theory and Empirical Examples." In *Competitive Ethnic Relations*, ed. Susan Olzak and Joane Nagel, pp. 47–68. Orlando, FL: Academic Press, 1986.

———. "The Immigrant Enclave: Theory and Empirical Examples." In *Majority and Minority: The Dynamics of Race and Ethnicity in American Life*, ed. Norman Yetman, pp. 319–32. Boston: Allyn and Bacon, 1991.

Portes, Alejandro, and Rafael Mozo. "The Political Adaptation Process of Cubans and Other Ethnic Minorities in the United States: A Preliminary Analysis." *International Migration Review* 19:1 (1990).

Portes, Alejandro, and Rubén G. Rumbaut. *Immigrant America: A Portrait*. Berkeley: University of California Press, 1990.

Portes, Alejandro, and Richard Schauffler. "Language and the Second Generation: Bilingualism Yesterday and Today." In *The New Second Generation*, ed. Alejandro Portes, pp. 8–29. New York: Russell Sage Foundation, 1996.

Portes, Alejandro, and Julia Sensenbrenner. "Embeddedness and Immigration: Notes on the Social Determinants of Economic Action." *American Journal of Sociology* 93 (1993): 1320–50.

Portes, Alejandro, and Alex Stepick. *City on the Edge: The Transformation of Miami*. Berkeley: University of California Press, 1993.

Portes, Alejandro, and John Walton. *Labor, Class, and the International System*. New York: Academic Press, 1996.

Portes, Alejandro, and Min Zhou. "The New Second Generation: Segmented Assimilation and Its Variants Among Post-1965 Youth." *Annals of the American Academy of Political and Social Science* 530 (1993): 74–98.

Portes, Alejandro, Luis Eduardo Guarnizo, and Patricia Landolt, ed. Special Issue on Transnational Migrant Communities. *Ethnic and Racial Studies* 22:2 (1999).

Poston, Dudley L., Jr. "Patterns of Economic Attainment of Foreign-Born Male Workers in the United States." *International Migration Review* 27 (1993): 478–500.

Pourat, Nadereh, et al. "Predictors of Use of Traditional Korean Healers Among Elderly Koreans in Los Angeles." *Gerontologist* 39:6 (1999): 711–19.

Powers, Mary, William Seltzer, and Jing Shi. "Gender Differences in the Occupational Status of Undocumented Immigrants in the United States: Experience Before and After Legalization." *International Migration Review* 32 (Winter 1998): 1015–46.

Pozzetta, George E., ed. *Folklore, Culture, and the Immigrant Mind*. Vol. 18. *American Immigration and Ethnicity*. New York: Garland, 1991.

Prashad, Vijay, "Culture Vultures." *Communalism Combat* (February 1997).

Prebish, Charles S. *Luminous Passage: The Practice and Study of Buddhism in America*. Berkeley: University of California Press, 1999.

Prebish, Charles S., and Kenneth K. Tanaka, eds. *The Faces of Buddhism in America*. Berkeley: University of California Press, 1998.

Prendergast, William B. *The Catholic Voter in American Politics: The Passing of the Democratic Monolith*. Washington, DC: Georgetown University Press, 1999.

"Prepare for the Future: Know Your Ancestors." *Consumer Reports on Health* (September 1999).

Price, C. *The Great White Walls Are Built*. Canberra: Australian National University Press, 1974.

Puri, Shivani, and Tineke Ritzema. "Migrant Worker Remittances, Micro-Finance, and the Informal Economy." Working Paper no. 21, Social Finance Unit, Enterprise and Cooperative Development Department, International Labor Organization, Geneva, 1999.

Purvis, Andrew. "Brain Drain from Canada to the U.S." *Time* (Canadian edition), May 11, 1998.

Qian, Zhenchao. "Breaking the Racial Barriers: Variations in Interracial Marriage Between 1980 and 1990." *Demography* 34:2 (1997): 263–76.

Quinn, Arthur. *The Rivals: William Gwin, David Broderick, and the Birth of California*. New York: Crown, 1994.

Radzilowski, Thaddeus, and John Radzilowski. "East Europeans." In *A Nation of Peoples*, ed. Elliott Barkan, pp. 174–99. Westport, CT: Greenwood. 1999.

Raijman, Rebeca, and Marta Tienda. "Immigrants' Socioeconomic Progress Post-1965: Forging Mobility of Survival?" Center for Migration and Development working paper, Princeton University, Princeton, 1998.

Raimes, A. *Techniques in Teaching Writing*. Oxford: Oxford University Press, 1983.

Rajagopal, Arvind. "Better Hindu Than Black? Narratives of Asian Indian Identity." Paper presented at the annual meetings of the Society for the Scientific Study of Religion and the Religious Research Association, St. Louis, MO, 1995.

Ramirez, David. "Performance of Redesignated Fluent-English Proficient Students." In *San Francisco Unified School District Language Academy: 1998 Annual Evaluation*. San Francisco: Language Academy, 1997.

Ramos, Henry A.J. *The American GI Forum*. Houston: Arte Publico, 1998.

Ranis, Gustav, and John C.M. Fei. "A Theory of Economic Development." *American Economic Review* 51 (1961): 533–65.

Ravenstein, E.G. "The Laws of Migration." *Journal of the Statistical Society of London* 48:2 (1885): 167–227.

Ravitch, Dianne. *The Great School Wars: A History of the New York City Public Schools*. New York: Basic Books, 1988.

Raz, Ram. *Essay on the Architecture of the Hindus*. 1834. Reprint. Varanasi: Indological Book House, 1972.

Ready, Timothy. *Latino Immigrant Youth: Passages from Adolescence to Adulthood*. New York: Garland, 1991.

Reed-Ward, Paula. "Chinese Aliens Found Hiding on Ship Docked in Savannah." *Savannah Morning News*, August 13, 1999.

Reich, Robert. *The Work of Nations*. New York: Alfred A. Knopf, 1991.

Reid, Joy M., ed. *Understanding Learning Styles in the Second Language Classroom*. Englewood Cliffs, NJ: Prentice Hall, 1998.

Reimers, David M. "Recent Third World Immigration to New York City, 1945–1986: An Overview." In *Immi-*

gration to New York, ed. William Pencak, Selma Berrol, and Randall Miller. London: Associated University Presses, 1991.

———. *Still the Golden Door: The Third World Comes to America.* 2d ed. New York: Columbia University Press, 1992.

———. *Unwelcome Strangers: American Identity and the Turn Against Immigration.* New York: Columbia University Press, 1998.

Reisler, Mark. *By the Sweat of Their Brow: Mexican Immigrant Labor in the United States.* Westport, CT: Greenwood, 1976.

Reitz, J. *Warmth of the Welcome: The Social Causes of Economic Success for Immigrants in Different Nations and Cities.* Boulder, CO: Westview Press, 1997.

Repak, Terry A. *Waiting on Washington: Central American Workers in the Nation's Capital.* Philadelphia: Temple University Press, 1995.

Reyes, Belinda I. *Dynamics of Immigration: Return Migration to Western Mexico.* San Francisco: Public Policy Institutes of California, 1997.

Reynolds, C.N. "The Chinese Tongs." *American Journal of Sociology* 40:5 (1935): 612–23.

Richey, W. "Many Seek American Dream—Outside America." *Christian Science Monitor*, March 19, 1997, pp. 9–12.

Richmond, Anthony H. "Return Migration from Canada to Britain." *Population Studies* 22:2 (1968): 311–35.

Rickets, Erol. "U.S. Investment and Immigration from the Caribbean." *Social Problems* 34 (1987): 374–87.

Riess, Steven A. *The American Sporting Experience: A Historical Anthology of Sport in America.* West Point, NY: Leisure Press, 1984.

———. *City Games: The Evolution of American Urban Society and the Rise of Sports.* Chicago: University of Illinois Press, 1989.

Rischin, Moses. *The Promised City: New York's Jews, 1870–1914.* Cambridge: Harvard University Press, 1962.

Ritsner, Michael, and Alexander Ponizovsky. "Psychological Distress Through Immigration: The Two-Phase Temporal Pattern?" *International Journal of Social Psychiatry* 45 (Summer 1999): 125–39.

Rivera-Batiz, Francisco, Selig L. Sechzer, and Ira N. Gang, eds. *U.S. Immigration Policy Reform in the 1980s: A Preliminary Assessment.* New York: Praeger, 1991.

Roberts, Bryan R. "Socially Expected Durations and the Economic Adjustment of Immigrants." In *The Economic Sociology of Immigration: Essays on Networks, Ethnicity, and Entrepreneurship,* ed. Alejandro Portes, pp. 42–86. New York: Russell Sage Foundation, 1995.

Roberts, James B., and Alexander G. Skutt. *The Boxing Register: International Boxing Hall of Fame Official Record Book.* Ithaca, NY: McBooks Press, 1997.

Roberts, Sam. *Who We Are: A Portrait of America.* New York: Times Books, 1983.

Rodriguez, America. *Making Latino News: Race, Language, Class.* Thousand Oaks, CA: Sage, 1999.

Rodriguez, Luis J. *Always Running: La Vida Loca: Gang Days in L.A.* Willimantic, CT: Curbstone Press, 1993.

Rodríguez, Néstor. "The Social Construction of the U.S.-Mexico Border," In *Immigrants Out! The New Nativism and the Anti-immigrant Impulse in the United States,* ed. Juan Perea, pp. 223–43. New York: New York University Press, 1997.

Rogin, Michael. *Blackface, White Noise: Jewish Immigrants in the Hollywood Melting Pot.* Berkeley: University of California Press, 1996.

Romero, Mary. "Chicanas Modernize Domestic Service." *Qualitative Sociology* 11 (1988): 319–34.

———. "Domestic Service in the Transition from Urban to Rural Life: The Case of La Chicana." *Women's Studies* 13 (1987): 199–222.

Romo, Ricardo. "Mexican Americans: Their Civic and Political Incorporation." In *Origins and Destinies: Immigration, Race, and Ethnicities in America,* ed. Silvia Pedraza and Rubén G. Rumbaut. Belmont, CA: Wadsworth, 1996.

Rosales, Arturo F. "Mexicans to Houston: The Struggle to Survive." *Houston Review* 3 (1981): 249–52.

Rosberg, Gerald. "Aliens and Equal Protection: Why Not the Right to Vote?" *Michigan Law Review* 75 (1977): 1092.

Rosenbaum, David E. "A Day of Spin Follows a Month of Hearings." *New York Times,* August 2, 1997.

Rosenberg, Morris. *Society and the Adolescent Self-Image.* Princeton: Princeton University Press, 1965.

Rosenblum, Marc. "Abroad and at Home: The Foreign and Domestic Sources of U.S. Migration Policy." Ph.D. diss., University of California, San Diego, 2000.

Rosenwaike, Ira. "Cancer Mortality Among Mexican Immigrants to the United States." *Public Health Reports* 103: 2 (1988): 195–201.

Rothenberg, Daniel. *With These Hands—The Hidden World of Migrant Farmworkers Today.* New York: Harcourt Brace, 1998.

Royko, Mike. *Boss: Richard J. Daley of Chicago.* New York: Signet, 1971.

Ruiz, Vicki L. "By the Day or the Week: Mexicana Domestic Workers in El Paso." In *Women on the U.S.-Mexico Border: Responses to Change,* ed. Vicki L. Ruiz and Susan Tlano, pp. 61–76. Boston: Allen and Unwin, 1987.

Rumbaut, Rubén G. "The Crucible Within: Ethnic Identity, Self-Esteem, and Segmented Assimilation Among Children of Immigrants." In *The New Second Generation,* ed. Alejandro Portes, pp. 119–70. New York: Russell Sage Foundation, 1996.

————. "The New Californians: Comparative Research Findings on the Educational Progress of Immigrant Children." In *California's Immigrant Children*, ed. Rubén G. Rumbaut and Wayne Cornelius. San Diego: Center for U.S.-Mexican Studies, 1995.

————. "Origins and Destinies: Immigration, Race, and Ethnicity in Contemporary America." In *Origins and Destinies: Immigration, Race, and Ethnicity in America*, ed. Silvia Pedraza and Rubén G. Rumbaut. Belmont, CA: Wadworth, 1996.

————. "Origins and Destinies: Immigration to the United States Since World War II." In *New American Destinies: A Reader in Contemporary Asian Immigration*, ed. Darrell Y. Hamamoto and Rodolfo E. Torres. New York: Routledge, 1997.

————. "Origins and Destinies: Immigration to the United States Since World War II." *Sociological Forum* 9 (1994): 583–21.

————. "Paradoxes (and Orthodoxies) of Assimilation." *Sociological Perspectives* 40:3 (1997): 483–511.

————. "Passages to Adulthood: The Adaptation of Children of Immigrants in Southern California." In *Children of Immigrants: Health, Adjustment, and Public Assistance*, ed. Donald J. Hernandez. Washington, DC: National Academy Press, 1999.

————. "Transformations: The Post-Immigrant Generation in an Age of Diversity." Paper presented at the annual meeting of the Eastern Sociological Society, Philadelphia, March 1998.

Rumbaut, Rubén G., and Wayne Cornelius, eds. *California's Immigrant Children*. San Diego: Center for U.S.-Mexican Studies, 1995.

Rumbaut, Rubén G., and Kenji Ima. *The Adaptation of Southeast Asian Refugee Youth: A Comparative Study*. Washington, DC: Office of Refugee Resettlement, 1988.

Rural Migration News. "California: Welfare, Development, and Options." http://migration.ucdavis.edu/Rural-Migration-News/Oct98RMN.html, January 29, 2000.

Russell, S.S., and M.S. Teitelbaum. "International Migration and International Trade." World Bank Discussion Papers, no. 160. World Bank, Washington, DC, 1992.

Sabagh, Georges, and Mehdi Bozorgmehr. "Population Change: Immigration and Ethnic Transformation." In *Ethnic Los Angeles*, ed. Roger Waldinger and Mehdi Bozorgmehr. New York: Russell Sage Foundation, 1996.

Sachar, Howard. *A History of the Jews in America*. New York: Alfred A. Knopf, 1992.

Safa, Helen. *The Myth of the Male Breadwinner: Women and Industrialization in the Caribbean*. Boulder, CO: Westview Press, 1995.

Sakala, Carol. "Migrant and Seasonal Farmworkers in the United States: A Review of Health Hazards, Status, and Policy." *International Migration Review*, Special Issue: Migration and Health 21:3 (1987): 659–71.

Salins, Peter D. *Assimilation, American Style*. New York: Basic Books, 1997.

Salt, John, and Jeremy Stein. "Migration as a Business: The Case of Trafficking." *International Migration Review* 35:4 (1997): 467–94.

Saltzinger, Leslie. "A Maid by Any Other Name: The Transformation of 'Dirty Work' by Central American Immigrants." In *Ethnography Unbound: Power and Resistance in the Modern Metropolis*, ed. Michael Buroway, pp. 139–60. Berkeley: University of California Press, 1991.

Salvo, Joseph, and Arun Peter Lobo. "Immigration and the Changing Demographic Profile of New York." In *The City and the World: New York's Global Future*, ed. Margaret Crahan and Alberto Vourvoulias-Bush. New York: Council on Foreign Relations, 1997.

Sampson, Robert E. and Janet L. Lauritsen. "Racial and Ethnic Disparities in Crime and Criminal Justice in the United States." *Crime and Justice: A Review of Research* 21 (1997): 11–74.

Sanchez, George J. *Becoming Mexican American*. New York: Oxford University Press, 1993.

————. "Face the Nation: Race, Immigration, and the Rise of Nativism in Late-Twentieth-Century America." *International Migration Review* 31 (1997): 1009–31.

————. "Race and Immigration History." *American Behavioral Scientist* 42 (June–July 1999): 1271–75.

SANDAG (San Diego Association of Governments). "Baja California Demographic Profile," *INFO Update Newsletter* (May–June 1992).

Sanders, G. "Aliens in Professions and Occupations: State Laws Restricting Participation." *I & N Reporter*, 1968.

Sanders, Jimy M., and Victor Nee. "Limits of Ethnic Solidarity in the Enclave Economy." *American Sociological Review* 52 (1987): 745–73.

————. "Social Capital, Human Capital, and Immigrant Self-Employment: The Family as Social Capital and the Value of Human Capital." *American Sociological Review* 61 (1996): 231–49.

Sanjek, Roger. *The Future of Us All: Race and Neighborhood Politics in New York City*. Ithaca: Cornell University Press, 1998.

Saphir, Ann. "Asian Americans and Cancer: Discarding the Myth of the "Model Minority." *Journal of the National Cancer Institute* 89 (1997): 1572–74.

Sassen, Saskia. *Cities in a World Economy*. 2d ed. Thousand Oaks, CA: Pine Forge Press, 2000.

————. "Economic Internationalization: The New Migration in Japan and the United States." *International Migration Review* 31 (1993): 43–72.

————. *The Global City: New York, London, Tokyo*. New updated ed. Princeton: Princeton University Press, 2000.

————. *Globalization and Its Discontents*. New York: New Press, 1998.

———. *Guests and Aliens*. New York: New Press, 1999.

———. "Immigration and Local Labor Markets." In *The Economic Sociology of Immigration*, ed. Alejandro Portes. New York: Russell Sage Foundation, 1995.

———. "Immigration Policy in a Global Economy." *Unesco Courier* (November 1998).

———. *Losing Control? Sovereignty in an Age of Globalization*. New York: Columbia University Press, 1996.

———. *The Mobility of Labor and Capital: A Study in International Investment and Labor Flow*. Cambridge: Cambridge University Press, 1988.

Sassen-Koob, Saskia. "The New Labor Demand in Global Cities." In *Cities in Transformation*, ed. M.R Smith, pp. 139–71. Beverly Hills, CA: Sage, 1984.

———. "New York City's Informal Economy." In *The Informal Economy: Studies in Advanced and Less Developed Countries*, ed. Alejandro Portes, Manuel Castells, and Lauren Benton. Baltimore: Johns Hopkins University Press, 1989.

Sayyid-Marsot, A.L. *A Short History of Modern Egypt*. New York: Cambridge University Press, 1985.

Schaefer, Richard T. *Racial and Ethnic Groups*. Upper Saddle River, NJ: Prentice Hall, 2000.

Schill, Michael H., and Samantha Friedman. "The Housing Conditions of Immigrants in New York City." Fannie Mae Foundation Working Paper, Washington, DC, 1998.

Schlosberg, Claudia. *Not-Qualifed Immigrants' Access to Public Health and Emergency Services After the Welfare Law*. Washington, DC: National Health and Law Program, 1998.

Schlosberg, Claudia, and Dinah Wiley. *The Impact of INS Public Charge Determination on Immigrant Access to Health Care*. Washington, DC: National Health and Law Program, 1998.

Schmeidl, Susanne. "Exploring the Causes of Forced Migration: A Pooled Time-Analysis, 1971–1990." *Social Science Quarterly* 78 (1997): 284–308.

Schmidley, A. Dianne, and Campbell Gibson. "Profile of the Foreign-Born Population in the United States: 1997." In *Current Population Reports*, pp. 23–195. Washington, DC: Bureau of the Census, 1999.

Schniedewind, Karen. "Migrants Returning to Bremen: Social Structure and Motivations: 1850 to 1914." *Journal of American Ethnic History* 12:2 (1993): 35–55.

Schoenberger, Karl. *Levi's Children: Coming to Terms with Human Rights in the Global Marketplace*. New York: Atlantic Monthly Press, 2000.

Schoeni, Robert E. "Labor Market Outcomes of Immigrant Women in the United States: 1970–1990." *International Migration Review* 32:1 (1998): 57–78.

Scholes, Robert J. "AF ISO WM: How Many Mail-Order Brides?" *Immigration Review* 28 (Spring 1997).

Schoof, Renee. "More U.S. Couples Adopting Abroad."

Associated Press News Service, Guangzhou, China, January 9, 1999.

Schuck, Peter H., and Rainer Munz. *Paths to Inclusion: The Integration of Migrants in the United States and Germany*. New York: Berghahn Books, 1998.

Schumann, Howard, et al. *Racial Attitudes in America: Trends and Interpretations*. Rev. ed. Cambridge: Harvard University Press, 1997.

Schumpeter, Joseph A. *Essays on Entrepreneurs, Innovations, Business Cycles, and the Evolution of Capitalism*. New Brunswick, NJ: Transaction, 1989.

Scott, Allen, and Edward Soja, eds. *The City: Los Angeles and Urban Theory at the End of the Twentieth Century*. Los Angeles: University of California Press, 1996.

Seager, Richard Hughes. *Buddhism in America*. New York: Columbia University Press, 1999.

Seccombe, Ian J. "Foreign Worker Dependence in the Gulf and the International Oil Companies." *International Migration Review* 20 (1986): 548–74.

Sekai Minzoku Mondai Jiten. *The World Encyclopedia of Race and Ethnicity*. Tokyo: Heibonsha, 1995.

Select Commission on Immigration and Refugee Policy. *U.S. Immigration Policy and the National Interest. The Final Report and Recommendations of the Select Commission on Immigration and Refugee Policy to the Congress and the President of the United States*. Washington, DC: Government Printing Office, 1981.

Seller, Maxine Schwartz. *To Seek America: A History of Ethnic Life in the United States*. Englewood, NJ: Jerome S. Ozer, 1977.

Seller, Maxine Schwartz, ed. *Ethnic Theatre in the United States*. Westport, CT: Greenwood, 1983.

———. *Immigrant Women*. Philadelphia: Temple University Press, 1981.

Sellin, Thorslen. *Culture Conflict and Crime*. New York: Social Science Research Council, 1938.

Senate Subcommittee on Human Resources. "The Impact of Immigration on Public Welfare Programs." Report. Washington, DC, November 1993.

Seshagiri Rao, K.L. "Encyclopedia of Hinduism: Questions and Answers." *India Post*, August 27, 1999.

Seward, Shirley. "Demographic Change and the Canadian Economy: An Overview." *Canadian Studies in Population* 14:2 (1987): 279–99.

Shai, Donna. "Cancer Mortality in Cuba and Among the Cuban Born in the United States: 1979–1981." *Public Health Report* 106 (1991): 68–73.

Shankar, Lavina Dhingra, and Rajini Srikanth, eds. *A Part, Yet Apart*. Philadelphia: Temple University Press, 1998.

Sheffer, Gabriel. "Ethnic Diasporas: A Threat to Their Hosts?" In *International Migration and Security*, ed. Myron Weiner. Boulder, CO: Westview Press, 1993.

Shimada, Haruo. *Japan's "Guest Workers": Issues and Public Policies*. Tokyo: University of Tokyo Press, 1994.

Shoop, Lyn G. "Health Based Exclusion Grounds in United States Immigration Policy: Homosexuals, HIV Infection and the Medical Examination of Aliens." *Catholic University Journal of Contemporary Health, Law and Policy* 9 (1993): 521–44.

Shuvall, Judith. T. *Immigrants on the Threshold*. London: Prentice Hall International, 1963.

Sicron, Moshe. *Immigration to Israel: 1948–1953*. Jerusalem: Falk Project and Central Bureau of Statistics, 1957.

Sider, Gerald. "The Contradictions of Transnational Migration: A Discussion." In *Towards a Transnational Perspective on Migration: Race, Class, Ethnicity, and Nationalism Reconsidered*, ed. Nina Glick-Schiller, Linda Basch, and Cristina Blanc-Szanton, pp. 231–40. New York: Annals of the New York Academy of Sciences, 1992.

Sierra, Christine Marie, Teresa Carrillo, Louis DeSipio, and Michael Jones-Correa. "Latino Immigration and Citizenship." *Political Science and Politics* 33:3 (2000): 535–40.

Simon, J.L. *The Economic Consequences of Immigration*. Oxford: Basil Blackwell (in association with the Cato Institute), 1989.

———. *The Ultimate Resource* 2. Princeton: Princeton University Press, 1996.

Simon, Rita J. *New Lives: The Adjustment of Soviet Jewish Immigrants in the United States and Israel*. Lexington: Lexington Books, 1985.

Simon, Rita J., and Susan H. Alexander. *The Ambivalent Welcome: Print Media, Public Opinion, and Immigration*. London: Praeger, 1993.

Simon, Rita J., and Margo Corona DeLey. "The Work Experience of Undocumented Mexican Women Migrants in Los Angeles." *International Migration Review* 18:1 (1984): 212–29.

Simone, Roberta. *The Immigrant Experience in American Fiction: An Annotated Bibliography*. Lanham, MD: Scarecrow Press, 1995.

Singer, Paul. "Dynamica de la Problacion y desarrollo." In *El Papel del Crecimiento Demografico en el desarrolo Economico*, pp. 21–66. Mexico: Editorial Siglo. XXI, 1971.

———. *Economia Politica de la Urbanizacion*. Mexico: Editorial Siglo XXI, 1975.

Singer, Shirley, Roger Kramer, and Audrey Singer. *Characteristics and Labor Market Behavior of the Legalized Population Five Years Following Legalization*. Washington, DC: Department of Labor, 1996.

Sjaastad, Larry A. "The Costs and Returns of Human Migration." *Journal of Political Economy* 70 (1962): 880–93.

Skeldon, Ronald. "Hong Kong: Colonial City to Global City to Provincial City?" *Cities* 14:6 (1997): 323–32.

———. *Population Mobility in Developing Countries: A Reinterpretation*. New York: Belhaven, 1990.

Skerry, Peter. *Mexican Americans: The Ambivalent Minority*. Cambridge: Harvard University Press, 1993.

Skinner, B.F. *Beyond Freedom and Dignity*. New York: Alfred A. Knopf, 1971.

———. "The Science of Learning and the Art of Teaching." *Harvard Educational Review* (1954): 86–97.

Sklair, Leslie. *Assembling for Development: The Maquila Industry in Mexico and the United States*. Boston: Unwin Hyman, 1989.

Smallwood, Betty Ansin. *Using Multicultural Children's Literature in Adult ESL Classes*. Washington, DC: National Clearinghouse on Literacy Education, 1998.

Smith, James R., and Barry Edmonston. *The New Americans: Economic, Demographic, and Fiscal Effects of Immigration*. Washington, DC: National Academy Press, 1997.

Smith, Judith E. *Family Connections: A History of Italian and Immigrant Lives in Providence, Rhode Island, 1900–1940*. Albany: State University of New York Press, 1985.

Smith, Kathryn Schneider, ed. *Washington at Home: An Illustrated History of Neighborhoods in the Nation's Capital*. Northridge, CA: Windsor, 1988.

Smith, Michael, and Luis E. Guarnizo. *Transnationalism from Below*. New Brunswick, NJ: Transaction, 1998.

Smith, Paul C., and Robert A. Warrior. *Like a Hurricane: The Indian Movement from Alcatraz to Wounded Knee*. New York: New Press, 1996.

Smith, Paul J., ed. *Human Smuggling: Chinese Migrant Trafficking and the Challenge to America's Immigration Tradition*. Washington, DC: Center for Strategic and International Studies, 1997.

Smith, Robert C. "Transnational Migration, Assimilation and Political Community." In *The City and the World: New York's Global Future*, ed. Margaret Crahan and Alberto Vourvoulias-Bush. New York: Council on Foreign Relations, 1997.

Smith, Timothy. "Religion and Ethnicity in America." *American Historical Review* 83 (December 1978): 1155–85.

Snowden, L. "Collective versus Mass Behavior: A Conceptual Framework for Temporary and Permanent Migration in Western Europe and the United States." *International Migration Review* 24 (1990): 577–90.

Sobel, Zvi. *Migrants from the Promised Land*. New Brunswick, NJ: Transaction, 1986.

Sofranko, A.J., and Khan Idris. "Use of Overseas Migrants' Remittances to the Extended Family for Business Investment: A Research Note." *Rural Sociology* 64:3 (1999): 464–81.

Soja, Edward W. *Postmodern Geographies: The Reassertion of Space in Critical Social Theory*. London: Verso, 1989.

Soloway, Lavi S. "Challenging Discrimination against Gays and Lesbians in U.S. Immigration Law: The Lesbian and Gay Immigration Rights Task Force." http://www.lgirt.org/html/about.html, 1996.

Soltes, Mordecai. *The Yiddish Press: An Americanizing Agency.* 1925. Reprint. New York: Arno Press/*New York Times,* 1969.

Sontag, Deborah, and Celia W. Dugger. "The New Immigrant Tide: A Shuttle Between Worlds." *New York Times,* July 19, 1998.

Sorensen, E., and E. Bean. "Immigration Reform and the Wages of Mexican Origin Workers: Evidence from Current Population Surveys." *Social Science Quarterly* 75:1 (March 1994): 1–17.

Sowell, Thomas. *Ethnic America: A History.* New York: Basic Books, 1981.

Spener, David. "Smuggling Mexican Migrants Through South Texas: Challenges Posed by Operation Rio Grande." In *Global Human Smuggling: Comparative Perspectives,* ed. David Kyle and Rey Koslowski. Baltimore: Johns Hopkins University Press, forthcoming.

Spener, David, and Frank D. Bean. "Self-Employment Concentration and Earnings Among Mexican Immigrants in the U.S." *Social Forces* 77:3 (1999): 1021–47.

Sreenivasan, Sreenath. "As Mainstream Papers Cut Back, the Ethnic Press Expands." *New York Times,* July 22, 1996.

Stalker, Peter. *The Work of Strangers: A Survey of International Labour Migration.* Geneva: International Labour Organisation, 1994.

Stark, Oded. "Relative Deprivation and Migration: Theory, Evidence, and Policy Implications." In *Determinants of Emigration from Mexico, Central America, and the Caribbean,* ed. Sergio Diaz-Briquets and Sidney Winetraub, pp. 121–44. Boulder, CO: Westview Press, 1991.

Stark, Oded, and David E. Bloom. "The New Economics of Labor Migration." *American Economic Review* 75 (1985): 173–78.

Statistics Canada. *Canada Year Book, 1997.* Ottawa: Statistics Canada, 1996.

Stefancic, J. "Funding the Nativist Agenda." In *Immigrants Out! The New Nativism and the Anti-Immigrant Impulse in the United States,* ed. Juan Perea, pp. 119–35. New York: New York University Press, 1997.

Stein, Leon. *Out of the Sweatshop: The Struggle for Industrial Democracy.* New York: Quadrangle, 1977.

Steinberg, Laurence. *Beyond the Classroom.* New York: Simon and Schuster, 1996.

Stepick, Alex, III, and Guillermo J. Grenier, eds. *Miami Now! Immigration, Ethnicity, and Social Change.* Gainesville: University Press of Florida, 1992.

Stepick, Alex, III, Guillermo Grenier, Hafidh A. Hafidh, Sue Chafee, and Debbie Drazin. "The View from the Back of the House: Restaurants and Hotels in Miami." In *Newcomers in the Workplace: Immigrants and the Re-*structuring *of the U.S. Economy,* ed. Louise Lamphere, Alex Stepick, and Guillermo Grenier, pp. 181–98. Philadelphia: Temple University Press, 1994.

Stern, Claudio. "Some Methodological Notes on the Study of Human Migration." In *International Migration Today.* Vol. 2, *Emerging Issues,* ed. Charles W. Stall, pp. 28–33. Perth: University of Western Australia for the United Nations Economic, Social, and Cultural Organization, 1988.

Stevens-Arroyo, Anthony. "Building a New Public Realm: Moral Responsibility and Religious Commitment in the City." In *The City and the World: New York's Global Future,* ed. Margaret Crahan and Alberto Vourvoulias-Bush. New York: Council on Foreign Relations, 1997.

Stinner, William, Klaus de Albuquerque, and Roy Bryce-Laporte, eds. *Return Migration and Remittances: Developing a Caribbean Perspective.* Washington, DC: Research Institute on Immigration and Ethnic Studies, Smithsonian Institution, 1982.

Stockton, Ronald R. "Recognize the Benefits from Our Arab Neighbors." *Detroit News,* April 3, 1994, p. 12A.

Suarez-Orozco, Marcelo. *Central American Refugees and U.S. High Schools: A Psychosocial Study of Motivation and Achievement.* Stanford: Stanford University Press, 1989.

Sue, S., and N.W. Zane. "The Role of Culture and Cultural Techniques in Psychotherapy: A Critique and Reformulation." *American Psychologist* 42:1 (1987): 37–45.

Sue, S., D. Fujino, L. Hu, D.T. Takeuchi, and N.W. Zane. "Community Mental Health Services for Ethnic Minorities: A Test of the Cultural Responsiveness Hypothesis." *Journal of Consulting and Clinical Psychology* 59 (1991): 533–40.Sullivan, Jake. "More Foreign Students but No More Foreign Aid." *Yale Daily News,* September 12, 1996.

Sumaya, Ciro V. "Major Infectious Diseases Causing Excess Morbidity in the Hispanic Population." In *Health Policy and the Hispanic,* ed. Antonio Furino, pp. 76–96. Boulder, CO: Westview Press, 1992.

Sun, Lena H. "The Search for Miss Right Takes a Turn Toward Russia: 'Mail-Order Brides' of the 90s Are Met via Internet and on 'Romance Tours.'" *Washington Post,* March 8, 1998.

Sundquist, James L. *Dynamics of the Party System.* Washington, DC: Brookings Institute, 1973.

Sundstrom, Eric. *Work Places: The Psychology of the Physical Environment in Offices and Factories.* New York: Cambridge University Press, 1986.

Sung, T.K. "Cross-Cultural Comparison of Motivations for Parent Care: Americans and Koreans." *Journal of Aging Studies* 8 (1994): 195–209.

Suro, Roberto. "Two California Judges Block Anti-Immigrant Measure at the Start." *Washington Post,* November 10, 1994.

Sutherland, Edwin H., Donald R. Cressey, and David E. Luckenbill. *Principles of Criminology.* New York: General Hall, 1992.

Sutter, Valerie O'Connor. *The Indochinese Refugee Dilemma.* Baton Rouge: Louisiana State University Press, 1991.

Swartz, Mimi. "Letter from Miami: The Herald's Cuban Revolution." *New Yorker,* June 6, 1999, pp. 36–63.

Swedberg, Richard, and Richard Granovetter, eds. *The Sociology of Economic Life.* Boulder, CO: Westview Press, 1992.

Sweeney, Maria. "Sweating the Small Stuff: Mickey, Michael, and the Global Sweatshop." *Radical Teacher* 55 (1999): 11–14.

Swinbanks, David. "Taiwan Welcoming Home Top Ph.D.s from U.S. Research Technology." *Management* 38:2 (1995): 3–4.

Tabora, B., and J.H. Flaskerud. "Depression Among Chinese Americans: A Review of the Literature." *Issues in Mental Health Nursing* 15 (1994): 569–84.

Taft, R., and D. Cahill. *Initial Adjustment to Schooling of Immigrant Families.* Canberra: Australian Government Publishing Services, 1978.

Takaki, Ronald. *A Different Mirror.* Boston: Little, Brown, 1993.

———. *Strangers from a Different Shore: A History of Asian Americans.* Boston: Little, Brown, 1998.

Tam, Tony. "Sex Segregation and Occupational Gender Inequality in the United States: Devaluation or Specialized Training." *American Journal of Sociology* 96 (1997): 1652–92.

Taylor, Barry. "Teaching ESL: Incorporating a Communicative, Student-Centered Component." *TESOL Quarterly* 17:1 (1983): 69–89.

Taylor, Ella. *Prime-Time Families.* Berkeley: University of California Press, 1989.

Taylor, J. Edward. "Differentiated Migration, Networks, Information, and Risk." In *Migration, Theory, Human Capital, and Development,* ed. Oded Stark, pp. 147–71. Greenwich, CT: JAI Press, 1986.

———. "Migration Networks and Risk in Household Labor Decisions: A Study of Migration from Two Mexican Villages." Ph.D. diss., University of California–Berkeley, 1984.

———. "Undocumented Mexico-U.S. Migration and Returns to Households in Rural Mexico." *American Journal of Agricultural Economics* 69 (1987): 626–38.

Taylor, J. Edward, and R.L. Martin. "The Immigrant Subsidy in California Agriculture: Farm Employment, Poverty, and Welfare." *Population and Development Review* 23 (December 1997): 855–74.

Tebeau, Charlton. *Synagogue in the Central City: Temple Israel of Greater Miami, 1922–1972.* Oxford, OH: Miami University Press, 1972.

Teitelbaum, Michael S., and Myron Weiner, eds. *Threat-ened Peoples, Threatened Borders: World Migration and U.S. Policy.* New York: W.W. Norton, 1995.

Teitelbaum, Michael S., and J.A. Winter. *Question of Numbers: High Immigration, Low Fertility, and the Politics of National Identity.* New York: Hill and Wang, 1998.

Thernstrom, Stephen, ed. *Harvard Encyclopedia of American Ethnic Groups.* Cambridge: Harvard University Press and Belknap Press, 1980.

Thomas, George M. "U.S. Discourse and Strategies in the New World Order." In *Old Nations, New World,* ed. David Jacobson. Boulder, CO: Westview Press, 1994.

Thomas, Wayne, and Virginia Collier. *School Effectiveness for Language Minority Students.* Washington, DC: National Clearinghouse for Bilingual Education, April 1997.

Thomas, Wendell. *Hinduism Invades America.* New York: Beacon Press, 1930.

Thrasher, Frederic Milton. *The Gang: A Study of 1,313 Gangs in Chicago.* Chicago: University of Chicago Press, 1927.

Tienda, Marta, and Leif Jensen. "Immigration and Social Program Participation: Dispelling the Myth of Dependency." *Social Science Research* 15 (1986): 372.

Tienda, Marta, and Audrey Singer. "Wage Mobility Among Undocumented Workers in the United States." *International Migration Review* 29 (1996): 112–38.

Tilly, Charles. "Migration in Modern European History." In *Human Migration, Patterns and Policies,* ed. William S. McNeill and Ruth Adams, pp. 48–72. Bloomington: Indiana University Press, 1978.

Tilly, Charles, and Charles H. Brown. "On Uprooting, Kinship, and Auspices of Migration." *International Journal of Comparative Sociology* 8 (1967): 139–64.

Tinker, Edward Larocque. *French Newspapers and Periodicals of Louisiana.* Worcester, MA: American Antiquarian Society, 1933.

Tizon, Alex, and Diedera Henderson. "Mail-Order Matchmaking Not Regulated." *Seattle Times,* March 12, 1995.

———. "The World of the Mail-Order Matchmaker: Blackwells Met via Bellingham Bride Broker." *Seattle Times,* March 12, 1995.

Todaro, Michael P. *Economic Development in the Third World.* New York: Longman, 1989.

———. *International Migration in Developing Countries.* Geneva: International Labor Office, 1976.

———. "A Model of Labor Migration and Urban Unemployment in Less Developed Countries." *American Economic Review* 59 (1969): 138–48.

Todaro, Michael P., and L. Maruszko. "Illegal Immigration and U.S. Immigration Reform: A Conceptual Framework." *Population and Development Review* 13 (1987): 101–14.

Tonry, Michael, ed. *Ethnicity, Crime, and Immigration: Com-*

parative and Cross-National Perspectives. Chicago: University of Chicago Press, 1997.

Torres-Gil, Fernando M. "Immigration's Impact on Health and Human Services." In *The California-Mexico Connection*, ed. Abraham E. Lowenthal and Katrina Burgess, pp. 164–75. Stanford: Stanford University Press, 1993.

———. *Politics of Aging Among Elder Hispanics*. Washington, DC: University Press of America, 1982.

Torres-Saillant, Silvio, and Ramona Hernandez. *The Dominican Americans: The New Americans*, ed. Ronald H. Bayor. Westport, CT: Greenwood, 1998.

Torrez, Adriana. "Immigrant Health Is Paradox." *Fort Worth Star-Telegram*, October 15, 1999.

Trafzer, Clifford E., and Joel R. Hyer, eds. *Exterminate Them! Written Accounts of the Murder, Rape, and Slavery of Native Americans During the California Gold Rush*. East Lansing: Michigan State University Press, 1999.

Tropman, John E. *The Catholic Ethic in American Society: An Exploration of Values*. San Francisco: Jossey-Bass, 1995.

Tucker, Robert S. "Isolation and Intervention." *National Interest* (Fall 1985): 16–25.

Tucker, Robert W., Charles B. Keely, and Linda Wrigley, eds. *Immigration and U.S. Foreign Policy*. Boulder, CO: Westview Press, 1990.

Turbin, Carole. *Working Women of Collar City: Gender, Class, and Community in Troy, New York, 1864–1886*. Urbana: University of Illinois Press, 1992.

Tuveson, Ernest Lee. *Redeemer Nation: The Idea of America's Millennial Role*. Chicago: University of Chicago Press, 1968.

Tweed, Thomas A. "Buddhists." In *American Immigrant Cultures*, ed. David Levinson and Melvin Ember, pp. 104–12. New York: Macmillan, 1997.

Tyack, David. *Turning Points in American Educational History*. Waltham, MA: Blaisdell, 1967.

Tyson, Lois. *Psychological Politics of the American Dream*. Columbus: Ohio State University Press, 1994.

Uchitelle, Louis. "I.N.S. Is Looking the Other Way as Illegal Immigrants Fill Jobs." *New York Times*, March 9, 2000.

Ueda, Reed. "The Changing Face of Post-1965 Immigration." In *The Immigration Reader: America in a Multidisciplinary Perspective*, ed. David Jacobson, pp. 72–91. Malden, MA: Blackwell, 1998.

———. *Postwar Immigrant America: A Social History*. Boston: Bedford Books of St. Martin's Press, 1994.

Ungar, Sanford J. "Coping with Diversity: The Magnitude and the Impact of Immigration Since World War II." In *The New American Immigrants*, ed. Sanford J. Ungar, pp. 91–114. New York: Simon and Schuster, 1995.

Upton, Dell. *Architecture in the United States*. Oxford: Oxford University Press, 1998.

U.S. Congress. *Border Violence*. Washington, DC: Government Printing Office, 1993.

"U.S. Says Truck Stowaways Not Much of a Problem." *Trucker's Electronic Newspaper*. http://www.ttnews/members/printEdition/0001158.html, October 29, 1999.

Vace, Nicholas A., Susan B. DeVaney, and Joe Witimer, eds. *Experiencing and Counseling Multicultural and Diverse Populations*. New York: Taylor and Francis, 1995.

Van Gendt, Rien. *Return Migration and Reintegration Services*. Paris: Organization for Economic Cooperation and Development, Manpower and Social Affairs Directorate, 1977.

Vander Zander, James. "Sources of American Minorities." In *Challenges to Education: Readings for Analysis of Major Issues*, ed. Judi Hurwist and Mary Sadler Tesconi. New York: Dodd, Mead, 1972.

Vanderpool-Gormley, Myra. "Exploring Church Records of Colonial America." *Colonial Homes* 25 (July 1999): 20–22.

Vega, William A., Bohdan Kolody, Ramon Valle, and Judy Weir. "Social Networks, Social Support, and Their Relationship to Depression Among Immigrant Mexican Women." *Human Organization* 50:2 (1991): 154–62.

Verba, Sidney, Kay Lehman Scholzman, and Henry E. Brady. *Voice and Equality: Civic Voluntarism in American Politics*. Cambridge: Harvard University Press, 1995.

Vernez, Georges. *Immigrant Women in the U.S. Workforce: Who Struggles? Who Succeeds?* Lanham, MD: Lexington Books, 1999.

Vernez, Georges, ed. *Immigration and International Relations: Proceedings of a Conference on the International Effects of the 1986 Immigration Reform and Control Act (IRCA)*. Washington, DC: Urban Institute, 1989.

Vertovec, Steven. "Conceiving and Researching Transnationalism." *Ethnic and Racial Studies* 22:2 (1999): 447–62.

Vigil, James Diego. *Barrio Gangs: Street Life and Identity in Southern California*. Austin: University of Texas Press, 1988.

Villa, Pablo. *Crossing Borders: Reinforcing Borders: Social Categories, Metaphors, and Narrative Identities on the U.S.-Mexico Border*. Austin: University of Texas Press, 2000.

Villareal, Roberto E., and Norma G. Hernandez, eds. *Latinos and Political Coalitions: Political Empowerment for the 1990s*. New York: Praeger, 1991.

Wagaw, Teshome G. *For Our Souls: Ethiopian Jews in Israel*. Detroit: Wayne State University Press, 1993.

Waldinger, Roger D. "From Ellis Island to LAX: Immigrant Prospects in the American City." *International Migration Review* 30:4 (1996): 1078–86.

———. "Immigration and Urban Change." *Annual Review of Sociology* 15 (1989): 211–32.

———. "Immigrant Enterprise: A Critique and Reformulation." *Theory and Society* 15 (1986): 249–85.

———. *Still the Promised City: African Americans and New Immigrants in Postindustrial New York.* Cambridge: Harvard University Press, 1996.

———. *Through the Eye of the Needle: Immigrants and Enterprise in New York's Garment Trades.* New York: New York University Press, 1986.

Waldinger, Roger D., and Mehdi Bozorgmehr, eds. *Ethnic Los Angeles.* New York: Russell Sage Foundation, 1996.

Waldinger, Roger D., and Michael Lichter. 1996. "Anglos: Beyond Ethnicity?" In *Ethnic Los Angeles*, ed. Roger Waldinger and Mehdi Bozorgmehr. New York: Russell Sage Foundation, 1996.

Waldinger, Roger D., Howard Aldrich, Robin Ward, and associates. *Ethnic Entrepreneurs: Immigrant Business in Industrial Societies.* Newbury Park, CA: Sage, 1990.

Walker, Alice, and Pratibha Parmar. *Warrior Marks.* New York: Harcourt, Brace, 1993.

Walker, Samuel, Cassia Spohn, and Miriam DeLone. *Race, Ethnicity, and Crime in America: The Color of Justice.* Belmont, CA: Wadsworth, 2000.

Walker-Moffat, Wendy. *The Other Side of the Asian American Success Story.* San Francisco: Jossey-Bass, 1995.

Wallerstein, Immanuel. *The Modern World-System: Capitalist Agriculture and the Origins of the European World Economy in the Sixteenth Century.* New York: Academic Press, 1974.

Ward, David. *Poverty, Ethnicity, and the American City, 1840–1925.* Cambridge: Cambridge University Press, 1989.

Ward, Kathryn. *Women Workers and Global Restructuring.* Ithaca: Cornell University Press, 1991.

Warner, R. Stephen. "Approaching Religious Diversity: Barriers, Byways, and Beginnings." *Sociology of Religion* 59 (September 22, 1998).

Warner, Sam Bass, Jr. *The Urban Wilderness: A History of the America City.* Berkeley: University of California Press, 1995.

Warner, Stephen R. "Work in Progress Toward a New Paradigm for the Sociological Study of Religion in the United States." *American Journal of Sociology* 98 (March 1993): 1047–1193.

(1993)Warner, William, and Leo Srole. *The Social Systems of American Ethnic Groups.* New Haven: Yale University Press, 1945.

Warnke, Christine. "Greek Immigrants in Washington, 1890–1945." In *Urban Odyssey: A Multicultural History of Washington, D.C.*, ed. Francine Curro Cary, pp. 173–89. Washington, DC: Smithsonian Institution Press, 1996.

Warren, R., and E.R. Kraly. "The Elusive Exodus: Emigration from the United States." *Population Trends and Public Policy* 8 (1985): 117.

Warren, R., and J. Passel. "A Count of the Uncountable: Estimates of Undocumented Aliens Counted in the 1980 U.S. Census." *Demography* 24:3 (1987): 375–93.

Waters, Mary C. "Ethnic and Racial Identities of Second-Generation Black Immigrants in New York City." *International Migration Review* 28 (1994): 795–820.

———. *Ethnic Options: Choosing Identities in America.* Berkeley: University of California Press, 1990.

———. "Immigrant Dreams and American Realities: The Causes and Consequences of the Ethnic Labor Market in American Cities." *Work and Occupations* 26:3 (1999): 352–54.

Waters, Tony. *Crime and Immigrant Youth.* Thousand Oaks, CA: Sage, 1999.

Wattenberg, Ben. *The First Universal Nation.* New York: Free Press, 1992.

Waxman, Chaim. *American Aliya: Portrait of an Innovative Migration Movement.* Detroit: Wayne State University Press, 1989.

Weatherby, Norman L., Virginia H. McCoy, and Keith V. Bletzer. "Immigration and HIV Among Migrant Workers in Rural Southern Florida." *Journal of Drug Issues* 27 (Winter 1997): 155–72.

Weiner, Myron. *The Global Migration Crisis.* New York: HarperCollins, 1995.

West, Thomas G. *Vindicating the Founders: Race, Sex, Class, and Justice in the Origins of America.* Lanham, MD: Rowman and Littlefield, 1997.

Whalen, Carmen. "Puerto Ricans." In *A Nation of Peoples*, ed. Elliott Barkan, pp. 446–63. Westport, CT: Greenwood, 1999.

White, G. Edward. *Creating the National Pastime, Baseball Transforms Itself, 1903–1953.* Princeton: Princeton University Press, 1996.

Williams, Duncan Ryuken, and Christopher S. Queen, ed. *American Buddhism: Methods and Findings in Recent Scholarship.* London: Curzon Press, 1999.

Williams, Raymond. *Religions of Immigrants from India and Pakistan: New Threads in the American Tapestry.* Cambridge: Cambridge University Press, 1988.

———. "Sacred Threads of Several Textures." In *A Sacred Thread: Modern Transmission of Hindu Traditions in India and Abroad*, ed. Raymond Williams, pp. 228–57. Chambersburg, PA: Anima Press.

Williams, William. "Immigration as a Pattern in American Culture." In *The Immigration Reader: America in a Multidisciplinary Perspective*, ed. David Jacobson, pp. 19–28. Malden, MA: Blackwell, 1998.

Williamson, Chilton, Jr. *The Immigration Mystique: America's False Conscience.* New York: Basic Books, 1996.

Williamson, John, ed. *The Political Economy of Policy Reform.* Washington, DC: Institute for International Economics, 1994.

Wilson, Franklin, and Alejandro Portes. "Immigrant Enclaves: An Analysis of the Labor Market Experience of Cubans in Miami." *American Journal of Sociology* 99 (1993): 295–319.

Wilson, Kenneth, and W. Allen Martin. "Ethnic Enclaves: A Comparison of the Cuban and Black Economics of Miami." *American Journal of Sociology* 88:1 (1982): 135–60.

Wilson, Melinda. "22 Stowaways Found off Detroit." *Detroit News*, August 25, 1998.

Wilson, William J. *The Truly Disadvantaged*. Chicago: University of Chicago Press, 1987.

Winter, O.O. *The Old Oregon Country: A History of Frontier Trade, Transportation, and Travel*. Stanford: Stanford University Press, 1950.

Wischitzer, Rachel. *The Architecture of the European Synagogue*. Philadelphia: Jewish Publication Society of America, 1964.

———. *Synagogue Architecture in the United States: History and Interpretation*. Philadelphia: Jewish Publication Society of America, 1955.

Wolfe, Gerard R. *The Synagogues of New York's Lower East Side*. New York: New York University Press, 1978.

Wong, Bernard. "The Chinese: New Immigrants in New York's Chinatown." In *New Immigrants in New York City*, ed. Nancy Foner. New York: Columbia University Press, 1987.

Wong, Sau-ling Cynthia. *Reading Asian American Literature: From Necessity to Extravagance*. Princeton: Princeton University Press, 1993.

Wood, Joseph. "Vietnamese American Place Making in Northern Virginia." *Geographical Review* 87:1 (1997): 58–72.

Woodrow-Lafield, K.A. "Viewing Emigration at Century's End." In *Migration Between Mexico and the United States: Binational Study*. Vol. 2, *Research Reports and Background Materials*, pp. 683–94. Mexico City: Mexican Ministry of Foreign Affairs; Washington, DC: U.S. Commission on Immigration Reform, 1998.

Woods, Robert A., and Albert J. Kennedy. *The Settlement Horizon*. New Brunswick, NJ: Transaction, 1990.

Woodsworth, James S. *Strangers Within Our Gates*. 1909. Reprint. Toronto: University of Toronto Press, 1972.

Wright, Gwendolyn. *Building the Dream A Social History of Housing in America*. Cambridge: MIT Press, 1981.

Wynar, Lubomyr. "The Study of the Ethnic Press." *Unesco Journal of Information Science* 1:1 (1979).

Wynar, Lubomyr, and Anna Wynar. *Encyclopedic Directory of Ethnic Newspapers and Periodicals in the United States*. Littleton, CO: Libraries Unlimited, 1976.

Wysocki, B. "On the Move." *Wall Street Journal*, January 1, 2000.

Yang, Philip Q. "Sojourners or Settlers: Post-1965 Chinese Immigrants." *Journal of Asian American Studies* 2:1 (1999): 61–91.

Yoo, Grace. "Federal Welfare Reform and Asian Pacific Islander Communities in Califomia: A View from the Grassroots." Paper presented at the Pacific Sociological Association Meetings, San Francisco, 1998.

Young, Rosalie F., et al. "Health Status, Health Problems and Practices Among Refugees from the Middle East, Eastern Europe and Southeast Asia." *International Migration Review* 21:3 (1987): 760–82.

Youseff, Nadia. *The Demographics of Immigration: A SocioDemographic Profile of the Foreign-Born Population in New York State*. Staten Island, NY: Center for Migration Studies, 1992.

Yung, Judy. "Chinese." In *A Nation of Peoples*, ed. Elliott Barkan, pp. 119–37. Westport, CT: Greenwood, 1999.

———. *Unbound Feet: A Social History of Chinese Women in San Francisco*. Berkeley: University of California Press, 1995.

Zahniser, Steven S. *Mexican Migration to the United States: The Role of Migration Networks and Human Capital Accumulation*. New York: Garland, 1999.

Zakai, Avihu. *Exile and Kingdom: History and Apocalypse in the Puritan Migration to America*. Cambridge: Cambridge University Press, 1992.

Zarate-Hoyos, German. "A New View of Financial Flows from Labor Migration: A Social Accounting Matrix Perspective." *EIAI* 10:2 (1999).

Zegeye, Abebe, and Julia Maxted. "Race, Class and Polarization in Los Angeles." In *Exploitation and Exclusion: Race and Class in Contemporary U.S. Society*, ed. Abebe Zegeye, Leonard Harris, and Julia Maxted, pp. 224–44. London: Hans Zell Publishers, 1991.

Zentella, Ana Celia. *Growing Up Bilingual: Puerto Rican Children in New York*. Malden, MA: Blackwell, 1997.

Zhou, Min. "Growing Up American: The Challenge Confronting Immigrant Children and Children of Immigrants." *Annual Review of Sociology* 23 (1997): 63–95.

———. "Segmented Assimilation: Issues, Controversies, and Recent Research on the New Second Generation." *International Migration Review* 31:4 (1997): 975–1008.

Zimmermann, Wendy, and Michael Fix. *Declining Immigrant Applications for Medi-Cal and Welfare Benefits in Los Angeles County*. Washington, DC: Urban Institute, 1998.

Zlotnik, Hania. "South-to-North Migration Since 1960: The View from the South." Paper presented at the International Population Conference, Montreal, 1993.

Zuber, Patrick L., Matthew T. McKenna, Nancy J. Binkin, Ida M. Onorato, and Kenneth G. Castro. "Long-Term Risks of Tuberculosis Among Foreign-Born Persons in the United States." *Journal of the American Medical Association* 278:4 (1997): 304–7.

Zubrzycki, Jerzy. "The Role of the Foreign-Language Press in Migrant Integration." *Population Studies* 22 (1958): 73–82.

GROUPS

Abelman, Nancy, and John Lie. *Blue Dreams: Korean Americans and the Los Angeles Riots.* Cambridge: Harvard University Press, 1995.

Abusharaf, Rogaia. "Sudanese Migration to the New World: Socioeconomic Characteristics." *International Migration* 35:4 (1997): 513–37.

Addelton, J. "The Impact of the Gulf War on Migration and Remittances in Asia and the Middle East." *International Migration* 29:4 (1991): 509–27.

Adepoju, Aderanti. "Migration in Africa: An Overview." In *The Migration Experience in Africa*, ed. Jonathan Baker and Tade A. Aina, pp. 87–108. Uppsala, Sweden: Nordiska Afrikainstitutet, 1995.

———. "Preliminary Analysis of Emigration Dynamics in Sub-Saharan Africa." *International Migration* 32:2 (1994): 197–217.

Africa Watch. *The Copts: Passive Survivors Under Threat.* New York: Human Rights Watch Publications, 1992.

Agbayani-Siewert, Pauline, and Linda Revilla. "Filipino Americans." In *Asian Americans: Contemporary Trends and Issues*, ed. Pyong Gap Min, pp. 95–133. Thousand Oaks, CA: Sage, 1995.

Allen, James Paul, and Eugene James Turner. *We the People: An Atlas of America's Ethnic Diversity.* New York: Macmillan, 1988.

Almirol, Edwin B. *Ethnic Identity and Social Negotiation: A Study of a Filipino Community in California.* New York: AMS Press, 1985.

Altankov, Nicolay. *The Bulgarian Americans.* Palo Alto, CA: Ragusan Press, 1979.

Altshuler, Mordechai. *Soviet Jewry Since the Second World War: Population and Social Structure.* New York: Greenwood, 1987.

Anderson, Robert N., with Richard Coller and Rebecca F. Pestano. *Filipinos in Rural Hawaii.* Honolulu: University of Hawaii Press, 1984.

Ansari, Abdolmaboud. *Iranian Immigrants in the United States.* New York: Associated Faculty Press, 1988.

Aponte, Sarah. *Dominican Migration to the United States, 1970–1997: An Annotated Bibliography.* New York: City University of New York, Dominican Studies Institute, 1999.

Appleyard, Reginald. *International Migration: Challenge for the Nineties.* Geneva: International Organization of Migration, 1991.

———. "IOM/UNFPA Project on Emigration Dynamics in Developing Countries." *International Migration* 32:2 (1994): 179–97.

Apraku, Kofi K. *African Emigrés in the United States: A Missing Link in Africa's Social and Economic Development.* New York: Praeger, 1991.

Araby, Kadri, et al. "Egyptian Muslims" In *The New Jersey Ethnic Experience*, ed. B. Cunningham. Union City, NJ: William H. Wise, 1977.

Asis, Maruja Milagros B. "To the United States and into the Labor Force: Occupational Expectations of Filipino and Korean Immigrant Women." Papers of the East-West Population Institute, no. 118, East-West Center, Honolulu, 1991.

Attah-Poku, Agyemang. *The Social-Cultural Adjustment Question: The Role of Ghanaian Immigrant Ethnic Associations in America.* Brookfield, VT: Avebury, 1996.

Auerbach, Susan. *Encyclopedia of Multiculturalism.* 6 vols. New York: Marshall Cavendish, 1994.

Bach, Robert L. "The New Cuban Immigration: Their Background and Prospect." *Monthly Labor Review* 103 (1980): 39–46.

Bakalian, Anny. *Armenian-Americans: From Being to Feeling Armenian.* New Brunswick, NJ: Transaction, 1992.

Balderrama, Francisco, and Raymond Rodríguez. *Decade of Betrayal: Mexican Repatriation in the 1930s.* Albuquerque: University of New Mexico Press, 1995.

Bariagaber, Assefaw. "Linking Political Violence and Refugee Situations in the Horn of Africa: An Empirical Approach." *International Migration* 33:2 (1995): 209–29.

Barkan, Elliott Robert. *Asian and Pacific Islander Migration to the United States.* Westport, CT: Greenwood, 1992.

———. *A Nation of Peoples: A Sourcebook on America's Multicultural Heritage.* Westport, CT: Greenwood, 1999.

Barrington, Herbert R., Robert W. Gardner, and Michael J. Levin. *Asians and Pacific Islanders in the United States.* New York: Russell Sage Foundation, 1993.

Barton, Josef J. *Peasants and Strangers: Italians, Rumanians, and Slovaks in an American City, 1890–1950.* Cambridge: Harvard University Press, 1975.

Bean, Frank, Barry Edmonston, and Jeffrey S. Passel. *Report of the Visa Office, 1991.* Washington, DC: Bureau of Consular Affairs, 1992.

———. *Undocumented Migration to the United States: IRCA and the Experience of the 1980s.* Washington, DC: Urban Institute, 1990.

Berrol, Selma Cantor. *Growing Up American: Immigrant Children in America Then and Now.* New York: Twayne, 1995.

Bickerton, Derek. "Creole Languages." *Scientific American* (July 1983): 116–22.

Bigman, Laura. "Contemporary Migration from Africa to the USA." In *The Cambridge Survey of World Migration*, ed. Robin Cohen, pp. 260–62. Cambridge: Cambridge University Press, 1995.

Bilge, Barbara. "Voluntary Associations in the Old Turkish Community of Metropolitan Detroit." In *Muslim Communities in North America*, ed. Yvonne Yazbeck Haddad and Jane Idelman Smith, pp. 381–406. Albany: State University of New York Press, 1994.

Binder, Frederick M., and David M. Reimers. *All the Nations Under Heaven: An Ethnic and Racial History of New York City*. New York: Columbia University Press, 1995.

Bonilla, Frank, and Ricardo Campos. "A Wealth of Poor: Puerto Ricans in the New Economic Order." *Daedalus* (Spring 1981): 133–176.

Bozorgmehr, Mehdi, ed. Special Issue on "Iranians in America." *Iranian Studies* 31:1 (1998): 3–95.

Bozorgmehr, Mehdi, and Georges Sabagh. "High Status Immigrants: A Statistical Profile of Iranians in the United States." *Iranian Studies* 21:3–4 (1988): 4–34.

Bozorgmehr, Mehdi, Claudia Der-Martirosian, and Georges Sabagh. "Middle Easterners: A New Kind of Immigrant." In *Ethnic Los Angeles*, ed. Roger Waldinger and Mehdi Bozorgmehr, pp. 345–78. New York: Russell Sage Foundation, 1996.

Bryce-Laporte, Roy. "Voluntary Immigration and Continuing Encounters Between Blacks." In *The Immigration Reader*, ed. David Jacobson, pp. 183–99. Oxford: Blackwell, 1998.

Bukowczyk, John J. *And My Children Did Not Know Me: A History of the Polish Americans*. Bloomington: Indiana University Press, 1987.

Bukowczyk, John J., ed. *Polish Americans and Their History*. Pittsburgh: University of Pittsburgh Press, 1996.

Bureau of the Census. *Characteristics of the Foreign-Born Population in the United States*. Washington, DC: Government Printing Office, 1990.

———. *Current Population Survey, March 1996*. Washington, DC: Government Printing Office, 1996.

———. *Current Population Survey, March 1997*. Washington, DC: Government Printing Office, 1997.

———. *Persons of Hispanic Origin in the United States*. Washington, DC: Government Printing Office, 1993.

———. "Series C 89–119. Immigrants by Country: 1820–1970." In *Historical Statistics of the United States*. White Plains, NY: Kraus International Publishers, 1989.

———. *Statistical Abstract of the United States: 1998*. Washington, DC, 1998.

———. *Statistical Abstract of the United States: 1999*. Washington, DC: Government Printing Office, 1999.

———. *We, the American Asians*. Washington, DC: Department of Commerce, September 1993.

———. *We, the Asian and Pacific Islander Americans*. Washington, DC: Government Printing Office, 1995.

———. *1990 Census of Population: Asians and Pacific Islanders in the United States*. Washington, DC: Government Printing Office, 1993.

———. *1990 Census of Population: General Population Characteristics, the United States*. Washington, DC: Government Printing Office, 1993.

———. *Census of Population. Persons of Hispanic Origin in the United States*. Economics and Statistics Administration. Washington, DC: Government Printing Office, 1990.

———. *1990 Census of Population and Housing*. Washington, DC: Government Printing Office, 1992.

Bureau of the Census, Housing and Household Economic Statistics Division. "Changes in Median Household Income: 1969 to 1996." Washington, DC: Government Printing Office, 1999.

Bureau of the Census, Population Division, Population Estimates Program. *Resident Population Estimates of the United States by Age and Sex: April 1, 1990 to November 1, 1999*. Washington, DC: Government Printing Office, 1999.

Caplan, Nathan S., Marcella H. Choy, and John K. Whitmore. *Children of the Boat People: A Study of Educational Success*. Ann Arbor: University of Michigan Press, 1991.

Caplan, Nathan S., John K. Whitmore, and Marcella H. Choy. *The Boat People and Achievement in America: A Study of Family Life, Hard Work, and Cultural Values*. Ann Arbor: University of Michigan Press, 1989.

Cardoso, Lawrence. "Labor Emigration to the Southwest, 1916–1920." In *Mexican Workers in the United States*, ed. George C. Kiser and Martha Woody. Albuquerque: University of New Mexico, 1979.

———. *Mexican Emigration to the United States, 1897–1931: Socio-Economic Patterns*. Tucson: University of Arizona Press, 1980.

Chaney, Elsa M. "Colombian Migration to the United States." In *The Dynamics of Migration, International Migration*, investigators Wayne A. Cornelius et al. Washington, DC: Interdisciplinary Communications Program, Smithsonian Institution, 1976.

Chervyakov, Valeriy, Zvi Gitelman, and Vladimir Shapiro. "Religion and Ethnicity: Judaism in the Ethnic Consciousness of Contemporary Russian Jews." *Ethnic and Racial Studies* 20 (1997): 280–305.

Chinchilla, Norma S., and Nora Hamilton. "Seeking Refuge in the City of Angels." In *City of Angels*, ed. Gerry Riposa and Carolyn Deusch, pp. 84–100. Dubuque, IA: Kendall and Hunt, 1992.

Chinchilla, Norma S., Nora Hamilton, and James Loucky. "Central Americans in Los Angeles: An Immigrant Community in Transition." In *In the Barrios: Latinos and the Underclass Debate*, ed. Joan Moore and Raquel Pinderhughes, pp. 51–78. New York: Russell Sage Foundation, 1993.

Choy, Bong-Youn. *Koreans in America*. Chicago: Nelson Hall, 1979.

Chung, E.C. "An Investigation of the Psychological Well-Being of Unaccompanied Taiwanese Minors/Parachute Kids in the United States." Ph.D. diss., University of Southern California, 1994.

Claymon, Deborah. "JoMei the Money." *Red Herring Magazine* (July 1998).

Colakovic, Branko M. *The South Slavic Immigration in America*. New York: Twayne, 1978.

———. *Yugoslav Migrations to America*. San Francisco: Ragusan Press, 1973.

Conniff, Michael L., and Thomas J. Davis. *Africans in the Americas: A History of the Black Diaspora*. New York: St. Martin's Press, 1994.

Constructing the New York Area Hispanic Mosaic: A Demographic Portrait of Colombians and Dominicans in New York. Claremont, CA: Tomas Rivera Policy Institute and NALEO Educational Fund, 1997.

Cook, Michelle Stem. "The Impossible Me: Misconstruing Structural Constraint and Individual Volition." In *Self and Identity Through the Life Course in Cross-Cultural Perspective*, ed. T.J. Owens. Stanford, CT: JAI Press, 2000.

Cordero-Guzman, Hector R. "The Socio-Demographic Characteristics of Return Migrants to Puerto Rico and Their Participation in the Labor Market: 1965–1980." M.A. thesis, University of Chicago, Department of Sociology, 1989.

Cornelius, Wayne A. "From Sojourners to Settlers: The Changing Profile of Mexican Labor Migration to California in the 1980s." In *U.S.-Mexico Relations: Labor Market Interdependence*, ed. Jorge A. Bustamante, Raul Hinojosa, and Clark Reynolds, pp. 155–95. Stanford: Stanford University Press, 1992.

———. *Mexican Migration to the United States: Causes, Consequences, and U.S. Responses*. Migration and Development Monograph C/78–9. Cambridge: MIT Center for International Studies, 1978.

Cose, Ellis. *A Nation of Strangers: Prejudice, Politics, and the Population of America*. New York: William Morrow, 1992.

Crocombe, Ron G. *The Pacific Islands and the USA*. Suva: Institute of Pacific Studies, University of the South Pacific and Pacific Islands Development Program, 1995.

Crouchett, Lorraine Jacobs. *Filipinos in California: From the Days of the Galleons to the Present*. El Cerrito, CA: Downey Place, 1982.

Cuddy, Dennis Laurence. "Australian Immigration to the United States: From Under the Southern Cross to 'The Great Experiment.'" In *Contemporary American Immigration: Interpretive Essays*, ed. D. L. Cuddy. Boston: Twayne, 1982.

Curtin, Philip. *Why People Move: Migration in African History*. Waco, TX: Baylor University Press, 1995.

Dallalfar, Arlene, "Iranian Women as Immigrant Entrepreneurs." *Gender and Society* 8:4 (1994): 541–61.

Daniels, Roger. *Asian America: Chinese and Japanese in the United States Since 1850*. Seattle: University of Washington Press, 1988.

———. *Coming to America: A History of Immigration and Ethnicity in American Life*. New York: HarperCollins, 1990.

Davis, Floyd James. *Who Is Black? One Nation's Definition*. University Park: Pennsylvania State University Press, 1991.

Deane, D. "Have Job, Will Travel; They're Called 'Astronauts' . . ." *Los Angeles Times*, March 31, 1993.

DeCesare, Donna. "The Children of War: Street Gangs in El Salvador." *NACLA Report on the Americas* 22:1 (1998): 21–43.

De Jong, G.E. *The Dutch in America, 1609–1974*. Boston: Twayne, 1974.

Delancy, Mark, et al. "Somalia." *World Bibliographic Series*. Oxford, UK; Santa Barbara, CA: Clio Press, 1988.

Department of City Planning. *Puerto Rican New Yorkers in the 1990s*. New York: Department of City Planning, 1994.

Department of Education. *Digest of Education Statistics, 1998*. Washington, DC: 1999.

Department of State. *Background Notes: Brunei*. Washington, DC: Department of State, August 1999.

———. *Background Notes: Cambodia*. Washington, DC: Department of State, January 1996.

———. *Background Notes: Indonesia*. Washington, DC: Department of State, August 1999.

———. *Background Notes: Laos*. Washington, DC: Department of State, August 1998.

———. *Background Notes: Malaysia*. Washington, DC: Department of State, August 1999.

———. *Background Notes: Singapore*. Washington, DC: Department of State, August 1999.

———. *Background Notes: Thailand*. Washington, DC: Department of State, August 1999.

———. *Background Notes: Vietnam*. Washington, DC: Department of State, August 1999.

———. *Report of the Visa Office, 1990*. Washington, DC: Bureau of Consular Affairs, 1990.

———. *Somalia: A Country Study*. Area Handbook Series. Washington, DC: Government Printing Office, 1993.

Dimbleby, David, and David Reynolds. *An Ocean Apart*. New York: Vintage Books, 1989.

Diversifying the New York Area Hispanic Mosaic: Colombian and Dominican Leaders' Assessments of Community Public Policy Needs. Claremont, CA: Tomas Rivera Policy Institute and NALEO Educational Fund, 1997.

Donia, Robert J., and John V.A. Fine, Jr. *Bosnia and Hercegovina: A Tradition Betrayed*. New York: Columbia University Press, 1994.

Douglass, W.A., and Jon Bilbao. *Amerikanuak: Basques in the New World*. Reno: University of Nevada Press, 1975.

Duany, Jorge. "Common Threads or Disparate Agendas? Recent Research on Migration from and to Puerto Rico." *Centro* 7:1 (1995): 67–77.

El-badry, Samia. "The Arab Americans." *American Demographics* 16 (January 1994): 22–30.

Espina, Maria E. *Filipinos in Louisiana.* New Orleans: A.R. Laborde, 1988.

Espino, Conchita M. "Trauma and Adaptation: The Case of Central American Children." In *Refugee Children: Theory, Research, and Services,* ed. Frederick L. Ahearn, Jr., and Jean L. Athey, pp. 106–24. Baltimore: Johns Hopkins University Press, 1991.

Fainhauz, David. *Lithuanians in the U.S.A.: Aspects of Ethnic Identity.* Chicago: Lithuanian Library Press, 1991.

Fathi, Asghar, ed. *Iranian Refugees and Exiles Since Khomeini.* Costa Mesa, CA: Mazda, 1991.

Fein, Isaac M. *The Making of an American Jewish Community: The History of Baltimore Jewry from 1773 to 1920.* Philadelphia: Jewish Publication Society of America, 1971.

Feingold, Henry L. *The Jewish People in America.* 5 vols. Baltimore: Johns Hopkins University Press, 1992.

Ferguson, James. *Venezuela: A Guide to the People, Politics, and Culture.* London: Latin America Bureau, 1994.

Fernández-Kelly, María Patricia, and Richard Schauffler. "Divided Fates: Immigrant Children in a Restructured U.S. Economy." *International Migration Review* 28:4 (1994): 662–89.

Fortuna, Juan C., Nelly Niedworok, and Adela Pellegrino. *Uruguay y la emigracion de los 70.* Geneva: United Nations; Montevideo: Ediciones de la Banda Oriental, 1988.

Friedman, Murray, and Albert D. Chernin, eds. *A Second Exodus: The American Movement to Free Soviet Jews.* Hanover, NH: University Press of New England for Brandeis University Press, 1999.

Frosch-Schroder, Joan. "Re-Creating Cultural Memory: The Notion of Tradition in Ghanaian-American Performance." *UCLA Journal of Dance Ethnology* 18 (1994): 17–23.

Fuchs, Lawrence. "The Reactions of Black Americans to Immigration." In *Immigration Reconsidered,* ed. Virginia Yans-McLaughlin, pp. 293–314. Oxford: Oxford University Press, 1990.

Funkhouser, Edward. "Mass Emigration, Remittances, and Economic Adjustment: The Case of El Salvador in the 1980s." In *Immigration and the Workforce: Economic Consequences for the United States and Source Areas,* ed. George Borjas and Richard B. Freeman, pp. 135–75. Chicago: University of Chicago Press, 1992.

Galens, Judy, Anna Sheets, and Robyn V. Young, eds. *Gale Encyclopedia of Multicultural America.* 2 vols. Contrib. ed. Rudolph J. Vecoli. Detroit: Gale, 1995.

Gall, Susan B., and Timothy L. Gall, eds. *Statistical Record of Asian Americans.* Detroit: Gale, 1993.

Gallo, Patrick. *Old Bread, New Wine: A Portrait of Italian Americans.* Chicago: Nelson-Hall, 1981.

Garcia, Maria Cristina. *Havana USA: Cuban Exiles and Cuban Americans in South Florida, 1959–1994.* Berkeley: University of California Press, 1996.

George, Rosemary Marangoly. "'From Expatriate Aristocrat to Immigrant Nobody': South Asian Racial Strategies in the Southern California Context." *Diaspora* 6 (1997): 31–60.

Georges, Eugenia. *The Making of a Transnational Community: Migration, Development, and Cultural Change in the Dominican Republic.* New York: Columbia University Press, 1990.

Gitelman, Zvi. *A Century of Ambivalence.* New York: Schocken Press, 1988.

Glenn, Evelyn Nakano. "Split Households, Small Producers, and Dual Wage Earners: An Analysis of Chinese-American Family Strategies." *Journal of Marriage and the Family* 1 (1983): 35–47.

Gold, Stephen J. *From the Workers' State to the Golden State: Jews from the Former Soviet Union in California.* Boston: Allyn and Bacon, 1995.

———. *Refugee Communities: A Comparative Field Study,* ed. J. Stanfield. Newbury Park, CA: Sage, 1992.

Gomez, R.A. "Spanish Immigration to the United States." *The Americas* 19 (1962): 59–77.

Gonzalez-Pando, Miguel. *The Cuban Americans.* Westport, CT: Greenwood, 1998.

Gordon, April. "The New Diaspora—African Immigration to the United States." *Journal of Third World Studies* 15:1 (1998): 79–103.

Gosine, Mahin. *Caribbean East Indians in America: Assimilation, Adaptation, and Group Experience.* New York: Windsor Press, 1990.

Goza, Franklin. "Brazilian Immigration to North America, 1994." *International Migration Review* (Spring 1994).

Graham, Pamela M. "An Overview of the Political Incorporation of Dominican Migrants in New York City." *Latino Studies Journal* 9 (Fall 1998): 39–64.

Grasmuck, Sherri, and Patricia R. Pessar. *Between Two Islands: Dominican International Migration.* Berkeley: University of California Press, 1991.

Greene, Victor R. *For God and Country: The Rise of Polish and Lithuanian Ethnic Consciousness in America, 1860–1910.* Madison: State Historical Society of Wisconsin, 1975.

———. *The Slavic Community on Strike: Immigrant Labor in Pennsylvania Anthracite.* Notre Dame: Notre Dame University Press, 1968.

Grenier, Guillermo J., and Alex Stepick. *Miami Now! Immigration, Ethnicity, and Social Change.* Gainesville: University Press of Florida, 1992.

Griswold del Castillo, Richard. *The Treaty of Guadalupe Hidalgo: A Legacy of Conflict.* Norman: University of Oklahoma Press, 1990.

Grueningen, J.R. von. *The Swiss in the United States*. Madison, WI: Swiss-American Historical Society, 1940.

Guarnizo, Luis E. "Los Dominicanyorks: The Making of a Binational Society." *Annals of the American Academy of Political and Social Science* 533 (May 1994): 70–86.

Guerin-Gonzales, Camille. *Mexican Workers and American Dreams: Immigration, Repatriation, and California Farm Labor, 1900–1939*. New Brunswick, NJ: Rutgers University Press, 1994.

Gutierrez, David G. *Walls and Mirrors: Mexican Americans, Mexican Immigrants, and the Politics of Ethnicity*. Berkeley: University of California Press, 1995.

Habenicht, Jan. *History of Czechs in America*. St. Paul: Czech and Slovak Genealogical Society of Minnesota, 1910. Reprint, 1996.

Haddad, Y. *The Muslims of America*. New York: Oxford University Press, 1991.

Hagan, Jacqueline Maria. "Social Networks, Gender, and Immigrant Incorporation: Resources and Constraints." *American Sociological Review* 63:1 (1998): 55–67.

Hakkert, R., and Franklin Goza. "Demographic Consequences of the Austerity Crisis in Latin America." In *Lost Promises: Debt, Austerity, and Development in Latin America*, ed. W. L. Canak. Boulder, CO: Westview Press, 1989.

Halter, Marilyn. *Between Race and Ethnicity: Cape Verdean American Immigrants, 1860–1965*. Urbana: University of Illinois Press, 1993.

Hamilton, D. "A House, Cash—No Parents." *Los Angeles Times*, June 24, 1993.

Haney Lopez, Ian E. "White by Law." In *Critical Race Theory: The Cutting Edge*, ed. Richard Delgado, pp. 542–50. Philadelphia: Temple University Press, 1995.

Hannasab, Shideh, and Romeria Tidwell. "Intramarriage and Intermarriage: Young Iranians in Los Angeles." *International Journal of Intercultural Relations* 22:4 (1998): 395–408.

Hansen, Marcus, and John Brebner. *The Mingling of the Canadian and American Peoples*. New Haven: Yale University Press, 1940.

Helweg, Arthur, and Usha Helweg. *An Immigrant Success Story: East Indians in America*. Philadelphia: University of Pennsylvania Press, 1990.

Hernandez, Ramona, and Francisco Rivera-Batiz. *Dominican New Yorkers: A Socioeconomic Profile, 1997*. New York: City University of New York, Dominican Studies Institute, 1997.

Hernandez-Alvarez, Jose. *Return Migration to Puerto Rico*. Population Monograph Series no. 1. Berkeley: University of California, 1967.

Hill, Richard, and Peter Hogg. *A Black Corps d'Elite*. East Lansing: Michigan State University Press, 1995.

History and Migration Task Force, Center for Puerto Rican Studies. *Labor Migration Under Capitalism: The Puerto Rican Experience*. New York: Monthly Review Press, 1979.

Hoffman, Abraham. *Unwanted Mexican Americans in the Great Depression: Repatriation Pressures 1929–39*. Tucson: University of Arizona Press, 1974.

Hofstetter, Richard R., ed. *U.S. Immigration Policy. Duke Press Policy Studies*. Durham, NC: Duke University Press, 1984.

Hondagneu-Sotelo, Pierrette. *Gendered Transitions: Mexican Experiences of Immigration*. Los Angeles: University of California Press, 1994.

———. "The History of Mexican Undocumented Settlement in the United States. In *Challenging Fronteras: Structuring Latina and Latino Lives in the U.S.*, ed. Mary Romero, Pierrette Hondagneu-Sotelo, and Vilma Ortiz. New York: Routledge, 1997.

Hondagneu-Sotelo, Pierrette, and Ernestine Avila. "I'm Here, but I'm There: The Meanings of Latina Transnational Motherhood." *Gender and Society* 11:5 (1997): 548–71.

Hong, G.K. "Application of Cultural and Environmental Issues in Family Therapy with Immigrant Chinese Americans." *Journal of Strategic and Systematic Therapies* 8 (1989): 14–21.

Hong, G.K., and M.D. Ham. "Impact of Immigration on the Family Life Cycle: Clinical Implications for Chinese Americans." *Journal of Family Psychotherapy* 3:3 (1992): 27–40.

Hong, L.K. "Japanese Pop Culture on the New Silk Road." *Japan Quarterly* (April–June 1998): 54–60.

Hurh, Won Moo. *The Korean Americans*. Westport: CT: Greenwood, 1998.

Immigration and Naturalization Service. *Annual Reports and Statistical Yearbooks for the Fiscal Years Ending 1965–1998*. Washington, DC: Government Printing Office, 1999.

———. "Illegal Alien Resident Population." http://www.ins.usdoj.gov/stats/illegalalien/index.html, June 22, 1998.

———. "INS Releases Updated Estimates of U.S. Illegal Population." News release, Department of Justice, Washington, DC, February 7, 1997.

———. "Legal Immigration, Fiscal Year 1998." Washington, DC: Department of Justice, 1999.

———. *Nicaraguan Adjustment and Central American Relief Act, 1997*. Department of Justice. Washington, DC: Government Printing Office, 1998.

———. *Office of Policy and Planning Annual Report*. Washington, DC: Department of Justice, 1999.

———. *Statistical Yearbook of the Immigration and Naturalization Service, 1996*. Washington, DC: Government Printing Office, 1997.

———. *Statistical Yearbook of the Immigration and Naturalization Service, 1997*. Washington, DC: Government Printing Office, 1998.

———. "Table 13. Immigrant Aliens Admitted by Country or Region of Birth, Years Ended June 30, 1945 to 1954." In *Annual Report of the INS for the Fiscal Year Ending June 30, 1954*. Washington, DC: Government Printing Office, 1954.

———. *1997 Statistical Yearbook of the Immigration and Naturalization Service*. Washington, DC: Government Printing Office, 1999.

———. *1980 Statistical Yearbook of the Immigration and Naturalization Service*. Washington, DC: Government Printing Office, 1982.

———. *1997 Statistical Yearbook of the Immigration and Naturalization Service*. Washington, DC: Government Printing Office, 1999.

Iritani, Evelyn. "In Silicon Valley, China's Brightest Draw Suspicion." *Los Angeles Times*, October 18,1999.

Jacobs, Dan N., and Ellen Frankel Paul, eds. *Studies of the Third Wave: Recent Migration of Soviet Jews to the United States*. Boulder, CO: Westview Press, 1981.

Jasso, Guillermina. "Have the Occupational Skills of New Immigrants to the United States Declined Over Time? Evidence from the Immigrant Cohorts of 1977, 1982, and 1994." Paper presented at the IUSSP Conference, Barcelona, 1997.

Jensen, Joan M. *Passage from India: Asian Indian Immigrants in North America*. New Haven: Yale University Press, 1988.

Jones, Maldwyn Allen. *American Immigration*. 2d ed. Chicago: University of Chicago Press, 1992.

Jones, O.L., ed. *The Spanish Borderlands: A First Reader*. Los Angeles: Lorrin L. Morrison, 1974.

Jones-Correa, Michael. *Between Two Nations: The Political Predicament of Latinos in New York City*. Ithaca: Cornell University Press, 1998.

Kamya, Hugo A. "African Immigrants in the United States: The Challenge for Research and Practice." *Social Work* 42:2 (1997): 15–65.

Karim, Persis, and M.M. Khorrami, eds. *A World in Between: Poems, Stories, and Essays by Iranian-Americans*. New York: George Braziller, 1999.

Karnow, Stanley. *In Our Image: America's Empire in the Philippines*. New York: Random House, 1989.

———. *Vietnam: A History*. New York: Foreign Policy Association, 1983.

Kasinitz, Philip. *Caribbean New York: Black Immigrants and the Politics of Race*. Ithaca: Cornell University Press, 1992.

Kass, Drora, and Seymour Martin Lipset. "Jewish Immigration to the United States from 1967 to the Present: Israelis and Others." In *Understanding American Jewry*, ed. Marshall Sklare, pp. 272–94. New Brunswick, NJ: Transaction, 1982.

Kean, Leslie, and Dennis Bernstein. "Aung San Suu Kyi." *Progressive* 61 (March 1997): 32–35.

Kelley, R., and Jonathan Friedlander, eds. *Irangeles: Iranians in Los Angeles*. Berkeley: University of California Press, 1993.

Kessner, Thomas. *The Golden Door: Italians and Jewish Immigrant Mobility in New York City, 1880–1915*. New York: Oxford University Press, 1977.

Kim, Illsoo. *New Urban Immigrants: The Korean Community in New York*. Princeton: Princeton University Press, 1981.

Kim, K. Chung, and Won Moo Hurh. "The Burden of Double Roles: Korean Immigrant Wives in the U.S.A." *Ethnic and Racial Studies* 11 (1988): 151–67.

Kipel, Vituat. *Belarusy u ZshA* (Belarusians in the United States). Minsk, Belarus: Belaruski instytut navuki i mastatsva, 1993.

Kitano, Harry H.L., and Roger Daniels. *Asian Americans: Emerging Minorities*. 2d ed. Englewood Cliffs, NJ: Prentice Hall, 1995.

Knight, Franklin W. *The Caribbean: The Genesis of a Fragmented Nationalism*. New York: Oxford University Press, 1990.

Knoll, Tricia. *Becoming Americans: Asian Sojourners, Immigrants, and Refugees in the Western United States*. Portland, OR: Coast to Coast Books, 1982.

Kolkin, Joel. *Tribes: How Race, Religion, and Identity Determine Success in the New Global Economy*. New York: Random House, 1993.

Kostash, Myrna. *All of Baba's Children*. Edmonton, Alberta: NeWest Press, 1977.

Krasnov, Vladislav. *Soviet Defectors: The KGB Wanted List*. Stanford: Hoover Institution Press, 1985.

Kruszka, Waclaw. *History of Poles in America to 1908*. 4 vols. 1908–11. Reprint. Washington, DC: Catholic University Press, 1993–2000.

Kuropas, Myron B. *The Ukrainian Americans: Roots and Aspirations, 1884–1954*. Toronto: University of Toronto Press, 1991.

———. *Ukrainian-American Citadel: The First One Hundred Years of the Ukrainian National Association*. Boulder, CO: East European Monographs, 1997.

La Brack, Bruce. "South Asians." In *A Nation of Peoples: A Sourcebook on America's Multicultural Heritage*, ed. Elliott Robert Barkan, pp. 482–504. Westport, CT: Greenwood, 1999.

Lado, Augustino. *Arab Slavery in Southern Sudan*. London: Pax Sudani Organization, 1994.

Laguerre, Michel. *Diasporic Citizenship: Haitian Americans in Transnational America*. New York: St. Martin's Press, 1998.

Lai, H.M. "The United States." In *The Encyclopedia of the Chinese Overseas*, ed. L. Pan. Singapore: Chinese Heritage Centre, 1998.

Lavoie, Yolande. *L'emigration des Canadiens aux Etats-Unis avant 1930: mésure du phénomène*. Montreal: Les Presses de l'Université de Montreal, 1972.

Le Espiritu, Yen. *Filipino American Lives.* Philadelphia: Temple University Press, 1995.

Lee, R.H. *The Chinese in the United States of America.* Hong Kong: Hong Kong University Press, 1960.

Lee, S.M. "Asian Americans: Diverse and Growing." *Population Bulletin* 53:2 (1998).

Lee, Sharon M. "Racial Classifications in the U.S. Census: 1890–1990." *Ethnic and Racial Studies* 16 (1993): 75–94.

Lee, Sharon M., and Marilyn Fernandez. "Trends in Asian American Racial/Ethnic Intermarriage: A Comparison of 1980 and 1990 Census Data." *Sociological Perspectives* 41:2 (1998): 323–44.

Leslie, Leigh A. "Families Fleeing War: The Case of Central Americans." *Marriage and Family Review* 19:1–2 (1993): 193–205.

Levin, Nora. *The Jews in the Soviet Union Since 1917: Paradox of Survival.* New York: New York University Press, 1988.

Levine, Barry B., ed. *The Caribbean Exodus.* New York: Praeger, 1987.

Levinson, David, and Melvin Ember, ed., *American Immigrant Cultures: Builders of a Nation.* 2 vols. New York: Simon and Schuster, and Macmillan, 1997.

Light, Ivan, Edna Bonacich, Carolyn Rosenstein, Georges Sabagh, Mehdi Bozorgmehr, and Claudi Der-Martirosian. "Beyond the Ethnic Enclave Economy." *Social Problems* 41:1 (1994): 65–80.

Lilwin, Howard. "The Social Networks of Elderly Immigrants: An Analytic Typology. *Journal of Aging Studies* 9 (1995): 155–74.

Liu, John. "A Comparative View of Asian Immigration to the USA." In *The Cambridge Survey of World Migration,* ed. Robin Cohen, pp. 253–59. New York: Cambridge University Press, 1995.

Liu, John, and Lucie Cheng. "Pacific Rim Development and the Duality of the Post-1965 Asian Immigration to the United States." In *The New Asian Immigration in Los Angeles and Global Restructuring,* ed. Paul Ong, Edna Bonacich, and Lucie Cheng, pp. 74–99. Philadelphia: Temple University Press, 1994.

Lobo, Arun Peter, and Joseph J. Salvo. "Changing U.S. Immigration Law and the Occupational Selectivity of Asian Immigrants." *International Migration Review* 32 (1998): 737–60.

Lopez, David E., Eric Popkin, and Edward Telles. "Central Americans: At the Bottom, Struggling to Get Ahead." In *Ethnic Los Angeles,* ed. Roger Waldinger and Mehdi Bozorgmehr, pp. 279–304. New York: Russell Sage Foundation, 1996.

Louder, Dean, and Eric Waddell. *French America: Mobility, Identity, and Minority Experience Across the Continent.* Baton Rouge: Louisiana State University Press, 1993.

Luebke, E.C. *Germans in the New World: Essays in the History of Immigration.* Champaign: University of Illinois Press, 1990.

MacKenzie, David, and Michael W. Curran. *A History of Russia and the Soviet Union.* Belmont, CA: Wadsworth, 1987.

Magosci, Paul Robert. *Our People: Carpatho-Rusyus and Their Descendants in North America.* 3d ed. Toronto: University of Toronto Press, 1994.

Mahler, Sarah J. *American Dreaming: Immigrant Life on the Margins.* Princeton: Princeton University Press, 1995.

———. *Salvadorans in Suburbia: Symbiosis and Conflict.* Boston: Allyn and Bacon, 1995.

Makinwa-Adebusoye, R.K. "Emigration Dynamics in West Africa." *International Migration Review* 33:3–4 (1995): 435–67.

Mangiafico, Luciano. *Contemporary American Immigrants: Patterns of Filipino, Korean, and Chinese Settlement in the United States.* New York: Praeger, 1988.

Mar, Don. "Another Look at the Enclave Economy Thesis: Chinese Immigrants in the Ethnic Labor Market." *Amerasia* 17:3 (1991): 5–21.

Markowitz, Fran. *A Community in Spite of Itself: Soviet Jewish Emigres in New York.* Washington, DC: Smithsonian Institution Press, 1993.

———. "Rituals as Keys to Soviet Immigrants' Jewish Identity." In *Between Two Worlds: Ethnographic Essays on American Jewry,* ed. Jack Kugelmass, pp. 128–47. Ithaca: Cornell University Press, 1988.

Massey, Douglas, Joaquín Arango, Graeme Hugo, Ali Kouaouci, Adela Pellegrino, and J. Edward Taylor. *Worlds in Motion: Understanding International Migration at the End of the Millennium.* Oxford: Oxford University Press, 1998.

Masud-Piloto, Felix. *With Open Arms: Cuban Immigration to the United States.* New York: Rowman and Littlefield, 1988.

Matsuoka, Atsuko, and John Sorenson. "Eritrean Canadian Refugee Households as Sites of Gender Renegotiation." In *Engendering Forced Migration,* ed. D. Indra, pp. 218–41. New York: Berghahn Books, 1999.

McCarus, E., ed. *The Development of Arab-American Identity.* Ann Arbor: University of Michigan Press, 1994.

McCunn, R. Lum. *Chinese American Portraits: Personal Histories 1928–1988.* San Francisco: Chronicle Books, 1988.

McSpadden, Lucia. "Ethiopian Refugee Resettlement in the Western United States." *International Migration Review* 21:3 (1987): 796–819.

———. "Negotiating Masculinity in the Reconstruction of Social Place." In *Engendering Forced Migration,* ed. D. Indra, pp. 242–60. New York: Berghahn Books, 1999.

McSpadden, Lucia, and H. Moussa. "I Have a Name." *Journal of Refugee Studies* 6:3 (1993): 203–25.

Mehdi, Beverlee Turner. *The Arabs in America: 1492–1977*. Dobbs Ferry, NY: Oceana, 1978.

Melendez, Edwin. *Los que se van y los que regresan: Puerto Rican Migration to and from the United States, 1982–1988*. New York: Center for Puerto Rican Studies, 1993.

Melendez, Edwin, and Clara Rodriguez. "Puerto Rican Poverty and Labor Markets: An Introduction." *Hispanic Journal of Behavioral Science* 14:1 (1992): 4–16.

Meltzer, Milton. *The Hispanic Americans*. New York: Thomas Y. Crowell, 1982.

Menjívar, Cecilia. *Fragmented Ties: Salvadoran Immigrant Networks in America*. Berkeley: University of California Press, 2000.

———. "Immigrant Kinship Networks and the Impact of the Receiving Context: Salvadorans in San Francisco in the Early 1990s." *Social Problems* 44:1 (1997): 104–23.

———. "The Intersection of Work and Gender: Central American Immigrant Women and Employment in California." *American Behavioral Scientist* 42:4 (1999): 595–21.

———. "Living in Two Worlds? Guatemalan-Origin Children and Emerging Transnationalism." Paper presented at the Conference on Transnationalism and Second-Generation Immigrants, Harvard University, Cambridge, April 1998.

———. "Religious Institutions and Transnationalism: A Case Study of Catholic and Evangelical Salvadoran Immigrants." *International Journal of Politics, Culture and Society* 12:4 (1999): 589–612.

———. "Salvadorans and Nicaraguans: Refugees Become Workers." In *Illegal Immigration in America: A Reference Handbook*, ed. David Haines and Karen E. Rosenblum, pp. 232–53. Westport, CT: Greenwood, 1999.

Menjívar, Cecilia, Julie DaVanzo, Lisa Greenwell, and R. Burciaga Valdez. "Remittance Behavior of Filipino and Salvadoran Immigrants in Los Angeles." *International Migration Review* 32:1 (1998): 99–128.

Menjívar, Cecilia, Eugenio Arene, Cindy Bejarano, Michelle Moran-Taylor, Edwardo Portillos, and Emily Skop. "Contemporary Latino Migration to the Phoenix Metropolitan Area." Report presented at the Center for Urban Inquiry, Arizona State University, Tempe, May 1999.

Metz, H.C. *Egypt: A Country Study*. Washington, DC: Library of Congress, Federal Research Division, 1991.

Miller, Kerby A. *Emigrants and Exiles: Ireland and the Irish Exodus to North America*. New York: Oxford University Press, 1985.

Miller Matthei, Linda, and David A. Smith. "Belizean 'Boyz 'n the Hood'? Garifuna Labor Migration and Transnational Identity." In *Transnationalism from Below*, ed. Michael Peter Smith and Luis Eduardo Guarnizo,

pp. 270–90. Vol. 6 in *Comparative Urban and Community Research Series*. New Brunswick, NJ: Transaction, 1998.

Min, Pyung Gap. "The Entrepreneurial Adaptation of Korean Immigrants." In *Origins and Destinies: Immigration, Race, and Ethnicity in America*, ed. Silvia Pedraza and Rubén G. Rumbaut, pp. 302–14. Belmont, CA: Wadsworth, 1996.

———. "Problems of Korean Immigrant Entrepreneurs." *International Migration Review* 24:3 (1990): 436–55.

Misir, Deborah N. "The Murder of Navroze Mody: Race, Violence, and the Search for Order." *Amerasia Journal* 22 (1996): 55–76.

Mitchell, Don. *The Lie of the Land: Migrant Workers and the California Landscape*. Minneapolis: University of Minnesota Press, 1996.

Monaghan, Jay. *Chile, Peru, and the California Gold Rush of 1849*. Berkeley: University of California Press, 1973.

Moore, J.H., ed. *Australians in America, 1876–1976*. St. Lucia, Queensland: University of Queensland Press, 1977.

Morawska, Ewa. "East Europeans on the Move." In *The Cambridge Survey of World Migration*. Cambridge: Cambridge University Press, 1996.

———. *For Bread with Butter: The Life Worlds of East-Central Europeans in Johnstown, Pennsylvania, 1880–1940*. Cambridge: Cambridge University Press, 1985.

———. *Insecure Prosperity: Small-Town Jews in Industrial America, 1890–1940*. Princeton: Princeton University Press, 1996.

Morning, Ann. "The Racial Self-Identification of South Asians in the United States." Unpublished manuscript.

Moskos, Charles. *Greek Americans: Struggle and Success*. New Brunswick, NJ: Transaction, 1988.

Naff, Alixa. *Becoming American: The Early Arab Immigrant Experience*. Carbondale: Southern Illinois University Press, 1985.

Naficy, Hamid. *The Making of Exile Cultures: Iranian Television in Los Angeles*. Minneapolis: University of Minnesota Press, 1993.

National Asylum Study Project. "An Interim Assessment of the Asylum Process of the Immigration and Naturalization Service." Immigration and Refugee Program, Program of the Legal Profession, Harvard Law School, Cambridge, 1992.

N'Diaye, Diana B. "Public Folklore as Applied Folklore: Community Collaboration in Public Sector Folklore Practice at the Smithsonian." *Journal of Applied Folklore* 4 (1998): 91–114.

Neher, Clark D. *Southeast Asia in the New International Era*. Boulder, CO: Westview Press, 1991.

Nelli, Humberto. *Italians in Chicago, 1880–1930*. New York: Oxford University Press, 1975.

Norman, Hans, and Harald Runblom. *Transatlantic Con-*

nections: Nordic Migration to the New World After 1800. Oslo: Norwegian University Press, 1987.

Nugent, Walter. Crossings. Bloomington: Indiana University Press, 1992.

Nyang, Sulayman. Islam in the United States of America. Chicago: Kazi Publications, 1999.

Oboler, Suzanne. "So Far from God, so Close to the United States: The Roots of Hispanic Homogenization." In Challenging Fronteras: Structuring Latina and Latino Lives in the U.S., ed. Mary Romero, Pierrette Hondagneu-Sotelo, and Vilma Ortiz. New York: Routledge Press, 1997.

Offoha, Marcellina U. Educated Nigerian Settlers in the United States: The Phenomenon of Brain Drain. Philadelphia: Temple University Press, 1989.

O'Hanlon, Ray. The New Irish Americans. Niwot, CO: Roberts Rinehart, 1998.

Okamura, Jonathan Y. Imagining the Filipino American Diaspora: Transnational Relations, Identities, and Communities. New York: Garland, 1998.

Olson, James Stuart. The Ethnic Dimension in American History. New York: St. Martin's Press, 1979.

"100 Most Influential Asian Americans of the Decade." A Magazine (October–November 1999): 79–122.

Ong, Paul, Edna Bonacich, and Lucie Cheng. "The Political Economy of Capitalist Restructuring and the New Asian Immigration." In The New Asian Immigration in Los Angeles and Global Restructuring, ed. Paul Ong et al., pp. 3–35. Philadelphia: Temple University Press, 1994.

Orleck, Annelise. The Soviet Jewish Americans. Westport, CT: Greenwood, 1999.

Ortiz, Vilma. "Changes in the Characteristics of Puerto Rican Migrants from 1955 to 1980." International Migration Review 20 (1986): 612–28.

Palmer, Ransford W. Pilgrims from the Sun: West Indian Migration to America. Twayne's Immigrant Heritage of America Series, ed. Thomas J. Archdeacon. New York: Twayne, 1995.

Pap, Leo. The Portuguese-Americans. New York: Twayne, 1981.

Park, Kyeyoung. The Korean American Dream: Immigrants and Small Business in New York City. Ithaca: Cornell University Press, 1997.

Parrillo, Vincent N. Strangers to These Shores. Boston: Allyn and Bacon, 2000.

Passel, Jeffrey S. "Undocumented Immigrants: How Many?" In Proceedings of the Social Statistics Section, Meetings of the American Statistical Association 1985, pp. 65–72. Washington, DC: American Statistical Association, 1985.

Pastor, Robert. "The Impact of US Immigration Policy on Caribbean Emigration: Does It Matter?" In The Car-

ibbean Exodus, ed. Barry B. Levine. New York: Praeger, 1987.

Patrick, T.H. Traditional Egyptian Christianity: A History of the Coptic Orthodox Church. St. Cloud, MN: North Star Press, 1996.

Pellow, Deborah, and Naomi Chazan. Ghana: Coping with Uncertainty. Boulder, CO: Westview Press, 1986.

Pessar, Patricia R.A. Visa for a Dream: Dominicans in the United States. Boston: Allyn and Bacon, 1995.

Petersen, William. Ethnicity Counts. New Brunswick, NJ: Transaction, 1997.

Pido, Antonio J.A. The Philipinos in America: Macro/Micro Dimensions of Immigration and Integration. Staten Island, NY: Center for Migration Studies, 1985.

Pinkus, Benjamin. The Jews of the Soviet Union. Cambridge: Cambridge University Press, 1988.

Piore, Michael J. Birds of Passage: Migrant Labor in Industrial Societies. New York: Cambridge University Press, 1979.

Pipic, George J. The Croatian Immigrants in America. New York: Philosophical Library, 1971.

Pitt, Leonard. The Decline of the Californians: A Social History of the Spanish-Speaking Californians, 1846–1890. Berkeley: University of California Press, 1966.

Popkin, Eric. "Guatemalan Mayan Migration to Los Angeles: Constructing Transnational Linkages in the Context of the Settlement Process." Ethnic and Racial Studies 22:2 (1999): 267–89.

Portes, Alejandro. "Los Angeles in the Context of the New Immigration." Newsletter of the Section on International Migration 4:1 (1997): 1–4.

Portes, Alejandro, and Robert L. Bach. Latin Journey: Cuban and Mexican Immigrants in the United States. Berkeley: University of California Press, 1985.

Portes, Alejandro, and Rubén G. Rumbaut. Immigrant America. Berkeley: University of California Press, 1990.

Portes, Alejandro, Robert L. Bach, and Alex Stepick. City on the Edge: The Transformation of Miami. Berkeley: University of California Press, 1993.

Price, Charles. "Migration to and from Australia." In Commonwealth Migration: Flows and Policies, ed. T.E. Smith. London: Macmillan; Atlantic Highlands, NJ: Humanities Press, 1981.

Pula, James S. Polish Americans: An Ethnic Community. New York: Twayne, 1995.

Puskas, Julianna, ed. Overseas Migration from East-Central and Southeastern Europe, 1880–1940. Budapest: Hungarian Academy of Science, 1990.

Radzilowski, John. The Eagle and the Cross: A History of Polish Roman Catholic Union of America, 1873–1998. Boulder, CO: East European Monographs, forthcoming.

Redden, Charlotte Ann. A Comparative Study of Colombian and Costa Rican Emigrants to the United States. New York: Arno Press, 1980.

Reichert, Joshua, and Douglas Massey "Guestworker Programs: Evidence from Europe and the United States and Some Implications for U.S. Policy." *Population Research and Policy Review* 1 (1982): 117.

Reid, Ira de Augustine. *The Negro Immigrant: His Background, Characteristics and Social Adjustment, 1899–1937*. New York: Columbia University Press, 1939.

Reimers, David M. *Still the Golden Door: The Third World Comes to America, 1943–1983*. New York: Columbia University Press, 1985.

Repak, Terry A. *Waiting on Washington: Central American Workers in the Nation's Capital*. Philadelphia: Temple University Press, 1995.

Rivera-Batiz, Francisco, and Carlos Santiago. *Island Paradox: Puerto Rico in the 1990s*. New York: Russell Sage Foundation, 1996.

———. *Puerto Ricans in the United States: A Changing Reality*. Washington, DC: National Puerto Rican Coalition, 1994.

Rodriguez, Clara. *Puerto Ricans: Born in the U.S.A.* Boston: Unwin Hyman, 1989.

Rodriguez, Nestor R., and Jacqueline Hagan. "Central Americans." In *The Minority Report: An Introduction to Racial, Ethnic, and Gender Relations*, 3d ed., ed. Anthony Gary Dworkin and Rosalind J. Dworkin. Dallas: Harcourt Brace Jovanovich, 1999.

Rodriguez, Richard. "Elian the First Cause That Could Unify Hispanics. *Jinn: the Online Magazine of the Pacific News Service*. http://www.ssc.msu.edu/~intermis/womv4nol/ porte_l.htm, 2000.

Ro'i, Yaacov. *The Struggle for Soviet Jewish Emigration, 1948–1967*. Cambridge: Cambridge University Press, 1991.

Root, Maria R.R., ed. *Filipino Americans: Transformation and Identity*. Thousand Oaks, CA: Sage, 1997.

Rosenthal, Mirra, and Charles Auerbach. "Cultural and Social Assimilation of Israeli Immigrants in the United States." *International Migration Review* 26:3 (1992): 982–91.

Rutledge, Paul James. *The Vietnamese Experience in America*. Bloomington: Indiana University Press, 1992.

Sachar, Howard M. *A History of the Jews in America*. New York: Alfred A. Knopf, 1992.

Saenz, Rogelio, et al. "Persistence and Change in Asian Identity Among Children of Intermarried Couples." *Sociological Perspectives* 38:2 (Summer 1995): 175.

Sanders, Jimy M., and Victor Nee. "Immigrant Self-Employment: The Family as Social Capital and the Value of Human Capital." *American Sociological Review* 61 (April 1996): 231–49.

Scourby, Alice. *The Greek Americans*. New York: Twayne, 1984.

Selassie, Bereket H. "Washington's New African Immigrants." In *Urban Odyssey: Migration to Washington, DC*, ed. Frances Carey. Washington, DC: Smithsonian Institution Press, 1996.

Sengstock, Mary C. "Iraqi Christians in Detroit: An Analysis of an Ethnic Occupation." In *Arabic Speaking Communities in American Cities*, ed. Barbara Aswad, pp. 21–38. Staten Island, NY: Center for Migration Studies of New York, 1974.

Shankar, Lavina Dhingra, and Rajini Srikanth, eds. *A Part, Yet Apart*. Philadelphia: Temple University Press, 1998

Shapiro, Gershon. *Under Fire: The Stories of Jewish Heroes of the Soviet Union*. Jerusalem: Yad Vashem, 1988.

Shelley, N. Mark. "Rebuilding Community from 'Scratch': Forces at Work Among Urban Vietnamese Refugees." *Sociological Inquiry* (Spring 2001).

Shukert, Elfrieda, and Barbara Smith. *War Brides of World War II*. Novato, CA: Presidio Press, 1988.

Silverstein, Ken. "A Kinder, Gentler Burma?" *Washington Monthly* (May 1988): 28–31.

Simanovsky, Stanislav, Margarita R. Strepetova, and Yuriy G. Naido. *Brain Drain from Russia: Problems, Prospects, and Ways of Regulation*. New York: Nova Science, 1996.

Speer, Tibbett. "The Newest African Americans Aren't Black." *American Demographics* 16:1 (1994): 9–10.

Stolarik, M. Mark. *Immigration and Urbanization: The Slovak Experience, 1870–1918*. Minneapolis: AMS Press, 1974; New York: AMS Press, 1989.

Sung, B.L. *Chinese American Intermarriage*. Staten Island, NY: Center for Migration Studies, 1990.

Suro, Roberto. *Strangers Among Us: How Latino Immigration Is Transforming America*. New York: Alfred A. Knopf, 1998.

Takaki, Ronald. *Strangers at the Gates Again: Asian American Immigration After 1965*. New York: Chelsea House, 1995.

———. *Strangers from a Different Shore*. Boston: Back Bay Books, 1998.

Takougang, Joseph. "Recent African Immigrants to the United States: A Historical Perspective." *Western Journal of Black Studies* 19:1 (Spring 1995): 50–57.

Tashjian, James H. *The Armenians of the United States and Canada: A Brief Study*. 1947. Reprint. Boston: Armenian Youth Federation, 1970.

Thernstrom, Stephen. "Central and South Americans." In *Harvard Encyclopedia of American Ethnic Groups*, ed. Thernstrom. Cambridge: Harvard University Press and Belknap Press, 1980.

Torres, Andres. *Between the Melting Pot and the Mosaic: African Americans and Puerto Ricans in the New York Political Economy*. Philadelphia: Temple University Press, 1995.

Torres-Saillant, Silvio, and Ramona Hernandez. *The Dominican Americans*. Westport, CT: Greenwood, 1998.

Trefousse, Hans, ed. *Germany and America: Essays on Problems of International Relations and Immigration*. Brooklyn, NY: Brooklyn College Press, 1980.

Tung, W.L. *The Chinese in America 1820–1973*. Dobbs Ferry, NY: Oceana, 1974.

Ueda, Reed. *Postwar Immigrant America: A Social History.* Boston: Bedford Books of St. Martin's Press, 1994.

———. "The Changing Face of Post-1965 Immigration." In *The Immigration Reader,* ed. David Jacobson, pp. 72–91. Oxford: Blackwell, 1998.

Urrutia-Rojas, Ximena, and Nestor P. Rodríguez. "Unaccompanied Migrant Children from Central America: Sociodemographic Characteristics and Experiences with Potentially Traumatic Events." In *Health and Social Services Among International Labor Migrants: A Comparative Perspective,* ed. Antonio Ugalde and Gilberto Cárdenas Austin, pp. 151–66. Austin: University of Texas Press, Center for Mexican American Studies, 1997.

Urza, Monique. *The Deep Blue Memory.* Reno: University of Nevada Press, 1993.

Varadarajan, Tunku. "A Patel Motel Cartel?" *New York Times Magazine,* July 4, 1999.

Vecoli, Rudolph J., and Suzanne Sinke, eds. *A Century of European Migrations, 1830–1930.* Urbana: Illinois University Press, 1991.

Virden, Jenel. *Goodbye Piccadilly: British War Brides in America.* Statue of Liberty–Ellis Island Centennial Series. Urbana: University of Illinois Press, 1996.

Waldinger, Roger. "Structural Opportunity or Ethnic Advantage? Immigrant Business Development in New York." *International Migration Review* 23:1 (1989): 48–72.

Wallace, Stephen R. "Community Formation as an Activity of Daily Living: The Case of Nicaraguan Elderly in San Francisco." *Journal of Aging Studies* 6:4 (1992): 365–83.

Watanabe, T. "'Child-Dumping'—Taiwan Teens Left to Struggle in U.S." *San Jose Mercury News,* March 26, 1989.

Weisskoff, Richard. *Factories and Food Stamps: The Puerto Rico Model of Development.* Baltimore: Johns Hopkins University Press, 1985.

Weyr, Thomas. *Hispanic U.S.A.: Breaking the Melting Pot.* New York: Harper and Row, 1988.

Wiener, Julie. "Russian Jewish Immigrants Go to the Head of the Class." *Jewish Telegraphic Agency.* http://www.jta.org, 2000.

Woldemikael, Tekle. *Becoming Black American: Haitians and American Institutions in Evanston, IL.* New York: AMS Press, 1989.

Wolkovich-Valkavicius, William. *Lithuanian Religious Life in America: A Compendium of 150 Roman Catholic Parishes and Institutions.* Norwood, MA: Corporate Fulfillment Systems, 1991.

Wortham, O.C. "Contemporary Black Immigration to the United States." In *Contemporary American Immigration: Interpretive Essays,* ed. D.L. Cuddy, pp. 200–219. Boston: Twayne, 1982.

Wyman, Mark. *Round Trip to America: The Immigrants Return to Europe, 1880–1930.* Ithaca: Cornell University Press, 1993.

Yanney, Rudolph. "Aspects in the Life of the Copts and Their Church in the U.S." *Coptologia* 10 (1989): 65–70.

Yoon, In Jin. *On My Own: Korean: Businesses and Race Relations in America.* Chicago: University of Chicago Press, 1997.

———. "The Changing Significance of Ethnic and Class Resources in Immigrant Businesses: The Case of Korean Immigrant Businesses in Chicago." *International Migration Review* 25:2 (1991): 303–31.

Yu, Eui-Young, and Earl H. Phillips. *Korean Women in Transition.* Los Angeles: California State University, 1987.

Zborowski, Mark, and Elizabeth Herzog. *Life Is with People: The Culture of the Shtetl.* New York: Schocken Books, 1952.

Zogby, John. *Arab America Today: A Demographic Profile of Arab Americans.* Washington, DC: Arab American Institute, 1990.

Zolatarev, Semeon. *Lyudi i Sydbi* (People and Fates). Baltimore: Vestnik Information Agency, 1997.

Zweig, David, and Chen Changgui. *China's Brain Drain to the United States.* Berkeley: Institute of East Asian Studies, 1995.

GENERAL INDEX

McCarran, Patrick, **1:**154, 182; **2:**505
McCarran-Walter Act. *See*
    Immigration and Nationality
    Act (1952)
McCarran-Walter Immigration and
    Nationality Act. *See*
    Immigration and Nationality
    Act (1952)
McCarthy, Joseph, **1:**154
McDonald White Paper (1939),
    3:1025
McDonald's, **1:**248
McKinley, William, **1:**247
McWilliams, Carey, **2:**621, 622;
    3:911
Media industry, **3:**795–797
    alternative media, **3:**797–798
    portrayal of immigrants. *See*
        Stereotypes
Median income statistics, **1:**361,
    362*t*
Medicaid, **2:**696–697; **4:**1447
Meissner, Doris, **4:**1437
Melanesian immigrants,
    4:1193–1197
Melting pot, **3:**997; **4:**1511*g*
Memorial of James Brown (1819),
    4:1470–1471
Mennonites, **1:**22, 94, 286;
    4:1511*g*
Mental health
    chain migration and, **1:**253
    children/adolescent immigrants,
        2:427–429
    counseling services, **2:**732
    depression, **2:**719–721
    elderly immigrants, **2:**434
    preventative measures,
        2:721–722
    self-help groups, **2:**719
    social networks and, **2:**717–718
Menzel, Gottfried, **4:**1480
Mex-America
    definition of, **4:**1511*g*
    demographics of, **3:**926
    economic restructuring of,
        3:926–927
    historical origins, **3:**922–926
    inequalities and identities in,
        3:927–928
    physical construction border,
        3:927

Mexican American Legal Defense
    Fund (MALDEF), **2:**541
Mexican American Political
    Association, **2:**538
Mexican American Youth
    Organization, **2:**539
Mexican Central Railroad, **2:**621
Mexican immigrants
    agricultural labor, **2:**621–627;
        3:1141
    Americanization of, **1:**170
    Bracero Program. *See* Bracero
        Program
    crime, **2:**495–496, 683
    demographics, **1:**195–196;
        3:1139–1140
    deportation, **1:**141, 154, 172;
        2:485
    Díaz era (1876–1911),
        3:1140–1141
    discrimination of, **1:**168, 170, 171
    education level, **1:**206; **2:**594, 595
    family relations, **2:**443–444
    fertility rate, **2:**595
    future of immigration,
        3:1143–1144
    gender roles, **2:**457–458
    Great Depression era,
        3:1141–1142
    health, **2:**712–713
    history of, **1:**170–172
    Immigration Reform and Control
        Act and, **3:**1142–1143
    literature, **2:**757
    occupation level, **1:**206
    politics
        activism, **1:**170–172; **2:**535–536,
            538–541
        exclusion from electoral, **2:**545
        homeland, **2:**554
    and poverty, **1:**208
    public opinion on, **2:**562–565
    remittances, **2:**597, 598, 599, 607
    repatriation, **1:**153, 170; **2:**485,
        545, 621, 623–625
    settlement patterns, **2:**415
        Houston, **3:**903–905
        Los Angeles, **3:**914–915
        rural America, **3:**958–959
    survival self-employment, **2:**582
    theater, **2:**765–766
    wages and income, **1:**171, 172

Mexican immigrants *(continued)*
    World War I, **3:**1141
    World War II, **1:**142, 153; **2:**538
Mexican Migration Project, **1:**252;
    2:405
Mexican Repatriation Program,
    2:485
Mexican Revolution, **2:**554;
    3:1140
Mexican-American War, **1:**17;
    2:620; **3:**909, 922, 1136
Mexico
    Bracero Program. *See* Bracero
        Program
    human smuggling, **1:**330
    Native Americans, **1:**12
    Spanish conquest of, **1:**14, 15, 17
Miami
    Cuban immigrants, **2:**416;
        3:931–933, 1112–1116
    demographics of, **3:**930–931
    future of immigration, **3:**935–936
    Haitian immigrants, **2:**674;
        3:933–934
    immigration policy and,
        3:934–935
    Los Angeles compared to,
        3:918
    settlement patterns, **1:**205, 289;
        2:411
    underground economy,
        2:673–675
Microenterprise, **4:**1511*g*
Micronesian immigrants,
    4:1193–1197
Middle Eastern immigrants,
    3:1186–1187, 1187–1192
Middle Immigration Series, **2:**393,
    396; **4:**1511*g*
Middleman minority theory,
    1:226–227; **2:**578
    See also Ethnic enclaves
Migration, circular, **2:**402
Mining, **1:**94
    California Foreign Miners Tax
        (1849), **3:**923
    Foreign Miners License Law,
        1:80
    Foreign Miners Tax (1850),
        3:1138
Ministry of Immigrant Absorption
    (Israel), **3:**1026

Numbers in bold indicate volume; g indicates glossary.

GEOGRAPHICAL INDEX

Numbers in bold indicate volume; g indicates glossary.

LEGAL AND JUDICIAL INDEX

8, Code of Federal Regulations sec. 214.2(o), **2:**707

8, US Code sec. 1101(a)(15)(f), **2:**707

8, US Code sec. 1101(a)(15)(j), **2:**706

8, US Code sec. 1101(a)(15)(m), **2:**708–709

8, US Code sec. 1101(a)(15)(q), **2:**707

8, US Code sec. 1481(a), **4:**1459

8, US Code sec. 1481(b), **4:**1459

8, US Code sec. 1153, **3:**837

8, US Code sec. 1153(b)(1), **2:**705; **3:**837

8, US Code sec. 1153(b)(2), **2:**705–706; **3:**839

8, US Code sec. 1153(b)(3), **2:**706; **3:**840

20, Code of Federal Regulations sec. 656.21, **2:**706

A

Act Banning Naturalization of Anarchists (1903), **4:**1288

Act Conferring United States Citizenship on American Indians (1924), **4:**1297

Act of Union (Great Britain), **1:**54

Act to Establish a Uniform Rule of Naturalization, An (1790), **4:**1277

Agricultural Act of 1949. *See* Bracero Program Act (1949)

Aguirre-Aguirre, I.N.S. v., **3:**1002

Alien Act (1798), **1:**51–52, 71; **2:**449, 484; **4:**1278

Alien Contract Labor Law (1885), **1:**344; **2:**502, 643; **3:**1139
  definition of, **4:**1505*g*
  text, **4:**1285

Alien Contract Labor Law (1887), **2:**502

Alien Enemies Act (1798), **1:**71, 140, 151; **2:**449; **4:**1505*g*

Alien Land Act (1913), **1:**162; **4:**1208, 1505*g*

Alien Registration Act (1940), **1:**141, 153, 345; **2:**505; **4:**1505*g*

Ambach v. Norwick, **2:**512, 520

Amerasian Children Act (1977), **4:**1330–1331

American Baptist Church (ABC) v. Thornburg, **1:**359; **3:**1101

American Competitiveness and Workforce Improvement Act (1998), **2:**646–647

Anarchists, Act Banning Naturalization of (1903), **4:**1288

Angell Treaty (1881), **4:**1282

Arms embargo bill (1914) proposal, **1:**138, 151

Atlanta Agreement, **4:**1352

B

Basic Naturalization Act (1906), **1:**345

Bastrop Independent School District, Delgado v., **1:**171

Bernal v. Fainter, **2:**512, 520

Bilingual Education Act (1968), **3:**815; **4:**1506*g*

Blaine Amendment, **3:**870

Board of Health Act (1892), **2:**667

Boutilier v. Immigration and Naturalization Service, **2:**446

Bracero Program Act (1949), **4:**1299

British Passenger Act (1803), **4:**1253, 1258

Burlingame Treaty (1868), **1:**74; **2:**502; **3:**1002; **4:**1282, 1506*g*

C

Cabell v. Chavez-Saldo, **2:**512, 520

Cable Act (1922), **3:**969

California, Oyama v., **2:**515

California Farm Labor Act (1975), **4:**1305–1312

California Foreign Miners Tax (1849), **3:**923

California Proposition 63, **4:**1388

California Proposition 187, **1:**231; **2:**573, 591, 696–697
  definition of, **4:**1513*g*
  injunction, **2:**507
  opponents, **2:**541, 543; **3:**972
  supporters, **2:**563, 591
  text, **4:**1389–1391
  voting patterns, **1:**231; **3:**917

California Proposition 209, **3:**972

California Proposition 227, **3:**815, 972; **4:**1392–1395, 1513*g*

California Sweatshop Reform Bill (1999), **2:**677

Campos v. FCC (1981), **2:**515

Canada-Quebec Accord (1991), **3:**1020; **4:**1506*g*

Chae Chan Ping v. United States, **3:**1002

Chavez-Saldo, Cabell v., **2:**512, 520

Chinese Exclusion Act (1882), **1:**81–82, 150; **2:**502, 621, 623; **3:**967, 1002
  definition of, **4:**1507*g*
  repeal of, **2:**505, 537; **3:**970; **4:**1298
  text, **4:**1283–1284

Chinese Immigration Act (1885) (Canada), **3:**1020

Civil and Political Rights, Covenant on, **3:**995, 996–997, 999